Mass Culture in
Soviet Russia

Mass Culture in Soviet Russia

Tales
Poems
Songs
Movies
Plays
and
Folklore
1917–1953

EDITED BY
James von Geldern and Richard Stites

INDIANA UNIVERSITY PRESS   BLOOMINGTON & INDIANAPOLIS

This book is a publication of

Indiana University Press
601 North Morton Street
Bloomington, IN 47404-3797 USA

http://iupress.indiana.edu

Telephone orders 800-842-6796
Fax orders 812-855-7931
Orders by e-mail iuporder@indiana.edu

The paper used in this publication meets the minimum require-
ments of American National Standard for Information Sciences—
Permanence of Paper for Printed Library Materials, ANSI Z39.48–
1984.

Manufactured in the United States of America

Library of Congress Cataloging-in-Publication Data

Mass culture in Soviet Russia: tales, poems, songs, movies, plays, and
    folklore, 1917–1953 / edited by James von Geldern and Richard
    Stites.
        p.   cm.
    Includes bibliographical references.
    ISBN 0-253-32893-4 (alk. paper).—ISBN 0-253-20969-2
(pbk. : alk. paper)
    1. Popular culture—Soviet Union. 2. Soviet Union—Civilization.
    I. Von Geldern, James.   II. Stites, Richard.
DK266.4.M38   1995
306'.0947'0904—dc20   94–47995

3 4 5 6 7 05 04 03 02 01

Contents

Note: Performances of entries marked with an asterisk
are on the accompanying cassette tape.

I. The Revolution and New Regime, 1917—1927

II. The Stalinist Thirties

THE CULTURAL REVOLUTION, 1928—1932

HIGH STALINISM, 1932–1936

THE PURGES AND PREPARATION FOR WAR, 1937–1940

III. Russia at War

IV. The Postwar Era

ACKNOWLEDGMENTS

Materials were first gathered for this collection as part of a seminar on Soviet mass culture supported by Stanford's Center for Russian and East European Studies. Later work was funded by the Center for Russian and East European Studies at the University of Illinois, by the Kennan Institute for Advanced Russian Study, and by a Joyce Grant from Macalester College. Many colleagues have offered useful suggestions for the content and format of the book, and we would like to give particular thanks to Allan Ball, Katie Clark, Iurii Druzhnikov, Robert Rothstein, and Jesse Sheppard, as well as to Vladimir Padunov, Nancy Condee, and the Study Group on Contemporary Culture for their encouragement.

Contents were collected through a process of extensive and often indiscriminate reading. We would like to thank the librarians of several fine collections for their kind advice and willing help: the wonderful reference librarians of Petersburg's Public Library, and others at the Hoover Institute, the music collections of Stanford University and the Library of Congress, and the Slavonic Library of Helsinki. Jeanne Stevens and Jean Beccone of Macalester College's Wallace Library were indispensable fact-finders.

Of all the people who helped put the book together, we would like to thank Lana Larsen for her good-natured and reliable assistance. Finally, we would like to thank our family members and loved ones for their patience and advice.

INTRODUCTION
James von Geldern

The Bolsheviks were journalists long before they were state leaders, and they never forgot the impact of a well-aimed message. Newspapers were the lifeline of the underground party. Formative ideological and political debates were conducted in them; reporters and deliverers evolved into party cadres; and readers became rank-and-file supporters. At times, newspapers smuggled from abroad kept the Party alive; and Lenin's editorials often forestalled factional division. Revolutionary struggle taught the Bolsheviks the value of mass media and confirmed their belief that culture is inherently partisan. In times of political turmoil, they exploited it skillfully. Illegal front-line newspapers helped demoralize troops and turn them against the Great War; effective propaganda helped win the Civil War. Yet the revolutionaries knew that the same weapons could be used against them—by newspapermen, vaudevillians, and others. Lenin and Trotsky had been lampooned: horns were drawn sprouting from their heads and barbed tails from their rears, and they were accused of treason, a sting they never forgot. When they took power, they protected themselves by denying the opposition access to public opinion; printing presses, theaters, movie houses were all eventually confiscated and placed under state monopoly. The Bolsheviks considered these measures necessary and just.

Soviet authorities were never ashamed of their monopoly on culture. They considered the policy progressive. Culture was a weapon of class struggle, available to acquaint people with the socialist program. Allowing the enemy access to mass media would have seemed criminally stupid, and neglecting propaganda a disservice to the people. To debate the ethics of censorship was a waste of time; the Bolsheviks' concern was to mold popular values, and they needed a way to reach the masses, reflect the wishes of the state, and censure alien ideals.

The Bolshevik seizure of power in October 1917 complicated rather than eased the task of propaganda. Before the Revolution, the main enemies had been apparent: landowners, tsarist bureaucrats, and bourgeois capitalists. The greatest challenge was to avoid the police. When they became masters of the state, the Bolsheviks were confronted by new adversaries, including the supposed ignorance of those whom they claimed to represent. To rule a socialist society, they had first to win over its citizens.

Building socialism was a frustrating task. For every triumph there was a setback, often delivered by the laboring classes themselves. The response to frustration was frequently brute force, which was evident in all aspects of government activity. In culture, the rare gestures at leniency which marked the first decade of Bolshevik power were offset by crude attempts at regulation. "Class-alien" artists found employment difficult to come by; polemical skirmishes became increasingly frenzied.

For this reason, discussions of Soviet mass culture have usually dwelt on its administration and rhetoric more than on its content and reception. This is unfortunate, because mass culture was a rare example of equilateral negotiation in Soviet society.

The culture gap could not be forced like a river crossing during war. The economy could be socialized by fiat; industry could be whipped into higher production; and citizens could be made, at tremendous cost, to behave as they should. But socialist society demanded that people not just say the necessary things, but also think them in private. Socialism had to be internalized. Many Bolsheviks saw art as the path from ideology to internal thought. It converted abstract phrases into concrete images. As Nadezhda Krupskaya, an old Bolshevik and director of the Committee for Political Education, said: "Workers usually think in images, and therefore artistic images are most convincing for the worker masses."

Propaganda demanded the cooperation of three groups: the Party and state, which provided the content; the artists, who made ideas into images; and the audience, which received and digested the images. Leaders, artists, and citizens all acknowledged the wishes of the others. The audience craved entertainment; the state needed its values represented by symbols; artists desired an arena for their creative energies (and a respectable living). One side—the audience—stayed mute about its thoughts, yet even at the height of tyranny, no mass audience could be forced to watch a movie or read a book.

Mass culture needed accommodation, which encouraged diversity of opinion (though not open-mindedness) even when ideological orthodoxy ran high. Styles varied, tastes fluctuated, schools contended for public approval. Ideologically correct songs competed with jazz tunes; radical activism struggled with political apathy; liberals and conservatives squared off. Echoes from distant times and cultures were heard at unexpected moments: revolutionary posters borrowed from commercial advertisements; socialist rituals mimicked Orthodox Christian rites. Outsiders often imagined Soviet society to be united and uniform, and insiders sometimes shared, even encouraged, the illusion. But it was not; unofficial anecdotes, ditties, and scabrous tales circulated despite official censure, offering a constant commentary on the culture of homogeneity. While they were not evidence of popular discontent, these undercurrents do attest to the fact that the world's first socialist society was mixed and varied—never the monolith of George Orwell's nightmares.

This anthology of Soviet Russian popular culture under Lenin and Stalin offers a unique entree into the mass culture that was sponsored by the regime and consumed by the millions, as well as the unofficial popular cultural forms that flourished beneath the surface. It brings together a rich array of documents, tales, poems, songs, movie scripts, plays, librettos, comic routines, and folklore from Soviet life between 1917 and 1953. The period covered encompasses the Russian Revolution and Civil War, the mixed economy and culture of the 1920s, the tightly controlled Stalinist 1930s, the looser atmosphere of the Great Patriotic War, and the grim but fascinating postwar era, ending with the death of Stalin. Much of the material appears here in English for the first time. The focus of the collection is not on great works of literary art, which have been readily available in translation for decades, but rather on the entertainment genres that both shaped and reflected the social, political, and personal values of the regime and the masses. Each entry is provided with a brief contextual introduction, giving its historical background and significance.

The anthology is divided into four sections: "The Revolution and New Regime, 1917–1927," "The Stalinist Thirties," "Russia at War," and "The Postwar Era." These unequal divisions reflect vast fluctuations in Soviet cultural and political life and the rules under which they were conducted. We have tried to select materials to reflect the spectrum of styles and schools present at each time and to catch the more popular themes. We have attempted to represent most of the leading trends in mass culture but acknowledge with regret that omissions are inevitable. Though all the mass media are represented, some are de-emphasized for obvious reasons (the socialist-realist novel for its size, and movies because they transfer poorly to print). We have included short excerpts from novels, which were the privileged genre of Soviet literature, but encourage interested readers to read the unabridged versions. For the musically minded, this volume is accompanied by an audio collection of popular songs and movie themes, which should also prove useful as a classroom supplement.*

The story of Soviet mass culture really begins before the Revolution (we plan to acquaint readers with prerevolutionary popular culture in a subsequent volume). The Bolsheviks reached their understanding of culture while still an underground party, and the struggle shaped their approach after the October Revolution, when they were embattled rulers. They always tried to communicate their ideas to the people, and they never lost the underdog's determination to ignore opposing viewpoints.

The Bolsheviks have been deemed the inventors of modern propaganda with good reason, yet there was a long pedigree to their practice. Russian intellectuals had a time-honored tradition of attacking the status quo with symbols (there were few other weapons available); and popular culture, like belles lettres, was never alien to political partisanship. Chapbooks, fairy tales, robber adventures, and melodramas had been used as educational vehicles for decades. Confounded by lower-class indifference to their program, radicals sought ways to bring their city-slicker ideas closer to the common folk. Small-scale theatricals dramatized the plight of the peasantry; utopian fantasy gave flesh to socialist ideals; and adventure tales made revolutionary struggle seem more exciting. Such efforts were not limited to leftists. Conservatives communicated their values in penny newspapers, religious calendars, and a wealth of other outlets where readers could be titillated by modern vices and edified by homespun virtues. Even before the Great War broke out in 1914, Russia had a rich tradition of mixing political discourse and popular entertainment. Habits and strategies prominent in Soviet times—the intelligentsia talking down to the people, and the people ignoring (or deliberately misinterpreting) condescending messages—were developed in these years.

---

*Listeners will notice variations between the lyrics printed in this book, which are the "canonic" texts, and the recorded lyrics, performed by popular contemporaries. Several songs were sung in many different versions.

Bolshevik propaganda was heavy-handed, yet judging by its success, much of the public did not resent the overbearing tone. Opponents on both the left and the right were no match for the Bolshevik blitz, and some, such as the Whites, showed a fatal disdain for public opinion. Though the losing side would later claim propaganda a distasteful and somehow radical activity, most factions of the artistic community acknowledged the practice in action (if not in theory). During World War I, many artists—painters from Leonid Pasternak to Kasimir Malevich, writers from Vladimir Mayakovsky to Fyodor Sologub, even the circus clown Vitaly Lazarenko—entertained Russian soldiers and boosted morale on the home front. Russians were subject to a steady barrage of anti-German propaganda. Variety theaters, nightclubs, and beer gardens provided patriotic entertainment for soldiers on leave; the film industry, succored by a shortage of Western films, produced such classics as *Under the Bullets of the German Barbarians, In the Bloody Glow of War,* and *Glory to Us, Death to the Enemy.*

The early twentieth-century media suited Bolshevik purposes. Short forms such as the newspaper report, poetic couplet, guitar song, street poster, and short movie were mobile and accessible to the masses. Under Bolshevik sponsorship, they spoke with one powerful voice, unweakened by dissent or excessive subtlety, unencumbered by complexity. Red propaganda depicted a world of stark contrasts: the sailors described by the renowned journalist Larisa Reisner were valorous and self-sacrificing; the Whites of Pavel Arsky's agitka *For the Cause of the Red Soviets* were cruel and debauched. It was not time for half-tones or self-conscious irony. Capitalism, the aristocracy, and the bourgeoisie (categories rarely differentiated) were viciously condemned, as in the fables of the red laureate Demyan Bedny. For those who preferred positive notes, there were utopian fantasies, paeans to socialist labor, and mass celebrations of brotherhood.

Controversy swirled beneath the seeming unanimity. Bolsheviks had split over the relationship between culture and politics even before the Revolution. One faction, led by Lenin, insisted that political power must precede culture-building. They believed the lower classes could lift themselves from ignorance only through educational enrichment, for which they needed the progressive intelligentsia and its cultural heritage. The working class, according to this view, could not create its own culture until it had mastered the past, which it would approach as both pilgrim and reformer. The other faction, inspired by the renegade thinker Aleksandr Bogdanov, considered proletarian culture the prerequisite of a worker state. These people invested their energies in Proletkult, an autonomous organization founded shortly before the October Revolution and funded by the state afterwards. Lenin's assumptions vexed Proletkult leaders; they considered the cultural legacy compromised by aristocratic and bourgeois origins. Workers, they believed, had a historical mandate for their own culture, which they would create themselves to express their own world-view. After October 1917, a third party to the dispute was formed by avant-garde artists who welcomed the Revolution. Their antipathy to the past was no less than Proletkult's. How, they wondered, could old forms express the needs of a new society: Could Raphael have painted a factory? Proletkult and the avant-garde agreed that the new society needed a new culture. But they disagreed over who should create it: pure but amateurish workers, or skilled but déclassé artists.

During the Civil War, each faction enjoyed the indulgent patronage of Anatoly Lunacharsky, the Commissar of Enlightenment. But as the war wound down and party leaders set to rebuilding the country, they became less tolerant of the loyal opposition. In November 1920, Proletkult and the avant-garde were hamstrung by the "Letter on the Proletkults," a Lenin-sponsored resolution. The letter accused radicals of overreaching their mandate: their "prolier-than-thou" attitude distanced them from the state-embodied revolution and made them incomprehensible to the masses. Withdrawal of state sponsorship made debate irrelevant: iconoclasts found access to the media cut off. Financial developments also swept them out of the public eye. The end of the Civil War and the advent of NEP (New Economic Policy) curtailed state cultural funding and unleashed small-scale market forces.

Radicals, lulled by the media monopoly into disregarding their audience, now had to compete for it. They soon found native commercial culture and Western imports imposing competitors. The aggravation was not new to Russian moralizers: Count Leo Tolstoy's *Tales for the People* had competed before 1917 with Pinkerton detective stories and the boulevard novels of Count Amori and Anastasia Verbitskaya. Prerevolutionary intellectuals had railed against commercial culture, but the audience blithely patronized cheap movie houses and dime novels. So it was during NEP: Bolshevik educators condemned commercial mass culture, but audience tastes persisted. Krupskaya banned Pinkerton and Verbitskaya from library shelves. But until appealing options appeared, the audience sought out these old books and entertainments.

Soviet mass culture operated under a double burden: it had both to entertain and to edify, not an easy task. Proletarian writers faded quickly; their rare successes, such as Dmitry Furmanov's *Chapaev,* combined socialist conventions with elements of adventure. Avant-gardists approached the NEP market with some success. During the Civil War, Mayakovsky had painted outdoor newspaper-posters (the ROSTA series) whose pithy rhymes and peasant stylization pleased popular tastes. He used similar techniques on NEP advertising posters, several of which were known throughout Moscow. However, when he turned to didactic long forms, such as the paean *Vladimir Ilyich Lenin,* reception was mixed; some of the poem's lines were known to Russians for decades, but that was due to compulsory classroom repetition. Other avant-gardists, who had created mass outdoor festivals during the Civil War, turned to objects of everyday use: porcelain, clothing, furniture. These objects can still be found in the world's finest museums, yet they never gained a mass market, because of prohibitive cost and reduced functionality.

Mass culture reached the mass audience only by compromising with its tastes. As Nikolai Bukharin told a national Komsomol gathering, Soviet writers needed their own "Red Pinkertons": stories that exploited audience-grabbing techniques and carried an ideological charge. Old genres such as serial adventure novels, detective stories, movie melodramas, and street ballads could be infused with revolutionary ideals. Marietta Shaginyan's *Mess-Mend* (1923), a novel of anticapitalist intrigue, used the formulas of detective fiction; the adventure film *The Little Red Devils* (1923) depicted three young people battling anarchist renegades; Innokenty Zhukov's *Voy-*

age of the "Red Star" Pioneer Troop to Wonderland combined science fiction and fantasy into a socialist children's story. Enthusiasts also brought their message to popular hangouts. Clubs showed propaganda skits and arranged "scripted trials" of enemies: NEP capitalists, loafers, drunkards (the effect was even greater when the audience, as sometimes happened, was not informed that the trial was pretend). In beer halls, Blue Blouse troupes accompanied vaudeville reviews of current events with gymnastics. Hybrids also yielded an occasional success: Pavel German's song "The Brick Factory" mixed motifs from the "cruel romance" type of urban ballad with a proletarian setting and happy ending; and icon painters in the village of Palekh applied their ancient techniques to revolutionary pictures.

There was a ceaseless struggle between what Bolsheviks thought should be read and what people wanted to read. Administrators and poets, avant-gardists and old-line intellectuals were united by a disdain for commercial culture: they railed against it, formulated alternatives, even tried to remove it from sight. Yet ultimately, old tastes flourished. Although Verbitskaya and Pinkerton could not be borrowed from libraries, they were still read. Blatant politics of any sort in fiction met with the people's indifference. Zhukov's sincere and correct science fiction never rivaled the popularity of Aleksandr Belyaev, who wrote deftly but without ideology. The young film industry produced socialist films such as Eisenstein's *Battleship Potyomkin* or Pudovkin's *Mother,* but they were trounced at the box office by *The Bear's Wedding,* which borrowed supernatural themes (a vampire) and the damsel-in-distress plot from old melodramas. The most popular movie stars in the USSR during the 1920s were Douglas Fairbanks and Mary Pickford.

The radical, often violent policies of the Cultural Revolution (1928–1932) changed things. They were fueled by hatred of NEP, with all its cultural compromises. The assault was launched by a reinvigorated proletarian movement led by RAPP (Russian Association of Proletarian Writers). These "proletarians" (who often had no working-class origins) proclaimed two objectives: to root out class-alien culture, and to create new art forms in its place. The first, at least, was achieved: former aristocrats, unsympathetic intellectuals, nonconformist artists, and other dangerous elements were denied access to presses, theaters, and museums. Cultural intolerance ruled. Prerevolutionary culture, ranging from Pinkerton to folk ensembles such as the Pyatnitsky Folk Chorus and the Andreev Balalaika Orchestra, was effectively banned. Popular culture came under attack: urban balladeers could find no song-sheet publishers; detective stories and science-fiction novels were condemned. Imports from the bourgeois West were automatically suspect. The campaign reached absurdity when dancing bears were banished from the streets of Moscow.

The Cultural Revolution, not the Revolution of 1917, altered the face of mass culture once and for all. Industrialization and collectivization almost destroyed folk and popular culture. The intelligentsia surrendered its independence; the peasantry and its culture almost ceased to exist; the urban audience was transformed. The disappearance of autonomous environments meant that local cultural production was replaced by centralized institutions. Cities, towns, and villages in the center and the provinces heard and saw approximately the same thing, aided by new expanse-shrinking technologies—foremost the radio. Soviet citizens had few unsupervised channels of communication, and none that could link more than several people at a time; and they had almost no contact with the creators of their culture.

The "proletarians" proved more adept at condemning culture than producing it. Clumsy initiatives, such as "collective" literature—represented by the shock workers' journal of a trip abroad or a collective account of the White Sea Canal—aped political more than literary attitudes. Establishment figures took up the proletarian theme, and made well-publicized pilgrimages to factories and kolkhozes to report on Russia's new life. Nonetheless the proletarian culture movement, whose writing about working life was stale and artificial, missed the popular audience. A more intriguing development was the "rabkor" or worker-correspondent movement, which encouraged workers to report on factory life themselves. Ideally an independent voice, rabkors often served as Party mouthpieces (note Panfyorov's article on collectivization in the Kuban); but capable and honest writers such as Ivan Zhiga provided an invaluable picture of life at the end of NEP.

Popular successes came in unexpected places. Though much of children's literature was hate-filled, the Marshak brothers (one writing under the pen name Ilin) provided diverting fare: *The Story of the Great Plan,* a socialist hornbook, and "Mister Twister," whose vilification of American capitalists was offset by magical sounds. Another productive strategy was to pack an ideological plot with action, usually from the Civil War, as when circuses used the Makhno campaign as backdrop for the traditional arts of horseback riding, trick shooting, and acrobatics.

In the early 1930s, civil war displaced revolution as the focus of mass culture. The Civil War generation was replacing its elders in power, and it wanted mass culture to reflect its experience. New leaders saw glamor in conflict, and had an impatience with procedure that inspired rough-hewn and iron-fisted solutions. Civil War mythology gave mass culture a spirit of implacable militancy. Communists were seen staving off an overwhelming enemy: rich peasants, leftover capitalists, priests and believers—almost anyone ambivalent toward the new society. The struggle was so fierce that even personal ties were disdained: industrial-novel engineers neglected their families to build factories; and a little boy, Pavel Morozov, denounced his own father.

By about 1931–1932, dogmatism led mass culture to a nadir of popularity. Most Soviet citizens were excluded by its rigid categories, and many watched in sullen silence. Their resistance eventually convinced state leaders that audience needs had to be acknowledged. The official response was a series of decrees in 1932 that banished cultural factionalism, blaming it on young hotheads. Literature and other arts were reorganized under umbrella groups. No longer were there proletarians, avant-gardists, or fellow travelers (non-Communists who accepted the Revolution), and no longer were independent artists at the mercy of politically adept colleagues. Artists and writers were invited into professional unions that were designed to be, like the society they represented, one harmonious family whose watchword was socialism and whose style was realism.

Socialist realism, a phrase coined by Maxim Gorky, would seem to have imposed a gray uniformity on Soviet culture. But from the inside, the 1930s—particularly the years 1932–1936—seemed anything but gray. Regulation did not eliminate variety:

newspapers printed both obsequious flattery and pointed satire; studios produced Hollywood-style musicals and Civil War pictures; the airwaves carried industrial marches and melancholy crooners. Hacks and opportunists thrived, but the most popular movie of the time, Grigory Aleksandrov's *The Happy-Go-Lucky Guys,* was written and produced by innovators who had broken into show business with the avant-garde.

The greatest contribution of socialist realism was not to create a single particular style—it never did that—but to legitimize the notions that socialist society needed a uniform culture and that variations in style implied ideological unorthodoxy. Soviet culture claimed for the first time the ability to describe the whole of reality. Fragmented realities did not suffice. Smaller genres—posters, poems, stories—made way on the canonic ladder for forms big enough to match new ambitions: the novel, opera, and feature film. That socialist realism was neither socialist nor realist did little to impede its effectiveness. Its other great contribution was to steer Soviet culture toward the mass audience. No longer was there an elite culture aimed at a select audience and a pulp culture for the masses; now all citizens—theoretically and, to a large extent, practically—shared one culture. The stylistic regime limited creative latitude, but it also made culture accessible to most citizens. Few consumers perceived socialist realism as oppressive or stultifying; the contemporary perception was likely one of gratitude. Not only did mass culture speak to the masses, it rejected the pious, hectoring tone of the Cultural Revolution.

Mass culture, as dictated in the 1928–1932 period, had been ruthlessly exclusive: it was not enough to accept the Revolution, one had to be an active and unswerving participant. Komsomol activists and dedicated Communists were the standard heroes, while peasants, the intelligentsia, homebody fathers and mothers—in short, most of the country—were objects of condemnation. New values of the 1930s offered these outcasts a chance for redemption. Tales of prisoners "reforged" by labor in *The Stalin White Sea–Baltic Canal,* or of waifs reformed by collective upbringing in Anton Makarenko's *The Road to Life,* were myths of social reintegration. New heroes arrived with the mid-thirties: simple-hearted but wise country folk, kind and fatherly professors, wives and mothers who stayed on the factory floor while they raised families. While their dedication to the cause was unimpeachable, it was no longer so ostentatious. Though they were, in the jargon of official criticism, "new Soviet people," they were also likely sources of identification for the mass audience.

Culture of the time was not gray, and neither was it grim. If it was marked by anything, it was unrelenting optimism. Young enthusiasts saw themselves at history's forefront, and they sang songs such as "Life's Getting Better" with conviction. People compared their lives not to the Western democratic ideal, and not to the radiant future promised by the Communist Party, but to the recent past, when famine and poverty, cruelty and bullying had been the norm. They seemed to be living in a time of relative latitude, inclusiveness, and opportunity. The Soviet land, inspired equally by its socialist creed and its leader Stalin, found no obstacle insurmountable. The great trans-Ural emptiness was conquered and industrialized with cities such as Komsomolsk-on-the-Amur; Soviet pilots, led by the daring Valery Chkalov, penetrated the polar regions; explorers—who were celebrities rivaling athletes and movie stars—pitched camp at the North Pole. According to the space pioneer Konstantin Tsiolkovsky, socialism would even make interplanetary travel feasible. As the popular air force anthem "Ever Higher" proclaimed: "We were born to make fairy tales come true!"

Mass culture of the mid-thirties flaunted a healthy and sanitized exuberance. A popular song industry rivaling Tin Pan Alley arose; songsmiths such as Dunaevsky, Isakovsky, and Blanter spun out tunes of chaste and virtuous love for girlfriend and motherland. The physical culture movement—useful in a country where public health had deteriorated—caught on among young people, and every national holiday—the November 7 anniversary, May Day, Red Army Day—would, weather permitting, feature thousands of scantily clad young men and women disporting in gymnastic vigor. Folk dancing and singing came back into style under Stalin's well-publicized patronage. Georgian dances, Russian choral singing, Central Asian horsemanship, and other neglected arts were pursued by millions. The young participants expressed their gratitude to the state and to its leader, Stalin, for the opportunity to channel their productive energies creatively. There was truly much to be glad for: the sickliness and self-hatred of earlier years were gone. When stunning revelations of treason were leveled against the Party's upper echelons late in the decade, much of the national collective retained its faith unshaken. The country, like any other healthy body, seemed to be purging alien germs.

The "Cult of Personality," or shameless adulation of Stalin, swelled to full vigor in the mid-1930s. The motive was, of course, to consolidate the Great Leader's power; yet ironically, it touched the hearts of millions with democratic themes. The mythology of democracy, in Russia and in the West, has often preferred symbols of plebeian advancement to the humdrum details of democratic governance. The "poor boy or girl made good" has a sweep and romance few myths can match, and its dream inspired many Soviet citizens. The mythology of opportunity had a strong base in fact: aggressive working-class promotion was a state policy. Positions once filled by the educated and experienced were given to factory workers. Men and women of simple birth saw limitless horizons: Aleksei Stakhanov could break world coal-mining records; Pasha Angelina could break tractor-driving records and inspire women across the country. Elaborate rituals supported the ethic and connected it to the person of the leader; each triumphant hero (in fact and fiction) was invited to the Kremlin, greeted and applauded by Stalin. Mass films featured simple heroes such as Chapaev, whose lack of education and polish was an asset rather than a handicap; and Aleksandrov's heroes (in *Volga Volga, Circus,* and *Radiant Path*) found that modest (or foreign) origins were no obstacle to fame.

In the mythology of the time, Stalin was merely the greatest of the country's favorite sons. He too was born into a humble family; he too overcame his origins with grit and determination; he joined the workers' party early on and rose to the top through courage and daring. If Stalin stood alone at the pinnacle of leadership, he represented many others who had followed similar paths. The popular audience did not reject the cult of Stalin as something directed against its interests, but accepted it as a myth of success available to anyone. National heroes were symbols of common endeavor, and their successes were shared by all.

Stalinist mass culture has often been interpreted as cynical manipulation of public ignorance. Of course, there was falsehood and deception, but the lies were not guileful. The currency of socialist realism was triteness and cliché: the boy-loves-girl-loves-tractor stories, the workers and peasants entwined in fraternal embrace were as false then as now. Any success needed consumer collaboration. For every silenced or silent critic of Soviet culture, there were many who welcomed a message of opportunity. The manipulation theory suffers further by crediting human insight to a ruling party notable for its ignorance of psychology. Many of the deceivers were also the self-deceived. Members of the new Soviet elite—ministry bureaucrats, ambitious workers, parvenu professionals and intellectuals—were avid consumers of mass culture; Stalin himself accepted the era's glossiest films as true coin.

The poverty of mass culture came less from falseness than from its uncut optimism. Citizens were asked to identify with the Soviet cause and show how it made their lives more fulfilling. Role models were plentiful: workers devoted to the national economy; mothers and fathers devoted to family; young people sharing a chaste and healthy love; heroes and heroines sacrificing themselves for the homeland. The onslaught of positive feelings masked insecurity, poverty, fear, and tragedy. The folklore movement screened the demise of an independent peasantry, and it simulated community warmth in a country where even families were scared to speak freely. Mass culture did not "report" the truth; its role, which was performed effectively, was to inspire and mold.

The reforms of 1932 created a powerful apparatus of conformity. It offered writers and artists of modest aesthetic ambition tempting perquisites: material security, access to a huge audience, and protection from the competition of the talented. The promissory note came due in the late 1930s, when internal Party divisions and external military threats prompted a cultural crackdown. Writers and artists who had served loyally suddenly found their fealty unappreciated. Anesthetized optimism no longer sufficed; culture had to join the struggle against enemies. Figures such as Boris Shumyatsky, the Soyuzkino chairman associated with happy mass-oriented movies, lost their jobs and often their lives. Sure paths to success—portraits of Party leaders, panegyrics to policy decisions, parodies of the prerevolutionary past—became dangerous when the leaders were shot, the decisions were reversed, and the past was reclaimed by Great Russian nationalism. Recent masters of the system were at a loss, while retired adepts regained prominence.

The first decade of the Revolution had allowed options for citizens unmoved by Soviet cultural offerings. If Soviet movies seemed dull, there were always foreign films; if mass songs seemed silly or heavy-handed, there were gypsy songs; if physical culture was too strenuous, there were the tango and fox trot. Most alternatives had been eliminated by the late thirties. The revival of national pride placed a black mark on things foreign; homegrown works whose politics had become suspect disappeared. Only the classics remained available, and even they were subject to revision and expurgation.

One can sympathize with writers and artists in search of a stable career. Willing to bend with the winds of time, they still had to satisfy two audiences with different tastes. Consumers wanted entertainment; officials demanded a graceless political orthodoxy. Sometimes both desires could be satisfied, but most cultural figures opted for pleasing the authorities—though the royalties were not so high, there was still room for mediocrity. The safest route was not political knife-throwing (knives could always turn into boomerangs) but flattery. The burgeoning cult of Stalin needed constant feeding. Party historians highlighted his role in the Revolution; bards composed epics of praise; sculptors carved gigantic monuments.

At a time when internal and external enemies posed a constant threat, the army and security organs provided mass culture with another source of acceptable topics (a police state is wise to make its policemen and soldiers feel at home). However reprehensible its sponsors, these themes achieved lasting popularity, as in Gaidar's *Timur and His Squad* or Blanter's "Katyusha." The martial motif even survived the bloody army purge of 1938. Since heroes of the Revolution and Civil War had been declared traitors, and enemies of the Cultural Revolution were now welcome citizens, soldiers profited from being the last topic of adventure untainted by controversy. Foreign intruders and internal traitors were the last unambiguous villains, and their vigilant foes became handy heroes. They represented the fatherland's new sons, Russian sons. They were not the Polish, Latvian, or Jewish Chekists of old, who inspired fear and alienation. They were simple but goodhearted Russian boys willing to defend the country they loved like a mother, without superfluous reflection.

These themes, first touched on in the late 1930s, would resonate deeply during the Great Patriotic War. Though a time of great fear, the 1930s were later remembered as they had been represented in movies and posters, as a time of peace and plenty. The fascist assault of June 1941, according to the myth, shattered a harmonious world and brought catastrophe upon a peace-minded population. The myth was unshaken by its blind spots or inaccuracies. What it reflected, rather than historical truth, was the fact that the war drew Soviet society—its diverse and often clashing nationalities, classes, and institutions—together for the first time. Myths that had been false when invented now created a welcome sense of togetherness, a true collectivity through shared suffering. Readers of leading war correspondents, such as Vasily Grossman, could share the burden of weariness and shame borne eastward by soldiers as they retreated in the early days of war. Even after the tide of battle had turned in Stalingrad, these reporters never forgot that war was mostly slogging through mud and snow. The finest Soviet reporting showed war as tedium and ugliness, rather than as a sporting match in which generals matched strategy and foot soldiers in a fight for glory.

Prewar and wartime culture were also bound by images of the enemy: the invasion redirected the poisonous hatred of the late 1930s toward a faceless aggressor. Skills acquired over the last decade came to good use in war. Poster artists such as Boris Yefimov and the Kukryniksy team, prominent during the purges, turned against the German invaders. Civil War artists such as Mikhail Cheremnykh and Viktor Deni returned to duty. The hatred was intensified by the notion that any empathy for Germans was somehow traitorous; categorical statements of good and evil, friend and enemy, flowed easily from their pens. In most wartime propaganda, Soviet citizens were kind and generous, capable of self-sacrifice in dire circumstances such as the Leningrad blockade; Germans were innately bad, gleefully slaughtering women and babies. Since most citizens shared these feelings, the illusory single audience that had inspired socialist realism in the 1930s finally came into being.

Wartime allowed writers and artists to exploit sentiment without pandering to political orthodoxy. Russians already knew why they were fighting; emotions moved them not because they were correct, but because they were strong and unadulterated. Wartime love songs resembled songs of the thirties in some ways: they were written by the same tunesmiths and featured the same sanitized love; yet their boys were not politically vigilant, and their girls did not drive tractors. Konstantin Simonov, author of the bloodthirsty "Kill Him," won renown as the author of "Wait for Me" and "Smolensk Roads," maudlin poems of faithful women and a sustaining motherland.

Unchecked sentiment has a way of defining its bearer. Sentimental love thrives best when men and women accept their traditional roles; patriotism is strongest when citizens accept traditional national identities. Hierarchical values—the patriarchal family and the Russo-centric state—that had been challenged by revolution recovered full status during the war and became the criteria for good and bad. German racism was contrasted to the multinational Soviet army. Russians, Ukrainians, Georgians, Jews, Uzbeks, and others fought side by side in the foxholes, wrote letters home to their parents and sweethearts, shared songs on lonely nights. They defended one great homeland in whose glory they shared. Russian soldiers indulged their comrades' ethnic eccentricities; and none hesitated to serve the almost exclusively slavic High Command. The women of mass culture were also subjected to older values. The Russian woman (ethnicity was rarely attributed to women) was strong, enduring, and simple; sexy and sophisticated women, such as the villain of the movie *Rainbow,* were often vain, sensual, and spoiled—likely collaborators. Mature women, mothers, and peasants were the favored heroines of wartime, distinguished by their patience and endurance. They suffered silently and waited faithfully for their men's return; sometimes they fought and died. Their contributions to the war effort were lauded, but in ways that circumscribed their social roles. The arena of their actions, with notable exceptions, seemed narrower and their personalities more predictable than before.

The new stereotypes should be understood in the context of upheaval. They belonged to a general call for national unity: the nation in which everyone plays an assigned role is a cooperative collective. Similar stereotypes could be found elsewhere. The once-irrepressible Komsomol bore new heroes such as Zoya Kosmodemyanskaya or the Young Guard of Fadeev's "Immortal": well-mannered, obedient, and respectful to elders. New types were created for front-line soldiers. The Russian Ivan was rarely sophisticated but always stoic and brave. The type was embodied in Aleksei Surkov's "Scout Pashkov" and Aleksandr Tvardovsky's *Vasily Tyorkin,* whose unsweetened view of soldiers' life won unrivaled fame in the trenches.

Foundations for the crumbling world were also found in Russia's past. Communists had once held Russian history at arm's length, seeing little to praise in slavery and exploitation. War blurred the boundaries between Russian and Soviet history.

A revival of national pride returned some distinctly unsocialist ancestors to favor, particularly state-builders such as Peter the Great and Ivan the Terrible who could legitimize Stalin's despotism. Posters depicted Soviet soldiers alongside Aleksandr Nevsky, Suvorov, and other guardians of monarchy. The strongest echo from the past came from Napoleon's invasion of Russia in 1812. Like the battle against fascism, it had been a "great patriotic war." Both featured arrogant foreign aggressors bent on domination; both began with enemy penetration deep into Russian territory. The turning point of both wars was the Russian winter (Generals Mud and Snow), which slowed enemy forces and forced them to retreat under partisan fire. Both wars created a myth of national unity. The myth was decisive in the dark early days of the war, when German Panzers raced toward Leningrad and Moscow. Though the German advance owed much to incompetent Soviet command, the example of Kutuzov's tactics in 1812—he had lured Napoleon forward to defeat—provided hope that the humiliating retreat of 1941 was a ploy. The hope was embedded in Tolstoy's nineteenth-century classic *War and Peace,* which was serialized over radio and read in foxholes; and in Aleksandr Dovzhenko's "The Night before Battle," which reworked its themes to fit the later war.

Comforting illusions of unity and tradition concealed deep-rooted conflicts that the war only exacerbated. Ethnic harmony was undermined by the enforced exile of entire nations; family roles were challenged by women who had spent the war upholding the home front; socialist ideals were questioned by soldiers who had seen the wealth of the West. Victory might have permitted society to address postponed issues, but the state leadership preferred instead to retrench power, preserving old mores and ignoring the demands of time. The canons of socialist realism, now fully ossified, were reinstated, and applied to a society that they no longer fit.

How different Soviet citizens were from their prewar selves. Returning soldiers faced wrenching displacements: they had seen a world forbidden to them, defeated the Germans, and tasted the fruits of victory. How different their country was: an emerging industrial power was now a wreck, its factories and cities in ruins, its fields pitted with craters, its population exhausted. Many men came back cripples, often to find their families gone; many women lost their homes, husbands, friends. Obviously, the country would never be the same; and the failure of postwar mass culture, the tragedy that left it deeply discredited, was that it ignored the nation's grief. Painters filled the countryside with sturdy peasants swinging scythes through fertile fields of grain. The returning soldier of Semyon Babaevsky's *Cavalier of the "Gold Star"* was greeted with open arms and given a job where his energies would not be wasted. The heroes of the movie *Cossacks of the Kuban* found their tables groaning with food and their hearts filled with song. All men, it seemed, were good, all wives faithful, and all children obedient. The fictional soldiers of postwar mass culture found their homes in order and their lives intact.

Postwar culture mimicked the distant illusion of prewar happiness. Values such as national pride, social hierarchy, and the traditional family that had once evolved from dynamic cultural processes, and had been sources of tension, were reimplanted after the war without the dynamism. Myths had never mirrored reality; but they had at least embodied popular aspirations. Now they represented the unimaginative tastes of Stalin, his vigilant lieutenant Andrei Zhdanov, and their minions. The Soviet society conjured by mass culture was reposed, frozen into a conflictless and actionless tranquillity; nary a worry furrowed the brows of its workers and kolkhozniks. Literature, film, and art were static and epic; their favored hero was the Great and Wise Leader Joseph Stalin. Radiant families moving into new apartments were painted hanging Stalin's portrait on the bare wall; steelworkers were portrayed writing a letter to Stalin (which aped Stalin's own favorite painting). Children's stories showed young citizens reflecting on Stalin's wise guidance, or thanking him for their happy childhoods; and war movies highlighted Stalin's martial genius. Symbolic of the eclipse of culture was the fate of the Pushkin Museum, whose fine collection of Western art was relegated to the basement in favor of gifts to Stalin from the peoples of the world.

Great Russian nationalism became ascendant in the postwar years, and its function changed. During the 1930s, it had helped rebuild the national self-esteem; during the war, it united the country against the Germans. After the war, nationalism fed on political and social division. It inspired bombast and concealed unmet needs. Patriotic Soviets would claim nothing less than first place for their country. A Russian was credited with inventing the telegraph, others were the fathers of aviation; if Russians were underfed at home, then the Western diet was said to be even worse. National pride was perhaps understandable from the conquerors of Berlin, but it often hid other agendas. The Russian botanist Ivan Michurin displaced Gregor Mendel in the scientific pantheon, and Western genetics was declared anathema. This bit of patriotic partiality aided the rise to power of Trofim Lysenko, director of the Agricultural Academy, whose campaign against "cosmopolitan" genetics ended many worthy careers and left Soviet science decades behind that of the West.

Nationalism inspired by internal considerations intensified the cold war. Methods born during the purges and honed during the war found new targets. The West was demonized as a gang of greedy capitalists plotting to destroy Soviet socialism. Cold war propaganda was not entirely uniform: Konstantin Simonov's *The Russian Question* portrayed American journalists as both honest and dishonest, and painted evil in shades of gray as well as black. But at its worst, propaganda deprived the enemy of all humanity, and reduced the complex cultures of the West to a few simple tones.

Effective propaganda stereotypes the enemy. An unspoken corollary is that it also stereotypes the maker. Discussions of class status before and during the war had demonstrated this, and their trivializations were echoed in postwar discussions of ethnicity and nationality, which were made sensitive by Soviet dominion over Eastern Europe. Mass culture dealt with the touchy relations between "fraternal" countries through the same rituals and gestures that were developed in the 1930s to ease class frictions. Encounters between nations and ethnic groups were elaborately framed; the roles of mentor and pupil were designated by a code of body placement and pose. National differences were positively depicted, but they were also seen as boundaries not to be transgressed. Hungarian workers gaze lovingly at their Russian instructor; a Kazakh ex-nomad develops a new millet strain by native instinct, but must consult Russians for scientific confirmation. Russians themselves were bound by abstract civic roles begotten by their own nationalism. The myth of the "new Soviet man" excluded sex (though not love), ambition, concern for one's own welfare, even individual struggle. Perhaps the most insidious facet of the myth was the equation of simple with good. The provincial values praised in Paustovsky's "In the Heart of Russia" took permanent root—and would, in fact, eventually provide the "village prose" school with the elements of a Russian identity.

The banalities of "Soviet humanhood" spawned an even more unfortunate corollary, tortuously termed "unconflictedness": if Soviet people were good and Soviet society had no problems, then art could show no conflict, only disagreements between the good and the better. The practical consequence of the doctrine was an absence of authentic contemporary heroes. Writers and artists looked to alternative sources. War stories, a staple of mass culture for decades to come, made their appearance, as did those about soldiers returning from the front. Old heroes from the 1930s were revived, as in Pavel Shchipachov's *Pavlik Morozov,* or recast, as in Boris Polevoi's adaptation of the Korchagin motif in *The Story of a Real Man.* Many of these heroes (with the prominent exception of Polevoi's Meresyev) found no resonance with the mass public. Leading icons and myths were quickly forgotten, and left little trace on the post-Stalinist years. Alternatives were few, but they attracted great popularity: favorite stars of the time were Johnny Weismuller as Tarzan, John Wayne the cowboy, or James Cagney the gangster (their movies were booty from the Nazis, who had also enjoyed them illicitly).

Even in these repressive years, there were alternatives—perhaps parallels would be more accurate—to Stalinist culture. The first signs were faint, and came from society's margins. The culture of prison camps—*blatnaya,* in the argot—was rough, direct, and rich in obscenity: qualities that had been cleansed from official culture. The attraction of prison culture was irresistible, and it has since inspired countless popular songs and beliefs. Another fertile source, one more ephemeral, was the "stilyaga" movement. The *stilyagi* were an anomaly: in a nation wrecked by war and oppressed by dictatorship, they listened to American jazz, flaunted Western wardrobe, and spoke in a willfully un-Soviet slang. This relatively small group, gathered mostly from children of the urban elite, created scandal mainly because no one else dared to be different. They never gained direct access to the media, and created no true culture of their own. Most had few political pretensions; but by denying the primacy of politics, they flouted the official conviction that culture must be ideological. Despite themselves, and through frequent and heavy-handed official condemnations, the *stilyagi* became icons of change.

Stilyagi were pioneers of the "unofficial" culture that would drag Soviet society out of stasis. Unofficial culture—which could range from informal youth groups to tape-recorded guitar songs to anecdotes—often achieved wider circulation than the official in post-Stalinist times; and because it did not bear the state imprint, it had more punch. State officials assumed reflexively that unofficial culture threatened social order. In doing so, they forgot (or perhaps remembered all too clearly) the "unofficial" origins of Bolshevik culture itself.

Though unofficial culture was in recent times identified with liberalization, the assumption was not always true. Rather than opposing the reigning order, it could challenge and force it to adapt. When new forms were brought in from the periphery, the official media, if they were to retain an audience, had to adapt the new forms to their own purposes. During NEP, pulp literature and gypsy songs were adapted; the thirties saw the successful modification of jazz, Hollywood musicals, and folklore. Unofficial culture was dynamic, vivid, often coarse. Its distinction from official culture did not always reflect divisions between the population and ruling apparatus or liberalism and conservatism. Rather, it carried on an internal dialogue within society (which we have tried to represent here by including anecdotes with the texts they critiqued). Staunch defenders of the system could tell anti-Soviet jokes; unofficial music could be imported by the privileged. Officials often resisted unofficial innovation, but then again, so did the workers. Proletarians of the 1920s protested the stylistic "mishmash" of the avant-garde; those of the early 1950s distrusted the *stilyagi;* and in the 1980s, Moscow's working-class toughs enjoyed smashing rockers' heads.

The *stilyagi* were only the first of many unofficial groups to undermine the Stalinist monolith. Unofficial culture continued to encounter powerful, often destructive resistance, but never would it be suffocated by Stalinism's grand assumption: that Soviet culture must be homogeneous, and that divergence from the norm was evil.

We hope that this anthology will bring readers closer to Soviet society as it was experienced from the inside. Mass culture offers unique insights into that distant way of life, because it embodied many of the unspoken assumptions underlying the system. Relations between the consumers, makers, and sponsors of Soviet culture mirrored other social relationships. The state monopolized political power; official mass culture monopolized the media. Communist ideology claimed exclusive right to the truth; official culture claimed to be the sole legitimate depictor of Soviet life. The state defended its power without mercy; the cultural apparatus did not tolerate dissent. Mass culture also shows how these rules were only partial truths, signals of intent more than of reality. The apparatus of cultural control could regulate artistic production by reward and punishment, but it had to compromise with audience tastes. Consumers could not be forced to read anything they found dull, they could not be forced to interpret it as the authorities intended, nor could they be forced to believe it.

Our readers should try reading these stories as they might have been read in their own time. Soviet cultural production under Lenin and Stalin often resembled medieval icons and saints' lives. Each type employed a cluster of symbols to reiterate a narrow range of themes, and they seem repetitive to outsiders; but they held a world of meaning for the insider, who was inured to generic conventions and paid great attention to slight deviations from the norm. Konstantin Fedin's "The Living Lenin" seems a standard political saint's life; the intended reader, however, might have noticed not the obligatory praise of Lenin but the implicit contrast between his style of leadership and Stalin's. One short piece, then, could really be two works of literature, dependent on the reader's inclinations—the believer saw orthodoxy where the skeptic saw a polemic.

Consumers, often oblivious of the state's guiding hand, were perhaps the determining factor in mass culture. The official apparatus could grind out all the pulp it liked, but if nobody noticed, did it matter? The desire to satisfy popular tastes was apparent: despite claiming an eternal and unchanging ideology, the makers of mass culture were constantly tacking with the sea breeze of fashion. This is demonstrated by the shifting outlines of the Chapaev legend, the most enduring of all. The story was based in fact: there was a Civil War fighter who gained fame for his exploits. This simple story was constantly rewritten to fit its time and audience, till its fate matched that of *Frankenstein* or *Moby Dick*—the original was unrecognizable in later versions. When Chapaev first appeared in Furmanov's novel of 1923, he was a head-strong partisan undergoing a difficult transition to Communism, and the peasant element in him was seen as negative. Chapaev had much to learn from city folk and commissars. By 1934, when the film was released, disdain for things peasant had softened, and Chapaev's peasantness seemed more positive: the didactic figure of the commissar was balanced by Chapaev's simple adjutant Petka. The film's popularity inspired attempts to shape audience response; a cycle of "folk" legends appeared that highlighted Chapaev's hatred for the rich and "corrected" his death with a happy ending. A cycle of unofficial Chapaev anecdotes (based on the movie, not the novel) appeared, contradicting the official legends: this Chapaev was coarse but canny, and his "peasant instincts" only diluted his socialism. The tradition of anecdotes continued up to the 1970s, when Chapaev was sent to Africa to aid the emerging nations, and thrived into the 1990s.

All this is not to deny that mass culture helped maintain the Soviet regime, but to insist that its role in society was complex. Whatever cultural bureaucrats believed, an anti-Soviet joke did not necessarily imply anti-Soviet attitudes, and ideological orthodoxy did not guarantee a proper audience response. Rather than searching mass culture for an ideology it often distorted, or for instruments of control it often failed to provide, we should let it expand our understanding of Soviet life. Mass culture shows us a society talking about itself the only way it could. Official voices spoke loudest, but not always most effectively. Soviet socialism was not the inflexible ideology it claimed to be: it was a set of social practices and cultural inclinations in constant flux, which hid its intentions not only from the outside world but from itself.

NOTE ON TRANSLITERATION

This anthology has several intended audiences, which complicates the matter of transliteration. In the texts, we have adopted a modified version of the Library of Congress system, with concessions to pronunciation, tradition, and common sense. Thus, Trotskii will be spelled Trotsky, the Enisei River will be Yenisei, Iaroslavskii will be Yaroslavsky. In the footnotes and bibliography, when transliterating Russian language documents, we will observe the Library of Congress system strictly. We hope this will meet the needs of all our readers.

Red Star, agitation boat during the Civil War.

A workers' club, 1920s.

"He who does not work,
neither shall he eat."
Porcelain plate, 1923.

The clown Vitaly
Lazarenko, sketch by P.
Galadzhev, 1920s.

P. G. Leonov, decorative
cotton, 1927.

I. I. Brodsky, *Lenin in
Smolnyi* (detail), 1930.

Vladimir Mayakovsky, poet
of the Revolution, 1930,
the year of his death.

Listening to the radio in
the Fergana Valley, Moscow
to Uzbekistan.

Palace of culture in the Proletarian District, a
Moscow neighborhood, 1930s.

Literature circle at the Moscow Automobile
Factory, 1932. Photo by V. Perelman.
Tretyakov Gallery.

Aleksandr Rodchenko,
photo of physical culture
demonstration, 1932.

Scene from the film
Chapaev, one of the most
famous shots in Soviet film
history.

Cover of sheet music for "Our Moscow," a
mass song by V. Kruchinin and V. Lebedev-
Kumach, 1935. Depicts the design for a
Palace of Soviets that was never built.

Poster of Stalin and Voroshilov by Gustav
Klutsis, 1935. Galeric Gmurzynska, Cologne.

Scene from the film *The Valiant Seven,* an epic of Arctic exploration, 1936.

Mayakovskaya Metro Station, Moscow, 1936.

Scene from the film *Circus,* a political
melodrama and musical comedy, 1936.

Yu. I. Pimenov, *The New Moscow,* painting, 1937.

S. V. Gerasimov, *Feast on a Kolkhoz,* painting, 1937.

Vera Mukhina, *The Worker and the Collective Farmer,* sculpture, 1937.

A. S. Deineka, *Future Flyers*, painting, 1938.

Lyubov Kuzmicheva and Vera Glebova,
performers of *chastushki*, 1939.

World War II poster by the
Kukryniksy, *Nevsky, Suvorov,
Chapaev,* recruited from
the dead.

T. A. Yeremina, *Partisans,
Take Revenge without Mercy!,*
poster, 1942. Collection of
Beate Fieseler.

M. G. Manizer, *The People's Avengers,* sculpture, 1944.

Kukryniksy, *We shall destroy the enemy without mercy!*, poster, 1941.

The Volga-Don Canal, Lock No. 1,
constructed with forced labor and
embellished as a triumphal arch, 1949–1952.

The Belorussian Pavilion at the USSR
Agricultural Exhibition, Moscow, 1954.

I.

The Revolution
and
New Regime,
1917—1927

We Grow Out of Iron

Aleksei Gastev (1918)[1]

GASTEV (1882–1941), A RADICAL LABOR ORGANIZER AND REVO-
LUTIONARY CULTURE FIGURE, WAS HIMSELF A FACTORY WORKER,
AND HIS VERSE POETICIZED THE ENVIRONMENT OF THE FACTORY
FLOOR. HE LATER BECAME THE LEADER OF THE TAYLORIST MOVE-
MENT TO INCREASE LABOR EFFICIENCY IN SOVIET INDUSTRY. HE
WAS EVENTUALLY PURGED BY STALIN AND DIED IN A LABOR
CAMP.

Look! I stand among workbenches, hammers, furnaces, forges, and among a hundred
    comrades,
Overhead hammered iron space.
On either side—beams and girders.
They rise to a height of seventy feet.
They arch right and left.
Joined by cross-beams in the cupolas, with giant shoulders they support the whole iron
    structure.
They thrust upward, they are bold, they are strong.
They demand yet greater strength.
I look at them and grow straight.
Fresh iron blood pours into my veins.
I have grown taller.
I too am growing shoulders of steel and arms immeasurably strong. I am one with the
    building's iron.
I have risen.
My shoulders are forcing the rafters, the upper beams, the roof.
My feet remain on the ground, but my head is above the building.
I choke with the inhuman effort, but already I am shouting:
"May I have the floor, comrades, may I have the floor?"
An iron echo drowns my words, the whole structure shakes with impatience.
    And I have risen yet higher, I am on a level with the chimneys.
I shall not tell a story or make a speech, I will only shout my iron word:
"Victory shall be ours!"

Translated in *A Treasury of Russian Verse,* ed. Avrahm Yarmolinsky (New York: Macmillan Company,
1949), p. 252.
1. Written in 1914.

The Iron Messiah

Vladimir Kirillov (1918)

KIRILLOV (1880–1943) WAS ONE OF THE "PROLETARIAN" POETS OF THE REVOLUTION WHO, WITH GASTEV AND GERASIMOV, EX-ALTED THE MACHINE AS THE SAVIOR OF RUSSIA. IN THIS PRO-METHEAN VISION, TECHNOLOGY BOTH DESTROYS WITH ITS "CLEANSING FLAME" THE CORRUPT AND SOFT "OLD WORLD" (IN-CLUDING THRONES AND PRISONS) AND CREATES THE DYNAMIC PROCESSES — MODERN LABOR AND MASS PRODUCTION — THAT WILL FREE MANKIND FROM THE FETTERS OF NATURE.

There he is—the savior, the lord of the earth.
The master of titanic forces—
In the roar of countless steel machines,
In the radiance of electric suns.

We thought he would appear in a sunlight stole,
With a nimbus of divine mystery,
But he came to us clad in gray smoke
From the suburbs, foundries, factories.

We thought he would appear in glory and glitter,
Meek, blessedly gentle,
But he, like the molten lava,
Came—multiface and turbulent...

There he walks o'er the abyss of seas,
All of steel, unyielding and impetuous;
He scatters sparks of rebellious thought,
And the purging flames are pouring forth.

Wherever his masterful call is heard,
The world's bosom is bared,
The mountains give way before him,
The earth's poles together are brought.

Wherever he walks, he leaves a trail
Of ringing iron rail;
He brings joy and light to us,
A desert he strews with blossoms.

Translated by George Z. Patrick, in *Popular Poetry in Soviet Russia* (Berkeley: University of California Press, 1929), p. 216.

To the world he brings a new sun,
He destroys the thrones and prisons,
He calls the peoples to eternal fraternity,
And wipes out the boundaries between them.

His crimson banner is the symbol of struggle;
For the oppressed it is the guiding beacon;
With it we shall crush the yoke of fate,
We shall conquer the enchanting world.

We

Mikhail Gerasimov (1919)

GERASIMOV (1889–1939), LIKE THE OTHER PROLETARIAN POETS,
COMBINED HIS TECHNOLOTRY OR MACHINE WORSHIP WITH A
GLORIFICATION OF THE COLLECTIVE — THE "WE" WHICH PER-
VADES SO MUCH OF THE REVOLUTIONARY POETRY OF THE TIME
(AND WHICH SUGGESTED THE TITLE OF YEVGENY ZAMYATIN'S
FAMOUS BUT LONG-SUPPRESSED ANTI-UTOPIAN NOVEL, WE
[1920]).

We shall take all, we shall know all,
We shall pierce the depths to the bottom.
And drunk is the vernal soul
Like May, golden with blossoms.

To proud daring there is no limit,
We are Wagner, Leonardo, Titian.
On the new museum we shall build
A cupola like that of Montblanc.

In the crystal marbles of Angelo,
In all the wonder of Parnassus,
Is there not the song of creative genius
That like an electric current throbs in us?

Orchids were cultivated,
Cradles of roses were swung:

Translated by George Z. Patrick, in *Popular Poetry in Soviet Russia* (Berkeley: University of California Press, 1929), p. 209.

Were we not in Judea
When love was taught by Christ?

We laid the stone of the Parthenon,
And those of the giant pyramids;
Of all the Sphinxes, temples, Pantheons
We have cut the clanging granite.

Was it not for us that on Mount Sinai,
In the burning bush,
The Red Banner glowed, like the sun,
Amid storm and fire.

We shall take all, we shall know all,
We shall pierce the turquoise of the skies;
It is so sweet to drink on a blossoming day
From the life-giving showers.

The War of Kings
(1918)

THIS ANTIWAR PAMPHLET, ISSUED BY THE COMMISSARIAT OF EN-LIGHTENMENT IN 1918, USED THE POPULAR TRADITIONS OF WOODCUT GRAPHICS (*LUBOK*) AND CARNIVAL VERSE (*RAEK*) TO DELIVER A MESSAGE ABOUT THE MONARCHICAL NATURE OF WAR AND THE SOLIDARITY OF COMMON PEOPLE AGAINST WAR — ALL IN REFERENCE TO THE STILL-RAGING EUROPEAN WAR OF 1914–1918.

Voina korolei, text by Iu. L. Obolenskaia, drawings by Iu. L. Obolenskaia and K. V. Kandaurov (Moscow: Teatral'nyi otdel Narkomprosa, 1918).

Come and hear this tale of cards,
That happened out in the big city—
A city decked out in spades and diamonds,
They'll be nothing new to you.
This here is a big-time king,
His role's the most important thing.

And this here fancy lady
Is the queen of the deck,
And this is the jack of-all-trades.
They've been around for centuries,
For every one of these dashing faces,
There's at least two number cards.

Here you see a whole stack of 'em,
They'd also like to be face cards,
But the most amazing tale of all,
Is that up till now they had no faces!
The dirty deuce, ditch-digger three,
Four and six gnaw dried breadsticks,
Seven and eight just flew the coop,
Nine and ten don't fast just on Lent.
Here comes comrade Petrushka
With his ears pricked up—
He listens to all the gossip,
Hears what they're up to,
He doesn't like to be stuck

Like a monk inside four walls.
And it's not like him at all
To say the same thing over again,
What ya didn't used to be able to say
Just seems funny when you say it today,
And tomorrow it'll be twice as funny.
You can listen to it bug-eared,
Or don't listen, if you like.
It's not the mansions that Petrushka
Tours with his sly tongue,
But he sends his words of wisdom
Over to the servants' wing.

Good day, respected public,
And the entire R.S.F.S. Republic!!!
It's me, Comrade Petrushka—
Your most uppity puppet!
I never palled around with rich folk,
Never made friends in palaces and
    mansions.
I mucked around in the back alleys,
And slipped through the back doors.
Back gates and sly words ain't safe!

For the first time, before you here
    today,
I'm telling a tale in my own words,
Brought to you by a free man,
How in a deck known to us all
All the kings lost hold of their crowns,
All the cardboard thrones were
    knocked down,
And all the houses of cards blown
    around.
All us Petrushkas are comics;
But when I hung it out for airing,
Then I felt even more merry!

I, the King of Spades,
Am not used to being crowded:
I want to rule a worldwide tsardom,
To be called the King of Trumps,

And to be tsar of all the planet,
And make the other tsars serve me,
And all the other suits
Would be under my boot!

The letter of the King of Spades:

Listen up, King of Diamonds,
You whose deck is new!
I declare war on you,
And occupy your land.

The King of Spades has schemed
To prop up his throne of bast
By splitting up my deck
And attacking my freedom.

But I'll cut him quite a caper:
Get all the diamonds up in arms
From the two up to the ten—
He'll scram without looking back.

Finally it's safe,
We can throw off our masks!
Madam, my lady,
How can I serve you?

Strike a chord up, balalaika,
I am now the mistress here—
A lady, a lady!
Now I'm my own mistress!

Farewell, girls, farewell, wenches,
We're not ready for you right now,
We're not ready for you right now,
They're herding us into the army!

Oh, you, Vanya,
You are such a dashing boy!
How far away
Will you be when you go off?
And who is it
That you're leaving me for, dear?

Spade: I will win a greater glory
When I pierce you with my spade.
Diamond: Ow, ow, ow, King of Hearts,
Step lively now and help me out!
I, a Red King, have been your
Ally from time immemorial.
Hearts: Together, we'll put the King of
    Spades
Between a rock and a hard place.

Spade: Ow, ow, ow, he fights like a lion:
Help me out, King of Clubs!
Club: Oh, sire, King of Spades,
Please release me from this war:
I have no gun, just this staff,
And on the staff my cross of clubs.

Hey, hey, stop, hold still,
That's what "our mighty foes" do.

I'm old, I shouldn't be fighting,
It's the King of Spades that started it.

I gotcha, King of Clubs, you oafish lout,
I'll make it hot for you, so kiss your heart goodbye!

Now I'm gonna stick ya good,
Just like the king says we should.
The king says so, but what of the soldier?
"How do you gain?" "You mean me?"

Hey you soldier, why ya goin'?
Why ya knockin' yourself out?
You'll never make an officer,
You'll have to make your way home
        barefoot!

March forward, forward
Working people!

Hey, he's talking to us!
Why are you looking away?

There's been enough fighting,
It's time we got to work.
We might be diamonds, you might be
    spades,
But we're all simple people.
Let's expel this world's kings,

So they won't bother us no more.
The deck won't be complete,
But then—we'll all be free.
March forward, forward,
Working people.

Spade: So, I'm finished with the hearts
And now your turn has come!
Diamond: Oh yeah? Then why are your
    soldiers
All dancing the trepak?
Just look, even the tens
Are dancing up a storm.
"What, I just don't get it—
We've lost the whole game!"

"It's all your and your wife's fault!"
"No, you and your war!"
"She danced your throne away!"
"No, the war was your undoing!"
But isn't life just a game?
But it wasn't whist we were playing.
We kept our trump cards in our hands,
And left the game all whist-ful.

Send Off: A Red Army Song
Demyan Bedny (1918)

BEDNY (REAL NAME YEFIM PRIDVOROV, 1883–1945) WAS THE
MOST POPULAR AND PROLIFIC OF THE REVOLUTIONARY POETAS-
TERS. HE SPECIALIZED IN MALICIOUS WIT AIMED AGAINST THE
REVOLUTION'S FOES. IN THIS RED ARMY SONG, WRITTEN DURING
A VISIT TO THE FRONT, ONE SEES THE FAMILIAR CONFLICT BE-
TWEEN TRADITIONAL VILLAGE VALUES (ESPECIALLY HOSTILITY
TO ALL RECRUITING) — HERE PRESENTED AS SHORTSIGHTED AND
IGNORANT — AND THE NEW POLITICS OF THE BOLSHEVIKS: TO
SWEEP THE LAND CLEAN OF ALL EXPLOITERS THROUGH COMBAT.
THE POEM WAS PUT TO MUSIC IN 1922, AND BECAME AN UNOFFI-
CIAL THEME OF CADETS OF THE ISPOLKOM MILITARY SCHOOL.

When my mother dear sent me
   Off to the army,
Then my kinfolk also came,
   Came a-running:

"Where are you going to, my lad?
   Where you going?

Vanya, Vanya, please don't go
   Into the army!

"The Red Army has enough
   Bayonets.
The Bolsheviks will get along
   Fine if you're gone.

"Provody," *Bednota,* 15 December 1918, p. 3.

"Are you going because you have to
    Or 'cause you want to?
Vanya boy, you'll be wasted
    For nothing.

"Your dear mother has gone gray
    Pining away for you.
In the fields and your hut there's
    Much to tend to.

"Nowadays things are going
    Mighty fine!
Look at all the land they've heaped
    On us all of a sudden!

"Nowadays there's not a trace
    Of the old hard times.
You'd be smarter off to marry
    With Arina.

"Live with your young wife, and seek
    No idleness!"
Here I parted with my mother,
    Bowed before her.

I bowed low before my kin
    At the threshold:
"Not a whimper from you, please,
    For love of god.

"If we all were scatterbrained
    And gaped like you,
What would happen to Moscow
    And our Russia?

"Things would go back to the old ways,
    Like those bad times.
They would take back what we have:
    Land and freedom;

"The lords would settle on the land
    As cruel masters.
In this nasty cabal's grip
    We'd be howling.

"I'm not going to a dance
    Or a feast,
This is what I leave for you,
    My old mother:

"I am marching off now with
    The Red Army,
Our deadly battle will be with
    Gentry rabble.

"We will give a talking to
    Priests and kulaks:
Our bayonets'll pierce the guts of
    Those bloodsuckers!

"Won't surrender? So you'll die,
    Go to hell then!
Paradise is sweeter when
    It's won in battle,—

"It's not the paradise of drunks
    Or bloodsuckers,—
But Russia, where our freedom reigns,
    A Soviet land!"

Solemn Oath on Induction into the Worker-Peasant Red Army (1918)

THE BOLSHEVIKS DISDAINED RITUALISM AS AN OLD-REGIME SU-
PERSTITION. BUT WHEN TROTSKY CREATED THE RED ARMY FROM
THE RUINS OF THE OLD, HE FOUND THAT RITUALS CONTRIBUTED
TO A BINDING ESPRIT. BELOW IS THE ARMY INDUCTION OATH,
WHICH ECHOED A SIMILAR OATH FROM TSARIST TIMES.

1. I, son of the laboring people, citizen of the Soviet Republic, assume the title of warrior in the Worker-Peasant Army.

2. Before the laboring classes of Russia and the entire world, I accept the obligation to carry this title with honor, to study the art of war conscientiously, and to guard national and military property from spoil and plunder as if it were the apple of my eye.

3. I accept the obligation to observe revolutionary discipline and unquestioningly carry out all orders of my commanders, who have been invested with their rank by the power of the Worker-Peasant government.

4. I accept the obligation to restrain myself and my comrades from all conduct that might debase the dignity of citizens of the Soviet Republic, and to direct all my thoughts and actions to the great cause of liberating the laboring masses.

5. I accept the obligation to answer every summons of the Worker-Peasant government to defend the Soviet Republic from all danger and the threats of all enemies, and to spare neither my strength nor my very life in the battle for the Russian Soviet Republic, for the cause of socialism and the brotherhood of peoples.

6. If I should with malicious intent go back on this my solemn vow, then let my fate be universal contempt and let the righteous hand of revolutionary law chastise me.

Little Apple

(1918)

Traditional four-line folk ditties (*chastushki*) reflected popular understanding during the Civil War. With or without the accompaniment of an accordion, they distilled complex political formulas into direct and pungent images. Based on an old Ukrainian verse, [1]

From *Krasnoarmeiskie pesni* (Moscow: Gos. voennoe izd-vo, 1937), pp. 75–76.

1. Roll, little apple. / Whither you may roll. / Give me in marriage, Papa, / Wherever I may wish.

ЯБЛОЧКО	LITTLE APPLE
Эх, яблочко, Да сбоку зелено, Колчаку за Урал Ходить не велено.	Hey you, little apple, Apple with the spot of green, Kolchak won't be allowed To get beyond the Urals.
Эх ты, прапор молодой, Золоты погоны,— Удирай скорей домой, Пока есть вагоны.	Hey you, ensign boy, With the golden epaulets, Beat it, get your butt on home While there's still a train for it.
Буржуи и кадеты, Гоните миллионы,— Теперь наши Советы, Теперь наши законы.	You bourgeoisie and you Cadets, Go on, take your millions,— Now the Soviets are ours, And the laws are ours too.

The Young Guard

Aleksandr Bezymensky (1918)

BEZYMENSKY (1898–1973) WAS AN ACTIVE AND STURDY PRACTITIONER OF THE "PROLETARIAN" SCHOOL OF SOVIET LITERATURE AND A LIFE-LONG SUPPORTER OF THE REGIME. HE BELONGED TO THE FIRST GENERATION OF POSTREVOLUTIONARY SOVIET POETS, AND HIS "YOUNG GUARD" WAS SET TO MUSIC AND BECAME THE THEME AND RALLYING CRY OF MILLIONS OF KOMSOMOLS.

Comrades in the struggle!
Go forward, meet the dawn,
With bayonets and grapeshot
We'll lay the road ahead.

From *Lirika 20-kh godov*, ed. V. Ia. Vakulenko (Frunze: Kyrgyzstan, 1976), pp. 508–509.

Go forward bravely, keep your step firm,
Loft the ensign of youth on high!
We are the Young Guard
Of the peasants and working class.

We have ourselves experienced
Indentured servitude.
Our youth passed by us unawares,
Ensnared in slavery's net.

We carried chains around our hearts—
The legacy of darkness.
We are the Young Guard
Of the peasants and working class.

Standing by our forges,
And bathing in our sweat,
We created with our work
Wealth for other men.

But that labor in the end
Forged fighters from us all,
Us—the Young Guard
Of the peasants and working class.

We lift high the banner!
Comrades, over here!
Come, you can build with us
The Republic of Laborers.

To make work the master of the earth,
And join us in one family—
To arms! Young Guard
Of the peasants and working class!

Letters from the Eastern Front
Third Letter: The Cruiser *Markin*
Larisa Reisner (1918)

REISNER (1895–1926) — PROTOTYPE FOR THE HEROINE OF VSEV-
OLOD VISHNEVSKY'S FAMOUS PLAY *OPTIMISTIC TRAGEDY* — WAS
BORN IN LUBLIN, POLAND, THE DAUGHTER OF A LAW PROFESSOR.

"Pis'ma s vostochnogo fronta. Pis'mo tret'e," *Izvestiia*, 24 November 1918, p. 2.

SHE WAS EDUCATED IN EUROPE AND RUSSIA, AND BECAME A PO-
LITICAL JOURNALIST FOR THE BOLSHEVIKS. BY ALL ACCOUNTS
SHE WAS A STRIKINGLY BEAUTIFUL WOMAN WITH A TASTE FOR
ADVENTURE. IN THE CIVIL WAR, SHE WAS HEAD OF INTELLI-
GENCE AND ESPIONAGE FOR THE VOLGA FLEET. SHE DIED OF TY-
PHUS IN 1926. THE HIGHLY ROMANTICIZED MEMOIR THAT FOL-
LOWS CAPTURES THE PATHOS OF BATTLE, THE NATURAL BEAUTY
OF THE BROAD RIVER KAMA, A TRIBUTARY OF THE VOLGA, AND
THE SENSE OF ADVENTURE SHARED BY THOSE WHO FOUGHT ON
THIS WATERY BATTLEFRONT.

Every morning the boatswain of the flagship *Twain* reports the Kama River's falling temperature with a satisfied smile. Today the thermometer stopped at one-half
degree Celsius (32° F)—zero degrees in the air. Lonely ice floes move along the
current; the water has become thick and sluggish. On its surface billows a constant
fog heralding frost. Ship crews who fought the long, tough campaign from Kazan
to Sarapul are heading for winter quarters, and with every day they grow cheerier,
anticipating a well-earned rest. Another day and the fleet will leave the Kama until
next spring.

And only now, when the hour of involuntary retreat draws near, does everyone
suddenly realize how these shores conquered from the enemy, every twist in the
river, every mossy spruce clinging to its steep banks have become cherished and
unforgettable.

How many hours of strained waiting, how many hopes and fears—not, of course,
for themselves, but for the great cause whose fate sometimes hung on the accuracy
of a shot or the courage of a scout—how many joyful moments of victory will be
left behind here on the Kama? Ice will cover the unforgiving waters battered by
shells and lined with tall ships; ice will forever conceal the depths that hide the
graves of our finest comrades and fiercest enemies.

Who knows where and whom we'll fight next year, what comrades will ascend the
bridges of these ships, so familiar and dear to each of us.

One of the transports departs for Nizhny Novgorod with a heavy thump of the
paddle, the signal lantern on its mast waving high in the dark.

The remaining ships send their departing comrade off with a wail of sirens that
goes on and on. Each siren is as distinct and recognizable as a friend's voice: the
shrill scream of the *Roshal*, the short, penetrating whistle of the *Volodarsky*, the deep,
deafening roar of the *Comrade Markin*.

Our saddest memories are bound up with this sailors' farewell. It is used by ships
in jeopardy. The unfortunate vessel *Vanya the Communist*, set on fire by an enemy
shell, ablaze with the icy river waters splashing around it, its rudder broken and

telegraph cut off, called for help in this way. How long, how ceaselessly its sirens howled! More and more fountains of water gushed up around it, black dots began flickering on the surface of the water—these were people who had jumped overboard to swim ashore—and the current carried along burning flotsam, some pails and nightstands. And the siren still wailed, shrouded in steam, charred by the fire, that horrible and insane siren of death. Misfortune came strangely and unexpectedly. Just the day before, the fleet won a significant victory over the White flotilla: after a two-day battle near the village of Bitka, the Whites had to retreat up the Kama, but our ships broke through their rear on both banks. The pursuit continued around the clock, and only on the morning of the third day did Raskolnikov's[1] fleet drop anchor in a wonderful stretch of the Kama's amber and sapphire blue waters lit by the clear November sun. It was decided to halt until the arrival of a landing force, because scouts had reported strong coastal defenses near the village of Pyany Bor that could not be taken from the river without infantry support. Furthermore, artillery supplies had been completely exhausted; our ships and barges had only eighteen to sixty shells apiece. While we waited for the marines, who were always late, motor launches went out on reconnaissance. Sailors watched from a distance with satisfaction as the Whites opened an absolutely useless hurricane of fire at the quick, elusive launches' trailing foam. A seven-colored arc shimmered in the pillars of water raised by the shelling, and every minute foamy, snow-white, and playful fountains swelled up and ebbed. A flock of frightened swans flew off a sandbar as a hydroplane buzzed past, and the air was filled with the shrieking of swans, the beating of white wings, and the propeller's bee-buzz.

Markin could not resist. Markin, commander of our finest steamboat, *Vanya the Communist,* was accustomed to danger and enamored of it like a little boy, and he could not just watch that morning's war games. He was tantalized by the high, sandy precipice, by Pyany Bor's mysterious silence, by the edge of the forest and what it concealed, and by the battery hidden onshore and waiting patiently.

Nobody quite remembers how they lifted anchor, how they slipped along the forbidding shore, how they left their moorage far behind. Suddenly very close, practically in front of him, Markin noticed a camouflaged emplacement and motionless gun muzzles aimed right at him. A single ship cannot do battle with a shore battery, but the morning after the victory was so intoxicating, so reckless, that the *Communist* did not retreat, did not hide, but drew defiantly close to shore, chasing the battery crew away from its weapon with a machine-gun. We sing the glory of valorous folly! But this time, fate did crown the exploit with success.

The minelayer *Nimble* came to the aid of the *Communist.* One might not believe in portents, but my God, everyone on the *Nimble* bridge was seized by gnawing worry. It was not fear—no one succumbed to that vile disease—but a special, singular, somehow oppressive anticipation that I have experienced only once, when the unsuspecting minelayer approached the *Communist.*

---

1. Commander of the Red Fleet and Reisner's husband.

A brief ship-to-ship communication was Markin's last. Comrade Raskolnikov asked by megaphone: "Markin, who are you shooting at?"

"The battery."

"What battery?"

"That one there, behind the trees; you can see its muzzles shining."

"Turn back at once!"

But it was too late. Hardly had the minelayer begun its furious retreat, hardly had the *Communist* begun to follow, when the Whites onshore, sensing that their catch was slipping away, opened a withering barrage. Shells poured down like hail. Port, starboard, and bow—all around the ship. They flew over the bridge with a deafening howl, rolling through and shattering the air like bowling balls. After several minutes the *Communist* was enveloped by a cloud of steam lit by a dancing and leaping golden tongue, and it tacked from shore to shore with a broken rudder. That was when the siren began wailing for help.

Despite the terrible artillery barrage, we turned back to the sinking ship, hoping to take it in tow and pull it to safety, as we had done for the *Tashkent* near Kazan. But there are conditions under which even the utmost bravery is powerless: the very first shell snapped *Vanya the Communist*'s steering hawser and telegraph antenna. The rudderless ship turned around in circles, and the minelayer, which approached at supreme danger to itself, could not take the dying ship in tow.

The *Nimble* made a sharp turn and had to sail away. Why the Whites let us get away is incomprehensible. They were firing pointblank, and only the minelayer's amazing speed and the barrage of its gun got it out of the trap. Oddly, two large seagulls flew right across the nose of the ship, not fearing the barrage, disappearing every minute behind the splashes of another shell. Among those saved was Comrade Poplevin, Markov's assistant. A quiet type, extraordinarily modest and brave, one of the fleet's finest, his face was pale to the point of blue for a long time after. Death's traces were particularly visible on him when the autumn sky was cloudless and bright, and the placid waters lapped against the ship. He paid the price for the loss of his friend and his ship. That night, when even the strongest had tired, Poplevin silently mounted the bridge and, alone beneath the starry sky, watched and listened, anticipating the night's slightest movement. His sacred vengeance never tired or weakened.

They waited for Markin all night. But Markin never returned, and they grieved for him, standing by the rudder: the silent helmsmen, the gunnery mates, sentinels by spyglasses that had become damp and murky from unshed tears.

Markin, with his fiery temperament, his sensitive, almost animal nose for the enemy, his savage will power and Viking pride, was a paragon of that class of people gifted with brilliant intuition and brilliant instincts.

In good and evil, in feverish creative work, in merciless annihilation; in the singularity of his powerful personality and its extraordinary range; in his isolation, almost alienation, from people; and in the foolish inclination to self-sacrifice that drove him to heroism "for everyone and every cause": this man remained forever larger than life, a force of nature, unbreakable.

And so *Vanya the Communist* had sunk, Markin had perished, the minelayer's cannon had almost no shells left, and the promised marines had still not arrived. At dusk on board the motor launch, the canvas was lifted from four long, dark objects laid side by side.

The flagship navigator, the captain, and the minelayers consulted a map for a long while, and when they came out of the cabin, they shook the hands of those leaving with a special firmness. Raskolnikov escorted four sailors and officers on deck, and in several minutes a destroyer loaded with "fish"-type mines was hidden by the island.

When it returned in the early morning, the long black mines resembling bewhiskered buckets were not to be seen on the poop deck. The only thing left was to wait patiently. And sure enough, on the next day the Whites, having celebrated the sinking of the *Communist* with a bacchanalia, went over to the attack. They came in a line ahead, with high pomp, as if on parade. Admiral Stark himself, commander of the White fleet, participated personally in the operation for the first time. He hoisted his flag on the *Eagle*. But drawing level to Green Island, the ceremonial parade came to a halt. The cruiser *Labor*, which sailed at the head of the formation, suddenly stood up, and its nose literally tore free from the body: the mines had done their job.

Now the charred and ruined hulls of two ships, *Vanya the Communist* and the White Guard *Labor*, lay almost side by side on the frozen banks of the Kama. And who knows, perhaps on the dark riverbed beneath the impenetrable surface of the river, the current has washed together Markin and the wretches who shot his drowning crew with machine-guns. Who can know? Leaving the Kama, perhaps forever, it was hardest of all to leave and forget the close-knit family of sailors. Nothing unites people so firmly as dangers shared, sleepless nights on the bridge, and those enduring exertions of the will and spirit, excruciating but unnoticeable from the outside, that prepare and make possible the long-awaited victory.

History cannot record or judge the true merit of the exploits great and small performed daily by the Volga fleet's sailors. Nor will it likely note the names of those who helped create the new navy with their ability to accept the discipline of volunteers and comrades, their fearlessness and self-effacement.

Of course, history is not made by individuals, but Russia has had so few great people and characters, and they have had to beat their way through a thicket of old and new bureaucratism—so much so that they have rarely found themselves in a true and testing battle instead of a battle of paper and words. And now there are such people, human beings, in the highest sense of the word, which means that Russia is healing itself and gathering its strength.

There are more than a few of them. In the places I had the chance to observe, there were many. They emerged from the general mass in crucial moments; they all showed themselves to be twenty-four-carat gold. They knew their heroic craft and raised the fickle and pliant masses to their own level.

How sadly I remember them now, and how alive they seem to me in Moscow, with its labyrinth of institutions, names, and ambitions. How I want to return to them, from Moscow's talk to their action, from the battle for political posts to the supreme endeavors of people who fear neither death nor disfigurement.

There is calm, laconic Eliseev, a wonderful gunner who can pick off a small boat with a long-range gun at a distance of eight miles, with his blue, lashless eyes, burned by a powder flash, that are always looking somewhere far in the distance.

There is Babkin, huge and always in a lather, with drunken eyes, who perhaps has little time left to live, and who squanders the treasures of his kind, carefree, and incomprehensibly staunch spirit like a tsar; it was he who laid out the minefield that blew up the Whites' mightiest cruiser, the *Labor.*

How many more names I could name, how many more deeds I could number.

For the Cause of the Red Soviets

A one-act play by Pavel Arsky (1919)

ARSKY, ONE OF THE ORIGINAL STORMERS OF THE WINTER PALACE, WAS A DRAMATIST WITH THE PETROGRAD PROLETKULT. THIS SHORT AGITATIONAL PIECE WAS USED IN PETROGRAD AND IN THE ARMY TO BUILD MORALE, DISCOURAGE DESERTION, AND CLARIFY THE EVIL NATURE OF THE ENEMY. NOTICE HOW THE AUTHOR GIVES THE WHITE COMMANDER A GERMANIC NAME, THROWS IN SOME ANTIRELIGIOUS MATERIAL, EXPOSES TRADITIONAL RUSSIAN PEASANT FATALISM, AND HAS THE MURDERED GRANDFATHER BARE HIS CHEST TO THE BULLETS — A DEVICE USED LATER AND MORE FAMOUSLY IN DOVZHENKO'S CLASSIC FILM *ARSENAL*.

CHARACTERS

Nikifor Rusanov, a Communist
Darya, his wife
Tanya, his sister
Agafon, his grandfather
Fekla, the Rusanovs' neighbor
Grabbe, a White Guard lieutenant
Zykov, a White Guard ensign

Mukhranov, a White Guard sergeant-major
First White Guard soldier
Second White Guard soldier
First Red Army man
Second Red Army man
Third Red Army man

"Za krasnye sovety. P'esa v odnom deistvii," *Pervye sovetskie p'esy* (Moscow: Iskusstvo, 1958), pp. 487–498.

A hut. Doors to the left and right. In the middle a large Russian stove. Agafon is on the stove. A table against the wall to the left. Tanya sits at the table and sews, quietly singing to herself.

Darya enters.

DARYA: Well, they fell asleep. Grisha kept asking when his father is coming home.

TANYA: He misses his father. He spoiled them pretty bad.

DARYA (*sighing*): I don't even know anymore if my Nikifor is coming back. He could be killed on the front... maybe he's dead already.

TANYA: That's enough now. Where did that come from? Nowadays everyone can get killed in the war.

DARYA: Whoever has luck gets to live. My man was always hotheaded, though. Whenever they go into battle, he's never left behind, he always has to be first. That's the sort of man I have, Tanya, brave and daring.

TANYA: Enough of bravery now. My Semyon, get this, hasn't written me for a month. Maybe something's happened to him too. Then we won't get married.

DARYA: All right now, our brave falcons will come back. Not everyone gets killed. You say so yourself. Maybe our men were born under a lucky star; we can't know in this world, maybe they'll return safe and sound.

TANYA: I don't believe that anymore. You wait and wait, and every once in a while something in your heart seems to snap—you're unhappy and the world seems all bad.

DARYA: So be a little merrier! Look at me: when I get up and set to work, time goes by so quickly you don't notice, and soon news from our men will come, and then they'll come themselves.

TANYA: But when? Not soon. Ours are retreating, and soon those people will come, may they rot. When they find out that your Bolshevik was boss of our soviet and even the chairman, you're a goner. Mark my words, my heart tells me misfortune will befall us.

DARYA: Nothing of the sort. Your fears are for nothing. How far from here to the station? Over a hundred versts! They'll never make it this far. And what haven't they seen here?

TANYA: Our village kulaks are furious at your man and everyone who sat on the soviet. When they heard that the Whites are coming, they celebrated, and when the soviet left town, they said: "Our people won, we'll show them." They'll vent their anger.

DARYA: Come now, they're people, not animals. Why would they kill my children and me? Are we guilty of anything?

TANYA: They're capable of anything. They're nasty as hounds. They don't like it when everyone can live live well and justly. They used to pillage and steal, and here they're under someone else's thumb, all the land has been made collective. Whatever harvest we don't need goes to the state. The new stuff isn't to their liking, and now they'll do whatever they want with us.

DARYA: Tanya, you're going overboard. Only your fears don't scare me; it's good that the night is so dark and thick. (*She looks through the window.*) The dogs are barking somewhere, like somebody's teasing them.

TANYA (*worried*): And...

DARYA: They're quiet now. It's all right, everything will turn out okay.

TANYA: But there's a pain in my heart. It hurts so I don't know. It's never hurt so bad.

DARYA: What's with you, girl, when did you become so sour and teary, like there was a dead man in the house? You should be ashamed. It's certainly not Grandpa Agafon—are you planning to die, to travel to the next world?

TANYA: Enough of that, I won't. (*She sews quietly.*) After lunch, Priest Nifont walked by our hut. He nodded his head in our direction and laughed. He shook his little goat beard, the redheaded scum, and he was with the old elder, paunchy as a fattened boar. When he looked at us he oinked and giggled. Watch out!

DARYA: Get outta here. Look there, Grandpa Agafon's all upset; he can't take your moaning and groaning.

AGAFON (*looking down from the stove*): Crickets! You could have given me some water to drink. And here all you do is chirp, chirp, like magpies.

TANYA: Right away, Grandpa. You shouldn't be getting yourself riled up, you're old and weak. It's bad for you, especially before you go to sleep.

AGAFON: I said give me something to drink, you cricket!

TANYA: It's coming. I'm running as fast as I can, Grandpa.

AGAFON: And what of it? Ah, now that's running, Cricket.

TANYA (*giving him the water*): Take it, Grandpa, drink to your health!

AGAFON: I'll drink it. There now, that's better. For that you deserve a good husband to provide for you. (*He drinks the water and gives the dipper back.*) Oh you—you cricket. It's time you went to sleep. (*He covers himself on the stove.*)

TANYA (*laughing*): Grandpa Agafon is rushing off to sleep again. And whenever the old man is going to sleep he starts cursing.

DARYA: And pretty good too. (*Agafon grunts on the stove.*) Shhh. He'll hear you and get mad.

TANYA: At you and me? Don't we do our best to please him? He's well fed and warm here. You'd think he had something to complain about.

DARYA: I know you're right. It's just he's awfully touchy. (*She pricks her ears.*) What's that? Like somebody's knocking. So it is. Go and open the door.

TANYA: God save you. What do you mean? And what if it's them. They've arrived in our village.

DARYA: So what? They won't hurt you and me. What did we do to them? My husband and your fiancé are fighting them, but we're just women. They won't kill us because of them.

TANYA: Just you watch. I'm telling you: something bad's going to happen. Okay, let's go open the door anyway. You can't have two deaths, you'll die from the first.

They go out to the entryway. Darya's voice: "Who's there?" Fekla's voice: "It's me, dear neighbors. Me... open up. Hurry. Wait till you hear what I have to tell you." *Darya's voice:* "What's with you, Fekla? You're not at all yourself." *They all come into the hut together.*

DARYA: So tell us what happened, tell us about it.

FEKLA *(frightened):* Oh, don't ask me, my loved ones. I don't know what we can do.

DARYA: What is it, tell us!

FEKLA: It's them... the Whites... in the village... Shooting, killing. My little boy was at Sofronikha's. He came running, says they're whipping her for some unknown reason. You could hear the screaming all over the village, didn't you hear?

TANYA: There you are, what did I tell you?

DARYA: Hold on, wait a minute. Why would they want to beat her?

FEKLA: I don't know. Her husband's in the Red Army. It's probably for that. Oh Lord! They'll beat us too. They'll come here too, no doubt. They'll probably take us with them, give us a good beating then flog us to death. We should have left with our own side instead of staying.

DARYA: Fekla, dearest! How can that be? It's impossible.

FEKLA: My boy saw it with his own eyes. He got out between the soldiers' legs. They didn't notice him. It was too dark.

DARYA: What is this. Are they men or beasts?

FEKLA: Beasts, they're beasts. We'd better flee to the barn, or into the woods.

DARYA: Come now, Fekla. I can't believe they'd touch us. What for?

FEKLA: Oh, I see we can't do anything with you. Well, as you wish. I'll flee by myself, with my boy. I'm scared of those devils worse than death. Oh you, my loved ones, poor little girls... Nobody is going to stand up for us.

TANYA: And God? Will he allow it?

FEKLA: I don't know. I don't know. Well, I'm off to hide. I'll run farther than you can see. Into the cold... Better to freeze outside in the snow than to fall into their mitts. Farewell. (*She runs off.*)

TANYA: God, what can we do? What can we do?

DARYA: Quiet! Don't worry. You'll wake up the children.

TANYA: I'm scared, Darya, I'm scared.

DARYA: So be it. What's with you anyway?

TANYA: You're husband's a Bolshevik, they'll take their revenge on us. Mark my words!

DARYA: Oh you, you're getting worked up over nothing. Everything will be all right.

TANYA: We should have gone with Fekla.

DARYA: You think they wouldn't have found us if we ran? Whatever is going to happen will happen. You can't avoid your fate. (*She sits down on a bench.*) I'm only sorry for the children if something happens... What are we doing? We should be ashamed, we'll wake Grandpa up again.

AGAFON *(poking his head out):* What are you doing out there? You give a man no peace. Crickets.

DARYA: Sleep, grandpa, sleep! We woke you up. Tanya and I were arguing. Sleep, we won't do it anymore.

AGAFON: Yikes, there's no peace with you around. I'll give you... Crickets. (*He covers himself on the stove.*)

DARYA: Somehow I can't believe it. Our people left only a week ago. Could they really get here so quickly? No, something's not right.

TANYA: They'll come, you'll see, if not now then later. Well, whatever is fated to be will be.

DARYA: So it is. Shouldn't we go to sleep? We'll get up early tomorrow.

TANYA: You lie down, I'll sit here a bit longer after the fire's gone out. I can't sleep.

DARYA: As you like. Wouldn't it be better to lie down than to grieve for nothing? Too many thoughts make your head ache and your heart dry up. Go to sleep. I'm going.

TANYA: May God give you rest! Go, I'll put the flame out. (*She extinguishes the light.*) No, wait, wait... voices... So it is. (*A knock is heard.*) They're knocking. Holy Mother of God, save us. Darya! Don't open the door. It's them. It's those beasts.

DARYA: Hold on, calm down. Quiet! If we don't open it they'll break the door down.

A knock on the window is heard. A voice: "Hey, who's there? Wake up, open the door! If you don't we'll break it down."

TANYA: Darya, dear. What should we do?

DARYA: We should go and open the door for them. Don't be frightened of nothing. (*She goes into the entryway.*)

TANYA: No, no, I won't let you do it. Let them break in like thieves. We won't let them in.

DARYA: They'll only get madder, let them in!

TANYA: No, I won't do it.

The outer entry-door falls in with a crash, and Zykov and Grabbe rush into the hut with lanterns in hand, wearing golden epaulets, holding lashes. With them are Mukhranov and two soldiers.

GRABBE: Aha! You lousy maggots, why don't you open the door? Well, answer me! (*He waves his whip. Darya and Tanya run into a corner. He chases after them, grabs Tanya, and tosses her on the floor.*) Who's your husband, where is he?

TANYA: I don't have a husband. I do have a fiancé. Who is he? A Red soldier on the front. Didn't you know?

GRABBE: Aha, there you are. (*He hits her with his whip. Then he turns to the soldiers.*) Hey you, take her away.

They lead Tanya off.

DARYA: Hangman, you damned monster. Why did you do that to her?

GRABBE: Aha, now it's your turn to talk. You God-damned doll! So tell us, where is your chairman of the friggin' soviet? Speak up or I'll bloody that mug of yours. Where is he?

DARYA: He left. A week ago. Where he went I don't know.

GRABBE: He messed things up and took off. Okay, where's the booty? Step lively, show us!

DARYA: I have nothing. What do you want from me?

GRABBE: We'll show you what we want. (*He tries to enter the door to the right.*)

DARYA (*shielding the door with her body*): I won't let you in. Monsters! Villains! The children are there—my children. You can kill me, but don't touch them! Don't you dare touch them, the poor little things!

GRABBE: A treasure of slight value, but we can use them to find out about many things. So, away from the door! Hey, Mukhranov, get her out of here!

MUKHRANOV: Plague of a wench. (*He moves to strike her with his bayonet.*)

Darya leaps to the side in horror.

GRABBE (*going through the door to the right with Zykov*): Let's take a look at the pups.

Children's frightened shouts and crying are heard.

DARYA: Damn you. Let me go. Pray to Jesus. Damned, damned monsters, what will they do with them? Lord. (*She goes through the door to the right.*)

AGAFON (*looking down from the stove cautiously*): Hey you, soldier. What is that you're doing? It's not godly. Stop it, I tell you. How can you, you damned robber?

MUKHRANOV (*yelping drunkenly*): You old dog. Hey, wait a minute (*aims his rifle at Agafon*).

AGAFON: What are you doing? The Lord will punish you for it.

MUKHRANOV: Take this (*clicks the rifle bolt*).

AGAFON: Really, now, what are you doing? Oh you, you tin soldier (*climbs down from the stove*). What is this—going to war with women? You murderers.

MUKHRANOV: Hey, hold your tongue, you old sod!

AGAFON: True enough that I'm old. Hard work made me old. I labored since I was little, earned bread for myself and my children with the sweat of my brow, lived honestly, did nobody harm. Not like you, beasts. Why did you come, what do you need, you damned devils?

MUKHRANOV: Shut up, I'll kill you.

AGAFON (*tearing the collar of his shirt open*): Here, kill me! I'm not afraid. You slob, you robber!

Grabbe and Zykov come back in.

GRABBE: What's going on?

MUKHRANOV: This old guy's playing soldier. Kicking up a real storm. (*He goes through the door to the right.*)

GRABBE: What are you doing, you old snake?

AGAFON: You should be ashamed of yourself. What are you doing—you've forgotten God! The things you're doing.

GRABBE: So, what else do you have to say?

AGAFON: That it's bad. I have to defend my family. What did you do with my granddaughter? You scared the children. Tyrants!

GRABBE: Do you see this? (*shows his revolver*)

AGAFON: I'm not afraid, I'm not afraid. For justice... I'll go anywhere. To my death... I'm not afraid.

GRABBE: So get over there, closer to the wall.

AGAFON (*stands by the wall, baring his chest*). Shoot! Shoot! I'm not afraid to die for the working people, for the red Soviets.

GRABBE: You dog. Take that! (*He shoots.*)

AGAFON (*falls with a moan*): Lord forgive me, have mercy.

GRABBE: We should burn out this nest. The Communist will be happy. We've rewarded his services.

> *Outside the door to the right, shouts and struggling are heard. Mukhranov's voice behind the door:* "Here you get it. I'll give you a holiday!" *Darya's voice:* "Oh, oh, save me. Help! They're killing me!"

(*Through the door*) Put those glasses on her, Mukhranov!

> *Mukhranov enters.*

MUKHRANOV (*smirking maliciously*): They're on.

ZYKOV: Now that was really a fine piece of work. The Cheka won't forget our deeds. Ha ha ha!

GRABBE: Yes. We have to burn this rotten den down. Wipe it from the face of the earth, so not a trace is left.

ZYKOV: We should burn the whole village, except for a couple of our people and the house where the priest lives.

GRABBE: So we shall. These bums will remember us for a long time.

> *The hammering of a machine-gun is heard in the distance.*

What's that? Oh, impossible.

> *A drum roll, the bugler's trumpet, the march of attack.*
> *A soldier runs in.*

SOLDIER: It's the Red Army.

> *The White-Guardists run out of the hut. Shots close by. Soon Rusanov enters with the Red soldiers, who carry Tanya in unconscious.*

RUSANOV: We're late. Damn! The murderers. Beasts! But where are they, where are my wife and children? They didn't?.. No... I'm scared just thinking. (*He runs through the door on the right.*)

RUSANOV'S MUFFLED CRY: Children. My children. You!.. What did they do to you!

(*Runs in*) Comrades, how is it possible? They're just not human. Beasts! Beasts. They... They even blinded her before they killed her. Damn them! (*Deep sobs*)

Red Soldiers come into the room on the right and quickly return, struck by what they have seen. Their eyes sparkle with rage.

RUSANOV (*standing up*): Comrades, we shall take vengeance on them for their atrocities. We shall take vengeance for the sufferings and torments of our close ones, our brothers who died in this terrible and unequal struggle with the enemies of the Revolution, with the enemies of poor people's power. We shall take vengeance for all the blood spilled by many thousands of innocent victims. There will be no pity or mercy for the malicious enemy. Before the spirits of all those executed and tormented, we vow not to lay down our arms until we have destroyed the enemies of Soviet power, until we smash and conquer the enemies of labor, the enemies of freedom. Let's swear, comrades!
RED SOLDIERS: We swear.
RUSANOV: Comrades, we may die, but we shall be victorious. Long live the Commune!
RED SOLDIERS: Long live Soviet power! Long live Comrade Lenin!

Curtain.

Toward a World Commune
Scenario (1920)

DURING THE REVOLUTION AND CIVIL WAR, PETROGRAD WAS THE SCENE OF NUMEROUS OUTDOOR PAGEANTS AND SPECTACLES IN WHICH THE BOLSHEVIKS ATTEMPTED TO MOBILIZE THE MASSES THROUGH MYTHIC VERSIONS OF REVOLUTIONARY HISTORY. THIS DOCUMENT IS THE SCENARIO FOR A MASS SPECTACLE PERFORMED JULY 19, 1920, IN PETROGRAD FOR THE SECOND

From P. Kerzhentsev, *Tvorcheskii teatr* (Moscow: Gosizdat, 1923), pp. 140–142.

CONGRESS OF THE THIRD (COMMUNIST) INTERNATIONAL OR
COMINTERN. NOTE THAT IT MAKES THE BOLSHEVIKS HEIRS TO
THE WORLD REVOLUTIONARY MOVEMENT.

PART I

Scene 1: Communist Manifesto

The kings and bankers who rule the world erect a monument to their own power, the power of capital, with workers' hands. Above, the bourgeoisie's sumptuous celebration; below, workers' forced labor. The laboring masses produce a group of leaders, founders of the First International. The Communist Manifesto. Clearly visible are the words "Workers have nothing to lose but their chains, but they have the whole world to win." "Workers of the world, unite!"

Only a small group of French workers answer the call to battle. They fling themselves into an attack on the capitalist stronghold. The forward ranks are met by shots and fall. The commune's red banner flies. The bourgeoisie flees. Workers seize its throne and destroy the monument to bourgeois power. The Paris Commune.

Scene 2: The Paris Commune and the Death of the First International

The Communards celebrate a merry holiday. Workers dance the *Carmagnole,* a dance created by the Great French Revolution. The Paris Commune decrees the foundations of a socialist order. New danger. The bourgeoisie gathers strength and sends the legions of Prussia and Versailles against the First Proletarian Commune. The Communards build barricades, defend themselves bravely, and perish in unequal battle, never aided by the workers of other nations still unconscious of their class interests. The victors shoot the Communards. Workers remove their fallen comrades' bodies and hide the trampled Red Banner for future battles. Women weep over their dead. The funereal black curtain of reaction envelops the fragments of the Paris Commune.

PART II

The Second International

The Reaction. The bourgeoisie triumphantly celebrates its victory. Below reigns the forced labor of workers. Above, the leaders of the Second International, socialist compromisers, noses buried in books and newspapers.

Nineteen-fourteen and the call to war. The bourgeoisie shouts: "Hurrah for the war. Death to the enemy." The working masses murmur: "We don't want blood." Their indignation grows. Again the red banner flies. Workers pass the banner from hand to hand and try to present it to the Second International leaders.

"You are our leaders. Lead us!" shout the masses. The pseudo-leaders scatter in confusion. Gendarmes, the bodyguards of the bourgeoisie, exult and tear the hated Red Banner apart. The horror and moans of workers.

The prophetic words of the people's leader[1] break the funereal silence: "As the banner has been rent asunder, so shall workers' and peasants' bodies be torn by war. Down with war!" A traitorous shot strikes the tribune. Triumphant imperialists propose voting for war credits. The Second International leaders raise their hands after a moment's hesitation, grab their national flags, and split the once unified mass of the world proletariat. Gendarmes lead workers away in different directions. The shameful end of the Second International and the beginning of fratricidal world war.

PART III

The Russian Commune

Scene I: World War

The first battle. The enthroned tsarist government of Russia herds long rows of bleak greatcoats to war. Wailing women try to hold departing soldiers back. Workers, exhausted by starvation and excessive labor, join the women's protest. Wounded are brought back from the front, and invalids crippled by war pass by.

The workers' patience is over. Revolution begins. Automobiles, bristling with bayonets, charge by flying red banners. The crowd, swept away by revolutionary wrath, topples the tsar, then stops dead in amazement. Before the crowd stand the new lords: the ministers of the Provisional Government of appeasers. They call for a continuation of the war "to a victorious conclusion" and send the workers into attack. Workers launch another courageous blow supported by an unstoppable stream of soldiers returning from the front, and sweep the appeaser government away. Above the victorious proletariat flares the Second Commune's red banner with emblems of the Russian Socialist Federated Soviet Republic, the hammer and sickle and slogans from the Declaration of Workers' Rights: "All power to the Soviets," "The Factories to the Workers," and "Land to the People."

Scene 2: Defense of the Soviet Republic—the Russian Commune

Having shed their weapons, workers and soldiers want to begin building a new life. But the bourgeoisie does not want to accept the loss of its supremacy, and begins an embittered fight with the proletariat. The counterrevolution meets with temporary success, manages to crush the unarmed workers, and the Commune is saved only by a great surge of heroism of the worker Red Guard. Foreign imperialists send the Russian White Guard and mercenaries into battle against the Soviet Republic. The danger increases. Workers answer their leaders' summons "To arms!" by creating the Red Army. Fugitives from areas razed by the Civil War appear. They are followed by workers from the crushed Hungarian Soviet Republic. The blood

---

1. A reference to Jean Jaurès, antiwar French socialist assassinated at the outset of the war.

of Hungarian workers calls for revenge. Welcomed by the people, lit by beams of the Red Star, the Red Army leads the heroic battle for Hungarian and Russian workers, and for workers of the whole world.

Red labor befits the Red Army: it battles against the dislocations of war. The Communist *subbotnik*.[2] Allegorical female figures representing proletarian victory rally workers of the world to the Third International's banner for a final and decisive battle against world capitalism. The first lines of the workers' hymn.

APOTHEOSIS

The Third International. World Commune

A cannon salvo heralds the breaking of the blockade of Soviet Russia and the world proletariat's victory. The Red Army returns and is reviewed by revolutionary leaders in a ceremonial march. Kings' crowns are strewn at their feet. Festively decorated ships carrying the Western proletariat go by. Workers of the entire world holding labor emblems hurry to the World Commune's holiday. In the sky flare greetings to the Congress in various languages: "Long live the Third International," "Workers of the world, unite."

A public triumphal celebration accompanied by the hymn of the World Commune, the "Internationale."

---

2. A Saturday of voluntary labor.

Mess-Mend
Marietta Shaginyan (1923)

SHAGINYAN (1888–1982) WAS AMONG THE FIRST AND MOST POPULAR SOVIET WRITERS TO COMBINE REVOLUTIONARY THEMATICS WITH POPULAR ADVENTURE IN ORDER TO REACH A WIDE READERSHIP. *MESS-MEND*, A CONTRIVED NAME WITH NO MEANING, CAME OUT AS A THRILLER SERIAL UNDER THE PSEUDONYM OF JIM DOLLAR. THE STORY IS ABOUT A CAPITALIST SCHEME TO UNDERMINE SOVIET POWER AND ABOUT THE RUSSIAN AND AMERICAN WORKER-HEROES WHO FOIL IT. UNDER THE TITLE *MISS-MEND*,

---

Excerpted from Dzhim Dollar, *Mess-Mend*, vyp. 1 (Moscow: Gos. izd-vo, 1924), pp. 15–19.

IT WAS A 1926 MOVIE DIRECTED BY BORIS BARNET AND F. OTSEP AND STARRING THE THEN FAMOUS PLAYERS BARNET, IGOR ILINSKY, AND ALEKSANDR KTOROV. THE PRESENT BRIEF SELECTION GIVES SOME INKLING OF THE POPULAR STYLE AND THE STEREOTYPES USED IN THIS GENRE.

CHAPTER 1

Arthur **Rockefeller**   Meets His Father

One fine morning in May, an automobile careened madly down Riverside Drive.

A young man dressed in white, seated next to a pensive and portly gentleman, shouted into his ear above the wind:

"My stepmother always thinks of me at the last moment. Her telegram has me worried. Just you wait, my father has run into trouble with the Polish loan, or something like that."

"Mister Jeremy is too smart for that, Arthur! There's no cause for alarm," answered the portly gentleman. "And besides, there's nothing unusual in the telegram: they are coming home on the *Torpedo,* and arriving tomorrow. You're overwrought, that's all."

"Hush, Doctor," the young man interrupted him. "Everything my stepmother and her mustachioed daughter initiate ends up in an unpleasant surprise. You know I've always hated women. But after my father's wedding, I hate them two, three, four times as much, and I derive pleasure from every demonstration of their baseness. I would even... I would do anything to trample them down, to defang them, humiliate them, even do away with them entirely!"

"Mister Arthur," laughed the doctor, "you sound delirious. I'm troubled, positively troubled by your love for your father. Filial attachment, of course, is commendable, but to such a degree. Get a hold of yourself."

Halt. The chauffeur took a sharp turn and braked the car. Before them spread Hudson Bay,[1] glittering under the bright sun, fed by thousands of slender canals and creeks. Countless ocean liners sat in the harbor, with their white smokestacks, colorful pennants, and cabin portholes sparkling. A myriad of small boats furrowed the water in all directions.

"The *Torpedo* has already docked," the chauffeur said as he turned to Arthur Rockefeller and the doctor. "We'll have to hurry to make the lowering of the gangplank."

Young Rockefeller leapt from the car and helped his companion out. The portly

---

1. In detective literature, American geography was traditionally cited more for local color than for educational purposes.

gentleman climbed out, huffing and puffing. He was the renowned Doctor Lepsius, an old friend of the Rockefeller family. His small, piercing, parrot-like eyes hid behind glasses; his upper lip was visibly smaller than the lower, and the lower shorter than his chin, which created the impression of a three-step staircase leading straight down from his nose.

As to the young man, he was most pleasant—the sort that was in greatest demand in moving pictures and novels. He was agile, self-assured, well-proportioned, well-built, well-dressed, and evidently not given to excessive hand-wringing. His whitish-blond hair was cut neatly and combed smooth, which did not impede the growth of a stubborn cowlick. Yet something glittered in his eyes that made this "Valentino" stand out from the rest. Mr. Charles Dickens would have directed his readers' attention to this flame as the hint of an ominous character flaw concealed within. However, Mr. Dickens and I belong to different schools of characterization.

And so, both climbed down to the ground and hurried to join the crowd of New Yorkers eyeballing the newly arrived ocean liner.

The *Torpedo,* an enormous ocean liner owned by the Douglass and Burley brothers, constituted a complete city, with its own internal government, warehouses, radio station, corps of engineers, newspaper, sickbay, and theater, its own intrigues and domestic melodramas.

The gangplank was lowered, and passengers began descending to terra firma. They included placid Yankees returning from their distant travels clenching pipes in their teeth and newspapers under their arms, as if only yesterday they had been filling an armchair in the New York Commercial Club. There were invalids who could barely move their limbs, beautiful women seeking their fortune in America, gamblers, world-famous adventurers, and con men.

"How odd!" the doctor hissed through his teeth, as he doffed his hat and bowed low to a robust military gentleman. "How odd to see Prince Hohenloh in New York!"

He was cut short when Arthur exclaimed: "Viscount, how unexpected!" The young man went swiftly toward a handsome dark-haired man, who was limping and leaning on his butler's arm.

"Viscount Montmorency," muttered Lepsius, doffing his hat and bowing yet again, though it went unnoticed. "It's stranger by the hour. What brings them to New York at this time?"

Meanwhile the crowd surging from the gangway separated them for a moment, and Lepsius lost sight of Arthur. The weather changed abruptly. Objects seemed lackluster, as if they had been washed over with ink. The Hudson waters turned a dirty grayish-yellow, accented by wisps of white foam. Seagulls shrieked along the shoreline, hovering in a great host near the wharf. The landing area quickly emptied as all the passengers rode off.

"Where are the Rockefellers?" the doctor asked himself, scanning the wharf. At that moment he spotted Arthur, deathly pale and staring off into space.

An odd procession descended down the deserted gangway. Several people dressed in black were slowly carrying a large zinc coffin draped in black velvet. Behind them walked two ladies pressing handkerchiefs to their eyes. They were dressed in deep mourning, and both were young, slender, and ginger-haired; despite the color of their hair, both had olive-dark complexions. Grief was etched on their faces.

"What does this mean?" whispered Arthur. "There's stepmother and Claire—but where's father?"

The procession moved on. One of the ladies, raising her gaze and spotting young Rockefeller, clasped her hands to her bosom and took a couple of steps in his direction.

"Arthur, my dear, be brave!" she intoned with great dignity.

"Be brave, brother!" exclaimed the second in an unexpectedly low voice, and she also approached Arthur. She was an unusually beautiful girl with two slight flaws: a deep bass voice and dark facial hair.

"Where's Father?" shouted young Rockefeller.

"Arthur, I'm afraid he's right here. Jeremy is here in this coffin. He was murdered near Warsaw."

Miss Elisabeth Rockefeller said this with a trembling voice. She covered her faced and broke out sobbing.

"Brother, let me take your arm," whispered beautiful Claire, hugging the immobile young man.

But Arthur staggered away from them and sank his fingers into the puffy hand of Lepsius.

"Ask them who killed Father," he whispered through bloodless lips.

Lepsius repeated the question.

"I can't now. It's hard for me to talk about it," murmured the widow.

"Why not tell him straight, Mama?" intervened Claire in her masculine bass. "There's no doubt that he was killed by the Bolsheviks."

The funeral procession moved further. Lepsius caught up the faltering Arthur and led him to the car. The dockside emptied, and rain began beating down like the fingers of a skilled typist.

Sputtering and spitting, their broad chests thrust forward, two sailors from the *Torpedo* ambled through the rain toward the docks. They hadn't had the chance yet, but they fully intended to tie one on. Both wore earrings, and their teeth glistened like pearls.

"Ain't no arguing, Dip, you're a dunderhead."

"Shut up, Dan, in my place you woulda clammed up too."

"Aw, git off it."

"I tell ya you'da clammed up."

"For that stupid thing? I wouldn'a even hiccuped!"

"Stupid! I tell ya, I'd sooner be ate up by a shark from my toes to the top of my head than go through that again."

"Through what? Some woman's magic trick?"

"You got it wrong, pal, that's no woman, that's a demon. If you had only seen her blubbering and sweet-talking the captain, and then she looks up dry-eyed and lets out a giggle—like she can't help it. Understand, she thought she was alone, but there I am behind the tarp—then you'd be scared to go out in daylight too."

"Fool, what's so terrifying about that?"

"Fool yourself, you just remember my words."

The rest of the conversation was lost in a stairwell leading down to the *Oceania*, which advertised "Hot food and strong drink especially for sailors." You and I, reader, should not go down there, particularly not at this moment, when, according to my calculations, the first chapter is coming to a close.

The Little Red Devils
P. Blyakhin (1923)

EXCERPTS FROM THE FILM SCENARIO

THE LITTLE RED DEVILS WAS ONE OF THE MOST POPULAR BOX-OFFICE MOVIE SUCCESSES OF THE 1920S, FAR SURPASSING THE CINEMATIC MASTERPIECES OF EISENSTEIN, PUDOVKIN, AND OTHERS IN TICKET SALES. DIRECTOR IVAN PERESTYANI, A VETERAN ACTOR OF PREREVOLUTIONARY TIMES, CAST YOUNG CIRCUS PERFORMERS — INCLUDING A BLACK SENEGALESE SAILOR WHO HAD DESERTED FROM THE FRENCH INTERVENTION FORCES — AS HIS TRIO OF YOUNGSTERS WHO OUTWIT THE ARMIES OF NESTOR MAKHNO IN THE CIVIL WAR. INTERTITLES, THEN USED IN SILENT FILMS, ARE INCLUDED IN THIS TRANSLATION OF THE SCENARIO FOR THE FIRST REEL OF THE FILM.

PART I

A motley detachment pitched camp in a big field next to a thick forest. People wandered among the tents in gaudy dress, riders galloped by at top speed, campfires burned, horses whinnied. Bivouac life seethed by the bonfires, in the tents, and under the shadowy trees.

Somebody was dancing to an accordion, and singing could be heard.

Title: **"HEY, LITTLE APPLE, WHERE ARE YOU ROLLING."**[1]

Excerpted from *Dramaturgiia kino* (Moscow: Tsekhdram, 1935), pp. 25–30, 39–40, 42–48, 50–53.

1. A folk ditty (*chastushka*) popular with Reds during the Revolution. See p. 15.

The camp buzzed like a giant beehive.

By the large gray tent at its center stood a small man girded with cartridge belts, and adorned with a long Caucasian saber in a silver scabbard. This was Ataman Makhno.[2]

Title: **SIRE.**

He was surrounded by a strange and ill-assorted retinue: fur caps sat on most of their heads like haystacks; several wore officers' hats, and some even wore German helmets.

Title: **MAKHNO'S STAFF INCLUDED GERMAN "WILHELMITE" OFFICERS, WHO WERE SAVAGELY OPPOSED TO THE REVOLUTION.**

The rabble crowding around the ataman slavishly listened to his orders.
Makhno stood deep in thought over a map.

*

The tracks of a railroad station were packed with empty cars. Broken locomotives sat on the rails like dead lumps. People swarmed around them.

Title: **DEPOT WORKERS HURRIED TO REPAIR TRAIN STOCK DESTROYED BY THE RETREATING WHITE ARMY. HAMMERS POUNDED, NUTS WERE SCREWED ON, WORK SEETHED.**

Then the whistle blew, announcing a break. Lunchtime.
The railroad workmen broke off work.

An elderly worker repairing a steam engine stopped work too. He slowly climbed out of the cabin. An adolescent, about fifteen years old, jumped to the ground behind him. He wore a torn shirt belted at the waist with a rope.

Title: **MASTER MECHANIC PETROV AND HIS SON MISHKA.**

Mishka was wiry, broad-shouldered, and strong as iron. Wiping their dirty hands with oakum, father and son set off along the railroad's right-of-way.

Reaching the switchman's hut, Mishka sat down on a bench and immediately lost himself in his book.

Title: ***THE PATHFINDER.*[3] JAMES FENIMORE COOPER'S STORY IS MISHKA'S FAVORITE HERO.**

---

2. Ataman means chief. Makhno was an anarchist peasant leader who fought against both Whites and Reds and was demonized in Soviet culture.

3. James Fenimore Cooper's Natty Bumpo (originally in *Last of the Mohicans;* nicknamed Pathfinder in an 1840 novel of that name).

As our hero became absorbed in Cooper's story, his surroundings started to fade away. The train station with its train wrecks disappeared; the machinist's helper in a torn shirt was no longer there. On a lush prairie, somewhere near the river rapids, a man in broad moccasins crawled through the high grass. It was Pathfinder, it was Mishka.

An Iroquois sat hiding in a tree over the river. He was naked and, as wartime customs demanded, painted in death paint. He held a bow and arrows in his hands.

The Indian aimed at Pathfinder when he spied him, but an accurate shot by the fearless Bumpo knocked the redskin from the tree.

Pathfinder threw up his hands in triumph. Suddenly and unexpectedly, laughter rang out close by. It was master Petrov laughing. The prairie, moccasins, and Indians disappeared instantly.

Mishka looked at his father in embarrassment. His father patted him on the shoulder and said:

Title: **OH, YOU READERS. DUNYASHA IS LATE WITH DINNER.**

She's probably reading, too.

And sure enough, a pretty girl, lithe as a steel spring, was slowly walking between two endless freight trains with a book in her hands. Her eyes did not leave the book for a moment. An orphaned bundle of food hung from her hands.

Title: ***THE GADFLY.*[4] VOYNICH'S NOVEL HAS CAPTURED DUNYASHA'S ATTENTION.**

Dunyasha leaned up against a lantern pole and lost herself completely in her reading.

She had a clear picture of Gadfly—the novel's hero—throwing a bomb into a passing automobile and panic-stricken people running from the explosion.

When she finally tore herself away from her book, Dunyasha remembered her father's dinner and lazily trudged off again with the book in her hands.

Title: **IN A NEARBY THICKET.**

The Makhno encampment prepared for a raid. Horses were hastily saddled, and weapons were readied for battle.

The ataman gave his final commands. Jumping on his horse, he drew his sword and gave his troops the signal.

The troops were already mounted.

Spurring his stallion, Makhno galloped around the field: his band hurried after him in a cloud of dust.

---

4. The American Ethel Voynich's *The Gadfly* (1897), a novel of national liberation set in Italy, is an all-time best-seller in Russian to this day, and at the same time a politically correct story of atheism and rebellion.

The frenzied detachment flew across the field and out to the road, and without slackening the pace galloped off down the highway toward a settlement visible in the distance.

In the settlement, Petrov and his son were seated peacefully on a bench waiting for dinner. Mishka continued reading *The Pathfinder.*

Dunyasha finally reached the place where they were. Even then she didn't take her eyes from her book.

Handing the bundle of food to her father, Dunyasha said to her brother:

Title: **GADFLY, FIGHTER FOR FREEDOM, GREETS
COMRADE PATHFINDER.**

This forced Mishka to break off his reading. Looking at Dunyasha, he answered:

Title: **PATHFINDER HAWKEYE GREETS HIS PALEFACE SISTER.**

The adolescents exchanged greetings, sat down together, and buried themselves in their reading again.

Title: **RAID.**

Makhno's band was already rushing along the railway. At the head of the detachment, whooping and brandishing his saber, rode the ataman himself. The band swooped down on the station shooting wildly.

The railroad workers quickly assessed the situation and began to prepare a defense.

Petrov also ran toward the shots firing. Only the frightened Dunyasha hid behind her brother's back.

Title: **LOYALTY TO DUTY.**

The workers took cover behind train wheels and piles of rail ties and shot back at the raiders.

Following the tradition of adventure novels, our young friends rushed off to meet the enemy. Leaping from railcar to railcar, they reached a hot spot of the battle.

The telegraph operator sent off an urgent telegram from the station:

Title: **YANTSOVO, YANTSOVO, YANTSOVO... MAKHNO, MAKHNO,
MAKHNO... HELP, HELP, HELP...**

That was mechanic Petrov's son, brother of our heroes.

Makhno's men raced up to the telegraph office. They leapt through the window and attacked the telegrapher. One of them hit him in the head with a pistol butt and then stomped on him after he fell. Other bandits helped.

Makhno's men wrecked the rail stock. One bandit wearing a German helmet put a stick of dynamite under the engine turnaround loop. From his hiding place on the train, he watched the Bickford fuse burn down and a deafening blast destroy the entire structure.

Meanwhile, our heroes had fled the enemy: a bandit with a pistol was chasing them.

But leaping from car to car, Pathfinder and Gadfly managed to avoid the danger.

The workers were still holding off the raiders. They lay in wait behind railcars, engine tenders, behind every corner.

Old Petrov shot at the bandits from his hiding place in a locomotive.

But the outcome of the unequal fight was preordained by Makhno's numerical superiority.

One of the raiders, noticing Petrov, stole up behind him and shot him point-blank. The wounded machinist clutched his chest and fell from the engine.

In flight from the bandits, Pathfinder and Gadfly jumped from a railroad bridge onto a freight train. Ceaseless running had worn them out. They collapsed, exhausted from their race across the train roofs.

The telegraph operator was brought beaten to the ataman. They dragged him to a spot not far from the tracks where Petrov lay wounded.

Seeing his battered son, Petrov tried to get up and help him, but his strength betrayed him and he fell to the ground in a dead faint.

The telegraph operator was dragged to Makhno. Tossing a brief glance at the prisoner, Makhno ordered:

Title: **SHOOT HIM.**

The telegrapher gathered his strength when he heard this, straightened himself up, and glared at the ataman with disdain...

Title: **HAT OFF. SON OF A BITCH. SHOOT HIM,**

Makhno shouted in a frenzy and stamped his feet.

The bandits fell on the telegraph operator again and dragged him off, barely alive, to be executed.

The raiders continued their wrecking: blowing up engines, breaking switches, ripping up tracks.

The battered telegraph operator was bound to a lantern post.

One of the executioners—the ataman's scribe—mocked the condemned man from atop his horse.

Title: **I SPIT ON YOU, SCUM!**

yelled the telegraph operator, but a Mauser bullet squelched his shout.

The murderer lifted his blue spectacles and laughed. The second executioner chuckled, too.

Pathfinder and Gadfly were still lying on the freight-car roof.

A Makhno horsemen rode by slowly below. He broke into a trot and began to steal alongside the train.

Mishka noticed the bandit stealing by and leapt on him from the roof. They rolled along the ground together.

Makhno's men were still demolishing the station. Setting a steam engine in motion, the man in a German helmet steered it toward a stationary freight train, leapt from the cabin, and fled.

The locomotive approached, gathering speed.

Mishka and his opponent were still struggling. They found themselves between two uncoupled cars. The chugging locomotive bore down on the two cars.

The exhausted Pathfinder could not overcome his opponent. He was visibly weakened. Mishka propped himself against a buffer and weakly warded off the blows.

Meanwhile, the locomotive was almost upon the freight train.

Dunyasha's attempt to help her brother failed, and she staggered away in horror. It seemed Pathfinder's end was near. But at the last moment he shoved his opponent, and both tumbled out from under the cars.

The locomotive smashed into the train. . . .

[The children returned to the station to find their father on the verge of death. Before he dies, they swear to avenge him.]

PART III

Title: **IN TOWN.**

The young dreamers reached a small settlement.

With unconcealed interest, they examined the wax figures topped by various wigs in a barbershop display. The shopkeeper watched these odd customers with a polite smile from behind the counter.

Pointing at the wigs, Mishka says to him:

Title: **MAKE US INTO OLD FOLKS.**

The friendly shopkeeper laid the entire selection of wigs out on the counter. He did not suspect what motives led our heroes to this unusual disguise.

Not far from the barbershop, a barrel organ was playing. The melancholy organ-grinder turned the handle of his simple instrument lazily. A trumpeter played along with him, blowing his horn for all he was worth.

Spectators surrounded the musicians.

Title: **TOM JACKSON, A NEGRO, JUMPED SHIP IN SEBASTOPOL AND BECAME A STREET ACROBAT.**

An acrobat on a small carpet was tumbling to the sounds of the unusual orchestra—the barrel organ and trumpet. Dark as coffee, he performed a variety of gymnastic routines. His mobile, muscular figure was a sharp contrast to the sleepy organ-grinder.

The street-show fans were in ecstasy over Jackson's deft routine.

Meanwhile, Misha and Dunyasha were choosing their disguise. They finally selected long gray beards and settled up with the shopkeeper.

The street show was over: Tom moved among the spectators, cap in hand, and he was paid handsomely for the pleasure he had given them.

Our adventurers left the barbershop. Their successful purchase had put them in excellent spirits. Laughing, they fastened on the beards, and instantly turned into decrepit old folks.

The wandering players had stretched out in a vacant lot. They were splitting the money they had gotten, reaping the fruits of their labors.

Title: **AN UNFAIR SPLIT.**

The organ-grinder was dividing up the profits. Not a trace was left of his drowsiness. He grabbed handfuls of money from Tom's cap. Taking the lion's share for himself, the organ-grinder gave most of the rest to the trumpeter. Tom was left with pennies. The offended Negro demanded his money. Things got tense.

The trumpeter got into the argument. He took the organ-grinder's side and gave Tom a powerful kick in the belly. The unexpected blow flipped Tom head over heels into a ditch, but collecting himself quickly, he snatched a stone from the ground and threw it at the trumpeter. A fight broke out.

A horde of urchins descended on them from nowhere. Without bothering to find out who was right or wrong, they attacked the Negro. Tom was in serious trouble. For all his strength, he could not beat them all.

Unexpected confusion gripped the enemy ranks. Two pairs of strong fists rained down on the urchins with the speed of a hurricane. Our adventurers had jumped into the fray. They foresaw the outcome of the argument and decided to stand up for Tom.

In a minute the gang of urchins had been put to shameful flight, which left only the organ-grinder and trumpeter, smartly beaten by Pathfinder, on the field of battle. The Negro was liberated. Rescued from misfortune, he gratefully shook his saviors' hands.

Title: **AND THUS THE THREESOME CAME TOGETHER DURING DAYS OF UNPRECEDENTED HORROR ON THE FERTILE UKRAINIAN FIELDS. . . .**

[The threesome hops a passing train taking Red cavalry units to the Civil War front. They decide to appeal to the leader, Semyon Budyonny,[5] for the right to join the revolutionary soldiers.]

Title: **THE GLORIOUS LEADER.**

Budyonny was sitting in a small shack. He was talking with an elderly, severe-looking regimental commander. The regimental commander was dressed in a Caucasian costume. He had long, luxurious mustaches which could probably hold a pood[6] weight.

The shack housed the headquarters of Budyonny's cavalry. A telephone operator was transmitting orders without taking his ear from the field phone. Commanders stood nearby.

Title: **BUDYONNY'S MEN.**

The cavalry troops guarding army headquarters had taken up position on the edge of the forest.

Title: **A PICKET.**

Sentries were patrolling a bridge near camp.

The friends, recently arrived from the front, ambled through the scrub.

Reaching the road, they approached the bridge. They looked suspicious in their shaggy wigs and long gray beards. When the sentry noticed the strange company, he shouted:

Title: **HALT, WHO GOES THERE?**

Red soldiers quickly surrounded the travelers. Our heroes were led to the village with their hands in the air.

The commanders and Budyonny were distracted from their work by the footsteps of the approaching group. One of the commanders stepped out of the shack and inspected the old people and the Negro coming toward headquarters.

Title: **WE CAUGHT THEM BY THE GUARDPOST. I BET THEY'RE SPIES,**

the headquarters sentry explained to the commander.

---

5. One of the most famous Red commanders of the Civil War. His horse army was made famous in Isaac Babel's *Red Cavalry.*

6. Approx. 36 pounds.

The apprehended friends were led into headquarters. Recognizing Budyonny, they pronounced a ceremonial greeting:

Title: **GREAT "RED ELK," SCOURGE OF THE PALEFACE DOGS. GADFLY AND PATHFINDER GREET YOU.**

The strange greeting surprised Budyonny.

Title: **WHAT ARE THEY, SIMPLETONS?**

he asked the commanders, who also looked at the prisoners with curiosity. The regimental commander eyed the alleged spies suspiciously. When he realized what was happening, he grinned, deliberately walked over to the "old folks," abruptly grabbed their beards, and yanked down. Our youthful heroes stood in all their glory before the stunned gazes of the commanders and Budyonny.

Headquarters broke out in laughter. The suspicious telephone operator even tried to wipe the "paint" from Tom Jackson's face.

Seeing the young faces of our friends, Budyonny also laughed.

The unmasked heroes had to tell all about their adventures.

Title: **DUNYASHA'S SAD TALE LASTED AN ENTIRE HOUR.**

She told the commanders about the death of her father and the loss of her elder brother, about the excesses of Makhno's band, and about many other things the reader already knows. After listening to Dunyasha's story, Budyonny told the regimental commander.

Title: **ALL RIGHT, WE'LL USE THEM AS SCOUTS.**

Pathfinder, Gadfly, and Tom met Semyon Mikhailovich Budyonny's words with shouts of approval.

Title: **HURRAY FOR COMRADE RED ELK!**

they shouted in chorus and hopped about the room. It did not even occur to them that they could soon find themselves in mind-boggling altercations they couldn't have dreamed of when they first made their plans.

Title: **NIGHTTIME.**

Tired out by the day's events, the young scouts fell asleep on a mat right in headquarters. Tom Jackson slept on the floor. He tossed in his sleep and muttered something. Finally he awoke, leapt up, and rubbed his eyes.

Title: **HE REMEMBERED BEING A SLAVE IN THE COLONIES OF "CIVILIZED" NATIONS.**

Carefully stepping around his slumbering friends, Tom drank a mug of water and began to stare intently at a portrait of Karl Marx on the wall.

Title: **HE UNDERSTOOD ONLY VAGUELY THAT RUSSIAN WORKERS AND PEASANTS STRUGGLING FOR SOVIET POWER WERE FIGHTING FOR THE CAUSE OF OPPRESSED PEOPLE ALL AROUND THE WORLD.**

PART IV

Title: **TIME FLEW.**

Our heroes got used to life in the Red Army.

Wartime, full of danger and adventure, tempered the young scouts through and through. By now they rarely deferred to the older soldiers. They were equipped like any other Red soldier, with a full uniform and dragoon rifle apiece. Fitted out like soldiers, the young people felt themselves true Budyonny warriors and were convinced that now nobody could stop them from fulfilling the tasks they set themselves, which the reader will soon discover.

The friends took up sports to help prepare for their exploits. They swung around a horizontal bar erected in a shady orchard near staff headquarters.

Skillful Tom Jackson directed the gymnastic exercises.

Title: **JACKSON DEVELOPED HIS FRIENDS' STRENGTH AND AGILITY IN THEIR LEISURE TIME.**

Following their dark-skinned friend's instructions, Pathfinder and Gadfly took turns doing vaults, rotations and stands on the bar.

Budyonny rode up on his horse and found the inseparable threesome at these exercises. Forgetting the horizontal bar, the young scouts ran over to the great Red Elk. Budyonny was not only a commander to them, but an older comrade who filled in for their father.

Title: **TWO MONTHS PASSED. SOMEHOW DURING A SCOUTING EXPEDITION...**

Our friends were carrying out a battle assignment. They rode through a field and surveyed the enemy from atop their well-fed horses. Coming to a halt, they surveyed the area with a sharp glance. A bare plain, intersected at several points by a gully, spread around them. Stunted brush leading to the edge of the road could be made out up ahead.

The scouts noticed something, spurred their horses through the fields, cut across a stream, and came out onto a hill near the road.

A long wagon train was moving slowly along a highway in the distance.

Title: **AT THAT TIME, THE WHITES WERE RETREATING TO THE SEA UNDER THE BLOWS OF THE RED ARMY.**

The White convoy riveted our friends' attention. They hurried down to the road and hid behind a stone wall.

The convoy slowly approached the ambush of Budyonny's young soldiers. An old uryadnik[7] rode at the head of the detachment. He calmly smoked his pipe and lazily lashed his mount.

Meanwhile Pathfinder, Gadfly, and Tom were sitting behind the wall and planning an attack on the convoy. They agreed on a plan and began to prepare the operation.

Title: **A DARING SCHEME.**

At first glance, their actions made no sense: for some reason, they began undressing Tom. They took his helmet, rifle, and greatcoat. The Negro took a seat on a rock and began to pull off his boots.

While they were undressing the Negro, Misha kept watch on the road from behind the wall.

The White Guard convoy with the uryadnik up front was already close by.

Tom's boots came off with Dunyasha's help.

Almost undressed, Tom ran out from behind the wall and lay down across the highway. Misha put his rifle down next to him. Pathfinder and Gadfly posed Tom like a corpse and returned to their hiding place behind the wall. Their black friend lay motionless.

The clever plan worked brilliantly. Misha was so satisfied that he chuckled to himself. Tom smiled, too, but a stern look from his friends made him play dead again.

The White convoy rode up to the wall. The uryadnik rode calmly ahead of it with his pipe in his teeth. When he noticed a man lying in the dust, he hurried up to him and said to the drivers,

Title: **TAKE A LOOK AT THE NIGGER.**

The White soldiers surrounded Tom.

Pathfinder and Gadfly watched anxiously, with bated breath, from behind the wall.

---

7. Cossack N.C.O.

The convoy soldiers were intrigued by the Negro. They poked him all over. But Tom gave no sign of life.

That was when our heroes leapt out from behind the wall with their rifles leveled. Yelling:

Title: **SURRENDER, YOU DEVILS,**

they threw the enemy into utter confusion.

Tom came to life and pounced on the uryadnik's throat. The two struggled in the dust of the road.

Tom strangled his opponent and returned triumphant to his friends. The perplexed White soldiers threw their rifles down and stood with their hands in the air.

It seemed that victory was assured, but the uryadnik regained consciousness, grabbed his revolver, and took a shot at the Red scouts. Fortunately the shot went wide... But the situation became tense again. The Whites might refuse to obey. Decisive action was needed. Mishka drew his pistol and shot the uryadnik.

Order was restored.

Title: **GIVE UP YOUR WEAPONS!**

the brave friends yelled at the Whites in unison, and they began to disarm their prisoners.

Gadfly quickly frisked the dead uryadnik. Dunyasha took his passport from his pocket. On it was written:

Title: **IVAN MELNICHENKO.**

Finally, the White soldiers were disarmed. They stood tamely before the brave scouts with their hands in the air.

Title: **MISHKA'S DECEPTION HAD WORKED.**

With their plan brilliantly executed, our friends returned home. The Whites were tied together with a long rope, and they walked downcast along the highway in single file. Pathfinder led the triumphal procession—he rode a horse at the head of the detachment. Dunyasha brought up the rear, urging the prisoners forward. And last but not least, Tom, radiant with happiness, closed out the procession and herded the convoy of booty.

Title: **CAPTURING THE CONVOY MADE THE TEENAGERS HEROES....**

*[Using the documents of Melnichenko and his son Pyotr, the friends
infiltrated an enemy camp.]*

PART V

Title: **THE MAKHNO ENCAMPMENT.**

Life was aboil on a large field next to a forest near Yekaterinoslav. Makhno's
troops had pitched camp. Canvas tents, evidently belonging to officers, could be
seen here and there; most people had just set themselves up on the ground. Campfires burned.

Near a black banner with a skull and crossbones,[8] a young Makhno soldier in a
fur cap stood guard. The cap almost completely covered the sentry's face.

A Cossack, dark as a Negro, stood near the banner in a cherkesska;[9] he was secre-
tively discussing something with a scribe dressed in a long-skirted frock coat.

Title: **THE ESAUL[10] ZARUDNY AND THE SCRIBE DOVBNYA.**

The scribe was more than a bit frightened. He listened to the esaul with his eyes
wide open. Zarudny was saying:

Title: **THEY GAVE IT TO OUR BOYS AGAIN. THERE'S A
TRAITOR AMONG US.**

Both looked around suspiciously.

Close by, near a large tent, stood the "little father's" familiar hammered-metal
trunk, and next to it on a velvet armchair was Makhno, half sitting and half lying
down. He was worried. His sharp gray eyes glanced around sullenly. There was a
note in Makhno's hands. He read it with alarm:

Title: **I'LL SHOW YOU, YOU SCOUNDREL, HOW TO ROB AND PLUNDER.
YOUR SCALP WILL SOON BE IN MY HANDS. PATHFINDER.**

and handed it to an approaching esaul. The Cossack spread his hands in consterna-
tion and looked around again.

But everything was quiet. Makhno's armed men sat around the campfires. The
black banner by the white tent flapped peacefully in the breeze. A sentry stood
motionless by the banner.

---

8. Black was the color of the anarchists.

9. A long, narrow, collarless coat, usually with cartridges sewn to the front, traditionally worn by Caucasian highlanders.

10. A Cossack rank equivalent to captain.

The confounded Makhno continued talking with the esaul. Suddenly he broke off what he was saying, stricken by terror and white as a sheet, and pointed at a small, folded triangle of paper lying in the middle of the table. Gasping for breath, he grabbed it with trembling hands and, after a frenzied reading, passed it to the esaul.

On the paper was written:

Title: **YOUR ATAMAN CHERNYAK WILL BE KILLED BY THE REDS TONIGHT. IT'LL BE HOT FOR YOU, TOO, SOON, SIRE OF THE DEVIL.**

Matters had taken a serious turn. Zarudny whispered in the ataman's ear:

Title: **MAYBE IT'S THE LATE MELNICHENKO'S SON PLAYING DIRTY TRICKS?**

Makhno thought for a minute and then resolutely rose from the trunk and strode into the tent.

The sentry stood by the banner as before. But then he stirred a bit and fixed his hair. The movement of his hand made his fur cap ride down on the back of his head: the sentry turned out to be Gadfly, who had used Melnichenko's papers to make her way to Makhno.

"Little Father" and the esaul walked over to the supposed Melnichenko. The ataman looked at the sentry suspiciously. But Makhno's steady gaze did not fluster Dunyasha; she purposely gave him a stupid smile. This dispelled Makhno's suspicions.

Title: **A COMPLETE IDIOT! WHAT COULD HE DO!**

he said to the esaul and left the sentry with a wave of the hand.

Dunyasha's face instantly became troubled. In deep thought, she said to herself:

Title: **TIME TO GO!**

Leaving the banner, she cautiously made her way to Makhno's chair, put a paper of some kind on the trunk, covered it with a revolver, grabbed the attaché case forgotten by the ataman, and ran.

Reaching the field where the horses were grazing, the false Melnichenko told the soldier guarding the horses in a commanding voice:

Title: **GIVE ME A PAIR OF HORSES, SEROSHTAN. LITTLE FATHER SENT ME.**

The bandit suspected nothing, and evidently knowing the sentry's face well, he chose fine horses and gave them to Dunyasha.

Dunyasha hopped agilely into the saddle and left the Makhno encampment at a round trot, leading the second horse by the reins.

She rode out onto the road and soon reached the guard watching over the camp. The sentry jumped out and said curtly:

Title: **PASSWORD!**

But Dunyasha knew the password. She calmly answered:

Title: **GULYAI POLE**[11]

and set off, leaving the sentry behind.

In camp, the ataman had returned to his chair. The paper under the revolver attracted his attention. Feverishly unfolding the note, Makhno read:

Title: **YOUR PLANS HAVE FALLEN INTO OUR HANDS. YOU'D BETTER TAKE CARE, YOU MONSTER, YOU MURDERER. GADFLY-MELNICHENKO WRITING FOR PATHFINDER.**

The ataman began tearing through the trunk like an infuriated beast, and when he could not find his attaché case, he shouted in a frenzy:

Title: **FIND THE BOY AND THOSE PAPERS EVEN IF YOU HAVE TO DIG THEM UP.**

The camp sounded the alarm. People ran from their campfires to saddle their horses. The scribe in his top hat jumped on a horse; the bandit in blue glasses galloped by. The posse was ready in several minutes.

The furious Makhno ran up to the detachment. Again he ordered that the fugitive be caught at any cost, and he even fired a shot in the air as a warning.

The esaul leapt on his horse, gave a signal with his hand, and the detachment flew away through the field. Coming out on the road, Dunyasha's pursuers rode by the sentry post and galloped away.

Makhno couldn't contain himself. He ranted, shouting left and right at his retinue.

Dunyasha was already far away. Reaching a copse, she reined in her horse and began to signal with a mirror.

A ray of light from a gully set off from the road flickered in answer. Mishka quickly clambered out, with Tom Jackson close behind.

The friends ran up to Dunyasha and happily embraced her. But Dunyasha deftly extricated herself from their embraces and said in haste:

---

11. Makhno's base of operations in Ukraine.

Title: **HURRY, THE POSSE IS COMING.**

The youthful scouts quickly jumped on their horses. With a significant gesture, Dunyasha gave Pathfinder the attaché case filled with papers, and our three heroes, mounted on two horses, galloped off along the road.

The posse chased after the fugitive.

The young friends rode full tilt into a stream, crossed it without slowing their pace, rode back onto the field, and soon reached the place where they had just met up.

Title: **THROUGH THE THICKET.**

The fugitives galloped through the woods, bending back the thick tree trunks.

Makhno's mounted detachment followed quickly in their tracks.

The young heroes spurred their horses on ceaselessly in an attempt to lose them, but the bandit detachment was relentlessly gaining ground on them.

The Red scouts' flight from their pursuers finally brought them to the edge of the forest. But the forest suddenly gave out onto a deep ravine. The road ahead was cut off.

It seemed our heroes had fallen into a desperate situation. However, giving up hope was not part of the young scouts' code. They hastily set to finding a way out.

Makhno's men whooped through the trees, brandishing their sabers. They raced toward the fugitives, cutting off all exits.

But Mishka suddenly discovered a way out. Grabbing a long rope, he unwound it and, holding on to one end, threw it across the ravine. The rope flashed over the abyss and wound itself tightly around the thick branch of a tree growing out over the precipice on the other side. It took Pathfinder only a moment to secure the line. Once everything was set, Mishka climbed up a tree, jumped out onto the rope, hung above the abyss, and began going hand over hand to the other side.

Meanwhile, cold-blooded Tom threw everything that hindered their crossing into the ravine. Their situation was perilous: the bandits' horses could already be discerned through the forest thicket.

Pathfinder successfully reached the opposite side, but Dunyasha and Tom hadn't even reached the middle of the rope yet.

The bandits rode up to the edge of the forest and noticed the horse abandoned by the little red devils. Running up to the ravine, they looked around and saw the fugitives crawling across the rope.

One bandit took out his rifle and aimed at Tom, hanging in the air. But he could not get off a shot: he was killed on the spot by one of Pathfinder's bullets.

Makhno's soldiers took cover behind the trees when they met resistance. A skirmish broke out. "Hawkeye's" well-aimed bullets took the life of a new enemy every minute. The dead bandits rolled toward the ravine's edge like sacks of potatoes and fell into the abyss.

Finally, despite the firefight, Tom made it safely across the rope. Dunyasha had already reached Pathfinder's hiding place and was shooting at the enemy with him.

It seemed our heroes—Pathfinder, Gadfly, and Tom—were already safe.
But the esaul commanding the detachment devised a plan to catch the fugitives.
Putting a stop to the aimless shooting, he began giving the bandits orders.

Title: **THE ESAUL KNOWS HOW TO GET AROUND THE SCOUTS.**

(End of first reel)

Buzzer-Fly
Kornei Chukovsky (1924)

CHUKOVSKY (1882–1969) IS MODERN RUSSIA'S MOST FAMOUS CHILDREN'S WRITER — STILL READ TODAY BY SCHOOLCHILDREN. CHUKOVSKY TRIED TO KEEP HIMSELF ALOOF FROM POLITICS (AS THIS POEM ILLUSTRATES) AND FOR THIS HE WAS PREVENTED FROM WRITING FOR CHILDREN AFTER THE 1930s. HIS DAUGHTER LIDIA CHUKOVSKAYA WAS A WELL-KNOWN WRITER AND DISSIDENT.

Buzzer-buzzer-buzzer fly,
Golden tummy, shiny eye,
Over fields she roamed and flew,
At the market, not so far,
She bought herself a samovar.
   "Listen, cockroaches, to me,
   Leave your holes
   And come for tea."
Came the cockroaches in masses,
And they drank from cups and glasses.
And the little ones drank, too.
Each three cups with milk—
Like you.
Each one had some cake and pie,

For the buzzer-buzzer fly
Had her birthday then.
With a present came the fleas:
High boots reaching to the knees
To protect the fly from cold,
All the snaps were made of gold.

To the party came the granny bee,
For the fly some honeycomb brought she.
   Suddenly,
   Without a word,
   Unseen,
   Unheard,
An old spider caught our fly:

Translated by Robert Magidoff in *International Literature,* no. 6 (1939), pp. 33–37. Originally published in *Mukhina svad'ba* (Moscow: Raduga, 1924).

"You shall die!"
"My dear guests, please help me, help me.
Stab the villain, dear guests, and free me,
For I dined you,
For I wined you.
In my hour of need don't leave me!"
    But the bugs and the worms
    Took to flight.
    Filled all cracks and all holes
    In their fright.
    The cockroach clan
    Into a pan.
    The clumsy bugs
    Under the rugs.
    The frightened fleas
    On their knees:
    "Don't fight,
    Plea—ease! . . ."
And none of them would help the fly.
    "Buzzer, buzzer,
    "On your birthday you will die."
And the grasshopper, the grasshopper!
    Like a little man
Jumps, jumps, jumps, jumps
    All he can.
Up, up, up, up—
    Stop!
Under bridge, under bush.
    Hush!
And the villain's getting ready.
He binds her steady, steady.
His teeth sink into her body.
They are near her heart already.
    The fly weeps,
    Screams for help
    Heartbreakingly.
    She's bound tighter
    Painstakingly.
Of a sudden comes on wings
Out of the night
A mosquito.
In his hand
Shines a searchlight bright.
"Where's the villain old and grim?
I am not afraid of him!"
To the spider straight he flies.

Draws his shining sword.
Cuts the spider's head in two
Like a paper cord.
Puts his arms around the fly:
"Darling-buzzer, don't you cry,
For I killed him, he is dead,
Darling-buzzer, don't be sad.
Let's be happy, buzzer-fly,
Let us marry, you and I!"
All the cockroaches and bugs
Left the cracks and left the rugs.
    "Glory to the hero,
    To the conqueror"
Then along came fire-flies,
Lit their lights and rubbed their eyes.
    Everyone was feeling good,
    Everyone was gay.
    Hey, centipede,
    Show some speed.
    Call musicians,
    Let us dance!
The musicians came a-running.
All the drums began a-drumming.
Boom! boom! boom! boom!
The bride is dancing with her groom.
Chirping, skipping, low and high.
The mosquito and his fly.
And the bed-bug jumps and hoots
In his patent-leather boots.
The little worms with the little bees.
The little moths with the little fleas.
    And the rich farmer-bug,
    Horned, handsome and snug,
    Waves his hat very high
    Dancing with the butterfly.
Hop-hop-hop! Hop-hop-hop!
Skip and trot without a stop.
    All are happy and gay.
    The fly is married today
    To the dashing fighting hero—
    The mosquito brave.
And the ant, and the ant
Holds his wife's dainty hand
And he dances
    and he skips
    and he winks

At the bugs
  And he sings:
    "Baby bugs,

Darling bugs,
Bu-bu-bu-bu-bugs!
Bu-bu-bu-bu-bugs!"

The Lady Aristocrat
Mikhail Zoshchenko (1923)

ZOSHCHENKO (1895–1958) WAS ONE OF THE MOST BRILLIANT SATIRISTS IN SOVIET LITERARY HISTORY, SO BRILLIANT, IN FACT, THAT HE RAN AFOUL OF THE AUTHORITIES MANY TIMES, MOST NOTABLY IN THE *ZHDANOVSHCHINA* OR CULTURAL PURGE OF THE IMMEDIATE POSTWAR PERIOD. BUT IN THE 1920S HIS POPU-LARITY AS A WRITER WAS RIVALED BY NO ONE EXCEPT MAKSIM GORKY. THIS PIECE, PUBLISHED LIKE MANY OF HIS IN A MASS-CIRCULATION NEWSPAPER, LAMPOONED THE CHANGING MORES OF A NEWLY EMPOWERED CLASS.

Fellows, I don't like dames who wear hats. If a woman wears a hat, if her stockings are fuzzy, if she has a lap dog in her arms, or if she has a gold tooth, such a lady aristocrat, to my mind, is not a woman, but just a void.

But there was a time when I felt the attractions of an aristocratic lady. When I went out walking with one and took her to the theater. It was in the theater that it all happened. There, in the theater, she unfurled her ideology to its full length.

I first saw her in the yard of our building. At a meeting. I saw such a stuck-up number standing there. Stockings on her feet. A gold tooth.

"Where are you from, citizeness?" I asked. "What's the number of your room?"

"I live in Number Seven," she said.

"Please," I said, "just go on living."

Immediately I took a terrible liking to her. Began calling on her in Number Seven. At times I would visit her in my official capacity. "How is it with the obstruc-tion in the water pipe and the toilet?" I would say. "Do they work?"

"Yes," she would reply, "they work."

And she wrapped herself in a flannel shawl, and not another murmur. Only slashed me with her eyes. And flashed the gold tooth in her mouth.

Translated by Hugh McLean in *Nervous People* (Bloomington: Indiana University Press, 1963), pp. 127–130.

I kept going to her for a month—she got used to me. Began answering in more detail. That the water pipe worked all right, and thank you, Grigory Ivanovich.

As time went on, we began taking walks along the street. We would go out into the street and she would order me to offer her my arm. I would take her on my arm and drag myself along like a pike swimming. I couldn't think of anything to say. I didn't know, and felt ashamed in front of people.

Well, once she said to me, "Why do you keep dragging me through the streets? My head's dizzy. Now, as my escort and as a man of position, you ought to take me somewhere, to the theater, for instance."

"That can be done," I said.

The very next day the Communist Party cell sent some tickets for the opera. I got one ticket, and Vaska, the locksmith, offered to give me his.

I didn't look at the tickets, but they were different kinds. Mine was for the orchestra and Vaska's up in the highest gallery.

So we went. Sat down in the theater. She sat in my seat and I in Vaska's. I sat up in the crow's nest and I couldn't see a damned thing. But if I leaned forward over the rail I could see her. Not very well, though.

I got more and more bored and then went downstairs. It was intermission. And during intermissions she takes a stroll.

"Hello," I said.

"Hello."

"I wonder whether the water pipes work here," I said.

"I don't know," she answered.

And traipsed off in the direction of the buffet. I followed her. She walked around the buffet and looked at the counter. There was a plate on the counter, and cakes on the plate.

I, like a goose, or an unclipped bourgeois, fussed around her and proposed: "If you wish to eat a cake don't be bashful. I'll pay."

"Merci." She slithered right up to the plate, with her sexy walk, and zup! grabbed a cream puff and started munching away.

And I had next to no money at all on me. At the most enough to pay for three cakes. She ate and I groped uneasily in my pockets, counting with my hand how much money I had. Not enough to put in your eye.

She ate up the cream puff and zup! grabbed another. I almost screamed. Restrained myself. Such bourgeois bashfulness overcame me. Here was I, a lady's escort, and no money!

I walked around her like a rooster. She laughed and angled for compliments.

I said, "Isn't it time to go back to our seats? Maybe the bell has rung."

She answered, "Nope," and grabs a third.

I said, "On an empty stomach—isn't that too much? They might make you sick."

"No," she replied, "I'm used to them."

And took a fourth.

Then the blood rushed to my head. "Put it back!" I cried.

She was scared. Opened her mouth. In her mouth the golden tooth shone.

By this time I was sore as hell. I don't give a damn, I thought; I won't be taking walks with her any more anyway.

"Put it back," I said, "you lousy bitch!"

She put it back.

And I said to the proprietor, "How much for the three cakes she's eaten?"

The proprietor acted nonchalant; he was playing it cool. "For the four cakes she's eaten," he said, "you owe so and so much."

"What do you mean, four?" I asked. "The fourth one is there on the plate."

"No," he replied. "It may be on the plate, but there's a tooth mark on it and it's been crushed by her fingers."

"What tooth mark?" I said. "Come on, now. That's all your imagination."

The proprietor was still playing it cool, circling his hands in front of his face.

Some people, of course, gathered around. Experts. Some said there was a tooth mark, others—not.

I turned my pockets inside out—all sorts of junk fell out on the floor—the bystanders guffawed. But it wasn't funny to me. I counted the money.

When I had counted it, I found there was enough for four cakes, right on the nail!

By God, I had started all this argument for nothing! I paid and then addressed myself to the lady. "Finish eating it, citizeness, it's paid for."

The lady didn't move. She was too bashful to go on eating.

At this point some old fellow butted in. "Let me have it," he said. "I'll finish eating it."

And he did, the son of a bitch. And on my money!

We went back to our places. Saw the opera to the end. Then home.

And when we got home she said to me, "That's all the lousy tricks I'll stand from you. People who ain't got money don't go out with ladies."

And I replied, "Happiness doesn't lie in money, citizeness, excuse the expression."

That's how we parted.

I don't like lady aristocrats.

Chapaev
Dmitry Furmanov (1923)

FURMANOV (1891–1926) WAS THE POLITICAL COMMISSAR OF THE FAMOUS CHAPAEV DIVISION THAT FOUGHT AGAINST THE WHITES IN THE URALS DURING THE CIVIL WAR. HIS NOVEL

Dmitri Furmanov, *Chapayev*, trans. A. Anichkova (Moscow: Cooperative Publishing Society of Foreign Workers in the USSR, 1934), pp. 78–97.

BRINGS OUT THE TENSION BETWEEN POLITICAL CONSCIOUSNESS, DISCIPLINE, AND CONTROL ON THE ONE HAND AND COMBATIVE SPONTANEITY AND INDIVIDUAL COMMAND ON THE OTHER — FUR- MANOV (KLYCHKOV IN THE NOVEL) VS. CHAPAEV. VASILY CHA- PAEV (1887–1919) IS ONE OF THE BIG HEROES OF SOVIET POPU- LAR CULTURE (AND THE SUBJECT OF HUNDREDS OF INDECENT JOKES). THE NOVEL INSPIRED THE MOST POPULAR FILM OF THE 1930S, WHICH SHIFTED EMPHASIS FROM CHAPAEV'S INTERNAL CONTRADICTIONS TO A MORE TRADITIONAL SWASHBUCKLING HERO. THE SELECTION BELOW ILLUSTRATES A BASIC LEVEL OF CHARM IN THE NOVEL: A TOUGH BAND OF HEROES FLOCKED AROUND A LOWER-CLASS, UNLETTERED, CHARISMATIC LEADER; AND IT ALSO EXPLORES THE TENSIONS AMONG THE PROLETAR- IAN, PEASANT, AND INTELLECTUAL MINDSETS, AS SEEN BY THE CONSCIOUS INTELLECTUAL.

CHAPTER V. CHAPAEV

ДМ.ФУРМАНОВ

ЧАПАЕВ

ГОСУДАРСТВЕННОЕ
ИЗДАТЕЛЬСТВО

Early in the morning, about five or six o'clock, somebody knocked firmly on Fyodor's door. He opened it and saw a stranger.

"Good-day, I'm Chapaev!"

Every vestige of drowsiness vanished, as if some- one had punched him and awakened him in an instant. He threw a quick glance at Chapaev and held out his hand—the gesture was somehow too fast, though he tried hard to keep calm.

"Klychkov's my name. Have you been here long?"

"Just came down from the station. My men are there. I've sent horses for them."

Fyodor was examining him rapidly with pierc- ing eyes; he was anxious to memorize every linea- ment of his face, to see and understand what kind of man he was.

"An ordinary, spare man, of middle height and not particularly powerful build, with delicate, al- most feminine hands; his thin, dark hair clings in wisps to his forehead; his nose is thin and sensitive; his eyebrows are narrow, they look as if they had been traced with a pencil; his lips are thin, his teeth clean and shining, his chin clean-shaven, his mustaches bushy like those of a noncom. His eyes... they are light blue, almost green—quick, intelligent, unblinking. His face is pale, but fresh, without spots or wrinkles. He wore a field-gray jacket, navy blue trousers, and top boots of deerhide with the fur on. His cap had a red band and he held it in his hand. There was a bandolier slung around his shoulders and a revolver hung on his right hip. He threw down his silver-hilted sword and long-skirted green coat on the table." That is what Fyodor wrote in his diary on the evening of the day he first saw Chapaev.

Everyone wants a drink of tea after a journey. But Chapaev declined the offer of tea and did not even sit down. He sent a runner to the brigade commander to tell him to go at once to headquarters, where he, Chapaev, would join him shortly. Soon the men who had come with him arrived, and noisily invaded Fyodor's room, depositing their baggage in all four corners; they littered the tables, chairs, and windowsills with their caps, gloves, and bandoliers, laid down their revolvers anywhere; some of them unslung the white, bottle-necked bombs they were carrying and shoved them recklessly down on the heap of caps and gloves. Their tanned faces looked stern and courageous; their hair was rough and thick; their gestures and speech were rude, free, uncouth, but impressive and convincing. Some had such a strange way of speaking that you might have thought they were simply swearing all the time; they questioned you in sharp, barking tones, and when questioned themselves they answered gruffly, as if in a rage. They shoved and threw things about every which way. The whole house echoed with their loud talk; they quickly invaded all the rooms with the exception of Yozhikov's, which he had locked from the inside.

They had not been there two minutes before one of them was sprawling on Fyodor's untidy bed, with his legs against the wall, lighting a cigarette and deliberately flicking the ash on Klychkov's suitcase, which stood beside the bed. Another leaned with all his weight against the rickety washstand, breaking one of its legs, so that it keeled over on its side. Another smashed the windowpane with the butt end of his revolver; yet another threw his filthy, stinking sheepskin on the bread that had been left on the table, so that it smelled loathsome when you came to eat it. With this horde, and as if heralding its coming, a gust of strong, noisy talk had come bursting into the room. It went on unabatingly, without changing in volume, a ceaseless din of shouting voices. That was the ordinary manner of speaking among these free people of the steppe. It was impossible to pick out who was chief and who subordinate among them. Nothing to distinguish the one from the other; they all behaved in the same forceful way, and had equally rough manners—the same colorful, assertive speech, primitive and wholesome as the steppe itself. They formed a united family! But there were no outward indications of any affection between one member and another, no vestige of considerateness, no bothering or caring about one another, even in the most trifling matters. And all the same you could see and feel that they were all indissolubly linked together. The bond between these men had been cemented by the perils of nomadic warfaring, by their courage, personal hardihood, contempt for privations and dangers, and by true, deep-rooted solidarity, unwavering loyalty to one another, by their arduous and varied life, lived together, shoulder to shoulder, in the ranks and on the battlefield.

Chapaev stood out among them. He had already acquired something of culture, looked less uncouth than his companions, and he knew some restraint. The others treated him a little differently. Have you ever watched a fly crawling across a window-pane? It crawls boldly, bumps into other flies, climbs over them or gets entangled with them, and it does not seem to mind; it disentangles itself and crawls on. But if it happens to blunder into a wasp, it starts away in terror and flies off. So it was with the followers of Chapaev. When it was just them, they felt entirely at their ease, could say anything that came into their heads, bang one another with their caps or spoons, kick, splash hot water out of glasses into each other's faces, but the moment they crossed Chapaev's path, such liberties ceased. Not from fear, not from a feeling of inferiority, but because of the respect he commanded. "He's one of us, to be sure, but he's something out of the ordinary; you can't quite put him on a level with us."

You could feel this subtle distinction all the time, however freely the men behaved in his presence, however much noise they made, however heartily they swore. The moment they came in contact with him, their demeanor changed at once. Such was the love and respect in which they held him.

"Petka, off with you to the commandant's office!" Chapaev told one of the men.

Petka jumped up at once and rushed off on his errand without a word. He was a thin little man, who was enlisted for "special assignments." "I start in two hours; make sure the horses are ready on time. Send the cavalry horses first, then a sledge for Popov and me. Be quick! Popov, you are coming with me." Chapaev nodded authoritatively to a sallow-faced, round-shouldered fellow of about thirty-five. He had kind, laughing gray eyes and a croaking voice, and he was powerful and thickset but had a strangely lithe and sinuous way of moving, like a girl.

"Wait, the commissar is coming too, and with him three mounted men. The rest will follow us to Talovka. Ride easy, spare the horses. Be there by evening!

"Listen, you." Chapaev turned around, then realized that the man he wanted was not there. "Yes, I sent him away. Well, Kochnev, you look in at headquarters. Tell me if they are all there." Kochnev left the room. Fyodor thought he looked like a professional athlete, he was so swift, light, supple, and sinewy. He wore a short quilted jacket with short sleeves, a very small cap pressed on the back of his head, boots, and puttees. He could not have been thirty, but his forehead was already furrowed with wrinkles. His eyes were light gray and had a cunning twinkle in them; he had a way of tweaking his broad, moist nose with his finger and assuming a mischievous air. His teeth were white and very strong, and when he laughed he bared them ferociously as though he were going to bite.

Then there was Chekov. He had extraordinary bushy eyebrows, a formidable mustache, a powerful jaw, high cheekbones. His thick lower lip hung down, his eyes were like coals; he was square-jawed and broad-chested. He must have been a little over forty years of age.

Ilya Tyotkin, a Red Army man with a fine record of service, a housepainter by profession, was busying himself with kettles, cutting bread into big chunks, shouting wisecracks back and forth, and laughing uproariously at his own jokes. He was very good-natured, noisy, popular with the other men, fond of songs and games, always performing all sorts of amusing antics. He must have been a little older than Petka—twenty-six or twenty-eight.

Next to Tyotkin, silently and patiently waiting to get his share of bread, stood Vikhor, a daredevil cavalryman, commander of the mounted scouts. The little finger of his left hand was missing, and this fact provided food for endless jokes.

"Give him a poke with your pinkie, Vikhor, he's getting fresh!"

"Show us your little finger, buddy, and I'll give you a smoke."

"Hey, you with the nine hoofs!"

Vikhor was not easily roused; it was his nature to be calm, and he remained calm, even in battle. He was living proof of the fact that great things can be done quietly!

The one who threw his weight around the most, and who swore and shouted the loudest, was Shmarin. He wore a sheepskin coat and knee-high felt boots (he was a sick man and always suffered from the cold); he had a croaking voice like Popov's, black eyes, and black hair. He was fifty, the oldest man there.

The young driver, Averka, had come in with the others. He stood leaning on his long-handled whip, eagerly watching preparations for eating and tea drinking. His face was purple, his nose the shape of an onion, his eyes watery from the cold, his lips cracked. A scarf, which he wore at night, was wound around his neck.

Then there was Leksey, the orderly, an old acquaintance of Chapaev and a clever, resourceful fellow. When anything was wanted, it was always Leksey who was commissioned to get it, and he would never return empty-handed. When food was short, when a saddle strap or a linchpin was missing, or when some homemade medicine was badly needed, everyone turned instinctively to Leksey for aid. He was the handyman of the company.

What a bunch!

Every face unique, worthy of an epic poem. No two fellows alike among the whole crowd, and yet they dovetailed together perfectly, like masonry. Theirs was a rock-like unity. They formed one common family, and what a glorious family it was!

Kochnev entered.

"The brigade commander is at headquarters."

All were astir. All eyes were riveted on Chapaev's face.

"Let's go!"

He gave a nod to Popov, crooking his finger in the direction of Shmarin and Vikhor. Spurs jingled; heavy boots with iron-rimmed heels clattered across the floor. Fyodor went out with the rest in a somewhat perplexed frame of mind. He thought that Chapaev was paying too little attention to him, putting him on a level with his "retinue." Somewhere, in the depths of his soul, lurked an unpleasant feeling. He remembered that there was a tale about Chapaev having horsewhipped a commissar. It was in 1918, in the heat of battle, when the enemy had surrounded our troops and the commissar was scared and did not know what to do. The memory of this incident rankled. Fyodor tried to persuade himself that the story was exaggerated, perhaps even invented, but all the same it might be true. Of course, times were different then, Chapaev himself was different, and perhaps the commissar was no good. Fyodor was walking behind the others, and this fact made him feel slighted.

Chapaev greeted the brigade commander hastily and abruptly, looking away from him as he spoke, whereas the commander was all amiability—he clicked his spurs and straightened himself up, as if reporting for duty. He had heard much about Chapaev, and most of what he had heard was about his bad side, his reckless hooliganism; at best, he knew him as a crank, had not heard of his real feats of valor, and did not believe the rumors of the steppe concerning his heroism.

All the doorways were crowded with curious onlookers. It called to mind an old-time festival in the house of a rich merchant when the shabbier members of the household would try to steal a glimpse of the honored guests. Evidently, it was not only the commander who had heard the rumors about Chapaev.

The apartment occupied by headquarters was unusually clean and tidy. The members of the staff were all sitting or standing in their places. Great preparations had been made; the staff did not want to make a bad show, and perhaps they were all a little apprehensive. This fellow Chapaev had a violent temper; who could foretell how he might behave?

The brigade commander spread out a beautifully drawn plan of the forthcoming attack on the table. Chapaev picked it up, silently admired the fine drawing for an instant, and laid it down again. He drew up a stool and sat down. Some of those who had come with him followed his example.

"Give me a pair of compasses!"

A shabby, rusty pair was handed to him. He opened them and turned them over in his hand with evident distaste.

"Vikhor, go and fetch me my compasses from Averka's satchel!"

In two minutes Vikhor was back again with another pair, and Chapaev began taking measurements on the plan. First he stuck to the plan; then he produced a map from his pocket and studied it closely. He kept inquiring about distances, the difficult parts of the road, about water, transport wagons, the early morning light, about blizzards in the steppe.

Those around him kept silent. Only now and again the brigade commander edged in a word or answered a question. Chapaev's eye saw more on the map than was traced upon it; he saw snow-covered valleys, the ruins of burned villages, columns of men marching in the dark, trundling baggage wagons—he heard the whine and whistle of the cold morning wind—he saw mounds and hillocks, wells, frozen streams, broken bridges, stunted bushes.

Chapaev was already leading the attack!

When he had finished taking measurements, he pointed out to the brigade commander the mistakes in the plan. Some distances that had to be covered were too great, some halts were ill chosen; the men would leave some places too soon or reach others too late. And he would jot down each of his remarks while he was measuring. The brigade commander did not agree very willingly; sometimes he seemed secretly amused at it all, but he gave in, took notes, made alterations in the plan. In some cases Chapaev turned as if for sympathy and support to Vikhor, now to Popov or Shmarin.

"What would you say? What do you think? Am I right?"

The men were not accustomed to air their opinions much in his presence; moreover, there was little to add—he always weighed and foresaw everything down to the minutest detail. The proverb "Two heads are better than one" had been changed by his followers into "One head is better than two."

There had been cases in the past when he had followed the advice of others, and he had always had occasion to regret it. He swore, burst into complaints, cursed himself for being a fool. His men would always remember a "conference" when in their excitement they had let themselves go and talked a lot of hot air. Chapaev had listened to them patiently, sometimes even encouraging them by throwing in a few words.

"Yes, yes... That's right... Very good..."

His followers had really imagined that he was in full agreement with them, and approved of all they were saying. But when they had finished:

"What we have to do," he declared, "is to forget all this nonsense you've been talking—get it right out of your heads. Now you listen to my commands."

And then he went on to give quite a different turn to the whole business, so that nothing was left of their suggestions.

Vikhor, Popov, and Shmarin had all three attended that whole conference, and now they were more diffident about putting themselves forward. They knew from experience when to speak and when to keep their mouths shut.

"Sometimes it may be wise to give advice, but sometimes a single word can spell disaster."

They were silent now. Fyodor, too, spoke but little. He was as yet ill acquainted with military questions; it was only later on, after months of experience on the field of battle, that he came to have any insight into these matters. For the time being he was still a mere "civilian," and what could one expect from him?

He stood by the table with his hands clasped behind his back and thoughtfully examined the map and the plan, frowning now and then or turning his head away to give a little cough, afraid to disturb so important a discussion. Outwardly he looked grave and self-possessed. An outsider might have thought that he was able to hold his own with the rest in the discussion.

Long before meeting Chapaev, Fyodor had made up his mind to be particularly cautious and diplomatic in his dealings with him. At first he would avoid conversations on military topics, in order not to show that he was a mere layman in these matters. He would turn the conversation to politics, because then all the advantages would be on his side. He would gain Chapaev's confidence, encourage him to speak frankly on all subjects, including intimate, personal peculiarities and minor details. He, Fyodor, would speak mostly about science, culture, general education—and here again Chapaev would be reduced to the role of listener. And later—later Fyodor would reveal himself as a brave fighter. That he must do, the sooner the better, because that was the only way to win the respect of Chapaev and the Red Army men. Politics, science, and personal qualities were of no avail without this. After having thus carefully approached Chapaev, and laid the foundations for more intimate relations, Fyodor would get to know him more closely, but for the present he must be on his guard. The danger now was that Chapaev might think Fyodor was playing up to him, behaving sycophantically toward a "hero." Chapaev, being so famous, having such enormous prestige, must know how ambitious countless people were about obtaining his friendship. Later on, when Chapaev was "captivated" by him, began to listen to him, and perhaps to seek enlightenment from him, it would all be smooth riding. However, no getting on your high horse! He must immediately establish simple and cordial relations, with a touch of the necessary rudeness. It was imperative that Chapaev not take him for a fastidious intellectual of the sort that was always treated at the front with suspicion and undisguised contempt.

This mental preparation produced results. It helped Fyodor to find his way by the simplest, quickest, and surest path into the environment in which he had to work, to merge with his surroundings, to become an organic part of them. He fully realized that Chapaev and his followers—this mass of semi-guerrilla fighters—were rather bewildering folk, people with whom one had to watch one's step. Beside the good elements among them, there were those who required careful handling, had to be constantly watched.

What sort of a man was Chapaev? What was Klychkov's conception of Chapaev, and why was he taking such elaborate pains to approach him in the proper way? Was it really worthwhile to do this?

While working in the rear of the revolutionary army, Klychkov had naturally heard and read a lot about "popular heroes" who had made a dazzling appearance on some sector of the Civil War front. He had noticed that they were mostly of peasant origin; only a few were townsmen and factory workers. The heroism of the worker was different from that of the peasant. Having grown up in a great industrial center, Klychkov had witnessed the well-organized struggle of the weavers, and he was therefore somewhat inclined to look askance at the semi-anarchic exploits of popular heroes of the Chapaev type. That did not prevent him from analyzing and studying them very attentively and appreciating their acts of real courage. But in the depths of his soul he slightly mistrusted them. Such was his attitude at the present moment.

"Chapaev is a hero," Fyodor thought to himself. "He embodies all the irrepressible and spontaneous feelings of rage and protest that have accumulated in the hearts of the peasants. But who can foresee what spontaneous protest will lead to? There are cases on record (and more than a few) where such glorious chieftains as Chapaev have suddenly taken a notion to bump off their commissars! Not some contemptible, despicable, cowardly commissar, but first-rate revolutionaries! Or they have suddenly gone over to the Whites with their whole 'spontaneous' detachment at their heels.

"Workers are different. Never, under any circumstances, will they desert to the enemy's camp—at least those who have consciously joined the struggle will not. Of course, workers include people who were peasants only yesterday; others are not fully class-conscious, and still others have become too 'intellectual,' and scorn hard work. But with workers it is easy to know what you are dealing with. Whereas there lurks an element of real danger in the devil-may-care attitude of Chapaev's reckless guerrilla fighters."

This feeling of mistrust made it all the more important for Fyodor to strike the right note when mixing with this new crowd. He did not want to be submerged in it; his aim, on the contrary, was to gain a proper influence over it. And he would begin with the head, the chief, with Chapaev himself. He would focus all his attention upon him.

Petka—that was what everybody called Isaev—poked his tiny, bird-like head in at the door, beckoned to Popov with his little finger, and gave him a note on which was written in an illiterate hand:

"Tell Chapaev that the horses and everything are ready."

Petka was aware that in some places and under some circumstances he was not allowed to butt in. In such cases he always wrote notes. His present message came at a very opportune moment, for all the orders had already been issued and signed, and would presently be sent to the regiments. Little or no time would be spent on formalities.

"I have come to take command," Chapaev had declared, "not to fuss around with papers. Clerks can do that."

"Vasily Ivanovich," Popov whispered to him, "I see you have finished. Everything is ready, we can start."

"Everything's ready? Let's go!"

Chapaev sprang to his feet.

Everybody made way for him, and he was the first to leave the room as he had been the first to enter it.

Outside, a crowd of Red Army men had gathered, having heard that Chapaev was in the house. Many of them had been his companions-in-arms in 1918; many knew him personally; all without exception knew him by repute. Craning their necks, their eyes lit up with enthusiasm and admiration, they grinned from ear to ear at the sight of Chapaev.

"Long live Chapaev!" yelled one of them as he appeared on the steps.

"Hurrah! Hurrah!"

Red Army men came swarming from all sides, followed by townspeople. The crowd swelled rapidly.

"Comrades!" said Chapaev.

In an instant complete silence reigned.

"I have no time to speak now. I am going to the front. We'll meet there tomorrow, for we've prepared something for the Cossacks that they won't relish, and tomorrow we're going to shove it down their throats. We'll talk later on, but for the present—goodbye to you all!"

A fresh burst of cheering followed his words. Chapaev seated himself in a sledge, with Popov at his side. Three mounted Red Army men were ready to escort them. Fyodor was given a spirited black stallion to ride.

"Off we go!" shouted Chapaev.

The horses started off; the crowd opened before them, cheering vociferously.

Chapaev's sledge sped away through an avenue of men that stretched to the very outskirts of the village.

The white expanse of bare steppe was monotonous and depressing. During the late thaw, all the hillocks had been stripped of snow till the bare ground was visible; now the wind had buried them under snow again. The whole steppe was crisp with frost. The horses sped on lightly and merrily. Chapaev and Popov were sitting in the sledge almost back to back, making it look as if they had quarreled. Each was pondering over the next day's difficult enterprise, and preparing himself for it. The sledge was followed at a small distance by the mounted escort, and that distance was never lengthened or shortened during the whole way. Fyodor kept apart from the others. Sometimes he would loiter behind, letting himself be outdistanced a whole verst, and then catch up with the party at a gallop. It was splendid to race over the steppe on a spirited horse.

"Tomorrow," he was thinking as he trotted along at an easy pace, "tomorrow will usher in a new life for me, a life of real fighting. And this life of warfare will go on and on—for how long? Who can tell what the issue will be? Who can foretell the day of our victory? Day after day will fly past in campaigns, battles, dangers, and anxieties. Will we survive, who are like puffs of down? Which of us will return to his native place and which will leave his bones here in some dark ravine or in the snowy waste of the steppe?"

Memories of everyday life and beloved, familiar faces arose before his mind's eye. He saw himself as a lifeless body, lying in the snow with his arms outspread, the blood oozing from a wound in his temple. He felt a twinge of self-pity. Some hours ago this feeling would have degenerated into melancholy, but now he shook himself free of it with a toss of his head and proceeded on his way, calm and serene, ready to laugh at the picture of his own death.

They had now been traveling for two hours and a half. Chapay,[1] evidently bored with sitting motionless so long, bade the driver to stop, got out, and told one of the mounted men to take his place in the sledge while he himself jumped on the man's horse. He rode up to Fyodor.

"So we two are going to be together, Comrade Commissar?"

"Yes, we'll be together," said Fyodor, and he noticed at a glance how firmly Chapaev sat his horse. Man and mount seemed molded into one. Fyodor himself feared he must look rather a bad horseman.

"With only a little more jolting and shaking I should lose my seat altogether," he thought to himself ruefully. "Chapaev, on the other hand, would never lose his seat."

"Seen much fighting, comrade?"

Fyodor thought he caught a smile on the man's face and sensed irony in his words. "He knows well enough that I'm a newcomer to the front and is trying to make fun of me."

"I am only a beginner."

----

1. His close friends usually just called him "Chapay."

"But you've seen service in the rear, I suppose?"

There was a sting in the question.

One must bear in mind that to a born fighter such as Chapaev, "the rear" was a place inhabited by a low, contemptible species of being. Fyodor had got some inkling of this before, and his recent conversation and trips with Red Army men and commanders had confirmed his suspicions.

"The rear?" he repeated, and added with feigned carelessness, "I was working in Ivanovo-Voznesensk."

"That's beyond Moscow, isn't it?"

"Yes, about three hundred versts beyond Moscow."

"Well, how are things there?"

Fyodor was pleased with the new turn the conversation was taking; he seized the opportunity to explain to Chapaev what a hard and hungry life the Ivanovo weavers were having. Why only the weavers? Were there no other inhabitants in the town to save them? Yet somehow when he spoke of Ivanovo-Voznesensk, Klychkov could picture only the serried ranks of the army of workers; he was proud of his nearness to this working-class army, and there was even a slight condescension in his mental attitude toward them.

"Seems as if they were having a hard time of it," mused Chapaev in a serious tone. "And all because of the famine. If it weren't for the famine, it'd be all right—things would be different then. Look at the stacks of food they gobble up, the sons of bitches, and they never think that."

"Who gobbles up food?" asked Fyodor uncomprehendingly.

"The Cossacks. They don't give a damn."

"Not all the Cossacks are like that."

"Yes, they are, all of them!" cried Chapaev. "You don't know, but I'll tell you they're all that way, every last one of them."

Chapaev chafed irritably in his saddle.

"That can't be," Fyodor protested. "There must be some, at least, who side with us. Wait a minute," he added in joyful excitement, "what about the mounted scouts in our brigade, aren't they all Cossacks?"

"In our brigade?"

Chapaev looked thoughtful.

"Yes, here in our brigade."

"Those must be town Cossacks. The ones here would never . . ."

Chapaev refused to let himself be convinced.

"I don't know whether they are town or steppe Cossacks, but that doesn't alter the fact that they are with us. You see, Comrade Chapaev, the Cossacks can't all be against us. It would be unthinkable, impossible."

"Why do you say that? When you've been with us bit longer..."

"However long I stay with you, I'll never change mind."

Fyodor's voice was firm and stern.

"I'm not saying there aren't one or two," said Chapaev, yielding a little. "Of course there are some—who says there aren't? But there are precious few of them—no, none at all."

"No, not only a few. You're mistaken. They've sent us news from Turkestan that Cossack regiments there have established Soviet power over entire regions. And in the Ukraine, too, and on the Don. There are more than you think."

"Don't you trust them! They'll soon show you."

"I don't trust them very much," explained Klychkov. "I know that there is much truth in what you say. The Cossack is a black raven, it's true—nobody denies it. That's why the tsarist government went out of its way to gratify them. But look at the young Cossacks, they're not of the old breed. And it's the young ones that join us. Of course, it's more difficult for an old graybeard of a Cossack to accept Soviet power. At least it's difficult for him now, when he hasn't come to understand what it means. All sorts of stories are told about us, and people believe them, too. How we convert churches into cowsheds, have common wives and common property, and make everybody eat and drink together and sit at the same table. How can the Cossacks be expected to like this sort of thing if they've been accustomed to go to church for generations and are fond of their rich, comfortable homes, of the free, wild life of the steppes, and of making other people work for them?"

"Ex-ploi-ters," pronounced Chapaev painstakingly.

"Exactly," said Fyodor, repressing a smile. "Exploitation is the very gist of the matter. Rich Cossacks do not merely exploit strangers and Kirghizians, they make no bones about exploiting their own people. And that brings discord. The old people, when they are oppressed, bow their heads and say that god has willed it so, but the youngsters have a simpler and bolder outlook, and that is why they are attracted to us. The old people can't be shaken in their convictions. It takes a bullet to get anything into their heads!"

"Yes, bullets, that's right," said Chapaev with a toss of his head. "But there's one thing that makes it hard for us at the front."

Fyodor could not see what Chapaev meant by this; nevertheless, he felt that there was a hidden meaning in these words. He remained silent, waiting for Chapaev to explain his idea.

"Our centers. They're no good," offered Chapaev vaguely.

Fyodor's curiosity was aroused.

"What's wrong with the centers?" he asked.

"They've packed them with all kinds of bastards," muttered Chapaev as if to himself, but quite audibly, obviously meaning for Fyodor to hear. "He used to keep me standing under guard in the frost for twenty-four hours at a stretch, the son of a bitch, and he gets treated with kid gloves. 'Please be seated, General; there's a padded armchair for you, General, sir. Sit down and issue orders. And be sure to please yourself; give us cartridges if you feel so inclined, or else let them fight with sticks!'"

That was Chapaev's sore spot—headquarters, with their generals, orders, and repressions for insubordination. Chapaev could not stomach them, and he was far from the only Red Army chief at that time who hated and despised headquarters.

"We can't manage without generals," said Klychkov softly. "You can't make war without generals!"

"We damn well can!"

Chapaev gave an impatient tug at the bridle.

"No, we can't, Comrade Chapaev. Boldness alone won't get us anywhere; we must have knowledge. And we haven't got it. Who, save the generals, can give us knowledge? They have studied and they must instruct us. In time we shall have teachers from among ourselves, but for the present we haven't. Admit that we haven't! You do? Very well, then, we must learn from others."

"Learn? Why, what the hell can they teach us?" Chapaev retorted hotly. "Do you think they can tell you your business? Not on your life! I myself entered the Academy, knocked about the damned place for two months, felt like a fish out of water, and then left for good. Came back here. It's no place for people like me. One of the professors there, a fellow named Pechkin—as bald as an egg—started asking me questions at the exam.

"'Do you know the river Rhine?' he asked me.

"I was all through the German war, and of course I knew about the Rhine. But why should I give him the answer he wanted?

"'No, I don't,' I said, 'and you, do you know the river Solyanka?'

"His eyes nearly popped out of his head. He wasn't expecting such a question.

"'No, I don't know it,' he said. 'What about it?'

"'Don't ask questions then,' I said. 'I was wounded on the Solyanka, crossed it back and forth five times. To hell with your Rhine, I don't want it. I must know every hillock and bush and tree near the Solyanka because we're fighting the Cossacks on its banks!'"

Fyodor burst out laughing, looked at Chapaev in amazement, and thought:

"What a childish way of reasoning this popular hero has!" Well, people have different tastes; some are attracted by knowledge, others repelled by it. This man had been at the Academy for two months and had understood nothing, found nothing good in it. And he was no ordinary man. Clever, beyond question, but raw and uncouth. He would not come around so soon.

"You didn't stay at the Academy long enough," said Fyodor. "You couldn't learn much in two months. It's too difficult."

"I might as well not have been there at all," said Chapaev with a contemptuous wave of his hand. "I don't need to be taught, I know everything."

"No, you must let yourself be taught," retorted Fyodor. "There are always things you can learn."

"There are, but not at the Academy," exclaimed Chapaev excitedly. "I know there are things to learn and I'm going to learn them. I'll tell you what, comrade. But what's your name?"

"Klychkov."

"I want to tell you, Comrade Klychkov, that I am almost totally illiterate. I learned to read only four years ago, and I am thirty-five! I have spent half a lifetime in ignorance, you might say. But enough of that, we'll discuss it another time. And just look yonder, that must be Talovka." Chapaev spurred his horse. Fyodor followed his example, and they rode up even with Popov. Ten minutes later they were entering the Cossack settlement of Talovka.

The Brick Factory

Valentin Kruchinin and Pavel German (1920s)

"BRICK FACTORY" (*KIRPICHIKI* IN RUSSIAN MEANS "LITTLE
BRICKS") WAS PART OF URBAN FOLKLORE IN THE 1920S. IT BE-
GINS WITH A TRADITIONAL FOLK FORM AS A WORKERS' LAMENT
AND ENDS AS A TRIUMPHANT HYMN TO SOVIET POWER. MILLIONS
OF COPIES OF IT WERE SOLD ON SHEET MUSIC, AND A MOVIE WAS
INSPIRED BY IT. IT ALSO SPAWNED HUNDREDS OF VARIANTS, AD-
APTATIONS, AND PARODIES — INCLUDING SOME INDECENT ONES.
FOR THIS REASON, IT WAS SUPPRESSED FOR DECADES.

КИРПИЧИКИ

На окраине где-то города
Я в убогой семье родилась,
Горе мыкая, лет пятнадцати
На кирпичный завод нанялась.

Было трудно мне время первое,
Но зато, проработавши год,
За веселый гул, за кирпичики
Полюбила я этот завод.

На заводе том Сеньку встретила.
Лишь, бывало, заслышу гудок, —
Руки вымою и бегу к нему
В мастерскую, накинув платок.

Кажду ноченьку мы встречалися,
Где кирпич образует проход...
Вот за Сеньку-то, за кирпичики
Полюбила я этот завод.

Но, как водится, безработица
По заводу ударила вдруг:

THE BRICK FACTORY

On the outskirts of some city
I was born to a poor family,
Oh the woe of it, at fifteen years old,
To the brickyard I went off to work.

At first working was difficult for me,
But when I had worked through my first
    year,
For its siren gay, for the bricks we made,
I came to love that old brickyard.

I met Senka there in that factory.
When the whistle blew and work was
    done,
I would wash my hands, throw on my
    old scarf,
And then run to him in the workshop.

Every evening there Senka and I met,
Where a passage is formed from the
    bricks
For my Senka and for the bricks we
    made,
I came to love that old brickyard.

But then suddenly unemployment hit
At our factory, like happened back
    then.

Iurii Sokolov, *Russkii folklor* 4 (1932), pp. 91–95.

Сенька вылетел, а за ним и я
И еще двести семьдесят штук.

Тут война пошла буржуазная,
Огрубел, обозлился народ,—
И по винтовку, по кирпичку
Растащали кирпичный завод.

После вольного счастья Смольного
Развернулась рабочая грудь,
Порешили мы вместе с Сенькою
На знакомый завод заглянуть.

Там нашла я вновь счастье старое,
На ремонт поистративши год,
По советскому, по кирпичику
Возродили мы с Сенькой завод.

Запыхтел завод, загудел гудок,
Как, бывало, по-прежнему он.
Стал директором, управляющим
На заводе "товарищ Семен"...

Так любовь моя и семья моя
Укрепились от всяких невзгод.
За веселый гуд, за кирпичики
Полюбила я этот завод.

Senka flew the joint, and I followed
    him,
With two hundred and seventy more.

Then the bourgeoisie started up their
    war,
The people got angry and rough,—
And so gun by gun, and brick by brick,
They tore that old brickyard apart.

After Smolny[1] gave us our bright liberty
The workers' chests swelled up with
    pride,
So then Senka and I decided to
Take a look at the old factory.

There I found again the joy I once
    knew.
After taking a year for repairs,
Senka and I did start the factory up
Like Soviet brickmakers should.

So the factory roared, and the whistle
    blew,
Just as it had done formerly.
The new manager, the new director of
The factory was "Comrade Semyon."

And so my love and my family
Grew stronger from all that we'd faced.
For its siren gay, for the bricks we made,
I loved that old brick factory.

---

1. Bolshevik headquarters during the October Revolution of 1917.

Bublichki

(1920s)

"Bublichki" (Hot Buns, or Bagels) was the most notorious of the "underground" songs of the NEP era. In stark
opposition to the bright visions of Communism that the

Variant from a private collection.

REGIME WAS TRYING TO PROMOTE, THE SONG WALLOWS IN PHYS-
ICAL AND FIGURATIVE DIRT—HITTING RATHER TOO CLOSE TO
HOME, I.E., THE REALITIES OF NEP STREET LIFE. FOR THIS IT WAS
BANNED IN THE USSR UNTIL THE LATE 1980s; BUT IT WAS
PASSED DOWN BY WORD OF MOUTH FOR DECADES, AND REACHED
THE PRESENT IN MANY DIFFERENT FORMS.

БУБЛИЧКИ

Ночь надвигается, она шатается,
Свет пробивается в ночную тьму.
Я неумытая, тряпьем прикрытая
И вся разбитая, едва брожу.

Припев:
Купите бублички, горячи бублички,
Несите рублички сюда скорей.
И в ночь ненастную, меня несчастную,
Торговку частную, ты пожалей.

Отец мой пьяница, он этим чванится,
Он к гробу тянется, ему лишь пить.
Сестра гулящая, а мать пропащая,
А я курящая, глядите вот.

Припев.

Вот у хозяина проклятье Каина
Потом на улицу меня прогнал.
Кормилась дрянею, ловилась нянею,
Теперь живу я да у кустаря.

Припев.

HOT BUNS

The night comes rolling in, it reels and
   it spins,
The light fights through the nighttime
   gloom.
I'm dirtier than sin, these rags are all
   I'm in,
And I'm so beat that I can barely move.

Refrain:
So buy these little buns, these little hot
   buns,
Bring all your rubles over here.
On this bitter night look at my bitter
   plight,
Take pity on a private peddler-girl.

My father drinks too much, and lords it
   over us,
The booze will be his grave—he doesn't
   care.
My sister walks the street, and Mom's a
   hopeless case,
I even smoke too much, but hey, that's
   life.

Refrain.

And there's my boss, he had the curse
   of Cain,
And then he chased me out into the
   street,
With only slop to eat, my nanny found
   me then,
And now I'm living in a craftsman's
   house.

Refrain.

Songs of the Underworld

(1920s)

BLATNAYA PESNYA (UNDERWORLD SONG) WAS A PREREVOLU-
TIONARY URBAN GENRE WHICH HAD NO RELATION TO POLITICS
OR PROTEST. SOME SONGS WERE VARIANTS OF "CRUEL SONG" FEA-
TURING LURID DETAILS OF CITY LIFE AND A SENTIMENTAL PLEA
FOR PITY; OTHERS (SUCH AS "RABINOVICH") REVEL WITTILY IN
THE CRIMINAL OR SEMICRIMINAL MILIEU (HERE ALSO WITH A
DASH OF POPULAR ANTI-SEMITISM). ALL OF THEM DEPICTED A
WAY OF LIFE THAT THE BOLSHEVIKS WERE OUT TO ELIMINATE,
OR WHOSE EXISTENCE THEY REFUSED TO RECOGNIZE. THOUGH
OUTLAWED THROUGHOUT MOST OF THE SOVIET PERIOD, THEY
WERE OFTEN HEARD AT PARTIES.

РАБИНОВИЧ

Раз пошли на дело
Я и Рабинович.
Рабинович выпить захотел.
Отчего не выпить бедному еврею,
Если у него нет срочных дел?

Выпить так уж выпить,
Закусить так надо.
Мы зашли в шикарный ресторан.
Там сидела Мурка.
Из-под юбки виден
Дробью был заряженный наган.

Рабинович стрельнул,
Стрельнул промахнулся,
И попал немножечко в меня...
Я лежу в больнице,
Сволочь-Рабинович с Муркой
Гуляет без меня.*

RABINOVICH

Once me and Rabinovich
Went to do some business.
Rabinovich stopped to get a drink.
So let the wretched Jew
Knock one back when he can
If his business can just wait a bit.

If you're gonna drink some,
You gotta have a snack too.
So we stepped into a swanky joint.
There's Murka[1] at a table.
And from her skirt is poking
A small-shot loaded pistol aimed at us.

Rabinovich fires, fires and he misses,
But the bullet nicks me up a bit.
Now I'm stuck in the hospital,
While the bastard Rabinovich
And Murka paint the town without me.

---

*Lyrics from a private manuscript.
1. Underworld slang: a moll.

МУРКА

Улики и воры, злые атаманы
Выбирали новый комитет.
Речь держала девка
Звали ее Мурка,
Строгая и смелая была.

Надо начать дело,
Выпить захотелось
И пошли в шикарный ресторан.
Там звенит гитара
И танцует пара,
Мурка, да какой-то юный Франт.

Я к ней подбегаю,
За руку хватаю—
Мне с тобою надо говорить.
А она смеется
Ближе к франту жмется:
Не могу с тобою больше жить.

В темном переулке
Костя встретил Мурку.
Здравствуй, дорогая, и прощай.
Ты зашухарила
Всю нашу малину
И за это жизнью отвечай.

Раньше ты любила
Сигарету «Тройку»,
А теперь не нужен даже и табак.
Раньше ты любила
Выпить с нами водку,
А теперь не нужен даже и коньяк.

Здравствуй, моя Мурка,
Мурка дорогая,
Ты зашухарила всю нашу малину,
А теперь маслину получай.

MURKA

The con men and the muggers,
And their wicked bosses,
Were electing new committeemen.
A girl took the floor then,
The girl's name was Murka,
And she was unyielding and bold.

To start the job off right,
It had to be toasted,
So they went off to a swanky joint.
There guitars were strumming,
And a couple was dancing—
Murka and her little pretty-boy.

So I go up to her,
And ask her for the next dance—
It was time we had ourselves a talk.
But she stands there laughing,
And pressed against her boyfriend:
I don't want to live with you no more.

In a dark back alley,
Kostya met with Murka.
Howdy, sweetcakes, now say your
        goodbyes.
You ratted on my buddies,
Now the gang's been busted,
And for that you'll answer with your life.

You used to like a good smoke,
"Troika" was your best brand,
But cigarettes won't do much good no
        more.
You used to like a good drink,
To knock back vodka with us,
But even cognac won't taste good no
        more.

So how ya doin', Murka,
Murka, you're a sweetheart.
You ratted on my buddies,
Now the gang's been busted,
And it's time that you paid up your
        dues.

Student, no. 8 (1967), p. 146.

Evening of Books
For Youth Clubs
Vitaly Zhemchuzhny (1924)

THIS IS ONE OF THE MANY POPULAR AND REVOLUTIONARY SKETCHES DONE FOR YOUTH AND WORKERS' CLUBS IN THE 1920S. ITS TARGET IS BOURGEOIS MASS CULTURE, WHICH HAD A LOCK ON RUSSIAN TASTES. THE SCENARIO WAS WRITTEN BY THE AVANT-GARDE PLAYWRIGHT, CRITIC, AND FILMMAKER VITALY ZHEMCHUZHNY; THE SETS AND COSTUMES ARE BY THE FAMOUS CONSTRUCTIVIST ARTIST VARVARA STEPANOVA.

THE CRYPTIC REFERENCES REQUIRE SOME IDENTIFICATION. ON THE ENEMY SIDE WE HAVE GOD; NAT PINKERTON, WHO SYMBOLIZES DETECTIVE FICTION; ANASTASIA VERBITSKAYA, A BESTSELLING AUTHOR OF ROMANTIC MELODRAMAS; TARZAN, THE HERO OF EDGAR RICE BURROUGHS'S JUNGLE ADVENTURES — ALL OF THESE STILL POPULAR IN REVOLUTIONARY RUSSIA AND THUS ANATHEMA TO THE BOLSHEVIKS, WHO WANTED TO PROMOTE THE "RIGHT" BOOKS. THEIR WRITING STYLES ARE PLAYFULLY MOCKED HERE.

ON THE "GOOD" SIDE IN THIS SKIT — ALSO PROVIDED BY AMERICAN POPULAR CULTURE — ARE GADFLY AND PATHFINDER, THE LITTLE RED DEVILS (FROM THE 1923 MOVIE OF THE SAME NAME: SEE ABOVE); JOHN REED, THE RADICAL AMERICAN JOURNALIST WHO WITNESSED THE RUSSIAN REVOLUTION AND WROTE A CLASSIC ACCOUNT OF IT; AND UPTON SINCLAIR, THE AMERICAN MUCKRAKER WHO EXPOSED THE EVILS OF INDUSTRIAL CAPITALISM EARLY IN THIS CENTURY.

Excerpted from *Vecher knigi v klubakh molodezhi (opyt massovoi khudozhestvennoi agitatsii za knigu)* (Moscow, 1924), pp. 40–61.

CONCLUSION

WORKER: What sort of books should we read? Anyone can find out by watching
the next scene, in which we judge good books and bad.
A moment's patience. Now let's start the show!
The characters are: the American writer Upton Sinclair; the elusive detective Nat
Pinkerton; Madame Verbitskaya, who has been greatly offended by Soviet
power; and the god Yahweh Sabaoth,[1] whom nobody has ever seen anywhere.
Without any tricks, we'll also show you the real live Tarzan, the little red devils
Gadfly and Pathfinder, and finally, the American journalist John Reed.

(Dark onstage. The god Sabaoth falls down from above. He gets up wheezing.)

SABAOTH: Yikes. I just flew straight down from heaven on an airplane. I thought
the final judgment was coming, so I had to hurry. I stand accused of swindling.
Before it was only peace and quiet. And now... Ah, it's not the good life you
run away from. I'm ashamed to say they've muddled the old man's head. What
a misfortune, you can't even tell the story. In *How Gods Are Born in General, and
in Particular Sabaoth,* the Communist Yaroslavsky[2] unmasked me, the god
Sabaoth, with poisonous phrases. The Narkomnats[3] are being reduced, so they
decide to make cutbacks on heavenly staff too. I thought that as director I
could hang on. But that wasn't the case. Dear brothers, the entire enterprise is
being liquidated. My hair fell out from grief. Grief—not a puddle, but a whole
ocean of it. Those ignorant Bolshevik writers yanked off my raiments and my
clothes. Now I'm spat on, laughed at, everyone's grown cold to me. I'm
unemployed, in a sense—bitten by the *Crocodile,* lit up by the *Projector,* mocked
by *The Godless,* Bukharins and Voronskys.[4] I weep at the Moscow River like the
Hebrews at the rivers of Babylon. My grief is too deep to be measured. Oh, I'll
sit down and think about how I can live alone in this world. *(He sits down
melancholically.)*
PINKERTON *(appearing through a trap door)*: A voice. A hair. Long. The question:
horse or dog. Footprints. A man. *(He crawls along sniffing the floor.)* Hands up!
(He aims his pistol.)
SABAOTH: A god, sir, a god. And who are you?
PINKERTON: Pinkerton. A billion readers. A billion subscribers. The King of
Detectives.
SABAOTH: And here I'm a god. It's just that I don't look so good right now. My
hair fell out from grief, so I had to become bald.
PINKERTON: Bald? New York, Dr. Duncan, 45 Fifth Avenue.
SABAOTH: Let's not waste words. My hair, if only it were my head. It's easy to live

---

1. The Hebrew Lord God of the Hosts.
2. Emelyan Yaroslavsky, an antireligious writer and leader of organized atheism.
3. Commissariat of Nationalities, just closing down in 1924.
4. *Crocodile, Projector,* and *The Godless:* satirical publications; Nikolai Bukharin: political leader and active
journalist; Aleksandr Voronsky: powerful critic and publisher.

without a head. (*Confiding*) The Bolsheviks don't want to have anything to do with holy books. May death and attrition come upon them—they took the holy books out of circulation.

PINKERTON: Yes. I've lived to see myself removed too.

VERBITSKAYA (*enters*): What's this I see? What a picture. Two men. An anguishing blackness torments my heart. To love two... I fear only dilation of the heart. . . .

PINKERTON: Madam, fortunately, we are comrades in misfortune. I am Pinkerton. I am the cousin of the Nick Carters, Holmeses, Lecoqs, and Listers, followed by their assistants: Dickies, Charlies, Rulands, and Patsys.[5] I am Pinkerton, who has billions of subscribers. I am the King of Detectives. I, Pinkerton, am Europe's detective-story miracle. A revolver, flashlight, and handcuffs, these are my faithful companions, and the thirty-two pages through which I catch and am caught are each a bucket of blood. They can seize and even kill me, but on page thirty-two I come back to life. It's the acme of the detective scene. Moreover, through my American bureau I secretly shadow worker organizations, strikes, and demonstrations. I catch the strike leaders, and receive a fat sum for my troubles. I, Pinkerton, am always cold-blooded, quick-witted, and best of all, alive on page thirty-two. I am the boulevard detective.

(*During his monologue, Pinkerton shows off his talents: waving his revolver, chasing Sabaoth, shooting, etc.*)

VERBITSKAYA: Interesting and eloquent.

SABAOTH (*to Verbitskaya*): And I, Madam, am a representive of the producers of the holy sacraments, which are a salvation from starvation, drought, and the Bolsheviks. And yet they decided to take me, the spiritual father, off the shelf.

VERBITSKAYA: That's just wonderful. You are the spiritual father, I am the spiritual mother, and they have resolved to take us off the shelf, so let us decide what we can do.

PINKERTON: Bah. I almost forgot my assistant (*he whistles*) Tarzan. An assistant without flaw, an ape-man.

(*Tarzan jumps onstage from the auditorium. During the following dialogue he acts like an ape—walking with a stoop, howling. Pinkerton introduces him to Verbitskaya.*)

PINKERTON: Tarzan will be devoted to us body and soul. Tarzan represents the satiated bourgeoisie tired of city life.

VERBITSKAYA: Fie on that. In our company! I haven't the slightest desire to mix with an ape, no matter how well mannered. They want to be beast not only in

---

5. Carter, Holmes, Lecoq, and Lister were detectives of Western birth who spawned their own Russian imitators; Dickie is Deadwood Dick, hero of Edward L. Wheeler's series; Ruland is Pinkerton's assistant, and Patsy is Carter's assistant.

the city, but also in the tropical forests, to live and love among the chimps. Hot love on the banks of the Nile.

PINKERTON: Oh, but Madam, read the fig leaf. Tarzan is no ape, he was born Lord Greystoke.

(With those words, Tarzan straightens up and bows gallantly like a lord.)

VERBITSKAYA: Ahh, the son of a lord. Well then (*giving her hand*), allow me. I'm Verbitskaya.

TARZAN: Ukh.

VERBITSKAYA: Ahh, took his breath away. What a fine one!

PINKERTON: Now, Madam. And so, there are four of us already.

(Everyone groups around Verbitskaya. The following scene is played as if they were plotting a robbery in the movies.)

VERBITSKAYA: Here's how it is, we will form an alliance on the basis of blood ties. There's no tsar anymore, but a soviet. Can we write like we used to?

PINKERTON: No.

SABAOTH: No.

TOGETHER: No.

VERBITSKAYA: If we write like before...

SABAOTH: They won't print us. . . .

VERBITSKAYA: We'll pour a stream of NEPism into the literary vat.

SABAOTH: By bribery.

VERBITSKAYA: Treachery.

PINKERTON: Penetrate all corners of publishing.

VERBITSKAYA: With the convolutions of love.

PINKERTON: With bloody detective stories. . . .

VERBITSKAYA: We'll earn our bread honestly.

PINKERTON: Gosizdat[6] will be ours.

VERBITSKAYA: So then...

TOGETHER: Lit-er-ar-y re-form.

VERBITSKAYA: Our platform.

TOGETHER: NEP.

VERBITSKAYA: Our motto.

TOGETHER: Bestseller. . . .

(John Reed enters. General panic. Everyone hides behind Pinkerton, who pulls out his pistol.)

REED: Am I bothering you?

VERBITSKAYA: Oh, you scared us.

––––––––––
6. The state publishing house.

PINKERTON: Hands up!

SABAOTH: What a scandal!

REED: Actually, I'm harmless. I'm not a criminal or a terrorist.

PINKERTON: Who are you?

REED: I'm John Reed, the American journalist...

PINKERTON: American journalist? Nothing to fear. On the contrary. All journalists in America have been bought off by Big Capital. I'm Pinkerton. (*He gives him his hand.*) We've formed an alliance that will be hard to break.

VERBITSKAYA: The Union of Writers of the Soviet Rococo.

PINKERTON: The Trust D. C.—Down with Communists![7] Against Communism under the banner of literary fascism. . . .

KOMSOMOL PRESS ADVERTISEMENT-PARADE

From five to ten newspaper workers run out with posters advertising Smena [Shift], The Young Guard, Young Leninist, etc.[8] *The following reading can be accompanied by gymnastics that connect the performers with the physical culture movement. Sections about how to subscribe can be inserted.*

> Open your ears, here's the news.
> Nope, we won't stop shouting.
> Extra, extra, read all about it.
> Read the Komsomol press.
> Listen, listen. Look, look.
> There's no time to think about it.
> The most important event here—
> Is the Komsomol paper.

———

> Read up, read the poetry and sketches.
> The life of the whole Komsomol.
> Everyone. Everyone. By radio and telephone.
> Every last one subscribe.

———

> Chronicle of knowledge, sports, and study,
> Letters, notes from all around.
> Remember our motto firmly, so that
> We sell millions of copies. Millions!

———

———

7. An ironic allusion to Ilya Ehrenburg's anticapitalist political novel *Trust D. E.* (The Give-Us-Europe Trust).

8. Communist Youth publications.

Open your ears, here's the news.
Hundreds of shouts to all the world.
Extra, extra, read all about it.
Millions of Komsomol papers.
(*Exit*)

Verbitskaya, Pinkerton, Reed, and Sabaoth enter, looking around fearfully.

VERBITSKAYA: There, did you see? Did you hear? Those are our enemies.

SABAOTH: Lord, save the lord.

PINKERTON: My plan is this: find and destroy.

VERBITSKAYA: Well, I'm with you on that.

SABAOTH: Isn't it dangerous? They're such a clever bunch that if you don't watch out you'll end up in heaven. Of course, that would be convenient: a free ride home, but what about the rest of the trust?

PINKERTON: There's no time to think about that. After them!

SABAOTH: Hold on a second. I'll go a bit slower, or else I'll lose. (*He hitches up his pants.*) You go on ahead, I'll catch up.

PINKERTON: No, we'll all go together. Reed will bring up the rear.

(*They steal away. The lights go out, and Gadfly and Pathfinder sneak onto the stage with flashlights.*)

GADFLY: Did you hear that?

PATHFINDER: I heard it.

GADFLY: And what does it mean?

PATHFINDER: As sure as my name is Pathfinder, they must die.

GADFLY: As sure as my name is Gadfly.

PATHFINDER: I swear by the beard of Gosizdat.

TOGETHER: As sure as we're little red devils.

(*Reed enters. They charge him with pistols aimed.*)

PATHFINDER: Aha, here's one.

GADFLY: Halt!

PATHFINDER: Get your hands out of your pockets!

GADFLY: Don't move!

PATHFINDER: Who are you?

GADFLY: Where you coming from?

REED: I'm John Reed, the American journalist.

PATHFINDER: Knock him out.

GADFLY: No, let him go.

PATHFINDER: My red-skinned brother made a mistake.

GADFLY: But that's John Reed.

REED: Yes, I'm John Reed, and I only latched onto the D. C. Company so I could describe how those four fools would meet the end of their D. C. campaign. Yes,

I'm John Reed, heart and soul with the Bolsheviks in October, their comrade by the light of history's fires, who in uneven prose described all the power of the country and people and the grandeur of those ten days that shook the world.

GADFLY: You can go without fear. You're free to do what you like.

(Reed exits.)

PATHFINDER: He'll tip them off and screw it all up.

GADFLY: Don't you know who John Reed is?

(A megaphone gives information about John Reed while it's dark. It would be good to show his portrait and the cover of his book on a screen.)

MEGAPHONE: John Reed was an American socialist journalist. One of the best reporters in the world. Traveled the whole world. Wherever there was a significant event, he was there. To publish one of John Reed's articles was an honor all the big newspapers competed for. In Russia in 1917 he observed the course of the Great Russian Revolution. He attentively followed the heroic struggle of the proletariat during the October days. He actively enlisted in the Communist movement and became one of the Comintern's most famous members. In his book *Ten Days That Shook the World,* he gave a wonderful description of the events of October. He died of typhus in Russia, and was buried on Red Square next to the Kremlin Wall. Lenin said: "I would like to see John Reed printed and distributed by the millions."

(When the megaphone is done, the lights come on again. Gadfly and Pathfinder are gone. Sinclair and a worker enter talking.)

WORKER: Well, Comrade Sinclair, how do you like it in Soviet Russia?

SINCLAIR: Wonderful. Wonderful. Life is bursting out anew. Everything is building and growing. It's just...

WORKER: Just what?

SINCLAIR: You're scatterbrained. And how can I say this...

WORKER: Muddle-headed. You can say it, don't be afraid.

SINCLAIR: Oh, that's not it! You're sensible enough. You have plenty of common sense, and you're quick on the uptake.

WORKER: Then what's the matter?

SINCLAIR: It's that with all your sense and quick wits, you're poor managers, and you're not organized enough. . . .

(The lights go out. When they come on again, Sinclair is alone. Pinkerton steals up to him.)

PINKERTON (*knocks Sinclair off his feet*): Don't move! Hands up! Handcuffs (*he puts them on*)... Well, buddy, I'll make things hot for you! You stirred up workers in

America with your exposés, and now you've shown up here with your writing. You want to open their eyes to America. (*He whistles.*) Hey, Tarzan! (*Tarzan appears.*) Call everyone in. (*Exit Tarzan.*) You've captured my attention. The honor will be great. You can try out my fist. (*Enter Verbitskaya, Sabaoth, and Tarzan.*) Ladies and gentlemen, the king of criminals, Upton Sinclair, has been apprehended.

TOGETHER: Long live Pinkerton!

SABAOTH: But if you'll excuse me. We're shouting "Long live," yet we don't know what part this scoundrel played in the international red gang.

VERBITSKAYA: Tell me, what part?

PINKERTON: Evidence? Proof? Allow me. My name isn't Pinkerton if this isn't Upton Sinclair, who, infected by socialist teachings, has decided to expose bourgeois society. In *100%* he portrayed a police detective, and he portrayed him so that oh-no! In *Jimmie Higgins* he divulged military secrets; *King Coal* is an extraordinary novel that tells all Europe how coal-miners are exploited. In a word, every last one of his works is directed against the capitalist order. And so there won't be any doubt of his crime, I'll show you the material evidence without delay. (*The titles and covers of Sinclair's books are shown on a screen or posters.*)

VERBITSKAYA: Oh, Lord, that's horrible.

SABAOTH: I think I'll exert myself and bind the heretic.

PINKERTON: Well, you won't be much help. Tarzan can do the work of two.

TARZAN: Ukh, ukh. (*He ties Sinclair.*)

PINKERTON: Okay, Verbitskaya will stand guard and we'll go after the enemy. We'll show them. . . .

(*Exit. Gadfly and Pathfinder sneak up on Verbitskaya.*)

PATHFINDER: Halt!

GADFLY: Don't move! (*He tosses a sack over Verbitskaya's head.*)

VERBITSKAYA: Oh, Lord.

PATHFINDER: Let's free Sinclair.

GADFLY (*untying Sinclair*): Done.

PATHFINDER: We got here just in the nick of time to free you.

GADFLY: We redskins are indebted to you, and now the hour has come to pay you back.

SINCLAIR: Thanks.

VERBITSKAYA: What right did you have to tie up my hands? The ropes are drawing blood.

PATHFINDER: The paleface squaw is telling the truth. Let's untie her.

GADFLY: And we'll put our enemies on trial. The great hour has come. (*To Sinclair*) Redskin chief, you preside, I'll be the prosecutor, and you, brother Pathfinder, be witness for the prosecution.

SINCLAIR: Name?

VERBITSKAYA: I am Verbitskaya.

SINCLAIR: Profession?

VERBITSKAYA: Spiritual mother.

SINCLAIR: Do you have anything else to say for yourself?

GADFLY: No. Let me speak now. The chief of the palefaces stands accused of shooting an arrow dipped in the poison of dimestore romance into young people's hearts. To put an end to such an epidemic, I demand before the great redskin chief that the paleface squaw be killed with a red tomahawk on the first new moon.

SINCLAIR: Witness Pathfinder, you can tell us everything you know without fear. When, where, and for what reason.

PATHFINDER: I confirm the testimony of my glorious redskin brother Gadfly.

SINCLAIR (*to Verbitskaya*): What do you say in your defense?

VERBITSKAYA: Permit me, you have completely misunderstood my novels. Are you in the least bit familiar with them? Why, *The Keys to Happiness* is a poem of love. . . .

SINCLAIR: Enough. The court, without wasting its strength on contemplation, has decided to consider the allegations proven. Within twenty-four hours Madame Verbitskaya is to be removed from all libraries and transferred to the archive.

(Pathfinder and Gadfly take Verbitskaya by the arms and legs and swing her back and forth, singing. When the song [sung to the tune of "Volga Boatman"] is completed, they toss her backstage.)

> Yo ho, heave ho, not a word said.
> Yo ho, lively, yo ho quickly.
> So that nowadays, of this trash
> Nothing remained, not a single trace,
> So this foolishness, silly senselessness
> Could not turn the head of the Komsomol.
> From the shelves of the libraries
> Once and for all
> Fly off quietly.

PATHFINDER (*to Gadfly*): You stay here on guard, and we'll go track down the rest.

(Pathfinder and Sinclair exit. Gadfly stays behind and is attacked by Pinkerton.)

PINKERTON: Hands up! We finally caught you too. Your Bolshevik notions have begun to look like detective novels. You pup, you Bukharin Pinkerton,[9] take a look now. Say goodbye to life. (*He aims his revolver.*) One, two.

PATHFINDER (*appearing suddenly, he knocks the gun from Pinkerton's hand*): Three...

(A fight. Pinkerton whistles. Tarzan races onstage from the audience to help him. Sinclair, brought back by all the noise, cuts him off. An all-out brawl. Tarzan is

---

9. Refers to a famous article by Nikolai Bukharin, "Red Pinkerton," in which he suggested that Soviet culture might do well to learn from the popularity of bourgeois mass culture. Blyakhin's *The Little Red Devils* and Shaginyan's *Mess-Mend* were inspired by the article.

knocked to the ground, but slips away and flees. Everyone jumps on him again and ties him up.)

PATHFINDER: Put the handcuffs on him.

GADFLY: Don't get angry.

PATHFINDER: Don't fight back, or else your head is going to hit the wall. They're your own handcuffs, only before you had them in your pocket and now they're on your wrists. . . .

GADFLY: Redskin brothers, I propose we put our prisoners on trial.

SINCLAIR: Your proposal is accepted. (*To Pinkerton*) Name?

PINKERTON: Pinkerton.

SINCLAIR: Profession?

PINKERTON: King of detectives.

SINCLAIR: Edition?

PINKERTON: Billions of subscribers.

SINCLAIR (*to Sabaoth*): And you? Are you dressed for *Crocodile*'s All-Soviet Idiot Contest?

SABAOTH (*embarrassed*): I'm... a writer... of the Soviet rococo.

SINCLAIR: Last name?

SABAOTH: I don't have a patronymic or last name. My name is Sabaoth.

SINCLAIR: When were you born?

SABAOTH: Depends how you measure it. Some say it was 1,923 years ago, but Yaroslavsky doesn't believe it.

SINCLAIR: Profession?

SABAOTH: Religious worship, absolution of sins, preparation of remains, miraculous cures, sanctifying of warfare. . . .

SINCLAIR: You may speak, prosecutor.

GADFLY: Pinkerton is accused of casting his detective novel net and catching young people, arousing their fantasy with absurd fairy tales; being hanged, stabbed, killed, but catching the crook for thirty-one pages, and coming back to life on page thirty-two. Even worse than absurd revival is that he spiritually scalped our youth. There is not one mitigating circumstance. I ask the court that his scalp be taken in return. Sabaoth stands accused of imprisoning all illiterate Russia. In light of the fact that his crimes were all premeditated, I recommend the whipping post for him. For three days and nights we will let his blood drop by drop, and prick him with a spear.

SABAOTH (*frightened, clutching at his hind parts, imagining how they will prick him*): Ow! Permit me a word about the living and the dead.

SINCLAIR: First let the witnesses speak. Pathfinder.

PATHFINDER: The paleface dog Pinkerton threw—I saw it myself—his fatal lasso at preschool, first-grade, and second-grade children, and dragged them off by his saddle. And not only young people, but adults, even old folks, went for his five-kopeck snares.

SINCLAIR: You may speak, Comrade Worker.

WORKER: Let me make a general point by the by. Here, they say, is our new life.

But where has it gone? How can it be when God has eaten into our life like rust? Our wives, sisters, and mothers are infected by religion, they read the holy books, the gospels, and psalter—the holy blisters. They believe some priest's nonsense about how the whole world and the people will perish in January of '25. It's ridiculous, but worker families have split up because of it. We have to make sure this sawed-off counterrevolution goes to hell. About that bride of Christ, give her a knee where she needs it.

SINCLAIR (*to Pinkerton*): What can you say in your defense?

PINKERTON: I won't dignify your words with an answer. I don't want anything to do with bandits, much less to confess to them.

WORKER: Take it easy, buddy, this isn't page thirty-two.

SINCLAIR (*writing*): The defendant refuses the right to speak in his own defense. Sabaoth, will we be hearing from you?

SABAOTH: I confess, I confess to everything. I repent. Just don't let me die, acquit me.

SINCLAIR: Acquit you? But you've confessed fully to everything.

SABAOTH: Don't let me die. Build your new life, I'll be useful and fit in somehow. I won't write anything, I never wrote a line—those idiot evangelists wrote everything for me. (*To Sinclair*) I beg you humbly, give me even the littlest thing. You can send me to Meyerhold[10] for cameo roles, just don't prick me with that spear.

SINCLAIR: Having heard the final testimony of the accused, the court rules: in light of the fact that Pinkerton is openly a literary bandit who has insulted even the court, his adventures must be burned immediately, to the last letter. Regarding the god Sabaoth, writer of the Soviet rococo, bearing in mind that his life is already bitter, and secondly, that he has now been consecrated in a Soviet manner and exposed by Yaroslavsky, so that nobody sees anything divine in him, we rule: let him go free.

SABAOTH: Lord. May god grant you good health. Long life to your mind and body. Now let's scram before they change their minds. (*Joyfully dancing, he exits.*)

REED (*writing in his notepad*): The D. C. Campaign is finished.

WORKER: The unholy alliance busted, but only thanks to the little red devils, who liberated Soviet literature and put an end to the literary NEP. Those guys are the first Soviet detective story. The first successful attempt. The author: Comrade Blyakhin, published in Kharkov. Here are the heroes of the little red devils: Gadfly and Pathfinder.

PATHFINDER: And now, whether you like it or not, the show is over.

GADFLY: To conclude, we appeal to you, our dear audience: the struggle was hard, almost the entire D. C. campaign has been liquidated—almost, because Tarzan got away. And so, esteemed audience, if someone happens to catch the ape Tarzan, bring the book to us; we'll abuse him so he'll never forget it, destroy a literary evil, and find the best use for the book in the scrap-paper mill.

TOGETHER: The end.

---

10. Soviet avant-garde stage director.

Blue Blouse Skit

(1924)

THE BLUE BLOUSE WORKERS' THEATER MOVEMENT WAS THE POPULAR STAGE EQUIVALENT OF THE RED DETECTIVE STORY AND FILM. COLLECTIVE TROUPES AND WORKSHOPS PUT ON "LIVING NEWSPAPERS," USUALLY ONE-HOUR SHOWS IN THE WORKPLACE OR CAFETERIA, ACTING OUT THE DAY'S NEWS AND COMMENTING SHARPLY ON CURRENT EVENTS THROUGH SONGS, DITTIES, AND SKITS. THE THEME OF ELECTRIFICATION WAS ONE OF THE MAJOR MYTHS OF BOLSHEVISM IN THE EARLY YEARS, SPRINGING FROM LENIN'S EXTRAVAGANT DREAMS ABOUT ITS POWER TO TRANSFORM HUMANKIND.

ELECTRIFICATION

We, the workers and the peasants,
Swept the tsarist throne away.
We twist a socket in the ceiling
And it shines the night away!

He blew away like a cloud of dust,
His imperial majesty.
We twist a socket in the ceiling
And there's electricity.

Dear heart, wait a bit, you'll see,
The whole world will turn around:
Lookit, there's a 'lectrical
Windmill working in our town.

In the hut of the widow Natalka,
Something's shining through the night
I'll be darned, I'll be darned,
Moonlight sure don't shine that bright.

Siniaia bluza, 1 (1924), p. 57.

Electricity and steam
Reap and mow and forge for us.
Soon electricity, not brains
Will do our thinking all for us.[1]

---

1. A joke of the time ran:
A man says to his neighbor, "Boy, I hate those living newspapers!"
"Why's that, you don't like the ideology?"
"Not at all, you just can't wrap anything up in them." [3:49]
Another joke, concerning the electrification drive, ran like this:
If Communism = Soviet power + electrification, then
Soviet power = Communism − electrification, and
Electrification = Communism − Soviet power. [5:132]

Note: Most of the anecdotes cited in this book are common knowledge, and there are several sources for many of them. Wherever possible, I have provided a source and page. [1] Eugene Lyons, *Moscow Carousel* (New York, 1937); [2] *Anekdoty pro tsaria Nikolia dikaria* (Petrograd, 1918); [3] *Sovetskie anektdoty* (Berlin: Chuzhbina [1928–1932]); [4] E. Andreevich, *Kreml' i narod* (Munich, 1951); [5] Dora Shturman and Sergei Tiktin, *Sovetskii soiuz v zerkale politicheskogo anekdota* (London, 1985).

Vladimir Ilyich Lenin
Vladimir Mayakovsky (1924)

MAYAKOVSKY (1893–1930) IS THE REVOLUTION'S MOST FAMOUS POET. HIS REPUTE MIRACULOUSLY SURVIVED HIS SUICIDE IN 1930 BECAUSE OF STALIN'S FONDNESS FOR HIS WORK, EVEN THOUGH MAYAKOVSKY'S POETRY FOUND DIFFICULT ACCEPTANCE AMONG WORKERS. THIS POEM CONTRASTS THE IRON CHARACTER OF THE BOLSHEVIKS WITH THEIR TEARFUL REACTION TO LENIN'S DEATH IN 1924.

A Bolshevik
  in tears?
Should a museum
  put him
    on display,
what a house

    he'd draw!
      Who ever saw
  a Bolshevik
    in tears!
Mamontov's rider
  sewed us

Excerpt translated by Isadore Schneider, in Vladimir Mayakovsky, *Vladimir Ilyich Lenin* (excerpts), *International Literature*, no. 1 (1939), pp. 39–45.

in sacks,
with branding irons
   fissured
      our backs.
The Japanese
   "pacifying"
      for the yen
fueled
   their locomotives
      with our men.
To make sure
   we were sealed
      as dead
They served us
   drinks of
      boiling lead.
"Curse Communism!"
   these gentlemen
      yelled
   while the lead pot
      heated.
Two words
   our last gasp
      formed,
two words
   our dying lips
      repeated,
"Live Communism!"

On January twenty-second
   this same
      human steel,
this fire-forged
   man iron
      met;
in patient rows
   sat down
the great
   soviet.
They finished off
   some routine
      bother,
then sat there
   looking
      at each other.
Chairlegs scrape,
   dig holes

in the floor.
It's time!
   It's time!
      What are they waiting for?
Why
   are their eyes
      raw red
         like meat?
Why
   can't Kalinin
      stand straight
         on his feet?
Is he ill?
   What's up?
      Tell me!
That?
   No.
      It cannot
         be!
A sudden
   night
      blackens
         the ceiling;
chokes on it
   pealing.
The lamps
   lose their
      light,
and our faces
   their
      life.
And lusters
   are shadows.
Self-mastered
  at last
      Kalinin
         stands straight.
but his streaked face,
   wet mustache,
      limp beard
and still weeping look
   betrayed
      a Bolshevik
         in tears.
Grief grips
   his lean hands,
Grief clots

his breast,
drives in his
    veins,—
"Last night
    ten minutes
        to seven
Comrade
    Lenin
        died!"

The stuff of centuries
    has crammed
        this year.
This black-bordered day
    will see many
        centennials.
We heard iron
    cry;
we saw grief
    strike sobs
        from the iron
            Bolsheviks.
The steadfast,
    the strong,
        with hearts
            iron-ahooped,
who'd faced
    death
        erect
met
    this death,
        stooped.
In its black drapes
    the Bolshoi
        Theater
tossed
    on the square,
        like a mammoth
            hearse.
Joy was a snail,
    but misfortune
        a horse;
galloping misfortune
    rode us
        down.
The sun is blank;
    ice cannot

glow
Sieved through black news
    this winter
        sheds
            black snow.
In the brain
    of the man
        at the bench,
the news
    rips
        like a
            bullet;
and his stare
    spills slowly
        like tears
            on glass.
A peasant, never moved
    by the faces
        and gestures
            of death,
tonight wiped his face
    and startled his wife
        with the mud
            his hand
                left on his cheek.
The stone stolid,
    the grim,
        the impassive,
tonight
    cracked their shells
        bit their lips
            wrung their hands.
Tonight
    children were like sober
        old men,
and sober
    old men
        wept like children.

    Like a steppe wind
over our lives
    howls
        our bereavement;
the stunned land
    cannot believe,
        cannot yet
            believe

that Moscow
  is a mortuary,
that there lies
  the coffin
    of the revolution's
      son and father!

One thought welds worker,
  peasant,
    Red Army man:
Lenin is gone.
  And hard now
    is the road
      of the republic
        without him!
But panting
  on mattresses
    never
      will smooth it.
Whom
  shall we set in his place
and how
  find him?
"A note,
  Comrade Secretary:
    Register tonight
the collective enrollment
  of our whole plant
    in the Communist cell."
The bourgeoisie
  shivers.
Straight from
  their benches,
    four hundred thousand
themselves
  bequeath;
four hundred thousand
  marching
    twining

Lenin's
    first party wreath!
"Listen,
  Comrade Secretary,
    enter this in the bank...
We will replace...
We must
  replace...
If I'm too old
  here's my grandson
    from the Komsomol!"
So Ilyich
  even in death
    remained
our best
  organizer.
A million arms,
  a sudden forest;
    the forest
      waves.
Red Square becomes
  a living
    red flag.
The line of march
  is its living staff.
From the immense
  living folds
    once more
Lenin
  living
    speaks:
"Draw up
  proletarians
    for the final clash;
slaves stiffen
  your backs,
    straighten
      your knees!"

  Popular reaction to Lenin's death was not always so reverent. Anecdotes of the time lost no piety on the topic:

  A Nepman buys a picture of the deceased Lenin and asks for the same kind of picture of all the leaders [1:323].

  Another ran like this:

  Two Petersburg thieves, having robbed a jewelry store, leave a note: "Lenin is dead, but his cause lives on" [3:76].

[For anecdote sources, see *Blue Blouse Skit,* above.]

Voyage of the Red Star Pioneer Troop to Wonderland

Innokenty Zhukov (1924)

POLITICAL UTOPIA AND SCIENCE FICTION — A WIDELY USED COMBINATION IN THE 1920s — JOIN UP IN THIS CHILDREN'S TALE OF EIGHT BOYS WHO LAND IN A BEAUTIFUL, BRIGHT COMMUNIST FUTURE OF ESPERANTO, GLASS CITIES, AND AEROBALL IN THE DISTANT YEAR 1957.

TO CAMP

Thinking of going to India? To the tropical countries? No need at all!

The "Red Stars" weren't headed for any wonderland. They were only going for a couple of days at the end of June to a forest camp on the banks of a small mountain stream flowing from the Ural foothills.

They left for the Pioneer camp on a most typical day and found themselves in wonderland, not some India or the tropics.

But then, everything should be told in order. First of all, let me introduce our travelers.

They are the "Red Star" troop of the Young Leninist Pioneers, Second Lysogorsk Detachment.

They're all nice children, friendly. The troop had just celebrated their first anniversary, which brought them even closer together.

Here are their first and last names: Kostya Chernyakov, Misha Surovtsev, Vanya Petenko, Kolya Saburov, Kolya Chernov, Seryozha Stupin, Monya Girsh, Grisha Stepanov, and their mascot, the dog Sharik (Balloon).

The Red Stars loved their leader Seryozha and would have followed him not only to the forest camp, but to the ends of the earth, if the earth were shaped like a plate and not a watermelon, which doesn't have an edge. . . .

Excerpted from *Puteshestvie zvena Krasnoi Zvezdy v stranu chudes,* Biblioteka iunogo lenintsa, no. 22 (Kharkov: Vseukrainskoe Ob-vo Sodeistviia Iunomu Lenintsu, 1924), pp. 3–4, 6–28, 31–36, 39–51, 62–69, 83–104.

The "Red Star" Pioneer Troop

As leader, Seryozha walked in front with the banner as the others followed in his tracks. They tried to sing "Kartoshka" (Potato), but that was hard to do on the move. They looked around from time to time. Everything behind them remained the same; while something new, unfamiliar, unknown loomed before them. In the leader's pocket were the Leadership Council's instructions: "Inspect the Kaidalovsky Sawmill, and also: how many tree species there are in the Kaidalovsky Forest, and gather their leaves; what insects live and work in these trees. Label the collection when you get back and exhibit it for the Pioneer club, and make a report about camp life and the troop's work."

The sun had already touched ground as our "Red Stars" entered the forest.

Everything instantly became cool and, in some new way, quiet. They halted. Seryozha took a map from his pocket and spread it out on the ground. They all lay down around him and for the tenth time began studying the route and familiarizing themselves with the forest roads and paths.

They were supposed to take a path through the forest depths to the banks of the Kaidalovka stream.

Having rested a bit, the troop set off on its way. The deeper they penetrated the forest, the darker, quieter, and gloomier it got. Night descended.

Sharik no longer bounded about the forest path, but silently and efficiently ran along the path ahead of the troop.

Kolya Chernov and Monya Girsh, the youngest members of the troop, were a little worried, but they tried to hide it.

"They say there used to be a lot of wolves around here, but now they're all gone: the hunters killed them off," said Seryozha. Things weren't so scary after that. Kostya even started whistling a march tune. Everyone began walking in step, and the hush of approaching nightfall was punctuated by their footfalls.

Suddenly Sharik stopped, pricked up his ears, and barked. He yapped once or twice and resumed his intent listening.

They took several steps, trying to walk more softly.

But what they saw around a bend in the path forced them to stop again.

A patch of ground before them was burning. That's how it seemed at first.

But there wasn't any smoke, and the light on the ground didn't move.

"Is a forest fire starting?" flashed through everyone's mind.

Their terror passed. The Red Stars raced after their leader to save the forest: this was how Leninist Pioneers of Soviet Russia should act.

There wasn't any fire, but whatever was there didn't yield to explanation.

For three arshins around, the ground was ablaze with an even, milky light. Pine-needle debris had formed weird designs on the glowing spot.

"What is it? A window underground??!" The "Stars" surrounded the glowing spot, leaned over, and tried to guess the cause of the mysterious light. Sharik's nose also took part in the investigation.

A brilliant opaque crystal surface shone through the debris, radiating a milky white light extraordinarily pleasant to look at.

Nothing could be seen through the opaque surface. But the investigation had yet to be concluded. First Sharik, snorting, began raking through the debris with his nose, then the others followed.

1957—four digits blazed blindingly bright on the surface of the mysterious circle.

1957. What does that mean? Is it a number or a year? But before anyone could make a guess, something new, unexpected, and improbable happened to the Red Stars. Their leader, Seryozha Stupin, disappeared.

He accidentally put both feet on the glowing circle and... and he was gone.

His disappearance was so incredible that their eyes refused to believe it.

He couldn't have fallen in, because the surface of the glowing crystal was intact.

"Seryozha! Seryozha! Where are you?" shouted the Pioneers. Was this one of his jokes... was he hiding in the bushes? They searched the bushes. Sharik took a zealous part in the search. But Seryozha wasn't anywhere to be found.

Vanya Petenko grabbed a rock and knocked several times on the glass with it. They waited for an answer, but the only response was the silence of that strange night.

"Let's break the 'window'!" someone suggested.

Vanya Petenko wound up and threw a rock for all he was worth, but not even a crack appeared in the glass.

They kept throwing things at it, but with no more success than before.

"Let's go home. We'll tell them—they'll get somebody out here," Kolya Saburov suggested.

Perhaps, readers, one of you would have found that proposal the most reasonable, but that's because you don't know just what Leninist Pioneers are. Was it really possible to abandon a lost leader and ask other people, outsiders, to search for him?

No, such behavior is not common among Pioneers and Leninists.

But what could they do? They stood on the path that had taken them into the enchanted forest and wondered what to do.

"There's only one thing left to do," the assistant leader, Misha Surovtsev, said decisively. "Follow him. Everyone stand on the circle, everyone disappear."

Everyone was scared by these words. . . .

"Seryozha!" yelled Monya Girsh with timid hope.

"Ser-yo-zha!" the whole troop shouted collectively. But the night was as silent as before.

Through a clearing above, they could see the sky sprinkled with glittering stars.

"Hey, hold up, guys!" said Misha.

Pallid and sober, they stood up where they had stopped at the command.

"At my command: One! two! three! Everyone into the circle! Get set! . . . Go!"
And the troop, headed by the courageous Misha, stepped into the circle.

THE SHINING BOYS

At first it seemed that nothing special had happened. The same forest surrounded them. They were walking along a path. Seryozha Stupin was in front of them, as before, and Sharik was still running ahead. Everything was as before, but the sky above the forest was completely different, and so was the path they were taking. The sky was illuminated by some sort of bright-orange light. They couldn't see the source of the light, but they felt it was somewhere beyond the forest's dark curtain.

The path was laid with bricks of a glass-like material and stretched ruler-straight, without a bend. And when they looked closer, the forest was completely different, too: there wasn't any brushwood or debris fallen from the trees, and there were no stumps. It seemed austere and efficient, not messy and unkempt, as before.

"I don't understand, where are we? said Monya Girsh, but nobody answered him. They couldn't have if they tried.

"Look! Look! What's that?!"

A light on the glass path appeared far in the distance.

The boys stopped. They could see the light moving toward them.

"Let's hide!" said Kostya.

"Take your positions for reconnaissance!" ordered Seryozha, and at his command everyone rushed off to hide in the bushes nearby.

What they saw was absolutely extraordinary. Eight boys dressed like them and carrying a troop standard approached and passed, but their flag and clothes shone with a green light, just like the light of a glow-worm at night.

"Are they ghosts?" little Grisha said fearfully.

"Be quiet! There's no such thing as ghosts!" Seryozha whispered sternly.

What they heard then also amazed them, and at the same time reassured them.

The shining boy walking in front said in the most ordinary Russian: "Site No. 117... It won't be far now. We can stop there till morning."

The radiant boys went by.

The Red Stars, enchanted by what they had seen and heard, followed them quietly.

Suddenly Sharik started barking.

Grisha, whose grandmother had muddled his head with silly ghost stories, got scared and started running away. Monya cowered. Vanya wanted to grab Sharik and hold his mouth shut, but Sharik jumped away and kept barking.

Suddenly Seryozha's short, jerky whistle was heard, and the boys ran to their leader.

It was as if time had stopped. The Red Stars waited for what would happen, ready for anything.

The light of the shining boys, boys like they had never seen before, went out. It was as if the black curtain of night had covered it.

The Pioneers listened tensely. Hearts beat faster in the troop members' chests.

And then the clothes of a glow-worm boy shone like a movie screen close by, and his voice, which had nothing terrible or threatening in it, could be heard asking: "Who are you guys, and where are you from?"

"From Lysogorsk," answered Seryozha, "Leninist Pioneers from the 'Red Star' troop. We're lost, we don't know where we are. Sharik!!! Shut up!! Kostya, get Sharik. And who are you, where are you from?"

"We're Leninist Pioneers from the 'Eternal Campfire' troop. Come with us to site No. 117, we can relax and talk some."

Our boys looked closely at the leader of the "glow-worms" now. He had a red Pioneer kerchief just like theirs on his neck, a shirt, shorts, and a backpack. It all radiated a bluish light.

There was a whistle, which seemed different, harmonic and pleasant, and both troops set off again along the glass path, with the light ones in front and the dark ones in back. Their footsteps echoed through the dark of night.

Within five minutes, a dark forest corridor to their left opened onto the site.

What happened then seemed like a fantastic dream to our boys:

First off, the "glow-worm" leader made the same pleasant whistle, which sounded like beautiful music. Then his voice: "Radiolight!"

Two shining boys left the troop and raced quickly about the clearing, scattering the trees and shrubs with something that looked like finely cut petals of paper. Two others spread a heap of these petals on the ground and raked them into a pile. Meanwhile, still another shining boy sat on the ground holding a box of some sort and waited for the leader's signal.

"Contact!"

"Contact!"

And then something happened that opened the Lysogorsk boys' eyes wide with amazement and surprise: the whole clearing and all the trees around sparkled with an extraordinarily pretty, colorful luster, and the pile of petals in the middle lit up with an orange fire that radiated warmth and light.

The Red Stars sat in silent admiration of what they were seeing. "Take a seat, guys," the leader of the "glow-worm" troop said in a simple, friendly manner.

The light and dark boys sat down together, and the light ones immediately turned dark. Their clothes stopped glowing.

When everyone was sitting around the orange fire, our boys started examining their new friends.

Boys like any other: nothing special. So it seemed to them at first, and only later did they discover there was a significant difference between them. But let's not race ahead.

"Guys, let's not waste time: there's an hour and a half until bedtime. First we have to get to know each other, then we have to send a radiogram by radiophonc to TsBYuP, Central Bureau of the Young Pioneers, reporting on the completion of our assigned tasks and our meeting with the Lysogorsk pioneers. Okay?"

"Okay!!!" the "glow-worms" answered in chorus.

"To save time, let's have each troop prepare questions for the other troop. I'll give three minutes for that. But first, let's find out everyone's name. I'll start. My name is Niputs Azhyores, leader of the 'Eternal Campfire' troop."

"I'm Vorubas Yalok," said one of the "glow-worms."

"I'm... I'm... I'm..." voices exchanged first and last names.

Then the troops broke apart and began to prepare questions.

A whistle brought both troops back to the campfire.

"You ask first," said the leader Niputs Azhyores.

"Okay," answered Seryozha Stupin. "Why did your clothes glow when we were walking along the path?"

This question was extremely shocking to the "glow-worms," and they looked at Seryozha with smiles and surprise.

"You don't know?! Tell them, Ashirg."

A TALK BY THE FOREST CAMPFIRE

Then Ashirg, the smallest Pioneer of the "Eternal Campfire," spoke up.

It was evident that he was used to expounding his thoughts, and he obviously considered himself a specialist on this question.

"Listen up. In August 1933 the radiophone announced to the whole world the news that a Scandinavian scholar, the Swede Ingrid, had discovered in her chemistry laboratory the secret of a glow-worm's light.

"The next few years saw thousands of factories the world over start manufacturing shining fabrics that were impregnated with a special chemical and connected to pocket batteries storing a special type of energy.

"The wireless transmission of this energy had been invented much earlier, and it made it possible for us to create such wonderful lighting here in the forest, or else... look here." He took a handful of thin, multicolored paper circles from a bag, threw them up in the air, pressed a button on the box standing next to him, and the paper petals circled in the air like hundreds of colorful glowing butterflies.

"How pretty!" Vanya Petenko exclaimed involuntarily. The glowing leaves were strewn about the grass and sparkled on the sitting boys' heads and shoulders.

"Like a dream. It's hard to believe . . . , Kolya Saburov said aloud. But what was that you said about the secret being uncovered in 1933? It's only 1924 now."

You can't imagine the merry laughter of the "Eternal Campfire" pioneers when Kolya Saburov spoke that phrase.

We readers would laugh the same way if someone told us with a straight face that it's only 1884 now.

We would think he was joking.

"Don't laugh: I'm telling the truth," said Kolya with an offended voice.

"That means you come from the beginning of 'The Great World Revolution?'" said Niputs Azhyores with a smile. "You come from 1924?.. Interesting. You, Vorubas, should give them a good questioning, you're the historian."

"But what happened after 1924?" asked Kostya Chernyakov with curiosity.

"Ask our 'Professor.' Really, Yalok, give us a history lecture."

These words were meant for the pioneer Yalok Vorubas, a fourteen-year-old boy with a large forehead and thoughtful, serious eyes.

The nickname "Professor" fit him perfectly.

He begged off out of modesty, but seeing serious interest and attention on the part of the Red Star troop, and perhaps flattered by the attention, he began telling of the working class's great heroic struggle for its liberation. At first he spoke haltingly, choosing his words carefully, but then his speech flowed smoothly and captured the attention of his listeners.

"Guys, you of course know that in 1924, the scarlet flag of social revolution flew only in Soviet Russia; only there did all power belong to the workers and peasants. The rest of the world was ruled by the heavy hand of the greedy bourgeoisie, who oppressed workers and peasants. But already by that year, worker rebellions were flaring up here and there in Western Europe and other countries, and the Communist Party, the leader of revolutionary fighters, was growing. Tens and hundreds of thousands of young workers, Komsomols, joined together under the red banners of revolution.

In the ensuing years, the flame of revolutionary fire spread to Germany, Belgium, France, Italy, England, and America.

The deadly and final battle of two giants, Labor and Capital, unfolded across the entire globe.

Soviet Russia (USSR), which had rebuilt its economy by then, Moscow, and the Kremlin were the citadel, the indestructible fortress, and the Comintern was the general headquarters of the worldwide army of rebellious workers and peasants.

The heroic Red Army, like a mighty armored fist, rained blow after blow upon the dwindling armies of capital's stooges.

Several more years passed in agonizing but heroic battle before the whole world was adorned with red banners, like red flowers.

The Great Union of Soviet Socialist Republics, founded in 1923, was joined voluntarily by all the peoples of the earth, and turned the world into a peaceful labor commune.

War on earth ceased forever.

Mankind, liberated, became master of the world. With the disappearance of oppression and violent force, enlightenment swept the world in a broad wave. Magnificent scientific discoveries and inventions gradually made mankind's life on earth easy and joyful—just like a holiday, yet not idle.

Perhaps you'll ask what Leninist Pioneers did in the era of revolutionary upheaval.

In 1924 there were only 90,000 of them in Soviet Russia, and about as many in Western Europe, but the children's movement, led by the Young Communist League, which had branches all over the world, grew like a snowball, and in the coming years its ranks would number hundreds of thousands and millions of boys and girls seized by the ardent desire to help their fathers and older brothers to fight and build.

They grew up into steadfast, courageous Komsomols, and then into members of the Great Communist Party.

During the revolutionary wars, many wonderfully disciplined detachments of our brother Pioneers not only served in the rear alongside women's organizations, they also rendered essential services to proletarian armies at the front.

"In the newspapers of that time you can find many descriptions of the exploits of Pioneer troops and individual Leninist Pioneers. A particularly remarkable exploit was accomplished by a Belorussian Pioneer troop, who delivered some vital documents and radio codes to Paris when it was blockaded by the fascists in 1929.

"But I'll tell you about that some other night, if you don't object to leaving tomorrow for a trip of several days. We'll show you our country and how we live now." . . .

I can't help telling you about one more incident. Its protagonist was Sharik. While Sharik was finishing his supper, one of the "glow-worms" was petting him.

Suddenly he jumped back in horror and exclaimed: "Ugh, fleas!" and with a squeamish look began wiping his hand. Not a minute had passed before two other "glow-worms" had grabbed Sharik and, despite his resistance and howling, dragged him away from the fire and tied him to a tree.

"What's this?" the indignant Niputs Azhyores asked our Lysogorsk pioneers. "How can a dog, and a Pioneer dog at that, have fleas?"

Our boys could have said that nobody in Lysogorsk pays attention to them, but for some reason nobody did. Instead, Seryozha said in confusion: "You mean your dogs don't have fleas?"

"Of course not. Long ago, about twenty years back, all domestic animals were liberated from parasites by the use of chemical baths. Some of these baths exist even today. Tomorrow we'll have to send your dog to the baths, or else you'll have to answer to the Municipal Committee on Pet Hygiene."

Sharik howled desperately and tried to get to his friends, but they couldn't help him. One of the "glow-worms" helped. He put a tiny tablet in a piece of sausage and tossed it to Sharik. Sharik ate it, and three or four minutes later he was sound asleep.

It was time for all the boys to go to sleep. Azhyores's whistle sounded unusually pleasant. The "glow-worms" started getting ready for bed, spreading out light, soft rubberized mattresses and pillows. Our boys also got ready. As they fell asleep, they heard and even saw Niputs Azhyores, bent over the radiophone receiver, talking to an unseen person: Site No. 117. Southeast. Report as follows: an extraordinarily interesting meeting: boys from 1924. Send a radioplane in the morning. Details tomorrow.

MORNING

It was already a fresh, bright, sunny morning when Niputs Azhyores's loud whistle forced everyone to wake up. Everything that had happened the day before seemed like last night's dream to the Lysogorsk pioneers. But wiping their eyes and looking around, they saw that it wasn't a dream. Around the clearing their new comrade Pioneers with the strange names were rising and getting dressed.

Sharik, tied up at the edge of the clearing, was howling, and in the middle of the field one of the "glow-worms" was gathering the strange campfire of last night into a sack. That's right, a sack.

He put the heap of papers that had radiated warmth and light yesterday into the sack, and where the campfire had been, the grass was as green as before.

It was time to get up. Monya Girsh and Grisha Stepanov—the smallest of our boys—loved to sleep late and lie around in bed at home, but though they had only recently joined the Pioneers, they felt awkward when they saw how quickly and smartly the "glow-worms" had risen and dressed.

So they got up quickly, too, and started dressing, grooming themselves, and brushing their teeth—they didn't want to disgrace their troop, though they could have—and how. All our boys felt that the "glow-worms" were made of different stuff. You could see it in everything: in how quickly and efficiently they worked, and how quickly and efficiently they mustered ranks when their leader blew his whistle ten minutes later.

Niputs Azhyores, who as the oldest took command of both troops, stepped out in front and said: "Guys, get ready! Yesterday I informed TsBYuP by radiophone of our interesting meeting with the Lysogorsk pioneers from 1924. Everyone is interested. A radioplane will be dispatched by 10 o'clock. We'll show our guests our city of Afu and everything interesting in and around it. That will be today's program, and then, if our new friends don't object, and if we receive permission from TsBYuP, we'll make a trip around the world by radioplane. But we can talk about that later. For now, a healthy charge of fresh air for our lungs. Let's stretch our muscles and take a dip in the river. Ready!"

Never in their lives had our boys enjoyed their gymnastic exercises as much as they did that fresh morning under the command of the gaily smiling Niputs Azhyores. Then both troops, forming a chain and walking in each other's footsteps, marched with a light, energetic step to the river for a swim. Only the "glow-worm" on duty stayed behind in the clearing, along with the plaintively howling and whining Sharik.

The river turned out to be quite close.

You can guess what went on at the river: they jumped from the bank into the water, swam, did flips, dived, splashed, blew water, huffed and puffed, rolled in the hot beach sand and dove into the water again, had swimming races, swam on their backs, on their sides, swam the crawl. And our boys were convinced again of their new friends' superiority: not one of the "glow-worms" was stooped, humpbacked, or narrow-chested, while some of the Lysogorsk Pioneers were.

All the "glow-worms" were well built, strong, and sturdy, as if they had been chosen specially. They all swam like fish, and knew all the best strokes.

Later the boys discovered that not only their new friends, but all the boys they had a chance to meet were just as sturdy, hale, and strong.

Liberated from capitalist slavery, the workers of the world had created a new,

At the river

healthy life on earth. Science had learned to defeat and prevent disease, and new people were born and grew as sturdy and strong as steel.

Daily physical exercise strengthened their muscles, straightened their spines, and made their lungs breathe freely and easily.

But our boys still hadn't seen and learned all this. They played merry games with the "glow-worms" in the water and onshore. Suddenly, they heard music in the air above them. Everyone lifted his head.

"What's that?" Grisha Stepanov asked curiously.

"A radioplane," the glow-worm Ashirg Vonapets answered calmly.

But before Grisha could ask what a "radioplane" was, a flying machine appeared in the sky from beyond the forest. It looked something like our airplanes, and it trailed musical sounds in its flight. Its wings were transparent, like a dragonfly's. Tracing a circle above the forest and river, it halted in the air for an instant and began a slow and unhurried vertical descent, during which you could see a propeller of special design working on its back. It landed on Site No. 117, where the Pioneers had spent the last night. . . .

Everyone rushed to the radioplane and began examining it.

"But where's the motor?" asked Misha Surovtsev.

"Oh, that's what they used to have on airplanes," said a "glow-worm" by the name of Vetsvorus Ashim.

"They don't exist anymore. This is what we have," and he pointed to a small box-like device—the energy-ray receiver.

"What was the pilot playing?" asked Monya, remembering the music they had heard in the sky when they were swimming.

"The propellers of old airplanes made an unpleasant, droning buzz when they cut through and hit the air. Nowadays the airstream is directed into a special device that makes musical sounds.

"That gives each radioplane its own voice, its own musical melody, which, incidentally, can be replaced by another if you wish. Our radioplanes can be tuned, just like your pianos used to be."

"But where's the pilot?" Monya asked again. He had looked over the radioplane and everything around it, but he didn't find the person who had flown it.

"The radioplane flew without a pilot. It doesn't need one."

"By the way, it seems that the first attempts to steer submarines and airplanes from the ground using length-modulated electrical waves were made in your time. By now, transmitting energy through the air has been the custom for a long time."

"But you'll soon see that yourself."

While the boys were examining the radioplane with such interest, the "glow-worms" on duty were making tea for everyone. Incidentally, this extraordinarily pleasant and nourishing beverage tasted like neither tea nor coffee, though it did resemble something our boys couldn't quite recall. The "glow-worms" called the drink "etalocohc."

Some of the delicious little cubes they had tried the night before and had liked so much were next to their glasses.

Before taking his seat, Grisha Stepanov remembered his friend Sharik, took some sausage and cheese scraps from his backpack, and brought them over to Sharik. One of the "glow-worms" followed him with a saucer full of "etalocohc" and several cubes.

After breakfast, everyone rushed to collect his belongings and take his place on the radioplane.

ON THE RADIOPLANE

When everyone had been seated in the radioplane's comfortable cabin, Azhyores Niputs took his pocket radiophone out and began speaking to an unseen person: "Southeast... Site No. 117. Direction Northwest, 2–73–45."

Then he pressed a button. The propeller on top began turning, quietly at first and then faster and faster. The machine lifted off the ground.

Suddenly a shrill and desperate shout from Monya cut through the propeller's melody: "Sharik! We forgot Sharik!" And in fact they could look down and see Sharik, tied to the tree, jumping desperately, howling and barking hysterically.

Niputs Azhyores threw a switch, and the radioplane began a slow return landing.

Hardly had the radioplane touched ground than Monya Girsh and Vanya Petenko rushed toward Sharik. But Niputs Azhyores blocked their way.

"No! Wait a minute, guys. You've forgotten he has fleas. We can't take him in the cabin. It would probably be better to leave him here. We can send a medical radioplane for him later."

"No, no," Monya said plaintively, "let's take him now!"

There was so much love and concern for Sharik in the tone of his voice that Niputs Azhyores didn't insist on his idea. But how could they carry him with all his dirty living baggage? Azhyores thought—but not for long.

"Guys, give me whatever ropes you have, and a kerchief."

This was done. Azhyores tied the ropes together, tied the kerchief around Sharik's stomach, fastened the rope to the kerchief, and secured its other end to the radioplane.

Monya and Vanya took their seats. Azhyores settled himself by the switch, pressed it, and the radioplane took off again, with the propeller's ear-soothing melody growing stronger and stronger. After the radioplane had left the ground, Sharik took off behind his friends, whimpering quietly.

Our boys felt sorry for Sharik flying beneath them with his paws flopping convulsively, but they had little time for pity.

Sharik flew off alongside the radioplane

They were already high above the earth, and with their heads stuck out the cabin windows, they watched the marvelous panorama below. It was like a huge geographical map spread out beneath them. A stream twisted through green fields like a silver ribbon. Patches of forest looked like perfect black squares. Mountains stretched in rows into the boundless distance.

Our boys were terrified and overjoyed, flying so high above the ground.

"Look! Look! All those birds! A whole flock!" Misha Surovtsev shouted and pointed ahead.

"And there and there too. A whole caravan!" added Monya Girsh.

"Those aren't birds," said one of the glow-worms with a smile.

And sure enough, they weren't birds, as our boys were soon convinced. They were small, one-seat radioplanes, mobile and agile, and large radioplanes holding hundreds of passengers and flying with the dignity of large, solid birds.

In 1924, airplanes were still a comparative rarity, and people traveled more by walking or riding, but by 1957 air travel had become the prevalent method of transporting people and cargo, as common as horses, bicycles, or cars are in our time.

But our boys didn't know that. With great interest and amazement, they watched thousands of planes flying in various directions, their transparent wings glistening in the blue July sky.

"Look—Brazilian planes!" yelled one of the "glow-worms."

A whole flock of glittering planes flew by and above them, with four letters on their wings: "BSSR," the Brazilian Soviet Socialist Republic, and with an Esperanto motto: "Estu preta!" which means "Be prepared" for the workers' cause.

"Yes, it's them! The delegation of Brazilian Leninist Pioneers flying in for the All-Ural Pioneer Jamboree," Niputs Azhyores said animatedly.

"What's that strange contraption on the mountain, with the tall masts and some sort of spheres on them?"

"That's the regional nimbofacturer."

"What's that?" our boys asked with interest.

"They didn't have it in your time. If I can use such an expression, it's a 'cloud factory,' a station that stimulates atmospheric precipitation: rain in the summer, snow in the winter.

"You probably made field trips to your own meteorological stations. You know that in your time atmospheric conditions, wind direction, and temperature were studied there, and that on the basis of these data scientists could make some predictions about the weather. But in your time they still couldn't make weather, though some experiments were done.

"In our time, the artificial evaporation of water basins and the artificial condensation of atmospheric water vapors enable our nimbofacturers to produce rain when it's needed, and scatter rain clouds that could damage our crops.

"Science has mastered the weather.

"There, look, those are our tractors working the fields."

The radioplane descended, and our curious boys observed gigantic tractors tilling the earth.

The mighty steel monsters moved along the ground at high speed and broke the soil.

"We plow in the spring, in April and May," said Misha Surovtsev.

"We've learned to accelerate the grain-growing cycle," answered Niputs. "The May crops have already been harvested. In July now there's another plowing and sowing."

"What's that? What's that?" shouted Kolya Saburov, pointing his finger.

The boys watched with surprise as one of the gigantic tractors, which had sprouted wings, climbed into the air and flew off like a huge beetle, filling the air with a buzzing hum.

"Do you have railroads and steamships?" asked Monya Girsh.

"They're still in some places, but nowadays we prefer the air to the ground and water," one of the "glow-worms" answered, smiling.

"Do you mean you don't have horses anymore?" Monya asked again with interest.

"Of course we do, but only in museums, zoos, and parks. We don't need animal labor anymore. Machines do everything better and faster."

The farther the radioplane went, the more animated was the movement of radioplanes through the air.

Niputs Azhyores took the radiophone receiver from his pocket, dialed a number, and said to someone: "Hello, comrade. You're returning already? Did everything go well with the troop?"

And our boys heard a voice from the other end of the receiver answer distinctly: "Everything went well, Comrade Niputs. We're flying in for the jamboree. But what sort of animal is that hanging from your plane by a rope?"

"That's a Pioneer dog from 1924. I'll tell you about it later."

The radioplane flew on with its soft, harmonic melody.

"Look, another flock of airplanes," pointed Seryozha Stupin.

A whole squadron of planes was flying up ahead in a perfect column.

"That's two thousand Ural workers flying on a trip to visit their brother workers in Italy.

"Do you see the greeting on the lead aircraft? 'Greetings to the Italian Soviet Socialist Republic from the Ural worker-comrades!' "

The squadron turned to the southwest. Hundreds of its harmonically tuned aircraft flew into the distance, wafting an orchestra of sounds.

Our boys watched this unprecedented spectacle with their eyes wide open, and below them the suburbs of Afu were already visible. What a city! Nothing at all like their Lysogorsk.

It glittered all over in the rays of the July sun, rolling in green gardens and parks and overflowing with specks of light. A city of glass and steel!

The Lysogorsk boys didn't know yet that in later years bulky and dangerous houses built of stone and wood had become history, and that people had learned to build houses of steel and opaque two-way glass. Such houses didn't burn or collapse; they were hygienic, comfortable in all respects, and served people for an immeasurably long time.

And here they were, flying the radioplane over just such a city. They could make out the city's tremendous street traffic; they saw a multitude of airplanes gliding onto its flat roofs and taking off from them. Everywhere there was movement and an intense bustle.

The radioplane descended. After several minutes it slowed down, stopped in the air, and began a vertical descent with the aid of tilted wings and a propeller mounted on its back. . . .

IN THE CITY

They descended along a broad staircase

They descended an enormous, broad staircase. In front and beneath them, two rapid currents of people ran left and right without merging. Particularly surprising was that the people were moving without moving their feet.

The moving sidewalks carried people standing on them like rivers. Different sidewalk belts moved at different speeds, which let passengers change speeds easily by crossing from one belt to another. The fastest belt was in the middle.

Enormous houses of glass

and steel. Steel, lace-like bridges thrown over streets and squares. Tall towers cutting into the blue July sky—all this raced past them with mind-boggling speed.

It all riveted their attention. Only later did they turn their attention to the passengers of this wondrous train, to the citizens of this new world.

They were all healthy, strong, and agile, men and women alike. There were no pale, exhausted faces, no stooped or hunched figures. Nobody was dirty or ragged.

But what our boys liked particularly after more contact with this new world of people was their especially good-spirited friendliness and sociability.

It was as if everyone on earth had become their friends.

The kind and simple word "comrade," which workers had used since the October Revolution, and even earlier, now expressed people's true attitude to one another. The world had turned into a single labor commune, and all people were united into a working family.

There was merry laughter, passersby smiled and bowed in greeting, and the air carried fragments of lively conversation.

"What are they listening to?" one of our boys asked Niputs Azhyores, pointing to the many passengers with radiophone receivers at their ears.

"They're listening to the city news, and also the world news. Radiophone stations keep us constantly informed of significant and important happenings the world over.

"Now we'll go to the Pioneer club, and I'll give you your own radiophone receivers. You'll not only be able to keep up with the world's most important events, you can also, if you wish, listen to symphonic concerts from Paris, London, New York.

"Wherever you are—the city, the fields, or the forest—you can connect yourself to the Central House of Literary Readings and hear stories or adventures at any time of the day or night.

"Our little children love to hook up to the Central House of Fairy Tales and Songs before they go to sleep.

"Radioscopes came into common usage fairly recently. They're little pocket devices that let you see not only whoever you're talking to on the radiophone, but pictures of nature hundreds or thousands of versts away."

"We're there! We're there!" shouted one of the "glow-worms." Everyone began to bustle about and, crossing from one belt to another, they headed toward a big, beautiful building, on whose facade they could read: "House of Young Leninist Pioneers."

THE HOUSE OF YOUNG LENINIST PIONEERS

It was an enormous building with hundreds of rooms. Beautiful, well-lit halls, dining rooms, bedrooms, workshops, rooms for games and physical exercise, and next door an enormous swimming pool, showers, and baths.

All this amazed and enraptured our boys when they toured Afu's House of Pioneers after their dinner in a bright, clean dining room.

Next to it was an enormous swimming pool

They especially liked the quiet and comfortable listening room, where hundreds of young Leninists seated in cozy armchairs were listening to the world news through their radiophone receivers.

Misha Surovtsev took one of the receivers, held it to his ear, and instantly heard: "Work on the broad canal uniting the Caspian and Black Seas is being completed.

"Yesterday an electro-thermal grid was successfully cast onto the summit of Mt. Kazbek to help thaw the permafrost. Soon, enormously powerful water turbines will begin working in the lower valleys.

"Laboratory 32 for the Study of Pacific Ocean Life completed the safe descent to a depth of eight versts. It will be opened for deep-water excursions in no sooner than a month. Its location is 22° latitude north and 178° longitude east (off Ferro Island)."

But our boys had no time to listen. Going from floor to floor, they finally came out onto a flat terrace roof, from which a wondrous view opened out onto the city.

In the waning rays of the setting sun, the city of glass and steel glittered with thousands of reflected suns.

The evening cool dispelled the heat of the July day. Our boys took deep breaths and watched with their eyes wide open. As in the morning, they saw hundreds of radioplanes with transparent wings aglitter flying and soaring in the air above the roofs.

Below, the moving streets moved like rapid streams. How small people seemed from atop an enormous multistory building!

"Where are they rushing to, those people?" asked Grisha.

"Home, to the garden cities that surround the city of Afu like a green ribbon. This is only the business center. Tomorrow we'll see the garden cities," said Niputs Azhyores. "That's where most of Afu's residents live. I want to introduce you to my parents." . . .

OUT IN THE COUNTRY

After a swim in the pool and some morning "etalocohc," our boys finished their tour of the Pioneer house, then went up to the terrace roof to admire the view of the city and wait for Azhyores...

Hundreds of radioplanes furrowed the sky in various directions, and at eleven o'clock on the dot one of the radioplanes stopped above them and began its quiet descent. This was Azhyores Niputs's radioplane. He greeted our boys merrily and invited them into the cockpit.

In a minute they were already flying over the city, circling and rising higher and higher. The city with its ray-like streets and the green ribbon of gardens around it were clearly visible.

Then the radioplane began a gradual descent toward the green garden cities.

Tens of thousands of tiny houses were drowning in the gardens' greenery. Here and there a lake glistened, and the moving steel roads carrying people from city to city flowed like rivers.

In many places, fountains rose above the canopy of green, freshening the stifling heat of the July day.

The radioplane started to glide, then stopped in midair and descended quietly to a landing pad amid the thick vegetation.

Azhyores and our boys left the plane and a minute later entered the pretty, opaque-glass house where Niputs Azhyores's parents lived.

A tall, beautiful woman met them on the terrace with a welcoming expression on her face.

"She looks so much like my mom," thought Seryozha.

Fountains bubbled in many places

"Hello, hello, boys. Azhyores told me about you. I'm glad to see you. I hope you made it here all right from such a distant year."

"She resembles my mama so much," thought Seryozha again. "Even her voice is the same. Only Mama's face was always tired, worried, and this woman's eyes are so shiny and friendly."

"Guys, let's see how my 'old folks' live." With these words Azhyores guided them into his parents' residence for a look.

"You mean you don't live with them?"

"No, I'm going to school. We live in a labor commune–camp on the slopes of Yamantau. Last summer mother and father lived there too, in this house."

"In this house on the slopes of Yamantau? How is that possible?" asked Grisha Stepanov.

"How is it impossible? After all, it's close, only several hundred versts away. The summer before last this house stood on the banks of the Nile River in Egypt. My mama is the director of Ural-African air transport."

Our boys looked at this woman, who held such an important position, with great respect.

They still were not aware that after the Worldwide Social Revolution, universal education and universal labor had made men and women complete equals. Public kitchens had gradually freed women from cooking, laundry, and petty household chores. Women stood straight and became men's comrades and collaborators in everything.

No less educated than men, women had contributed equally to the creation of a new world, to the improvement of humanity's life on earth. Creative labor for the common good had banished tiredness from mothers' faces and smoothed the wrinkles that constant want, worry, and woe had put on them. Mothers' faces had become as affable as the face of Niputs Azhyores' mother.

She walked ahead of our boys and acquainted them with the layout and furnishings of their small home's several rooms. Everything was practical, clean, and attractive.

Afterwards, everyone sat at a table on the terrace-veranda and breakfasted.

Our boys had never eaten with as much appetite as they did that day on the veranda of the glass house.

The water in a pretty vessel on the table boiled as soon as they dropped a radio-receiver disk into it, and Niputs's mother made them a drink more delicious than they had ever tasted before. It was not only delicious, it was nourishing.

After the Worldwide Revolution, the preparation of food products was recognized as an extraordinarily important matter. Making food nourishing and delicious, and freeing it from all harmful bacteria—the attention of an entire army of learned biologists, bacteriologists, and hygienists had striven for this goal. And they had dealt with the task successfully. Food factories manufactured thoroughly top-quality products for everyone.

Our radio freight planes are tremendously powerful

The public dining rooms of the world food trust (Mirpit) served all humanity, and women no longer fussed over food preparation in their apartments' dirty kitchens.

This is what Azhyores and his mother told our boys.

After breakfast everyone went out to a shady garden surrounding the house.

As they were coming down from the veranda, Grisha said, turning to Azhyores: "I keep thinking: how is it possible to live in this house for one summer in the Urals and another in Egypt? Do you mean the house can be taken apart and shipped?"

"No, it can't be taken apart, but it can be moved easily from one place to another. There on the roof you can see a ring for an anchor lowered from a heavy-freight plane.

"Your airplanes couldn't lift heavy objects. They had to taxi along the ground before they took off, and it made sense not to tie a heavy load beneath them.

"In that respect, our radioplanes are like eagles or kites, which seize prey sometimes as big as themselves and climb up into the air with it. Our heavy-freight planes possess an enormous lifting capacity, and transporting a house as small as ours isn't hard."

"Like it lifted Sharik yesterday?" recalled Grisha Stepanov with a smile. Everyone laughed at the comparison.

"Were you inside your house when it flew through the air like Sharik?" Grisha asked again.

"Yes, of course, it's more comfortable inside than in the radioplane cabin," answered Azhyores's mother.

After a walk through the garden, Azhyores suggested flying to the aerodrome, where aerogames were supposed to take place that day.

Of course, how could they turn down such a suggestion? They said good-bye to Azhyores's mother.

Again they boarded the radioplane. Again the steel bird flew high above the ground with its melodious music.

THE AEROGAMES

Colorful tethered balloons marked the boundaries of the airfield where the aerogames and contests were to take place.

Outside the airfield boundaries, thousands of airplanes with tens of thousands of spectators hovered motionless in the air. Tens of thousands also watched from the ground, and the moving sidewalk belts brought hundreds and thousands of new spectators from the city.

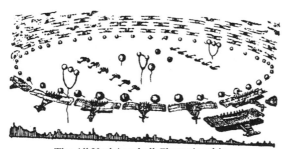

The All-Ural Aeroball Championship

And you could understand why. The All-Ural Aeroball Championship was on the day's program.

Our boys flew in right at the start. The powerful but harmonic sound of a signal horn rang out from the referee's plane, and instantly, six red radioplanes entered the field from one side and six orange planes from the other. They lined up opposite one another.

The signal horn blew again, and two red and two orange balloons held level by ballast hung from thin cords that almost touched the ground rose slowly to the middle of the airfield.

Then, at each end of the field rose three small balloons tied together and anchored to the ground by colored ribbons.

They formed two goals, as on a soccer field. A third goal of smaller dimensions rose in the middle part of the field.

The distance between the large goals was at least 1½ to 2 kilometers.

A sharp whistle signaled the start of the aeroball game. Play began.

The radioplanes, with long bars fronting their propellers alternately red and white, flew up to the balloons and, using the bars, tried to push them through the middle goal, and then through the large goals at opposite ends.

The red and orange balloons were knocked across the field by the radioplanes. They bumped together or jumped through the goals to the deafening applause of the hundreds of thousands of spectators.

The game was reminiscent of croquet.

Our boys followed the new game with keen interest.

Suddenly they all felt the radiophone receivers in their pockets ticking.

They had been given them that morning.

Putting the receivers to their ears, they all heard the same thing: "The Brazilian Pioneers invite the 'Red Star' troop to a meeting tonight after the aerogames to choose a route for tomorrow's trip around the world."

Seryozha answered for everyone: "We'll be there! Thank you!" And so, when the aeroball game finished to thunderous applause—in honor of the orange victors—our boys flew back to the city in the middle of a flock of large and small radioplanes.

This is what Azhyores Niputs told them in the cockpit: "Guys, you already know that our radioplanes differ from your aeroplanes in that they don't use motors to produce their power energy. Energy flows in through receivers. But the difference in speed is even greater. What was the speed record in 1924?"

Misha Surovtsev, who considered himself an expert in aviation questions, answered: "403 kilometers per hour."

"There, you see, nowadays it's 840, and we'll soon attain the muzzle velocity of a bullet."

"But how can you breathe at that speed? It will take your breath away," said Kolya.

"The cabin is hermetically sealed, and an oxygen generator completely eliminates the danger of suffocating at high speed. The radioplane cabin turns into something like a high-speed projectile."

"How soon will we get to Brazil?"

"You can fly across the Atlantic Ocean in about fourteen hours, and it takes three times longer to get to Brazil."

Of course, that's if you don't stop anywhere.

CHOOSING A ROUTE

The Pioneer House was abustle. After dinner in a magnificent dining room, our boys went to the Council Hall to meet with the Brazilian Pioneers about the next day's flight.

The magnificent monument to Lenin

The Brazilians had already gathered, and they gave our Lysogorsk boys a friendly welcome.

Everyone took his seat. An Esperanto translator sat with our boys.

This is what the chairman said to our boys to open the meeting: "Dear Comrades! The choice of our route to Brazil depends on you: do we fly to the east or the west?

"We would like to show you the places most interesting in all respects. There are many of them in both the east and the west. Our boys have split into two parties: the easterners and the westerners.

"Representatives of both parties will lay out their plans for you.

"The floor goes to the westerners' representative, Kimo Rudzho. Let Kimo Rudzho come to the podium."

"Dear brothers! We should fly to the west. We cannot bypass Moscow; we must see Berlin, Paris, Madrid, where there are so many fine monuments to the heroes of great proletarian battles.

"Don't you want to see what Moscow has become, her new parks and magnificent glass buildings, and finally, the grand monument to Lenin on the hills that in your day were called the Sparrow Hills? You must, of course, visit Ilich's tomb on Red Square and see the Palace of Labor next to it.

"In the West you will see wonders of technology: gigantic mountain drills and great canal-digging plows. And the Rhine, Garonne, and Ebro Rivers! You won't recognize them now: they are filled with water flowing from the gorges of snow-capped mountains, where thermal grids melt the eternal ice and where gigantic dynamos drive the whole of Central Europe.

"We'll fly over the ocean. From our height we will see the deep bottom of the sea, and by evening we will see a flowering shoreline and the city of Rio de Janeiro.

"Let's fly to the west! To the west! That's all I have to say."

"Comrade Batalio Grande, representative of the easterners, will now take the floor."

"No, no, my friends, we will of course fly to the east!

"The road is long, but the longer it is, the more interesting it will be.

"Before you is the Soviet Chinese Republic, an enormous anthill of creative energy. What in your times was the Gobi Desert is now an enormous blue inland sea filled by electrothawed snows and icecaps.

"And Tibet? What was once an uninhabited plateau is now a gigantic agent of electrical energy giving warmth and light to Asia. There is a huge monument to Lenin in the Himalayas raised by millions of workers from Soviet India under the direction of the Central Bureau for Global Improvement. Grand steel bridges built across the Malay Archipelago, deep-water laboratories for the study of the ocean floor, enormous underwater whale pens, the utilization of bubbling lava from the Mauna Loa and Manua Kea volcanoes of Tahiti,[1] and many more interesting things.

"My friends! Let's not hesitate to head to the east tomorrow. The choice is clear. Choose! Thank you."

The Brazilian Pioneers turned their gazes to our boys.

The chairman said: "Talk it over and tell us your opinion."

They began talking. The boys went over both arguments, and when they voted, they also split into easterners and westerners.

Then someone proposed splitting up: the westerners could go west, and the easterners east: "We'll all get to Rio Janeiro anyway."

To this, Seryozha Stupin responded: "No, if we're going to go, we'll go together. Let's choose one thing." And the arguments began again. Who knows how long they would have continued if the smallest of our boys, Grisha Stepanov, hadn't said: "Let's go to Brazil by the west, and come back by the east. That would be around the world. Then we'd see everything."

This simple suggestion was agreeable to everyone, and when the chairman asked them which way they wanted to travel, Seryozha answered for everyone with three words: "Around the world."

"Then we can see everything!" added Vanya Petenko.

The Brazilians' orderly applause expressed their approval for this wise decision. Departure was set for ten o'clock the next morning.

DOWN WITH CHRISTIAN NAMES

The boys had this conversation when they returned to their dormitory:

"Still, it's awful we don't know Esperanto; it's indispensable for international jamborees."

"I studied it some last year," said Misha Surovtsev. "Kimo Rudzho means Red Kim—that was the first speaker's name.

"Batalio Grande means, I think, Great Battle.

"I like their names, and I don't like our names at all: Vanya, Monya, Seryozha. The priests gave them to us when we were baptized. Let's change our names."

"Let's give ourselves names connected to the Revolution and its heroes," suggested Kolya Chernov.

"I hear they've been doing it for a long time in Leningrad, Moscow, and the Ukraine, but in Lysogorsk we're still living like old times."

"I'll call myself 'Red Kim' too."

"I'll be Krasarm (Red Army)."

"I'll be Yul, which means Young Leninist."

"I'll call myself Revmir (Worldwide Revolution)."

"I'll be Spartacus, because I admire his heroism."

---

1. Mauna Loa and Mauna Kea are actually located on the island of Hawaii.

"I'll be Vladlen, in honor of Ilich."

"And I'll be October," said Seryozha Stupin, and added: "We'll forget our old Christian names forever."

There was a merry shout, and Seryozha shuddered happily and opened his eyes.

It was early morning. The sun was already up on the other side of the forest. Dew glittered with diamond sparkles in the trees. A light fog spread over the plain and over Lysogorsk.

The boys were asleep. Only Sharik, lying next to Monya Girsh with his head up, was pounding his tail against the ground. Then he got up and yawned. Monya woke up and put his arm around his neck.

"Don't touch him, Monya, he has fleas," said Seryozha.

"Boy, did we sleep well! Well, in two hours we'll be at the lumber mill," said Monya and began looking at the map that had been on the ground since last night.

"Tonight by the campfire I'll tell you about Niputs Azhyores," Seryozha said in a minute.

"What's that?" asked Monya, but Seryozha was lost in thought and didn't answer. Two minutes went by before Monya suddenly smiled and said: "I know what it is: you have to read it backwards."

Seryozha read it backwards and was surprised. Then he said, "Don't call me by my Christian name anymore. My name is October," he said austerely. "You weren't there when we changed our names."

"When?!" asked Monya, but Seryozha was again lost in thought and didn't answer.

The other boys began stirring and waking up.

Sharik was furiously scratching and biting a flea on his side.

The End

V. I. Ulyanov (N. Lenin)
Childhood and Grade School
A. I. Ulyanova (1925)

ANNA ULYANOVA-ELIZAROVA (1864–1935) WAS THE OLDER SIS-
TER OF LENIN. SHE WROTE MUCH ABOUT HER FAMILY LIFE WHEN

As excerpted in F. A. Fridliand and M. F. Robinson, *Chtenie* (Moscow: Uchpedgiz, 1950), pp. 9–10, from A. I. Ulianova, *V. I. Ulianov (N. I. Lenin). Detstvo i shkol'nye gody* (Moscow: Detgiz, 1925).

THE YOUNG VLADIMIR WAS GROWING UP. IN EACH PIECE SHE ALSO SET A MORAL LESSON, HERE CLEARLY ON DISPLAY IN THE FINAL PARAGRAPH. THIS EXCERPT IS TAKEN FROM A SOVIET FIFTH-GRADE TEXTBOOK.

Behind the house was a long, green courtyard with gigantic slides built for us, and a fairly large orchard that led out onto Pokrovskaya Street. There was a gate in the garden fence, and we would go out through the garden: in the winter to skate, in the summer to swim in the Svyaga River.

Most of the trees in the orchard were fruit trees: apples, cherries, and various berry bushes. There was also a pretty flower bed. Mother, who loved gardening, took care of it all. And each of us helped.

I remember the evenings after dry, hot summer days, and how we would all take watering cans, buckets, pitchers (anything that would hold water), pump water from the well, and travel back and forth to the garden and beds. I remember how quickly Volodya[1] would hurry back with his empty watering can.

We stuffed ourselves with as many berries and fruits as we wanted. But we did not do it in a disorderly fashion; even in this there was a certain discipline. When the apples had ripened, we were allowed to gather and eat the fallers, the apples that had fallen to the ground and were spotted with wormholes, but we could not pick apples from the trees. And then there were other rules: which apples spoiled quickly and should be eaten first, which should be gathered for jams and for the winter.

As a result we could eat to our heart's content during the autumn months and have enough for the entire winter.

I remember how we were all annoyed by one guest, a girl who demonstrated her daring by biting an apple on the run while it was still on the tree. We found such hooliganism alien and incomprehensible. It was exactly the same with the berries: we were shown the strawberry patches, blackberry bushes, or cherry trees where we could "graze," and which ones we should leave untouched because they would ripen later or go for jams. I remember how family friends were amazed that three beautiful cherry trees near the gazebo where we had our evening tea in the summer stood covered with berries until July 20 (our father's nameday), and that despite the availability and abundance of the berries, the children did not touch them.

"The children can eat berries on the other side of the garden, but I asked them not to touch these trees until the twentieth," said Mother.

Our mother knew how to maintain discipline without ever being too strict. She allowed us just enough freedom so that it never impinged upon the freedom of others. This had a tremendous significance in our upbringing.

The sensible discipline and caution that Vladimir Ilich showed in his personal

---

1. A nickname for Vladimir, i.e., Lenin.

life, and which he demanded from all his comrades in the building of the Soviet state, were absorbed by him in his childhood.

Heard in Moscow
Radio-Newspaper Correspondence Report No. 285
7 November 1925

ON THIS DAY THE ANNUAL PARADE AND CELEBRATION, INCLUD-ING SPEECHES BY MIKHAIL KALININ AND KLARA ZETKIN, WERE BROADCAST LIVE FROM RED SQUARE. THIS WAS SOVIET RADIO'S FIRST LIVE DIRECT BROADCAST, WHICH BEGAN A LONG HOLI-DAY TRADITION.

Comrade workers, peasants, and everyone else listening to this radio-newspaper in near and distant cities and villages of our Union. You are sitting by your radio receivers and loudspeakers and listening to Moscow. You want to know how Moscow is celebrating the eighth anniversary of the October Revolution. We won't be transmitting all of today's speeches, because they were already broadcast from Red Square and you've heard them. But we will tell you how Moscow is abuzz and enjoying itself today.

Let's begin from early morning. The day started out cloudy. There was a drizzle. But that had no effect on the mood. The city was sparkling with bright posters, fresh greenery, fiery flags, and the portraits of revolutionary leaders.

Life began early on the outskirts. Building decorations were hastily completed in several places. Every factory, every club, every cooperative was painstakingly decorated with bright-red cloth, slogans, and garlands of green.

Decorations in the Red Presnya and Rogozho-Simonovsky districts were particularly beautiful. The Red Presnya Raikom[1] was the center of the district festival. The Raikom building is drowning in greenery and posters. The letters USSR are aflame on both sides of the building. The slogans proclaim: Every Soviet, every Ispolkom,[2] every judicial institution must be the faithful guardian of revolutionary legality. "May the union of workers and peasants grow and expand, may its roots in Communist Party leadership grow stronger."

From *Istoriia sovetskoi radio zhurnalistiki. Dokumenty, teksty, vospominaniia, 1917–1945* (Moscow: Izd. Moskovskogo universiteta, 1991), pp. 115–118.
1. District Party Committee.
2. Executive (state administrative) Committee.

The building facade is adorned by white marble busts of Lenin and Marx.

A poster spans the street by the Rogozho-Simonovsky Raikom: "Greetings to millions of Young Communists and Pioneers." The building itself is painted colorfully with the slogan "Long Live the Russian Communist Party—Builder of Socialism!"

AMO, Dynamo, and other factories are decorated with slogans that summon laborers to the consolidation of production and the raising of labor productivity. Clubs, cooperatives, and other institutions and organizations are adorned with a multitude of posters demanding clear and defined tasks for the present.

Workers began to gather for the demonstration at ten in the morning. Joyful laughter, merry jokes, and the cheerful exchanges of thousands of workers, Pioneers, and Young Communists cut through a thick shroud of light rain. The human mass swiftly arranged itself in rows and columns.

By eleven o'clock, the streets and squares of Moscow were overflowing with people. Automobiles filled with children honked ceaselessly. Huge masses of people streamed into the center from the outlying districts. The merry chatter of the marchers was mixed with the happy hum of children's voices and cheerful orchestral strains. The air was filled with the Great Holiday's triumphant noise. Moscow came to life. On Serpukhov, Sukharev, and other squares, by Red Gate and Red Presnya Gate, loudspeakers attracted large masses of workers: everyone wanted to hear the speeches from Red Square. The holiday atmosphere was joyful.

Now let's take a look at the main streets leading to Red Square. Here the stream of people gets thicker. Endless columns of people go by. They stretch from all ends of Moscow, and it seems that no power can stop this endless stream.

Plants, factories, institutions, organizations, and schools are all marching toward Red Square. Banners and posters flutter in the air. The children are especially animated. Hundreds of trucks transport them all over the city. The kids wave red flags and shout greetings to the passing columns. Joyful exclamations and anniversary salutations can be heard from every side street. Gaily decorated automobiles drive by. Here comes the Grain Products automobile. Built onto it is a float made of posters with slogans and drawings. The posters say "Down with Grain Wreckers."

The grain wreckers are huge insects with the heads of foreign capitalists. Interspersed with the professional organizations are military units playing music and singing revolutionary songs.

The demonstration halts in front of the Moscow Soviet building. Shouts and congratulations are heard, then everyone marches on toward the Kremlin and the mausoleum[3]—the heart of Moscow.

Comrades, we're coming up on Red Square.

What a tremendous stream of people. A mighty, great power, the power of October, is moving this stream. There are no sad or cloudy faces. The holiday belongs to all workers; they feel close to it and have a heartfelt understanding of it.

A holiday for workers and their children. Here a worker-mother is holding her tiny son up high. He has a firm grip on a tiny red banner.

We're next to Lenin's tomb. A megaphone booms: "Long live the worldwide vic-

---

3. Lenin's mausoleum is located on Red Square.

tory of workers!" The little red flag quivers, and the proletarian tot yells in a bell-like little voice: "Hurrah!"

The head of the column has long ago skirted Red Square, but its tail is still far away, by the Tver Gate about two or three versts away. Hundreds of bands fill the space with the waves of marches. Singing is heard everywhere. It flares up without prompting in one group, then another. Today the sea of millions glorifying October includes everyone for whom the banner and victory of proletarian revolution are not just words, but a cause they are prepared to defend at the slightest enemy provocation. That's why there is no end to the sea of humanity on Red Square. And there's no end to the joy felt by workers of the proletarian land.

The sky begins to clear around noon, the storm clouds scatter, sunlight floods the squares and streets of Moscow, and the holiday becomes even brighter and happier.

Now, comrades, we'll describe the central moment of the celebration on Red Square.

At ten sharp, Comrade Uglanov, standing on the tribune, declared the demonstration open. Comrade Tomsky, chairman of the All-Union Central Trade Union Council, greeted everyone who had gathered.

You've heard this speech on the radio.

Then, the German Union of Red Front-Line Soldiers handed their banner over to Moscow workers. The banner was handed over to the tune of the "Internationale." After the investiture of the banner, columns of demonstrators from the outskirts entered Red Square. The tribune and columns exchanged slogans and salutations. Comrades Kalinin, Tomsky, Yaroslavsky, Enukidze, Mikhailov, Bubnov, Rudzutak, and others are on the tribune. On the mausoleum's right-side tribune stands a guest delegation of Moscow Province peasants, along with Comrade Rykov, members of the Danish and Norwegian delegations, members of a German Youth delegation, and the German Union of Red Front-Line Soldiers.

One after the other, representatives of the Communist Party, the government, trade unions, and the Red Army on the tribune addressed the marchers with slogans of welcome, which you, comrades, have already heard on the radio. Peasants waving their caps congratulated Moscow workers in the name of the peasantry.

Funny figures appeared among the banners and posters. There was a garbage wagon driven by a Red soldier. Several people in the uniforms of various West European armies were seated tightly together on it. These were the defenders of the capitalist system. The legend on the garbage wagon said "Dump the Western European bourgeoisie in the trash." Another poster depicted a fur shop signboard. It said "The Moscow State Fur Factory takes receipt of the pelts of Chamberlain, Scheidemann, Hindenburg, Vandervelde, and other predators. Exceeds prewar quality."

Groups of marchers representing the Red Army appeared in the columns. They were met with thunderous exclamations and a mighty "Hurrah!"

Comrade Mikhailov greeted the new Comissar for Military and Naval Affairs, Comrade Voroshilov, with another "Hurrah!" The masses in their thousands took up the "Hurrah!"

The appearance of the aged Clara Zetkin[4] on the tribune was greeted with thunderous applause by the entire square. Dense columns of people continued streaming onto the square. The masses were marching. Slogan after slogan caught up by the thousands-strong mass rained down from the mausoleum tribune.

"You can see that our elder, Mikhail Ivanovich,[5] is happy," says the crowd. "A happy smile keeps playing over his face. And then it was especially radiant." That was when the county[6] peasant delegations went by.

An old, old peasant jumped out of the ranks and ran almost right up to the mausoleum, waving his cap high in the air and shouting for all he was worth: "Glory to our dear leader, Comrade Kalinin."

A reconnaissance plane appeared above the square, did several loop-the-loops, and then flew away again. It then returned with a whole squadron buzzing loudly over the square.

The holiday continued. There is no way to tell you everything, comrades.

---

4. German Communist leader and frequent visitor to Soviet Russia.
5. Kalinin.
6. Uyezd.

The Long Road (Those Were the Days)
K. Podrevsky and B. Fomin (1926)

THIS SONG WAS DONE IN THE STYLE OF PREREVOLUTIONARY "GYPSY" SONGS, A GENRE CLOSER TO RUSSIAN "CRUEL ROMANCES" OR URBAN LAMENTS THAN TO AUTHENTIC GYPSY TABOR CULTURE. IT GAINED GREAT RENOWN IN THE VERSION RECORDED BY THE PREREVOLUTIONARY AND THEN ÉMIGRÉ SINGER ALEKSANDR VERTINSKY. THOUGH HEARD ON IMPORTED RECORDINGS IN THE 1930s, IT BECAME LEGAL ONLY AFTER THE SINGER'S RETURN TO RUSSIA IN 1943. A FAMOUS WESTERN REVIVAL WAS MADE BY THE BRITISH SONG STAR MARY HOPKIN IN THE 1960s AS "THOSE WERE THE DAYS."

Variant from a private collection.

ДОРОГОЙ ДЛИННОЮ

Ехали на тройке с бубенцами,
А вдали мелькали огоньки
Эх, когда бы мне теперь за вами,
Душу бы развеять от тоски!

Припев:
Дорогой длинною, погодой лунною,
Да с песней той, что вдаль летит звеня,
И с той старинною, да с семиструнною,
Что по ночам так мучила меня.

Да, выходит, пели мы задаром,
Понапрасну ночь за ночью жгли.
Если мы покончили со старым,
Так и ночи эти отошли!

Припев.

В даль родную новыми путями
Нам отныне ехать суждено!
Ехали на тройке с бубенцами,
Да теперь проехали давно!

Припев.

THE LONG ROAD

Driving on a troika decked with
    sleighbells,
With lights aflicker far away ahead,
Oh, if I only could drive off with you,
And let my longing heart wave in the
    wind.

Refrain:
Along a distant road beneath a moonlit
    sky,
And with that song that flies afar and
    rings.
And that guitar of old astrung with
    seven strings
That brought me anguish in my
    younger nights.

We were fated to sing all for nothing
Burning brightly night by night in vain.
If we put an end to all that had passed,
We also left those nights behind at last.

Refrain.

Our fate from now on is to drive forever
Along new roads toward a distant home.
Driving on a troika decked with
    sleighbells,
But long ago our destination's passed.

Refrain.

Anecdotes

THE SOVIET JOKE OR ANECDOTE (*ANEKDOT*) IS A PECULIAR CUL-
TURAL PHENOMENON THAT BEGAN TO FUNCTION ON THE EDGES
OF THE OFFICIAL WORLD SOMETIME DURING THE CIVIL WAR,
THOUGH POLITICAL JOKES DATE FROM BEFORE THE REVOLUTION.
THEY SERVED AS THE SCRIPT IN THE PRIVATE THEATER OF

For anecdote sources, see *Blue Blouse Skit*, above.

FRIENDS IN SMALL GROUPS, AN OUTLET FOR THE SATIRICAL IM-
PULSE NOT PERMITTED ON THE STAGE, AND A SAFETY VALVE FOR
DAILY FRUSTRATIONS.

During the Civil War, a villager shouts hurrah for the incoming troops; and to the question "Whose side are you on?" he answers: "The ones coming in." [1:323]

A doomed man wishes to become a communist before he dies so that there will be one less communist in the world. [1:323]

An elderly man, distressed with Soviet conditions, utters the mournful sigh "oi!" on a tramcar. His wife hushes him and says: "Fool, don't talk counter-revolution in public!" [1:323]

"I was married in a civil ceremony. But now everyone lives in legal matrimony. So I decided to divorce my legal wife: I didn't want to be like everyone else. I want to live in illegal matrimony."
"Illegal matrimony?"
"Right, I stole my neighbor's wife." [2:4]

And as a comment on the continuing failure of the Comintern, a lifetime job is advertised: to climb a tower and look out for the dawn of world revolution. [1:323]

Bim and Bom were the most popular clowns in revolutionary Moscow.
Bim came out with a picture of Lenin and one of Trotsky. "I've got two beautiful portraits," he announced. "I'm going to take them home with me!"
Bom asked, "What will you do with them when you get them home?"
"Oh, I'll hang Lenin and put Trotsky against the wall." [2:5]

A common thought about the two main Soviet newspapers, *Pravda* (Truth) and *Izvestiya* (News): There's no truth in the *News,* and no news in the *Truth.* [2:6]

A doctor, an engineer, and a Communist were arguing about who was the first person on earth.
Doctor: "I was the first person, for without me, nobody could have made Eve from Adam's rib."
Engineer: "No, I was first, because without engineers, the world couldn't have been built from chaos."
Communist: "And who do you think created chaos?" [3:9]

A student of noble origin, who has also been guilty of Menshevism in the past, is questioned for entrance into the university.
"What are your social origins?"
"The same as Lenin's."
"Which side were you on before the October Revolution?"
"The same as Trotsky." [3:33]

A speaker at a rally: "Comrades, for three hundred years, the government poured slop on your heads, and you were silent. Now's the time to open your mouths!" [4:26]

A Chekist has to execute a Russian, a Jew, and an Armenian, and before he shoots them, he promises to grant each one wish.
The Russian asks to speak to a priest. The request is granted.
The Jew asks for some raspberries.
"But it's December. Where can I get raspberries?"
"No problem, comrade, I can wait."
The Armenian asks to be accepted into the Communist Party.
"That won't help, we're still going to shoot you."
"But it's better to kill a bastard than a decent man." [3:40]

In 1924, the first Soviet silver money was coined to ensure the purchase of agricultural products. When the coins are delivered to the village, the peasants surround it and cross themselves. The priest asks: "Why are you crossing yourselves? It's Soviet money."
"The money might be Soviet, but the silver is sure the church's." [5:58]

"Old lady, why are you looking at the calendar?"
"My daughter just named my granddaughter Industry, and I'm seeing when her saint's day will be." [3:51]

An NEP reader tells a proletarian writer: "Your novel isn't realistic at all!"
"Why's that?"
"It's four hundred pages long, and the hero gets married only once." [3:64]

In a tailor's shop: "Why isn't my suit ready? You said it would take a week. God created the whole world in a week."
"And do you like it?" [5:413]

The dark of night. An automobile glides up to the apartment of a Moscow Nepman. Some men rip out the bell and pound at the door.
Pandemonium in the apartment. The residents scurry about like rats, hiding books, burning letters, throwing money out the window, stuffing gold in the mattress.
Suddenly, a shout from outside the door: "Hey, don't worry, we're not here to search you, we're only here to rob you." [3:50]

Question: Can a snake break its own spine?
Answer: Only if it slithers along the General Line. [5:110]

II.

The Stalinist Thirties

THE CULTURAL REVOLUTION, 1928–1932

Leninist Fairy Tales

The first tale, a charming blend of class analysis and folklore, was recorded in 1918 by Lidia Seifullina from a woman in an isolated village of the steppe. It reprises a prerevolutionary legend featuring Ivan the Terrible. The second tale, a similar example of "Soviet folklore" reconciling old notions and the new politics, was collected in a village of Vyatka Province. Told no earlier than 1925, it echoes a motif common long before the Revolution, in which the tsar wandered secretly among the people. Note the peasantisms and rustic spellings in both (rendered roughly here in translation).

HOW LENIN AND THE TSAR DIVIDED UP THE PEOPLE

AN ORENBURG FAIRY TALE

Once Tsar Mikolashka[1] was approached by his most important general. "Once upon a time, your Royal Highness, in a faraway kingdom, there appeared a man who knew everything about all things. His rank was unknown, he had no papers, and he was called Lenin. And this very same man threatened: 'I will go against Tsar Mikolai, make all his soldiers mine with one word, and all the generals, all the directors, all the noble officers, and you yourself, Tsar Mikolai, I will grind into dust and throw to the winds. I have a word that can do all that.'"

Tsar Mikolashka was frightened. He jumped to his feet, threw up his hands and shouted: "Go right away and tell this man Lenin without rank or pedigree that he

---

Lenin v russkoi skazke i vostochnoi legende (Moscow: Molodaia gvardiia, 1930), pp. 23–27, 40–43.

1. A variant of Nikolai, i.e., Tsar Nicholas II.

should not go against me with his word, or grind me into dust, nor my generals, my directors, my noble officers—and for that I will give this man half my kingdom!"

Right off the tsar's learned men came running, caught their breath, honed the points of their quills, and wrote to this Lenin: "Now, Lenin, don't use your word against Tsar Mikolai, and he will give you half his kingdom without a fight or harsh words."

It might have been too early, might have been too late, but soon an answer came from this man Lenin without rank or papers. And Lenin wrote Tsar Mikolashka: "I agree, Tsar Mikolashka, to take half your kingdom. Only let me tell you how we'll split it. Not by province, not by region, not by district. But here's how, I tell you, I'll agree to split your kingdom—and no arguments, please. You take for yourself, Tsar Mikolashka, all the blue bloods: your generals, your directors, your noble officers with all their honors, with their ranks, their crosses, and the epaulets you gave them, their noble spouses and their blue-blooded children. Take the manor lords with all their riches, their silk clothes and velvet, their silver dishes and gold, their spouses and progeny. Take the merchants with their wares, their countless treasures, and let them take all their worldly goods from the bank. Take all the factory owners with their money, with their machines and all their factory riches. You give me all the lowborn: the peasants, the soldiers, the factory workers, with all their simple belongings. Just leave us the livestock, the grassy fields, and mother earth for plowing."

Tsar Mikolashka read the letter, broke into a joyful dance, clapped his hands with pleasure, and ordered his generals, officers, and directors: "Send my unconditional agreement to Lenin right away. What sort of know-it-all is he, what sort of secret word does he know, if he refuses my countless treasures, the merchants' wares, and the landowners' holdings, and takes only no-good commoners for himself. We'll use our treasury to buy other commoners, make them into soldiers and live in peace and plenty again."

Once again the tsar's learned men came running, caught their breath, honed the points of their quills, and sent this Lenin the tsar's consent. But not a peep about all the laughing, so that Lenin wouldn't rethink and attack the tsar with his secret word.

Maybe it was too soon or too late, but anyhow quickly Lenin snuck off to his soldiers, peasants, and factory workers. The tsar and his blue bloods had already gone off far away. The peasants, soldiers, and workers look, and see that a simple peasant has come and says: "Greetings, comrades!" As far as the eye could see, he took their hands and said in a loud voice: "It will be the same for me as for you, since we're comrades now. Only do as I tell you; I know everything about all things, and I wouldn't teach my comrades anything bad."

The soldiers say in their soldier way: "Yes, sir, Comrade Lenin, at your command." The factory folk, who had picked up some smarts in the city, also did like he said. But the peasants were angry that he had made a bad deal; they raised a din and clamor: "Why did you let countless riches and money out of your hands? You should have given it to us, we would have done well in our work."

Here Lenin laughed, shook his head, and said in reply: "Don't kick up a fuss, don't scold me, just take the land and livestock and get to work. There you'll see what happens. There wouldn't have been enough money for everyone; there's thousands of you and only a few hundred of the blue bloods. I don't quite know the word yet that will get the blue bloods off the face of the earth. I still have a bit to figure out. But I do have another trusty word for the commoners of all the world. Whenever I say it, the blue bloods won't be able to find themselves soldiers or laborers. Everyone will come over to me and say no to the blue bloods. And since they're not breadwinners but spongers, they won't be long for this world."

And it might have been too slow, might have been too fast, but still, just what he said would happen soon happened. A horseman rode up to Lenin with a message from Tsar Mikolashka. Tsar Mikolashka said in this message: "So, Lenin, you tricked me. You took the commoners for yourself, and you didn't leave me any breadwinners, just spongers. My generals and noble officers are like old horses without their soldiers. They only drink, eat, and chew the fat. The manor lords have already finished up their provisions, worn out the clothes from their trunks, tattered and soiled everything without a thought for the future. My merchants are ruined; without peasants there's nobody to sell their old goods to. My factory owners have wrecked and ruined the machines. They can't do anything; they know everything by the book but can't even screw in a screw. And the foreign commonfolk won't come to work for us; they came over to your side, to your secret word. The way it turns out, even if I lie down and die, my generals and noble officers are going to war against you to win back the common folk."

And that's when the war between the blue bloods and commoners started. But the blue bloods won't last for long, since the generals and noble officers are used to shouting orders at the soldiers, moving their armies here and there, but they're not used to fighting themselves, because their blood runs thin. And they won't be long for this world.

ILICH WILL WAKE UP SOON

A FAIRY TALE FROM VYATKA

Once Lenin was sitting in his office after dinner reading through some books and newspapers. No matter what paper he looked at, no matter what book he opened, he found something about himself:

"It says we have nothing to fear from the Entente, nothing to fear from America as long as we have Vladimir Ilich Lenin."

Lenin thought this odd. He got up from his bentwood chair, paced around the office a bit, and said to himself: "All right, I'll do it."

And after that he sends a messenger to the head Soviet doctor. The doctor comes, and Lenin tells him: "Can you make it so that I die, but not completely, just so it looks like I did?"

"I can, Vladimir Ilich, but why?"

"Just so," he says, "I can see how things will go without me. For some reason everyone heaps all the blame on me; they shield themselves with my name."

"Well," answers the doctor, "it can be done. We'll put you in a large room instead of a grave, and for decency's sake we'll cover it with glass, so nobody can touch you, or else they will."

"One thing, Doctor, make sure this stays a big secret between us. Only you and Nadezhda Konstantinovna[2] will know."

And soon Lenin's death was announced to the people.

The people moaned and groaned, and even the Communists couldn't stand it—they broke into tears. Everyone sets to thinking, their hearts aflutter: what will we do now? Pretty soon the English and French will come poking around.

And the oldest of the old, Kalinin,[3] beseeches: "What can you do. It isn't ours to change. You won't fix misfortune with tears. We've cried our fill; all right, now, let's get down to work."

They laid Lenin in this big barn called a marsoleum, and put a guard at the door. A day passes, then two... a week, a month, and Lenin gets tired of lying under glass.

So one night he sneaks out of the marsoleum by the back door and goes straight to the Kremlin, to the main palace, where they hold all sorts of commissar meetings.

He was let through the doors because he still had his lifetime pass in his pocket, and he pulled his hat down so nobody would recognize him.

Lenin gets there, but the meeting is already over, and the servants are washing the floor. Lenin asks: "Is it over?"

"Yup."

"Do you know what they talked about?"

"All sorts of things. I hear the English want to make friends with us, and some other big countries too. But I only heard it through the keyhole with the tip of my ear. I didn't understand everything."

"Did they mention Lenin?"

"Of course they mentioned him. Here," they say, "Lenin is dead, but then there are twice as many Communists as there were before.[4] Let the Entente try something now!"

"And there's not a peep from the Entente?"

"Not a word from them, not even now."

"Good, good," Lenin agreed and bid the servants farewell.

He went back to the marsoleum, lay down under the glass, and thought: "So it's okay after all, they can work without me. Good. I'll check in a couple more places. Tomorrow I'll drop in on the factory workers."

Next day Lenin went to a factory. They didn't stop him there either; he was taken straight to the inner workings. Not many people worked the night shift, only

---

2. Krupskaya, Lenin's wife.

3. Mikhail Kalinin, president of the Soviet Republic, whose peasant origins were well known, was often called the "All-Russian Elder."

4. After Lenin's death in 1924, the Party began mass recruitment of working-class members, which was called "the Lenin Enrollment."

enough to make sure the steam didn't die out. They kept a machinist, a greaser, a stoker, and also a guard, so that spies couldn't mess anything up.

"They'll be enough," thought Lenin. "After all, I'm not organizing a rally, I only need to ask a few questions."

"Hello, comrades."

"Hi."

"Well, how are things?"

"Not bad... Everything's all right."

"You're not Party members?"

"We weren't until Lenin died, but now we're Communists. Leninists."

This soothed Lenin's heart greatly.

"No obstructions in your work? Do you produce many goods?"

And slowly he began to wear them out with questions.

"Soon we'll be doing as well as in peacetime."

"Well, keep working, all in good time, and for now goodbye."

"Everything's all right here," thought Lenin on the way back to the marsoleum, "and now I only have to find out from the peasants how they're doing!"

The third night, Lenin got up earlier: he had to make it to the train station, then ride the train a while, and then he'd have to walk from a backwoods station to the village.

He went to the poorest village he could find, so he could see how people really live. A light was shining in the window of one hut. Lenin walked over.

"Can I rest a bit here?"

"Sure."

Lenin walks in and is amazed. No icons. Red posters all over. Portraits. Lenin asks deliberately: "What are you, nonbelievers?"

"We, comrade, are citizens; there is a reading room in our home, and our Lenin Corner is over there."

"They remember me even here," thought Lenin.

"Well, how are peasants doing nowadays?"

"Not much you can't endure, but it's like things are still sorting themselves out. They say now they're turning their face, not their rear, to the countryside.[5] Lenin told his Communists long ago about linking the city and the country, and now it seems they've started to think about it. It's about time."

Lenin left the hut happy, went back to his marsoleum contented, and he's been lying there many days since his wanderings were over.

He'll probably wake up soon.

That will be a joyous occasion.

Words cannot tell about it, and pen cannot describe it.

---

5. Reference to a party slogan of the time: "Face to the countryside"—i.e., an appeal to pay more attention to the peasantry.

The Thoughts, Cares, and Deeds of the Workers
(Diary of a Rabkor)
Ivan Zhiga (1928)

THE WORKER CORRESPONDENT (RABKOR) MOVEMENT ORIGI-
NATED IN THE 1920S TO GIVE WORKERS A DIRECT PUBLIC VOICE.
RABKORS PROVIDED ACCOUNTS OF WORKER LIFE AND OFFICIAL
CORRUPTION, AND MADE POLITICAL LEADERS AWARE OF PUBLIC
OPINION. THE MOVEMENT, HOWEVER, WAS EVENTUALLY CO-
OPTED BY THE PARTY, AND IT SERVED AS AN ENTHUSIASTIC DE-
NOUNCER DURING THE PURGES. THE CELEBRATED MURDERS OF
SEVERAL RABKORS AND POPULAR CONTEMPT FINALLY UNDER-
MINED THE MOVEMENT COMPLETELY. BUT WHILE IT THRIVED,
SKILLED CORRESPONDENTS SUCH AS ZHIGA COULD GIVE A VIVID
PICTURE OF WORKER LIFE IN TRANSITION.

One day at a worker correspondent meeting we were arguing about how to describe workers' lives. The question is tremendously important to us rabkors, because we've never read a description of our life nowadays as workers that was broad or complete.

True, you run across individual bits and scraps of worker life in the newspapers. Sometimes our life is described so that workers live like the bourgeoisie used to, or sometimes so that our life is flat-out filth.

These descriptions really upset us. We're furious at the writers and, of course, even more so at ourselves. Who the hell knows what's going on! Some people don't know how we live, but they write. We do know, but writing is beyond us. We could just cry! That's why we decided to get together and figure out how to describe our lives ourselves.

We read the notices published in newspapers, selected passages from books, and compared the bad remarks with the good, the true with the false. It was very interesting work, and we had no disagreements. But toward the end of our talk, the secretary of our circle, Comrade Krasny,[1] raised a new question. He said, "Now, guys, instead of discussing 'how to write,' let's discuss 'what to write about.'"

Excerpted from I. Zhiga, *Dumy rabochikh, zaboty, dela (zapiski rabkora)* (Moscow: Zemlia i fabrika, 1928), pp. 7–10, 13–28.

1. Comrade Red.

"That's a strange question," the rabkors said, "'what to write about': about workers' lives, of course."

"For instance?"

"Well, for instance, what do workers do in their factories?"

"Who doesn't know that? Everyone knows that at a certain hour the whistle blows, at a certain hour workers get up and go to the factory, work for as long as they're supposed to, go home: they eat, drink tea, do some work around the house. What's there to write about?"

"So then let's describe how the worker lives," the rabkors answered.

"How does he live?" asked Krasny. "He sleeps, eats, smokes, works, goes to meetings, drinks beer and vodka, swears, fights, beats his wife, reads books, goes to the club, studies. What's interesting here?"

"Well, there's your problem! According to you we have nothing to write about," said the excited rabkors.

"There is something to write about," answered Krasny, "but there are some bad, evil things left over from the past in our life, and there are many good things the Revolution gave us. We have to decide what to write about most: the good or the bad?"

And here the circle split into four.

Some said: "We should write about the good mainly. For instance, forty-year-old working women are starting to learn to read. Old-time workers are joining the Party; workers volunteer to work three machines and four benches. Or else: new housing and public cafeterias are being built, workers are raising their level of education. We should write about all that, because we have a lot of good things, but we don't notice them and they're wasted."

Others objected: "On the contrary, we should write more about the bad things in our life, because the good is good, it will stay with us, nobody can take it away now, while the bad things in our life... we shouldn't just write about them, we should scream about them from every street corner so they disappear, so that they don't stop the good from developing."

A third group objected to the first and second: "If we write only about the good, then we'll embellish our life just like other writers do, and nobody will believe us. And if nobody believes us, then we don't have any reason to write; let the other writers do that. And if we exhibit only the bad side, then it will come out again like the writers, and again it won't be right, because there are good things in our life.

"So if we want to be truthful, then we have to write about the good and the bad in equal measure."

"Allow us," objected the fourth group. "How can you write about the good and the bad in equal measure? Suppose it turns out there's more bad? And what if there's absolutely nothing good about some part of our life, or else there's so little that it would be embarrassing to compare it with the bad? What then? Should we not write at all? We think," they said, "that before you write about workers' lives you should expel any thoughts about good and bad sides from your head. There are no good and bad sides, there's only a single, many-sided workers' life, and if we describe it, then let's describe it just like it is. Let's take our plant, for example. Twelve thousand people work there. We see the established life of an enormous collective before us. Well, let's not describe this life from one side or the other, but say, let's jump straight into the thick of it, look at it from top to bottom, let's tell about what we see there. Let the people we tell it to decide whether there's more good or bad."

"That's right," said several rabkors. "If we were writing about someone else's life, then, of course, we could lie out of ignorance, just like those writers lie about us, but here we'll be telling about ourselves!"

"But telling what about ourselves!" exclaimed Krasny.

Then the renowned rabkor Aspid got up and said: "Here's what, comrades. We might be rabkors, but it's evident we don't know our own life. Let's take a good look and feel around ourselves, then maybe we can stop arguing?.. Here's my idea: let's get together on our first day off and start investigating our life. Let's tour the barracks for starters: we'll see who lives how. Then we can write it down and everything will become visible, like in a mirror. Okay?"

We were overjoyed at Aspid's idea. We accepted it gladly and resolved: "Begin investigation on the first day off." . . .

I

The Barracks

Besides the three-story stone quarters, the factory owns old wooden barracks. They were built by the previous owner and served as a filter for new workers. Every worker joining the factory settled there if he couldn't find an apartment, and lived there for a year or two—until he proved his loyalty to the owner.

The filter has been eliminated, but the barracks remain, a clear reminder of the past. Squat, coated with mud, they stand half-buried in rows twenty meters apart. Piles of peat and murky slop puddles are all around. The latrines are between the buildings, and whether it's daytime or nighttime, winter or autumn, workers living in the barracks have to go outside. But the latrines are wrecked. One half—the men's—is broken, only the women's are left, and they have to be used in turns. There's stinking bilge on the latrine floor; it leaks outside and poisons the air.

The barracks are filled with dirt and stench. There's a huge Russian stove by the entrance. Narrow corridors stretch off from the stove, which lead to tiny rooms like prison cells. The floor is wooden, with holes in it. A draft comes through the floor, and the barracks are cold. Little kids crawl around the hallways, screaming, fighting, crying. A four-year-old tyke, dark-eyed, as pot-bellied as a pitcher, plucks a piece of dry clay from the stove and gnaws it with relish, like a nut. Of course, none of the children use the latrine. They do it wherever they are, and that makes such a smell in the barrack that a newcomer loses his breath.

We enter one of the tiny rooms. It's five steps long and an arm's breadth wide. A family of four lives there. It's furnished with a bed, a small table, and two stools. The family was eating dinner when we entered; the worker and his wife were sitting, and the children ate standing. In a corner across from the table gaped a hole so big that a dog could have crawled in. The windows weep. The sills have rotted. The room is filled with dirt, damp, and stench.

"So this is how you live?" the Komsomol Kryuchok asked sadly.

"This is how we live," the worker grinned.

"Take a look: that beam is warped, it's going to fall down soon," said the rabkor Chuma.[2]

"We know," the worker said indifferently.

"You'll be crushed!"

"Well, and what can you do?"

"You have to ask them to give you a new room."

"And who are you?"

"We're rabkors!"

"You're not the one giving out rooms," the worker muttered gloomily.

The next-door neighbor heard our conversation. He came over and asked us to look into his room. We went to his room and tried to open the door, but it wouldn't give.

The floor was swollen. We slipped into the room with difficulty, and the worker, thin, dark, constantly coughing, told us: "Here, comrades, you can see how we live. There are six people in my family, and the room is six by five arshins. That's nothing in itself; we can stand it in the summer, but the winter is a calamity. You come home from work, sit in your outer clothes, sleep without undressing, don't take off your boots, and the children just plain freeze. How can we keep going like this?"

The barrack residents mistook us for a commission. They yanked us into their rooms for a look, complained about their living conditions, said they were completely lost and had nowhere to turn. One woman was particularly insistent that we see how she lives. We opened the door. The room was completely dark. The woman walked forward quickly, pulled a blanket from the window, and we saw a half-rotted frame without glass, and a tiny infant sucking hard at its hands on the bed.

"So how can anyone live here?" this worker asked us. "How can my baby and I stay healthy?"

"Have you notified the authorities?"

The woman waved her hand hopelessly.

"They promise everything," and she covered the window with the blanket again.

When we walked out of the barracks, the rabkor Yazva said: "Brothers, that's living death!"

"But what can you do? There aren't any apartments!"

"So what! Does that mean we shouldn't do anything?"

"Well what? Do you have a suggestion?"

Yazva fell silent and sank into thought.

There was a crowd of womenfolk by the entrance to another barrack. They were whispering animatedly, staring into the hallway. Children had gathered around, and they looked into the barracks' dark maw curiously.

---

2. This and the other rabkor names are related to pain and sickness.

Suddenly a woman's wild wail rang out from inside; feet tramped, and four men struggled outside with a corpse on a canvas stretcher.

The womenfolk made way for them and watched the dead man silently, like cows looking at blood and ready to break out howling. Wrapped in a filthy gray sheet on the stretcher, the man rolled from side to side, showing his dirty gray toenails, and behind him, with her hands covering her face, walked an emaciated, stooped woman who was either crying or laughing.

"Somebody's gone 'home,'" Aspid muttered gloomily.

"We'll all be there someday," said Chuma. But Kryuchok, a young rabkor and Komsomol, flared up and said: "This, brothers, is where everyday life begins! Let's write about how this worker lived, lived and worked, worked and when his time came he's gone in a flash."

"Well, that's nothing to write about," Zanoza objected. "That's how we'll all live and die: that's not life, it's death."

Aspid walked away, went over to the women, and asked who had died. The women answered indifferently: "The Lord has taken Uncle Nikita."

"What was his room?" Aspid asked.

"Number twenty-five."

Aspid took out his notebook and wrote it down.

"Why'd you do that?" asked the rabkors.

"Just in case it's useful," Aspid answered evasively. "A rabkor should note down everything."

The Women's Barracks

We went to the Roza Luxemburg[3] Dormitory. The wenches' quarters, as they used to be called, were a long, two-story building that looked like an old-time merchant's trunk.

The staircase was neat and clean. There wasn't even any dust in the hallway, and sitting a while in the huge dorm rooms was pleasant. The clean beds were piled high with thick pillows and quilts. Pillowcases competed with each other for whiteness, and lace bedspreads were stretched over them. Embroidered towels, mirrors, and photographs hung on the wall next to each bed. Icons hung in several places, with portraits of Lenin, Clara Zetkin,[4] and Krupskaya nearby. On the wall were occasional glimpses of soldiers from the tsarist war, with their sabers, cutlasses, and tilted caps.

The place of honor right next to the soldiers was occupied by young men, slicked down, their hair combed, or simple village lads in peasant blouses.

You could tell by the photographs who their owner was. Widows of husbands killed in the war live here, along with village girls who came to work at the factory and old women who either lost or were never able to start their own family. And all

---

3. Communist, heroine, and martyr of the German Revolution, killed in 1919.
4. Another German Communist.

this is reflected on the walls, on the towels, on the lace bedspreads and the photographs.

When we toured the rooms, some women were sitting next to a window sewing, others were knitting, and yet others were in the kitchen cooking dinner. The barracks were quiet, peaceful, pleasant.

We were received like guests. We were surrounded and showered with questions: Why and for what should we study worker life? When we told them, they praised us, willingly answering our questions. Each one happily told us about herself, about her life, her joys and sorrows.

"Everything here is different," said the amazed rabkors.

"Don't you think women know how to live?" a worker woman answered sharply. "Go around other barracks, see if they're as clean as we are."

Others shouted, "Show them the red corner!"

They dragged us over to the red corner.

Two semi-basement rooms had been made into one. Living in those rooms was impossible: they were damp and cold, so they were outfitted as a red corner. The smaller room was a stage, and the bigger was for the audience. Benches were set against the walls of the five-square-sazhen hall, and a table was placed in the middle for newspapers and magazines. The walls of the room were decorated with posters and portraits of our national leaders. The Lenin Corner was placed on a windowsill for lack of space. The Atheists' Corner was actually put in the corner, and was abloom with colored pictures. An enormous wall newspaper spread along the wall, and a small shelf with books hung across from it. Garlands cut from colored paper were stretched across the whole room from threads hung below the ceiling, and there were paper lanterns. The women had done it all themselves; they had decorated their corner and made it bright and colorful, just like they were.

They told us proudly how they had begun building the corner, how volunteers were found, how they had spurred on backward women, pooled resources, bought material for the curtain, hired a carpenter, and forced everyone to work on the red corner. "Take a look!" said the red-cheeked young worker woman who ran the corner as she drew back the curtain.

The stage opened before us. If you climbed onstage, your head hit the ceiling—it holds no more than five people.

"But the things we can do here—ay-yay-yah!" the woman said gaily. "We have our own drama circle, and we give shows not only here but in other barracks. Today, for instance, we're playing Ostrovsky's *At the Jolly Spot* in the New Barrack. Do you want to go?"

"Do you perform here often?" asked Chuma.

"Every Sunday, and the other evenings we have antireligious lectures, lectures on maternity and infants, on hygiene—and all that with magic lantern slides."

"There's something going on here every night," another woman informed us.

"We have a circle for liquidating illiteracy, with sixty people registered," a third says.

"There's Auntie Dunya, she's fifty-five, she's learning to read and is the hardest-working student!" yells a fourth.

"Auntie Dunya, Auntie Dunya!" they shouted around the barracks. A strong and spritely old woman came and was surrounded by young women, who led her like a blind woman to the wall, stood her in front of a poster, and began vying with each other to shout, "Auntie Dunya, read it, Auntie Dunya."

The old woman laughed good-naturedly, wiped the sweat off with an apron, latched onto the largest letters, moved her lips, and then, turning to her friends, said joyfully: "It says: Sov-i-et power."

"That's right, Auntie Dunya, that's right!" the women shouted together, young and old. They were all sincerely glad for their friend, and all of them, like children caught up in a good game, gaily told us of their own progress.

"But how it used to be, how it used to be!" the red corner director told us. "It used to be that young fellows would come over in the evenings; the men would bring vodka with them, accordions, they'd start dancing, then fighting, and knives would come out. It used to be you couldn't sleep or relax, and there was nowhere to get away from it. Every day there were jealous arguments, constant yelling, uproar, swearing, and all sorts of trouble. But now we've come together like friends, redirected our work, built a red corner, gotten everyone reasonable jobs. And you see, our life changed. Everyone likes it now. Now we have a choral circle for whoever wants to learn to sing; somebody else does the wall newspaper, another is in the drama circle, yet another is liquidating illiteracy. And when you want to go for a stroll with your sweetheart, please, you can do whatever you like outside the barracks, but inside the barracks—beg your pardon."

"And we did it all ourselves," said a woman. "We created the red corner, and it began a whole revolution here. Even the male workers treat us differently. Before, whenever they found out that a girl lived in this dormitory, they considered her lost, but now, you see, they treat her with respect, they invite her to their barracks to act, and they point at us and say, 'Now that's the way it should be done!'"

Together with the worker women, we were shining with happiness.

The Red Army Barrack

A huge three-story building. Each floor is dissected by a wide corridor lined with closely packed room doors. The corridor is of poured cement—it is smooth and glittery, like a roadway.

The barracks hum like a factory. When you climb the stairs to the second floor, a shaggy Karl Marx greets you, on the third floor an apathetic Engels, and on the fourth the slyly squinted eye of Ilich.

We go straight to the kitchen. A huge Russian stove with stoke holes on both sides is at the end of each corridor, and on the walls around it are dish shelves, cupboards, and cooking counters. It's stuffy near the stove. Blue-gray smoke can be seen in the windows. Women bustle back and forth. Almost all of them have their sleeves rolled up to their elbows. Several wear aprons that are so greasy they seem to be made of rawhide leather. Every woman is carrying something in her hands: one a pot of cabbage soup, another hot potatoes, yet another freshly baked pies or steaming wheat cakes.

"Hey, ladies, did I get some flour!" boasts an elderly woman. "Yesterday I put it down wet, and today I look—it's pushed the lid open and spilled over the lip, so hard it got the towel all cruddy."

"Where'd ya get the flour?" asks the woman standing next to her and stirring potatoes in a frying pan.

"At that retailer's called '4–0,' and you can also get American wheat, so it's better not to take this: it's thin as water."

The women roll the dough, cut it up, and show off their cooking to each other. Pretzels, pastry, "cuklets," stewed potatoes, soup with pork.

Maria doesn't back off from Darya, and Darya doesn't want to let Agafya see her flop. How could they—it would be a disgrace!

The steam oven doors slam continuously; the women throng around the fire-breathing stove. The truce comes to an end.

"Hey, you, dearie, why'd you take my soup off the heat?"

"I'll put it back again as soon as I move my potatoes, don't you worry."

"Don't touch it and I won't worry."

"My, my, your ladyship: can't even touch it."

"Here's where you and that ladyship can go," says the worker woman, pointing at her rear end.

"I can see it, you pockmarked devil."

"Hey, bitch, still barking?"

"What are you yapping about, you mangy carcass!"

"I'll knock your teeth out with my frying pan for talking like that."

"Just touch me and I'll bend your ugly snout out of shape."

"Your old man might, but he's not here now, the long-assed snake."

"Oh, you god-damned devil, you and your kids are bogeymen."

"And yours have the plague."

The women start to wrestle, aim frying pans at each other, shove, lose their tempers. Someone spills something, someone gets cracked with a kettle, someone shoves someone—and as a result, the frying pan falls to the floor.

Cursing...

"You so-and-so, you thief, you drunk."

"Oh, you god-damned mangy devil!"

They call each other bad words, contrive to find fault not only with their foes but with their husbands and children. The kitchen roars like a factory.

On the other side of the stove an elderly worker woman, Akulina Utka[5] by name, is frying pancakes in butter on the hot coals. She says dreamily: "Hey, ladies, it'll soon be time to get the slop money from the cow maids—we can tie a good one on! In the old days, remember, we'd carry the tables out into the hall, wine, snacks, accordions, and then crank it up!"

"Look out, your pancakes are burning," her neighbor said.

Akulina slowly took the pan from the stove, flipped the singed pancakes with her fingers, put the pan back in the stove, this time off to the side, and started

---

5. Duck.

talking again: "Well, how's it gonna be, ladies, do we drink up the slop money or not?"

"The men will start fighting," muttered a young woman who hadn't said anything.

Akulina was transformed. Forgetting her pancakes again, holding a rag in one hand, she leaned against the stove and loudly, so everyone could hear, yelled: "You'd think they were lords! Keep quiet and they'll do even worse. Just look at my Prokhor there, he doesn't dare let out a squeak; when he gets up his gumption I just take my rolling pin and show him—he shuts up right away."

"Well, your Prokhor is ready for a monastery. Just you try talking that way to my man and he'd take that rolling pin to your head."

"Oh shut up, the men will be riding you like a horse," Akulina answered, now with more heart in it.

"They already do, Auntie Utka," shouted a Komsomol boy walking by from the cellar with a dish of pickles.

"Get wherever you're going!" Utka snapped back. "All sorts of trash stick their noses in other people's business."

Akulina, muttering, took the pancakes from the stove and turned to the women, saying keenly: "So, does that mean we won't be having any fun? We could buy some wine, invite an accordion, and have some drinks! Come on, Vanka, I'm going." And Akulina, a rag made from her husband's trousers in one hand, frying pan in the other, jauntily turned on her heel.

"What sort of relaxation is drinking?" the young woman objected.

"What, are we supposed to live without whooping it up once in a while?"

Some other women came into the kitchen, and a hot argument started.

It was noisy. Little children scurried around the adults and whined, tugging at their mothers' hems: "Mommy, gimme cake."

"Bug off, brat," wailed the flustered mothers, caught up in the argument. "You little buggers are such pests! There's no peace from you anywhere. Why don't you go drop dead."

As they waited for the hot and fragrant cakes and pies, the working men sat in groups in the hallway, smoking, passing on the news, reading fresh newspapers, laughing. The women ran by them with the pies and, calling their husbands, entered their rooms.

In one group, a worker who was still young said with sadness in his voice: "I was a quiet, hard-working boy. I was my parents' only child, and look what happened!— I'm a good-for-nothing. I see myself that I'm a drunk. True, I didn't love my mother, I couldn't take her because of her swearing. What didn't she do! When you wanted to study, she'd chase you out of the room so you wouldn't bother her or block the light. And it would be just awful when she started to swear—I never heard men curse like that. I grew up and went off to work. I earned twice as much as my mom and pop together, and it still was no life: my mother was screwing around."

"I would have left, but I felt sorry for my father. He was drinking hard. Guzzling it by the fifth. Oh, was he drinking. He'd drink, lie down in bed, stack the pillows high, and say to me: 'Vasya, pour me another!'"

"There weren't any shotglasses. I'd pour out a big glass and go over to him, and he'd be lying all pale with his eyes shut. 'Pour it,' he'd whisper. 'Pour it, Vasya, straight in my mouth. I want to drink.'"

"And he drank it like water."

"Those evil days stretched on locked up in that box, and I didn't know what to do. Sorrow took me too, and like my father, I began to drown my sorrow in wine."

"At first it disgusted me, but still I drank. I had nobody to open my heart to. Back then there was none of that Komsomol, no meetings, no classes to go to. And I got used to it, brothers, how I got used to it. I drowned myself in that habit."

"I became a drunk, brothers, and destroyed myself. Here I'm sitting with you and my guts are on fire—I want a drink. I'm lost!"

The workers listening to the drunk's confession were quiet and gloomy, and who knows, maybe they were remembering their own lives; maybe theirs had been no better than Vasya's, and only desperate resistance had saved them from destruction. The workers listened silently to their comrades' tale, and a spark of pity glowed in their eyes for someone close to them they could understand.

Others were laughing at a worker clowning around at the other end of the hall.

"Markelych!" they called a balding old man over.

"What's the matter?"

"Sit down a while."

Markelych smiles guiltily.

"No, guys, I can't."

"Take a seat, what do you need over there—we have to talk about something very important."

Markelych smiles, sits, and begins a story that everyone has heard a hundred times.

"Life's tough, brothers, tough," the old man drawls.

The workers wink at each other and put on a serious air.

"Aren't you lying, Markelych? You're probably salting something away in your piggy bank. Oh, you're a sly one, you rogue!"

Markelych gets angry: "What piggy bank? Where'd you get that? I get my thirty rubles and—flash, they're gone! And don't wait for the wife's salary, it all goes for grub."

"Hold on, Markelych, you said yourself that your wife earns fifty rubles."

"So what, fifty... It's chicken feed."

The workers chuckle and egg him on.

"Well then, but you say..."

Markelych runs for his union booklet and, showing it, shouts irritably: "You don't believe me? There, take a look!"

The workers look over the book for a long time, and suddenly one asks unexpectedly: "Does your wife bring all her money home?"

You could have knocked Markelych down with a feather.

"I don't know. Maybe not all of it," he mutters fearfully.

"Well, there, I don't know. How can you tell us for sure that you're not putting anything in the piggy bank? Not you, maybe, but your woman. Look out, brother, you'd better lock the door tight at night."

Markelych gets upset, turns red, and walks away with a baffled smile.

The women had settled things in the kitchen. They wore themselves out, strained their nerves, cursed and talked their fill, and teatime started. They drink and eat. Then everyone who likes to sleep goes to bed; others go "visiting," or else take a seat on a bench in the sun.

The women take the men's place in the hall. They sit on benches or right on the floor—they let their hair down, search each other's heads for lice, catch them, squash them, and pass sentence: "Now there's a fat one, like Lyubka Yegorova."

"This one's like Zinka Garyukhina—a real nit."

"Did you hear, ladies?" says one. "Manka, the slut, had a baby."

"Well, and what?"

"I swear to god, girls. Only I don't know who knocked her up; the stinker won't tell."

"It'll be Zhenka's turn soon," another proclaims prophetically. "She was humming away all last night with some guy under the staircase."

"It'll come down on her," the others agreed with conviction.

A finely dressed lady walked by the women.

"My, all dressed up!" the women comment. "And where do they get it? The furniture in their room glitters, they eat all sorts of delicacies and throw parties. They must be pilfering."

Somewhere below an accordion strikes a plaintive chord, and outside under the windows a girl's deep voice rings out:

> From this feast of the lazily idle,
> Who dip their red hands in the blood,
> Take me away to the camp of those fated
> To die for the wondrous cause of love.*

The barracks hum like a factory. Little kids crawl up and down the stairs. Barely dressed, shoeless, wearing only their shirts, most of them pantless, they sit their bare bodies straight on the asphalt floor, yell, shriek, and wail.

The young people—guys and girls—have gathered at the end of the hall; a balalaika plays, and they sing ditties. Sometimes the guys and girls open the hall windows on all three floors, go out to the balconies, and roar to the music! Who's better? Who's louder? Who's the most interesting? The noise of the accordion roars through the barracks and echoes in a wave to the woods beyond the factory.

Zanoza said: "It's a typical story here. You even get sick of it."

"Everything's like it used to be," Aspid confirmed. "I used to be just like that little boy crawling on all fours along the hallway, and then when I grew up some, I also made noise. Nothing has changed here."

---

*These sketches of life in the Red Army barrack belong to rabkors [author's comment].

Makhno's Band ("Gulyai-Pole")

An Aquatic Pantomime in Three Scenes
with a Prologue and Apotheosis
Performed by the Leningrad State Circus, Spring 1930
Theme and Production by Williams Truzzi
Scenario by Vladimir Mass

THIS CIRCUS SCENARIO, PERFORMED IN THE FORMER CIRCUS CINIZELLI, ILLUSTRATES ONCE AGAIN HOW POLITICAL OPPONENTS WITH A CERTAIN POPULAR APPEAL HAD TO BE DEMONIZED IN SOVIET CULTURE. NOTICE THE SIMILARITIES WITH THE FILM SCRIPT FOR *THE LITTLE RED DEVILS*. *MAKHNO'S BAND* WAS ALSO THE INSPIRATION FOR AN OPERETTA OF THE 1930S AND A 1960S FILM, BOTH CALLED *WEDDING AT MALINOVKA*.

CHARACTERS

Red Staff Officers:
  Brigade Commander Denisov
  Kurkov
  Sergeev
Obukh, a railroad activist
Klavdia, his wife
The Stationmaster
Passengers caught at the station:
  Madam Gireau
  Her husband

A priest
A grammar school student
Perepelitsyn, Councillor of State
Makhno
Makhno's Assistants:
  Ferz
  Shchus
  Hun
Ataman Grigoriev
His adjutant

Extras:
The Red Army. Makhno's band. Peasants, female workers, female street traders, solid citizens. In the apotheosis: Red soldiers, sailors, Young Communists, swimmers, rowers, boxers, gymnasts.

The plot is taken from the Ukrainian Civil War. It takes place in 1920 in "Gulyai-Pole," a little village in the Dnepropetrovsk district, center of the kulak peasant movement that formed around Makhno. This anarchist outlaw group, which arose at the end of 1918 as a result of complex relations within the Ukrainian peasantry, was an expression of wealthy peasants' hatred for the city and their dissatisfac-

---

Makhnovshchina ("Gulyai Pole") (Moscow: Teakinopechat, 1930).

tion with the new ruling powers. Deprived of most of the peasantry's support, the Makhno movement was destroyed from within by the activity of poor peasant committees and liquidated by the Red Army. Thus, without attempting to reflect Makhno as a socioeconomic phenomenon, which would be beyond the capacity of the present-day circus, the show aims to re-create individual episodes from that era with the specific features of circus art, artificially combining events of the Civil War and the Red Army with the era of socialist construction and sociopolitical slogans of our day.

PROLOGUE: RED HEADQUARTERS

The field commanders of a Red Army brigade are discussing the timeliness of liquidating Makhno's band. A railroad worker, Obukh, informs them of a sudden raid by Makhno's men, who have blown up the tracks near their camp so they can capture an approaching supply train. The commanders cannot contact the necessary military unit to order a detachment sent out, because Makhno has cut the telephone wires. Obukh decides to use a bypass to stop the train and deliver the order to the army unit to attack Makhno immediately.

SCENE I: THE RAILROAD STATION

Obukh meets his wife Klavdia at the station, shows her the order, and tells her about the assignment he has taken on himself. Vatrushkin, a speculator who is also stuck at the station waiting for the train, overhears them. He immediately races across the platform to his companions, middle-class denizens who are likewise stuck at the station, to share the news with them, but he can't get the story straight. The stationmaster runs up to announce that a mounted detachment of Makhno's men is coming, which causes panic among the passengers. Makhno's horsemen charge in. Pointing at Obukh, who is running by the platform, Vatrushkin turns him in to the Makhnovites as an underground Bolshevik. As they wait for their chief to come, they tie Obukh to a post and start interrogating the people left in the station. Vatrushkin convinces them that they are all actors leaving on tour. Makhno rides in and orders the Communists and bourgeoisie put to death immediately. When he finds out that some actors have chanced to be in the station, he orders Vatrushkin to put on a play. During the improvised show, where everybody does whatever comes into his head, Obukh's wife flirts with the men guarding her husband. She manages to distract the sentry and untie Obukh and tries to flee with him. Obukh succeeds in hiding, but Klavdia remains in the hands of Makhno's men. Makhno's adjutant Ferz, who has taken a fancy to Klavdia, decides to take her to Gulyai-Pole.

A train approaches the station. According to the calculations of Makhno's men, it's the very supply train they have been aiming for. However, Red cavalry unexpectedly spring from the train. A battle scene ensues which results in Makhno's retreat. The Reds pursue them. Peasants and railroad workers aid the wounded. One of the wounded Red soldiers gets up and walks off, leaving his horse, which was shot in the crossfire. The horse gets to its feet and limps off after him.

SCENE II: "GULYAI-POLE"

Gulyai-Pole is celebrating with a drunken bash. Makhno rides in with his squadron, bringing plundered goods. Scenes of sorting and dividing the booty are interrupted by the arrival of Ataman Grigoriev, summoned by Makhno for negotiations. Makhno calls an impromptu rally. Differences between Makhno's and Grigoriev's "programs" lead to the ataman's murder by Makhno's men. A drunken debauch starts, during which Makhno remembers Klavdia, abducted by Ferz at the station. Makhno proposes an immediate wedding for Ferz and Klavdia. Klavdia is brought in. But at that moment Obukh, disguised as one of Makhno's men, distracts them, lifts Klavdia onto his saddle, and puts the spurs to his horse. Makhno's men rush off in pursuit. The approach of a Bolshevik train is announced. Makhno orders his band to attack the Bolsheviks from the rear. His men gather and ride off.

SCENE III: SABOTAGING A BRIDGE ON THE OUTSKIRTS

A bridge outside town. Anarchy in town. A group of local residents prepare to meet the Reds. Suddenly the rumor circulates that the Whites are approaching. The citizens appropriately change their colors. Makhno's men unexpectedly burst into town. General pillage ensues. Anyone caught is tossed into the water from the bridge. The Red cavalry bursts in. A battle scene follows. As he retreats, Makhno orders the bridge blown up. The destruction of the bridge follows. Calamity strikes. The Reds are cut off. The cavalry halts before the dynamited bridge section. After several seconds of indecision, the cavalry wades into the water and, riding up to the other side of the bridge, attacks Makhno. There is confusion in the bandit ranks. Makhno's men flee, pursued by the Reds.

APOTHEOSIS

The apotheosis takes the spectator from the time of the Ukrainian Civil War back to the present. A structure built in the arena symbolizes a large power plant, providing energy to a series of industrial complexes and transmitting its current to the countryside (on stage). The Red Army, faithful guardian of the gains of the October Revolution, is situated on balconies suspended in the air all around the circus. Sailors stand on masts that are hung from the big top. There is a celebration of mass physical culture, one of the foundations of the country's defense capabilities. Radio and slogans underline the sociopolitical objectives of the apotheosis.

Swell the Harvest
(*chastushki*)
Shock Brigade of Composers and Poets (1930)

Brigades of composers, artists, cinematographers, poets, and others were part of the "Cultural Revolution" scene in the years of the first Five-Year Plan and collectivization. Songs were adapted to the target audience — in this case to peasants who were used to singing short two- or four-line rhymed doggerel verses with a rustic theme (*chastushki*). Here, the main message is: ditch the archaic equipment and take up the new agricultural machines provided by kolkhoz authorities.

Hey, Fyodor and Malania,
And Avdotia and Pakhom,
Let's strike up a merry song
About the sowing season.

Hey you, Vanya, best stretch out
That accordion past your ears.
Why should you be sowing from
Your grandpa's basket in these years.

Take a gander in the barn—
Ain't it mighty nifty
How that newfangled machine
Sorts the grain so swiftly.

Hey you, basket, blow away,
Like some measly weevil,
Cuz we got ourselves a drill—
A fancy city seed-drill.

It ain't nothing like you are,—
It'll dance a pretty dance,
Each seed drops out where it should,
Not a single one askance.

From *Umnozhai urozhai. Kolkhoznye pesni i chastushki,* rabota pervoi udarnoi brigady kompozitorov i poetov pri teakinopechati (Moscow: Teakinopechat, 1930).

Rammed It Through
(Notes on the Road)
Fyodor Panfyorov (1930)

PANFYOROV (1896–1960) WAS A WELL-KNOWN SOCIALIST REAL-
IST WRITER WHO CAME FROM THE PEASANTRY AND WROTE
ABOUT IT IN THE OFFICIAL MANNER. HE ALSO EDITED THE IM-
PORTANT JOURNAL *OCTOBER* FOR THIRTY YEARS. HIS MOST FA-
MOUS NOVEL, *BRUSKI* (1928–1937), AN IDEALIZATION OF RURAL
LIFE DURING COLLECTIVIZATION, WAS REPRINTED MANY TIMES.
THIS PIECE REFLECTS OFFICIAL HESITATION ABOUT THE AU-
THORITARIAN COLLECTIVIZATION CAMPAIGN (REFLECTED ALSO
BY STALIN'S "DIZZY FROM SUCCESS" SPEECH) AND THE ATTEMPT
TO BLAME IT ON LOCAL ACTIVISTS.

Prochnookopsk village in the northern Caucasus is well off. At one time there
was a Cossack officer school here. In 1918 and 1919, townspeople crept out and
sang "Hey, Kuban, You Are My Homeland."[1] The neighboring non-Cossack village
of Sibilda burned to the ground.

Sibilda no longer exists. There is an old kolkhoz, Red Fields, that still bears traces
of a fire and pogrom: even now, many live in earthen dugouts and scraggly mud
huts. On the other hand, Prochnookopsk glitters with electric lanterns by night,
and by day boasts houses of stone, wood fences, orchards, tiled roofs. People still
walk with dignity, bearded and festooned in lace and braid. But the Red Fields
kolkhoz conducted its sowing campaign with great success and encroached on
Prochnookopsk fields across the river.

"Let them be ashamed—they burned us out in '19, and now in '30 we go to help
them. Let them be ashamed," one partisan, the chairman of Red Fields, told us
sternly, waving his hand at Prochnookopsk.

"And what will they do, say thanks?"

"They won't bat an eye."

Today is the Sabbath. Comrade Khramov (deputy director of the Khutorok sovkhoz) and I have agreed on a trip to Prochnookopsk; they plan on switching over

---

Fedor Panferov, "Provernuli (Putevye zarisovki)," *Pravda,* 25 May 1930, p. 3.

1. An anthem of the Cossack separatist movement.

to the new regulations, a sovkhoz tractor column is working there, and Khramov is worried that when they switch to the new regulations, the kolkhoz will explode.

"It's a restless village," he complains.

Here we are in Prochnookopsk. We roll onto the main street with great trepidation. The street is packed with strollers. Many are drunk. A drunken Cossack sways in the middle of the road. He chuckles and, spreading his arms, tries to catch our car like it's a rooster. The driver makes a sharp turn and speeds by. The Cossack watches us drive away in surprise and yells something. On the corner is a stone house with broken steps, chipped, with a twisted gate that's always open: these are signs that the house belongs to the local communal sector. Villagers are stretched out along the fence. Evidently, there's a meeting going on.

Khramov explains: "The Prochnookopsk kolkhoz is split into three districts. The first and second are the most unreliable. Let's take a look at the first!"

"Let's!"

We take a look.

About forty people are crowded around a table in a small courtyard. At first we are surprised by the fact that there are so few of them, then by the fact that they are talking peacefully, cracking sunflower seeds, and stretching out in the warm rays of the sun. A grain farmer (eaten away by pockmarks) is sitting at the table and, hands clasped, persuading everyone softly: "It's the most useful thing for our village."

We don't understand a thing. We make our way closer to the table. The voice of the same grain farmer reaches us: "These pots are the most useful thing for our village."

It turns out that the first district has already passed the regulations and the talk now is about pottery. They want to organize the manufacture of clay pots.

We find out from the village soviet chairman that the second district has also passed the regulations.

It's funny: we came for a fight and get only pots. I ask the chairman: "How is it that everything went so peacefully?"

The chairman, a young, energetic, dashing and manly fellow (he lacked only a horse to ride), didn't answer immediately: "They were going to kick up a row some. So we rammed the question through!"

"And why are so few people at the meeting?"

"They went home," answered the chairman and turned away.

The third district—the peaceful one—gathered in the village soviet auditorium. There were about two hundred people. This was still far from a quorum. But, they said, many were working the fields, many had gone to Armavir, and that had to be taken into consideration. We do, and stay "in case of a fire." A member of the administration opens the meeting. On the agenda are the new regulations. An item is added about weeding the winter wheat (to be done by each individually).

"The agenda is approved unanimously," says the chair and opens the floor to the report of a Communist from the neighboring village of Kubansk.

The speaker reads the new regulations point by point. Then he explains them. He explains them ably and well. People listen on the edge of their seats, and nod their heads in approval. The cows should not be collectivized—good. They can all work their private plots of land as they wish—good... But then a dark shadow creeps up: The new regulations say that the land of anyone leaving the kolkhoz goes to the state; kolkhoz lands are not to be chopped up. They've clamped down. There's not a crack to slip through just in case. Well, what of it... once you've joined the kolkhoz, there's no thinking about cracks.

On the front benches everyone listens attentively, but in back the "local party," about fifteen people, are crowded together. There's an old, old guy with them. His hands are improbably big, particularly his palms. I look at his hands and think: "How many heads were cut off by that Cossack's hands?"

But what's this? There's some turmoil. The villagers get up in bunches, hop across the benches, and clump together in back. Aha. The report is finished. The chair asks if there are any questions. Silence. The chair presses them: "Well, what's this— it's like you're holding water in your mouths."

Finally a young fellow in a black jacket gets up. Everyone can see that he is being egged on. He is completely inexperienced and looks like a young hound. He wants to leap into the fray but is scared.

"I," he begins, hiccuping and getting confused, "as a poor peasant, want to make a proposal. We grain farmers gave all our inventory to the kolkhoz, but the white collars—like the school workers—gave only their allotments. We sweated, built up an inventory, while they kept their hands folded and gave furniture and furs. My opinion is let's take those furs and furniture and sell them."

"And use the money to buy shirts for the poor," the old man supports him with his huge hands. "Otherwise the teacher contributes a ten-ruble share and gets a thousand rubles a year."

The speaker protests: "You order the scholars to be equal to us uneducated people, but science says be equal according to learning. He studied, and he's contributed his means and abilities."

"Hey, hey," people shout from all over. "He contributed his abilities? Equal according to that? That's what we want... Here they've come to our kolkhoz, so we say wear your furs, but let us have our ten rubles too."

The same young fellow shouts through the ruckus: "There are people who lived high on the hog, but in my time I did myself in—didn't see a single day of the good life."

"You did what?" the young fellow's neighbor says in surprise. "In your time? The snot under your nose hasn't even dried. Right here," and he runs his finger under his nose. The young fellow has gone overboard. Even his own people are laughing at him. But they won't retreat.

From the middle of the "local party" a woman's voice rings out: "Each and every one of us wants to do our weeding by ourselves. Each and every one of us! Why don't you say anything? Around the corner you were whispering, but here you're silent."

"You will do your weeding by yourself," the chair says to calm them.

"Of course," rings out the Cossack woman's voice. "Since we sowed by ourselves in the fall, we'll weed by ourselves. I won't take a step off my own strip of land."

"Let me say something." A young man with furrowed eyebrows steps forward from the back rows. A villager (clearly the leader of the "local party"). "Let me say this—of course, we'll weed on our own. But I want to say this. The old regulations promised us that any extra inventory—live or dead—and any goods we dumped into the kolkhoz would come back in cash. For instance, I contribute 300 rubles' worth, and my share is 25. That means I get 275 rubles cash. The new regulations say I get nothing back. I contribute, and my money's thrown away. That's what we want—cash back. How can we do this voluntarily? There can't be any force."

"Cash?!" yells the village soviet chairman. "Who promised you cash?"

"Everyone did when they were ripping us off. So, they didn't promise... and that's what we want, cash."

"So."

"That's what we say."

"You want to force us?"

"Voluntary."

"Why should we be silent?" The leader's words are echoed, and the glass of the auditorium's windows almost bursts from the racket.

The uproar continues for almost two hours.

"Well, I'm voting," the chair cuts off the racket. "That's enough of that... Who's for the new regulations—please raise your hands."

Silence. Not a single hand. Light laughter.

"I don't understand," someone kicks in.

"What's not to understand? Whoever's for the new regulations is for them, whoever's against is against."

"Understood. Vote," advises the leader.

And the chair votes. Twenty hands go up for the new regulations. Eighteen are against, and the remainder, about 160 people, aren't for or against. Nobody asked them what they thought.

"The regulations are passed by a majority," announces the chair.

An explosion. The scraping of benches. Protest carries from the back like a trumpet. They demand a new vote. Only the authorities are sitting on the front benches. The village soviet chairman leaps up from the bench and abuses the villagers. The villagers are in an uproar. A group of about thirty people tear themselves away from the back rows and leave the auditorium. And in the hall, amid the noise and ruckus, the chair protests:

"I, as the chair, have allowed a mistake. A mistake!" he shouts.

Everyone falls silent.

What sort of mistake?

"My mistake was that after the vote, I allowed discussion. The question was decided by a majority. Going on to the next item on the agenda, about weeding the wheatfields."

And again an uproar.

Khramov and I split up. I run after the people who left the auditorium. They are clustered by the village soviet, shaking like horses after a swift run. They shake and can't say a word, they're so angry.

"Why are you against the new regulations?" I ask. "After all, the old regulations didn't even apply to you."

"Out of malice," someone shouts. "Out of malice!"

In the dark, I can't make out the face of whoever shouted, but I imagine how distorted it is, how his lips are quivering.

"Out of malice!" he shouts again. "They brought me into the kolkhoz, and now they don't want to talk with me. I'm no master. Filka's the master. Filka would pour soup in a plate for two dogs, and it's Filka that's commander over us. What are we, manure?"

"But about that, getting cash for inventory? What was that?"

"That was out of malice too. Once they start shoving, let them fork over the cash," says the leader and stretches out his hand.

We talk for a long time.

I understand their seething peasant spite, the spite of a petty property owner. I understand that it was aroused by incompetent leadership, confusion in the field, and the fact that methods of persuasion gave way here to methods of coercion. I understand that kulak kerosene has been poured on the peasants' spite (the demand of cash for inventory, the attacks on school workers); it crackles in the peasants' anger and bursts in all directions.

But what do the people running the kolkhozes see? Why do they have such satisfied and benevolent looks on their faces? Whom do they want to deceive, to lead on? "The regulations are passed by a majority." The majority didn't even vote. Tomorrow they'll go to the kolkhoz with the new regulations, and the kolkhozniks will say, "We didn't vote." Who needs that, and for what?

Aha, here they come. The meeting is over.

"Well, how did it go?" I race over to the village soviet chairman.

"Rammed through," he says and smiles with satisfaction.

"How? Everything stayed the same—twenty for, eighteen against—and the other 160?"

"Stayed the same."

"Was that what happened in the first two districts?"

"Almost," he says, and only here did his eyebrows barely quiver.

"Who are you kidding, Comrade Chairman?"

MARGINAL NOTES

I. It's untrue that the peasants were forced into the kolkhozes. There was pressure, methods of coercion, and bunglers overdid it. But that wasn't enough to drag the many-million-strong peasant masses into kolkhozes. Everyone knows that in recent years the majority of poor and middle peasants have come to the conclusion that life in the peasant community is impossible with individual farming; the fields get more and more spoiled every year, the harvests grow smaller. The masses of middle and poor peasants joined the kolkhoz out of conviction. But somebody wanted to gallop ahead, to give quick orders to property owners who have their own deeply rooted habits ("The power of habit of millions and tens of millions of people is the most terrible power"—V. I. Lenin), to turn them into Communists.

In the village of Kurgan, an initial total of about two thousand households were turned into twenty-five kolkhozes. Each kolkhoz has its own administration and soviet, so that about five to six hundred people were directly involved in creating kolkhozes. Tiny kolkhozes. They decided to combine them into one. They combined them. They chose their own administration, their own soviet; they pushed the immediate members of the kolkhoz aside, and the kolkhoz fell apart with incredible speed. Leaders don't see that the misfortune is hidden precisely in the fact that kolkhozes are being built by bureaucratic fiat, and anyone who raises his voice about blunders is considered a "socially harmful element, a demoralizer."

II. Still worse is the question of labor organization within the kolkhoz. The matter is new and very important. Nobody has any experience in it. Piecework payment, well developed in the old communes and kolkhozes, has been turned into a genuine daywork system.

III. If local kolkhoz leaders continue to act like this, massive failure must be expected for the harvest campaign.

IV. Several thousand higher Party workers must be immediately mobilized to help the 25000ers.[2] In August, probably, Party workers will be mobilized for the grain-procurement campaign. Why not do that now? Let them come right away and set the correct line: organize the poor, enlist the middle peasant directly in running kolkhozes, straighten out those who are used to ramming through important decisions, adjust work within kolkhozes, and organize the masses for the harvest campaign and fall sowing.

This has to be done immediately.[3]

---

2. Politically active industrial workers recruited to help collectivize the countryside in 1930.

3. Collectivization was the source of many anecdotes, aimed mostly at its "voluntary" nature. One, which appeared in many variants, ran: Stalin complains to Kalinin that there are mice in the cupboard. Kalinin advises him to hang a sign outside: *Stalin Collective Farm.* Then half the mice will die of hunger and the other half will run away.

Bread
Vladimir Kirshon (1930)

KIRSHON (1902–1938) WAS A PLAYWRIGHT FAMOUS FOR DRAMA-
TIZING THEMES OF THE CULTURAL REVOLUTION (*HUM OF THE*

This excerpt is translated in *VOKS*, no. 10–12 (1931), pp. 158–163, with some corrections.

RAILS, WINDY CITY, THE TRIAL). BREAD, HIS MOST FAMOUS
WORK, WAS PRODUCED BY THE BOLSHOI DRAMATIC THEATER IN
LENINGRAD AND THE MOSCOW ART THEATER AT THE HEIGHT
OF COLLECTIVIZATION. HE TOOK PART IN THE CAMPAIGN AS A
VOLUNTEER, AND HIS WORK IS A POLITICAL PASSION PLAY IN
WHICH CHARACTERS EMBODY TYPES OF GOOD OR EVIL. KIRSHON
WAS LIQUIDATED BY THE STALIN MACHINE IN 1938.

PRINCIPAL CHARACTERS

Mikhailov, secretary to the district Party
    committee, 35–40 years old
Olga, his wife, 25–27 years old
Raevsky, mandatory for the grain supplies,
    30–35 years old
Romanov, peasant and former Party
    member
Proshkin, kulak
Kvasov, kulak, 55–60 years old
Kotikhin, kulak

Zubov, kulak
Mikhail, Kvasov's son
Petka, his friend
Mokrina, a nun
Shilov, peasant
Sotin, farm laborer, Party member
Olkha, peasant
Grunkin, poor peasant
Pasha, Kvasov's daughter.

TENTH SCENE. SECOND EPISODE

*Absolute darkness. Singing and accordion playing behind the scene. The scrape of a
hatch, followed by the creaking of an opening door, and footsteps.*

MIKHAIL (*whispering*): Close the door, or else he'll run away.
PROSHKIN: He will not.
PETKA: Where do we have to go?
MIKHAIL: Be quiet!
PROSHKIN: I'm walking toward the bed. We should strike a match.
PETKA: Better not.
MIKHAIL: Shall I give you some light, lads? (*A pause.*) I say, shall I give you some
    light?
PROSHKIN: Don't. We will find you without it.
MIKHAILOV: Ah-ah! Is it you, Proshkin? Why do you come at so late an hour?
PROSHKIN: You recognize me?
MIKHAILOV: Of course! Well, what news?
PROSHKIN: We have brought two thousand poods. Take them!
MIKHAILOV: This is good! And I thought this might be another note.
MIKHAIL: We have not settled the first yet.

PROSHKIN: We will! Where are you? (*He advances and stumbles against a bench, which falls over.*) Damn you!

MIKHAILOV: Be careful! Don't hurry, you have time yet to kill me. Why are you doing it, lads? (*A pause.*) Why, I ask you?

PROSHKIN: Because you deserved it.

MIKHAILOV: But still?

PROSHKIN: I want to hear you give up the ghost.

MIKHAILOV: Maybe you'll spare me? I am young!

PROSHKIN: Enough talk, Mikhailov! Come around Mishka. You, Mikhailov, don't shoot. If you are quiet you will have an easy death. If you shoot we will make it hard for you. I speak in earnest!

MIKHAILOV: No, why should I shoot? Let me give you some light. (*He strikes a match and lights a candle.*)

The izba is illumined and there are seen, along the walls, in the corners, and next to Mikhailov behind the table, peasants and Komsomol members standing with the barrels of their guns directed at the kulaks. The music and the singing behind the scene become more audible in the silence.

MIKHAIL: Oh, you... (*He drops the revolver.*)

MIKHAILOV: Take them! (*The kulaks are encircled. Sotin approaches Proshkin and takes him by the chest with both hands.*)

SOTIN: I have long been waiting for you, Sofron Kuzmich! (*He shakes him inexorably and fiercely, first slowly, then ever more strongly.*)

The izba turns slowly, leading into the

THIRD EPISODE

Before the izba. The singing dies down. The kulaks are standing close to the door.

SHILOV: Good lord, what is going on there?

KVASOV: They are slow.

ZUBOV: You can't hear anything.

A LAD (*looking through a peephole in the shutter*): They have made light.

GRUNKIN: What is that out there? (*The group is crowding round the window.*)

LAD: Oh, dear! Ivan Gerasimovich, but there's the whole Komsomol! Our fellows have got into a scrape!

SHILOV: Let us run away, brothers! (*The group rushes away from the izba.*)

KVASOV: Stop! Where to? Who are you running away from? Stop!

KOTIKHIN: We must do something. How cunning is the district chief?

KVASOV: Not more cunning than we are. Be ready, villagers! Nobody will leave the izba. Take the logs, block up the door, prop up the windows! (*They rapidly seize the logs. There begins a knocking at the doors and windows.*)

PASHA: Ah-ah! Keep knocking! You wanted to burn the house, well, burn it!

KVASOV: I will burn it! You won't outwit me, Mikhailov! Pour the gasoline! (*One of the lads runs up to him, splashing the gasoline. The alarm bell begins to ring. Broken window-glass tinkles; the kulaks prop up the logs.*)

MOKRINA: Burn them, Christians, burn them with fire, let them writhe with pain, them who are cursed by God!

KVASOV: Quick, quick! Do you not hear? They're ringing the alarm bell!

KOTIKHIN: Ivan Gerasimovich, your son is in there.

KVASOV (*suddenly remembering*): In there...

PASHA: Father, you wanted to burn! Are you afraid? (*Within the izba they try to knock out the shutter with a butt. The kulaks lean against the logs.*)

ZUBOV (*leaning out of the gate*): What is the matter here? People are running to the alarm.

KVASOV: Mother of God! Burn, burn all the same!

SHILOV: Stop, Ivan Gerasimovich! How can you burn people alive?

GRUNKIN: Citizens, citizens, what are we doing?!

1ST PEASANT: Stop!

2ND PEASANT: What are we doing, villagers?

MOKRINA: Burn them!

GRUNKIN: Stop, citizens, the drunkenness is passing!

KVASOV: I'll kill you like a dog! Hush!

3RD PEASANT: What's it all about, villagers?

ZUBOV (*showing his head*): People are coming here, led by Kolka.

KVASOV: Burn!

2ND PEASANT: Don't you dare!

GRUNKIN: Ivan Gerasimovich, I bow my thanks to you for the vodka (*he bows*), but I won't let you set the house on fire!

KVASOV (*wildly*): You won't?! (*A group of peasants advances against Kvasov. Kulaks and lads group themselves around him.*)

2ND PEASANT: Hold him! He will kill him!

Zubov shoots from behind the gate. Kvasov strikes Grunkin in the face; the latter falls. The peasants advance against the kulak group. A scramble. The shutters are knocked out. At one window appears Mikhailov with a gun, at the other Sotin with a cudgel. Kolka jumps over the wattle with a revolver in his hand, followed by his "guard," the peasants. The wattle falls down. Komsomol members jump out of the izba and join the fighters. The kulak group is hard pressed.

MIKHAILOV: Bind them all! (*The kulaks are being bound. Sotin twists Kvasov in tying the rope.*)

SOTIN: I'm not bothering you? Just say the word, Ivan Gerasimovich, and I'll let go.

KVASOV (*between his teeth*): It's all right, thanks!

OLGA (*shouting over the fence*): Where is Raevsky?

MIKHAILOV: I haven't found him. (*A pause. Movement in the crowd.*)

GRUNKIN: Oh, him. There he is!

Romanov unties Raevsky with the help of one of the Komsomol members.

ROMANOV: Dear, why did you lie down here?

MIKHAILOV (*aloud*): Why didn't you cancel the order?

RAEVSKY: We will speak later.

MIKHAILOV: Yes, we'll talk later. You are dismissed from your work. Please leave immediately for the district.

OLKHA: He risked his life to save you, he has attacked the crowd by himself, for your sake... and you have found only these words for an answer!

MIKHAILOV: Thank you, Pasha! But you will be tried all the same. (*Sharply*) Excuse me, Olga, but I have no time to talk to you now.

OLKHA (*approaching Kvasov*): Well, citizens, this is what has come from our shouting. We all shouted as loud as we could, and Ivan Gerasimovich Kvasov has just set the Soviet government on fire.

SHILOV: This is true, Vasily Pavlovich, this is true.

OLKHA: And we others? Does this mean that we others stand aside? This is wrong, quite wrong, villagers. We must have our say. I promise to bring thirty poods, on the cart at once, and call for all the others.

SHILOV: Right, Vasya! Citizens, I told him. Why, I said, are you doing this, Ivan Gerasimovich? I give fifty poods!

GRUNKIN (*approaching Kvasov*): Villagers! Citizens! I have some grain! Ivan Gerasimovich Kvasov has put it in my house. Say that this is yours, he said. Well, if it is mine, I will give it to the Red wagon train. I am bringing a hundred poods!

SHILOV: We must start at once, then we will be in town in the morning.

ROMANOV: To town, let's go to town. What a life! Our line is ringing! Mikhailov, what shall we do with the kulaks?

MIKHAILOV: Lead them along!

KVASOV (*to Mikhailov*): You rejoice too soon. All the same, either you or we shall not live.

MIKHAILOV: I am afraid that you won't. Comrades! Ivan Gerasimovich has made a false reckoning. He wanted to kill Mikhailov, thinking that Mikhailov was alone, but look how many Mikhailovs there are! There are the Mikhailovs! (*pointing at the people around him on the stage*). And there too are Mikhailovs! (*pointing to the audience*). We can't be burned!

Curtain.

Pavlik Morozov
Excerpted from *A Poem about Hate*
Mikhail Doroshin (1933)

PAVLIK MOROZOV WAS A HERO OF THE PIONEERS, THE COMMUNIST CHILDREN'S ORGANIZATION. IN 1932 HE DENOUNCED HIS FATHER TO THE SECRET POLICE FOR HIDING GRAIN SUPPLIES. THIS GRAIN—MOST LIKELY THE NEXT YEAR'S SEED—WAS DEEMED EVIDENCE OF KULAK SYMPATHIES. WHEN THE FATHER WAS GIVEN A SHOW TRIAL AND SUBSEQUENTLY DISAPPEARED INTO THE GULAG, PAVLIK'S MALE RELATIVES EXACTED REVENGE ON THE BOY AND HIS BROTHER. DOROSHIN'S POEM WAS THE FIRST IN A HAGIOGRAPHIC CAMPAIGN. PAVEL BECAME A MODEL OF ORTHODOX BEHAVIOR FOR GENERATIONS OF SOVIET CHILDREN, AND THE BANE OF UNORTHODOX ADULTS.

Pale lakes
And
The taiga woods.
From the country, the city
Is as far off as heaven.
There's no place remoter
Around the Urals.
It was here,
Pavlusha,
Your life ran its course.

You crack the door open
And beasts barge in
For a visit
With a litter of cubs.
With a friendly roar:
"Hi!"
They're back in the woods.
But the village predators
Have sharper teeth.
His uncle's army hat

"Pavlik Morozov. Iz *Poemy o nenavisti*," *Pionerskaia pravda*, 29 March 1933.

Make his head feel too small.
But still Pashka
Has big things to do.
Pavlik neatly chops
Firewood for Mother.
Pavlik learns new words
For school.
He plays hide-and-seek
Or leapfrog,
But his notebooks
Are heavy
With all his thoughts.
Outside the village
The sunset is settling
In its nest
Like a bird,
But Pavlusha is rushing
Off to his Pioneer troop.
Then he hears
The trumpet's
Muted wail.
"What should we do, Pavlusha?
What should we do?"
Pavlik gives the boys
A spirited answer:
"I will be
The leader,
Since there's nobody else!"
In his calm and simple manner
He calls them into ranks:
"Line up by height,
And march off after me!"

The swamp's all around—
He's scared to take a step.
Then someone blocks
The Pioneer's path,
Like a fog,
Or shadow,
And whispers
Like a deaf-mute:
"Get down
On your knees!"
Maybe it's the wind,
Or maybe—No,
Pashka sees
His granddad.

Kulikanov stands
Right behind his back,
And the men surround
Pavlik like a wall.
"Listen to your elders!
Chuck the Pioneers!"
And they point their fists
At Pavlik.

And just like they're singing:
"Pavlik! Pashka! Pash!
No matter what, you will be
Ours! Ours! Ours!"
They wave their fists at him
Like a big oak club.
"If you don't become ours,
Then we'll kill you."
Let them roar
Like thunder.
Pavlik Morozov
Can't be scared off
By his enemies' threats.

They look around.
The village sleeps.
At a table in the soviet
The chairman sits.
By the window Pashka
Looks into the depths.
The chairman writes papers
For the kulaks.
The words are a flourish,
The seal is a wheel.
Again they can steal
And not answer for it!
It's all right to embezzle
Again.
"Stop! Don't!"

Pavlik could scream...
The soviet's empty.
How can he find
The traitor's
Just deserts.
If his very own
Father
Is chairman.
All around
Are lakes
And the taiga forest.
From the country, the city
Is as far off as heaven.
And Pavlik decides:
I'll go to the raikom
And force my father
To answer the court.
Let father tell us
What protection
He gave kulaks
In the village soviet.
Let him say
Straight out
How he helped
The enemy
Dig pits
For the grain.
"Judge him, uncles!
My words are simple!
Answer, parent!"

The court is in session!..
Rise!..

The boys hung up
On a rough-hewn fence
Slogans and posters
That proclaim:
"For shame!"
The house
Is branded
With burning
Shame.
Everyone knows
The fences, and
Which hides
A thief.

Kulikanov
Can see
Them dance
In a circle,
And everyone's
Finger
Is pointed at him.
Their merry laughter
Angers
And wounds him.
They're all
Even singing
The very same song.
And all of their shirts
Are abloom with red ties:
"Pashka! Pashka! Pashka!
Here! There! Everywhere!"

They gathered nicely
In a neighborly way
Good times, Danila!
Have a good time!
That prewar brew
Is some pretty strong stuff!
And hey, sing a song
For the funeral day!
And while the fool
Cranked up the crowd,
Pavlik and Fedya
Went out to the woods.

Danila's head
Was spinning
With wine.
Danila
Can't feel
His hands
Or feet.
His uncle
Sergei
Burns
For revenge.
He blesses Danila:
"God be with you!
Don't get chicken!
Kill him!"
The knife was on fire

Like it
Was drunk too!
What happened?
What's that?
Pavlik, what's wrong?
"Oh, no!"
He cries out
And falls:
"Fedik!
Run!
They're not kith—
They're vipers!
They're not kin—
They're enemies!
Run!"
Grandpa grabs little Fedya:
"Stop,
You're not going anywhere!"
The blade of the knife
Catches in his thin shirt.

The branches shake
On a mossy pine tree,
Two brothers lie still
At the foot of the tree.
The pine is touched

By their awful peace:
"What's this?"

Silence.

Muter and muter
Stand the woods round the boys.
Pavlusha won't be going
To the Pioneers anymore.
Joyful and curly,
He won't come to school.
But his great glory
Will outlive everything.
"Pavlik is with us,
Pashka the Communist!"
Out in front, like a banner,
Friendly and merry.
(That's how
Everyone should live).
How much
Every schoolchild
Resembles him
Somehow.
All of their shirts
Are abloom with red ties:
"Pashka! Pashka! Pashka!
Here! There! Everywhere!"

The First Cruise

Shock Workers (1931)

AT THE END OF 1930, 257 SOVIET SHOCK WORKERS WERE GIVEN
A CRUISE AROUND EUROPE IN REWARD FOR THEIR HIGH PRODUC-
TIVITY. THEIR FACTORIES ALLOWED THEM TIME OFF WITH FULL
PAY AND FINANCED THE CRUISE. THE WORKERS WERE DULY DIS-
MAYED BY THE STATE OF THE CAPITALIST WEST, AND DURING
THE CRUISE MOST OF THEM APPLIED TO JOIN THE COMMUNIST
PARTY. ON THEIR RETURN, THE SHOCK WORKERS RECORDED

Excerpted from *International Literature*, no. 1 (1932), pp. 3–15, trans. Anthony Wixley.

THEIR IMPRESSIONS. THE BOOK EXEMPLIFIED THE NEW "PROLE-
TARIAN" LITERATURE; IT WAS A COLLECTIVE COMPOSITION
(THOUGH EACH ENTRY WAS SIGNED); AND IT INSTILLED PROPER
POLITICAL ATTITUDES IN ITS READERS. PUBLISHED WITH GREAT
FANFARE, THE BOOK WAS A MODEL FOR SOVIET LITERATURE.

Moscow, November 8, 1930

Today the shock-brigade workers are making their first "sortie" into Europe.

Promptly at nine o'clock the engine gave a short, sharp whistle, and our train glided out of the brightly-lit station into the darkness. I sat by the window. A few of my comrades, I could see were wiping their eyes. Their mouths quivered suspiciously.

The train raced onward, lights flashed past the windows, telegraph poles sailed by.

Somebody began singing and that was enough to start the whole lot going. Soon the train rang with voices of young and old. Folks from the Ukraine, from the Urals, from Ivanovo-Vosnesensk. They sang for a long time.

We did not go to sleep till late that night. I lay awake listening to the monotonous sound of the wheels. They seemed to chant—"To Europe—to Europe—to Europe!"

F. KOROLEV

On the journey we roved from one compartment to another, making friends.

There were the "Dynamo" people, the leaders of the shock-brigades, Gavrilov and Popov, the foreman Bashlikov, and the engineer Rickman. They were worrying about how the production plans were going to be carried out without them. Gavrilov said that he had left a lot of pupils there at the works. They would have no one to guide them now. Would the program of work be spoilt, he wondered.

Night. Conversation was at a low ebb. Some of the old shock-brigade workers were already snoring. And the express went tearing along full speed ahead. The engine driver never slackened his pace. He knew that he was carrying 300 of the best workers in the Soviet Union, and was trying to land them, at a shock-brigade rate...

A. SALOV

November 10, 11, 12.

The Excursion Bureau organized a committee out of the leaders of the group. The question of our work on board was discussed, of the leaders' duties and the publication of the wall-newspaper. A number of worker-correspondents volunteered to take up this work. We discussed the plan of reports to be read on the countries that we were to visit, Germany, Italy, and Turkey.

We passed the shores of Sweden. The islands Gotland and Aaland. On our left was Latvia. We caught a glimpse of Reval.[1]

A. SALOV

We glided up the Kiel Canal. Before we got up to the lockgate, somebody pointed out a launch coming in our direction. There were about five people on it, and they waved their hats to us. They were employees from the Hamburg and Berlin Soviet trade delegations.

We shouted "Hurrah" to them in reply. Eight policemen were already waiting on the quay.

Two German boys from the Young Communist League, who had found out that the shock-brigade workers from the Soviet Union were coming, tried to come on board to speak to our Young Communists. The police would not let them. One Young Communist got through somehow, though. He ran on board the *Abkhazia* shouting "Rot Front!" (Red Front).

Along the gangway came a group of Soviet people working in Germany. They were headed by Comrade Krumin, our consul-general in Hamburg. The Soviet colony in Berlin sent its representative, too.

Our Soviet Diplomats and Trade Representatives turned out to be former workers from the Moscow and Leningrad factories—Comrades Krumin and Bayat as well. They began to tell us about Germany. We sailed up the Kiel Canal as far as Hamburg.

A. SALOV

After dinner our excursion bureau gave a lecture over the wireless on Germany, Hamburg in particular.

Along the shores of the Kiel Canal stand houses, factories and schools. The festive appearance of the *Abkhazia* as it sailed slowly up the Canal under its red flag, and the songs that rang out from its deck, drew all eyes. Heads popped out of windows, and here and there a clenched fist—the sign of "Rot Front"—was raised, and the words "Rot Front" floated across to us.

V. SHILIN

Hamburg

Two tug-boats came out and took us to the quay. We had no sooner arrived than we heard the greetings of the longshoremen: "Rot Front! Rot Front!" And one German worker called out in broken Russian—"Long live the shock-brigade workers of the Soviet Union!"

We replied and cheered. The police who came down to "welcome" us were not

---

1. Now Tallin, capital of Estonia.

particularly pleased at this exchange of greetings. They went up to the workers and started a dispute about something or other.

A. SALOV

The port of Hamburg gives the impression of being well thought out and well equipped. The loading and unloading of boats is fully mechanized. There are fine port railways. The pavement is diabase, and this allows immense platform-cars to be moved easily with the help of small tractors. The tractors have a very large production capacity. I admired the mechanized loading of bricks—no wheelbarrows, no gangways and not one brick broken in the unloading. The unloading of the *Abkhazia* was carried on in the same way. We saw floating docks, beautifully mechanized, great shipyards, colossal warehouses, scores of giant steamers. We had read in the papers all about the crises in capitalist countries, but mere printed paper is not as convincing as the sight before one's eyes. It was not Sunday and there was no strike on, and yet—the great warehouses stood empty and silent as if frozen. That was how they looked at home during the civil war. Only here, on the spot, can one realize the meaning of that capitalist catastrophe that is called the industrial crisis.

We were put ashore at one of the huge shipyards where 7,000 workers used to be employed. Now only about 800 are engaged there. But even these workers, who are exceptionally highly skilled, are kept going with a great effort.

At present they are working eight hours a day, but very soon the working day and the working week will be shortened, with corresponding reductions in wages.

Why? Because there is no work. There is a crisis.

All the workers wear tarpaulin overalls—their own—they are not provided by the employers.

V. SHILIN

In the sheet-iron department the different processes of preparing iron are carried on. The equipment is very old. We had this sort of equipment 40 years ago, but now most of it has been scrapped. The machine shops occupy a tremendous area. There are many lathes here, doomed to idleness on account of lack of work. Only in one corner of the huge workshop are the lathes working. We notice gearing that was got rid of long ago in the best Leningrad works as it was uneconomical and hindered the movement of the cranes. We did not see anything new in the patternshop—the usual benches. Some very simple patterns were being made by an ancient pattern-maker. There were no young folks to be seen. The workers wore very dirty clothes. Almost all of them had pipes in their mouths. The heads of departments smoked cigars.

During the dinner-hour we saw how uncomfortable the workers were. They ate standing at their lathes, amid all the noise and hurry. The better-off workers ate at dining rooms in the shipyards. As we left the shipyard, we saw opposite the head office, several score painted booths, made of thin boards. They had tiny windows.

We thought, in our simplicity, that they must be dog kennels or pigeon coves. What was our surprise, then, to learn that they were summer "cottages" rented by some of the better-off workers.

V. SHILIN

When we had finished inspecting the shipyard, we sailed away in the launch to our *Abkhazia*. After a good dinner we went to see the sights of Hamburg. The Trade Delegation gave us a guide to show us around.

From the port, dark, narrow streets led to the center of the town. We divided up into groups of 20 each with a leader. There were 15 groups. Sometimes the groups bumped into each other, and then together with the German Young Communists who were trying to explain things to us, we presented a whole procession. People turned to look at us in astonishment; others ran out of shops to see what had happened.

And we were something to look at! There were young lads and lasses amongst us, and grown-up men and women, and old gray-haired people. All differently dressed. Some wore ordinary caps or hats, some caps with shiny peaks. The women wore red kerchiefs and shawls on their heads, Soviet fashion. Some were in shoes, others in high Russian boots. We all had Soviet badges in our button-holes, and we held our heads high and smoked our Soviet cigarettes.

Yes, with heads held high we walked through the streets of Hamburg.

After all, we had come to visit the workers of Germany in our own ship and not just anyhow.

We had come to the German workers—not as slaves, but as the masters of our country, the land of the Soviet that is building up socialism.

The sense of their own dignity could be seen even in the way our folks walked. I was not surprised, therefore, that the policemen were unusually polite even when we crossed the streets at points where it was not allowed. They did not stop us, but the traffic. The policemen held up their white gloved hands, and all buses, motor-cars, and bicycles stopped to let us pass. We saw streets flooded with light, electric signs, arresting placards. We saw the great windows of smart shops with wax figures in them and live people, too, who took the place of the wax figures. There was everything that science could invent, everything for every need, for eating or wearing. In some windows hung the carcasses of pigs or oxen beautifully done up. The butchers and confectioners were loaded with every delicacy. The drapery and shoe-shops were full of goods. Everything shone, everything had a price on it, from the cheapest to the dearest. There was plenty of everything. Shops and goods and salesmen.

Only one thing was absent: customers.

We walked about "free" Hamburg all day, for many a long mile, but we never saw a customer. And it was easy enough to understand why; the economic crisis had deprived scores of thousands of workers of their wages and therefore of their purchasing power.

V. SHILIN

The police were hand-picked men, well-built, young, clean-shaven. They wore good uniforms, helmets and beautiful leather leggings. They were each armed with a revolver, a short sword, and a baton on a strap.

V. Shilin

The class contrasts between the various quarters of the town struck one at once. Luxurious residences lined the shores of the lake. These belonged, of course, to the upper bourgeoisie. Then there were the districts, where the intelligentsia and middle classes lived, and last of all, a labyrinth of dark tunnel-like lanes and alleys, some of them not more than six feet wide. This was where the workers lived, the creators of the world's wealth.

And how did the rich live, those who wring the last drop of blood from the workers?

The shore of the lake where the bourgeoisie took their ease and enjoyed life, was divided up into lots; each lot was fenced off in a different way. Trees had been planted along the streets which were spotless. These were palaces, not houses. They were all built differently from one another, all two-storied. There were decorative plants and flowers in the gardens. The entrances and drive-ways were beautiful, the windows glittered like diamonds.

We entered the working-class district, and walked up one of the streets. I went first, stood with my back flat against the wall, and in four steps was already at the opposite wall. We went on further. All the windows were either broken or open. The buildings were so rickety and in places leaned over at such an angle, that they seemed to be only about three feet across the street from one another. In fact, it was rather terrifying to go up a street like that at all.

We turned into a lane. I measured its width—two steps. We looked into one of the yards. Great iron rubbish bins stood in it. Under each window there were wooden brackets with ropes across on which washing was hanging out to dry. There were no wash-houses, or attics for drying the clothes. The people washed their clothes at home, dried them under the windows, and lived in the attics themselves. These, then were the streets and alleys of the Hamburg proletariat. No sunlight here. Only eternal gloom.

V. Shilin

It was terrible to see workers living like this. Rickety houses, ready to tumble down any minute. An awful stench, mingled with the odor of carbolic acid, came from them. Poverty peered from every crack. We saw children with pale, drawn faces. Although the weather was cold, they ran about barefoot, in ragged garments.

We wanted to find out more about the workers' lives, so we wandered slowly from street to street. Hundreds of heads popped out of windows, hundreds of eyes stared after us, unable to understand why tourists should have come to their filthy alleys. They asked us who we were, and when they learned that we were Soviet workers, they showed the German communist sign of the clenched fist and shouted, "Rot Front!" The children ran after us. They also clenched their little fists. The lane rang with their cries of "Rot Front!"

At a cross-roads we saw placards with the number 4 on them. They were the lists of communist candidates. The whole district had voted for them...

And then up came a squad of police. The "Dynamo" engineer Rickman said: "See how soon they sniffed us out! They learned there was a landing party and are ready to meet the enemy."

A. SALOV

Germans from the Young Communist League and other organizations were waiting for us at the quay. The police were really alarmed this time at the behavior of the unemployed, who tried to show their friendliness to us. Many of them were hungry; our shock-brigade workers shared their sandwiches with them. They devoured them like starving people.

In the evening I went round the town with a few comrades and a German stevedore, a communist, who had been unloading our boat. This man took us to a little room, and told us how the stevedores' union functioned. He showed us various cards and forms. From there we went to the working-class district, where he was well-known for his work in the trade union and the Party.

It was cold and pouring rain. But in spite of the weather, on either side of the street women were standing. They were of all ages, and wore all kinds of clothes, but all had painted lips. One of them, a timid, neglected woman, glanced about, searching for a client. Others, bolder, would tug at the sleeve of some passer-by, offering themselves for sale.

We got to the home of a worker-communist, who had been eleven months out of work. It was on the second floor. We were warmly welcomed. As soon as the inhabitants of the flat knew why we had come, they revealed to us all the miseries of the German worker's life. It was a small flat of three tiny rooms. The floor was uneven and rotting. We went up to the attic where people had been driven, by poverty and need, to live. The roof let in the light, the wind, and the rain.

"This is supposed to be a good flat," we were told. "As a rule the rooms and dwellings of the workers are much worse."

V. SHILIN

Five of us Young Communists went for a stroll around the working-class district of Hamburg. A German house-painter came with us. He took us to slums beside which even our old "Prolomka" would look like a fine, clean district. In one of the narrow lanes we went straight from the street through an open door into a room that looked like a barn. It was furnished with a bed, a table and two chairs. We were warmly greeted by a man and a woman, both still young. The wife, Maria, wanted to run out to buy something for us with what was probably her last penny. We would not let her go. We stayed there talking for a whole hour. They told us how terribly hard it was for workers to live in Hamburg.

We made our way along the market-gardens, now quiet, that surround the town. The dark silent outlines of huts became more frequent. At the door of one of the huts we stopped. A young man lifted the latch and let us into a very chilly room. In a moment a candle was lit and we could see a small room. There was nothing but wooden benches and a small table in it. Huts like these are inhabited by paupers, petty thieves, prostitutes, and unemployed workers who cannot afford to pay rent for flats.

We returned to the *Abkhazia*. We were silent all the way, oppressed by what we had seen.

G. BEBCHUK

How the Steel Was Tempered
Nikolai Ostrovsky (1932–1934)

THIS *BILDUNGSROMAN* BY OSTROVSKY (1904–1936) BECAME THE CLASSIC NOVEL OF SOCIALIST REALISM — AND INDEED WAS SINGLED OUT BY THE AUTHORITIES AS A MODEL FOR THE GENRE. IT HAS BEEN STUDIED AND REPRINTED AGAIN AND AGAIN. MILLIONS OF PEOPLE HAVE READ IT IN THE DECADES SINCE ITS PUBLICATION. THE PROTAGONIST, PAVEL KORCHAGIN, IS THE QUINTESSENTIAL POSITIVE HERO, A LOWBORN, UNCARED-FOR BOY, BOLSHEVIK HERO, AND MARTYR. THE FILM VERSION OF 1956 BY ALOV AND NAUMOV IS SUPERIOR TO THE BOOK IN EVERY WAY.

For a year now Pavel Korchagin had travelled up and down his native land, riding on machine-gun carriages and gun caissons or astride a small grey mare with a nick in her ear. He was a grown man now, matured and hardened by suffering and privation. The tender skin chafed to the raw by the heavy cartridge belt had long since healed and a hard callus had formed under the rifle strap on his shoulder.

Pavel had seen much that was terrible in that year. Together with thousands of other fighting men as ragged and ill-clad as himself but afire with the indomitable determination to fight for the power of their class, he had marched over the length and breadth of his native land and only twice had the storm swept on without him: the first time when he was wounded in the hip, and the second, when in the bitterly cold February of 1920 he sweltered in the sticky heat of typhus.

The typhus took a more fearful toll of the regiments and divisions of the Twelfth

Translation excerpted from *How the Steel Was Tempered,* trans. R. Prokofieva (Moscow: Progress Publishers, 1973), pp. 175–178, 181–185, 194–195, 234–238, 240–243, 264–266, on the pattern of "The Heart of a Bolshevik," *International Literature,* no. 11 (1935), pp. 9–31.

Army than Polish machine guns. By that time the Twelfth Army was operating over a vast territory stretching across nearly the whole of the Northern Ukraine blocking the advance of the Poles.

Pavel had barely recovered from his illness when he returned to his unit which was now holding the station of Frontovka, on the Kazatin-Uman branch line. Frontovka stood in the forest and consisted of a small station building with a few wrecked and abandoned cottages around it. Three years of intermittent battles had made civilian life in these parts impossible. Frontovka had changed hands times without number.

Big events were brewing again. At the time when the Twelfth Army, its ranks fearfully depleted and partly disorganized, was falling back to Kiev under the pressure of the Polish armies, the proletarian republic was mustering its forces to strike a crushing blow at the victory-drunk Polish Whites.

The battle-seasoned divisions of the First Cavalry Army were being transferred to the Ukraine all the way from the North Caucasus in a campaign unparalleled in military history. The Fourth, Sixth, Eleventh and Fourteenth Cavalry divisions moved up one after another to the Uman area, concentrating in the rear of the front and sweeping away the Makhno bandits on their way to the scene of decisive battles.

Sixteen and a half thousand sabres, sixteen and a half thousand fighting men scorched by the blazing steppe sun.

To prevent this decisive blow from being thwarted by the enemy was the primary concern of the Supreme Command of the Red Army and the Command of the South-western Front at this juncture. Everything was done to ensure the successful concentration of this huge mounted force. Active operations were suspended on the Uman sector. The direct telegraph lines from Moscow to the front headquarters in Kharkov and thence to the headquarters of the Fourteenth and Twelfth armies hummed incessantly. Telegraph operators tapped out coded orders: "Divert attention Poles from concentration cavalry army." The enemy was actively engaged only when the Polish advance threatened to involve the Budyonny cavalry divisions.

The campfire shot up red tongues of flames. Dark spirals of smoke curled up from the fire, driving off the swarms of restless buzzing midges. The men lay in a semicircle around the fire whose reflection cast a coppery glow on their faces. The water bubbled in mess tins set in the bluish-grey ashes.

A stray tongue of flame leaped out suddenly from beneath a burning log and licked at someone's tousled head. The head was jerked away with a growl: "Damnation!" And a gust of laughter rose from the men grouped around the fire.

"The lad's so full of book-learning he don't feel the heat of the fire," boomed a middle-aged soldier with a clipped moustache, who had just been examining the barrel of his rifle against the firelight.

"You might tell the rest of us what you're reading there, Korchagin?" someone suggested.

The young Red Army man fingered his singed lock and smiled.

"A real good book, Comrade Androshchuk. Just can't tear myself away from it."

"What's it about?" inquired a snub-nosed lad sitting next to Korchagin, laboriously repairing the strap of his pouch. He bit off the coarse thread, wound the remainder round the needle and stuck it inside his helmet. "If it's about love I'm your man."

A loud guffaw greeted this remark. Matveichuk raised his close-cropped head and winked slyly at the snub-nosed lad: "Love's a fine thing, friend," he said. "And you're such a handsome lad, a regular picture. Wherever we go the girls fairly wear their shoes out running after you. Too bad a handsome phiz like yours should be spoiled by one little defect: you've got a five-kopeck piece instead of a nose. But that's easily remedied. Just hang a Novitsky 10-pounder* on the end of it overnight and in the morning it'll be all right."

The roar of laughter that followed this sally caused the horses tethered to the machine-gun carriers to whinny in fright.

Sereda glanced nonchalantly over his shoulder. "It's not your face but what you've got in here that counts." He tapped himself on the forehead expressively. "Take you, you've got a tongue like a stinging nettle but you're no better than a donkey, and your ears are cold."

"Now then, lads, what's the sense in getting riled?" Tatarinov, the Section Commander, admonished the two who were about to fly at each other. "Better let Korchagin read to us if he's got something worth listening to."

"That's right. Go to it, Pavlushka!" the men urged from all sides.

Pavel moved a saddle closer to the fire, settled himself on it and opened the small thick volume resting on his knees. "It's called *The Gadfly*,[1] Comrades. The Battalion Commissar gave it to me. Wonderful book, Comrades. If you'll sit quietly I'll read it to you."

"Fire away! We're all listening."

When some time later Comrade Puzyrevsky, the Regimental Commander, rode up unnoticed to the campfire with his Commissar, he saw eleven pairs of eyes glued to the reader.

In the neighbouring village a group of Budyonny cavalry had formed a wide circle on a hill outside the schoolhouse. One giant of a fellow, seated on the back of a machine-gun carrier, his cap pushed to the back of his head, was playing an accordion. The instrument wailed and blared under his inept fingers like a thing in torment, confusing the dashing cavalryman in unbelievably wide red riding breeches who was dancing a mad *hopak* in the center of the ring.

Eager-eyed village lads and lasses clambered onto the gun carrier and fences to watch the antics of these troopers whose brigade had just entered their village. "Go it, Toptalo! Kick up the earth! Ekh, that's the stuff, brother! Come on there, you with the accordion, make it hot!"

But the player's huge fingers that could bend an iron horseshoe with the utmost ease sprawled clumsily over the keys.

"Too bad Makhno got Afanasy Kulyabko," remarked one bronzed cavalryman

---

*The Novitsky grenade was used to demolish barbed-wire entanglements.
1. Ethel Voynich's 1897 novel, which we have already seen in *Little Red Devils*.

regretfully. "That lad was a first-class hand at the accordion. He rode on the right flank of our squadron. Too bad he was killed. A good soldier, and the best accordion player we ever had!"

Pavel, who was standing in the circle, overheard this last remark. He pushed his way over to the machine-gun carrier and laid his hand on the accordion bellows. The music subsided.

"What d'you want?" the accordionist demanded with a scowl.

Toptalo stopped short and an angry murmur rose from the crowd: "What's the trouble there?"

Pavel reached out for the instrument. "Let's have a try," he said.

The Budyonny cavalryman looked at the Red infantryman with some mistrust and reluctantly slipped the accordion strap off his shoulder. With an accustomed gesture Pavel laid the instrument on his knee, spread the sinuous bellows out fanwise and let go with a rollicking melody that poured forth with all the lusty vigor of which the accordion is capable:

> Ekh, little apple,
> Whither away?
> Get copped by the Cheka
> And that's where you stay!

Toptalo caught up the familiar tune and swinging his arms like some great bird he swept into the ring, executing the most incredible twists and turns, and slapping himself smartly on the thighs, knees, head, forehead, the shoe soles, and finally on the mouth in time with the music.

Faster and faster played the accordion in a mad intoxicating rhythm, and Toptalo, kicking his legs out wildly, spun around the circle like a top until he was quite out of breath.

On June 5, 1920, after a few brief but furious encounters Budyonny's First Cavalry Army broke through the Polish front between the Third and Fourth Polish armies, smashed a cavalry brigade under General Sawicki en route and swept on toward Ruzhiny.

The Polish command hastily formed a striking force and threw it into the breach. Five tanks were rushed from Pogrebishche Station to the scene of the fighting. But the Cavalry Army bypassed Zarudnitsy from where the Poles planned to strike and came out in the Polish rear.

General Kornicki's Cavalry Division was dispatched in pursuit of the First Cavalry Army with orders to strike at the rear of the force, which the Polish command believed to be headed for Kazatin, one of the most important strategic points in the Polish rear. This move, however, did not improve the position of the Poles. Although they succeeded in closing the breach and cutting off the Cavalry Army, the presence of a strong mounted force behind their lines which threatened to destroy their rear bases and swoop down on their army group at Kiev, was far from reassuring. As they advanced, the Red cavalry divisions destroyed small railway bridges and tore up railway track to hamper the Polish retreat.

On learning from prisoners that the Poles had an army headquarters in Zhitomir (actually the headquarters of the whole front was located there), the commander of the First Cavalry Army decided to take Zhitomir and Berdichev, both important railway junctions and administrative centers. At dawn on June 7 the Fourth Cavalry Division was already on its way at full speed to Zhitomir.

Korchagin now rode on the right flank of one of the squadrons in place of Kulyabko, the lamented accordionist. He had been enrolled in the squadron on the collective request of the men, who had refused to part with such an excellent accordion player.

Without checking their foam-flecked horses they fanned out at Zhitomir and bore down on the city with naked steel flashing in the sun. The earth groaned under the pounding hoofs, the mounts breathed hoarsely, and the men rose in their stirrups.

Underfoot the ground sped past and ahead the large city with its gardens and parks hurried to meet the division. The mounted avalanche flashed by the gardens and poured into the center of the city, and the air was rent by a fear-inspiring battle-cry as inexorable as death itself.

The Poles were so stunned that they offered little resistance. The local garrison was crushed.

Bending low over the neck of his mount, Pavel Korchagin sped along side by side with Toptalo astride his thin-shanked black. Pavel saw the dashing cavalryman cut down with an unerring blow by a Polish legionary before the man had time to raise his rifle to his shoulder.

The iron-shod hoofs grated on the paving stones as they careered down the street. Then at an intersection they found themselves face to face with a machine gun planted in the very middle of the road and three men in blue uniforms and rectangular Polish caps bending over it. There was also a fourth, with coils of gold braid on his collar, who levelled a Mauser at the mounted men.

Neither Toptalo nor Pavel could check their horses and they galloped toward the machine gun, straight into the jaws of death. The officer fired at Korchagin, but missed. The bullet whanged past Pavel's cheek, and the next moment the Lieutenant had struck his head against the paving stones and was lying limp on his back, thrown off his feet by the horse's onrush.

That very moment the machine gun spat out in savage frenzy, and stung by a dozen bullets, Toptalo and his black crumpled to the ground. Pavel's mount reared up on its hind legs, snorting with terror, and leapt with its rider over the prone bodies to the men at the machine gun. His sabre described a flashing arc in the air and sank into the blue rectangle of one of the army caps.

Again the sabre flashed upwards ready to descend upon a second head, but the frantic horse leapt aside. Like a mountain torrent the squadron poured into the streets and scores of sabres flashed in the air.

It happened on August 19 during a battle in the Lvov area. Pavel had lost his cap in the fighting and had reined in his horse. The squadrons ahead had already cut into the Polish positions. At that moment Demidov came galloping through the bushes on his way down to the river. As he flew past Pavel he shouted: "The Division Commander's been killed!"

Pavel started. Letunov, his heroic commander, that man of sterling courage, dead! A savage fury seized Pavel. With the blunt edge of his sabre he urged on his exhausted Gnedko, whose bit dripped with a bloody foam, and tore into the thick of the battle.

"Kill the vermin, kill 'em! Cut down the Polish *szlachta!* They've killed Letunov!" And blindly he slashed at a figure in a green uniform. Enraged at the death of their Division Commander, the cavalrymen wiped out a whole platoon of Polish legionaries.

They galloped headlong over the battlefield in pursuit of the enemy, but now a Polish battery went into action. Shrapnel rent the air spattering death on all sides.

Suddenly there was a blinding green flash before Pavel's eyes, thunder smote his ears and red-hot iron seared into his skull. The earth spun strangely and horribly about him and began to turn slowly upside down. Pavel was thrown from the saddle like a straw. He flew right over Gnedko's head and fell heavily to the ground. Instantly black night descended.

Upstairs as soon as the outsider was gone, thirteen heads bent closer over the large conference table. "See here," Zhukhrai's finger jabbed the unfolded map. "That's Boyarka station. The timber felling is six versts away. There are two hundred and ten thousand cubic meters of wood stacked up at this point: a whole army of men worked hard for eight months to pile up all that wood, and what's the result? Treachery. The railway and the town are without firewood. To haul that timber six versts to the station would take five thousand carts no less than one month, and that only if they made two trips a day. The nearest village is fifteen versts away. What's more, Orlik and his band are prowling about in those parts. You realise what this means? Look, according to the plan the felling was to have been started right here and continued in the direction of the station, and those scoundrels carried it right into the depths of the forest. The purpose was to make sure we would not be able to haul the firewood to the railway line. And they weren't far wrong—we can't even get a hundred carts for the job. It's a foul blow they've struck us. The uprising was no more serious than this."

Zhukhrai's clenched fist dropped heavily onto the waxed paper of the map. Each of the thirteen clearly visualised the grimmer aspects of the situation which Zhukhrai had omitted to mention. Winter was in the offing. They saw hospitals, schools, offices and hundreds of thousands of people caught in the icy grip of the frost; the railway stations swarming with people and only one train a week to handle the traffic.

There was deep silence as each man pondered the situation. At length Fyodor relaxed his fist. "There is one way out, Comrades," he said. "We must build a seven verst narrow-gauge line from the station to the timber tract in three months. The first section leading to the beginning of the tract must be ready in six weeks. I've been working on this for the past week. We'll need," Zhukhrai's voice cracked in his dry throat, "three hundred and fifty workers and two engineers. There is enough rails and seven engines at Pushcha-Voditsa. The Komsomols dug them up in the warehouses. There was a project to lay a narrow-gauge line from Pushcha-Voditsa to the town before the war. The trouble is there are no accommodations in Boyarka for the workers, the place is in ruins. We'll have to send the men in small groups for a fortnight at a time, they won't be able to hold out any longer than that. Shall we send the Komsomols, Akim?" And without waiting for an answer, he went on: "The Komsomol will rush as many of its members to the spot as possible. There's the Solomenka organisation to begin with, and some from the town. The task is hard, very hard, but if the youngsters are told what is at stake I'm certain they'll do it."

The chief of the railway shook his head dubiously. "I'm afraid it's no use. To lay seven versts of track in the woods under such conditions, with the autumn rains due and the frosts coming," he began wearily. But Zhukhrai cut him short.

"You ought to have paid more attention to the firewood problem, Andrei Vasilievich. That line has got to be built and we're going to build it. We're not going to fold our hands and freeze to death, are we?"

Tokarev came back from town fuming. He called a meeting of the leading Communists in Kholyava's room and told them the unpleasant news. "Nothing but obstacles all along the line. Wherever you go the wheels seem to be turning, but they don't get anywhere. Far too many of those White rats about, and it looks as if there'll be enough to last our lifetime anyway. I tell you, boys, things look bad. There are no replacements for us yet and no one knows how many there will be. The frosts are due any day now, and we must get through the marsh before then at all costs, because when the ground freezes it'll be too late. So while they're shaking up those fellows in town who're making a mess of things, we here have to double our speed. That line has got to be built and we're going to build it if we die doing it. Otherwise it isn't Bolsheviks we'll be but jelly-fish." There was a steely note in Tokarev's hoarse bass voice, and his eyes under their bushy brows had a stubborn gleam.

"We'll call a closed meeting today and pass on the news to our Party members and tomorrow we'll all get down to work. In the morning we'll let the non-Party fellows go; the rest of us will stay. Here's the Gubernia Committee decision," he said, handing Pankratov a folded sheet of paper.

Pavel Korchagin, peering over Pankratov's shoulder, read: "In view of the emergency all members of the Komsomol are to remain on the job and are not to be relieved until the first consignment of firewood is forthcoming. Signed R. Ustinovich, on behalf of the Secretary of the Gubernia Committee."

The kitchen barracks was packed. One hundred and twenty men had squeezed themselves into its narrow confines. They stood against the walls, climbed on the tables and some were even perched on top of the field kitchen.

Pankratov opened the meeting. Then Tokarev made a brief speech winding up with an announcement that had the effect of a bombshell: "The Communists and

Komsomols will not leave the job tomorrow." The old man accompanied his statement with a gesture that stressed the finality of the decision. It swept away all cherished hopes of returning to town, going home, getting away from this hole.

A roar of angry voices drowned out everything else for a few moments. The swaying bodies caused the feeble oil light to flicker fitfully. In the semidarkness the commotion increased. They wanted to go "home"; they protested indignantly that they had had as much as they could stand. Some received the news in silence. And only one man spoke of deserting.

"To hell with it all!" he shouted angrily from his corner, loosing an ugly stream of invective. "I'm not going to stay here another day. It's all right to do hard labor if you've committed a crime. But what have we done? We're fools to stand for it. We've had two weeks of it, and that's enough. Let those who made the decision come out and do the work themselves. Maybe some folks like poking around in this muck, but I've only one life to live. I'm leaving tomorrow."

The voice came from behind Okunev and he lit a match to see who it was. For an instant the speaker's rage-distorted face and open mouth were snatched out of the darkness by the match's flame. But that instant was enough for Okunev to recognise the son of a gubernia food commissariat bookkeeper.

"Checking up, eh?" he snarled. "Well, I'm not afraid, I'm no thief."

The match flickered out. Pankratov rose and drew himself up to his full height. "What kind of talk is that? Who dares to compare a Party task to a hard-labour sentence?" he thundered, running his eyes menacingly over the front rows. "No, Comrades, there's no going to town for us, our place is here. If we clear out now folks will freeze to death. The sooner we finish the job the sooner we get back home. Running away like that whiner back there suggests doesn't fit in with our ideas or our discipline."

Pankratov, a stevedore, was not fond of long speeches but even this brief statement was interrupted by the same irate voice.

"The non-Party fellows are leaving, aren't they?"

"Yes."

A lad in a short overcoat came elbowing his way to the front. A Komsomol card flew up, struck against Pankratov's chest, dropped onto the table and stood on edge. "There, take your card. I'm not going to risk my health for a bit of cardboard!"

His last words were drowned out by a roar of angry voices:

"What do you think you're throwing around!"

"Treacherous bastard!"

"Got into the Komsomol because he thought he'd have it easy."

"Chuck him out!"

"Let me get at the louse!"

The deserter, his head lowered, made his way to the exit. They let him pass, shrinking away from him as from a leper. The door closed with a creak behind him.

Pankratov picked up the discarded membership card and held it to the flame of the oil lamp.

The cardboard caught alight and curled up as it burned.

The cherished goal was in sight, but the advance toward it was agonisingly slow, for every day typhoid fever tore dozens of badly needed hands from the builders' ranks.

One day Korchagin, returning from work to the station, staggered along like a drunkard, his legs ready to give way beneath him. He had been feverish for quite some time, but today it gripped him more fiercely than usual. Typhoid fever, which had thinned the ranks of the building detachment, had claimed a new victim. But Pavel's sturdy constitution resisted the disease and for five days in succession he had found the strength to pick himself up from his straw pallet on the concrete floor and join the others at work. But the fever had taken possession of him and now neither the warm jacket nor the felt boots, Fyodor's gift, worn over his already frost-bitten feet, helped.

A sharp pain seared his chest with each step he took, his teeth chattered, and his vision was blurred so that the trees seemed to be whirling around in a strange merry-go-round. With difficulty he dragged himself to the station. An unusual com-motion there caused him to halt, and straining his fever-hazed eyes, he saw a long train of flatcars stretching the entire length of the platform. Men who had come with the train were busy unloading narrow-gauge engines, rails and sleepers. Pavel staggered forward and lost his balance. He felt a dull pain as his head hit the ground and the pleasant coolness of the snow against his burning cheek.

Several hours later he was found and carried back to the barracks. He was breath-ing heavily, quite unconscious of his surroundings. A doctor's assistant summoned from the armored train examined him and diagnosed pneumonia and typhoid fe-ver. His temperature was over 106°. The doctor's assistant noted the inflammation of the joints and the ulcers on the neck but said they were trifles compared with the pneumonia and typhoid which alone were enough to kill him.

Pankratov and Dubava, who had arrived from town, did all they could to save Pavel. Alyosha Kokhansky, who came from the same town as Pavel, was entrusted with taking him home to his people.

With the help of all the members of Korchagin's team, and mainly with Kholyava acting as battering ram, Pankratov and Dubava managed to get Alyosha and the unconscious Korchagin into the packed railway carriage. The passengers, sus-pecting typhus, resisted violently and threatened to throw the sick man out of the train en route.

Kholyava waved his gun under their noses and roared: "His illness is not infec-tious! And he's going on this train even if we have to throw out the whole lot of you! And remember, you swine, if anyone lays a finger on him, I'll send word down the line and you'll all be taken off the train and put behind the bars. Here, Alyosha, take Pavel's Mauser and shoot the first man who tries to put him off," Kholyava wound up for additional emphasis. The train puffed out of the station. Pankratov went over to Dubava standing on the deserted platform. "Do you think he'll pull through?" The question remained unanswered. "Come along, Mityai, it can't be helped. We've got to answer for everything now. We must get those engines un-loaded during the night and in the morning we'll try to start them going."

Kholyava telephoned to all his Cheka friends along the line urging them to make sure that the sick Korchagin was not taken off the train anywhere. Not until he had been given a firm assurance that this would be done did he finally go to bed.

The Story of the Great Plan
M. Ilin (1930)

Ilya Marshak (pseud. M. Ilin) was a trained engineer from a famous family of children's writers (his brother was Samuil Marshak). *The Story of the Great Plan* (1930) provides lyrical and dynamic descriptions of the great construction epics of the first Five-Year Plan. Ilin's language appealed to children and adults alike, and this book helped to generate the romance of construction that so caught the imagination of Soviet youth around 1930 and which suffused so much of the mass culture of the decade. The English translation was at one time widely read in the United States.

CHAPTER VIII

Iron Workmen

1. What Machines Are Most Essential?
Metal for machines we shall have.
Energy too.
But what machines are we going to construct?
We shall need all kinds of machines. Many machines. For every type of work a machine has been invented. There are machines that sew boots, machines that weave, machines that churn butter, machines that make paper, machines that count. And there are machines that make machines.
There are tens of thousands of machines. Which of them are most essential?
The most essential machines are the machines that make machines. The reason for this is quite clear: if we have these machines, we can have all the others also. If we have iron blacksmiths, locksmiths, and lathe-grinders; if we have drillers, grinders, and polishers, then we shall be able to make any machine for any factory.

Excerpts based on a translation by George S. Counts and Nucia P. Lodge (Boston: Houghton Mifflin, 1931), pp. 83–94, 143–162.

And that is the whole point.

Up to now we have had few such machines. We had automobiles, but we had no machines that make automobiles. We had tractors, but we had no machines that make tractors. And that is why we were forced to buy automobiles, tractors, and many other machines from abroad and to pay European and American capitalists large sums of money.

This is bad. Our country works according to a plan, and the success of this plan must not depend on whether a certain Mr. Fox wishes or does not wish to sell us machines.

Foreign capitalists do not like our plans; they would like to hamper us in every possible way. They realize that we are building socialism, and that socialism will bring an end to profiteering. But why, then, do they sell us machines at all? Only because they need buyers, because they need to dispose of their goods. "It is difficult," says Ford, the American millionaire, "to refuse today's dollar for the good of tomorrow."

We must not depend on the calculations of European and American capitalists. And that is why we must first of all construct those machines that make machines.

2. Things That Make Things

At one time man made everything with his own hands. Now things make themselves. Man placed an instrument in the iron hand of a machine and ordered the machine to work.

Did you ever see a turning lathe?

What makes it work? A tool, a sharp-edged chisel. But the chisel is clenched not in a human hand, but in an iron holder.

And the thing that the turning-lathe shapes is also not held by the hand of a worker. The lathe itself holds and turns it.

You often hear people say about a machine: it works just like an iron man.

But this is not right; this is nonsense. If a machine could work only as well as a man, building it would be unprofitable. A machine should work better than a man. It should be, and can be, a hundred times more agile, more accurate, and more powerful than a man.

Man has only two hands. We can give a machine as many hands as we want.

Man cannot work with two tools at the same time: a machine can work not only with two, but with tens of tools simultaneously.

Man cannot do two things at once. He cannot at the same time saw, chop, hammer, and plane. But a machine can.

There are automatic lathes. The worker feeds iron rods into the machine, and the machine does the work. First with three "rough" chisels it grinds a bolt out of the rod, and then with three "finishing" chisels it finishes the bolt.

Thereafter a "form-tool" fashions a little head at one end and a "screw-cutting" tool cuts threads at the other. And now everything being ready, the turn comes for the ninth tool. It is a "cutting" tool and cuts the finished bolt from the rod. All of this is done so quickly that you can hardly follow the movements of the lathe.

There's a machine for you! It uses nine tools. And do not imagine for a moment

A drilling lathe   A grinding lathe   A six-charge automat

that one tool rests while another works. They all work at once. While the cutting chisel is removing the bolt from the first rod, the figure and screw-cutting tools are busy with the second, the finishing chisels are occupied with the third, and the rough chisels have begun on the fourth.

What human being could work like that?

No, a machine is not an iron man.

And the speed that it works with! Sometimes the chisel cuts so rapidly that it gets red-hot. For such work chisels must be made of specially tempered steel.

And precision! Have you ever seen how blacksmiths work?

They work in twos. One hits the forge lightly with a small hammer to show where the real blow should be struck. The other, wielding a heavy sledge, strikes with all his might. But is it possible for a man to swing a sledge with all his might precisely where he should? The stronger the blow, the greater the chance of missing.

But the iron blacksmith—the steam hammer—never misses. The sledge it strikes with glides between two iron rails. The stroke is exactly aimed and calculated. There can be no mistake.

Rapidly and with precision the iron smith labors.

And what does the human worker nearby do? He merely brings the material and removes the finished product. He is to the machine what a helper is to a skilled workman. But here the helper, not the workman, is in command.

3. Two Leningrads and Three Urals

We need first of all lathes, steam hammers, steel forges, presses, scissors, saws.

But if these machines are to work, we must have engines: steam and water turbines, diesel engines, electric motors.

Do we have them?

Very few. We lack engines probably even more than lathes. By the end of the Five-Year Plan, we must make six times as many lathes as now. And steam turbines must be increased elevenfold. We shall also need water turbines in great numbers: we must build them nine times faster than at the start of the Five-Year Plan.

This is a tremendous task. But we must achieve it.

Otherwise the entire Five-Year Plan will crash.

Just think how many water and steam electric stations we have contrived to build! And each one of them will need turbines.

And steam boilers? We do not have enough of them either.

Even those that we do have should be replaced. In our factories many of the boilers are old-timers made last century. Three out of every ten are more than twenty-five years old.

A machine does not live as long as a human being. A twenty-five-year-old boiler is an old man.

Let the old guys retire! We shall melt them down in our open-hearth furnaces. And their places will be taken by new boilers, sound and strong.

We still need many machines.* We must have locomotives, ships, lifting cranes, conveyers, electric cars, and elevators to transport and raise loads; pumps and ventilators to drive water, air, gasoline, and oil through pipes; building machines, railroad machines, excavators, hewing machines, chemical apparatus, combines, threshing machines and tractors. But can you list all of them? We need a vast army of machines—coal miners, ore miners, loaders, carriers, builders, farmers, weavers, chemists, cobblers, millers, butter-makers. Some of these machines will procure raw materials for us—ore, coal, sand, and stone. Some will transport raw materials to the factories. Others will work in factories and make finished articles out of the raw materials. Yet others will labor in sovkhozes and kolkhozes and produce bread for us.

Every one of our factories for the construction of machinery must make thousands of machines every year. Many machines we have never made in the past, but now we will. Heretofore we have not constructed combines, automobiles, hewing machines, electric cars, disk planters, tractor plows, typewriters, railroad machines, pneumatic hammers. We shall have to build hundreds of altogether new enterprises. And this is not so easy. We must learn a new job from the beginning.

There are, then, two difficult tasks ahead of us: to organize new industries and to increase the output of machines manyfold.

All of the Leningrad factories taken together cost 700 million rubles. For the repair of these enterprises and the building of new ones in the city we shall spend during the next five years about 700 million more. That means that in five years we shall have created a second Leningrad. We shall then have two Leningrads, three Urals, and two Ukraines.

4. A Factory Is an Automaton

To every new machine we build we assign a definite task, a definite program: so many products an hour, so many a day, so many a year.

Also the whole factory must work according to a plan.

If the tractor factory in Stalingrad should give us not fifty thousand tractors a year, but only twenty thousand, the deficiency would be felt at once on another part of the front—in the sovkhozes and kolkhozes. If the blast-furnaces should produce not 12 million tons of pig iron a year, but only 6 million, half of our machine construction factories would be forced to close.

---

*According to the Five-Year Plan, machine production should have grown 3½ times. Now the assignment has been changed. Machine construction must be increased 8 to 9 times over five years.

Each factory has its little plan. And of these little plans the large plan is composed—the Five-Year Plan. In order to fulfill the large plan, all the little plans must be achieved.

Every factory must work like an automaton.

But what must we do to make every factory turn out machines with the precision of an automaton? A machine is not a train ticket. You cannot drop a coin into a slot and expect a finished machine to jump out.

A large factory is a whole city in itself. Something is always certain to be out of order. Here the water has stopped, there a light has gone out, in a third place a worker is loafing, in a fourth a tool has broken.

All of these things certainly occur, and yet a factory can be made to work like a machine, like the automaton that throws tickets out of a slot.

Take, for example, the tractor factory in Stalingrad. Every six minutes a new tractor will come out of the assembly plant. Every day seventy carloads of raw materials will enter the factory gates. And every day seventy-five platforms carrying tractors will leave the factory.

How is that different from an automaton!

But how are we to do this? How can we achieve this?

A tractor is not a trinket; it is composed of five thousand separate parts.

Each part must be carefully prepared, cast out of metal, forged from iron, finished on a lathe, ground, polished, drilled, and planed.

And then all these parts must be assembled and attached to each other. Suppose they do not fit. Suppose someone has made a mistake: the opening is not where it should be or the bolt does not go into place. Anything like this may happen.

And if it does happen, if a mistake is made in one place, in another, in a third, then the plan of the factory miscarries and the entire Five-Year Plan is endangered.

The tractor internationale. The Stalingrad Factory has begun to make
30-horsepower tractors like this.

No, there must be no mistakes. We must arrange matters so that mistakes cannot happen.

5. How They Work without Machines

Imagine a huge hall. Across the center stand many rows of lathes, like the houses of a city.

Turning lathes, drilling lathes, planing lathes, bolt-cutting lathes, bur-cutting lathes, milling lathes, polishing lathes—1,360 lathes.

Between the lathes run streets, hundreds of streets.

Along the streets in long chains move, not people, but things—parts, details of a tractor.

In this city, of course, there are no streetcars, no buses.

Light things move over ball-bearing roads and glide along inclined grooves. Heavy things go in carts on railways, or slowly creep along moving platforms—conveyer belts. They all go, run, and ride in one direction—toward the city's main street. And on their way they stop at each lathe as if at a house. Here they are planed, there they are ground, in a third place they are polished. When a detail reaches the main street, it is in order, finished, and ready to become a part of a tractor.

On the main street the tractor is assembled from these parts.

Imagine yourself watching the main street, an assembly line. The tractor nearest to you does not even resemble a tractor yet. It has neither wheels nor steering wheel nor fenders. The box that axles protrude from on either side is the frame. One worker attaches the kerosene tank. Another puts on the motor and the radiator.

The next tractor already looks more like a tractor. The fenders are on. And soon it will have a steering wheel: you can see it being put in place.

The tractor still doesn't have wheels. As it enters a tunnel, however, it is almost entirely completed. There stand painters wearing eye goggles. They paint, not with brushes, but with an atomizer: a device that sprays paint on the body of the car. It works much more rapidly than a brush.

Then the tractor, painted and dried, descends from the conveyer, and for the first time stands on its own legs, or, we should say, on its own wheels.

Thus works the assembly department of a tractor factory.

There will be no mistakes.

A definite task is assigned each machine and a definite time for the job: so many minutes, so many seconds. To each detail a definite time on the belt, a definite schedule of arrival and departure. On the way between lathes a few extra details will always be attended to—in case there has been any delay. Before being mounted on the tractor, every motor is checked in a testing station.

There will be no mistakes. Six minutes for each tractor, not seven and not eight, but just six.

CHAPTER XII

New People

1. A Fragment from a Book to Be Written Fifty Years Hence

They lived in crowded dwellings with little windows, with dark, dirty corridors, with low ceilings. Of every five or six persons one had to sweep and scrub the floors, cook the food, go marketing, wash clothes, nurse the children. With rare exceptions this work was done by women, "the so-called 'housewives.'" At that time there were already on the market such inventions as mechanical potato peelers, meat choppers, dishwashers, clothes cleaners, and other devices. But in spite of this millions of housewives continued to work with their hands. Small wonder that toiling fifteen or sixteen hours a day they were still unable to finish their work. Rooms were cleaned thoroughly only twice a year, on the eve of important holidays. Children were always unkempt and ragged. Food was prepared carelessly, was tasteless and unnourishing. Not a single housewife knew how many calories were in a kilogram of cabbage or a liter of milk. Food was cooked in a "kitchen," that is, a small, crowded room. Steam kettles were altogether lacking and food was cooked over an open fire. An unheard-of amount of wood was consumed in the process—in those days they still used wood for fuel.

The food often burned, and suffocating smoke spread through the rest of the house. Here in the kitchen also was a garbage pail to hold the wastes of production: potato peelings, herring tails, bones, and so on. During the day this refuse poisoned the air: not until evening was it emptied into a kind of half-covered garbage pit in the yard. No one thought of turning the kitchen wastes into glue, fertilizer, or to some other useful purpose.

Every room in the house was heated separately. Very few homes were equipped with central heating systems. Even in the United States as late as 1930 there were 30 million open fireplaces and stoves. All of these heaters burned enormous quantities of fuel.

This might be the nightmare of a housekeeper after a day's work

The furniture in the rooms was heavy, clumsy, and uncomfortable. Light metal furniture was then almost unknown. The most popular chairs and sofas were covered with cloth and filled with hair or sawdust. To raise a great cloud of dust, all you had to do was to tap a chair seat lightly. On the floor they laid pieces of thick carpet. On the walls they hung little shelves and pictures. The windows, besides being small, were screened by curtains which shut out most of the light. All these were done as if purposely to collect dust. Yet dust had already been established to be a source of infection. If you examine dust under a microscope, you will find that it contains the germs of various diseases, particles of human skin, tiny bits of clothing, etc. Yet no one seemed to realize that dust is a social calamity as terrible as flood or fire.

The houses in which people lived were completely unsuited to rest after work. In one crowded apartment they read, cooked their food, prepared for examinations, washed their clothes, received their guests, nursed their children. When they returned home exhausted from their labors, they were unable to find the rest they needed to renew their energy and vigor for the following day.

In the majority of families children had no care during the entire day because their mothers were at work outside the home or busy with household duties. Every large building boasted a yard that was somewhat like a well surrounded by four stone walls. In this yard there was usually a hole to receive the refuse from the kitchen. And this dark place, without sunlight, without trees, and without grass, was the children's playground.

People lived still worse in the villages. One writer and political leader wrote at the beginning of the twentieth century:

"Most peasant huts are eighteen by twenty-one feet. In such a hut are housed on the average about seven people, but there are huts—little cages—no larger than twelve feet square. The stove occupies about one-fifth of the total air space. The stove plays an enormous role in the home-life and even the economy of the family. Not only do the peasants warm themselves on it, but they also sleep on it and use it for drying clothes, shoes, grain, hemp. Not only do they bake and cook on the stove, but they also depend on it for steam baths. And under the stove chickens, calves, and sheep are often protected from the winter frosts. Not infrequently, the cow is also brought into the hut at calving time. Practically the only furniture is a table that serves for both cooking and eating. On this table too all kinds of housework are done, harnesses repaired, clothes made and mended. A common saying among the peasants was: 'We're so poor that we can't even feed the cockroaches.'"

That's how millions of people lived. And the remarkable thing is not that they lived, but that they didn't all die.

2. New Life and New People

All this will be written about us a few decades hence.

We live badly and stupidly. We change Nature, but we have not changed our own selves. And this is the most essential thing. Why did we conceive this tremendous labor which will last not five, but fifteen, twenty, and perhaps more years? Why do we mine millions of tons of coal and ore? Why do we build millions of machines? Do we do these things merely to change Nature?

No, we change Nature so that people can live better.

We need machines so that we can work less and accomplish more. By the end of the Five-Year Plan the factory working day will be reduced by 50 minutes. If we consider that the working year consists of 273 days (not counting rest days and holidays), a worker will work 227 hours a year less than he did at the beginning of the plan. And 227 hours equals almost 32 7-hour working days.

Workers will work less and yet accomplish more. During seven hours in the factory they will do what now requires eleven and a half hours.

And if this is so, his wages will be raised by more than fifty percent. Compared to conditions before the Revolution, every worker will labor three hours less a day and yet will receive twice as much pay.

But that is not all. Work will be made easier. No longer will there be bent backs, strained muscles, inflated veins on the forehead. Loads will travel not on people's backs, but over conveyers. The heavy crowbar and pick will give way to the pneumatic hammer and compressed air.

Instead of dark, gloomy shops with dim, yellow lamps there will be light, clean halls with great windows and beautiful tile floors. Not the lungs of men but powerful ventilators will suck in and swallow dirt, dust, and shavings from the shop. Workers will be less fatigued after a day's labor. There will be fewer "occupational" diseases. Think of all the people who perish now from these ailments! Every metal worker has lungs eaten up by metal dust. You can at once recognize a metalworker by his pale face, a stoker by his red, inflamed eyes.

After we build socialism, everyone will have equally healthy faces. Men will cease to regard work as a punishment, a heavy obligation. They will labor easily and cheerfully.

But if work will be a joy, time off will be a double joy.

Can one rest now in a crowded and noisy home amid the hissing of oil burners, the smoke of the kitchen, the drying of wet diapers, the filth of dim windows, dirty furniture, spittle-covered floors, and unwashed dishes on the table?

After all, man is not just muscles for working. He is not a machine. He has a mind that wants to know, eyes that want to see, ears that want to hear, a throat that wants to sing, feet that want to run and jump and dance, hands that want to row and swim and throw and catch. And we must organize life so that not merely certain lucky ones but all may be able to feel the joy of living.

After socialism is built there will no longer be dwarfs—people with exhausted, pale faces, people reared in basements without sunshine or air. Healthy, strong giants, red-cheeked and happy: such will be the new people.

But to accomplish this we need new cities and new houses. We must remake our whole life down to the last kitchen pot.

Down with the kitchen! We shall destroy this little domestic penitentiary! We shall free millions of women from housekeeping. They want to live and work like the rest of us. In a factory kitchen one person can prepare from fifty to one hundred dinners a day. We shall force machines to peel the potatoes, wash the dishes, cut the bread, stir the soup, crank the ice-cream maker.

Down with dark, small, and crowded dwellings!

We shall build large communal houses with light, spacious rooms. Let us understand once and for all that it is impossible to work, rest, study, cook, and receive guests in the same place. There must be separate rooms for rest, for play, for reading, for dining, for receiving guests. And children must have rooms of their own. Adults frequently complain that children interrupt their sleep, their study, their conversation. But let not the grown-ups annoy the children and interfere with their noise and games.

Already we have such houses. The newspaper *Pravda* writes that in Moscow on Khavsky Street a "Commune House" has recently been built.

It is a huge building. On the first floor there is a light and spacious dining room; on the second an auditorium with a balcony for lectures, entertainments, and moving pictures. Next to the auditorium are several rooms for club circles, libraries for noisy and quiet relaxation, rooms for the receiving of guests. The third floor is a many-roomed gymnasium. The roof is flat. Benches will be placed there and flower beds arranged. In summer people will rest and take sun and shower baths here. In winter the roof will be converted into a skating rink, and merry skaters will cut figures on the ice high above the streets of Moscow.

For little children several rooms are reserved on the first floor. Here are play-rooms (make as much noise as you please!), and classrooms and workshops and verandas.

All the rooms are light and cheerful.

Colors are selected so that they may delight and not tire or hurt the eyes.

But we need not just new houses: we need new socialistic cities.

The old city is a huge pile of gloomy and crowded houses, a cheerless world of stone walls and pavement. Only here and there in the center may be seen the little islands of green squares. But the farther you go from the center of the city—toward the workers' quarters—the dirtier and darker become the streets. For those who can get themselves out of this stone hell at least once a year, life is not so bad. But there are people who never leave the city.

I recall that once in our class we laughed at a boy who had never seen a sheep. This little boy was born and reared on Borovoi Street. There he died. Not once during his whole life was he fortunate enough to walk through a forest or a field.

Down with these abominable old cities! Like huge lichens they have grown and spread over the earth. We must make them over and build new socialistic cities.

A socialistic city will be entirely different from the city that we know.

A new club for commune dwellers in Moscow

A Storm off Hope

Aleksei Garri (1928)

FROM ICE AND PEOPLE, ONE OF THE MANY EPICS OF ARCTIC TRAVEL AND EXPLORATION IN THIS ERA (THE ISLE OF HOPE LIES OFF SPITSBERGEN NEAR THE ARCTIC OCEAN). THE DANGER AND EXCITEMENT OF THE VOYAGE PROVIDED THE APPEAL; THE GLORIES OF TECHNOLOGY AND SOVIET HEROISM PROVIDED THE MESSAGE. THE AUTHOR, GARRI (1902–1960), WAS ARRESTED IN 1938 AND SPENT SIXTEEN YEARS IN CAPTIVITY.

For a month and a half the sun didn't set over the *Malygin*. I saw amazing polar nights as bright as day, their beauty incomparable. People lost count of the hours, the days, the weeks. Those who stared at the bright polar snow without special glasses paid for their curiosity brutally, with snow blindness. They would be in bed several days, even weeks, with bandaged eyes, blind and sick. Only a person born there can look at the polar radiance with impunity.

Several hours before we reached the edge of the icecap, the first navigator showed us the arctic sky. On the horizon above the water, sunlight reflecting from the snow traced a dazzling white streak in the sky. Soon, solitary ice floes began coming our way. They swirled around the *Malygin* and were sucked underwater by its whirlpool. The ice floes were grayish-blue, partly melted, as if they had just been knocked into the water from a Moscow roof. Then came the finely crushed ice. It swelled and ebbed with the waves. Ice floes scraped against the ship sides, and sleep was impossible. We approached the edge of the ice. The expedition leader, Professor Vize, called all the journalists on deck and showed us the first polar bear. To kill it, however, was forbidden: this would bring bad luck.

Sailors still haven't overcome their superstitions and prejudices. When we left Arkhangelsk, part of the crew grumbled that we were casting off on the thirteenth. In the same way, killing the first bear was forbidden—it would come to no good. The bear ran alongside our vessel on the ice. He was greenish-yellow, like a grease stain on a clean tablecloth. From time to time he stopped, sat on his haunches, and gazed at us with curiosity. Then he would lope off again as if he had urgent and important business—catch the ship no matter what.

Then came the large chunks of ice. They moved in sheets that were miles long, perfectly smooth, dazzling, white, and imperturbable. The *Malygin* shuddered slightly from the ice's resistance, and its nose broke through as easily as a saber. We began to move slower and slower. Sometimes we had to back up, take a running

---

From *Vchera i segodnia* (Moscow, 1960), vol. 1, pp. 111–121.

start, and charge the ice. In such instances, the icebreaker would rear up with half the vessel sticking out of the water. The *Malygin* would lie on the ice and crush it with its weight. To sail a sea of ice you must know how to dare. The watch was manned by the second navigator, Aleksandr Petrovich, a man of daring, with the soul of a great seafarer, and with the average Russian sailor's ability to make history without even knowing it. Aleksandr Petrovich had sailed the seas for twenty-five years, and ten of those were spent sailing the ice. He was considered the finest arctic navigator in northern ports. When he stands watch, we go twice as fast. The *Malygin* creaks and groans. The captain's chair in the wardroom rolls back and forth along the floor. People fall from their berths; anything not fastened down in time shakes loose and flies to the deck. But the ice snaps like sugar.

There are ice ridges we have to hit twenty-five times before breaking them. On such occasions, the captain sneaks out on the bridge all wrapped in furs and tarps, looking monstrously big and heavy like the magic whale in a provincial production of the opera *Sadko*. He climbs the ladder without holding the railing, and the bridge seems to sway beneath him.

"Vachman," he says, mangling the English "watchman"—head of the watch—with incredible nonchalance. "Vachman," he repeats, "stop this rocking, this damn rocking; you're giving me a headache."

His unshaven bristle trembles with indignation. The captain walks up to the compass and stares at it for a long time, as though perplexed.

"How long have you been ramming it, Petrovich?" he asks. "We're on course and have run into an ice ridge. There are twenty-five sazhens in that ridge. Come on, let's hit it again." Then the captain goes to a corner of the bridge, stands by the binocular case, and we begin ramming the ice again.

The only thing known about the Isle of Hope in the English pilot book's navigational description is that it doesn't lie where it's marked on the map. It also indicates that no man has ever set foot on the island. And in conclusion it says that vessels with a draft of more than fifteen feet are categorically forbidden to go closer than ten miles.

I read the English instructions, written by a wise old admiral, when we were on the *Malygin,* only two miles from the Isle of Hope with a draft of twenty-one feet. The ice, always disdainfully calm, changed its mood this time. The air was crackling many times louder than combined rifle and artillery fire. The ice squeezed us tighter and tighter. The wind grew stronger. Icebergs butted up against each other, breaking, crumbling with deafening cracks. When the fog rolled back, the Isle of Hope appeared to us in all her untouched beauty—a sharply outlined ridge of black cliffs and dazzlingly blue glaciers.

The *Malygin* was drifting swiftly toward the reefs. The old English admiral was right after all. Much later, reading a wireless transmission the Swedish pilot Lundborg addressed to his king, I understood that ice has a certain property that slipped a Moscow journalist's attention. Lundborg telegraphed:

"It's impossible to work in this latitude with this ice. Only Russians or madmen can fly here."

Still, Lundborg took General Nobile on board with his white dog, which was seeing the polar ice a second time. He didn't want to fly anymore after that. The pilot Babushkin had been absent three days when a cruel arctic storm blew us toward the Isle of Hope's cliffs. And although we were already stowing fresh water and food on the *Malygin*'s lifeboat, and radio operators were figuring out how to save our only transmitter, we couldn't help thinking about three half-starved and exhausted people somewhere in the distant ice and mist, trying to wrest a tiny duralumin bird—their only salvation—from the storm.[1]

Others, however, thought differently. When Babushkin came on board two days later, unbent by five sleepless days, and mounted the captain's bridge, asking only, "Well, is everyone still in one piece, mates?" the governor of Spitsbergen, a man quick on the uptake, telegraphed the Norwegian government:

"The pilot Babushkin, returning to the icebreaker *Malygin* after a five-day absence, found all alive and well."

The governor of Spitsbergen believed the storm wouldn't break Babushkin, yet he also believed the English pilot book and thought it impossible to go where it wasn't possible to go.

Babushkin brought back an airplane with one broken ski, a pail of bear meat, and a heap of broken illusions. For the first time we felt the overwhelming difference between the seventy-seventh parallel and the Moscow aerodrome. But that happened later. Here's what happened earlier.

The ice spun the *Malygin* like a top. The icebreaker listed on its side, reared up on the ice, and fell back again. As in a movie, the fog would show us the Isle of Hope's dazzling peaks and then hide them from us again. There were long moments when we didn't know where we were being carried: toward or away from death. At the most terrifying moment, when the captain ordered us to release the steering rope—that is, to free the rudder so it wouldn't break—the telegraph operator came in from the radio room. You couldn't say he walked to the bridge—he crawled. Every second he was thrown from the deck into the cabin walls. He fell, rolled backwards, and crawled forwards again, holding a white sheet of paper folded in four. According to merchant fleet instructions, he was obliged to deliver a telegram immediately if it was urgent. The storm was no concern of his—he was carrying out some regulation, number twenty-seven, it seems. But an unexpected obstacle blocked his path. The cameraman Valentei's tripod burst unassisted through the cabin door onto the spar deck. It slid along the deck, the sharp metal tips of its legs striking sparks. Catching it was impossible: who would willingly jump on a storm-swept spear point? The tripod skewered the radioman like a piece of

---

1. The Italian general Umberto Nobile was a polar explorer, who successfully flew over the North Pole with Amundsen in 1926. A 1928 flight ended in a crash, and Nobile was rescued from the ice by a Soviet expedition, which became a source of national pride. A joke of the time ran: "During the search for Nobile's wreck, all the post offices in the USSR were ordered to accept correspondence relating to the mission free of charge. An Odessan telegraphed Moscow: 'Abramovich, save Nobile; if you can't, send forty sacks of sugar.'" [4:39]

[For anecdote sources, see *Blue Blouse Skit*, above.]

shishkabob, and both almost went overboard. But the radio operator won out, and the tripod was folded up and stored away.

Just at that moment the *Malygin* listed, and thick layers of broken ice climbed up the starboard side. The radio operator fell again for one last time, yet still he delivered the urgent telegram to its addressee. The radiogram was meant for Ostrovsky, a correspondent from one of the Moscow newspapers. The message said literally: "In connection with the conclusion of your leave, report immediately to the editorial office." With signature.

It was a very serious moment. During the entire month-long voyage through the ice, the *Malygin* had never come closer to becoming a rescuee instead of a rescuer, but still we all laughed like children. There was an endless amount of genuine humor in the newspaper's stern message, whose author was evidently sticking to the contract. At any rate, Captain Chertkov laughed incredibly.

The arctic storm buffeted us for a day. Then the wind began to die down, but the movement of the ice didn't cease. The fog lifted completely. The Isle of Hope was right next to us; we had almost gone completely around it, and it was hard even to accuse it of anything, so disdainfully majestic were its dazzling peaks. The reefs were somewhere right nearby. The English chart knew only that the Isle of Hope was marked where it wasn't located; it had nothing to tell us about the reefs.

As I gazed at the Isle of Hope, I puzzled long over what had inspired the black humor of the man who had given such an ominous place that name. Afterwards an old book on polar travel cleared up my uncertainty. The island was properly called "Abandon All Hope." "Hope" was just an abbreviation.

There was one more unforgettable moment. Right in front of where the ice drift had carried us, two giant icebergs appeared—two glacier fragments sliding into the sea. The icebergs had run firmly aground. They were terribly blue and shiny, as though the sun were filtering through them. On a foggy night off the Newfoundland coast, a similar iceberg had sent the oceanliner *Titanic* to the bottom.

Captain Chertkov stood on the bridge with his arms folded across his chest. The rudder was unmanned; the engines stood ready but weren't running. The ice was stronger than the icebreaker, and steering it was impossible. Then something happened like an episode in an American stunt movie: A girl is sitting on the railroad tracks and the mail train rushes down on her. The train goes by the viewer, and then the girl rises slowly from the ground. She's unharmed. Just as in the American stunt film, we drifted between the two icebergs. The cameraman Valentei stood on the starboard bulwark cranking the handle madly. Next to me Aleksandr Yakovlev, the writer, stared fixedly and greedily at the iceberg's blue ice and kept whispering: "My Lord! It's so beautiful!"

When this beauty was finally behind us, the captain shouted something into the megaphone, and the propeller started working again after many hours of inactivity. We had entered a belt of ice where it was possible to travel. Then we were squeezed against a large ice field. Birds could be seen on the Isle of Hope with the naked eye.

Babushkin flew in at dawn. When the noise of propellers was heard, a calico red signal flag was spread out on the snow to show him the direction of the wind. But the pilot Babushkin had two living people with him who had fought death for five days, and he was flying a plane entrusted to him by the government for rescuing Nobile's crew. He didn't believe us landlubbers—the Junkers made five big circles in the air above the island and the *Malygin*. Then Babushkin landed not where we had placed the signal, but over to the right; it was better there.

Slogging over the thawed ground, racing each other and shouting incoherently, we ran over to greet him.

ABOVE THE ICE

Babushkin was too big for his plane—they're made on the wrong scale for each other. When the pilot stands next to the plane, the disproportion is glaringly apparent. Even the flight mechanic Groshev, who is short, looks like a giant crab crawling into a small shell when he works on our Junkers.

Groshev looks after his airplane like the peasants of a horseless village look after their only horse, which they've just bought from gypsies at the bazaar with their last grain reserves. I think that if Groshev owned a horse in similar circumstances, he still wouldn't handle it as lovingly as he treats the Junkers—it would be too tiresome.

On terrible stormy days when, after hours on end of fighting death, people lie on their berths like corpses, oblivious to the tossing or the storm's approach, Groshev can't stay in his cabin. He's long unshaven. His face is deathly pale—conditions on the *Malygin* affect even the strongest of us. Groshev goes out on deck, fastens his leather jacket tighter, puts on his polar glasses, and goes to his plane on the stern deck, tossed by the rocking vessel from bulwark to deckhouse walls.

There is a lot of work for him there. He has to check how soundly the ropes are holding, whether the wind has blown the tarpaulin back, whether the wind is buffeting the motor, and so on.

The watchman usually walks over to Groshev. He's also very tired and wants to sleep because he came on guard duty right after a storm watch. They light up from each other's cigarettes on the lee side, observing varied and numerous forms of smokers' etiquette that would make them the envy of any diplomat. Sailors, especially those at sea, are demonstratively courteous people. I had frequent occasion to become convinced of that on the *Malygin*. Groshev's cigarettes and the watchman's matches finally emerge triumphant, and they begin discussing aviation.

The mechanic talks and the sailor listens. And whenever he's explaining some particularly complex nuance of flight technique, the watchman spits over the bulwark with great proficiency and says:

"So that's how it is; we're not just living, we're sailing along."

When our plane and the other flying machines have been dismantled down to the last piece, Groshev circles the Junkers one more time and his proprietary eye gives it the once-over. Then he returns and, before going to bed, drops by the wardroom for a glass of water with cranberry extract. After only two weeks at sea, something happened to the hot water system: sea water leaks in, so we drink salty tea, salty coffee, salty water. Drinking it straight without cranberry extract is impossible.

If Professor Vize, our expedition leader, who is also a light sleeper, is sitting in the wardroom, Groshev, pouring water for himself from a decanter, says to no one in particular, "Went up to the stern. Well, the plane's still standing, everything's shipshape."

Then without saying goodbye, the mechanic goes to his cabin to sleep, only to wake again in two hours.

When a storm on the Barents Sea blew us around, and huge waves rolled across the spar deck in mockery of man's attempts to conquer the elements, we held the airplane with our hands for two days in a row so that the waves wouldn't wash it away. These days were so full of various memories, from an underwater leak to an uninhabited lifeboat thrown into the sea by shipwrecked seamen, that it is hard to remember every detail of that remarkable page from the history of the *Malygin*'s voyage. The only thing I remember firmly was that Groshev wasn't relieved even once. His leather jacket turned white from a crust of sea salt. His unshaven bristle was also covered with sparkling white crystals. But, gripping the hawsers powerfully, the mechanic held onto his airplane. And the face of this man, probably carrying out not the first heroic feat of his life, was so childishly peaceful that we would have felt awkward being relieved and going to the warm wardroom.

The part of Babushkin's plane I hate most is the fuselage. Junkers, the talented designer of a multitude of various flying machines, probably never thought that madmen on the seventy-seventh parallel would drag one of his creations—the Ju-13—on their shoulders from ship to ice. Therefore, the disassembled shell of the plane was covered with protuberances, bolts, and hooks that cut painfully into the body. If the fuselage is carried on the shoulders—and ten to fifteen people are carrying it—black-and-blue marks form on the body after one such trip down to the platform. If the airplane is loaded and unloaded several times a day, the black-and-blue marks turn into sores. If the fuselage is held by hand, blood appears under the fingernails in a moment. It's generally a tricky business.

When we have to take the plane out, we lay down a platform and drag the separate parts of the Junkers out with our hands. Babushkin always goes in front; because he is very tall, the fuselage tail slopes backwards, and the men walking in back have to crawl along the platform supporting the tail on their backs. This is very painful. Babushkin's face isn't young anymore—probably the air has aged it—but his eyes are absolutely youthful; with such eyes you can fly wherever you want. Babushkin goes in front. The front end of the fuselage is on his shoulder; one hand is free. He waves this hand in rhythm and shouts from time to time, "One, two, heave! One, two, heave!" And we lift. At such moments I remember the ancient Vikings, who are said to have discovered not only Spitsbergen but also America. Their techniques on the arctic ice were probably just as primitive as ours.

Carrying the wings out to the ice and loading them back onto the ship is considerably easier. But even they conceal a tiny unpleasantness—the steering rudders. If a finger gets caught between a rudder and the wing frame, it will be all black-and-blue for the next ten days. More than anything else, I like to unload the tail plane—

the depth rudder; one person can carry it, yet the job is still crucial. The slightest dent in the tail plane can deprive the airplane of maneuverability in the air.

And then there are the skis. They can just be rolled down the platform. I know only one thing about the skis—if all the foreign airplanes rescuing Nobile had them, and if the pilots knew how to use them, they could have landed right next to the general's tent long ago. We have only one such pair of skis with us, and we treat them like babies. The Ju-13 inspires a generally pitiful impression. When it was assembled on the ice for its first trial flight, our deck ensign walked up to the plane, touched it, and said to Babushkin with obvious distrust: "You're going to fly this thing? She's not worth a damn. One puff of wind and there won't be anything left."

I have flown in this very same plane with Babushkin several times and am convinced that the tiny duralumin bird is actually worth a great deal. But her appearance, especially when she's dismantled and carried down the platform on someone's shoulders, does not instill confidence. If you grab the special handle on one of the wing's edges with both hands and give it a strong tug downwards, the whole airplane rocks, even if the fuel tanks are full, or even if three people are sitting in it. As I later discovered, this feature helped the plane break away from the ice.

The ice is covered with a blanket of snow at this latitude. As soon as the airplane lands, the skis settle into the snow and freeze to the ground a bit. Just to give the airplane a chance to build up some speed, you have to grab the wing and rock it until the other ski rises above the blanket of snow. Incredible, but true.

When the takeoff is from our base, it's only half-bad. Usually no less than half the population of the *Malygin* sees us off, and everyone is ready to help us lift off from the ground.

But if it is done from the ice, in the fog, several hundred kilometers from base—who the hell knows exactly where, because we can't determine where we are ourselves—then things are a lot trickier.

The pilot and mechanic sit up front by the motor. In the cabin sits the radio operator, who's also navigator, passenger, and observer. To break away from the ice, the third person has to rock the plane loose and then hop in before Babushkin taxies faster than a man can run.

For a Muscovite who's not even used to jumping on streetcars, this is a far from easy task. However, Babushkin gave me a friendly warning: "If you miss when you jump, fall flat on the ground. Remember the tail plane will be coming up behind, and judging by your height, it's going to hit you right in the back of the head. And what will I do without a tail plane? Then we'll be sitting on the ice like fools."

I followed Babushkin's advice with reverent precision. When the airplane set out along the ice, I decided to outwit the laws of physics. I did not let go of the wing but went around it, trying not to fall behind the airplane. At that moment the Junkers hopped over a chunk of ice and I crawled into the cabin on my belly, squinting and blinded by the propeller's backstream of air and snow. The laughing Babushkin grinned through the window. He probably couldn't understand how it was possible to crawl into the cabin in such a strange manner. After the flight, he explained to me at length that there were steps on the wings and that the job really wasn't all that difficult. I don't know—maybe.

And then this other thing happened too. The third person on the plane was the ship's radioman, Fominykh. He was also rocking the plane loose and wanted to outwit the laws of physics. But the ice under the Junkers cracked, and Fominykh fell into the water. Babushkin noticed the third person's absence in time and shut off the gas before we had gained full speed on the ice. Fominykh scrambled out onto the ice, repeated his experiment, and three hours later returned to us, along with the pilot and the mechanic. This took place two hundred kilometers from the *Malygin.*

The radio operator crawled out of the cabin, and all of his clothes froze on him. When we asked him how he liked his first flight, Fominykh muttered through his teeth, "Curse it!"

But the next time he asked to fly again.

———•—•———

Once we were flying without Groshev. We were testing a new motor. The sea pilot Sergeev was sitting to Babushkin's right as copilot. Groshev didn't leave us until the last moment. He ran around the airplane with a particularly anxious expression, tightened some screws, and pounded the side with a wrench. Then he crawled out onto the wing and fiddled with the motor for about fifteen minutes; his whole expression suggested that flying without him was insane. I don't know which he felt more: apprehension for our well-being or for the plane's. In any case, I remembered the horseless peasant again and thought he'd look about the same if he lent his horse to a neighbor.

Groshev cranked the propeller with his own hands. He probably wouldn't have let anyone else do it, even under cannon fire. Then he crawled out onto the wing once again and glanced into the engine, checking the rotation speed. When I saw the ice close to the cabin window for the last time, Groshev was rocking the airplane wing with his own hands to help us break free from the ground. He yelled something to Babushkin, frowning—whether it was a farewell or advice, who knows—and I felt vividly how close a man could be to a machine entrusted to his care.

Babushkin tugged the wheel back several times. The skis just could not break away from the snow pack. We rose a meter, fell back, hopped along the bumps, rose again and fell back again, and finally took off, gaining altitude. The moment of final separation from the surface went completely unnoticed. You experience nothing like it taking off from wheels, from pontoons, or even with a flying boat. When I finally realized that we were in the air, Babushkin was circling and the *Malygin* looked like a just-lit cigar stamped out on the sidewalk by a drunken heel. Everything else around was dazzlingly white. We flew at an altitude of approximately one kilometer. The visibility was so exceptional that I saw the peaks of King Charles Island crowned with caps of fog. A tiny stream of smoke trailed from the motor. This was the only blemish on an otherwise dazzling background of ice and sky.

Below, our shadow ran along the ice behind us. We flew very high and it was invisible to the naked eye, but through binoculars this fantastic shadow glided along the snow in all its fairy-tale beauty. I have never seen anything so beautiful in my life, and I don't think that anyone who hasn't flown above the ice has. The absence of anything visible on the ground, the absolute freedom, the tremendous open space, when the blindingly bright ground almost imperceptibly becomes the blinding bright horizon—human words cannot describe these things.

Minutes seemed like seconds. Babushkin began to descend. At first I saw a thick black trail of smoke, then I saw the *Malygin*. Fog was moving in from the north, and the firemen were doing their best—they were afraid that we wouldn't spot the vessel in time.

The airplane touched down so delicately that the binoculars I had hung on the cabin wall didn't even sway. Groshev the mechanic ran to meet us, wallowing through the snowdrifts. He climbed onto the wing first, opened the hood, and began tinkering with the motor.

As we climbed the ladder to the vessel, I stepped aside to let this remarkable man go by. But Groshev didn't notice me. Spinning some kind of wrench in his hands, he spat on it, blew on it, wiped it on his sleeve, and blew on it again. He was busy.

The Stalin White Sea—Baltic Canal
The History of Its Construction (1934)

THIS BOOK, WRITTEN BY A COLLECTIVE OF THIRTY-SEVEN WRITERS[1] FOR THE HISTORY OF FACTORIES SERIES, IS ONE OF THE MOST NOTORIOUS APOLOGIAS FOR SLAVE LABOR CAMPS EVER MADE. ONE WOULD HAVE TO IMAGINE A FRENCH GOVERNMENT TOURIST BROCHURE DESCRIBING THE PEDAGOGICAL JOYS OF DEVIL'S ISLAND OR A NAZI TRAVELOGUE ABOUT AUSCHWITZ TO GRASP THE CONTRAST BETWEEN REPRESENTATION AND REALITY THAT MARKED THIS BOOK—AND STALINIST CULTURE IN GENERAL. ALTHOUGH THOUSANDS DIED IN THE CONSTRUCTION OF THE WHITE SEA—BALTIC CANAL (COMPLETED IN 1933), IT WAS LAUDED AS AN EXPERIMENTAL COLONY FOR THE REHABILITATION OF WAYWARD PERSONS, HAILED AS A GLORIOUS SOVIET

Translation by Amabel Williams-Ellis (London: John Lane, 1935), pp. 116–140, excerpted with minor changes.

1. L. Auerbach, B. Agapov, S. Alimov, A. Berzin, S. Budantsev, S. Bulatov, S. Dikovsky, N. Dmitriev, A. Ehrlich, K. Finn, E. Gabrilovich, N. Garnich, G. Gausner, S. Gekht, K. Gorbunov, Maksim Gorky, V. Ivanov, Vera Inber, V. Kataev, Z. Khatsrevin, G. Korabelnikov, B. Lapin, A. Lebedenko, D. Mirsky, L. Nikulin, V. Pertsov, J. Rikachov, L. Slavin, V. Shklovsky, A. Tolstoy, B. Yassensky, N. Yurgin, K. Zelinsky, and M. Zoshchenko, and edited by Maksim Gorky, L. Auerbach, and S. G. Firin. This particular segment is the work of Mikhail Zoshchenko.

ACHIEVEMENT, AND MEMORIALIZED IN THE NAME OF THE MOST
FAMOUS BRAND OF CIGARETTE (OR *PAPYROSA*): BELOMORKANAL.

CHAPTER XII. THE HISTORY OF A MAN REFORGED

ROTHENBURG'S STORY

"My name is Abram Isaakovich Rothenburg. I was born in Tiflis. I am now forty years of age. My father was a worker, employed by his own brother. This brother was a rich man while my father had nothing at all. He used to address his younger brother respectfully as David Isaakovich.

"My father had five sons and two daughters. I was the eldest of the family. My mother handed me over to a Jewish charitable organization, where I received free tuition. It was really a respectable sort of school. We had meat pies, boiled milk, buns and sausages for breakfast. At home, though, I often found there was nothing to eat.

"My father was a gambler by nature. He would spend the whole day playing dominoes and usually lost everything. My mother had so many small children to look after—life was hard for her, she suffered a good deal.

"My father's brother, that is, my uncle, had not a care in the world. He never knew what it was to want, and his children gorged on grapes and apples every day.

"I could only watch and lick my lips.

"I felt at the time that fate was unkind to me. I began to steal books from school and sell them. I bought myself sweets with the money, thinking to myself all the while 'I'll get my own back, anyhow.' But once I was caught at this dirty work.

"They sent for my mother and said to her: 'Your son is always up to mischief. Take him away from our school.'

"After that my father beat me with a stick, but my mother cried, 'He'll never do it again.'

"So I stopped going to school, and began to go about the bazaars, and saw everything that was to be seen there, how frauds were committed and how stolen goods were sold, and what various things people did so as to get money for their support and to have a better time.

"I was a boy of about fourteen when I first took to the thorny path. At the bazaar I became friendly with a man called Akop. One day he gave me a fake gold watch and a bracelet to sell as stolen goods, and he himself pretended to be bargaining with me. Some greedy fool passed by, saw him bargaining, and was glad to buy them from me.

"After this success, I was given other business to transact. I did the work given me, but got a mere trifle in payment. 'Hold your tongue,' they told me, 'or we'll give you a good beating, and if you don't look out, kill you, maybe.'

"Once I was arrested, but my uncle's firm was well known, and no one could believe that his nephew would do this kind of thing. The Justice of the Peace, Prince

Tseretelli, believed it, I think, but he just laughed at me, saying that although I was so little, I was already impudent and daring enough to cheat grown-up people. Then I was released. Soon after that I was arrested for another affair.

"I sold an officer, a colonel, a 'gold' watch for forty rubles. 'If you can get any more like this,' he said, 'bring them to me every time.' When he saw what kind of a watch it was, however, he was very angry and reported it to the police. Then I was caught and got six weeks in prison.

"My father never came to see me, but my mother did. She was very fond of me, you see, and my being in prison upset her a great deal.

"No sooner was I released than I got caught again, and was sent back to prison for another six weeks. When, after my release, I was arrested for the third time, they sent me up before the district court as a repeat offender.

"I was sentenced to six months. I thought I must be specially unlucky to have been caught so often, but I was told it was the usual thing.

"I was a bright lad and most people liked me. I was taken on in the prison drugstore to deliver medicine. While I was taking the medicines around the cells, I made the acquaintance of a very interesting and pretty girl. She was in for the same offense as I. She was a thief, and 'worked' the shops—a 'shoplifter,' in a word. She fell in love with me at first sight and wrote to me about it. She was a Cossack girl from the Kuban district, and her name was Maria Kornienko. She was a beauty. She attracted the attention of everyone, they would look at her and think—'How pretty women are, after all.'

"A love affair began between us, but I had only a month left to serve, while she had four. We arranged that I should wait for her to come out, no matter what happened. I was released at last and went back to my old trade.

"I was very fond of Maria, and tried to earn more than ever before. I would buy her twenty or thirty rubles' worth of food and things—I had to take a cart to carry the stuff to the prison. Everybody was surprised to see how much I brought her.

"I dressed very well and was a good-looking boy, and I was so lavish with gifts to her that without noticing it, she grew very fond of me. She was only terrified that I might deceive her and not wait for her release, but I loved her so much that I waited the whole three months.

"At last she was free, she came out, and we lived together as man and wife.

"The war with Germany broke out, and I had to hide so as to avoid being conscripted to the army.

"My father—what a queer fellow he was—went against his own flesh and blood and informed the police of my whereabouts.

"I was caught once but escaped, and went on living with Maria as usual. I had to pay enormous sums of money to people to hide us. Still Maria and I went on with our trade as before.

"It was over one of these 'deals' that I got caught the second time, and was sent to Kutais. I ran away again. Maria and I started on our thieving expeditions at once and made a good bit of money. I used to wear a soldier's coat and everyone thought that the things I sold were stolen. They all bought them, though, and we lived very well. I helped my mother. She never wanted for anything now, nor Maria either.

"Then I got caught—and all over a trifle. I was wearing my soldier's uniform, and once when I met a sergeant-major, I did not salute him. He gave me such a whack across the jaw that it nearly knocked me off my feet. He arrested me and sent me to the commandant. The cat was properly out of the bag then. They found out all about how I came to be in uniform, and what I was doing. They sent me up to the military court. I was in prison for eleven months before I came up for trial.

"Maria was sorry for me. She remembered how the things I had brought her when she was in prison helped, and she began to do the same for me now. She outdid me at that, though, but still I thought she did very well, and I appreciated it. Her own line was shoplifting, but she loved me so much that she turned her hand to anything, so as to be able to give me all I wanted.

"Then the trial came up. I was sentenced to eight years' hard labor. My mother fell down in a dead faint when she heard it, and Maria burst into such terrible sobs that my heart stood still. I was led away into a separate room, and the two ladies were brought in to say goodbye to me, and for some reason a priest came in, too, and tried to soothe my mother, telling her not to cry. He gave me some sandwiches, 'to take the sharp edge off my hunger,' he said, but I would not take them.

"Then Maria, putting all her hopes in her beauty, went up to the cavalry general. Kneeling down before him, she told him who she was, and who I was, and what she wanted him to do. 'He'll go to the war,' she said, 'and make up for what he's done. He'll try to deserve it, I swear, if you'll only give him another chance.'

"The general said: 'I'm surprised at you. You a Cossack woman, pleading like this for a dirty Jew. Very well, then, I'll try to do something for him.' But he did nothing at all. I was put in chains and left to await my bitter fate, and be sent far away from everyone.

"Then all of a sudden there came a turn in the tide of events. Our February Revolution broke out. All at once I heard the prisoners breaking their chains and shouting. We were all let out into the yard. Everyone shouted and threw the chains over the fence. Then I took an axe and smashed my fetters to bits and flung them over the fence too.

"A man in uniform came and said to us: 'What are you doing here? Why do you stay? Even those who have spent twenty years in the city jail have left it. You are the only people who are waiting and doing nothing.' We wanted to go at that, but just then the chairman of the Executive Committee arrived. 'Wait a bit,' he said, 'I've sent a telegram to Kerensky. He'll let us know by tomorrow what we have to do with you.'

"We called a meeting and gave a pledge to the Provisional Government that we would not follow our old trades any longer if they let us out. Just after that the Chairman of the Executive Committee arrived and said: 'Here's a telegram from Kerensky. You're all set free. You can go. I trust you.' We said: 'We'll do our best now.'

"You can imagine the joyous welcome that was waiting for me when I got home. My mother fainted clean away with joy. I was even afraid she would die. Maria and all our friends came; it was just like a wedding. There were such tender, loving words spoken that day, and the samovar stood on the table. We all sat around it and marveled at the strange turns life takes.

"No, the February Revolution made no great impression on me. I had not lost my fondness for my profession yet. Of course, I had promised the Provisional Government to cut loose from the old life—but what of that? I had to look out for myself, hadn't I? . . .

[Nine years passed.]

"At that time I knew very little about the Soviet Union and what sort of a country it was. I had never thought about politics. I had just carried on my trade—a usual enough trade in other countries. My conscience never troubled me. So I went to the U.S.S.R.

"I was an experienced thief, an expert indeed. I thought that no matter what country I was in, and wherever there were people, I would be able to live by my trade. From Jaffa we went straight to Odessa. We were going to a country where a social revolution had taken place. I did not know yet what that was, nor why it had come about, but I had been told that people lived very badly there.

"We were approaching Odessa. You can imagine what sort of a mood I was in. I was glad to see my own country again, but I was terrified of the unknown. Then I gave myself up to the captain of the boat and told him who I was. I don't care to beat about the bush. 'You'll have to go to Odessa now,' I was told. 'We'll hand you over to the G.P.U. there, and let them find out what sort of a bird you are.'

"We arrived at Odessa on the 9th of January, 1926.

"I was handed over to the G.P.U. in Odessa. 'You may be a spy,' they said. 'You come under Point 6 of Article 58.' Then I told them all about myself, the whole truth, absolutely everything. Then I was taken to Tiflis for identification purposes. The G.P.U. banished me for three years to the Baraba District in Siberia. I was left free to live where I liked within that district. I lived there in the house of a tailor. I nearly married a young Communist girl—V. I took a great fancy to her, as she did to me. But the secretary of her Komsomol cell had his eye on her too. . . .

"He went to the local prosecutor and said: 'We can't have such characters chasing after Komsomol girls.' (He thought I was a banker instead of a thief.)

"So the prosecutor banished me to the village of Nazimovo, in the Turkhansk district of the Yenisei region. The Komsomol secretary got banished too, and I don't even know where. Wherever it was, he didn't stay there. He never did get the chance to take up with that little V.

"They let me go after a year. I wanted to go join V., but I found out she had betrayed me.

"So I left for the Caucasus instead of going to see her. As we say in the underworld, what's not meant to be won't be.

"I returned to Tiflis and my old trade. Things were not to my liking there, so I left for Batum, but even in Batum I had no luck. I began to think that my luck had deserted me for good. Then I saw that it was not a question of luck, but of something quite different. I could find no customers of the old kind, and there was not the same eagerness to buy from me. Something could be earned, of course, for there are always simple trusting fools to be found everywhere, but it just wasn't the same.

"Then I left Batum for Poti. I was arrested over a little deal in Poti and got six months. After that I went back to Tiflis, and worked a whole year without being arrested. Things were slow, though, and I got no big jobs to do.

"It was 1929. I was living in Tiflis. There was a lady living there, too, a nice, educated sort of person. She was a whore, but I didn't know it, and of course, she didn't mention it to me. I met her just as I might have met anyone else. A love affair began between us. No one would dream, to look at her, that she was a whore. As a matter of fact she was the most abominable trash in all Europe. I could not even describe her to you.

"Absolute trash. A whore who had lost all sense of decency and had no conscience. People like her have no place in our Soviet Union and in our future. I knew nothing of all this then. I lived with her and she pretended she loved me. All she wanted was money, nothing else. She kept a fancy man. I did not know anything about that either. I was simple enough to let her hook me.

"She got to know everything about me. She drew me out and I told her all my sins, things I would not have confessed to my own mother.

"Then I got into a reformatory. I was given a year for a little deal of mine. I managed to live quite decently there, though. I could move about freely. I was sent on errands and delivered parcels. I got paid for it, too, so there was really nothing much to complain about.

"Paulina, that was the woman's name, often came to see me and I would give her money. I never turned her down. At last my mother came to see me. 'This Paulina of yours is trash,' she said. 'There are no words bad enough for her. She's a prostitute. What do you mean by bringing harlots and suchlike into our house?' And even my pals said: 'You should be ashamed of yourself. She's been following the trade for years. You must have been blind not to see it.'

"Soon I was set free. They counted up all my working days in prison, and I was released. I went home and said to the woman: 'I'll give you half my things and all my money—but you must clear out of Tiflis. I don't want to even breathe the same air as you.' She took the money from me and gave it to her fancy man. 'I'm not going away,' she said, 'I'm all right here.' Then I took her by the arm and said: 'Come on, I'll buy you a railway ticket and you'll clear out.' 'All right,' she agreed, 'I'll go, then.'

"We were going into the railway station, when all of a sudden she began to scream: 'Look out, there's a bandit coming. A thief. See him—he's an international crook, he should be shot, that's what he deserves.'

"A crowd gathered round. I said to them: 'There's nothing to see, so clear out, if you please. There's nothing interesting going to happen at all, absolutely nothing. It's just a little quarrel between husband and wife.' But she went on screaming: 'He's a desperate bandit, I tell you. He's done things that would make you shiver to think of. I turn all sick when I see him, I'm just ready to faint. Hold him, all of you, else he'll run away.'

"Then a couple of Chekists came up and arrested us. She told them all about me, all she knew. I was sent to prison, and they let her go.

"The Board of the Georgian G.P.U. sentenced me to three years' hard labor. That was on the 29th of April, 1932.

"So in April, 1932, I was sent by the G.P.U. to work on the canal that was being constructed between the White Sea and the Baltic. I was horrified when I got to the place. It seemed to me that now my life was over, that I was a lost man here, and that I would never see Tiflis again.

"I did not fancy the spot at all. Although it was springtime, the snow lay thick everywhere. The place looked withered and lifeless. I felt so depressed. I could see no way out. The three years before me seemed to me worse than anything else in the world. I was sent to section 7, a small station called Sosnovetz. The camp began there.

"I arrived there feeling as if I were coming to a cemetery. It was raining. The trees were mean, shriveled little things, and there was not even a blade of grass to be seen. Stones stuck up out of the ground all over, and I thought I would very likely die here on these stones and never live to see anything else.

"This is the state of mind I was in when I was sent off to work on the rocks at Lock No. 14. The rocks had to be broken and blasted, and the work was very hard. The worst of it was I had never worked in my life. I regarded hard labor as a crime and a disgrace.

"The first few days there I only turned out thirty, and even twenty, percent of what was expected, and the foreman, Bufius, a German, said: 'Fancy a big, strong hulking fellow like you not being able to work. You should be ashamed of yourself.' I thought that was ridiculous, and told him off. 'It's only fools and horses that work,' I said, 'and I'm neither the one nor the other, and if you're so fond of work, come and do mine. Let's see what sort of a fool you are. A German, too.'

"He told Tryaskov about it. Tryaskov was our head foreman. A busy, energetic chap. He tried to talk to me, but I would not listen. I cursed him and told him to clear out.

"So that was how things went on. I hardly did thirty percent, just enough, in fact, to keep me from falling asleep. I was thinking all the time about Greece and my trade and my past. It seemed to me like a fairy tale now.

"Then the chief, Sapronov, passed by. The foreman rushed out and told him about me. The chief said: 'That's odd. Everybody works here. It hardly ever happens that anyone refuses. Our work is very urgent. I'm surprised to hear you refuse. Very likely there's something you don't understand!' So he went on talking to me, but I did not take much interest in what he said.

"'I'm accustomed to seeing the results of my work,' I said. 'I've always worked for myself and I could always see whether my living conditions improved or not, but who's going to get anything out of what I'm doing now—I don't know. And as for you, you're just a government official who's been put in charge here and you say whatever you've been ordered to say.'

"He seemed astonished and went away.

"Soon after that our reform instructor, Varlamov, came up and said to me: 'Go and see Sapronov after work. He wants to speak to you. He's surprised at you, can't understand you at all.' I went to Sapronov. The table was laid for tea, and there were biscuits and caramels and a good brand of cigarettes.

"I smiled to myself as I went in. Aha, I thought, he takes me for a child, does he? Thinks he'll win my confidence this way? We sat down and fell into conversation. We talked a long time. He was interested in my past, and I told him everything. He was awfully surprised at the way I had lived. We drank our tea and ate the biscuits, and I could see he was a decent guy, the kind one could talk to.

"'Well,' he said, 'you've been everywhere and you've seen what sort of reform they go in for abroad. They clubbed you and punched you in the face. Of course, we aren't asking you to work in return for behaving decently to you. It's hard, I know, it's no paradise here, but then, if it was like paradise everybody would be committing crimes so as to get sent here. We don't want that. We demand work because we're working for ourselves, and not for the capitalists. We want our country to develop and be prosperous.'

"He gave me a cigarette, and I went home to the barracks. I wondered all the way home about the new fashion in prisons and hard labor.

"Next day, more out of a sort of liking for that fellow than anything else, I did eighty-seven percent.

"The day after that Prokhorsky, the head of the department, came by with Sapronov. 'I can't understand you at all,' said Prokhorsky. 'Why don't you want to work? We aren't doing it for anyone except ourselves. We're working to make our own country a better one, and if things are better here, it'll better for you, too. You're not a counterrevolutionary, are you? Socially, you're close to us. If you meet us halfway, we'll look after you. If you work well, we'll release you sooner, and we'll teach you a trade, a better one than your own. You'll get such splendid qualifications that every door will be open to you when you're set free.' That was how he spoke to me. Then he said goodbye and went away.

"Well, I thought to myself, that's the limit. What are they bothering me for every day? I can't get rid of them now. Wanting to make a worker out of a thief.

"Three days or so later, the reform instructor, Varlamov, came up to me. 'Prokhorsky and Sapronov are asking for you again,' he said. I went off to see them. We had a talk over our tea and biscuits. They started telling me about the new State where there are no capitalists, nor property owners. They drew me a picture, as you might say, of the work to be done and of a life—such as we had never even dreamed of.

"'It's interesting,' I said, 'to hear that there aren't going to be any more thieves in your State. That's very interesting.' 'Of course there won't be any thieves,' they said. 'Nobody will have any need to steal, and who'll they rob? It's the seamy side of capitalism that produces thieves.'

"We talked a lot about that, and about other things as well. Prokhorsky told me I was wrong, that there was another life before me now, and that thieves would have to learn another trade. That struck me as funny. I thought, well, if it's like that, I really suppose one should work, particularly as I had already felt something was going wrong, way back in Tiflis.

"So I went home and next day I did a hundred and forty percent of the work expected of me. Anybody who has ever worked on rocks knows what that means. It's the very devil. The day after that I did the same amount. I started in to work. Then I thought about my old life and what I had been. It wasn't that I was sorry for having been a thief. Life had driven me to it. Prokhorsky himself said it was the seamy side of life. Then it turned out it wasn't really my fault. It would be my fault, though, if I had the chance at another life and still went on thieving.

"Funny thing, my conscience began to worry me. I wanted to work then, I didn't need any driving or encouragement. Once I reached a hundred and fifty percent. Everyone in our brigade began to do over a hundred percent. We were glad when this happened. We went around feeling really pleased with ourselves, and after that we were able to get anything we wanted at the camp store. I got some good clothes and boots.

"When I saw the decent way I was treated and cared for, I was ready to work my fingers to the bone to please them, and I said to the brigade: 'Let's do our best.' 'Yes of course, we will,' they all agreed. So we worked like devils and had no time to think of anything. Sometimes Maria Kornienko came into my head and then something would catch at my heart.

"Yes, we certainly worked conscientiously. There was no reason why we shouldn't. We could not do otherwise, after Comrade Firin's order came into force. This order said that all criminals coming under Article 35 of the Code, all social miscreants and women, were to receive the best and most humane treatment. We were not bullied, and not only that, no one dared even to lay a finger on us. No one had the right to raise his hand to us.

"If ever Comrade Firin saw that anything was not just as it should be, pity the official who had failed to carry out his instructions.

"We beat all records. We got up to a hundred and fifty percent. You would hardly believe the way we ran around with those wheelbarrows of rocks. Actually ran with those loaded wheelbarrows. We did things that it would be hard to tell about. Every one of us was trying his best, without stopping. We could see it was important work. It wasn't any of your silly stone-breaking like they had given us to do in the Occupation Forces' prison. We had a goal now, and it goaded us on.

"We wanted to reach our goal as soon as possible. Besides, our work was noticed and we were properly looked after.

"We started to help the ones that lagged behind. We did social work. I was elected a member of the Production Committee of Three. Our brigade turned out to be the best. We were transferred to work on concrete. They wanted to teach us a trade, and we learned it. We turned out a hundred and eighty mixings. The head foreman, Martynov, noticed us. Sapronov and Prokhorsky said: 'You're doing well. We've come to admire your work.'

"One fine morning these two officials, Sapronov and Prokhorsky, came up to me and said: 'Some of the "Article Thirty-five" men have refused to work. You ought to go and talk to them. Make them go to work. They're starting a row, those who have not gotten their sentences reduced for the anniversary of the Revolution.'

"I went off. All the Article Thirty-five men were collected in the barrack. There were cutthroats and thieves—old hands at the game, crooks and swindlers of all kinds. They jeered at me when I came in. 'First you were totally against work, and now you're in with the bosses. Clear out of here.'

"Then I said: 'Just let me say two words.' Some of them said: 'All right, spit it out, but hurry up—we want to sleep' (it was still daytime).

"They were all lying flat on their backs on their bunks. It didn't look as though there would be any swaying them.

"'Listen, gentlemen,' I began. 'We've got to look at the social improvements. We're thieves, that's what we are, but it seems there aren't going to be any soon, in this State.' A good many of them burst out laughing and said: 'How're you going to manage that?' Then I got up on one of the bunks, and by that time all the men were as curious as anything, and I said: 'We're all living together here like one family. For years and years we carried on a common business together—robbing and thieving. This brought us all close together, as close as a tie of blood, and as for me, I'm not sucking up to anyone, but I can see the changes that have come about and it's because of them that I've taken to work, and that's why I've come here now.'

"'What changes?' they asked. 'Gentlemen,' I said, 'our world, that is, the criminal world, is going to pot. You ought to be able to see that yourselves, and get it into your heads. If there are any greenhorns here, new to the business, let them stick to their hopes, but people like me—with experience—they understand no end of things and feel like I do. The underworld is going to pot. I won't say as much for other countries, but it looks like this at home, and even if it isn't so just now, it soon will be.'

"Some of them said: 'It certainly does look a bit like it.' Others said: 'No way.' I painted them such a picture of life and work that they simply gasped.

"'Who shall we steal from,' I said, 'if there are no rich folk and nobody has any property?'

"Then they said: 'Even if there are only poor folk left, and no rich, people will steal just the same. But if they are all pretty well off, and there are no poor, then the criminal world really will go to pot.' 'That's very likely what will happen,' I said. 'And so we ought to learn another trade. We're bound to work, and it'll all be put down to our credit soon.' But they wouldn't go out to work that day. They shouted and argued awhile and they went back to sleep. Next day I had another talk with them.

"'Come on, gentlemen, let's get to work,' I said. 'How do you do it?' they said. The third day I wanted to ask for tea and biscuits to be given us, so that we could have a good talk, but it wasn't necessary after all.

"They all turned out to work and were quite set to be reforged.

"Then I was appointed assistant reform instructor. I organized six working collectives. We worked splendidly. During the 'Storm Days' one of my collectives turned out two hundred and twenty percent of the work set for them. None of the others did less than a hundred and twenty. Practically all of their sentences have been remitted.

"I carry quite a bit of weight now in the Punishment Isolation Houses. The masses have begun to respect me. I was entrusted with the feeding of the men in the prison camp. I did a good bit of work among the national minorities. I put an end to free feeding and stealing in the kitchen.

"We used to read the papers. We got together a godless circle and set about liquidating illiteracy.

"I was appointed commissar of Section 5, and head reform instructor.

"People worked for me like devils, although I never laid a finger on them. At present I am chief of the Punishment Isolation House, and an instructor. At the time of writing this, I have only a few days left to serve. I have been eighteen months in the camp. I am leaving it with a feeling that there is no gloomy past behind me, but only a bright future."

This ends the story of Rothenburg's life. In the autumn of 1933 he was awarded the Order of the Red Banner of Labor. It was as a free citizen that he went to the construction work on the new canal—one linking the Volga and Moscow Rivers. He spent a month there, and then asked leave to go to Tiflis. He wanted to see his mother, whom he had left grieving over him.

I can imagine his feelings when he arrived at his birthplace, and the quiver of pride and ecstasy with which he opened the door and greeted his parents.

I wish you every success, Comrade Rothenburg, in your new life. May all your hopes be realized.

You must send this story to Cairo, to Maria Kornienko, the Cossack woman.

So that is the end of our interesting story. Now we'll try to scrape the superficial tissues a little, as they say, with the surgeon's knife.

A skeptic who was accustomed to have his doubts about human emotions, might feel dubious on three points.

The first would be—had Rothenburg's character really undergone a change after all he had passed through, and had he, on coming into contact with the proper system of reform, yielded to its influence and become a different man?

Or was he simply trying a new "con"?

Or, being by no means a stupid fellow, had he taken everything into consideration and made up his mind that the end of the underworld was approaching and that the best thing for a thief to do was to learn a new trade? If he had come to this conclusion, then the skeptic might say his behavior was prompted not by normal considerations but by necessity.

I have placed these three theories in the scales of my professional capacity for understanding people's motives, and I have come to the conclusion that the change in Rothenburg was due to proper treatment, that he reformed his own character, taking into consideration, of course, the changes in the life of today in this country. I am as certain of this as I am of myself. If it is not so, then I am but a naive fellow, a dreamer, and a simpleton—things that I have never been accused of in my life.

I would be prepared to vouch for this man leading a new life now. Perhaps that is saying a little too much; I mean that I would answer for it under our noncapitalistic conditions.

Once more, I wish Rothenburg every happiness; I would like to tell him in his own words: "Your criminal underworld is going to pot."

I want to live in a country where there are no locks on the doors and where such sad words as thief, robbery, and murder will soon be obsolete.[2]

2. An anecdote of the time ran: Question: Who built the White Sea–Baltic Canal? Answer: The right side was built by those who asked, the left by those who answered.

Mister Twister
Samuil Marshak (1933)

SAMUIL YAKOVLEVICH MARSHAK (1887–1964) WAS ONE OF THE MOST BELOVED OF ALL CHILDREN'S TALETELLERS, AND "MISTER TWISTER" WAS ONE OF HIS MOST ENDURING WORKS, TRANSLATED INTO MANY LANGUAGES AND PRINTED IN MILLIONS OF COPIES OVER THE DECADES. ITS INVENTIVE RHYMES AND CATCHY RHYTHM REINFORCED THE STRONG POLITICAL MESSAGE.

1

Tourists
Abroad
Do their touring
Through Cook.
Whenever
The wanderlust
Moves you
To book
A trip
Round the world
All its wonders to see—
The tower of Pisa,
The Kremlin, Paree—
Cook
In a flash—
Should you relish
The notion—
Will charter a ship

For a sail
On the ocean,

Translated by Sam Raphael Friedman in *Soviet Literature*, no 1. (1948), pp. 7–19, and corrected against S. Marshak, *Mister Tvister* (Moscow: Molodaia gvardiia, 1933).

Or furnish a plane
For your personal use,
Or send you
A camel,
Or maybe
A moose;
Reserve you
A room
In the finest hotel,
With breakfast in bed
At the touch
Of a bell.

To highlands,
And lowlands,
To East
And to West—
To all lands
Cook
Takes you,
Each dressed
In its best.

2

Mister
Twister
Quondam
Minister,
Mister
Twister,
Millionaire,
Banker and broker,
Owner of stocks,
Newspapers, steamers,
And real-estate block,
Opined that he needed
A rest from his labors,
A trip round the wide world
Without all his neighbours.

And so
He decided
To trek with his wife

And Suzie,
His daughter,
The light of his life.
His Suzie
Was willing,
And likewise his wife.

"Let's go!"
Whooped Suzie.
"Call James!
Where's the car?
Lct's all go and visit
The U.S.S.R.!"

"But darling daughter,"
Her fond parent said,
"Who planted
Such nonsense
In your pretty head?

"There's Spain to visit,
There's bullfights to see..."
Said darlingest Suzie:
"Then go
Without me!
I want something different:
Fresh caviar
And shchi,
And loll
In the shade
Of a cranberry tree."[1]
Old Twister,
He pleaded
And fumed,
Cried "Pshaw!"
But Suzie
Was firm,
And her word
Was law.

3

Anon
Rings the phone

---

1. Shchi is cabbage soup. The "cranberry tree" is a Russian expression for foreign misconceptions about Russia.

At Cook's:
"M'lad!
Reserve
Four staterooms:
New York—
Leningrad.
With a bath
And a pool,
And a garden,
Begad!
And listen,
Be sure
The crowd
Isn't low-brow,
No Negroes
Or Hindos,
Or riffraff
From "Ho-chow"!
Old Twister,
He's touchy
Concerning
Dark faces.
He can't stand the sight
Of those colored races."
Answers Cook
At the telephone:
"Oh yes, Sir!
Okay, Sir!
We're glad to oblige you!
We'll do as you say, Sir!"

4

In exactly
Ten minutes
The boat was to sail,
When along came
The Twisters
And climbed through the rail.

With his spouse
In her travelling clothes.
Her tortoise-shell glasses
Perched high on her nose;
He came
With his Suzie,

Bewitchingly dressed,
Her marmoset monkey
Pressed close to her breast;

He came
With a mountain
Of trunks all in tags,
He came
With four giants
With forty-four bags.

5

The steamer is sailing,
A-sailing
The sea,
To the S.U. a-
sailing—
The U.S. a-lee.
Its course
Lies due eastward
As your crow ever
flies;
Its wake
Churns and gurgles
As onward
It plies.

Mister
Twister
Quondam
Minister,
Mister
Twister,
Millionaire,
Banker and broker
And newspaper king,
While on the briny
Decided he'd try
To learn
To play tennis
To keep himself spry.

On deck
In a garden
Fenced in by a net,
He leaps for
A ball
In a wild pirouette;
All shaded
By palms
From the sun's blazing rays,
He chases
A ball
Like a bull in a maze.

Then laved
In a lather
And pleased as Punch
He jumps
In the pool,
Where he has his lunch.
Refreshed,
He makes
For the billiard hall,
Where he "takes his cue"
From a stand
By the wall.

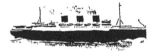

And the ship
Sails on
As a ship should sail—
Like a palace fair
From a fairy tale.
And all
Of his playmates
Are folk of his nation—

No Negroes
Or Chinese
But gents of his station.
The Negroes
And Chinese
In making the trip
Were packed

All aboard
In a far different ship.
The Negroes
And Chinese
Were packed in a freighter;
The sea waves
Or fumes
Floored them sooner
Or later.

6

Mister
Twister
Travelling far,
Is tourist bound
For the
U.S.S.R.

The hustle,
The bustle
Of Leningrad nears.
Off to the starboard
The skyline appears.
On steely gray water
Ride boats
By the score,
And workshops unending
Extend from the shore.

Clutching
Their hats
As they strut down the plank,
The Twisters
Are soon
Strolling over the
bank.

Then,
With a glance
At a golden-tipped spire
They turn
To their auto
And test every tire.

The ladies
Are seated,
The luggage

Is stowed,
The car with a rush
Roars off down the road—
The driver
In front,
Where a driver should be,
Old Twister
In back,
With a bag on his knee;
His spouse
At his left,
Her umbrella clutched tight,
The monkey
And Suzie
Squeezed in at his right.

7

Mister
Twister,
Quondam
Minister,
Mister
Twister,
Millionaire,
Drives up

And enters
Hotel Angleterre.

Chewing
Away at his gold-band
Cigar,
He cries
(Speaking English),
"Well, folks,
Here we are!
Porter!
My bags!
Hi, clerk!

How're tricks?
Get all the cables
I sent you?—
All six?
My suites—
Are they ready?
We're all feeling blown.
I'm dying for victuals.
I'd welcome
A bone!"

"Your rooms, Sir,
Are ready—
The second floor, right.
It's cool there
And quiet,
With plenty of light."

8

Past mirrors,
Round corners,
With slow measured pace,
They marched on
And onward—
Like snails in a race.

In front
Strode the porter
In gold-braided gear,
Behind him
Came Twister,
"A flea in his ear,"
Behind him
His spouse
Looking quite *comme il faut,*
Behind her
The maiden,
The monkey in tow.

All
Of a sudden
The Twisters
Stopped dead.
They gaped
And they goggled,
"Lord help us!"
They said.

Along
The hall
From a suite
Near theirs,
Came a Negro
Calmly
Bound for the stairs.

From the suite
Near theirs
Came
The dark-skinned man;
He was big
And strong
And dressed spick and span;
And he puffed
His pipe

As he strolled along,
And he smiled
To himself
As he hummed
A song.

And the numerous
Mirrors
That covered
The walls
Reflected
A picture
Of numerous
Halls,
And along
Each hall
From a suite
Near theirs
Came a Negro
Calmly
Bound for the stairs.

Mister
And Mrs.
(The maiden too),
Wished they were back
In Kalamazoo.

"What's this!"
Roared Twister
"Does he live here?

I'd rather live
With a racketeer!
"Gangway!"
Roared Twister,
And turned in his tracks—
"We'll find a place
Where there ain't no blacks!"
Then back through the
Hallway
In single file,
Dashed Twister
And daughter
(neglecting all style!)
Her monkey rushed
Headlong,
His wife
Scuttled
Fast;
The porter
Alone
Walked
Leisurely,
Last.

They tore down
The stairway
At break-neck speed,
They tore
Through the door
In a mad stampede!
They rushed
To their auto,
Piled in with a crash!
And in frumious silence
Drove off like a flash.

The porter
Thought hard,
As they sped
Down the street,
Then went
To the telephone
Next to his seat.

He dialed
A number:
Four 2's and an 0—
"Hotel Astoria?

Is that you,
Joe?
"This is Peter
The Porter...
Uh-huh, that's me.
Now listen old boy,
It's like this:
You see—

A party
Of tourists
Are headed for you:
A man, wife and daughter,
And monkey—
Some crew!

"They're the kind
As talk big—
With their dough
And white faces.
They won't stand the sight
Of the coloured races.

"They'll ask
For a room, Joe,
Just shoo them away!
You said it!
So long, Joe,
Be sure they don't stay!"

He dialed
Again:
Four 4's
And a 2—

"Hotel Sicilia?
Steve,
Is that you?
"This is Peter
The Porter...
Uh-huh, that's me.
Now listen, old boy,
It's like this:
You see—
A party
Of tourists
May come your way:
A man, wife and daughter,
And monkey—
Today!

"They're the kind
As talk big—
With their dough
And white faces.
They won't stand the sight
Of the coloured races.

"They'll ask
For a room, Steve,
Be sure they don't stay!"

This time
He dialed
Three 5's
And a 10—

"Hotel Europa?
Is that you,
Ben?
"This is Peter
The Porter...
Uh-huh, right you are.
Now listen, old boy,
It's like this..."
et cetera...

9

Up
Every avenue—
Quiet and clean—
Down
Every avenue
Whizzed a machine,

Hotel Astoria,
Gogol Street;—
"No,"
Said the porter,
"Nary a suite!
We're full up
And booked
Till I don't know when.
The cotton-field farmers
Are meeting
Again."

Hotel Sicilia,
Pestel Gate:
"No,"
Said the porter,
"You're just too late,
We're full up
And booked
For a month
In advance—
It's a congress
Of breeders
Of mulberry
Plants."

Hotel Europa,
Pushkin Place:—
"No,"
Said the porter,
"Sorry no space!
We're full up
And booked
For a week
Or so.
A Tatar troupe's here now
To put on
A show."

Up
Every avenue
Whizzed the machine,
"Jumping"
The red lights,
"Racing" the green.

All of a sudden
A tire blew out.
Little by little
The fuel gave out.

10

Mister Twister,
Quondam Minister,
Mister Twister,
Millionaire,
Arrives
Again
At Hotel Angleterre.

With him
His spouse
In her travelling clothes,
Her tortoise-shell glasses
Now low
On her nose;
With him
His Suzie
All rumpled and mumpish
Her marmoset monkey
Decidedly dumpish.

He entered
The lobby
Demanding his suite.
He wanted
A shower
And something
To eat.
The clock
Struck 12—
High time for bed.

From his post
Came the porter
With leisurely tread.
"You're late,"
Said the porter.
"Your rooms,
Sir,
Are taken!"
"The devil!"
Cried Twister,
Now thoroughly
Shaken.

"You see,"
Said the porter,
"We're packed
to the ceiling."

"Again,"
Whispered Suzie,
"Go automobiling?
"I won't!"
She wailed.
"It's a wild-goose chase.
If we can't

Get a suite here,
Then buy out the place!"

"With pleasure,"
Said Twister,
And dolefully sighed,
"Or a house on the Neva!
With pleasure!"
He cried.

"But, darling,
Remember,
You're not in Chicago
Or even,"
He added,
"In old Santiago.
In Leningrad
People
Just simply don't sell—
You can't buy a house,
Let alone
A hotel!"

"Look!"
Gruffed the banker
And owner of stock
To the Leningrad porter,
Who looked
At the clock,
"Wangle
A place
For the ladies and me,
And hang the price!"
Quoth the porter:
"You see,
Money

Can't get you
A place here tonight!
Our rooms
Are all taken
By black folk and white!"

"My darling,"
Growled Twister,
"It looks pretty bad.
Let's go find
A park bench,
We'll sleep there, begad!"

11

His Suzie
And spouse
Stood aghast
At the notion.
The Leningrad porter
Soon stilled the commotion.
He offered
Them cots—
"Proletarian fare!"
And the Twister
He brought
A "luxurious" chair!

The ladies
Turned in
And were soon counting.
"Ho-hum!"
Yawned Twister,
"Me for some sleep!"
And so off to dreamland—
Lodged in a chair,
That stood near the door
Of Hotel Angleterre—

Dropped Mister
Twister
Quondam Minister,

Mister
Twister
Millionaire.

12

He slept...
While sleeping
He smiled and he scowled.
He dreamed
A dream.
And he laughed
And he howled.

He dreamed
He was homeless,
Alone in a town.
Tramping the avenues
Up and down,
When all of a sudden
Who should appear
But Cook
In a plane—
From a sky that seemed clear!

Twister
Was tickled,
As tickled
As could be:
"You're just
The guy
I wanted to see!"

The airplane landed
And Twister
Stepped in.

The plane
Climbed high,
And it flew and it flew
Till it reached his mansion
In Kalamazoo.

Then out
He jumped
And he rushed
To the gates.
"No plathe,"

Lisped the butler,
"For you in the Th-tate-th!"—
And slammed the door
With a sneer
And a glare.
And Twister awoke
In Hotel Angleterre—
Awoke in a sweat
In an angular chair—
Mister Twister,
Quondam Minister,
Mister Twister,
Millionaire.

13

Bright and early
The bootblack
Appeared,
Collected
The footwear
And mightily smeared.
He smeared on the polish
And warbled
A lay.
He smeared on the polish
And polished away—
At others
Marked Soviet
German and French,
British, Bulgarian,
Made at the bench,
Czechoslovakian,
Danish
And Dutch.
He polished
And smeared
With a masterly touch.

He finished the lot
With a flick
And a snap!
He whistled a tune
As he pulled on his cap;

When lo
And behold!

From a well-screened chair
Rose a foreigner
Yawning
And smoothing
His hair,
And out of the office
Headed for him
Came Peter
The porter,
Neat and trim.

"We have,"
Said the porter
"A three-room suite,
With a bath
And a sun parlor
All complete.
I'll show you
The place,
If you like,
Although—
Perhaps
There's something
You ought to know:
In the room to the left
There's a Bengalese,
In the room to the right
A Singhalese;
In the room above
There's a Japanese,
In the room below
A Javanese;
Across the hall
An Annamese
Together with
Some Siamese.
Up the hall
There's a girl from Malay
Down the hall
A girl from Tokay;
Not to forget

The folk from Tibet,
The Abyssinians
And Palestinians,
The Indonesians
And Polynesians.
Along the hall
There's a Hindu
And Zulu."
Old Twister,
He chuckled
And slapped his thigh.
"Okay! my boy!"
He roared in reply,
"Give us the keys
And make it
Snappy!"
He whistled a tune—
He was thoroughly
Happy.

Then grabbing
His Suzie
And monkey
And all,
And followed by Mrs.,
He danced down the hall.
With a skip
And a hop,
Like a prancing bear,
Upsetting
The calm
Of Hotel
Angleterre.
Went Mister
Twister,
Quondam
Minister,
Mister
Twister,
Millionaire.

Anecdotes

What's the difference between Stalin and Moses?

Moses took the Jews out of Egypt, while Stalin took them from the Central Committee. [3:12]

Rumor has it that Point Number 20 of the Party membership application, which asks whether the applicant has ever been arrested, and for what, will be followed by a new Point Twenty-one, which asks: If not, then why? [3:13]

A customer pushes his plate back in disgust and asks the waitress: "Do you serve garbage like this every day?"

"No, we're closed Mondays." [4:24]

A Jew stops a well-known Communist at an ostentatious funeral and asks with amazement how much the whole thing is costing the state.

"Very expensive. I think it cost about one hundred thousand," the Communist answers with a touch of pride.

The Jew's indignant answer: "And what about the economizing policy? For half that price, I can bury the entire Central Committee. And with pleasure." [3:11]

A little boy at the zoo asks: "Why is that stork standing on one leg?"

His father: "What can he do? It's the economizing policy." [3:11]

"There aren't any more absentee workers in our factory."

"Great."

"No, not really. There's none in the factory because they're all sitting in the bar." [3:25]

A professor asks a worker-student, "What's the Donbass?"

"A Spanish nobleman, Comrade Professor." [3:30]

The Soviet censor reviews *Popular Astronomy for the People*, published by Gosizdat. A day later, Gosizdat receives this telegram: "I direct your attention to an unforgivable oversight. Destroy the edition. In the next version, the planet Jupiter[1] must be called Ju-lenin." [3:31]

Bekhner's famous book *Ants* is banned by the censor, in view of the fact that ant society is recognized to be counterrevolutionary and study may prove harmful to Komsomols. [3:31–32]

Let's go full speed ahead to socialism—and you can drop me off in Warsaw. [3:32]

For anecdote sources, see *Blue Blouse Skit*, above.

1. Piter: old nickname for St. Petersburg, renamed Leningrad in 1924.

An agitator assures a meeting that after a few five-year plans, not only will most Soviet citizens have their own cars, they'll have their own airplanes.

A listener is so carried away with the idea that he whispers to his wife: "Won't that be the life, Manka, we can take the plane anytime we hear they're selling cabbage in Moscow." [4:48]

Even before the district was completely collectivized, they started building a radio relay station in one kolkhoz. A peasant approaches it timidly and asks: "Comrade, does this thing really send messages without wires?"

"Absolutely."

"And you'll be able to hear it all over?"

"Absolutely."

"Even across the border?"

"That's right."

The peasant races up to the microphone and shouts: "Help! Thief!" [4:49]

The corpse of a drowned man was discovered in the Moscow River. No signs of force were found on the body except for two state lottery tickets. [3:47]

The speaker at a meeting is talking on the theme "We will catch the capitalist countries."

An audience member asks: "When we catch them, can we stay there?" [4:45]

A foreigner asks a Soviet Communist with amazement: "How do you get everyone to sign up for the bond drive voluntarily?"

"It all depends on your approach. For instance, in your country, no cat would eat mustard on its own, but in our country it will."

"How's that?"

"Easy, just smear the mustard under its tail, and the cat will eat it voluntarily." [4:19]

HIGH STALINISM, 1932—1936

Granddaddy Sebastian Went Godless
Gr. Bortnik (1934)

MARXISTS WERE ATHEISTS BY CONVICTION, AND THE BOLSHE-
VIKS SOUGHT TO ABOLISH RELIGIOUS BELIEF BY PROPAGANDA.
THE STATE-SPONSORED *BEZBOZHNIKI* (GODLESS ONES) AT-
TACKED RELIGIOUS "SUPERSTITION" WITH PERSONAL AGITATION
AND IN THE PAGES OF THEIR JOURNAL, FROM WHICH THIS AC-
COUNT IS TAKEN. SOME WORKERS *HAD* LOST THEIR FAITH IN GOD
BEFORE THE REVOLUTION BECAUSE OF CORRUPT PRIESTS OR
NATURAL DISASTERS; BUT THIS EXAMPLE SEEMS CONTRIVED—
THOUGH IT WAS CERTAINLY REPRESENTATIVE OF "GODLESS" TES-
TIMONIALS OF THE 1920S AND 1930S. NOTE ALSO HERE THE IN-
FLUENCE OF THE URBAN SON UPON THE RURAL FATHER.

Just a year ago, Granddaddy Sebastian Andreevich Demkov was one of the most pious old men in
the village of Shkryabin.

And then Granddaddy Sebastian changed. You
wouldn't recognize him now.

"I was going to visit his hut for some reason," says
Praskovya Stebunova, his neighbor, in amazement,
"and what do you think?" He's taken down all the
icons in his hut, and says that he's burned them in
the stove. He says why should those carved idols
waste room. They had their time on the wall, so enough with 'em."

Recently I dropped by Granddaddy Sebastian's for a chat.

I asked him to talk a bit about himself—how he became an atheist, so I could
write about it in *The Godless.*

"Ded Sebast'ian stal bezbozhnikom," *Bezbozhnik,* no. 12/10 (October 1934), p. 16.

Demkov grinned. He rolled a rough cigarette, took a long drag, and said: "Well, if that's what you want, I'll tell you why I gave up religion in my old age." He cleared his throat and went on: "My story is modest. My wife, Anna, died last year. Back then I followed the religion and observed all the rites. I asked Father Lebedev to bury my wife.

"'Father,' I say, 'my wife just died, please give her a Christian burial.'

"'Sure,' answered Father Gregory, 'but Sebastian Andreevich, do you have any money? You'll have to pay me twenty rubles plus four loaves of bread.'

"'No, Father,' I say, 'I can't get my hands on that much money right now. Here's five rubles, and I'll also give you a loaf.'

"'What a cheapskate,' snapped the priest. 'You can go find yourself a priest at the bazaar for that price.'

"He wouldn't even talk to me. What a calamity, I think. There's no money, and my bread is all gone, and I can't bury my wife without a priest. So I begged the priest to take half the money and bread now for the funeral. But no, he was stubborn. That was when I lost my temper: 'You're a bloodsucker, not a priest! All you want is to live off other people's misfortunes. Here I've believed in you priests for seventy years, and wouldn't even listen when something bad was said about you.'

"So I returned home from the priest's that day," Granddaddy Sebastian continued his story, "and buried my wife without a church ceremony. The neighbors helped. My faith was shaken forever that day.

"When my grandson Kondrasha came on his vacation (he runs a club in the Donbass, for the Sherbinovsk Mine Administration, Shaft No. 41), he brought a year's worth of *The Godless* along with him. I enjoyed reading it so much that I didn't leave a page unread. From that time on I've been an atheist.

"I ask my fellow godless," he added, "that when I die, they bury me to either violin music or an accordion."

Nine Girls

Sergei Tretyakov (1935)

TRETYAKOV (1892–1939) WAS ANOTHER OF THE DEDICATED
REVOLUTIONARY WRITERS DESTROYED IN THE STALIN PURGES. A
PARTICIPANT IN PROLETKULT, BLUE BLOUSE, AND LEF, HE
ACHIEVED FAME THROUGH POLITICAL THEATER AND ATTRACTED
THE ATTENTION OF BERTOLT BRECHT. IN THE 1930S TRETYAKOV
LED SKETCH WRITERS WHO JOURNEYED TO WORKPLACES TO

From *Vchera i segodnia* (Moscow: Khudozhestvennaia literatura, 1960), pp. 305–316.

WRITE ABOUT "REAL" SOVIET PEOPLE. HE SPENT TWO YEARS ON A KOLKHOZ RESEARCHING THIS PIECE.

PASHA ANGELINA (1912–1959), FROM A DONETSK OBLAST PEASANT FAMILY, IN 1935 ORGANIZED A WOMEN'S TRACTOR BRIGADE WITH THE SLOGAN "MY 100,000 GIRLFRIENDS, GET ONTO THE TRACTORS!" HER SUCCESSES MADE THE WOMAN TRACTOR DRIVER A PERMANENT CLICHÉ IN POPULAR ENTERTAINMENT.

She sits and leans forward slightly.

Her tense, extended hands are joined on her lap—it's the same grip used to steer a tractor when it jerks through frozen clods of autumn soil.

The transparent tangle of her bangs falls into her eyes, which glisten through the hair, concentrated, with a cold, unwavering gleam.

That's how they watch a furrow at night, when the "Bat" lantern flickers in the wind, but the job has to be done right.

She doesn't jest. Doesn't stumble in her speech. Her words flow, measured and serious. In her restrained and muffled voice a metallic ring sometimes appears—that's when she remembers old insults and hardships overcome in pain. Sometimes a surprisingly gentle softness is woven into her voice—she's talking about friendship or something fun—and then her lips confirm what she's said with a smile. Only the lips. Not the voice or the eyes.

Eight girls sit next to her in a row. They have strong hands, accustomed to grappling with iron, and eyes of such clarity that it seems they've been washed by the rain. There is a great calm in their silence. They know—whatever Pasha Angelina said must be true.

They're used to it. The behavior that the brigade learned at work has gone beyond the boundaries of the job. Sometimes even Pasha smiles, remembering how scared they were of losing her, their leader, in Mostorg.[1] They held hands as in a round dance and walked up the staircase, past the stalls, toward the cashiers, and through the entrance to the bus.

"Like ducklings," I remark.

A calm smile touches their faces. They take the comment without humor. Yes, just like ducklings. Each is wearing the same jacket, the same collars folded back on their blouses.

"What can I do with them!" exclaims Pasha, as if flustered, but actually proud. "I buy something, and they buy it too."

"We were visiting Comrade Sarkisov, president of the Don Regional Committee," she continues. "He begged one, then another to eat. They bow, thank him, but just sit there without moving. So I say, 'OK, girls, let's eat'—and right away they begin."

---

1. A large Moscow department store.

Pasha speaks a pure Russian. But if she's moved by her memories or the heat of the moment, strange intonations sneak into her speech. It's a Greek accent.

Out of the nine girls in her famous tractor brigade, five are Greek.

"Nei kuricha," one of them says. That's Greek for "nine girls."

"There are Hellenic Greeks," Pasha specifies, "but Vera Mikhailovna here is a Tatar Greek, and we generally speak Tatar Greek."

And truly, if they're talking about private, unofficial matters, they quickly begin to speak Tatar.

Ancient Greece has come to the Soviet Five-Year Plan!

How many centuries has mankind been amazed by the statues of beautiful white heroines, brave young men, and commanders it has dug from the earth. One glance at them makes for the legend of mankind's beautiful springtime.

Verses traced on parchment telling of battles and exploits, of friendship and hatred, of voyages and wars, fly across the centuries from that age to ours. A magnificent era, which to this day is a lesson to man.

But take a look here! A volcanic eruption has wrenched the earth, and these Greeks emerged from the black soil of the Ukraine, unearthed from the coal dust and factory grime of the Donbass mining region. They come to us not with blind eyes of marble, but with the energetic gleam of Komsomol eyes; not with the silence of stony lips, but with the piercing melody of a ditty; not with the smooth gesture of a petrified hand, but with the firm grip of a skillful fist clenching the wheel of a tractor, a manager's pencil, the shoulder of a Komsomol dance partner; not in the pampered nakedness of a goddess begotten by the foam of warm seas, but in the buttoned jacket of a proletarian girl who knows the discipline and joy of work, the joy of someone who has worked a twenty-hour shift on a frozen iron tractor seat, and strolls away in her thick cotton workpants, hands in pockets not because of the cold but to hold the pants up, and there and then breaks into a dance—a dance not just to warm up, but to show the happiness of work successfully completed, show it proudly to friends, neighbors, the field, the motherland, the world. The language of singing and dancing.

In these strong, quiet girls with their beautiful, calm faces Greece has been resurrected, with its myths of people who fear no encounter with the savage monsters and phantoms. Great tales of battles, remembered through centuries, come back to life in the story of these nine girls who conquered the earth in this true springtime of mankind. These girls, of whom the oldest is twenty-two, the youngest not even sixteen.

"Besh" means five in Greek. The village of Starobesh near Stalino has that name because five Greek families moved there from the Crimea in the time of Catherine the Great, and by our day they have grown to more than a thousand households.

Pasha grew up in the village. Her father, Nikita Vasilievich Angelin, was a farmhand. Her mother worked for the kulaks whitewashing huts.

"Mother nursed all us children herself and yet never quit working," says Pasha in a conversation about whether a tractor driver should quit work when she has a baby. And she remembers an incident from when her older brother was still nursing.

Leaving for the fields, her mother tied the baby to a cart wheel so he wouldn't crawl away. She returned to feed him and saw that the baby had stretched the string tight and was playing with something springy, black, and quick. A poisonous snake. He inched his fingers toward it, pouted his lips, and goo-gooed. And the snake was twisting peacefully near his hands, so that her mother was scared to make a step—frighten it and it'd bite.

She ran for the father and her blood ran cold. When they raced up, the snake was gone. It hadn't touched the baby.

A real Mowgli of the steppe.

The Angelins lived poorly in a one-room hut thatched with ancient reeds, where it was worse than outside when it rained.

"How often," Pasha remembered, "I cried angrily by the stove in the winter, after I had to run home through the snow from school barefoot, in my summer jacket."

But Nikita Vasilievich never got mad. He was even-tempered, steady, and extraordinarily firm-willed. Himself illiterate, he set aside his pennies so that his children might become something (and there were eight of them).

The family grew up Bolsheviks. The family of a true Soviet celebrity. Her older brother is a regional agronomist; another finished the Communist Institute of Journalism and became Party secretary of a regiment stationed in the Far East; a third is a Black Sea sailor; the fourth is a tractor driver and Party organizer. Of her sisters, one works as a market gardener in the kolkhoz brigade, another studies at the Industrial Workers' School. She'll become a metallurgical or mining engineer. A third is the leader of a Pioneer troop. The fourth is Pasha, a Komsomol member and the most famous girl in the Soviet Union.

Even in elementary school the kulak pups teased her and called her a "commie." Sometimes they beat her up. She cried rarely and quietly. She was stubborn even then, unbendable like her father. She didn't know how to snap back, and she didn't know how to be soft.

The benighted customs of Greek families dictated that girls be quiet and veil their faces up to the eyes. Against their will they grew up shy, scared even to talk with a boy. They'd tar your gates if you did.

In 1927 Pasha's father organized the first kolkhoz in Starobesh, and her brother delivered the first tractor.

Pasha liked the machine very much, and the way you drove it. She pestered her brother to explain better how it was made. But he didn't know. Only knew how to turn the wheel.

From that time on, Pasha would dream about the tractor. She hung a picture clipped from a magazine on the wall—a tractor driver plowing.

Her mother saw it and said: "It won't happen. Become a doctor. It's better."

The kolkhoz slowly got stronger. Pasha's father fought for it against overt and covert kulaks. Pasha also learned to fight, by her work in the brigades.

The year 1930 arrived. The kulaks fought back savagely; radicals took policies too far. Lamps kept going out at meetings, and Party organizer Angelin and his children were pelted with corncobs.

The kolkhoz came out of that year's scrape very small and weak, with only twenty-three households, and the fields unweeded. But Pasha's father didn't give up, and his children were in the front ranks of the weeders that saved the Bolshevik harvest.

And when a kulak with a Party card, a member of the kolkhoz board, tried to undermine Nikita Angelin, Pasha rushed to the Regional Party Committee, unmasked the scoundrel, and made sure he was put on trial.

It was then that a leaflet from the tractor courses arrived in the village. But the young men were needed for field work; nobody wanted to let them go. That's why they sent Pasha, so that the spot in the courses didn't go to waste.

One sixteen-year-old girl among a hundred young men. Everybody mocked her. They noticed that cursing made her blush, and the language got three times fouler. You could hear: "Long of hair, short of brains!" "You should be barefoot and pregnant, not on a tractor!" If she passed through a crowd of boys on her way to class, they'd always shove her, make her fall in the snow—and that so it hurt.

She tried to stay away. She never ate with any of them. Always ate after everybody else was done. And always in the corner, hiding behind her kerchief after every bite.

When she came home from school, it wasn't any easier. Her mother didn't believe she'd learned anything; the kolkhoz members laughed: "What good will come of you?"

She worked in a men's tractor brigade. But what she managed to produce was swamped in the prevailing leveler's stew. People continued to laugh at her. She just stayed silent and knit her brow. But she noticed that there were other female tractor drivers in the area, and that they were having a tough time too.

From there comes that angry tenacity with which she holds to her purely female brigade, refusing to dilute it with men. As if saying: "You mocked 'women's work'—take a look now, be ashamed, just try and match us."

In 1933 the Politsection was formed. The organizer sensed in Pasha one of his first allies among the village youth of the time. And most important, a selflessly conscientious person who loved her work more than herself.

The Politsection director, Kurov, whose name she remembers gratefully to this day, once invited her to his office.

She came with her frowning face buried in her collar.

"Have a toothache?"

"No."

"Why are you hiding?"

"Just because."

"You're a good worker. Let's organize a women's brigade. Let's show how important women are to the kolkhoz."

Her face popped out of the collar and lit up. Her dream was coming true.

All the kolkhozes were laughing: "They sent girls. We don't need girls—they'll ruin the fields."

Kolkhoz director Afenkin greeted them with vulgarities and chased them away. It was no easier in other kolkhozes. No huts were set up for them to sleep in, they had to beg for food, they had to drink from a stream, there were hitches in fuel delivery, the tractors kept breaking down—and nobody helped them find a mechanic.

But how she worked! Furious, gritting her teeth. The girls were a bit green and timid. One got a tractor and she raised a ruckus. Pasha ran up—the girl wouldn't budge: "Who the hell thought up this damned machine. Take it, I'm leaving!"

And it seemed tougher to budge the girl than the dead machine. Pasha pushed her, pushed, gave her a pep talk, explained things, and then she herself got so angry that she too started howling—so they cried together. They cried themselves out, and when they settled down, they again set to conquering the "damned machine."

The girls had a tough time getting used to tractors; they were scared.

They would drive over a gully and quit right there: "No further! We're scared!" The brigade leader herself would get into the saddle and guide each tractor, one after the other, across the gully.

The first seven days, when they weren't given anywhere to sleep, they worked without leaving their tractors. They slept right there, in the furrow, while the mechanic fixed the machine. Or right in the iron saddle, if their inflamed eyes couldn't make out the furrow anymore, with their oozing, shaking fingers slipping off the wheel.

After seven days Pasha went to Kurov to tell him about their work. She said three words and fell silent. The Politsection director looked at her, and she was asleep on the couch.

But still she fulfilled her Plan. And Pasha is vain and stubborn as hell about the Plan—don't mind that her last name is angelic.

That was when the brigade's fame first began. The kolkhozes began fighting one another to have it. Even Afenkin begged its pardon and invited them to work. But Pasha cut him off: "We won't go to Afenkin!"

Pasha doesn't remember personal insults, but she never forgives an insult to her cause.

Pasha also remembers how she hauled coal with tractors from the mines to the Tractor Station. In a blizzard, in freezing weather, when even the young men refused to drive, she went with an improvised girls' brigade.

The mine director refused to give them coal.

"Bring lumber first, then I'll give it to you."

In such a storm? Pasha wouldn't agree to the artful dodger's idea. And it was already late, almost evening. The girls let the water out of the radiators so that the freezing pipes wouldn't burst. They huddled together on their tractor benches against the cold. There they slept in the blizzard.

And Pasha drove back all night to complain to the Politsection director. She arrived and covered the machine with her own shawl so that it wouldn't freeze. And she ran off in her summer jacket. By the way, she saw nothing special in this. Most important to the girls were their machines, and more than once they took their coats off to wrap the tractors.

The Politsection director went to let the mining bureaucrat have it. Pasha didn't sleep that night, shivered the whole time. She drove back to bring food to the girls—they hadn't eaten for days.

The coal was brought. But by then the girls were in no condition to work.

Then the personnel director, a certain Serdyuk (Pasha remembers his name very well), ordered her to deliver it with a brigade of men.

But she just couldn't anymore. She could barely rise from the bench.

"If you don't go," said Serdyuk, "we'll raise the question of your exclusion from the Party."

It was like a knout blow. Pasha couldn't tolerate it. She stood and went over to the machine, swaying. Her eyes were green circles, her face like ashes. The mechanic saw her and announced that he wouldn't let her go. He brought her back, and she fell down without getting up for a month and a half. Pneumonia.

Sickness is not as terrible as human callousness. Disease might not leave a trace. But the blow of a callous word will always leave a wrinkle around the mouth or the scar of an insult in the heart.

From her hospital bed she went straight back to the tractor seat. Her fame swept through the region. She already sensed the ability of herself and her friends and knew that for the honor of their tractor brigade they'd go through fire and water, without mercy for themselves.

They challenged Anastasov's tractor brigade to a competition. And beat them. The men did 4 hectares per shift, Pasha's brigade did 5.6. And there was more. She took Anastasov into the brigade as a student. As an exception. By the end of the summer, Anastasov was amazed: "I earned five hundred rubles for the year in my brigade, but under Pasha's leadership, I earned twelve hundred in five months."

Already two of Pasha's girls lead brigades of their own: Stepakina and Anastasova. The Starobesh Tractor Station already has three women's brigades.

It was hard for them to leave Pasha! Not only did they break into tears when they said goodbye, but later, whenever they'd see Pasha's brigade from a distance, there'd always be tears.

You look at this quiet, serious girl in a Moscow hotel room and think: Where did this disciplined strength, these fine leadership qualities come from?

She runs into the room and speaks hurriedly, because there isn't much time. She speaks precisely, in detail. But her hand works independently: it smooths the rumpled dress hanging on the headboard of the bed, puts the pen near the inkwell, covers some carelessly unwrapped packages. Unconsciously, she puts everything in order.

Pasha has a law for the brigade: If you can't take care of yourself, you can't take care of your machine.

That's why the girls never step into their field cabin without first examining their machine, cleaning it till it shines, and washing themselves properly.

How could you enter that cabin dirty—it's first-rate, whitewashed on the inside! Folding beds along the walls, chests for their linen, suitcases, flowers, 150-book library, pictures, a gramophone.

Pasha's drivers look out not only for themselves, but also for the nearby truck drivers' cabin. They make sure the truckers wash, don't curse, read, and wear their work clothes, not street clothes, on the job. And study their machines well.

Incidentally, it's a bit tougher with the truck drivers. There are always different drivers, depending on which kolkhoz the brigade is working.

What makes the brigade so strong? It maintains a strict discipline that is entirely voluntary, it is faultlessly clean, it has a sharp sense of political responsibility, and it strives to justify the honor of high norms for female labor.

But its strength comes not only from Pasha's knowing her tractor like her own hand and caring for it like a mother cares for her child. Not only because she ceaselessly searches for fuel, or for parts, or for food, breaking down the barriers of human sluggishness, ignorance, bureaucratic callousness, or the simple vileness of enemies.

The tremendous power of the brigade, besides all that, comes from the closeness of the girls, living heart to heart, looking after one another, worrying and caring for one another.

Not only for business, but for any personal problem they go to their brigade leader. If it's something happy, they laugh together; if it's sad, they cry.

"Which tractor driver," I ask Pasha, "is the most careful? Who works hardest? Who likes to read most? Who's the best dancer?"

Pasha doesn't like the question. She frowns.

"They're all the same. They all work just as hard, dance just as well, read just as much."

A stern answer, in which you don't know whether there's more solicitude for the members of her team, or a unique "psychological leveling."

Of course, each is different. And of course, Pasha treats each differently. It's called "the distribution of strengths."

Take Natasha Radchenko. Broad-faced, quiet, doesn't raise her eyes. But actually the merriest. She dances on the way to dinner, dances as she gets off the tractor. The best *chastushka*[2] singer in the brigade.

> Little apple, little apple,
> What a nation.
> Satellites, loafers, carburetion.

Or jauntier still:

> I didn't love the tractor boy,
> And wouldn't drive a tractor.
> Then I loved a tractor boy,
> And became a tractor girl.

She puts *chastushki* together herself, or takes an old one and changes it:

> If I was, if I was,
> If I was a parakeet,

---

2. A folk ditty, like a limerick.

In my loved one's pocket,
I'd weave myself a nest.

She gets on her tractor with a painful hop. During the winter break she married the president of the workers' committee, a railroad worker. Come spring, she returned to her tractor, and he began to treat her badly.

"What the hell use are you to me in the brigade? Stay home and cook my dinner. Otherwise, who will feed me and darn my socks? I won't let you go!"

Natasha was ticked off.

"I won't live with such an idiot!"

She left her husband as if she were leaving a prison. She got on her tractor and, literally in a fury, began to cut the earth, putting into her work the entire supply of maternal energy that found no outlet in her failed marriage. Now Natasha is a brigade leader finished in Pasha's school. And on her strong, broad chest is the Order of Red Labor.

Marusya Radchenko, no relation, is entirely different. A calm-eyed hulk, capable, hard-working, but so imperturbable that when you see her serenity you want to jostle her, just so she'll flare up!

Each is her own girl. Hot-tempered Marusya Tokareva takes the most pleasure in life; she's never unhappy when others frown: "Oh, the weather's bad. Will we fulfill the Plan?"

But Marusya had some bad luck: she dislocated her arm cranking up her tractor. True, it was her own fault: some guys were checking her out, she wanted to impress them, and cranking a tractor—not a subtle piece of machinery—should be done carefully, particularly by a girl.

"Why is it that people who start a tractor carefully never get hurt?" asks Pasha.

"Because they're spoiled"—Marusya needed another forty-nine hectares for her award.

And Natasha Radchenko had to work double for her partner.

How Pasha looked after Marusya Tokareva! When the brigade received a pass to a sanatorium, she gave it to Marusya, supplied her for the journey, told her how to dress, wrote to her all the time, and when she ran out of money, dug some up and sent it to her.

Vera Zolotopup,[3] the brigade Komsomol organizer, next in line after Natasha to run a brigade, has slowly but steadfastly changed from an extremely shy, hesitant girl into a competent leader and lecturer. More than anything she wants to change her last name.

"I'll go back to the regional center and fix everything up there," she says.

And then there's the stern face of the silent Greek girl Vera Mikhailova, who, unlike Natasha, knew how to bring her husband, the commander of a tractor brigade, to reason when he insisted that she chuck her machine and stay home. Very easily confused. She complained to me about her illiteracy.

---

3. Golden-navel.

The brigade's fussiest member, and its most avid reader, despite her semi-literacy, is Marusya Balakai, a person with a bright and welcoming heart, who never gets mad at anyone.

Light-haired Vera Kosse, also Greek, whose eyes are opened wide with surprise to the world, dreams of sailing the distant seas.

And finally there's the youngest, restless Nadya Biits, whom Pasha made editor of the wall newspaper and then taught her that she must put her brigade leader through the wringer as well. And in the beginning, for show, she even wrote critical notes about herself, if there was a break in the fuel supply or not enough food.

Once at a meeting Nadya got a note from a boy she didn't know: "Hey, I like you, let's get to know each other!"

She took the note to Pasha. The brigade leader decided: drop it, you're too young. Then she hunted down the boy and gave him a dressing-down.

"It's a monastery," the regional Komsomol secretary, Pasha's husband, smiles. "There was some agitation in the brigade when they found out that their leader had married me. They decided: he'll take her away to the big city; the brigade'll be done for."

He also chides her gently for the fact that the girls still don't read much. He tells of how much effort it cost Pasha herself to quit being an unsociable Amazon of the steppe who never climbed out of her dust-bitten work clothes, and to speak with people freely. Back in 1933, when she walked onto the tribune for her first big speech, Pasha stood silent for ten minutes before she got out the first word.

"Do you think it was easy to train you out of your work coat and into a dress?" her husband jokes, and continues to tease: "Will you tell him what you want to call our boy?"

Pasha flares up: "You idiot!"

"What idiot? I can imagine him clearly. He'll be a real pistol."

"I don't know what you're talking about. I'm a tractor driver. I'm not interested in children."

Then the young Communist's voice becomes terribly sly: "And who was that choosing a baby blanket in Mostorg?"

And then Pasha falls face first into her hands. And for a long time she doesn't take her hands from her brightly blushing cheeks.

But quickly, leading the conversation back to the Don steppe, she tells how this autumn the brigade harvested the very last hectare just to keep the promise Pasha had made to Stalin at the Second Congress of Kolkhoz Shock Workers: to give 1,200 hectares per tractor.

Everything was fine. They had already done 1,180 per tractor, and the brigade had saved twenty tons of fuel, when a hard frost set in. The ground became boggy. It stuck to the tractor treads and forced them to stop for cleaning. It slowed their pace to a crawl. One more week, and the soil would become iron.

Pasha walked about silently, with a pencil and paper, calculating something. The tractor drivers didn't bother her with questions. If Pasha's thinking, she'll think up something.

And Pasha thought up something.

To save time on fueling the tractors and passing them on from shift to shift, she proposed that the brigade go from a ten-hour shift to twenty hours and fill up the tractors only when the gas tanks were almost empty. According to her calculations, they would complete their work victoriously by the twentieth.

The plows bucked, and fingers were frozen. Working twenty hours straight wasn't easy. But the work was fun, because the entire country was watching!

And nine girls, overcoming their dreary kerchiefs and their decrepit, dirty living quarters, and the kulaks' mockery, and bureaucratic callousness, and the oddities of their machines, and the weariness of their muscles, defeated the weather.

Four days before time was up, they tallied what they'd done, and it turned out that each tractor had completed 1,225 hectares.

And for those days the best worker had been little Nadya Biits.

Nine girls had conquered the earth.

Then came the long-awaited Moscow. It was like a holiday, but a little frightening. Particularly frightening was the subway—the doors closed without asking, and could snatch away one who got flustered from the other eight and abandon her in the glittering underground passage. True, Pasha explained that the doors close on a rubber strip and that even a finger stuck in won't hurt—all the same it was frightening.

The streets were packed with people, and riding the tram was even more complicated than driving a tractor downhill.

But this was eclipsed by the most important thing.

Nine girls could be seen by the whole country. The conquerors were called to microphones, to factory clubs; celebrations were arranged in their honor. Their hands were shaken, glowing words were said, they were showered with gifts, photographers caught them on staircases, at the sight of them reporters pulled out their pencils.

Stores guided them from counter to counter. They tried on jumpers and chose shirts for their brothers. And not only their brothers. They found bicycles for themselves—true, the brigade already had some, but they were the heavy type. They read record labels and shrugged their shoulders, because there wasn't anything they didn't already have in their cabin in the steppe.

But the most important thing lay ahead: the gathering in the Kremlin, where Stalin would be, to whom they had made a promise and kept it.

It was evening. The tractor drivers, happy and excited, left the writer's apartment. A shiny Lincoln awaited them at the entrance of the tall building. Hurriedly, one after the other, chattering in a whisper, they got into the car. The door slammed shut, and the olive Lincoln set off. And suddenly from inside a many-voiced song of the steppe rang out, so piercing that passersby reeled, stood stock-still, and smiled.

When Pasha mounted the tribune of the Kremlin Palace, Stalin stood up applauding, and with that motion he pulled up all three thousand people in the audience.

Pasha stood in her bright-green beret, seizing hold of the tribune as if it were a tractor, and directed her speech into the fertile furrows of the rows of humanity, through a storm of greetings that blew in her face. Then she leaned into the rostrum and shouted: "Comrades!"

She shouted to the very horizon, as they yell to a distant tractor in the steppe to drown out its rumbling.

She shouted for the entire country, the entire world, throwing her words to the Pamir plateaus, where the warm sheep graze, and to the frozen strait across which America can be seen from our territory, and to the Moldavian gardens above the murmuring Dnestr, and to the shoreline where the Red Navy distrustfully and guardedly watches the expanse of the Pacific Ocean.

Amazement and a ringing pride were in her hurried tale: That's what I am, and that's what we girls are.

Her pride was not conceited: just take a look what I've done; nobody else could have done it. No, it was comradely: work intelligently and happily, as we do—you'll do the same.

It was a challenge to a duel.

Eight girls watched her from the first row and learned how to be proud and to work people up.

"I will take it upon myself this year to organize"—Pasha shouted and gathered her breath before a leap—"ten women's brigades. I will sacrifice my girls to other brigades, take new ones for myself, and give per tractor"—here there was no pause; this figure had been noted and marked down long ago—"1,600 hectares!"

And then she fell silent. She wiped her brow with her hand and, leaning to the side, said quietly, like a little girl:

"Working is easier than talking..."

The Road to Life
Anton Makarenko (1932–1934)

MAKARENKO (1888–1939) WAS THE MOST FAMOUS PEDAGOGUE IN SOVIET HISTORY. THROUGH HIS WORK WITH CHILDREN IN WORK SCHOOLS AND COLONIES AND THROUGH HIS WRITINGS ON UPBRINGING AND COLLECTIVE WORK (SEE ALSO *THE PARENTS' BOOK*), HE ACHIEVED INTERNATIONAL RENOWN IN THE 1930S. HIS MOST FAMOUS WORK, *PEDAGOGICAL POEM,* WAS TRANSLATED AND WIDELY PUBLISHED ABROAD AS *THE ROAD TO LIFE*

Translation from *The Road to Life (An Epic of Education)* (Moscow: Foreign Languages Publishing House, 1951), vol. 1, pp. 41–54.

AND IS ONE OF THE FEW WORKS ON THE SUBJECT OF TEACHING THAT BECAME A PERENNIAL BESTSELLER. THE THEME OF TRANSFORMING DELINQUENTS INTO PRODUCTIVE CITIZENS THROUGH DISCIPLINE, COLLECTIVE COOPERATION, AND SOCIAL CONSTRAINT HAD A BROAD RESONANCE IN SOVIET POPULAR CULTURE (CF. THE 1934 MOVIE *START IN LIFE* [*PUTEVKA V ZHIZN'*], RELEASED IN THE WEST AS *THE ROAD TO LIFE*).

OPERATIONS ON THE HOME FRONT

In February, a bundle of notes almost equivalent to my six months salary disappeared from one of my drawers.

At that time my room was office, teachers' room, accountant's office, and pay desk, since I fulfilled the corresponding functions in my own person. The bundle of crisp banknotes had disappeared from a locked drawer which bore not the slightest traces of having been forced.

I informed the boys of this the same evening, asking them to return the money, pointing out that I could adduce no proof of theft, and might easily have been accused of embezzlement. The boys heard me out in grim silence, and dispersed. After this meeting I was waylaid in the dark courtyard on the way to my room in the wing by two of the boys—Taranets and a slight, agile lad named Gud.

"We know who took the money," whispered Taranets, "only we couldn't say so in front of everyone; we don't know where it's hidden. And if we peached, he'd run away with the money."

"Who was it?"

"There's a guy—" began Taranets, but Gud shot him a lowering glance, obviously not approving of his tactics.

"What's the good of talking? He ought to have his mug pushed in."

"And who's going to do it?" retorted Taranets. "You? He could knock you into a cocked hat!"

"Why not tell me who it was. I'll speak to him myself," I said.

"That wouldn't do!"

Taranets was all for a conspiratorial secrecy.

"Well, just as you like," I said, shrugging my shoulders. And I went off to bed.

The next morning Gud found the money in the stable. Someone had stuffed it between the bars of the narrow window, and the notes lay scattered all over the place. Gud, in a frenzy of joy, came running up to me with his fists full of crumpled banknotes in wild disorder.

In his ecstasy Gud capered all over the colony; the other boys were radiant, and kept running into my room to have a look at me. Only Taranets strode about, his head held proudly erect. I refrained from questioning either him or Gud about their activities subsequent to our conversation of the previous night.

Two days later someone wrenched the padlocks off the door of the cellar, and made off with a few pounds of lard—our entire stock of fats—and the padlocks themselves. A day or two later the storeroom window was taken out, and some sweets we had been saving up for the anniversary of the February Revolution, together with a few jars of cart grease, were missing. The cart grease was worth its weight in gold to us.

Kalina Ivanovich, the groundskeeper, actually began to lose flesh; turning his wan visage upon one boy after another, and puffing smoke into their faces, he tried to reason with them:

"Look here! It's all for you, you sons of bitches! You're robbing yourselves, you parasites!"

Taranets evidently knew more about it than anyone else, but would say nothing outright, it apparently not being his style to give the show away. The boys expressed themselves freely about it, but it was the sporting aspect which appealed to them. They could not be brought around to the view that it was themselves who were being robbed.

In the dormitory I shouted at them in bitter rage: "Who do you think you are? Are you human beings, or are you—?"

"We're gangsters!" called a voice from a bed at the other end of the room.

"Gangsters—that's what we are!"

"Shucks! You're not gangsters! You're just sneak thieves, stealing from each other! Now you don't have any lard, and the heck with you! There'll be no sweets for the anniversary. No one's going to give us any more. You can go without—I don't care!"

"But what can we do, Anton Semyonovich? We don't know who did it. You don't know yourself, and no more do we!"

I had known all along that my urgings would be useless. The thief was obviously one of the bigger boys, of whom all the rest went in fear.

The next day I took two of the boys with me into town to try to wangle another fat ration. It took us several days, but in the end we did get some lard. They even issued us a fresh supply of sweets after haranguing us at length about our inability to hold on to what we had already been given. When we got back, we spent the evening in exhaustive narration of our adventures. At last the lard was brought to the colony and stored in the cellar. The same night it was stolen.

I was almost glad when this happened. Now, I thought, the common, collective nature of our interests will assert itself, and arouse greater zeal in the matter of clearing up the thefts. As a matter of fact, though all the boys seemed downcast, there was no special display of zeal, and after the first impression had passed, they fell again under the spell of the sporting interest: Who was it that worked so adroitly?

A few days later a horse collar was missing, and now we couldn't even go into town. We had to go from house to house begging the loan of one for a few days.

Thefts had become everyday occurrences. Every morning something or other would be found to be missing: an axe, a saw, a pot or a pan, a sheet, a saddle strap, a pair of reins, provisions. I tried not going to bed, pacing the yard with my revolver handy, but of course I couldn't keep this up more than two or three nights. I asked Osipov to stand guard for one night, but he showed such terror at the prospect that I never brought it up again.

My suspicions fell on many of the boys, not excluding Gud and Taranets. But I could produce no evidence whatsoever, and was compelled to keep my suspicions to myself.

Zadorov, laughing uproariously, asked me facetiously:

"Did you really think, Anton Semyonovich, that it would be all work, work in a labor colony, and not a bit of fun? Just you wait—there's more to come! And what d'you mean to do to the one you catch?"

"Send him to prison."

"Is that all? I thought you intended to beat him up."

One night he came out into the yard, fully dressed.

"I'll walk up and down with you for a bit."

"See that the thieves don't have it in for you, that's all!"

"Oh, they know you're on watch tonight, and they won't go out stealing. So that's all right."

"You're afraid of them, Zadorov, aren't you? Own up, now!"

"Afraid of the thieves? Of course I am! But me being afraid or not isn't the point—you know yourself, Anton Semyonovich, that it's not the thing to peach on one's pals."

"But it's you yourself who is being robbed."

"Me? There's nothing of mine here."

"But you live here."

"You call this living, Anton Semyonovich? Is this life? Nothing will come of this colony of yours. You might as well give it up! You'll see, as soon as they've stolen all there is to be stolen, they'll run away. You should simply hire a couple of hefty watchmen with rifles."

"I'm not going to hire any watchmen with rifles."

"Why ever not?" asked Zadorov, astonished.

"Watchmen have to be paid, and we're poor enough as it is; and what is more important—you've got to learn to realize that you yourselves are the owners."

The idea of hiring night watchmen was suggested by many of the boys. There was a regular debate held on the subject in the dormitory.

Anton Bratchenko, the best of our second batch of boys, argued as follows:

"While there's a watchman on guard, no one will go out stealing, and if anyone does, he'll get a load of shot you-know-where. And after walking around with it for a month, he won't try any more tricks."

He was opposed by Kostya Vetkovsky, a good-looking boy whose specialty in the world-at-large had been searching people's rooms with forged warrants. His was but a secondary part in these searches, the chief roles belonging to adults. Kostya himself, as attested in his "record," had never stolen anything, his interest in these operations being purely theoretical. Thieves he had always despised. I had long noted the subtle and complex nature of this lad. What amazed me was the way he got on with the roughest of the boys, and his acknowledged authority on political matters.

"Anton Semyonovich is right," he insisted. "There mustn't be any watchman. We don't all understand yet, but soon we shall realize that there must be no stealing in the colony. Even now lots of our guys understand that. Soon we will begin to stand guard ourselves. Won't we, Burun?" he exclaimed, suddenly turning to Burun.

"Why not? There's no harm in standing guard," replied Burun.

In February our housekeeper resigned her post in the colony, I having found her a place in a hospital. One Saturday Laddie was driven up to her doorstep, and all her former cronies and the participants of her philosophical tea parties began busily piling her innumerable bags and boxes on the sledge. The good old soul, swaying serenely atop her treasures, set out at Laddie's habitual two kilometers per hour to take up her new life.

But Laddie returned late the same night, bringing back the old woman, who burst sobbing and crying into my room: she had been robbed of almost all her worldly possessions. Her cronies and other helpers had not put all her boxes and bags on the sledge, but had carried some off—it was a flagrant case of robbery. I at once aroused Kalina Ivanovich, Zadorov, and Taranets, and together we thoroughly searched the colony. So much had been stolen that it had not been possible to hide everything properly. The housekeeper's treasures were found among bushes, in the lofts of outhouses, under the steps of a porch, and even simply pushed beneath beds and behind cupboards. And she certainly was a rich old woman: we found about a dozen new tablecloths, a quantity of sheets and towels, some silver spoons, various little glass receptacles, a bracelet, some earrings, and trifles of all sorts.

The old woman sat weeping in my room, which gradually filled with suspects— her former cronies and allies.

At first the boys denied everything, but after I shouted at them a bit the horizon began to clear. The old lady's friends turned out not to have been the principal thieves. They had restricted themselves to a few souvenirs, such as a napkin or a sugar bowl. Burun was found to have been the chief actor in the whole business. This discovery amazed everyone, especially me. From the very first, Burun had seemed the most reliable of all the boys, invariably grave, reserved, but friendly, and one of the best and most painstaking of our scholars. I was overwhelmed by the scope and thoroughness of his proceedings: he had stowed away the old woman's property by the bale. There could be no doubt that all the previous thefts in the colony had been the work of his hands.

At last I had arrived at the source of the evil. I brought Burun before a "People's Court"—the first to be held in the history of our colony.

In the dormitory, seated on beds and tables, were ranged the ragged and grim-visaged jury. The rays from the oil lamp lit up the tense faces of the boys and the pale countenance of Burun, who, with his heavy, awkward frame and thick neck, looked like a typical American gangster.

In firm, indignant tones I described the crime to the boys: to have robbed an old woman, whose only happiness consisted in her wretched possessions, to have robbed one who had shown more affection for the boys than anyone else in the colony, just when she had turned to them for aid—surely anyone capable of this must have lost all human semblance; he must be, not simply a beast, but a skunk!

A man should be able to respect himself, should be strong and proud, and not rob feeble old women of their few possessions.

Whatever the cause—whether my speech made a great impression, or whether the boys were sufficiently aroused anyhow—Burun became the object of a united and vehement attack. Little, shockheaded Bratchenko extended his arms toward Burun:

"Well! What can you say for yourself? You ought to be put behind bars, you ought to be thrown in jail! All because of you we've gone hungry—it was you who took Anton Semyonovich's money!"

Burun made a sudden protest. "Anton Semyonovich's money? Prove it if you can!"

"Don't you worry about that!"

"Prove it then!"

"So you didn't take it—it wasn't you?"

"So it was me, was it?"

"Of course it was you!"

"I took Anton Semyonovich's money? Who's going to prove it?"

From the back of the room came the voice of Taranets: "I am!"

Burun was thunderstruck. Turning toward Taranets, he seemed to be going to make a rebuttal, but changing his mind, only said:

"Well, what if I did? I put it back, didn't I?"

Somewhat to my surprise, the boys burst out laughing. They found the altercation highly entertaining. Taranets bore himself like a hero. Stepping forward, he declared: "But still he shouldn't be expelled. We've all of us done what we oughtn't to. But there'd be no objection to giving him a thorough licking."

Everyone fell silent. Burun let his unhurried glance travel over the pockmarked face of Taranets.

"I'd like to see you do it! What are you trying so hard for, anyway? You'll never be made manager of the colony, however you try! Anton will give me a licking, if necessary, and it's none of your business."

Vetkovsky jumped up. "What d'you mean 'none of our business'? Fellows—is it, or is it not our business?"

"It is, it is!" shouted the boys. "We'll beat him up ourselves, and we'll do it better than Anton could!"

Someone was already making a rush at Burun. Bratchenko was shaking his fists right in his face, bawling: "You ought to be flogged!"

Zadorov whispered in my ear: "Take him away, or they'll beat him up!"

I dragged Bratchenko away from Burun. Zadorov shoved two or three of the other boys out of the way. With difficulty we put a stop to the commotion.

"Let Burun speak! Let him tell us!" cried Bratchenko.

Burun hung his head.

"There's nothing to tell. You're right, all of you! Let me go with Anton Semyonovich! Let him punish me as he thinks fit!"

Silence. I moved toward the door, fearing to allow the rage welling up within me to overflow. The boys dispersed to right and left to make way for me and Burun.

We crossed the dark yard, picking our way among the snowdrifts in silence, I in front, he following.

My state of mind was deplorable. I regarded Burun as the very scum of humanity. I did not know what to do with him. He had been sent to the colony as one of a gang of thieves, most of whom—the adults—had been shot. He was seventeen years old.

Burun stood silently just inside the door. Seated at the table, I restrained myself with difficulty from throwing some heavy object at him, and thus putting an end to the interview.

At last Burun lifted his head, looked steadily into my eyes, and said slowly, stressing every word, and scarcely able to repress his sobs:

"I... will... never... steal... again!"

"You're a liar! That's what you promised the Commission!"

"That was the Commission! And this is you! Give me any punishment you like, only don't expel me from the colony."

"And what is it you like about the colony?"

"I like it here. There's the lessons. I want to learn. And if I stole, it was because I was always hungry."

"Very well! You'll stay under lock and key for three days and get nothing but bread and water. And don't you lay a finger on Taranets!"

"All right!"

Burun spent three days shut up in the little room next to the dormitory, the same room in which the tutors had slept in the former reform school. I didn't lock him up, he having given his word not to leave the room without my permission. The first day I did send him nothing but bread and water, but the next day I took pity on him and sent a dinner to him. Burun attempted a proud refusal, but I shouted at him:

"Come off it—I won't have any of your airs!"

He smiled faintly, shrugged his shoulders, and took up his spoon.

Burun kept his word. He never stole anything again, either in the colony or anywhere else.

March of the Happy-Go-Lucky Guys
(From the lm *Happy-Go-Lucky Guys*)
Vasily Lebedev-Kumach and Isaac Dunaevsky (1934)

WRITTEN BY THE MAJOR COMPOSING TEAM OF THE DECADE, THIS SONG BECAME A COLOSSAL HIT. ITS POPULARITY WAS TIED TO THE ROMPING MUSICAL COMEDY FILM *HAPPY-GO-LUCKY* GUYS (1934), STARRING THE JAZZ BANDLEADER LEONID UTESOV AND THE SONGSTER LYUBOV ORLOVA. THE JOYFUL ELEMENT IN THESE SONGS WAS EASILY TRANSFERRED OVER TO SONGS OF PATRIOTISM AND PRODUCTION, SOME OF WHICH FOLLOW BELOW. LEBEDEV-KUMACH (1898–1949), THE MAJOR LYRICIST OF THE STALIN ERA, GOT HIS START AS AN AGITATIONAL POET IN THE CIVIL WAR. LATER A JOURNALIST, POET, AND WRITER OF SONG LYRICS, HE WAS A FREQUENT COLLABORATOR WITH DUNAEVSKY, THE KING OF SOVIET SONGWRITERS UNTIL HIS DEATH IN 1955. TOGETHER THEY DID THE SONGS FOR GRIGORY ALEKSANDROV'S BIG-TIME MUSICALS *HAPPY-GO-LUCKY GUYS*, *CIRCUS*, AND *VOLGA, VOLGA*.

МАРШ ВЕСЕЛТЫХ РЕБЯТ

Легко на сердце от песни веселой,
Она скучать не дает никогда.
И любят песню деревни и села,
И любят песню большие города.

Припев:
Нам песня строить и жить помогает,
Она, как друг, и зовет и ведет.
И тот, кто с песней по жизни шагает,
Тот никогда и нигде не пропадет!
И тот, кто с песней по жизни шагает,
Тот никогда и нигде не пропадет!

MARCH OF THE HAPPY-GO-LUCKY GUYS

Merry singing fills the heart with joy,
It never will let you be sad.
The countryside and villages love
    singing,
And big cities love singing too.

Refrain:
A song helps us building and living,
Like a friend, it calls and leads us forth.
And whoever goes through life singing,
Will never ever fall behind.
And whoever goes through life singing,
Will never ever fall behind.

From *Russkaia-sovetskaia poeziia: sbornik stikhov 1917–1953* (Moscow: Khudozhestvennaia literatura, 1954), pp. 380–381.

Шагай вперед, комсомольское племя,
Шути и пой, чтоб улыбки цвели!
Мы покоряем пространство и время,
Мы—молодые хозяева земли.

Припев.

Мы все добудем, поймем и откроем,
Холодный полюс и свод голубой!
Когда страна быть прикажет героем,—
У нас героем становится любой.

Припев.

Мы можем петь и смеяться, как дети,
Среди упорной борьбы и труда,
Ведь мы такими родились на свете,
Что не сдаемся нигде и никогда.

Припев.

И если враг нашу радость живую
Отнять захочет в упорном бою
Тогда мы песню споем боевую
И встанем грудью за Родину свою!

Припев.

Stride forward, clan of Young
    Communists,
Sing and joke, and make smiles bloom.
We are taming space and time,
We are the young masters of the earth.

Refrain.

We'll grasp, discover, and attain it all,
The cold North Pole and the clear blue
    sky,
When our country commands that we
    be heroes,
Then anyone can become a hero.

Refrain.

We can sing and laugh like children,
Amid our constant struggle and toil,
But that's how we were born into the
    world,
Nowhere and never to relent!

Refrain.

If our enemy decides to start a battle
To take our living joy away from us,
Then we'll strike up our song of battle,
And leap to defend our motherland.

Refrain.

Sportsman's March

Vasily Lebedev-Kumach and Isaac Dunaevsky (1936)

THEME SONG OF TIMOSHENKO'S POPULAR MOVIE GOALKEEPER (1936), A COMEDY, THIS MARCH EMBODIED THE DETERMINED GOOD CHEER AND HEALTH OF THE MID-1930S. THE MOVIE'S PROTAGONIST IS AN ATHLETE SET ON INDIVIDUAL GLORY, WHO EVENTUALLY LEARNS TO BE A TRUE TEAM PLAYER AND FINALLY MAKES THE NATIONAL TEAM.

From *Russkie-sovetskie pesni* (Moscow: Khudozhestvennaia literatura, 1977), pp. 184–185.

СПОРТИВНЫЙ МАРШ

Ну-ка, солнце, ярче брызни,
Золотыми лучами обжигай!
Эй, товарищ! Больше жизни!
Поспевай, не задерживай, шагай!

Припев:
Чтобы тело и душа были молоды,
Были молоды, были молоды,
Ты не бойся ни жары и ни холода,
Закаляйся, как сталь!
    Физкульт-ура!
Физкульт-ура-ура-ура! Будь готов!
Когда настанет час бить врагов,
От всех границ ты их отбивай!
Левый край! Правый край! Не зевай!

Ну-ка, ветер, гладь нам кожу,
Освежай нашу голову и грудь!
Каждый может стать моложе,
Если ветра веселого хлебнуть!

Припев.

Ну-ка, дождик, теплой влагой
Ты умой нас огромною рукой,
Напои нас всех отвагой,
А не в меру горячих успокой.

Припев.

Эй, вратарь, готовься к бою,—
Часовым ты поставлен у ворот!
Ты представь, что за тобою
Полоса пограничная идёт!

Припев.

SPORTSMAN'S MARCH

Hey you, sunshine, shimmer brighter,
Make us glow with your golden rays!
Hey you, comrade! Liven up there!
Keep up, step up, don't hold us back!

Refrain:
To make our hearts and bodies younger,
Become younger, become younger,
Do not fear the coldness or the heat.
Harden yourself, like steel.
    Physicult—hurrah!
Physicult—hurrah—hurrah—hurrah!
    Be ready!
When the time comes to beat the
    enemy,
Beat them back from every border!
Left flank! Right flank! Look sharp!

Hey you, breeze there, make our skin
    smooth,
Freshen up our head and our chest!
Everyone can make himself younger
If he takes a merry mouthful of the
    wind.

Refrain.

Hey you, raindrop, full of warm
    moisture,
Wash us with your mighty hand,
Fill us all up with your courage,
And cool down the hotheads.

Refrain.

Hey you, goalie, prepare for battle!
You're a watchman by the gate!
Just imagine, that behind you
The borderline must be kept safe!

Refrain.

Life's Getting Better

Vasily Lebedev-Kumach and Aleksandr Aleksandrov (1936)

THE LYRICS OF THIS SONG, BY LEBEDEV-KUMACH, WERE IN-
SPIRED BY STALIN'S COMMENT DURING PREPARATIONS FOR THE
1936 CONSTITUTION, WIDELY DISCUSSED AND PUBLICIZED IN
JUNE AND FORMALLY ADOPTED IN DECEMBER 1936. THE TITLE
FORMED THE WATCHWORD OF THE STALINIST MYTHOLOGY OF
THE 1930s. MUSIC BY THE PROLIFIC FOUNDER AND LEADER OF
THE RED (LATER SOVIET) ARMY ENSEMBLE, GENERAL ALEK-
SANDR ALEKSANDROV.

ЖИТБ СТАЛО ЛУЧШЕ

Звонки, как птицы, одна за другой
Песни летят над Советской страной.
Весел напев городов и полей—
    «Жить стало лучше,
    Жить стало веселей!»

Дружно страна и растет и поет,
С песнями общее счастье кует.
Глянешь на солнце—и солнце светлей!
    «Жить стало лучше,
    Жить стало веселей!»

Всюду простор для ума и для рук,
Всюду находишь друзей и подруг.

LIFE'S GETTING BETTER

Beautiful as birds, all in a row
Songs fly above the Soviet land.
The happy refrain of the cities and
    fields:
    "Life's getting better
    And happier too!"

The country is growing and singing as
    one,
It forges everyone's joy with its songs.
Look at the sun—the sun's brighter
    too!
    "Life's getting better
    And happier too!"

There's room everywhere for our minds
    and our hands,

From *Pesni sovetskoi molodezhi* (Moscow, 1937), pp. 156–157.
Two contemporary anecdotes:
    "Did you hear that Stalin said, 'Life's getting better, and happier too!'
    "Yeah, but he didn't say for whom." [4:66]

Top Party leaders from Moscow are inspecting a psychiatric hospital in the provinces. They step into
one ward. The patients all stand as one and shout: "Life's getting better, and happier too!"
    The leaders are happy—even lunatics know the slogan. But then they notice a gloomy fellow standing
alone in the corner without saying anything. They ask him, "Why didn't you shout that life's getting
better?"
    "Sorry, I'm not insane, I just work here." [4:66]

[For anecdote sources, see *Blue Blouse Skit,* above.]

Старость—теплее и юность—смелей,—
  «Жить стало лучше,
  Жить стало веселей!»

Wherever you go you'll find you have
    friends.
Old age feels warmer, and youth braver
    still—
  "Life's getting better
  And happier too!"

Знай, Ворошилов, мы все на—чеку,—
Пяди одной не уступим врагу.
Сидушка есть у отцов и детей,—
  «Жить стало лучше,
  Жить стало веселей!»

Know, Voroshilov, we're all standing
    guard—
We won't give the enemy even a yard.
There is a saying for folks old and
    young:
  "Life's getting better
  And happier too!"

Хочется всей необъятной страной
Сталину крикнуть:—Спасибо, родной,
Долгие годы живи, не болей!
  «Жить стало лучше,
  Жить стало веселей!»

Let's let the whole gigantic country
Shout to Stalin: "Thank you, our man,
Live long, prosper, never fall ill!"
  "Life's getting better
  And happier too!"

The Stakhanov Movement Explained

By Its Initiator Aleksei Stakhanov (1936)

ALEKSEI GRIGORIEVICH STAKHANOV (1906–77), A COAL MINER,
WAS A MAJOR FIGURE OF SOVIET MYTHOLOGY IN THE 1930S AND,
IN AN ATTENUATED VERSION, BEYOND. HIS MYTHIC IMPORTANCE
LAY NOT SO MUCH IN HIS VAUNTED WORK NORMS, BUT IN HIS
ROLE AS A SUCCESSFUL MODEL FOR SOVIET YOUTH AND HIS EXAL-
TATION IN THE MEDIA. "STAKHANOVITE" ENTERED THE SOVIET
LEXICON IN 1935. IT IS TO THIS DAY AN IRONIC NICKNAME FOR
AN INDUSTRIOUS PERSON, AND THE SOURCE OF MEAN-SPIRITED
RUMORS AND ANECDOTES.

A powerful movement for more efficient methods of organizing work has been
developing in the Soviet Union. This movement has brought in its wake an improve-

---

Aleksei Stakhanov, *The Stakhanov Movement Explained by Its Initiator* (Moscow: Foreign Literature, 1939).

ment in labor productivity equal to two, three, and even ten times the performance heretofore. Its cradle was the coal industry, whence it spread with lightening speed to other branches of industry, and also to agriculture. It has become a mass movement that has everywhere shattered the old, now antiquated estimates of rates of output and production capacities.

How is it that this vast movement of Soviet working people for high labor productivity has been named after me, a plain hewer of coal? What is my method of work?

Before answering these questions, I should like to sketch my life in brief.

I am thirty-three, born into a poor peasant's family. My childhood years were bleak and joyless. At the age of nine I was already working as a hand on a rich peasant's farm, where I got no pay except my keep. Then I was a shepherd for three years, and after that again a farmhand. Under the Soviet government I got a job in a mine.

I went to the Central Irmino Colliery in Kadievka (now Sergo), where nearly thirty men from my village were employed. There I was broken in in the usual way: first I was a brakeman, then a pony-man, and finally I came to hew coal myself.

As time went on, I grew attached to the colliery and the people that worked there; the work became my most vital interest.

When I first started hewing with a pneumatic pick, it took me a while to get the knack of handling the tool. I kept at it, trying my level best, until my perseverance was rewarded. I gradually acquired the technique of the business and my performance steadily increased. While the standard daily rate of output was five tons, which meant covering about three yards, I would often make eight tons, covering as much as five yards. In a year's time I was sent to take a special course in coal-hewing with pneumatic picks. This course helped me a great deal, and I began to hew as much as ten tons in one shift. But I did not want to stop there; I wanted to keep increasing my output, for even then I realized that eight or even ten tons of coal in a day's work was a long way from what could be got out of a pneumatic pick.

My observations, calculations, and reflections brought me to a number of conclusions and practical ideas for increasing output. The coal face I was working was divided into eight small sections. There were ten hewers in every shift, and even if one of us had the makings to produce more, there was no chance to do so, for lack of elbow room. The small sections were so crowded with people that they got in each other's way. Besides, the work in general was so organized that the picks were used only about three to three and a half hours a shift, or even less. The rest of the time went into timbering, for we did both the hewing and the timbering ourselves, and while we timbered, the picks lay idle.

When these handicaps were removed, I hewed 102 tons of coal in a single six-hour shift. Such performance was absolutely unheard of; 7, 8, and 9 tons had been the maximum output in our pits. This output of 102 tons was a world record. Even in the old coal fields of the Ruhr district, with all their accumulated experience, a worker's average daily output is only about 17 1/2 tons of coal.

Such was the result of the new system of production that swept away every obstacle in the path of the worker's initiative and industry.

And what happened after I made my record? The very next day Dyukanov arranged his work so well that he hewed 115 tons in his shift. The day after, Terekhin hewed 119 tons, and a few days later Kontsedalov hewed 125 tons and Savchenko as much as 151. In quite a short time I was able to hew 200 tons in one shift. This might really have seemed the maximum. However, Nikita Izotov hewed 240 tons, and Artyukhin 310, scoring 536 tons only a little later. All around me I saw my fellow workers eager to get more and more coal from their sections, from their picks. Scores and hundreds of people began forthwith to adopt my method, perfecting it all the time. No more than a few weeks elapsed before miners hewing 200, 300, or even more tons of coal with every shift could be counted by the dozen.

So this first record due to proper planning and rational organization of production gave rise to ever new records, each more remarkable than the last, first in the pits of that one colliery, and later in other collieries and other coal fields. The movement spread like wildfire to other economic fields—it took firm root in the transport system, in the factory, in agriculture; in fact, it embraced every sphere of economic activity.

So it was that the first Stakhanovites made their appearance, and now they number in the millions.

The ranks of the Stakhanovite army are swelling irresistibly. By the middle of 1938 there were in the Donets basin over 350,000 miners holding certificates of master coal-hewers (senior and junior grades). The record for the iron and steel industry is as follows: in the Central Regions, the Stakhanovites make up over 25 percent of the total number of workers, and in the South as much as 30 percent. Over a third of the workers in the heavy machinery industry are Stakhanovites, 33 percent in the medium machinery, the transport machinery, and the tractor industries, 34 percent in the electrical machinery industry, and about 50 percent in the oil-refining industry. Thus, in a number of industries from a third to half of all the workers employed are Stakhanovites, that is, people who possess a high degree of proficiency at work, who have shattered the old, now out-of-date ideas of what could be got out of machinery.

Naturally, such a spread of the Stakhanov movement, such a mass increase in labor productivity, was bound to have a very favorable effect on the country's whole economic life, and that is the clue to the successful fulfillment and overfulfillment of our national economic plans and the rapid increase in output in every field.

During the period of the Second Five-Year Plan, the average output per worker in the coal industry (coal-face workers only) has increased by 70 percent.

In 1932 the average coefficient of volumetric efficiency of blast furnaces was 1.75; in 1938 it improved considerably, going down to 1.14, and at times almost touched 1. In some of the mills the results of Stakhanovite work are even more striking. For instance, at the Stalin Mill in the Kuznetsk Basin, the coefficient in 1938 was 0.95, and for one of the furnaces—No. 2—as low as 0.72. The coefficient of the Krivoy Rog Mill was 0.98 in 1938.

In 1933, 2.8 tons of steel was the average rate per square meter of hearth. In 1938 the average was 4.64 tons, while some Stakhanovite smelters have achieved 12 tons and more.

The increase in labor productivity in large-scale industry during the period of the Second Five-Year Plan (1933–37) has amounted to 82 percent, as against the 63 percent envisaged in the plan. In every industry the development of the Stakhanov movement has led to a marked increase in efficiency.

The coal-hewers' pneumatic picks are working faster, more productively; the smelting of iron is taking less time; the machinery in the factories is running more smoothly and swiftly; on the railways, trains are running at greater speed.

How is it that this mass movement for proficiency in production, arising in one spot, spread so fast, with such overpowering force, throughout the country? Perhaps it was to some extent accidental? Perhaps the sudden appearance of the movement implies that it will be a temporary, transitory phenomenon? Far from it. Any such view of the movement would be profoundly mistaken.

The Stakhanov movement did not develop gradually; it swept the Soviet Union with whirlwind speed. And the reason it could spread so rapidly was that its roots lie in the very nature of Soviet life today, that the time for the movement was ripe and it needed only a touch-off, an initial stimulant, to break out and begin to spread far and wide.

The Stakhanov movement had its origin among the rank and file—in the pits, at the work benches, in the shops. It arose and developed on the initiative of the masses themselves. To many industrial establishments the Stakhanovites were able to achieve their remarkable results only after overcoming the resistance—at times very obstinate—of those managers and engineers who would not part with the old ideas of what were possible production capacities and rates of output.

The Stakhanov movement is a product of the will and high public spirit of the Soviet working people, who are moved by the great desire to employ to the utmost their initiative, resourcefulness, energy, and personal capacity for the sake of improving their work, of achieving better results. There are several factors underlying this desire, underlying the development of the Stakhanov movement.

In the first place, it was possible for the Stakhanov movement to become a mass movement because the Soviet people know that they are not working for the capitalists but for themselves, for the more and more complete satisfaction of their needs. In a country where the entire national income is employed for the benefit of the working people, where all the means and instruments of production, all the mills and factories, together with what they produce, as well as the land and its mineral deposits, are the property of the working people, the whole community, every improvement in the work of the individual contributes to the general welfare. The Soviet people know, they see and realize that the better work progresses, the wealthier the country becomes and the greater is the prosperity of its inhabitants. That is the reason why the Soviet people put their heart and soul into their work, why they exert every effort, use their abilities to the utmost—to enhance the prosperity of their country. Loving their homeland, they love their machines, their factories, their work.

When Stakhanovites are asked why they strive to score records, they reply as a rule that they have a real interest in their work and that the good results achieved are the natural consequence. This reply voices the general sentiment of the Soviet people.

In May 1936 our mining town of Gorlovka, in the Donets Basin, was visited by a delegation of French miners. On their return, they published their impressions in *The Miner*—a newspaper appearing in the city of Briey. I shall quote a passage:

> We could hear the muffled sound of pneumatic picks. There were four men in the gallery, plainly distressed at our appearance on the scene.
>
> After we were introduced, however, the Soviet comrades' attitude changed at once. When they raised their lamps, we could see four smiling black faces.
>
> "We are interfering, aren't we?" I asked.
>
> "That's all right," one of them replied. "You see, you are our guests, and we thought at first it was some of our boys."
>
> "Don't you get paid if you have to stand idle?"
>
> "Yes, we do," replied Yermachok, who had been pointed out to us as one of the best Stakhanovite hewers.
>
> "So why worry?"
>
> "What do you mean? Any time that's lost means less coal, and we need coal."
>
> When he said "we," it sounded as if he owned the mine.
>
> I asked him squarely:
>
> "Don't you have enough coal?"
>
> He waved his hand impatiently: "I mean the country, and you're talking about me. People work with a will, they take joy in their work. And that is the source of everything."

There is yet another very important cause for the development of the Stakhanov movement in the Soviet Union: the country has been equipped with up-to-date machinery, and numerous operatives have mastered this machinery. The Soviet people have learned to promote the technique of production, to get twice, three times, ten times as much out of their machinery as before. Many of the Stakhanovites may rightly be called masters of their craft—so well do they know their business, so thoroughly are they initiated into all the secrets of high labor efficiency.

Finally, a most important factor contributing to the rise and development of the Stakhanov movement has been the greater welfare of the people. A life of security and happiness brings with it a new pace of work. There is more teamwork and energetic application to one's job. When life is good, work is smoother, faster, more productive.

Such are the causes that gave rise to this popular movement, the Stakhanov movement, whose members have come to be the notables of the Soviet land, enjoying universal respect and admiration. They are a direct outcome of the Soviet order, of the socialist system of society in the Soviet Union. They explain why the Stakhanov movement is developing so confidently; they hold the key to its power and might.

There are some who think that the Stakhanov movement is a variety of the Taylor system. Such a view is profoundly mistaken. Taylor proceeded on the supposition that workers are naturally lazy, that they will always try to work slower than they could. When he established his rates of output, Taylor would take the hardiest workers, time their movements, and require the same output of all the rest. His system amounts to taking the result of the utmost exertion of effort by the strongest worker as the standard of output for all the others, lowering rates of pay at the same time.

Naturally, under the Taylor system only young workers can be employed, people possessed of powerful constitutions and great physical strength, capable of withstanding enormous exertion of effort for a certain length of time. It is a system which can be saddled on the workers only by force, against their will.

The Stakhanov movement, on the contrary, is a voluntary movement of the masses, who are themselves interested in the results of their work. Stakhanovite work does not call for physical overexertion. It requires only a public-spirited attitude toward one's work and a thorough study of one's machinery and its technique.

Stakhanovite work is a combination of manual and mental work. It enables the Stakhanovites to show their mettle, to display their faculties, to give free rein to their creative ideas; it signifies the victory of man over machine.

The Stakhanovite movement is significant, for it is the first token of the nascent rise of every worker to the cultural and technical level of an engineer or technician. Such progress by the working class will obviously mean still higher labor productivity, a degree of proficiency in production that will provide the universal abundance which the Soviet people are working to achieve, since that is the essential prerequisite to effect the transition to the new Communist social system, under which every member of society will receive all products according to his needs, the needs of a culturally developed human being.

Such is the significance and such the outlook of the Stakhanov movement.

Chronicle of Komsomolsk-on-the-Amur
The Beginning of a City
Yury Zhukov and Roza Izmailova (1937)

THE SAGA OF RAISING A NEW CITY IN THE MIDST OF A DISTANT WILDERNESS RESOUNDED THROUGH HIGH AND POPULAR CULTURE THROUGHOUT THE 1930s — IN SONG, STORY, AND MOVIE — AND ANIMATED THE YOUNG COMMUNIST (KOMSOMOL) MOVEMENT. TRAINLOADS OF VOLUNTEERS MADE THE MONTH-LONG TREK ALONG THE TRANS-SIBERIAN RAILROAD OUT TO THE FORESTED SITE ON THE BANKS OF THE AMUR RIVER. THE THEME ALSO INSPIRED A FAMOUS MOVIE OF THE TIME, *KOMSOMOLSK* (1938), WHICH FEATURED A SABOTEUR BAND'S PLOT TO WRECK THE CONSTRUCTION.

From *Vchera i segodnia* (Moscow: Khudozhestvennaia literatura, 1960), vol. 1, pp. 344–360.

Far to the east, in one of the taiga's wildest and most remote corners, where the Amur rolls swift and broad through the hills on its way to the ocean, stands a new city. Young Communists dispatched east by Party planners founded it in 1932. There on the banks of the Amur, surrounded by wild forests, bogs, and swamps, rose mighty factories, palaces of culture, theaters. Upon its birth in the autumn of 1932, the city was named for the Young Communist League: Komsomolsk-on-the-Amur.

Year by year, the city's fame spreads further across the land. Young people think of it as their own, like family. Volunteers come by the hundreds, and they write thousands of letters: "Tell us what you did back then, what you accomplished, how you built a city, what help you need." In 1937, when the Komsomol celebrated the fifth anniversary of its city, delegations of young workers, kolkhozniks, engineers, artists, and musicians streamed in from all over the country. People traveled ten thousand kilometers to meet their peers who were building a new cultural center for the Far East in the remote, impenetrable taiga.

We, two reporters for *Komsomol Pravda,* were fortunate enough to visit Komsomolsk-on-the-Amur for the occasion. The journey turned out to be so interesting that we are publishing some quick notes we jotted down along the way.

. . . An old, two-stack steamboat, its ridiculous paddles splashing the water, floats steadily along the current of the big, deep-bottomed river. The distant banks loom a murky blue on the horizon. The crowns of steep, angular mountains are painted scarlet by a flaring sunset. The violet dusk thickens above hilltops overgrown with hazelnut bushes. The wondrous river reaches a width of several kilometers in these parts. Tossing off sparks and frantically bellowing smoke, the steamboat crashes through heavy foam-crested waves. The vast expanse of water, where real sea gales sometimes rise, makes it look like a toy boat.

Residents of European Russia have never seen such rivers. The Amur does not even resemble a river. Many water currents are diabolically interwoven. They rush several thousand kilometers to the ocean, flowing together, then parting and spilling their waters on the broad floodplains. The Amur has deposited huge lakes and swamps where weeping willows and soft grasses grow.

The captain of the steamboat *Ilich* is an old sailor, who has sailed the Amur more than thirty years. He willingly shares his recollections of customs and laws that once ruled these waters.

"Who traveled the river back then? Merchants. Fish buyers. Kulaks—whoever had the money. Mercenary gold prospectors. Officers. There weren't many passengers. After all, most of the settlers and workers were brought in on barges.[1] Once I went through something I'll never forget.

"We were heading for Nikolaevsk. The tugboat was pulling three barges: two with dead weight, one with living weight—prisoners. The *Mermaid* was taking them to Sakhalin.

"All of a sudden, a terrible storm swooped down on us. I wanted to head to shore

---

1. A standard form of prison transport.

to wait it out, but the cops pushed us on. A wave caught the *Mermaid* and flipped it over. In a minute my hair was gray: there were seventy people, all behind bars. Not a one was saved."

The captain nervously snapped a rosemary twig and tossed it overboard.

"It's hard to think of it without getting worked up. Tsarism turned our entire land into a prison camp. It did everything to make people hate these hills, this sky, the Amur. But can you really?"

The steamship siren sounded a drawn-out toot to greet an approaching vessel, the steamship *Karl Marx*, hurrying south through the waves. A long, mournful Volga song reached us from the stern. A hand waved a white kerchief in farewell, and a girl's laughter rang above the river.

"From Komsomolsk," the captain said quietly.

It grew dark. The silhouettes of distant peaks seemed to come alive like huge prehistoric lizards. The last gleam of sunset dusted their snowy peaks gold. The intoxicating fragrance of cherry blossoms reached us. All around, as far as the eye could see, it was deserted.

Suddenly a distant bonfire flared. Many bonfires. Flickering fires stretched along the banks in a chain.

These were the fires of Komsomolsk. In the taiga backwoods, among stony hills on the banks of this tremendous river, our eyes could hardly believe that tens of thousands of fires suddenly ignited to light the streets, when the bright "eyes" of building-site floodlights and the colored lanterns of docked ships appeared. They seemed right next to us. But the steamboat kept moving, the electric glow grew brighter, and the trip continued on.

"The port of Komsomolsk," the captain repeated. "My daughter works here. At the machine factory... The city... Factories... The port..."

"I've sailed these shores for thirty to forty years," continued the captain, "and I see the changes taking place in this area better than anyone else. Here's Sofievka, it was a commonplace village. Many captains never even dropped anchor here. And now it's a city!

"And the Jemgi nomad camp? There were no more than thirty fanza[2] before. And now there's a first-class factory and a settlement. It's a suburb of Komsomolsk. We never halted ship before at Permsk village, where the city is now. Once in a while you'd pick up a couple passengers—usually the Kuznetsovs, who were kulaks, when they traveled from Permsk to Khabarovsk to sell pelts. That was it. And now..."

The captain saluted and went over to the bridge.

"Starboard rudder!"

The steamboat shuddered, churning the waves, and turned to shore. The golden fires on the embankment rocked as they came nearer. The funny little tugboat with a disproportionately tall smokestack sputtered and sparked. A steam engine whistled somewhere on shore. Automobiles drove along the embankment with blazing headlights.

---

2. A Korean peasant hut.

Silhouettes of buildings and construction sites peeked through the murky darkness. Red signal flares glowed atop tall masts.

Yes, a real city! Anchor chains rattled, the sloop oars splashed, and a floodlight shone on the gangplank leading to the river bank.

"We don't have a floating landing stage yet, and our wharf has put us in a tight spot. It's lost," a slightly sarcastic voice said. We looked around. A hale and hearty fellow puffed abstractedly on a hand-rolled cigarette. He was hatless and the wind rustled his soft hair. He seemed immediately likable and acted somehow homey— like he was standing in front of his own house, saw some friends, and was inviting them in. That's how it actually happened. The stranger introduced himself warmly:

"Lesha Kuchumov from Komsomolsk-on-the-Amur. You've come for the anniversary, of course?"

"You guessed it!"

"Excellent!"

Thus we met one of Komsomolsk's old-time residents.

"The old-timers of 1932" these ardent city patriots were called.

Lesha Kuchumov became our indispensable companion. Although he was a native Leningrader and had lived only five of his twenty-seven years in Komsomolsk, he had managed to become a living chronicle of the new city. It turned out he was on vacation, and therefore he readily agreed to wander around with us for a few days.

Next morning, after we had gotten a decrepit Ford (born the same year as the city) from the municipal Komsomol committee, we took off. Pasha Mozgovoi, the committee's ex-chauffeur, dashingly steered his car through piles of crushed stone, mounds of wet sand, lathes, wood chips, and scrap metal.

Here are some notes on our first impressions: The city begins on a big, broad highway, which has the temporary construction name of "Brigade." We drive by tiny houses with merry sharp-cornered red roofs and cozy top stories, by the large wooden "Komsomol Settlement," all the buildings of which are painted a fresh pink, by a new "Gastronomy" store with mirrored display windows.

"Old" and "new" Komsomolsk are neighbors, but they squeeze each other. Directly in front of us were some primeval long-houses. Only someone lost in the woods would make such a place to live. Back then, a thick wall of pine had stood on the new city's territory. These first long-houses were built in clearings slowly cut from the forest. The human habitat was simple in 1932! Three stakes. Birch bark on top. Weave vines all around.

But the gloomy, primitive long-house city was gradually overwhelmed by the expanding construction site. It was crowded out by buildings of stone, brick, and wood. A huge Sixteenth Anniversary of the Revolution Club was built next to the long-houses. A bit further on—two big, beautiful new garages. A broad avenue led to a cluster of unfinished two-story homes. They say that doctors will soon move in. They try to set them up comfortably. The hospital is also nearby. It's an entire city. The maternity hospital is comfortably situated as well. The doctor who runs it is very busy; on the average, 250 infants are added to Komsomolsk per month.

In a couple of blocks there's another big red building. A tall portal. Big, pretty windows.

"What is it, a theater?"

The chauffeur turns around and chuckles: "Not quite. It's our new bathhouse! When they finish it, 500 people will be able to wash at the same time."

The streets we're traveling have unusual names: Bruschatka, Firemen's Settlement, Accidentville. They were named in the haste of construction. Pasha Mozgovoi, looking ahead, says: "It'll all be done soon. I read in the *Komsomolsk Shock Worker* that the city soviet is getting new names ready for the streets. We already have eighty-two streets."

"Well, how do you like the city?" Lesha Kuchumov interrupts him impatiently, pointing proudly to the new three-story Sergo Ordzhonikidze Grade School.

A muted crack rings out somewhere.

"Kopai-grad[3] is closing up," Lesha explains. "I'll take the photographer there tomorrow. It'll be a historical snapshot!"

We drive along the riverbank.

. . . The dust, scraping, and cracking get nearer. There it is, the "historical picture" that Lesha promised. "Kopai-grad" is in its death throes. Its dark underground burrows are living through their final months. Scraps of roofing paper, clods of dirt, plywood remnants, scrap iron, shards of glass: how fantastically rich are these half-blind dens that first sheltered humans against the severe Amur winds.

Patchwork hovels are being torn to pieces. The axe and crowbar are terminating the existence of these earthen shelters. But three or four of them will be preserved as visible witnesses to bygone days, museum exhibits that remind amazed passersby: thus lived man!

The embankment that we're driving along with Lesha Kuchumov is still called Permsk, the name of the remote taiga village nestled on this shore five years ago. Its small gray huts remain in a few places. They cling to uneven earthen mounds, darkening the magnificence of the steep, proud bank with their meager façades, their wooden posts, their rotted porches.

In the early dusk on the river bank, the translucent Amur landscape wins your heart. You want to stand long on the embankment and watch the hills cloak themselves in smoky fog against the chill. Their half-round wooded silhouettes slowly turn a deep blue. It seems as if the sun only just dropped behind the gray mountaintop, leaving behind three streaks of soft, dying flame. Against this cloudy watercolor, the dying shades of old Perm village seem pitifully sad.

. . . A wooden parachute tower and the magnificent, graceful slipways of the Amur shipyard loom above the city. Its new docks are still scaffolded, but an orderly row of tall columns already sketches their future outline. From these docks, ships will depart for the broad Amur expanses.

Komsomolsk will be a city of great factories.

---

3. Digsville.

But for now, how scattered it is, this city! We wander through the woods, stopping before signs nailed right to the trees—"Victory Village," "Nekrasov Street," "Red Street"—and inspect the big factory workshops. Lesha Kuchumov is plainly happy that Komsomolsk impresses guests as a big, lively, growing city.

"And that's not all," he says with a certain self-satisfaction. "You should come in a year. This summer we'll build another twenty stone buildings, sixty two-story wooden houses, a stadium..."

Our companion tells us of new plans. He is literally in love with his city and doesn't seem to notice that it is chaotic, muddy, inhospitable.

One evening we mentioned this to Lesha. He laughed:

"Of course I'm in love. How could it be otherwise? Don't you know what an old-timer's patriotism is like? It's... Anyway, I won't talk about it. Better let's drop in on the Komsomol dormitory some weekend. It's in the Bruschatka Settlement. The guys will get together and talk about old times. Then a lot of things will become clearer to you."

We remember that evening in Bruschatka well. The dorm residents were popular in the city. After all, they had arrived on the first voyage of the steamboat *Columbus*. They were the founders and first citizens of a new city. Their stories helped us see the origins of Komsomolsk's birth.

TRAINS LEAVE FOR THE EAST

The year 1932 was rich in events, a year of apprehension but also of tremendous enterprise. Worrisome news was in the paper every morning. Cannon roared on the fields of Manchuria; Japanese divisions fought their way closer to the Soviet border. Days were dark in Berlin; brown-shirted regiments marched while Hitler wailed hysterically about how Germany needed the Ukraine.

Everyday life was full of hardships: food lines in state stores, hundreds of people sleeping in train stations waiting for trains that were late. And still, life moved forward purposefully in the direction of tremendous changes.

The West was amazed to discover that new blast furnaces were being fired up in the Urals, and that conveyor belts had started running in the Stalingrad and Kharkov tractor factories. The turbines of Dneprostroi[4] had been installed, and in Gorky the automobile factory was nearing completion. And everywhere young, strong, energetic people were needed.

 . . . Three friends, Young Communists, left for work without coats on a warm March day near the banks of the Dnepr (that's how they begin the story of this memorable period). Their comparatively recent arrival at the hydro-power station had been a special assignment that made each of them very proud. They were tagged the "towboat brigade," and their task was to transfer to the Dneprostroi project the experience of a renowned Komsomol battalion that had set a world record for concrete pouring at the Kharkov tractor factory site.

---

4. A dam on the Dnepr River.

A swarthy youngster with thick, tangled eyebrows and an unkempt mop of hair clambered up the scaffolding to the top of the huge iron-alloy factory. Here, at a height of thirty-four meters, the shock brigade of female cementworkers he was to direct was at work. They were to finish laying cement for the last bunker that day. The young brigade leader didn't look too reliable: his puffy, almost childlike cheeks betrayed his youth. But the Kharkov construction site had been an excellent school, and his name was known throughout the Soviet Union. Pictures of the mop-headed cement-layer were plastered all over the newspapers. When construction of the Tractor Factory was completed, he had received what was then a remarkable and unusual prize: with a group of shock workers, he was awarded a trip around Europe on the steamship *Ukraine*. So Panchenko had been in Berlin, London, Naples, Istanbul, and had only recently returned to the Dnepr, to the greatest construction site of the south.

"Panchenko-o-o!"

The dark-eyed cement-layer glanced down below. What's that? His friends Zhuk and Zvantsev, who should have been at work already by his calculations, were standing at the base of the tower and waving desperately.

"Sasha! Come here!"

Evidently something unusual had happened.

"Guys! Why the hell'd you stop working? Couldn't you wait for break?"

The brigade leaders were taken aback, but tongue-tied by excitement, they told him of an extraordinary happening. Half an hour ago Zvantsev had been mobilized to the Far East. Why, nobody knew! And soon the army would be taking Zhuk. And it wasn't even his year yet!

"Pretty soon you'll be the only rooster in this henhouse."

Panchenko grew sad. But then he found a way out of the problem:

"We can probably stay together if we go to the Far East..."

"You know, we're needed more there. We finish the cement work today. Let's try, what do you say? First let's go to the Komsomol committee, and then to the Military Board about Zhuk."

Next day, the three friends left for Kharkov. Draftees were gathering there for transport. A throng of Komsomols saw them off. The sun was shining brightly, and the young grass was turning green. Here in the south, spring was in full bloom. Everything was coming back to life and young. Only the train seemed unattractive—the Komsomols called it the "Veal Express." They quickly erected cast-iron stoves, made wooden bunks, hung up iron lanterns in the freight cars.

The dirtiest car of all was very noisy. The Komsomols, it turned out, had gotten a coal car that was just unloaded. Someone complained: "The Krivorozhie organization doesn't deserve such an affront! Krivorozhie fulfilled the Five-Year Plan in three years!"

The young man flew off the handle, and a fluffy-haired girl wearing a man's jacket stopped him. She brandished some rags and implored:

"No time. I tell you there's no time for this. Don't make a ruckus, take a rag, we'll get things clean right away. Otherwise the train'll start and it'll still be filthy."

Panchenko wanted to butt in and help the girl, but suddenly he saw a teenager in a neatly pressed uniform and howled joyfully: "Krikun! Kolya... how'd you get here?"

The meeting was unexpected. Two years ago Panchenko had seen him for the last time in the Ukrainian backwater Orekhov. Krikun was a student in the Central Institute of Labor School, and Panchenko was its Komsomol secretary. They became friends. Then fate dispatched them to separate construction sites, and now...

"You're going to the Far East?"

"Exactly. And you?"

The locomotive whistled, and the long train set off. It turned out that the train held a whole group of old friends from Orekhov. It was simply wonderful. An entire company of old buddies was heading east.

The train traveled slowly. At stops, Komsomols raced car to car and struck up friendships. The only bad thing was that there were no girls; one for the whole train, and she was wearing a man's jacket.

Semyon Vinokurov, a Komsomol with merry blue eyes, warned: "Don't fool around with Tishchenko; she's worth two guys. By day she was a carpenter, and she worked nights in the mineshafts running coal cars."

Tishchenko straightened her pretty hair in confusion. Some smart alecks from Kiev tried to tease her. She took the hand of one scoffer and squeezed his fingers so hard that he lost any desire to babble about fragile girls.

The train was filled with Ukrainian Komsomols exclusively. Entire organizations were going. A car from Kiev, one from Odessa, one from the Zaporozhie... As they traveled they printed newspapers, played chess, gave lectures, washed their linen. When junction stops dragged on, the Komsomols would inspect everything. The train left some of them behind, and they had to catch up by courier train. These incidents were severely condemned at all-car meetings.

Panchenko loved to travel. He kept the complete run of a curious newspaper, whose editorial board changed its address daily. The first issue heading read: Baltic Sea. The second issue came out with a new address: Kiel Canal. The third read: Pas-de-Calais–Lamanche, the fourth: the Bay of Cadiz (Spain). The paper was called *The Second Voyage,* and it wandered around Europe with its readers aboard the steamship *Ukraine.*

When rain drizzled from the sky and car residents slid the doors shut, already sick of the Siberian plains, Panchenko took the papers from his suitcase and the Komsomols gathered around the stove. Although they knew beforehand what he was going to read, they still watched the brigade leader with curiosity: he had seen a hell of a lot in his short life. Panchenko cleared his throat and began significantly:

"Log entry. August 21. We gazed at Italy's bright-lit shores until midnight. At 6:30 we docked. The Soviet colony meets us. The fascist port police scramble up on deck. Headquarters is working out a plan for our visit to Genoa.

"August 22. At nine in the morning some shock workers get in a bus and ride off to see the city, others leave for the artillery factory "Ansaldo" in a charter tram.

"August 23. After breakfast all the shock workers, some off-duty crew members, along with the Soviet colony, take a train to Rappalo. There, at the international spa, the bourgeois public dropped their jaws at the sight of Soviet shock workers.

"August 24. At 6:00 we separate: some go to Milan, others to Turin, to the Fiat factory."

And the train kept going further east. The portents of spring were disappearing, and it got colder every day. The provident Dneprostroi workers pulled on new boots and wrapped themselves in warm blankets. The careless Odessans, who had departed their hometown in summer clothes, froze desperately and cursed the dry, cold climate of the East. Lena Tishchenko was also shivering from the cold, but she wouldn't let on, and bellowed Ukrainian songs.

Beyond Lake Baikal the first quarrels began: Klochko, an Odessa metalworker, read some morbid poetry out loud and said that in this climate the poetic gift might abandon him. His friend, the boilermaker Ilyushin, made sarcastic cracks about cowardly poetasters.

. . . March passed. Soon it would be a month since the train had headed east. Conversation died out in the cars. The singing stopped. One could sense an orphaned anguish; they had strayed into far and unaccustomed lands, not at all like the warm and pleasant south.

Sanya Panchenko and Nikolai Krikun acted more courageously. They loved adventure, and the journey pleased them immensely. Kolya dreamed of one thing: finding a rifle and hunting wild boar. There were said to be tons of them. But for some reason the train-station stalls didn't trade in boar meat or tiger skins. The Far East looked a good deal more prosaic than it had seemed from the Ukraine.

When the train reached Khabarovsk on the thirty-fifth day, Kuchumov sent them straight to Voronezh wharf, where the young people were put on the first steamboat headed for Permsk settlement.

Funny that the steamboat was called the *Columbus*. Ilyushin from Odessa, who loved allegories, proved to his friend Klochko that there was a special meaning in the name: the *Columbus* was going to discover a new world. Klochko agreed sluggishly and gazed sadly over the side of the boat. He didn't like the strange river, where ice flows till the fifth of May. In his hometown of Odessa, he would have been able to swim by May.

The dilapidated steamboat crawled along the current. The paddlewheel blades slapped the water lazily. It was dry and cold. A dank fog hung over the Amur. The Komsomols hid in the hold and warmed themselves packed together on the bunks.

At ten in the morning the *Columbus* and another steamboat, the *Comintern*, gave long toots on their whistles. Dogs could be heard barking from the steep bank. Thirty plank huts stood on the slope. A bare forest stripped of foliage rustled beyond. Finally the long journey was ending.

In five years, the memory of this time would evoke a warm smile.

In five years they would be experienced managers, Party workers, qualified specialists.

They would live on the very same slope, but amid a big city, driving automobiles along its paved roads, spending evenings in the theater, reading the city's daily paper in the morning.

Five years later, on a warm evening in May 1937, it would be hard to recognize the young sailor of 1932 in Vagarshap Guloyan, a municipal Party committee instructor strolling along the embankment with a throng of Pioneers and telling them: "That's how we came to be here."

VAGARSHAP AND KUZMA BUILD A SMITHY

Work began in mayhem and misery. You can't chop down the taiga without axes. It seemed that order would not come to this chaos soon.

Directors and leaders were still hard to pick out among the barrels, crates, and pallets marked "Moscow," "Rostov," "Odessa," or "Nizhny Novgorod." Everyone was giving commands and orders at the same time. Superintendents were accosted from all directions. "Where are the axes? Where do we start digging? How do we sharpen our saws? When are you handing out boots?"

An electrician from Rostov, the communist Pyotr Tkach, figured out with amazement that hard efforts had scraped up a mere twenty-three axes and thirteen saws over the entire construction site. The Komsomols went to work in the forest as they had come, in light clothes and canvas shoes. The sneakers fell apart at first contact with the thick and sticky taiga mud. Tkach angrily remembered the foolish advice he had gotten from some Rostov volunteers: "Travel light. Don't take any work clothes or tools. Everything will be ready when you get there."

Now it was clear that such talk was scatterbrained. But how to repair the damage? You can't have every construction worker order boots and canvas pants from Moscow. And when would they get here?

It turned out they had even forgotten to build a bakery, and that a powerful steamboat had to be sent to Khabarovsk for five tons of baked bread.

Vagarshap Guloyan found it amusing at first: he had always liked life to be complicated. But adventure seemed more demanding here in the primitive taiga than it had in books. They had to spin their wheels for days. Crawl through attics in search of "free space," then set up a cafeteria in a former church, then go with a committee to dekulakize[5] the wealthy Romanov family, which kept the entire village in collusion, or wander the taiga and collect registration cards from Komsomols—it was time already to make a duty list of the organization. Then he had to equip the machine shop. That was an urgent assignment. There was still no electric light, no blacksmith's, no metal shop. It's easy to say: open a workshop! But how do you do it if there's nowhere to put it, no tools, no materials?

Vagarshap Guloyan and Tkach remembered the hardships of Robinson Crusoe more than once. First they found a shop—or so they called the big barn. They had to buy it from a local fisherman for a half-crate of candy and a half-crate of cookies. Then in cargo dumped straight down by the huts they searched out sixteen machine vises, parts of a lathe, and a small motor. The barn stood a good distance down along the Amur current. How could the loads be hauled? Too much to carry. Then Vagarshap came up with an idea: "Some Robinson Crusoes we are! Tkach, remember how he got his crates ashore!"

---

5. A euphemism for murdering or sending to a Siberian prison.

Tkach smiled. He liked the idea. The guys quickly tied a few logs together and hauled the machine vises onto the improvised raft. Then they grabbed a rope and pulled the raft along the shore like barge-haulers.

When the "machine shop" was ready, Tkach stayed behind to get work started, and Vagarshap began to set up the blacksmith's. That was even more complicated. The supply depot had completely forgotten that a smithy would be needed, and they hadn't brought any equipment from Khabarovsk. The chief mechanic goaded Vagarshap:

"I know you Komsomols. If you want to you'll even dig one out of the ground. Do what you want, but make sure there's a smithy in five days."

Vagarshap wandered gloomily along the Amur bank. Another idea came to his head: it can't be possible that the village doesn't have a blacksmith. Find him, and then...

By evening they had actually found him. It turned out he had already liquidated his shop and was packing his trunk. Vagarshap begged from him an old, torn bellows, which the blacksmith was too lazy to drag very far.

Together with Kuzma, a hammerer from Nizhny Novgorod who came to help, they mended the bellows with the leather uppers of Vagarshap's boots. What can you do, you have to sacrifice! They found an anvil on the *Klara Zetkin*, a boiler-barge. They got an iron cart axle from the Forest Products Division, and forged pincers from it.

Thousands of people were already living on the shore in long-houses and earthen huts. They needed a post office, a hospital, a school, a bakery, and a steambath. However strange it may seem, in the woods they had already laid the foundation of a temporary talking-picture theater, though if truth be told it was only a canvas stretched between two birches; and the Komsomols, swatting the persistent mosquitoes away, watched movies standing up. The post office was stuck in a little barn. The people that had been sent didn't know what they were doing yet, and a pile of letters and telegrams was stacked in the corner. Everyone had to dig through the stack of soiled envelopes to find his or her own letters.

A big event was the sawmill opening. But still the untamed taiga was as frightening as ever, and in the long-houses at night, tempers flared more than once. To some it seemed that no city could be built on this accursed spot, and that they should flee. Others restrained them and said they should wait and see what would come of it.

. . . However, some began to run away. Datyuk, from Kiev, disappeared. Then an entire group of Komsomols was guided into the taiga by a suspicious old man who had taken money from them.

The eighteen-year-old Komsomol Kalachev was depressed by his nickname, Pupsik,[6] which he got because he was short. That was denigrating, and Pupsik wanted to prove that he was a real man any way he could. But how? He fell in with a gang of inveterate debauchees and cardsharks whose "god" was Zhorka Konovalov,[7] and

---

6. Little Belly-Button.
7. Cattle-Rustler.

painstakingly copied their manners. Konovalov was a smart card player. Soon he had twenty thousand rubles. And then he proposed to Pupsik: "Pupsik! Listen up. Let's go to Moscow."

Kalachev turned red and lied: "I don't have any money!"

"A trifle. I'll take care of you."

Kalachev got angry: "I'm a Komsomol, Zhora!" He wanted to leave right then, but it was a pity to ruin his reputation just like that. He tried to make excuses: "Zhora, somebody here has to work!"

"God" shrugged. "Idiot. In Moscow you'll work in a joiners' shop; it's good, warm, and you're a joiner! Here you have to dig up birches. Why?"

"But we'll build our own joiners' shop here. I'll be making ships."

"You'll croak first; there'll be nothing left of you but superphosphates."

"You're not a Komsomol, Zhora, you're only out for yourself. I gave my word to the Frunze Regional Committee that I'd build a factory. Got it?"

"God" made fun of him: "Wow, how principled. We wanted to save the jerk and he puts the noose around his own neck."

Konovalov and his buddies split. Kalachev stayed at the site.

The Komsomol Committee was located at the time in an old steambath on a double-decker plank bed. Here the Komsomols kept deserters caught in the forest or on the steamboat, and talked with them. Protocols of these conversations were sewn into a tattered binder with the melancholy title: "Fugitives from the Construction Site."

The protocols looked like this:

"1. Sham-Uli. Born 1915. Komsomol from 1930. Worked in the second sector in Fisakov's brigade. Reason for escape: grub stinks, pooped, stomach sick. Resolved: send to the doctor.

"2. Bortovoi. Born 1913. Komsomol from 1932. Worked in the fourth sector in Cheremisov's brigade. Announces: I'm sick of this life. I escaped and will run away again, won't work. Resolved: organize a public trial, expel from the Komsomol, and ban from the construction site."

People were tired. Many weren't used to the climate, to the cruelty of nature. And when some suspicious old guy started a rumor about bears coming out of the forest to hunt, desertions increased.

Panchenko and Guloyan crawled through attics, roamed the huts, ran through the taiga stopping people, talking with them. The committee created antidesertion patrols, ran meetings for absentees, unmasked local kulaks who incited the deserters. Every day the work was different. Political instruction was conducted in the long-houses. They collected the children of workers who came to the site and created the first Pioneer detachments. They confiscated cards and switchblades. Wrote appeals. Organized the repair of torn boots and shoes. Collectively they gathered berries and mushrooms in the taiga.

Tkach left to secure vegetable supplies from the Tambov region. Andreev went to Nikolaevsk to buy fishing equipment: the Komsomols had decided to start a fishing industry at the site. Of course, by doing these things the Komsomols were taking the place of cooperatives.[8] But they had decided to do anything to keep workers satisfied. The committee didn't lose spirit and thrived with the multitude of worries.

Animated conversations could be heard in the long-houses at night. Zak, a Rostov Komsomol, found some kerosene, made an oil lamp from a jar, and read lectures in the evening about what life would be like under Communism. The guys began to study the history of the Party. They collected whatever books anyone in the huts owned and made the first taiga library.

The physical-culturalists met on a tiny field near the village church. They owned a ball, and began to train for the regional Spartak Games, where they wanted to send a delegation of athletes from the new city. The workers themselves had already begun to call it Komsomolsk. Everyone liked the name. It was a successful idea. Komsomolsk—the first Komsomol city in the world—that's what was built here in the taiga. Many sectors asked the Komsomol committee to send the government a letter asking that the city be given the honorary name of Komsomolsk.

The city of youth has carried its new name for five years now. That distant address is cherished by all Soviet young people. From Moscow a train left, filled with girls who had decided to resettle in the taiga capital. A letter from the wife of the mayor of De-Castri Bay, Valentina Khetagurova, inviting girlfriends to go to the Far East, inspired many, and postmen dragged bales of telegrams and letters to the Regional Komsomol Committee: "Telegraph need mechanics and gardeners arrive stop Donbass October Krindachevka 56 Khodorovka Dronova."

"My girlfriend engineer coming Komsomolsk stop offer services arts director Park of Culture or theater director stop Moscow 37 Park of Culture Director Maltsev."

"Komsomolsk. Municipal Komsomol Committee. Comradely greetings! We live at a time when anyone can do anything, and so permit me to go on. But I'm unacquainted with you both, and one has to know with whom is he speaking. Here's who I am: my name is Pyotr Andreevich Kulkov. I'm 24. My father was a railroad mechanic. I'm a member of the Komsomol from 1929. From 1926, when I finished school, I was an absolute orphan, after which I fell in with hooligans and began to go bad.

"But then I tore myself away from that, began to study again in the factory night school, and finished with the rank of assistant railroad mechanic. I was a driver, a mechanic, a watchmaker, and secretary of the factory Komsomol organization. I was frequently given production awards. In 1936 they finally sent me to summer school. But then something bad happened—they dismissed me from the school because of an illness, and that was terribly sad.

"Then I decided to come to you with my wife (forgive me, let me introduce you)—Klavdia Semyonovna Kulkova, a Komsomol and work-process technician (she also lived four years in an orphanage, where she came into my life). We want to be useful to the labor front. We chose your new city of youth. But since we don't

---

8. I.e., engaging in nonsocialist forms of economy.

know it, and the distance is so great, we're turning to you for advice. If you think we would be useful people and our professions would come in handy, then write us your answer to Kazan. We send all your Komsomol organization our greetings and firmly shake all your hands.

"P. A. and K. S. Kulkov, spouses."

. . . The long-awaited steamships arrived on a clear spring evening. The city was living its usual life. Somewhere on the other side of the river, dynamite was exploding in a rock quarry. A locomotive whistled merrily as it rushed along the small-gauge rail on the embankment. A noisy pack of little kids ran out of the school. And suddenly someone's high, pure voice rang out over the river:

"I see-ee it! Smoke around the bend!"

People followed the shout to the very same bank where exactly five years before the *Columbus* and the *Comintern* had set anchor.

The silhouettes of the steamships floating along the current grew more distinct.

"Lesha, see it? Our *Comintern.*"

Pressing through the crowd, Panchenko, holding up the construction banner, emotionally embraced Lesha Kuchumov. They both watched the steamship that had brought the first construction Komsomols into the isolated taiga five years ago as it broke through the Amur ice.

Today girls from the capital were descending the steps to the shore. They smiled shyly at the suntanned, broad-shouldered builders and excitedly listened to Vagarshap Guloyan as he delivered the speech he had spent so much time preparing.

"Dear girls! Your ships have moored at the city of youth, about which so many young men and girls of the Soviet country have dreamed. This meeting moves us: today is our anniversary. Exactly five years ago this very same *Columbus* and *Comintern* brought here, into the taiga backwoods, the first Komsomol detachment, and I greeted them too. In those days things were dark, gloomy, and a little scary. Perhaps to some it seemed that the experiment could not succeed. However, they turned out to be wrong. I want to tell you today that everything came out right, and how much there is in our young city, only five years old.

"On the site of the Victory settlement there are foundations for 40 new buildings, and 82 roofs are already up. Today in our 12 schools there are 6,208 pupils. Komsomolsk residents can borrow 111 books from the Ostrovsky Library, including Goethe's *Faust,* Mendeleev's *Foundations of Chemistry, The Shipbuilder's Encyclopedia,* Rustaveli's *Knight in a Panther Skin,* Flaubert's *Salammbo.* The Central Bookstore sold 300 books and 270 brochures yesterday. The theater has begun to rehearse a new play. Almost a thousand workers are taking night courses in high-schools and the workers' college. In the municipal military soviet over 600 people are being trained by sport-shooting and sailing instructors. Our radio network serves over 980 points. Tonight there will be a local broadcast, and you'll hear an old Komsomolsk resident, the technician Kuchumov, read his sketch "Trains Head for the East." He'll tell about the new builders of the city. What else can I tell you? What about this—our trade organizations made 573,000 rubles today. The shipbuilding factory's clinic served 286 patients and made housecalls to another 32. The municipal clerk registered 6 newborns and 1 marriage.

"Yesterday at 23 hours 15 minutes a goods and passenger train arrived from Khabarovsk. It brought 470 passengers, and some girls arrived: 19." Guloyan waved to them and added: "Of course, this isn't the capital. I won't hide that things will also be tough on you. But all the same we have accomplished something in these last five years and, as they say, be happy for the riches you have!"

The girls joyfully applauded and shouted "Hurrah!" Guloyan hopped off the truck and busily began to explain their new apartment addresses to them. Their suitcases were loaded onto cars, and a friendly column of many thousands moved off the shore.

A new shift of Komsomols had arrived in the East to help our first city of youth grow and flourish on the banks of the Amur.

Ever Higher

Pavel German and Yuly Khait (1920)

THE AGGRESSIVE OPTIMISM OF THIS SONG SPEAKS FOR ITSELF. NOTE ITS FOLKLORIC STYLE. THOUGH WRITTEN IN 1920 (WITH WORDS FROM THE LYRICIST OF "THE BRICK FACTORY," ALSO IN THIS VOLUME), IT WAS THE EMBLEM FOR PEOPLE WHO WERE YOUNG IN THE 1930s AND ESCAPED ITS HORRORS. THE AIR FORCE CHOSE IT AS AN ANTHEM. OTHERS HAVE FOUND IT FALSE AND REPUGNANT. AN UNDERGROUND PARODY OF IT APPEARED IN THE 1960s, OPENING WITH THE WORDS "WE WERE BORN TO MAKE KAFKA'S NIGHTMARE COME TRUE."

ВСЕ ВЫШЕ (АВИАМАРШ)

Мы рожденны чтоб сказку сделать
    былью,
Преодолеть пространство и простор.
Нам разум дал стальные руки—крылья,
А вместо сердца пламенный мотор.

EVER HIGHER (AVIATORS' MARCH)

We were born to make fairy tales come
    true,
To conquer the distances and space,
Our minds made steel wings for our
    hands,
And throbbing engines take the places
    of our hearts.

From a private collection.

Все выше, выше и выше
Стремим мы полет наших птиц,
И в каждом пропеллере дышит
Спокойствие наших границ.

Бросая ввысь свой аппарат послушный,
Или творя невиданный полет,
Мы сознаем, как крепнет флот
    воздушный,
Наш первый в мире пролетарский флот.

Наш острый взгляд пронзает каждый
    атом,
Наш каждый нерв решимостью одет.
И верьте нам: на всякий ультиматум
Воздушный флот сумеет дать ответ.

Все выше, выше и выше
Стремим мы полет наших птиц,
И в каждом пропеллере дышит
Спокойствие наших границ.

Ever higher, higher and higher
We aim the flight of our birds,
The tranquility of our borders
Breathes in each propeller.

Throwing our willing planes into the
    heavens,
Or making unprecedented flights,
We feel how our air force is growing
    stronger
Our workers' air force, the first in the
    world.

Our keen glance pierces every atom,
And resolution clads every nerve,
Believe us: to every ultimatum
Our air force will give the right
    response.

Ever higher, higher and higher
We aim the flight of our birds,
The tranquility of our borders
Breathes in each propeller.

Radio Speech of K. E. Tsiolkovsky
1 May 1935

TSIOLKOVSKY (1857–1935), PIONEER EXPERIMENTER WITH SPACE TRAVEL AND ROCKETS, BECAME AN ICON OF RUSSIAN SCIENTIFIC INVENTIVENESS IN THE AGE OF AVIATION. ONE OF HIS LAST SPEECHES WAS BROADCAST BY RADIO—A MAJOR VEHICLE FOR THE CONVEYANCE OF POPULAR SCIENCE AS WELL AS CULTURE AND OFFICIAL POLICIES. IT WAS FEATURED, ALONG WITH SPEECHES BY THE ACADEMICIAN A. E. FERSMAN AND THE TRACK-STAR BROTHERS ZNAMENSKY, IN A MAY DAY PROGRAM TRANS-

From *Istoriia sovetskoi radio-zhurnalistiki. Dokumenty, teksty, vospominaniia, 1917–1945* (Moscow: Izd. Moskovskogo universiteta, 1991), pp. 175–176.

I permit myself to address ardent fatherly greetings to the May Day proletarian and kolkhoz columns from the quiet, modest city of Kaluga. Greetings to you! I imagine how the capital's Red Square looks today. Hundreds of steel dragonflies hover above marchers' heads. Cigar-like dirigibles—a dream of my youth—float low, so low. A fulfillment of my cherished and fervid fantasies, and perhaps even a result of my early work. There will be less room for the birds in the air. And this has become possible in our land only now, in recent years, when our party, and our government, and our laboring people, when every worker of our Soviet homeland, everyone has joined together to realize humanity's most audacious dream—conquering the altitudes beyond the clouds. An unprecedented ascent. There has been nothing like it before. It's no wonder that Soviet pilots have flown higher than anyone else into the enigmatic stratosphere. All the other altitude records can be understood too, and we can easily explain our parachute jumpers' world records, the flight-time records, and many other examples of heroism shown by our glorious conquerors of the air. Now I am absolutely certain that my other dream, interplanetary travel, which I have proven theoretically possible, will become a reality. I worked for forty years on reactive propulsion and was sure that the first people would stroll on Mars within a few hundred years. But times change. I cannot refuse myself the wish to share my latest news, which is my joy. I recently made a discovery as a May Day gift to you, which will perhaps allow you, who are responsible for the May Day celebrations, to witness the first transatmospheric voyage. The implementation of my discovery will undoubtedly quicken the pace. It is the active participation of millions in conquering the upper altitudes. Young fliers, as I call those chubby little boys with model airplanes, children with gliders, young men in airplanes—there are tens of thousands of them in our land.

I rest my most daring hopes on them. They will help realize my discoveries. They will provide us with talented designers for the first interplanetary ship. These heroes and daredevils will establish the first routes through the air, routes like Earth-Moon orbit, Earth-Mars orbit, and even Moscow-Moon, Kaluga-Mars.

Orchestras on the square are probably playing "Ever Higher." Beautiful music, good and remarkably true words. Verily, ever higher climb the Bolsheviks for the benefit of all humanity, so that people can breathe easier and live more happily. So that every proletarian, be he German, Japanese, Chinese, or Negro, might live as boldly and joyfully as you, might celebrate the May Day holiday.

My heartfelt greetings to you!

Valery Chkalov

B. Galin (1937)

CHKALOV (1904–1938), THE MOST FAMOUS OF SOVIET AVIATORS, WAS FROM A WORKING-CLASS BACKGROUND. HE BECAME A MECHANIC AND THEN A FLYER. HE WAS GROUNDED FOR DISOBEDIENCE AND STUNT FLYING UNDER A BRIDGE ON LENINGRAD'S NEVA RIVER. RESTORED TO THE PILOT SEAT, HE MADE PIONEERING FLIGHTS TO KAMCHATKA IN 1936 AND TO VANCOUVER IN 1937. HE WAS KILLED IN A TEST FLIGHT IN 1938. HIS LIFE WAS THE THEME OF A POPULAR FILM, *VALERY CHKALOV* (1940).

I

They arrived at the Kremlin at four. On the desk in Stalin's office they spotted a model of their red-winged plane. Chkalov nudged Baidukov in the ribs. They exchanged merry winks, and Chkalov whispered:

"Yegor, our plane!"

They were met warmly, like old friends.

"What, the world isn't big enough for you again?" asked Stalin with a smile. "Planning another flight?"

Chkalov answered simply and seriously: "The time has come, Comrade Stalin. It's time."

He reported on everything: how they had stripped the plane and re-covered it with canvas, how they painted it and flew it. Stalin laughed. Such hotheaded and impatient lads!

"We've abandoned our wives since February," continued Chkalov heatedly, "we abandoned our children. We live by ourselves, Comrade Stalin, and think of only one thing."

The government gave its permission to fly across the North Pole to America.

Chkalov was excited and anxious. He bade everyone farewell, got ready to leave, then unexpectedly turned and went over to Comrade Stalin to give him a firm handshake.

"Thank you, Comrade Stalin, thank you very much."

Stalin held onto his hand.

"It's we who should thank you when you get there."

They walked out of the Kremlin at dusk, excited and hushed. Chkalov glanced over at Baidukov.

Pravda, 21 June 1937, p. 3.

"Yegor!" Chkalov winked at him mischievously, like a little boy. "It's over the North Pole for us, eagle!"

Chkalov went over all the details of the Kremlin meeting in his mind. The airplane model on the desk. Stalin's lively and inquisitive eyes. His first question, asked as a joke: "What, the world isn't big enough for you? Planning another flight?" And Stalin's proposal obliging the crew to land immediately if the situation was inauspicious.

That particular decision somehow touched Chkalov. "People," he thought about Stalin, "in Stalin's eyes people are always the most important thing." It seemed to Chkalov that he still had not done enough for the country, for the Party, and for Stalin, who had raised him and whom he, like Baidukov, Belyakov, and thousands of others, owed everything.

He raced, or better yet flew, up the steps to the third floor and drummed furiously on the door of his apartment. His wife opened the door. By Valery's happy, shining eyes and by his sharp movements, she understood that the results of the Kremlin visit were good.

"Everything's set," he thundered in his scratchy bass voice.

Laughing, she pointed to the door of the children's room: they were asleep.

"A-OK," he said, lowering his voice, "let them sleep. It's all right!"

He walked over to his room, threw open the window, and approached the map of the world that covered almost the entire wall. The names of islands, rivers, and cities along the Canadian shore were mysterious, unfamiliar.

A deeply rooted pilot's custom made Chkalov call everything—large and great— he had done in his life a test. And now before him stood the task of passing a new test, of justifying the hopes of the Party, Stalin's faith, of preparing for the flight and doing it in such a way that the motherland would say: there they are, raised by the Bolshevik Party, people of the Age of Stalin, who fear no hardship but confront it and overcome it in the name and glory of Communism.

Despite the late hour, he had Baidukov and Belyakov come over—they all lived in the same building—and drank a bottle of cognac with them.

"Our last bottle," he told his wife. "From tomorrow we drink only Narzan."[1]

With quiet solemnity the friends clinked glasses. Valery said calmly in his Volga accent: "Well, guys, it's all up to us now. It's to work in the morning. You, Sasha, rustle up maps tomorrow. Yegor and I will go to the aerodrome."

II

From the moment that the ANT-25 airplane returned to Moscow from Schast'ye Gulf, Chkalov had lived with one thought: to continue the Stalin Route, to make a nonstop flight over the North Pole to America.

A pilot of concentrated will and great character, Chkalov, like his two friends, combined daring, courage, and a willingness to take risks with the knowledge and

---

1. A popular mineral water.

ability to exploit technology's most recent achievements. He had no thought of resting on his laurels. On the contrary, last year's flight had given him an irrepressible desire to perfect his knowledge of flying, to solve new aviation problems that posed intriguing complications.

All autumn and winter Chkalov worked at his usual job: testing new airplanes. He was as before the factory's chief pilot, attentively following the birth of new fighter planes, testing them in the air and putting them through difficult, head-spinning flights. Advanced-speed planes attracted his particular interest. He studied how to fly each new fighter, analyzing the complex tasks of airplane construction thoughtfully and thoroughly.

It was difficult work, full of risk and value for the country. And all these test flights did not distract him from the main thing—that for which he lived during those days and months.

It was precisely now, after the great flight along the Stalin Route, that new ideas were born in his consciousness, that new plans emerged. Sometimes he would sit around until dawn with Baidukov. They would go over details of last year's flight, and for the hundredth or thousandth time discuss a new variant, the thought of which gave them no peace.

Once in a workers' club, an ecstatic young man asked Chkalov about his dream.

"My dream?" Chkalov repeated and half-jokingly, half-seriously said, "To have a pile of kids. Best have six. Not less."

He loves children with all his heart. He can play for hours with his little puffy-cheeked daughter, make up complicated and mischievous games with his son, turn the whole apartment topsy-turvy. But about the planned flight, Chkalov did not let a word slip. He could talk about that only with Yegor and Belyakov.

There was only one other person they let in on their secret: Stoman, chief engineer of TsAGI.[2] Yevgeny Karlovich got caught up by the idea.

Chkalov came to the aerodrome several times over the winter. The ANT-25 was parked there. Yevgeny Karlovich had put it on skis. Just in case. Maybe they'd want to take a flight.

And Chkalov couldn't restrain himself; he took the airplane up. Baidukov flew with him. Chkalov told Yevgeny Karlovich: "I'm flying for old time's sake. I can also give the new heating system a check."

Stoman understood what the real point was. He didn't ask many questions. Somehow it came out that they agreed to prepare the plane for a flight.

III

Chkalov possessed a highly developed sense of collectivism at work. He never said "I'm going to fly," but always "We're going to," or "Our crew is planning such and such." There was no false modesty in that. Relations between the three friends were built on a principle of mutual respect, faith, and cohesion.

---

2. The Central Aero- and Hydrodynamics Institute (Moscow).

"Of course," Chkalov would say, "each of us has some value by himself. But together we don't do three times but ten times more than alone."

Each of them knew the others' value perfectly. They had got to know each other truly, deeply, and forever during the 56 hours 20 minutes of last year's flight.

Chkalov remembered the most difficult moments of the flight from Moscow to Schast'ye Gulf. The experience of 1936 had to be of use in 1937. Everything had to be considered: the takeoff, running into a cyclone, the danger of icing up, landing in perilous conditions.

They had flown into a cyclone over Severnaya Zemlya. They were above Victoria Island 16 hours and 15 minutes after leaving Moscow. From there the route went directly to the North Pole. Chkalov, without taking his hands from the controls, turned to Yegor and, smiling, pointed toward the Pole: straight across the Pole to America. Yegor laughed. Chkalov turned the plane to the east and set course for Franz-Josef Land.

What they had been wary of suddenly crashed down on the plane. With incredible speed, the patches of fog floating before them grew into a threatening wall that blocked the sun.

The airplane slowly crept upward. At an altitude of three thousand meters, everything was still dark. A grayish murk enveloped the plane. The thermometer showed minus eleven degrees centigrade. The wings were covered with thin ice. The airplane plunged down. Below there was also darkness. The plane turned south. Fog was there too.

In the gray semidarkness, Belyakov entered into the log: "Flying blind, socked in from above, shaking, have decided to fly around from the north."

Chkalov had a cramp in his legs. He called Yegor and turned the controls over to him. It was a complicated, brief, and ludicrous operation. Chkalov moved to one side in the pilot's seat and freed one pedal, keeping his hands on the rudder. Yegor deftly stuck in his feet and took a corner of the seat. Then he grabbed the rudder with one hand. Chkalov removed his hand and crawled off to the side.

Flying blind, the pilot began to gain altitude, trying to break through the clouds. It seemed to him that the plane was not flying properly. This was the dangerous sensation of contrarotation. He had to fight off the false sensation, which demanded steering the plane exactly by the instruments.

The plane reached an altitude of 3,850 meters. Belyakov made a brief notation in the log: "Going through clouds. Flying blind. Icing up." The plane changed course nineteen times. First it would go up, then dive down in search of a ray of light. And when, finally, they broke loose from the ice, Baidukov radioed Moscow: "Everything A-OK."

They iced up twice over the Tatar Strait. The plane was tossed about sharply. Chkalov flew at a height of twenty to forty meters. The low cloud cover pressed the plane toward the raging waves. Chkalov banked steeply over the water, trying to tear free from the clouds.

A mountain suddenly appeared in front of the plane. With truly superhuman self-control, Chkalov managed to turn the plane aside in an instant. (That was when the arts of aerobatics and test-piloting came in handy!) Valery sighed with relief.

His lips were parched, and he was tormented by thirst. He looked ahead without moving his eyes—at any moment the plane could tear into a fog-shrouded hill.

He was the commander of an airship. He had to make quick and precise decisions. The thought that he should turn back toward the strait and break through the cloud cover came through his hands from the rudder. Slowly he circled up higher and higher. He could see no end to the clouds. The rain whipped down as before. A light ice began to form on the strong wings. That was the most terrifying thing. Vibrations and jolts confirmed that the plane was icing up.

Chkalov turned and met Yegor's eyes. He understood everything. At 9 hours 25 minutes Baidukov radioed Khabarovsk: "Fog all the way to the ground. Icing up in the fog." Chkalov took the plane to a lower altitude. The wind and rain stripped the ice from the wings. The vibrations stopped.

Their altitude was twenty to thirty meters. Raging waves beat beneath the wings. Moscow ordered them to land. Valery resisted. He made several more attempts to break through, but they came to nothing. Every time he went up, the plane started to shake again.

The crew commander looked back at his comrades and, without taking his hands from the controls, pointed down with a nod of the head. Baidukov and Belyakov silently nodded in agreement. Chkalov pointed the nose down to land. Yegor began lowering the undercarriage. The ground below was uneven, pitted with gullies.

Pilots say that Chkalov has a "light touch," that he is brilliant at "three-point" landings. At Schastye Gulf, at the very last moment, a water-filled gully suddenly glistened before them in the dark. Chkalov's "light touch" momentarily gave some gas, pushed the iced-up plane over the gully, and landed on a sandbar. Belyakov opened the plane's rear hatch.

One after the other, the pilots jumped to the ground. Baidukov, tired, with his eyes shut, leaned against the wing. Chkalov crawled under the plane to inspect the undercarriage. The wheels were mired in sand. The plane was whole, without a single scratch. Chkalov yelled loudly, merrily: "A-OK, friends."

IV

This is why Chkalov values his crew and the ANT-25 so highly. And despite the fact that he and his friends know the plane very well, when they were preparing for the flight they trusted neither the plane nor themselves and subjected it to a series of brutal tests. Everything started over from the beginning, as if they were learning the remarkable plane for the first time.

Chkalov arrived at the Moscow Aerodrome on June 1. It was drizzling, and tiny clouds floated in the sky. Stoman met Chkalov at the entrance to headquarters. They exchanged greetings. Looking at Stoman, Chkalov broke into a smile. Yevgeny Karlovich's face confirmed that preparations were going full speed ahead—he had grown thin, he was tanned, and his eyes were sunken from sleepless nights.

Belyakov was asleep on the office couch. Flight maps were spread on the floor. Chkalov went over to the window and looked out at the field. The plane was parked on a side road. Its wingspan was thirty-four meters. A remarkable plane with wonderful wing extension! Chkalov gazed at it for a long time.

"Hey, my beauty," he said quietly, not to wake Belyakov, "fly away, fly away..."

He went downstairs. A heavy tractor brought the plane out onto the concrete main runway. Last year's inscription stood out on the fuselage: "The Stalin Route." Chkalov thought: "It will be continued. The Stalin Route will be continued."

The plane was towed up onto a concrete mound. The motor was started. Chkalov and Stoman silently listened to it working. It was a good, clean sound. Chkalov turned the brim of his cap around. He climbed into the plane by a narrow stepladder. The ailerons moved for the first time. Chkalov checked the steering. The plane slipped down the runway, built up speed, and lightly broke away from the ground. Chkalov made a masterfully steep low-altitude turn.

"That devil," Stoman said in admiration.

The airplane went off to Shcholkovo.[3] There, Chkalov and Baidukov subjected it to lengthy tests in thorough preparation for the flight.

"My job," said Chkalov, "is to take off smoothly and to land the plane successfully."

He gave the takeoff particular importance, because the flying weight of the plane exceeded eleven tons. Mastering the takeoff was not the least important part of the control-testing program.

Chkalov was taciturn and irritable in those days. Yevgeny Karlovich Stoman, even thinner than before, listened to him attentively and accepted his comments. Baidukov and Belyakov also knew that side of Chkalov's character. Chkalov became withdrawn and even irascible right when dozens of details had to be resolved and fixed, when the flying of the plane had to be studied as thoroughly as possible.

The doctor demanded that Chkalov and his friends maintain a strict health regime, sleep more, muster their strength. But Chkalov relaxed best when he was strolling through the woods. He would wander through the pines for hours and return home happy, energetic. Sometimes he left for a night of fishing. The only fish that came were tiny, humdrum, but Chkalov would sit on the river for hours in his boat. Toward dawn the sky would grow light, fog would creep over the water, and sometimes the silence would be broken by the roar of airplanes.

One night in the middle of June, Chkalov came to Moscow. His son was leaving for Pioneer camp. Chkalov brought Igor to the train station, put him on the train, and, hugging him, gave him some words of fatherly advice.

"All right," Igor said impatiently, "I'll learn to swim, I'll be part of the collective, I'll obey the group leaders. I'll do everything. But you tell me, tell me this—how's it going with your flight?"

The son was like his father in many ways: gray eyes, white-blonde hair, strong hands, his noisy way of moving.

"Everything is A-OK," Chkalov said amicably, "preparations are going full speed ahead. Only the weather is fouling us up."

He looked at the sky and sighed. Igor kissed him and said quietly: "Good luck!"

---

3. A Moscow airport.

Around six in the morning, Chkalov made a test flight. His course lay to the north. The ANT-25 was like a flying laboratory. Everything was put to a final, decisive test.

It was a dress rehearsal. The motor worked faultlessly; the plane flew beyond reproach. Chkalov tested his materials again and again, checking his previous observations, his flying reflexes.

The day before takeoff was particularly trying. The crew went to bed early. At two in the morning, Chkalov woke up and lifted his head. Dawn showed blue outside the window.

"Yegor! Sasha!" he called in a whisper. "It's time!"

Dinner at the Pole
A Radio Sketch by I. T. Spirin (1938)

ON-THE-SCENE REPORTAGE OVER THE AIRWAVES FROM EXOTIC PLACES BROUGHT EXCITEMENT AND ADVENTURE INTO THE HOMES OF ORDINARY PEOPLE EVERYWHERE IN THE 1930s — THE USSR WAS NO EXCEPTION. HERE, THE EXOTIC IS COMBINED WITH PRIDE IN SOVIET SCIENTIFIC-TECHNICAL ACHIEVEMENT AND HUMAN DARING. THE REPORTER, SPIRIN, WAS AN ARCTIC PILOT AND POPULAR WRITER ABOUT AVIATION.

People's appetite turns out to be no worse at the North Pole than at the middle latitudes. Anyone who travels there can easily confirm the veracity of this statement. As for us, the first settlers, we made this scientifically important discovery immediately upon our arrival at the Pole.

We had not yet felt the full grandeur of the historical moment or managed to unbosom our exaltation and mutual congratulations when we became aware of a prosaic, everyday detail: we, the courageous argonauts, conquerors of the polar axis, were most unpoetically hungry. We were so starved that we were ready to tear the first seal to happen upon us to shreds.

It was then that Ivan Dmitrievich Papanin demonstrated the full splendor of his talents. While we were pondering just what we could eat, he unloaded his culinary instrumentation onto the ice, ignited the hellish flame of a now legendary "Pa-

From *Istoriia sovetskoi radio-zhurnalistiki. Dokumenty, teksty, vospominaniia, 1917–1945* (Moscow: Izd. Moskovskogo universiteta, 1991), pp. 197–202.

panin" primus, and, performing a series of mysterious manipulations over some tubes, packets, and boxes, prepared a lavish meal, which would have done honor to any cook in the capital. His virtuosity evoked such rapture that there and then we awarded him the title of the world's finest polar chef.

Ivan Dmitrievich bore his sonorous title with pride, and for several days fed us with sundry and appetizing victuals. But our felicity soon came to an end. Molokov arrived, and after him came Alekseev and Mazuruk. The encampment grew, and Papanin could no longer cope with the burden of such, as he grumbled, a "horde." Our much-decorated chef handed in his resignation. At that point we held a conference and decided to go over to a decentralized system of provender. Henceforth, everyone was obliged to dine on his own airplane, and each was to take turns cooking for all the rest.

And what meals they were! Not a single restaurant, not a single menu offered dishes like those we invented then. There were the most fantastic combinations of soups and stews, milk noodles and meat sauce, and other peculiar mixtures, which received the name "dietary drivel."[1]

All this was made from concentrates that had fallen into hands unaccustomed to working with the newest intricacies of contemporary culinary art. Each experimented at his own risk, and we thus had frequent occasion to eat fried what has since time immemorial been properly eaten boiled, and vice versa. The debuts of our chefs du jour were usually crowned by failure and, although the unsightly inventions of their culinary imagination were swallowed to the last crumb, there was no avoiding reprisal. Once the last morsel had disappeared from the table, the luckless cook was bombarded with enough ridicule to drive him from the Pole.

All this seemed amusing until my turn came. I acknowledged my duty notification without undue ecstasy and, foreseeing the inevitable dénouement, tried everything to relieve myself of the task, volunteering to make any flight or do any excruciating astronomical calculation rather than the already hated kitchen duty. But it was all in vain: the polar lodgers were implacable.

The cook on duty was allowed an assistant—"a mess hand." I chose the mechanic Petyonin. His composure and reliable disposition instilled trust. "With him, I'll get through it somehow," I thought. Evidently he thought the same about me, and we commenced preparing dinner with an air of having done this and nothing else all our lives.

"Well, what shall we cook?" I asked my mate nonchalantly.

"What would you like?" he answered in the same tone, and began pouring gasoline into the primus.

"Should we cook cabbage soup?"

"We had that yesterday."

"Then perhaps Ukrainian borsch would do?"

"There's not much difference between cabbage soup and borsch. Maybe another soup would be better."

---

1. Drivel, *sumbur* in Russian, was the tag used to discredit modernism in music and other arts.

"What good is soup?" I objected. "There's only water in it. Nobody will eat it."

"Depends on which soup and how you make it," the mechanic answered, and looked at me like he was talking about something he had dedicated his whole life to studying.

I became interested and inquired curiously how this soup was cooked.

"In the usual way," answered Petyonin without the slightest embarrassment. "Take some meat, potatoes, fresh onion..."

I lost patience when he got to the sour cream. "That's fine, but soup alone won't be enough," I interrupted him calmly. "They say that there are some remarkable grouse beyond those ice hills. Why don't you go and shoot some for the entrée."

Petyonin gave me a perplexed look and turned away. Then we both broke out laughing, and with a sigh, we set to studying the possibilities offered by our concentrates. They were the same old "Ukrainian borsch," "cabbage soup," and ragout, crammed into paper packets, boxes, and tubes. Suddenly we came upon an unlabeled packet. We shook it. There was an unknown, rose-colored powder.

"We'll have to go see Papanin," said Petyonin, noticeably intrigued.

But speaking of the devil, Papanin himself showed up. He was making his normal rounds of the encampment just then, checking the airplanes for anything he might be able to use after we had flown home. We rushed over to him with our find.

"Ivan Dmitrievich, what sort of concoction is this?" began Petyonin.

"You're a concoction yourself," shot back Papanin. "That's powdered chicken, a remarkable thing. The dietary institute prepared it by my special order. From that jar you can make..."

Once he was on his favorite subject, Papanin began an inspired enumeration of how many calories and how many real live chickens the jar could replace and what remarkable dishes could be made from it. For instance, chicken cutlets."

Chicken cutlets? We caught fire.

"That's it!" shouted Petyonin. "That's no Ukrainian borsch. We'll outdo them all!"

After some hasty questions about how the first delicacy uncovered at the Pole was to be prepared, we energetically set to the task.

Petyonin took upon himself responsibility for mixing the powder with water. He performed the rites with such pomp that it seemed he expected the mixture to yield an alloy of gold and silver at the very least. He entrusted the dressing of the forcemeat to me. I successfully negotiated this complicated task, and soon the fruits of our creative labor were gaily hissing on a huge skillet in the form of appetizing chicken cutlets.

But we didn't have long to admire the spectacle. Our cutlets behaved most mysteriously. They suddenly swelled, fell apart, and merged into one big panful of a strange, watery porridge. We watched the metamorphosis horror-stricken.

"Something's not right here." I finally came to myself and shot a searching glance at the clearly dismayed Petyonin. He was studying the consequences of the catastrophe silently, poking a knife thoughtfully into the skillet's contents.

"Well, what is it?" I interrupted his philosophical meditation. "Did you forget to add something?"

"Bread cubes," he muttered in gloomy reply. "I forgot the bread cubes."

We didn't have any bread cubes. We had to pound them out of biscuit. We sat down across the table and started diligently hammering away at the biscuit, cursing the unfortunate moment when we had conceived of tangling with the ill-fated cutlets. Finally the bread cubes were ready. It was then we discovered that neither Petyonin nor I knew precisely what we were supposed to do with them. We reasoned that the most correct approach would be to pour them into the remains of the perished cutlets. Our reckoning proved accurate: the meat porridge grew thicker, but... the new cutlets collapsed on the skillet even faster than the previous ones.

Matters took a menacing turn. Dinnertime was nearing, but we could only contemplate the rabidly gurgling cutlet mash helplessly and curse the caprices of culinary art, before which the secrets of black magic seemed as simple and comprehensible as the alphabet.

Babushkin "himself" found us at this occupation. He glanced into the skillet and, after a tortuous pause, said scathingly: "One must study, young people.[2] The cutlets must be heaped around the bread cubes first, and only then fried."

Again, for a third time, we set to making the loathsome cutlets. This time we piled them onto the skillet with the firm intention of chucking them out at the first sign of failure. But Babushkin turned out to be right. The critical moment passed, and the cutlets held firmly to the skillet, neat and massive, as if carved from wood.

We were saved and, sighing with relief, we had a pleasant smoke some distance from the primus stove.

Suddenly my assistant froze with the cigarette almost touching his lips, then let out a desperate string of curses and dashed toward the primus. The ill-starred cutlets weren't cooking. The primus had gone out. All the gasoline had burned.

Mute with fury, we liquidated the new misfortune like lightning. We filled the primus to the brim and primed it so hard that the primer almost bent. The cold cutlets frisked about again, desperately smoking and crackling, threatening to become coal before our eyes. Rushing to lower the flame, I lifted the skillet, put it next to the primus, turned the knob and... barely managed to jump back: a fountain of gas splashed from the overfilled reservoir and splattered the cutlets.

"That's it," Petyonin said in a terrible voice.

I could only shrug.

It was dinnertime. In the "officers' mess" (that's what we called the airplane passenger cabin that passed for a dining room) on two boards stacked up on crates, the dinner table was "set." Schmidt, Shevelev, Vodopyanov, and the other starving residents of "N-170" noisily took their seats and began eating caviar, tinned goods, and fish. They ate quickly. The terrible moment approached. We had to decide whether to confess all our mishaps or serve the cutlets with gasoline. While everyone was eating, we kept arguing and deliberating in the "kitchen."

"I don't understand why you're worried," Petyonin implored in a villainous whisper. "Vodopyanov once drank a whole mug of pure gasoline and nothing happened. Gasoline is harmless."

---

2. A favorite phrase of Lenin's, repeated constantly in the 1930s.

"Hey, cooks!" Shouts from the "dining room" interrupted us. "Pick up the tempo! We don't see any dinner here!"

Petyonin shrugged, grabbed the skillet, and carried it to the table with an unperturbed look. The appearance of the cutlets inspired a storm of rapture. Everyone leapt up from his seat and burst into exclamations and shouts of approbation. Petyonin and I humbly seated ourselves at the end of the table, trying not to look at one another and preparing for the oncoming scandal.

Finally, Otto Yulevich took the first large earth-colored cutlet. He took a bite, chewed it thoughtfully, and with a gallant bow in our direction, exclaimed: "Bravo, no different than the best restaurants!"

The others then reached for the cutlets. I understood absolutely nothing. The devil only knows! I had never seen food disappear so quickly. The officers' mess snatched up the cutlets and gobbled them down with such avidity and delight that I simply began to envy them.

"Why aren't you eating?" Vodopyanov asked me suddenly when he noticed my strange behavior.

"Thanks, but I don't feel like it," I mumbled indistinctly and, turning away quickly, began an animated conversation with Shevelev. But Mikhail Vasilevich would not back off and kept shouting across the table.

"Cut out playing noble or else we won't leave any for you."

"Hey, yeah, why aren't you eating?" someone else said, badgering Petyonin this time.

"We've already eaten. We must have eaten at least ten of them while we were cooking," said my helpless assistant in his own defense.

I was ready to kill him with a glance. He lost his head and continued to talk some nonsense that gave us away. Some people at the table began to exchange suspicious glances and whispers. This was our downfall. There were two cutlets left in the skillet. One of the diners got up and laid them before Petyonin and me with a resolute gesture. Silence reigned.

"Eat," said a threatening voice.

Further resistance was unthinkable. We looked at each other and, barely containing our laughter, sank our teeth despairingly into the accursed cutlets, anticipating the sweetish, repulsive taste of gasoline. The crew did not take their eyes from us. We chewed and stared into each other's eyes. What miracle was this? The cutlets were wonderful and had no smell. After swallowing the last mouthful, I fixed my gaze on Petyonin.

"Well?" was the only thing I could say.

"The smell's gone," Petyonin replied gloomily. "Completely gone. What a waste we didn't eat. What a pity."

And we told the whole story.

The whole honorable company chuckled over our tragic story for a long time. And we sat hungry, sadly contemplating aviation fuel's astonishing ability to evaporate from chicken cutlets without a trace, which played such a dirty trick on us.

Song of the Motherland

Vasily Lebedev-Kumach and Isaac Dunaevsky (1935)

WRITTEN FOR A MOVIE STARRING LYUBOV ORLOVA, *CIRCUS*, THE POPULARITY OF THIS SONG WAS SO IMMENSE THAT THE MELODY BECAME THE BROADCAST SIGNAL FOR RADIO MOSCOW IN THE 1930s. ITS OPTIMISTIC AND PATRIOTIC WORDS WERE EVEN CITED BY ONE OF STALIN'S PURGE VICTIMS AT HIS TRIAL THE DAY BEFORE HE WAS EXECUTED. THE LYRIC RESEMBLES AN OLD RELIGIOUS SONG THAT BEGAN "OUR NATIVE COUNTRY — GREAT AND DEAR — / IT IS A KNIGHT IN STRENGTH. / FROM END TO END, A HEMISPHERE / IT IS IN BREADTH AND LENGTH."

ПЕСНЯ О РОДИНЕ

Припев:
Широка страна моя родная,
Много в ней лесов, полей и рек.
Я другой такой страны не знаю,
Где так вольно дышит человек!

От Москвы до самых до окраин,
С южных гор до северных морей
Человек проходит как хозяин
Необъятной Родины своей.
Всюду жизнь и вольно и широко,
Точно Волга полная, течет.
Молодым—везде у нас дорога,
Старикам—везде у нас почет.

Припев.

SONG OF THE MOTHERLAND

Refrain:
O, my homeland is a spacious country:
Streams and fields and forests full and
    fair.
I don't know of any other country
Where a man can breathe a freer air!

From great Moscow to the farthest
    border,
From the Arctic seas to Samarkand,
Man can walk and feel that he's the
    owner
Of his own unbounded Motherland.
Here our life can flow as freely, broadly,
As the Volga—brimming and
    unchecked.
Here the young will always have clear
    roadway
And the old are always shown respect.

Refrain.

From *Pesni strany sovetov,* ed. Boris Turganov (Moscow: Khudozhestvennaia literatura, 1940), pp. 108–110. Translation revised and adapted from *Modern Russian Poetry,* ed. Vladimir Markov and Merrill Sparks (Indianapolis–New York: Bobbs-Merrill, 1967), pp. 739–741.

Наши нивы глазом не обшаришь,
Не упомнишь наших городов,
Наше слово гордое—товарищ—
Нам дороже всех красивых слов.
С этим словом мы повсюду дома,
Нет для нас ни черных, ни цветных,
Это слово каждому знакомо,
С ним везде находим мы родных.

Припев.

За столом у нас никто не лишний,
По заслугам каждый награждён,
Золотыми буквами мы пишем
Всенародный Сталинский закон.
Этих слов величие и славу
Никакие годы не сотрут.
Человек всегда имеет право
На ученье, отдых и на труд.

Припев.

Над страной весенний ветер веет,
С каждым днем все радостнее жить,
И никто на свете не умеет
Лучше нас смеяться и любить.
Но сурово брови мы насупим,
Если враг захочет нас сломать,—
Как невесту, Родину мы любим,
Бережем, как ласковую мать.

Припев.

You can't see the end to all our fields,
Or recall the names of all the towns
    you've heard,
Most precious of all words is
    "Comrade,"
It means more to us than any other
    word.
With this word we are at home all places
And with this word we always
    comprehend:
There are no longer black or colored
    races,
For with it—the whole world is your
    friend.

Refrain.

There is none unwelcome at our table,
Whoever merits gets his just reward.
In golden letters we now write the stable
Law of Stalin in a calm accord.
The passing of the years will not
    extinguish
The grandeur and the glory of these
    words:
Every man will have these rights forever:
He has the chance to study, rest and
    work.

Refrain.

The breeze of spring is blowing o'er our
    homeland,
Every day we live more joyfully.
And in the world you won't find any
    people,
Who know better than us how to laugh
    and love.
If an enemy should wish to crush us,
We shall set our faces stern and hard.
Like our bride, we love our homeland
    dearly;
And o'er our tender mother we stand
    guard.

Refrain.

Autumn

Vadim Kozin (1930s)

THIS WAS A SONG TYPICAL OF THE REPERTOIRE OF VADIM KOZIN, THE MOST POPULAR MALE CROONER OF THE 1930S, WHO SPECIALIZED IN ROMANTIC BALLADS AND GYPSY SONGS. HE WAS ARRESTED DURING WORLD WAR II—FOR REASONS STILL UNKNOWN—AND STILL LIVES AS OF THIS WRITING IN MAGADAN.

ОСЕНЬ

Осень, прозрачное утро,
Дали, как-будто в тумане.
Небо—в тонах перламутровых,
Утро—холодное, раннее.

Где ж наша первая встреча,
Яркая, жгучая, тайная,
В тот светло-памятный вечер,
Милая встреча, случайная.

Не уходи, тебя я умоляю.
Слова любви стократ я повторю.
Пусть осень у дверей—я это твердо
    знаю—
И все ж не уходи—тебе я говорю.

Наш уголок нам никогда не тесен.
Когда ты в нем, то в нем цветет весна.
Не уходи—еще не спето столько песен,
Еще звенит в гитаре каждая струна.

AUTUMN

Autumn, translucent morning,
The distance is shrouded in mist.
The sky is mother-of-pearl,
The morning is early and cold.

Where has our first meeting gone to—
Radiant, burning, mysterious.
On that bright and memorable evening,
Our sweet meeting was by chance.

Please don't leave me, I beg of you.
Over and over, I'll say the words of love.
What if autumn's at the door—I know it
    surely—
All the same I say, please don't leave
    me.

Our little corner's never too small for
    us.
Whenever you are there, it flowers like
    spring.
Don't leave me—many songs must still
    be sung,
And the strings of my guitar still ring.

From a private collection.

In Praise of Modesty

Mikhail Koltsov (1936)

KOLTSOV (REAL NAME MIKHAIL YEFIMOVICH FRIDLYAND; 1898–
1942?), A FAMOUS SOVIET JOURNALIST, WAS EDITOR OF OGON-
YOK FROM 1924 TO 1938, AND FOR A WHILE OF CROCODILE.
AFTER SERVING AS A JOURNALIST (SOME CLAIM AS AN NKVD OP-
ERATIVE) IN SPAIN, KOLTSOV, LIKE MANY OTHER PARTICIPANTS
IN THAT WAR, WAS ARRESTED. HE DIED IN CAPTIVITY, AL-
THOUGH HE HAD BEEN A FAVORITE OF STALIN. HIS BROTHER,
BORIS YEFIMOV, WAS WELL KNOWN AS A STALINIST CARTOONIST.
BOTH WERE TALENTED AND IRONIC COMMENTATORS ON THE
TIMES. THIS PIECE EXEMPLIFIES A FAVORITE TARGET (AND THE
TACIT LIMITS) OF SOVIET SATIRE IN THE 1930s: RIDICULE THE
MIDDLE-LEVEL OFFICIAL, BUT DON'T LOOK ABOVE.

It seems four tailors lived next to each other on Prolomnoi St. in Kazan.

There weren't many customers, and competition was fierce. So to get a leg up on his rivals, the tailor Makhotkin put out a sign: "Executor of Gentlemen's and Ladies Fashions, finest in the City of Kazan."

Then the second up and printed: "Master Edward Weinstein, Russia's Finest Clothier, at most moderate Rates."

The third had to take an even more elevated tone. He ordered a huge canvas on tin-plate with the sumptuous figures of knights and ladies: "The world-renowned Professor Ibrahimov, *le derriere cri* of Europe and Africa."

What was left for the fourth to do? He outsmarted them all. His sign was brief: "Arkadii Korneichuk, bestest tailor on the block."

And the public, as the old story goes, the public flocked to the fourth tailor.

And, judging by common sense, they were right.

Sometimes a gallant and manly regiment will be marching down the street. In front is the commander. In front of the commander the band. In front of the band the drummer. And in front of the drummer, yelping mightily, is a little barefoot boy, with the white tail of his shirt sticking out of his pants.

The little boy is leading. Try and dispute that.

With a running start and a huge push, powerful muscles tensed, teeth clenched, physical and moral strength concentrated, our country, which used to be backward,

---

Translated from *Classics of Soviet Satire* (London: Redwood Press, 1972), pp. 85–89.

has leapt ahead and is heading for first place in the world, first place in all divisions—in production, in consumption, in the health and well-being of its people, in culture, in science, in art, in sports.

The route is locked in. It's an equation without variables. The socialist system, its lack of exploitation, the tremendous national revenue its planned economy produces and above all, the owner of that revenue, the powerful and energetic Soviet people, its Party, young people, its Stakhanovite workers, its Army, its confidence in itself and its future—what can withstand its onslaught?

Though the contest's outcome is preordained, the contest itself is no laughing matter. The struggle is hard, much effort is needed, there can be no indulgence or lenience—you can send lenience to hell. Let facts decide the dispute, as they have until now.

What's so annoying and offensive is when the little boy's yelps drown out the call to battle, when a pop gun strays into a fire fight.

Wherever you look, wherever you turn, whoever you listen to, whatever anyone is doing—it's always the best in the world.

The world's best architects are building the world's best buildings. The world's best cobblers are sewing the world's best boots. The world's best poets are writing the world's best poems. The best actors are doing the best plays, and the best watch-makers are producing the world's finest watches.

The very expression "world's best" has become an inalienable part of every loud-mouth's verbal repertoire on any topic or any field, of every Party yea-sayer or trade-union minstrel. They can't say a word without "the world's best," even if they're talking about collecting empty bottles or a tax on dogs.

Recently we visited one of Moscow's district libraries. It was relatively clean, tidy and well-ventilated. We also praised their courtesy to visitors. The comments made little impression on the director. She haughtily answered: "Well, of course. Our work-place is the best organized in the world. Some foreigners were here, they said so themselves."

Who could counteract this stream of vainglory and conceit. Many even encourage it. Particularly the press. Everything is described in either black or gold ink. Either the store is bad—it isn't worth anything, the manager is a drunkard, the clerks steal, the goods are junk—or the store is good—then it's the best in the world, and nowhere, not in Europe, not in America, is there or will there be anything like it.

An enterprise hasn't even been started up, a hotel hasn't been opened, a building not built, a film not shown, yet already the nightingales are chirping from newspaper branches:

"The new bathhouse will be equipped along new lines perfected by Engineer Vatrushkin [Cheesecake], namely: they will possess hot as well as cold water. For the first time, the supply of each customer with an individual sheet will be introduced. Steam rooms will be the first in the world equipped with radios and telephones, thanks to which patrons can listen to a course in personal hygiene, take care of any matter by telephone or subscribe to any magazine while washing."

"As concerns the arrangement of the hotel, it is equal to the finest examples of American hostelries, though it surpasses them in many ways. Each hotel room will be provided with its own individual key. Every lodger can summon a taxi by phone. Using the postal box specially installed on the hotel building, residents can sent letters to any point in the USSR or abroad."

"Soviet clock factories have a firm hold on the world lead in grandfather clock production."

"Once facades have been painted and arc lights installed, Petrovka can assume its position amongst the first rank of the world's most beautiful streets, surpassing Unter den Linden, Broadway, the Champs d'Elysées and Nanking Road."

And, receiving a reporter at home, the cinema master wearing chic guano-colored breeches booms in a confident bass: "Our world-leading movie industry as embodied by its best outstanding representatives is ready to release new great films. In particular, I personally am intensely contemplating a scenario for my upcoming epic. A plot has not been found yet. But one thing is clear: its novelty will be unprecedented. The filming location and cast have also not been yet selected; but we have an agreement: the district where we film will be the most picturesque in the world, and the acting will leave behind everything in the present century."

If the director of some middle-sized pants-pressing megaplant is behind the times and slow on the uptake, the selfsame reporter, like an animal trainer in the circus, will smartly point out the necessary terminology to him.

"Do you reconstruct trouser creases by the 'express' method?"

"Unquestionably. How else? Pure express."

"Interesting ... Chicago on Pliushchikha St.... We grow, we overtake... And what's that? There on the stool?"

"That? It looks like a newspaper, the Evening News."

"Uh-uh, a small reading room for the convenience of visitors. Clever! And a potted flower next to it. A small, cozy reading room with greenery gives an edifying lesson to American steam iron magnates about serving the growing needs of laborers and their extremities. That so?"

"Unquestionably. How else?"

This idiotic pop-gun fire is even more annoying because next door there's a real battle for world supremacy going on, achieved authentically with authentic facts and figures.

It is after all a fact that our country leads the world in the production of tractors, combines and other agricultural machinery, of synthetic rubber, sugar, peat, and many other materials and machines. Isn't boasting about first place in grandfather clock output ludicrous?

We've reached second place in the world in cast iron, gold and fish.

Concentrating all the resources of his young head, Botvinnik[1] took first place in the world chess championship. But he had to share it with a Czechoslovak. And still Botvinnik is gathering his strength, preparing new battles for the international, the world championship.

Our proletarian soccer team did battle with France's best bourgeois team. They

---

1. M. M. Botvinnik (1911–), Russian world chess champion.

lost for now—that's a fact. But the loss was more than respectable. We're sure they'll win next time. But even that will be recognized only on the basis of hard facts: the figures on the scoreboard will show it, and nobody else.

The Soviet Union's parachute jumpers took the world championship by their incomparable daring. Three young heroes broke the balloon ascent record, but they paid for it with their lives. Doesn't the conceit and bragging of those who call their own work "the world's best" without checking the records insult their memory?

We should begin verifying world-class quality on our very own street.

The Moscow Metro, by the admission of authorities on the question, is incomparably superior to any other subway on earth. But it is good in and of itself, here in Moscow, for the residents of Moscow's streets. A Muscovite might doubt his subway's world-class quality if riding it caused him pain.

Imagine this:

A clock store. A customer walks in, looks like a foreigner, solid, respectable, upright. He asks for a pocket watch. As long as it's the best.

"Would you like an 'Omega'? A wonderful watch, an old Swiss brand."

"I know. No thanks. Something better."

"Perhaps then a Longines?"

"Better."

"What then? Perhaps Moser, the latest model?"

"No, better. Do you have any of your own watches, Tochmekh?"[2]

"Of course. But mind you, they're very expensive."

"It's worth it if they last you a lifetime. I can get any of those Swiss bulbs at home. But I want to take a genuine Tochmekh home from Moscow."

We await the day when this fairy tale will be a common fact. Until then—we will, among other things, hold onto first place in the world in modesty.

---

2. Short for "Precision Mechanisms."

Uncle Steeple
Sergei Mikhalkov (1935—1939)

MIKHALKOV (1913–) IS FAMOUS AS A CHILDREN'S WRITER OF GREAT VERSATILITY. HE COULD COMPOSE DELIGHTFUL STORIES SUCH AS "UNCLE STEEPLE," WHICH HAD SEVERAL SEQUELS; HE

Excerpted from a translation by Dora Rothenberg in Sergei Mikhalkov, *A Choice for Children: Poems, Fables, and Fairy Tales* (Moscow: Progress, 1980), pp. 74–81.

WAS COAUTHOR OF THE SOVIET STATE ANTHEM (SEE PART III), AND HE COULD WRITE TURGIDLY CORRECT VERSE FOR SOVIET SCHOOLBOOKS (SEE PART IV). HE IS THE FATHER OF TWO WELL-KNOWN FILM DIRECTORS: THE RUSSIAN, NIKITA MIKHALKOV, AND THE AMERICAN, ANDRON KONCHALOVSKY. STALIN PRIZE WINNER AND HEAD OF THE RUSSIAN REPUBLIC'S WRITERS' UNION, MIKHALKOV IS A VIRTUAL ICON OF HARD-LINE CONSERVATISM IN LITERARY POLITICS TO THIS DAY.

On our street a young man lived,
Known to all the local people;
Because this citizen was tall,
He was nicknamed Uncle Steeple.

Now, his last name was Stepanov,
And his first name was Stepan;
Of the giants in the district,
He was quite the tallest man.

And because he was so tall,
He was loved by one and all;
Coming home at close of day,
He'd be seen a mile away.

Firm his measured footsteps beat,
As Stepan came down the street;
And his shoes were number fifty—
Few are men who have such feet.

He'd seek shoes at shops and fairs,
Asking for the biggest pairs.
He'd buy coats so long and wide,
You and I could hide inside.

When at last a suit he'd buy,
Which had struck his fancy's eye,
One quick turn before the mirror—
And apart the seams would fly.

Over any fence or wall
He could peep, he was so tall:
Dogs would loudly bark in warning,
Thinking thieves had come to call.

At his mealtimes he would eat
Double portions, as a rule;

And at night he'd stretch his feet
From the bed on to a stool.

When he'd go to see the pictures,
He'd be told by quite a few,
"Sit upon the floor, young fellow,
It is all the same to you."

When to stadiums went he,
They would let him enter free,
For they thought that Uncle Steeple
Surely must a champion be.

And the neighbors, near and far,
Every grown-up, every kid
All could tell you where he lived
Where he worked, and what he did.
For when kites would catch and dangle
High above, from wires or trees,
Who but he could disentangle
Them so quickly, with such ease?

And the very smallest fry
At parades he lifted high,
Because everyone should see
When our troops go marching by.

Everyone loved Uncle Steeple.
And respected Uncle Steeple,
For he was the friend of children,
Of the kids in every yard.

When towards his home he strolled,
"Greetings!" shouted young and old:
When he sneezed they'd shout in chorus.
"Uncle Steeple, don't catch cold!"

Very early Steeple rises,
Opens all his windows wide
Does his daily exercises,
Takes a shower in his stride.
Not to brush his teeth each morning
Is a thing he can't abide.

Someone's riding on an ass
Feet a-ploughing through the grass;
Why, that someone's Uncle Steeple:
People stare, as he rides past.

And they all shout to Stepan:
"Try a camel, little man!"
So a camel Steeple tried;
People laughed, until they cried.

Someone made a clever crack,
"You will break the camel's back!
Camels, friend, will never do,
Elephants were made for you!"

On the tower, Steeple's waiting
For his turn to take a jump,
He stands with his parachute,
And his heart goes thump, thump, thump.
While below him laugh the people,
"See the Steeple on a steeple!"

Into shooting-galleries,
Uncle Steeple'd barely squeeze;
To the keeper he would cry,
"Let me shoot at targets, please."

But the puzzled man would stand
And, with twinkling eye, demand,
"Surely, you don't need to shoot them
You can reach them with your hand."

In the park, this Saturday,
'Twill be very bright and gay;
There'll be music all night long,
Dancing, laughter, merry song.

At the entrance Steeple asks,
"Will you, please, show me some masks
I want one that will disguise me,
So that none will recognize me."

"What's the point," they say in jest,
"Even though you do your best,
Anyone will recognize you:
You're much taller than the rest."

What's the matter; Why the tumult?—
"Schoolboy's drowning!" people shout.
"He has fallen in the river,
Hurry up and pull him out!"
While the people stood about,
Uncle Steeple got him out.

"This is perfectly fantastic,"
All the people shout with glee.
"See, the water in the middle
Doesn't reach above his knee!"

Frightened, wet, but safe and sound,
Stands the schoolboy on the ground;
Uncle Steeple saved the schoolboy,
Saved a boy who might have drowned.

All the people, for his deed,
Wish to shake him by the hand;
"Ask for anything you need,"
He is made to understand.
"I don't need a single thing,"
Answers Steeple, coloring.

Chapaev

Written down from a recital by the storyteller Korguev,
a sherman of the shery-collective Karelia (1936)

IN ACCORDANCE WITH THE POLICY, ADOPTED IN THE MID-1930S, OF INVENTING SOVIET FOLKLORE, BARDS WERE ENCOURAGED TO CREATE NEW TALES DEALING WITH CONTEMPORARY ACHIEVEMENTS, HEROES, AND LEADERS. THE STORYTELLER KORGUEV, A MEMBER OF FISHERY COLLECTIVE IN KARELIA (A MAJOR CENTER OF TRADITIONAL FOLKLORE TO THIS DAY), SPUN THIS VERSION OF THE CHAPAEV LEGEND. NOTE THE FOLK LANGUAGE, THE FORMULAS, THE INVOCATION OF THE NUMBER THREE, THE MAGIC RING, ETC. IN IT CHAPAEV ASSUMED SOME OF THE SUPERNATURAL POWERS ATTRIBUTED TO OLD REBELS SUCH AS STENKA RAZIN IN FOLK POETRY AND SONG.

Not in a kingdom somewhere, not in a state far away, but in this country where you and I live, there was a peasant named Ivan. Three sons he had, the eldest named Ivan after him, the second Peter and the youngest Vasily—Vasily Ivanovich Chapaev.

They were poor. They owned neither drift nets nor boats for fishing. Of his great poverty died the father Ivan, and lonely and hard was the lot of the widow and her three small sons.

When the children grew up, war broke out. They took Ivan and Peter. Vasily they spared, but not for long. They took even the very young: those who had strength enough to hold a rifle straight were taken. So, soon Vasily was taken. He says good-bye to his mother and goes to the front.

As he walks through the village he passes the house of his aunt. "I must bid farewell to my aunt too," thinks Vasily, "for who knows if I shall come back from this war or not." So he went in to say farewell.

"How are you, Auntie?" he asks.

"How are you, nephew, and where are you off to?"

"I am going to the war to join my brothers."

And she tells him: "Listen, nephew, take this ring. It was left me by my dead husband. He got it in the Turkish war. The ring has magic power. He who wears it is safe from lead and from steel. Bullets cannot go through him and swords cannot

---

Translated in *International Literature*, no. 12 (1937), pp. 45–47.

cut him. But mind its power is good only on the land. On the water its power leaves it."

So he took the ring and he went off to war. He came to the army and was drilled. When he was a trained soldier they sent him into battle. He was strong and daring and quick, and he understood everything; so they made him a corporal. The ring protected him from lead and from steel. For three years he was in the war and remained alive. Then the war ended and he went home.

At home there was only his mother now. Peter and Ivan, his brothers, had been killed in the war. "Mother," he said, "I will take a wife so that I won't be alone." "Yes, son, take a wife," said his mother.

He took a wife from the same village, a peasant's daughter. They had a big wedding and Vasily Ivanovich began to live with his wife. Two years they lived together and they had two children.

Then Vasily Ivanovich heard that evil men, Kolchak and Denikin, had power. He heard that the rule of the Whites was spreading and that they were persecuting the free Bolshevik people and taking their powerful guns.

Vasily was sad. He thought of it in the field and he thought of it when he rested. Must the toiling people perish? Must the White rule come to our village? This was his decision. "It will be better to go to war again than to let my fatherland be ruined. No bullet can harm me."

So he says to his mother: "Dear mother, I must go to war again to defend the toiling people and the Soviet power."

His mother weeps. "Oh, son! You are the last hope of my old age. Three sons I had. Two have laid their heads in the earth and you will lay your head in the earth too if you go to war again."

"Still, mother, I must go," said Vasily Ivanovich. "Promise me you will look after my children if I am killed in the war."

Then he said farewell to his mother and his wife and his children. He saddled his black horse. He rode to the Red Army.

He comes to the Soviet troops. He bows to the Red Commanders.

"Health to you, Red Soviet Commanders. I want to serve in the Red Army. I will frighten Denikin and Kolchak. They will run off. The toiling people and the fatherland will be free."

The commanders said, "Good! But who are you, lad? There are all kinds of people. Some talk big and make big promises. But when the time comes to keep them they are gone."

"I'm not that kind," said Vasily Ivanovich. "After this I will not say anything but will let my deeds speak for me. I am from the village so-and-so, Vasily Ivanovich is my name."

"Welcome then into the Red Army, Vasily Ivanovich. Be a brave fighter and help the fatherland."

A bloody battle began. Chapaev jumped on his black horse and rode into the middle of the enemy. Like a reaper he cut down the men of Kolchak and Denikin. Some he stuck with his spear; some he sliced with his sword. And some he shot with his revolver. For six hours he slaughtered them. He covered the field with their corpses. Kolchak was frightened and ran away with his soldiers.

Then the Red Army believed him; the Red Commanders believed him for they had seen what he had done with their very own eyes. The soldiers said: "Let Chapaev lead us. We will go into battle with him anywhere. With him we will not perish."

Well, Kolchak was angry. He collected more men and they were twice as many as before. Again he led them against the Red Army. And again Chapaev jumped on his black horse and rode into the midst of them, even where Kolchak himself was standing. He beat the White soldiers the second time as badly as the first time. Some he stuck with his spear; some he sliced with his sword. And some he shot with his revolver. Back and forth he went like the wind. For twenty-four hours he slaughtered them. And his soldiers helped him. The field was covered with corpses but hardly any of them were his men. Almost half of Kolchak's soldiers were killed that day. Many were captured. Kolchak himself just had time enough to run away.

Then they rested. They ate and they drank. Later Chapaev went to Frunze. Frunze said to him: "Chapaev, young hero, here is an army. You have Kolchak on the run. Go chase him out. Lead your army to the other front where Kolchak is again rallying his forces."

Chapaev led his troops to the White River. They encamped near a village. Where was the enemy? He didn't know. He had to find out. He had to locate Kolchak's staff. So Chapaev says to his men: "Listen, boys, who'll go along with me to find out where Kolchak is hiding himself? When we find where he is we'll bring the army and finish him."

You couldn't have counted all who volunteered, but Chapaev only picked out between fifty and a hundred and went ahead with them.

On the road they meet a woman.

"Auntie, where are you going?"

"I'm going to pay a visit to my husband in the Red Army. I lost my way. For two days I have been on my feet wandering around like a blind woman, and eating nothing. If you don't want to see me die help me and give me something to eat."

"We'll give you something to eat, Auntie," said Chapaev. He ordered the men to give her food, and the woman went with them. But the woman was a Pole and a Kolchak spy and she deceived Chapaev.

They reached a village. It was on the banks of the White River. The peasants there told him Kolchak's army was nearby, only a few versts, about ten, further along. Then Vasily Ivanovich said to his bunch: "Well, boys, we found them. Now turn in and get a good night's sleep and tomorrow we'll bring the army here and finish them off."

The men went to sleep. Chapaev went to sleep. They wanted to have a good rest before the battle. Only the sentinels on watch were awake.

But the Polish woman did not go to sleep. She waited for Chapaev to fall asleep. Then she ran to Kolchak. She told Kolchak where Chapaev and his men were. She told him that Chapaev had only a few men with him and that they were fast asleep. You can be sure that was good news to Kolchak. Then he was not afraid of Chapaev. He commanded his generals to get Chapaev dead or alive.

The generals called all their soldiers. They came up in the darkness. They surrounded Chapaev's men on three sides. Only the river-front was free of them. They overpowered the sentincls. When the Whites reached the house where Chapaev was sleeping he jumped to his feet. He shouted: "There's been treachery, boys! Get up!"

They got up. They grabbed their rifles. But what was the use? They were only a few against an army. Well, the men held out as long as they could. They stood off the Whites as long as they had cartridges. But the cartridges gave out and Chapaev shouted to them: "We're cut off by land, boys, but we can get through by water. To the river, boys."

They broke through the White lines and jumped into the river. When Kolchak saw Vasily Ivanovich and his men jump into the river he shouted to his generals: "Don't let them cross alive. If they get across and then bring their army it will be our finish."

Kolchak's people fired and fired into the water. Vasily Ivanovich's ring had no power in the water. A bullet wounded him in the arm, but he did not stop swimming. All around him bullets were flying. Many beside him were shot. On the bank was Kolchak, jumping up and down and shouting: "You're letting him get away. Kill Chapaev. Don't bother about the others. Shoot only at Chapaev."

A second bullet struck Vasily Ivanovich. At last his head sank down under the water. That was how Vasily Ivanovich died. He was near the opposite bank already and his army was coming to help him.

They rallied. They avenged Chapaev. They struck Kolchak and Denikin. They smashed Kolchak. They drove him out of the Soviet land.

Vasily Ivanovich became famous.

Everywhere they talk about him: but that won't bring Vasily Chapaev back to us.

Anecdotes

THE COMPLETE PROHIBITION OF GENUINE PUBLIC SATIRE IN THE STALIN PERIOD CREATED A VOID FOR SOME PEOPLE, WHO FILLED IT BY MEANS OF ILLICIT JOKES. THE CURRENCY OF SUCH JOKES WAS VERY LIMITED; PEOPLE WERE THROWN IN JAIL FOR MUCH LESS THAN RECITING ONE OF THEM.

Question: What is a line?
Answer: The Communist approach to shop counters. [5:71]

For anecdote sources, see *Blue Blouse Skit,* above.

Trade Commissar Mikoyan brags to Health Commissar Semashko: "When you took over, malaria raged and it still does; when I took over, there was bread, meat, and sugar—but no more!" [5:71]

Atheist shops are now opening with ungodly prices.[5:71]

Kolkhozniks from the sticks are touring Moscow. The guide is reciting standard materials about the "accomplishments of the Soviet system," about its "concern for the human being," about the "expanding needs of Soviet people" and the "abundance of consumer goods."

One of the kolkhozniks says: "Comrade Leader, I spent the whole day yesterday walking around the city, and I didn't see any of the things you're talking about."

The guide replies with irritation: "You should spend less time walking around and more time reading newspapers!" [4:56–57]

Somewhere in the provinces, a bridge was built across a stream. Since strategically positioned bridges must be guarded, the local authorities put a guard on it. A cashier was hired to pay his salary. To make sure the accounts were calculated correctly, an accountant was hired. A director was hired to ensure proper personnel policies were observed. But then the order came down to reduce payroll. So the guard was fired. [5:47–48]

A good factory director is like a malaria mosquito: he makes you quiver. [3:77]

At a meeting, the kolkhoz director announces prizes for the best shock workers. One milkmaid is given a radio receiver, another gets a gramophone, and a third gets a bicycle.

Everyone claps, and the milkmaids are happy.

The director gets up again and announces with great ceremony: "And now, comrades, we award first prize to the very best shock worker, who is politically conscious, worked without taking days off or holidays, and set a record for raising pigs; she is an example for everyone. I hereby present our leading pig-tender, Darya (and here the director's voice quivered)... with the complete works of our beloved Comrade Stalin!"

The meeting fell silent. A voice from the back said:

"Just what the bitch deserves." [4:54]

A Soviet Communist, after showing a foreigner the Exhibition of Economic Accomplishments, in Moscow, says: "Well, now you see that socialism can be built in one country."

"Sure, that's true, but why would anyone live there?" [4:65]

During the campaign to improve service in shops, clerks were ordered to be polite to all customers. A persnickety lady walks into a textile shop and asks to see some cloth. She rejects it. She asks for another bolt, and turns that one down too. Finally she's gone through all the store has, and still hasn't found what she wants.

The clerk bends overs and whispers: "Please, dear Citizeness, you come stand on my spot, and I'll go to hell." [4:83–84]

A Moscow influence peddler trying to get into the movies for free steps into the administrator's office. "Hey, pal, gimme a couple of freebies," he says offhandedly, flipping his overcoat open, and showing a tag that looks like an important medal.

"We're not allowed to give out complimentary tickets."

"The hell you're not. I'll give the Kremlin a call right now."

He picks up the phone and dials a number. "Give me Molotov. What? Thank you. Hey, Vyachik, why can't the 'Dawn of Revolution' movie theater give out freebies? What? I can use your name? Thanks, buddy."

The administrator hisses, "While you're at it, could you please use your high connections to get that phone fixed? It hasn't worked for two months." [4:69]

A peasant is asked, without much chance for refusal, to sign up for a two-hundred-ruble bond. He scratches his head: "Who guarantees the bond?"

"Our beloved leader Stalin."

"And if something should happen to him . . . ?"

"The Communist Party."

"And what if something happens to the Party?"

"Wouldn't that be worth a measly two hundred to you?" [4:69]

THE PURGES AND PREPARATION FOR WAR, 1937–1940

Tale of the Pole
Marfa Semyonovna Kryukova (1937)

MARFA KRYUKOVA (1876–1954) WAS A FOLKTALE-TELLER FROM NORTH RUSSIA WHO MADE A SOVIET CAREER BY ADAPTING TRADITIONAL FOLK FORMS TO THE POLITICAL PURPOSES OF THE REGIME WITH "FOLK SONGS" ABOUT LENIN, STALIN, CHAPAEV, VOROSHILOV, AND OTHERS. THOUGH KRYUKOVA'S PEASANTISMS WERE MEANT TO REFLECT POPULAR PRIDE IN SOVIET POLAR EXPEDITIONS, THEY WERE ALSO EDITED BEFORE PUBLICATION TO CONFORM TO LITERARY STANDARDS.

> The great chieftain Stalin summoned all his men unto a meeting,
> He hailed them all for meetings and discussion,
> He summoned all the wise men and the scholars,
> The glorious hero of the ice Ivan Longbeard,
> He called together his brave eagles, the arctic pilot heroes,
> And he spoke to them this speech:
> "Hail to ye, my champions brave and hero pilots,

Note from *Komsomol Pravda* (24 June 1937), p. 2: This tale of the polar expedition was written down from the words of the famous northern storyteller Marfa Semyonovna Kryukova (village of Lower Zolotnitsa, Primorsky District of the Northern Region).

Kryukova not only recalls the "legends of ancient times" with her exceptional memory, she responds to the events of our era with poetic tales. Poetic talent, a love of reading (she is literate and reads quite a bit), and a thirst for knowledge have enabled Kryukova to create in her own unique manner several new works of folktale narrative, including this tale of polar exploration.

The tale was recorded by Viktorin Popov in June of this year in Arkhangelsk, where Kryukova was summoned by the Northern Arts Administration to participate in the regional Folk Art Olympics.

Fly ye off to yon country in the distance,
To yonder country, yon cold country,
The cold country, yon northern country,
Whereto brave eagles heretofore have never flown,
Whereto our champions brave have never fared,
Where our good folk have never found abode,
A country of great moment to us.
For thence the fits of weather descend
All across our native land!
Reconnoiter and inquire
Wherefore the morning sun arises,
Wherefore the blustery winds blow thence—
Is not their cause the frosty breath of ice?
We must know all that might be known about the weather,
When and whence the blustery winds blow forth,
When and whence the gentle rains do fall,
And when the cruel drought does occur.
On our fields and in our work
We must know all that might be known.
Fly ye off to yon country cold,
To the cold country, yon country of the ice,
Build ye there a dwelling of the ice,
A house of ice with a lofty tower,
Gaze ye from yon lofty tower, survey,
Write down all ye behold in a ledger,
Send me a dispatch and a speedy deposition
How goes your work and what your eyes have seen!"
Many people from foreign countries
Had journeyed to the midnight land
To the land in the north in the ice,
Thereto, the pillar of the globe,
A wondrous pillar there to see.
It looms out of the earth, from the ocean.
One man journeyed there from foreign parts,
He wished to cross the icy fields
But could not cross yon frozen fields,
And he perished on his journey far,
In the cold, in the bitter cold.
Many were the years before we knew
Where this valiant traveler met his death.
Many times and many years did pass
Before yon fishermen sat fishing
By the White Sea, wherein they cast their nets.
In their nets they found a wondrous wonder,
A wondrous wonder, a most confounding wonder:
They found the boot from his right foot,

And in yon boot they found a note laid there:
"In my searches I have met with mishap,
My most cherished dream did not come true."
When another man from foreign parts did journey
Across the sea-bound route, across the ice
To the upright pillar of the world,
He wearied of his journey and grew tired,
And sought his respite on the route,
And thereat, at the very moment,
The polar bears fell upon him,
Polar bears, very ravenous bears,
Tore him into pieces, tiny bits,
Ate him up, swallowed the last trace,
Leaving from him nary a small bone,
By the sea, by our great White Sea.
Our hunters journeyed there to do their hunting
For the seal and the sea beasts.
Once in their hunting they shot down a beast,
Not the seal, but a polar bear,
A polar bear wandered far from home.
When they began to flay, to skin the bearhide,
When they began to cleave the carcass,
They found a wondrous wonder, most confounding:
They found a spy glass left in its entrails,
A wanderer's spyglass, the spyglass of yon traveler
And on a note laid in the spyglass written:
"In my searches I have met with mishap,
My most cherished dream did not come true."
When men from foreign parts again did journey
Across the sea-bound route, across the ice
To the upright pillar of the world,
They came upon their downfall there,
They met with great misfortune,
A savage hunger started up among them.
They started eating, to consume each other.
A Soviet ship arrived posthaste
And saved all the survivors, whomsoever was alive.
Many people journeyed there from many countries,
But they had not the wherewithal to cross,
The ability it took and the wisdom,
They had not the courage or the knowledge.
Our brave eagles flew there too,
Our brave eagles, our hero arctic pilots,
They flew across the lofty mountains, icy mountains,
And flew across the oceans deep,
They flew yonder to the land of cold,

The land of cold, to the pillar of the globe,
But ice blocks float all around that pillar,
The ice blocks float, circle round and round,
They carried the wise men on their wings,
Men of wisdom, men of valor,
From their wings they set them down
Onto the frozen ice block, the floating ice block,
And on that pillar of the earth they hung
The glorious Soviet flag,
And built a house on the block of ice,
A house of ice with a lofty tower.
They went down to the bottom of the sea,
To the bottom of the bottomless sea,
They touched the ocean depths,
They looked, they saw that the earth spins round,
That the earth spins round and turns,
It spins around that pillar,
To warm everyone with the sun,
So everyone knows when the day comes,
And the dark of night goes by,
And that the earth doesn't rest on three whales,
As old people said of yore,
And the earth doesn't shake because
The whales stir from their dreams.
The earth turns round an upright pillar,
The earth is skewered through by the pillar,
And that is why our mother earth shakes.
Because that wondrous pillar is shaking in the wind.
On that selfsame pillar of the earth,
That sticks up like a tall spear to the heavens,
The glorious Soviet banner flies.
And Ivan Longbeard himself stands by the banner,
The wind ruffles his black beard,
And he gives all sorts of orders,
How things should be done, and how to make the weather,
And they stay on that moving block of ice,
Our Soviet heroes, those wondrous knights.
They stand at the outpost, the frozen outpost,
They live and survive by yon upright pillar,
By the glorious Soviet flag.
The polar bears came to them as helpers,
The polar bears bowed low before them,
They came to befriend the heroes,
To make friends and pass the time of day,
To be neighbors, the closest neighbors,
To be comrades, the most loyal comrades.

The heroes live on the ice block and do their deeds,
Do their deeds, look through and at all things,
Whenever the blustery wind starts blowing.
They make walls of ice for protection,
To stop the blustery winds from blowing on our fertile lands,
The trees from bending in our orchards,
And to help our Soviet ships sail on calm seas.
When storm clouds gather they hold them back,
Hold them in their hands and get their feel,
And then they let it go in the direction
Where the land needs rain right away.
The ice block floats the heroes around the ocean,
They know not what direction they are headed,
Fires of all sorts burn on the ice block,
Flowers bloom on it, blue as the sky.
Yet it is no wonder, there is no marvel to it:
For now the weather is made for our homeland
By Soviet heroes with their wisdom,
Their wisdom made great by knowledge!

The Living Lenin
Konstantin Fedin (1939)

FEDIN (1892–1977), A MODERATELY EXPERIMENTAL WRITER OF
THE 1920S WHO GAINED WIDE FAME OUTSIDE THE USSR, LATER
BECAME A MEMBER OF THE LITERARY ESTABLISHMENT. A STALIN
PRIZE WINNER AND OFFICER OF THE WRITERS' UNION, HE WAS
INSTRUMENTAL IN BANNING SOLZHENITSYN'S CANCER WARD IN
1968. THE FOLLOWING STORY WAS A CONTRIBUTION TO THE
VAST FLOW OF LENIN HAGIOGRAPHIES; IT MIGHT ALSO HAVE
SUGGESTED — TO CRITICAL READERS — AN ALTERNATIVE TO STA-
LIN'S STYLE OF LEADERSHIP.

Pravda, 21 January 1939, p. 4.

I

Early in 1919 in Moscow I saw Lenin for the first time. After recovering from serious wounds inflicted by the counterrevolutionary assassin, Lenin had begun going out again.

Lenin was waiting for Nadezhda Konstantinovna Krupskaya at Narkompros, in the building of a former lyceum near the Crimean Bridge. He was in a fur coat, without a hat, and was pacing in the narrow part of the vestibule between the front door and the stairs. The doorman was sitting near a small desk.

Lenin's head was easy to see from above—it was large, unusual; memorable from first glance. Curls of bright yellow hair fell onto his fur collar. Of all his features, the sweep of his forehead, the top and back of his head were oddly predominant: they were unknown in any other figure of history or modern times, unique to this person—Lenin. Clutching his hat behind his back, he moved back and forth methodically, with small steps, concentrating intently and only occasionally looking up.

Although work had long since finished and only a few of the staff remained in the building, I remember how typists came running from their offices to watch Lenin—they leaned over the balustrades and scurried back if he looked up.

The fact that Lenin was pacing near the doorman, who busied himself with boiling the water, and the fact that the staff, overflowing with burning human curiosity, poked their noses in and out of their offices, first won my heart over to Lenin—he was manly, approachable, and a shining example of simplicity.

II

In July of 1920 in Petrograd, the Second Congress of the Communist International opened.

Lenin entered the hall of Uritsky Palace[1] at the head of a multiethnic group of congress delegates. A wave of thunderous applause rolled forward to meet him, drowning everything with its din. At this moment baskets of red carnations were brought in from all around the hall, and the flowers were handed out to the delegates.

Lenin hurried through the entire hall, tilting his head forward as though cutting through a strong headwind and as if trying to hide from view and stop the applause. He stepped up on the presidium bench and stayed out of sight while the ovation continued.

When the applause died down, he abruptly reappeared in the auditorium and began climbing rapidly up through the amphitheater between the benches. He was noticed immediately, and as soon as he had been spotted, everyone resumed their applause and clogged the aisle he was dashing along. Lenin came alongside an old man and, with a friendly smile, held out his hand to him. I have no idea who the

---

1. The Tauride Palace had been renamed after the assassinated director of the Cheka, M. S. Uritsky (1873–1918).

old man was. Judging by the sobriety and dignity of his greeting, it was one of Lenin's dear old peasant friends.

Lenin had to endure a third and, perhaps, most ecstatic, overwhelming ovation when he mounted the tribune to speak. He spent a long time rifling through his papers on the podium then, raising his hand and shaking it, tried to calm the frenzied hall. Reproachfully and sternly he scrutinized the auditorium and, suddenly taking out a watch, showed it to the auditorium, angrily tapping the watch face, but nothing helped. Then he examined and shuffled through his papers again. The rumble of applause did not soon subside.

Lenin the orator coordinated his gestures and his words. The contents of his speech were communicated plastically, with his entire body. It seemed as though molten metal had been poured into a pliant form, so exactly did his movements match his words and so tempestuously did the fiery logic of his speech flow. Lenin glanced frequently at his notes and cited many figures, but he remained a great tribune, not for a moment sounding like a monotonous professor.

When he asked the hall why were there "disturbances" throughout the world, as the bourgeois government of England delicately put it, his entire body demonstrated ironically how awkward and ticklish these "disturbances" were for the bourgeoisie, and world politics were transformed instantly into a striking, sarcastic picture.

Next to me in the press box sat an artist. Probing Lenin's figure with his dogged eyes, he tried to convey Lenin's vitality on paper. But neither the gestures nor the movements of Lenin could be captured. The artist moved to another seat. Then I saw him move to a third, then a fourth. The lenses of still and moving cameras joined the artist in trying to capture the elusive, living Lenin.

After the session, Lenin and Gorky left the palace with a crowd of delegates. Right there by the exit they were photographed. Hence the famous portrait *Lenin and Gorky by the Palace Columns*.

III

The sky was a dazzling blue. People were carrying three-meter wreaths of oak twigs and red roses over their heads. On the Square of Martyrs they were to be placed at the graves of those who in life had been as unbending as oaks and as beautiful as roses in bloom.

Lenin walked up front with the congress delegates. The people alongside him kept changing—foreigners and Russians, old and young.

He walked without an overcoat, with his jacket unbuttoned, moving his hands between his back and waist pockets. It was as if he weren't outside, amid huge, heavy buildings, but in a cozy room, maybe in his own home. He found nothing extraordinary in the masses surrounding him, and felt unconstrained by the people's yearning to be with him.

During the procession, Lenin had a wonderful conversation with a certain man.

But allow me a short digression. Petrograd was visited by a German who for three days had headed the "independent" republic of Braunschweig,[2] which was subsequently crushed by Noske.[3] I met him in the Palace of Labor. From the balcony we looked onto the bleak square, which preserved traces of the recent heroic defense of Petrograd from Yudenich.

The Braunschweiger was upset by Soviet procedures for goods distribution. Hunching his shoulders, he suddenly raised his long arm over his head and, with anguished despair, surveyed the entire square.

"But why in the world did you close the small shops? If I were to lose a button, where would I buy one?"

This Braunschweiger republican was a tailor by profession.

And this Braunschweiger turned up among Lenin's companions on the walk to the Square of Martyrs.

Lenin cocked his head to one side, to hear his shorter companion better. At first Lenin was serious. But then he began to smile, to squint, curtly shaking his head. Then he stepped back, abruptly waving his hand as though to say, "Nonsense, rubbish!" The Braunschweiger, gesticulating, continued to argue something. Lenin took his elbow and said two or three phrases—short, as though final and irrevocable. But the Braunschweiger objected furiously. Then suddenly Lenin clapped him on the shoulder lightly, thrust his hands into his waistcoat, and began to laugh and laugh, shaking, and hastening his step.

Had this failure of a Braunschweiger mentioned a button? It's possible, of course.

This scene, lasting all of two or three minutes, gave me a chance to see the jovial Lenin, Lenin with a belly laugh, to observe him in a lively argument—with the quick changes of expression, with crafty squinted-up eyes, with gestures full of meaning, passion, and willpower.

These three precious moments impressed the brilliant, eternally living Lenin in my imagination and my heart.

---

2. Brunswick in English, a small state in Weimar Germany.
3. Head of the German police.

I Heard Lenin
An Old Worker of the Bolshevik Factory (1939)

ONE OF MANY TESTIMONIALS OF VETERANS OF REVOLUTION WHO "SAW" OR "HEARD" LENIN. THE "BOLSHEVIK" (FORMERLY OBU-

---

From *O Lenine* (Moscow: Khudozhestvennaia literatura, 1939), pp. 577–578.

KHOV) FACTORY, WHERE THE AUTHOR WORKED, WAS MADE FA-
MOUS IN 1901 IN THE SO-CALLED OBUKHOV DEFENSE, A PROLE-
TARIAN ACTION AGAINST THE POLICE. THE SCENE OF LENIN
SPEAKING IN A FACTORY TO THE WORKERS WAS OFTEN CAPTURED
IN GRAPHIC ART AND IN THE MOVIES, FOR EXAMPLE *MAN WITH
A GUN*. IN THIS SELECTION, THE MENSHEVIKS ARE PRESENTED
AS IN OFFICIAL HISTORY, FALSELY AND MALICIOUSLY, AS "BOUR-
GEOIS LICKSPITTLES."

It was in April [1917], soon after Lenin's arrival in Petrograd. The Mensheviks
and S.R.'s were trying to undermine his authority among workers, and had started
nasty rumors about Lenin. But attempts to shake the people's faith in their leader
ended in complete failure.

Attempts to blacken Lenin's name were also made at the Obukhov Factory (now
the "Bolshevik"), but the Obukhovites weren't easily fooled.

Once during a hot argument with us Bolsheviks, the Mensheviks, those bourgeois
lickspittles who grew fat on the war, announced that Lenin was scared to come to
the factory because nobody would come hear him.

We laughed at the liars and thought: "It would be nice to invite Vladimir Ilich to
visit us! Then we'd show those lying dogs who the workers will listen to: Lenin, who
told the workers the truth, or the Mensheviks, who deceived them."

After we talked things over, we sent delegates to see Ilich. V. I. Lenin received our
emissaries very warmly. He asked about the factory, about how the Obukhovites
live, about some old friends, and he promised to come.

Finally, the day arrived. A rally was scheduled for the New Tower workshop still
under construction. In those days there weren't many Bolsheviks at the factory. We
were very worried and watched the Mensheviks' petty intrigues with alarm. They
wanted to spoil Lenin's appearance at any cost. They even started a rumor that
Lenin could promise all he liked, but he wouldn't come. But the workers believed
Lenin's word. Everyone knew that once Lenin had made a promise, it meant he
would come. Many workers gathered to hear him speak. Workers came not only
from the Obukhov and Semyannikov factories, but from the textile plants and the
railroad workshops. Many people came who had already met Lenin in workers'
circles. They all wanted very much to see Lenin again and hear his voice. There
were more people than could fit in the workshop. People found room where they
could: some climbed up on a crane, some on planks, some on girders.

The steam engines were howling. At first we thought it was by accident, but then
we guessed it was the Mensheviks trying to drown out Lenin's words. Vladimir Ilich
wasn't flustered. He waited for the right moment and began his speech. He was
listened to with great attention. The workers' faces were lit up, their eyes glistened.
Everyone was moved. Lenin spoke for thirty to forty minutes, and when he finished,

we noticed that the Mensheviks had gone off somewhere to hide. How we wanted to shout at them:

"See how the workers listen to Lenin!"

One of the Menshevik leaders, who had come to the factory specially, tried to speak, but nobody wanted to listen to him.

The workers were packed tightly around Lenin and carried him back to his car on their shoulders.

Goose Gets a Transfer
A Folk Tale
Lazar Lagin (1937)

THIS ADAPTATION OF FOLKLORE TO POLITICS BY LAZAR LAGIN WEDS THE FAMILIAR ANIMAL TALE, WITH ITS REPETITION AND ACCUMULATION OF ENCOUNTERS, TO THE ENDURING PROBLEMS OF SWOLLEN BUREAUCRACY, NEPOTISM, AND UNCTUOUS DEFERENCE TO POWER. SUCH SATIRE, WHICH WAS WITHIN THE BOUNDARIES OF ACCEPTABLE *SAMOKRITIKA* (SOCIALIST SELF-CRITICISM) EVEN AT THE HEIGHT OF DICTATORSHIP, FILLED THE PAGES OF HUMOR MAGAZINES SUCH AS *CROCODILE*.

Once upon a time in a district capital there lived a fairly important bird, a Goose, it seems. One day the Goose was transferred to another district. The Goose received a discharge from the appropriate office; he received his traveling expenses and packed his things. He built himself a most elegant carriage, harnessed it to twelve rabbits in tandem, and set off. He rode along, singing a song, breathing the air, communing with nature, sniffing the flowers.

Along the way the Goose met a rooster, one of his close colleagues.

"Hello, Goose."

"Hello, Rooster."

"Where are you going, Goose?"

"To Pleasantville, Rooster."

"Take me along with you, Goose."

"And what do I need you for, Rooster?"

Krokodil, 7 March 1937, p. 3.

"What do you mean, what for? I can compile notes for your reports, prepare theses for your speeches, and select quotations."

"All right, Rooster, get in."

The Rooster got into the cart and they rode off. The Goose was singing his songs, breathing the air, communing with nature, sniffing the flowers. The Rooster was preparing a welcoming resolution from the laboring people of Pleasantville on the occasion of Goose's arrival at his new post. At that moment they came upon the Hare.

"Hello, Goose."

"Hello, little Hare."

"Where are you going, Goose?"

"To Pleasantville, Hare."

"Take me with you, Goose."

"What the devil can you do for me, Hare?"

"How's that? I'll come to visit you, and I can invite you to visit me; we can play preference."

"All right, get in."

Hare got into the cart and they set off. Goose was singing his songs, breathing the air, communing with nature, sniffing the flowers. Rooster was preparing a welcoming resolution from the laboring people of Pleasantville on the occasion of Goose's arrival at his new post. Hare was mulling over which jam he would serve Goose in Pleasantville and how he could most conveniently and elegantly lose at cards. They drove along. And there alongside the road they saw a lumbering bear asleep in a sun patch in a field. He was the manager of Goose's communal holdings.

"Hello, Goose."

"Hello, Misha."

"Where are you going, Goose?"

"To Pleasantville, Misha."

"Take me along, Goose."

"What do I need you for, Misha?"

"I'll come in handy, Goose. Oh, how handy I'll be! I can't stay here without you. The self-critics will chew me up."

"All right, get in."

Bear got into the cart and they set off. Goose was singing his songs, breathing the air, communing with nature, sniffing the flowers. Rooster was preparing a welcoming resolution from the laboring people of Pleasantville on the occasion of Goose's arrival at his new post. Hare was mulling over which jam he would serve Goose in Pleasantville and how he could most conveniently and elegantly lose at cards. And Bear was calculating what it would cost to build Goose a dacha, which apartment residents he would evict for Goose, Rooster, Hare, and himself, and how he could do it. At that moment they met a heifer on the bridge, a most kind and affectionate heifer.

"Hello, Goose."

"Hello, Brown Cow."

"Where are you going, Goose?"

"To Pleasantville, Brown Cow."

"Take me along with you, Goose."

"What do I need you for, Brown Cow?"

"That's a strange question, Goose. When you need it, I'll play dumb for you. When it's your will, I will liberally edit a newspaper for you, glorify you, and free up a pedestal for you."

"All right, get in."

Then and there, everyone began to protest. Rooster said: "In an emergency, I can double as newspaper editor." Hare said: "I'm also rather affectionate." And Bear said: "I have nothing against Heifer personally, but it's just that I built the bridge we're on now and can take no responsibility for it."

Goose didn't listen to Bear, sat the Heifer in the cart, the bridge snapped, and everyone tumbled into the water.

The twelve rabbits harnessed in tandem climbed out of the water and said: "We knew that this was disgraceful nepotism long ago, but we weren't comfortable saying it to Goose."

Narkom Yezhov
Dzhambul Dzhabaev (1937)

DZHAMBUL DZHABAEV (OR JAMBOUL JABAEV; 1846–1945), A KA-ZAKH FOLK POET AND SINGER WHO GAINED RENOWN DURING THE 1930S FOLK REVIVAL, WAS THE MOST FAMOUS AND LONG-LIVED OF THE "ETHNIC" TELLERS WHO LAUDED THE SOVIET ORDER, ITS LEADERS, AND ITS LAWS. HIS TRANSPARENTLY EULOGISTIC SONGS WERE DONE UP IN LOCAL TRADITIONAL STYLE, FEATURING GOD-LIKE LEADERS BATHED IN NATIONAL IDIOMS AND FIGURES. EXALTED FOR HIS PAEANS TO LENIN AND STALIN, DZHABAEV HERE PRAISED NIKOLAI YEZHOV, PEOPLE'S COMMISSAR [NAR-KOM] OF INTERIOR AFFAIRS, WHO AT THE MOMENT WAS CON-DUCTING THE BLOODY PURGES.

> In a flash of lightning we came to know you,
> Yezhov, eagle-eyed and keen Narkom.
> The hero Yezhov was nurtured for battle

Dzhambul, "Narkom Ezhov," trans. K. Altaiskii, *Pravda,* 20 December 1937, p. 2.

By the wisdom and words of the Great Lenin.
Yezhov heard with his heart, heard with his blood
The fiery summons of the great Stalin.
When the dawn of October first glimmered,
He stormed the Winter Palace with valor in his gaze.
When the horizon reflected war's glare,
He saddled his steed and rode off to the front.
Class struggled with class. The land was ablaze.
The blood of the motherland flowed in those days.
The enemy squeezed us tight in its ring
Of iron and steel, fire and lead.
I remember the past. In a sunset of crimson
I see through the smoke Commissar Yezhov.
Baring his cutlass, he daringly led
The great-coated people into attack.
He battles, with great batyrs[1] as his models:
Such as Sergo,[2] Voroshilov, and Kirov.
With his men he is tender, but stern with his foes,
Courageous Yezhov, who was tempered in battle.
When the sun of the east rose over the steppe,
And the Kazakh people straightened their backs,
When the chabans[3] rose up against the bais,[4]
Lenin and Stalin sent Yezhov to us.
Yezhov arrived and, dispersing the haze,
Raised Kazakhstan to fight for its fate,
Rallied the auls[5] to the Soviet banner,
With the strength and wisdom of Kremlin decrees.
Leading the Kazakh people behind him,
He led the campaign against beks[6] and the bais.
The people went on the attack with Yezhov.
And their golden visions began to come true.
He drove the bloodsuckers off past the hills,
Seized all their herds, their flocks, and their droves.
The lies of the bai are all gone forever,
Spring is abloom in the Kazakhstan steppes
More splendid and lovely than the best dreams of old.
Here everyone loves you, Comrade Yezhov!
The aryks,[7] the ponds, the blue-watered lakes
Turn to your figure their adoring gazes.

---

1. A traditional Kazakh folk hero.
2. Ordzhonikidze.
3. Landless Kazakh peasants.
4. Rich landowners.
5. Central Asian villages.
6. A middle-ranking official.
7. Central Asian irrigation canals.

Here each blade of grass, each reed and each flower,
The snow on each peak and each mountain stream,
The limitless steppes from border to border,
Remember you, they have not forgotten.
The long prairie grass sings of you songs.
In the movement of wind we hear your breathing.
The akyns[8] of the steppe sing their lays of you,
Like the music of waterfalls, or the marvel of aryks.
And the people repeat it as they gather round:
Greetings to you, companion of Stalin!
But the foe is alert, angered and cruel.
Listen closely: the enemy creeps in at night,
Creeps through the gullies, and the infidels
Carry pistols and bombs, and cholera bacillus.
But they are met by you, powerful and stern,
Yezhov, who is tried in the fire of battle!
The enemies of our way, the enemies of millions,—
The Trotskyist bands of spies crept up on us,
And the Bukharinites, those cunning swamp snakes.
The furious mob of the nationalists.
They were rejoicing as they brought us our chains,
But they fell into the traps of Yezhov:
Devoted friend of the mighty Stalin,
Yezhov destroyed their traitorous ring,
The brood of the enemy snakes was exposed
By the eyes of Yezhov—the eyes of the people.
Yezhov lay in wait for the poisonous snakes,
And smoked the vipers from their lairs and their dens.
The scorpion brood was entirely crushed
By the hands of Yezhov—the hands of the people.
And the Order of Lenin, burning with fire,
Was given to you, Stalin's companion.
You are a sword, bared calmly and fiercely,
A fire that burns out the nests of the snakes,
You are a bullet for scorpions and vipers,
You're the eye of the nation, brighter than diamonds.
Gray-haired annalist, witness of the epoch,
Who has absorbed all woe and rejoicing,
And lived for an age, the ancient Dzhambul
Heard the rumble as it came from the steppe.
A sonorous word, voiced by the millions,
Flew from the peoples to the batyr Yezhov:
Thank you, Yezhov, that you beat the alarm
As you stand on guard for your nation and leader.

---

8. Kazakh folksinger (whose tradition was followed by Dzhabaev).

Two Purge Poems

(1937)

Bedny and Bezymensky never regained the popularity they enjoyed in the revolutionary era. Bedny in particular suffered in the 1930s when his play *The Folk-Knights* (*Bogatyri*) was attacked for mocking Russia's sacred past. Still, they could be enlisted to write doggerel for the Stalinist regime — in this case an apologia for the terror trials of the 1930s. Both works are drenched in hatred, primitive images of creatures, filth, and implacable evil set over against the joyful images of a worker's state.

WE DEALT THE ENEMY A CRUEL COUNTERBLOW

DEMYAN BEDNY (1937)

Monstrous! I can hardly put in words
That thing my head can find no place for,
For which no name would do, such an awful evil
That it's hard to find a word to fit its horror.
How despicable is the hissing voice of spies!
How disgraceful the sight of enemies among us!
   Shame to the mothers that gave birth
         To these dogs of unprecedented foulness!
         These vicious dogs, whose fury is before us,
         Whose abominable names
Will join the ranks—for ever and all times—
   With the vilest names on earth.
What dogs! Mad dogs leave home
        And flee the pen
        Where they were born—But these!..
The poison oozes from their fascist gut.
When they stuck their snouts in the fascist trough,
They meant to bring misfortune to their homeland!
        A nest of spies has been uncovered!
        The spies remanded to the court!

"My nanesli vragu zhestokii kontr-udar," *Pravda*, 12 June 1937, p. 3.

All those Feldmans, Yakirs, Primakovs,
Putnas and Tukhachevskys—common rabble!
They tried to put the fascist fetters
On our Union, the country of their birth.
The vile spies were working with a plan:
The spies were salesmen, their homeland was their ware.
Unmasking them was fortunate for us:
What a joy to realize that we dealt
       The enemy camp a cruel counterblow!
Nary an ash will remain of these loathsome vermin!
Let the vicious fascist choir sing their requiem.

The Soviet land has grown, gained strength, and flourished
       In defiance of its evil foes.
Despite its foes, it will get even stronger,
Equally great in battle and at work.
Didn't we study in the school of Lenin?
Heading with Stalin toward our radiant destiny,
Standing together in our unconquerable will,
       Haven't we forged our power?!
Yes! Along the road our Revolution chose,
We will arrive at worldwide victory.
       And none of these damned traitors will bar the way!!

THE LAW OF MILLIONS

ALEKSANDR BEZYMENSKY (1937)

We close our ranks around a single will
And there is no limit to our power.

Our path is clear
   In the struggle with the enemy,—
Spies
   and traitors to the country
Deserve one thing:
      To be shot.

Such is our unshakable law.
The law of struggle,
   powerful and simple.
Like two times two,
   entered in our laws
And confirmed
   unanimously.

The fascist horde
   on the road of degenerates,
The rot of Tukhachevskys
   Korks and Yakirs
Was led
   into the awe-inspiring hall
Of Soviet justice,
   without their masks and greatcoats.

The court can see
   that these are villainous men,
The "Your Honors"
   of the days of old.
Noblepersons,
   murderers and liars.
A bourgeois pack
   of loathsome miscreants.

"Zakon millionov," *Pravda*, 12 June 1937, p. 2.

Steeped in blood,
    and crawling in the mud,
They wanted—
    these gentlemen and thugs—
To kill everything
    that cannot be destroyed,
And take away all that
    no power can.

We'll use these traitorous villains'
    vile knife
To devastate
    the enemy band's desires.
The land of labor,
    this giant of a land
Will crush
    that bunch of pygmies
        beneath its heel.

All our people
    have rallied round their leader.
No matter how the enemy
    hides his tracks,
He will be found
    wherever he's concealed,
By the sword of our Bolshevik Marat.

Yes,
    the enemy will be wiped
        from the face of the earth.
He will find
    salvation
        nowhere.

Such is the law,
    the unshakable law.
And we
    will execute it fully.

Timur and His Squad
Arkady Gaidar (1938)

Arkady Gaidar (Golikov; 1904–1941) was one of the enduring Soviet children's writers. He was killed in World War II. His works praised the values of good citizenship and respect for elders, which were shared by Makarenko (and the long-banned Boy Scouts). They also tried to project the public's deeply ingrained esteem for the military at a time when its leadership was being wiped out by the purges.

The boys settled themselves on the sack-covered straw around Timur, who had spread out in front of him a map of the estate.

A lookout was stationed on a rope swing suspended in front of a hole in the wall above the window. From his neck dangled a pair of dented opera glasses.

Translation excerpted from Arkady Gaidar, *Timur and His Squad* (Moscow: Progress Publishers, 1960), pp. 26–30, 33–36, 49–52, 55–57, 62–70.

Zhenya sat not far from Timur and gave all her attention to the proceedings of the conference of this top-secret headquarters. Timur was speaking:

"At daybreak tomorrow, while everybody is still asleep, Kolokolchikov and I will repair the lines she (he pointed to Zhenya) broke."

"He'll oversleep," gloomily interjected the bullet-headed Geika, who was wearing a striped sailor's jersey. "He wakes up only for breakfast and lunch."

"That's a l-lie!" Kolya jumped up and stuttered. "I g-get up with the first r-ray of sun."

"Well, I don't know which is the sun's first ray and which the second, but I do know he'll oversleep," Geika retorted stubbornly.

At this juncture the lookout on the swing whistled. The boys sprang to their feet.

A mounted artillery battalion was galloping down the road in a cloud of dust. The powerful horses, in heavy harness of leather and metal, were pulling their green ammunition wagons and tarpaulin-covered cannon at a spanking pace.

The suntanned, weatherbeaten postilions took the bend in dashing style without swaying in their saddles, and, one after another, the batteries disappeared into the woods. Soon the entire unit was out of sight.

"They're headed for the station to board a train," Kolya explained importantly. "I can tell by their uniforms. I can tell when they're out on drill, on parade, or on anything else."

"You just keep your eyes open and your mouth shut!" Geika stopped him. "We've got eyes too. You know, boys, this windbag wants to run away to the Red Army!"

"You can't do that," Timur intervened. "It won't wash."

"Why not?" asked Kolya, flushing. "How come boys always used to run away to the front?"

"That was before! Now the officers and other bosses have strict orders to kick out all the kids."

"How do you mean, kick 'em out?" cried Kolya, turning a deeper red. "You mean—their own side?"

"That's right!" Timur heaved a sigh. "Their own side. And now, fellows, let's get down to business."

The boys resumed their places.

"Unidentified boys have been stealing apples from the garden of No. 34, Crooked Lane," Kolya announced sullenly. "They broke two branches and trampled all over a flower bed."

"Whose house is that?" Timur glanced at his notebook. "It's Kryukov the soldier's. Now, which of you is an ex-specialist on other people's gardens and apple trees?"

"Me," muttered an embarrassed voice.

"Who could have done this job?"

"Kvakin and his assistant, the chap they call Figure. They picked out a Michurin tree;[1] it grows Golden Sap apples."

---

1. After Ivan Michurin (1855–1935), plant breeder, predecessor of the notorious Trofim Lysenko. See V. Lebedev, "Michurin's Dream" (1950), below.

"That Kvakin again!" Timur reflected a moment. "Geika! Did you talk to him?"

"I did."

"Well?"

"Got him on the jaw twice."

"What'd he do?"

"Well, he got me once or twice, too."

"All you can say is 'I got him and he got me.' And a fat lot of good it does! Okay! We'll make Kvakin a special case. Next?"

"The son of the old milkwoman who lives at No. 25 has been called up into the cavalry," a boy in the corner reported.

"Some piece of news!" Timur shook his head reproachfully. "We've had our sign on the gate for two days now. Who put it there—you, Kolokolchikov?"

"Yes."

"Then why is the upper left point of the star all wavy like a leech? If you take on a job, do it properly. People'll laugh when they see it. Next?"

Sima Simakov jumped up and rattled off his report.

"A goat's been lost at No. 54, Pushkaryov Road. I was walking along when I saw an old woman beating a girl. I yelled out, 'Missis, beating's against the law!' She says, 'She's lost the goat, blast her hide!' 'Where was it lost?' 'Over there, in the gully back of the woods. Chewed through her rope and made off, you'd think the wolves'd clean swallowed it.'"

"Wait a minute! Whose house?"

"Pavel Guryev's—he's in the army. The girl's his daughter. Her name is Anya. It was her grandma who was beating her. Don't know her name. The goat's gray, with a black back. They call it Manka."

"Find that goat!" ordered Timur. "Take a squad of four—you, and you, and you. Well, fellows, is that all?"

"There's a girl always crying at No. 22," Geika submitted reluctantly.

"Why does she cry?"

"I've tried asking her but she won't say."

"You ought to have asked her better. Perhaps someone beats her—or treats her badly."

"I asked her, but she wouldn't say."

"A big girl?"

"She's four."

"There's a real tragedy for you! If she'd been a person... but—four years old! Just a moment, though—whose house is that?"

"Lieutenant Pavlov's. The one who was killed at the frontier not long ago."

"'I've tried asking her but she won't say,'" Timur mocked, obviously disappointed in Geika. He frowned and thought a while. "All right. Leave that one to me."

"Kvakin's in sight!" cried the lookout. "He's walking down the other side of the street, eating an apple. Timur, let's send out a squad to give him the bumps!"

"No. Remain where you are. I'll be back soon."

He climbed down the ladder and disappeared into the bushes. Now the lookout continued his running commentary:

"A good-looking girl just came into my field of vision. Name unknown. Standing at the gate with a jug and buying milk. She must be from the house."

"Is it your sister?" asked Kolya, tugging at Zhenya's sleeve. Receiving no answer, he warned her with an important and rather offended air: "Better not try calling to her from here."

"Shut up!" retorted Zhenya derisively, jerking her sleeve free. "I'm not having you order me around!"

"Better leave her alone," Geika teased Kolya, "or she'll clock you one."

"Who? Me?" Kolya was stung to the quick. "What's she got? Nothing but nails! Me, I've got real muscles. Here, look at these biceps! Feel that? And calves too!"

"She'll clock you one anyway—muscles or no muscles. Hey, fellows, watch out! Timur's going up to Kvakin."

Idly swinging a branch which he had broken off one of the trees, Timur was making to cut across Kvakin's path.

Kvakin saw him and halted. His vacant features registered neither surprise nor fear.

"Hiya, Commissar!" he said quietly, cocking his head on one side. "Where you off to in such a hurry?"

"Hiya, Chief!" Timur replied in the same tone. "I was off to meet you."

"Glad to see you. Pity I haven't anything for you. Except this..." He fumbled in his shirt and produced an apple.

"Stolen?" asked Timur, biting into it.

"That's right," Kvakin said. "Golden Sap. Only trouble is, it's not really ripe yet."

"Sour as vinegar!" Timur made a face and tossed the apple away. "Look here: did you notice a sign like this on the fence of No. 34?" Timur pointed to the star embroidered on his blue shirt.

"Well, and what if I did?" Kvakin was on his guard. "Brother, I keep my eyes peeled day and night."

"Then take my advice, and when you see this sign anywhere, day or night, run like a scalded cat."

"Say, Commissar, you're a bit of a fire-eater!" drawled Kvakin. "That'll do—enough said."

"Say, Chief, you're a bit of a mule," answered Timur without raising his voice. "This is our last parley, so keep it in mind and pass it on to your gang."

Nobody watching this scene would have thought that those two were anything but the best of friends. So it was not surprising that Olga, standing at the gate with her milk jug, should have asked the milkwoman whether she knew the boy who was talking to that ruffian Kvakin.

"No, I don't," said the milkwoman vehemently. "I suppose he's just another one of them hoodlums. I've seen him hanging around your house lately. Watch out they don't go knocking your little sister about, dearie."

At daybreak the shepherd blew his wooden horn. The old milkwoman opened her gate and drove her cow out to join the herd on the common. She had scarcely turned the corner when five boys jumped out from behind an acacia shrub and scuttled over to the well, trying not to make a clatter with their empty buckets.

"Pump it!"

"Let's have it!"

"There!"

"Take it!"

One after another, the boys rushed into the yard, cold water spilling on their bare feet as they ran, emptied their buckets into the oak barrel, and dashed back to the well.

Timur ran up to Sima Simakov, who was wet from exertion, and asked:

"See Kolokolchikov anywhere? No? Then he has overslept. Hurry! The old woman'll be back any minute."

Timur stole into the Kolokolchikovs' garden, stood under a tree, and whistled. Without waiting for an answer, he climbed the tree and peered into the room. All he could see from his perch was the end of a bed standing by the window and a pair of blanket-covered legs.

He threw a piece of bark onto the bed and called softly:

"Kolya, get up! Kolya!"

The sleeper did not stir. Then Timur pulled out his pocketknife, sliced off a long, thin switch, sharpened the end, and threw it into the window. He hooked the blanket and tugged.

The light blanket slipped out over the windowsill. A hoarse shout issued from the room.

His sleepy eyes almost starting out of his head, a gray-haired gentleman clad only in his pajamas leapt from the bed and, grabbing the retreating blanket, rushed up to the window.

Finding himself suddenly face to face with this venerable old man, Timur dropped to the ground.

The old gentleman, however, flung the recaptured blanket onto his bed, snatched his double-barreled gun off the wall, hastily put on his spectacles, poked the gun through the window, and, pointing the muzzle skyward, closed his eyes and fired.

Timur was so frightened that he did not stop running until he reached the well. There had been a misunderstanding. He had taken the sleeper for Kolya, and the old gentleman had, naturally, taken him for a burglar.

Just then Timur saw the milkwoman going through the gate with her water buckets.

He dived behind a clump of acacias and settled down to observe what would happen next.

When she returned from the well, the old woman lifted a bucket and poured the water into the barrel. The next moment she sprang aside, because the water splashed back at her out of the already brimming barrel.

Gasping and peering round in bewilderment, the old woman inspected the barrel from all sides. She plunged her hand into the water and sniffed it. Then she hurried over to the porch to see if the lock on her door was in order. Then, finally, not knowing what to think, she tapped at her neighbor's window.

Timur laughed and came out of his hiding place. He had to hurry. The sun was already rising. Kolya had failed to turn up, and the lines still had to be repaired.

There was still plenty of work to do, but the chief thing now was to draw up an ultimatum and send it to Misha Kvakin.

Nobody knew how to draw up an ultimatum, so Timur asked his uncle.

His uncle expected that each country had its own way of drawing up ultimatums, but that courtesy obliged you to wind them up with the following words:

"Please accept, Mr. Minister, the assurance of my highest esteem."[2]

After this the ultimatum should be tendered to the head of the hostile country by an accredited ambassador.

But this did not appeal to Timur or to any of the others. First of all, they had no intention of conveying any kind of esteem to that hoodlum Kvakin; secondly, they had neither a permanent ambassador nor even an envoy accredited to Kvakin's gang.

After discussing the point, they decided to send a simpler ultimatum, like the one the Zaporozhye Cossacks sent the Turkish sultan. They had seen a picture of the Cossacks writing their ultimatum, and they had read about how the brave fellows fought the Turks, the Tatars, and the Poles.[3]

On a daisy-covered green off Maly Ovrazhny Lane, behind the chapel whose peeling murals depicted stern, bearded old men and clean-shaven angels, and somewhat to the right of the picture of Judgment Day with its cauldrons, boiling oil, and darting devils, Kvakin's gang was playing cards.

They had no money, so they played for "backbreakers," "flicks," and "revive the stiff." The loser's eyes were bound, he was forced to lie on his back on the grass, and he was given a "candle," that is, a long stick. With this stick he was supposed to repel his kind brethren, who out of pity for the dead man would do everything they could to revive him by energetically lashing at his bare shins, calves, and heels with nettle.

The game was at its height when the shrill call of a bugle came from the other side of the fence.

Timur's envoys stood there.

Kolya Kolokolchikov, the staff trumpeter, gripped a shiny brass bugle in one hand, while the barefoot Geika, his face stern, held a big envelope made of wrapping paper.

"What kind of circus act is this?" asked the boy they called Figure, leaning over the fence. "Misha!" he yelled over his shoulder. "Drop the game, there's some sort of delegation here to see you!"

"Here I am," said Kvakin, hoisting himself up on the fence. "Hiya there, Geika! Who's that shrimp you've got with you?"

"Take this envelope." Geika handed over the ultimatum. "You have twenty-four

---

2. An old-regime bureaucratic formula.
3. Painting by Ilya Repin, reputed to be Stalin's favorite, and often imitated by socialist realists.

hours to think it over. I shall come back for your answer at the same time to-morrow."

Annoyed at being called a shrimp, Kolya Kolokolchikov raised his bugle and, blowing out his cheeks, sounded a furious retreat. The two envoys then departed in dignified silence under the inquisitive stares of the boys strung along the fence.

"What's this, anyway?" said Kvakin, fingering the envelope and looking at the gaping boys. "Here we were, minding our own business, and then bugles, threats! No, fellas, I can't make head or tail of it!"

He tore open the envelope and, perched as he was on the fence, began to read:

"'To Mikhail Kvakin, Chief of the Gang for the Mopping-up of Other People's Gardens.' That's me," he explained in a loud voice. "Full title and all the trimmings. 'And his,'" he continued, "'inglorious assistant Pyotr Pyatakov, otherwise known simply as Figure.' That's you," he explained with satisfaction to Figure. "Sounds good, 'inglorious'! Too high-sounding, though, if you ask me; they could have called the fool something simpler. 'And likewise to all the members of their infamous band—an ultimatum.' What that is I don't know," announced Kvakin sarcastically. "Most likely a swearword of some sort."

"It's an international word. Means they're going to lash us," explained the boy who was standing next to Figure, a close cropped lad called Alyosha.

"Then why don't they say so!" said Kvakin. "Now we come to Article One:

"'In consideration of the fact that you make night raids on the gardens of peaceful inhabitants, not sparing houses bearing our sign—a red star—or even those bearing the star with the black border of mourning, we order you, you cowardly scoundrels...'

"Can you beat it? Just listen to how they swear—the dogs!" continued Kvakin, forcing a smile. "And look at all the fancy words and commas! Boy!"

"'We order you, Mikhail Kvakin, and that altogether inglorious individual, Figure, to appear at the place indicated by our messengers at a time not later than tomorrow morning, bringing with you a list of all the members of your infamous band.

"'In the event of a refusal, we shall consider ourselves at liberty to take any further action we may think fit.'"

"What do they mean—'at liberty'?" Kvakin pondered. "We never locked them up anywhere, did we?"

"It's another of those international words. Means they're going to lash us," the close-cropped Alyosha explained again.

"Then why don't they say so?" Kvakin said with annoyance. "Too bad Geika's gone; looks like he hasn't cried for a long time."

"He won't cry," Alyosha said. "His brother's a sailor."

"So what?"

"His father was a sailor, too. He won't cry."

"What's it to you, anyway?"

"My uncle's a sailor, too."

"Cut it out, will you!" Kvakin flared up. "Father, brother, uncle, what's it all mean, anyway!" Better let your hair grow, Alyosha—looks like you've got sunstroke. And what are *you* mumbling about?" he turned on Figure.

"We've got to catch those messengers tomorrow and give that Timur and his lot a licking," said Figure sullenly, nettled by the ultimatum.

They left it at that.

Withdrawing to the shade of the chapel, the chief and his assistant stopped by a painting depicting agile and muscular devils dragging howling and resisting sinners toward the everlasting furnace. Kvakin asked Figure:

"Look here, was that you in the garden where that girl lives, the one whose father was killed?"

"That's right. What about it?"

"You see, it's like this," Kvakin muttered glumly, poking his finger at the mural. "I don't give a darn for Timur's signs, and I can make mincemeat of him any day."

"Okay," agreed Figure. "So what're you poking your finger at the devils for?"

"Because," replied Kvakin with a crooked grin, "even though you're a pal of mine, Figure, you're not human; you're more like this dirty fat old beast of a devil."

At 11 A.M. Geika and Kolya set out for the reply to the ultimatum.

"Walk straight," Geika growled at Kolya. "You ought to walk with a light and firm step. But you go hopping along like a chicken trying to catch a worm. Your get-up's fine—pants, shirt, and everything—but you still look like nothing on earth. Don't go taking offense—I'm talking sense to you. Now why do you have to lick your lips as you go along? Stick your tongue back in your mouth and keep it where it belongs. And what are you doing here?" Geika asked Sima Simakov, who had just popped up in their path.

"Timur sent me to act as liaison," Simakov rattled off. "It's okay even if you don't know what it's all about. You've got your assignment and I've got mine. Kolya, let me blow your bugle—just once. Boy, aren't you looking important today! Geika, you nut! You might have put a pair of boots or shoes on when you're on a mission! Ever see a barefoot ambassador? Well, so long—you go that way and I go this way. Be seeing you!"

"What a chatterbox!" Geika shook his head. "Shoots off a hundred words where four would do. Sound your bugle, Herald, here's the fence."

"Bring up Mikhail Kvakin!" Geika told the boy whose head appeared above the fence.

"To the right, please. You'll find the gate open to welcome you," Kvakin called from the other side.

"Let's not go," Kolya whispered to Geika, tugging at his hand. "They'll beat us up."

"You mean all of them against us two?" Geika said contemptuously. "Blow your bugle, Kolya—louder! We go wherever we choose!"

They walked through the rusty iron gate and found themselves face to face with a group of boys. In front stood Figure and Kvakin.

"Let's have the answer to our letter," Geika demanded firmly.

Kvakin was smiling, Figure scowling.

"Let's talk this over," Kvakin offered. "Sit down a while, what's the hurry?"

"Give us the answer to the letter," Geika insisted coldly.

"We can talk afterwards."

It was hard to tell whether he was play-acting, this upright, sturdy chap in the sailor's jersey, at whose side stood the puny, now pallid bugler. Or whether he was really demanding an answer as he stood there, barefoot and broad-shouldered, his gray eyes mere slits, confident that justice and power were on his side.

"Here, take it," said Kvakin, handing him a note.

Geika unfolded the sheet of paper. What he saw was a crude drawing of a thumb to a nose captioned with a dirty word.

Geika calmly tore the sheet in two; not a muscle of his face moved. And at that moment the two boys were seized by the arms.

They did not resist.

"You deserve a black eye for delivering ultimatums like that," said Kvakin, coming up to Geika. "But we don't want to be too hard on you. We'll lock you up till nighttime in here"—he pointed to the chapel—"and during the night we'll clean out the garden at No. 24."

"Oh, no you won't," replied Geika, unruffled.

"Oh, yes we will!" cried Figure, hitting Geika in the face.

"You can hit me a hundred times," said Geika. He shut his eyes tight and then opened them again. "Kolya," he grunted encouragingly, "keep your courage up. I've got a feeling there'll be a No. 1 general rallying signal today."

The captives were shoved into the small chapel with its closed iron shutters. Both doors were then locked, bolted, and barred from the outside.

"Well," Figure shouted at the door through cupped palms, "how are things going now, your way or ours?"

From inside came a hollow, scarcely audible answer:

"No, you bums, from now on things'll never go your way again!"

Figure spat in disgust.

"His brother's a sailor," the close-cropped Alyosha explained morosely. "He and my uncle serve on the same ship."

"So what?" Figure asked menacingly. "Who are you, the captain or what?"

"You hit him when he couldn't use his hands. Is that fair now?"

"I'll sock you one, too!" Figure snarled and swung his fist at Alyosha.

The two boys rolled over and over on the grass. The others grabbed them by the arms and legs and tried to pull them apart.

Nobody noticed Sima Simakov's face appearing briefly in the thick foliage of a lime tree which grew near the fence.

Sima slipped to the ground and sprinted across the vegetable patches toward the river, where Timur and the boys were swimming.

At the chapel, the boys had gone off after arranging to meet again later near the garden of No. 24.

Only Figure remained behind. He was perplexed and angered by the silence inside the chapel. The captives neither yelled, nor pounded on the door, nor responded to his taunts and questions.

He then tried a ruse. Opening the outer door, he entered the stone-walled vestibule and held his breath.

While he was standing there with his ear glued to the keyhole, the outer door suddenly closed with a bang, as though someone had hit it with a log.

"Hey, who's there?" he demanded angrily, springing to the door. "Hey, cut out the tricks or I'll sock you one!"

No one replied. He heard strange voices outside. Then he heard the shutters creaking. Someone began to talk to the captives through the bars of the window.

Then the boys inside the chapel burst out laughing. The sound of that laughter made Figure feel uneasy.

At last the outside door was thrown open. Timur, Simakov, and Ladygin stood in the doorway.

"Open the second door!" Timur ordered without stirring from his place. "Open it yourself, if you don't want things happening to you!"

Figure reluctantly drew the bolt. Kolya and Geika came out of the chapel.

"Now take their place!" Timur ordered. "Get in, you swine, quick now!" he shouted, clenching his fists. "I've no time to waste talking to you."

Both doors were slammed shut on Figure. A heavy bolt was shot through the iron loop and a padlock fixed to it.

Then Timur took a sheet of paper and scribbled on it with his blue pencil:

"Kvakin, no need for a sentry. I've locked them up and am taking the key. I'll come straight to the meeting place this evening."

They ran off. Five minutes later, Kvakin came through the gate.

He read the note, fingered the lock, grinned, and retraced his steps to the gate while Figure pounded frantically at the iron door with his fists and heels.

At the gate Kvakin turned around and muttered indifferently:

"Pound away, Geika! You'll have plenty of time to get tired of it before evening!"

Just before sundown, Timur and Simakov made their way to the market square. At the edge of a straggling row of stalls dealing in soft drinks, vegetables, tobacco, groceries, and ice cream stood a rickety empty booth where cobblers worked on market days.

Timur and Simakov spent a few minutes in that booth.

At dusk the helm in the loft went into action. One after another the wires tightened, conveying the right signals to the right places.

Reinforcements poured in. Quite a large number of boys had already gathered— about two or three dozen. And more kept creeping noiselessly through gaps in the fences.

Tanya and Anya were sent away. Zhenya stayed at home, too. Her assignment was to keep Olga from going out into the garden.

Timur stood by the helm.

"Repeat the signal over the sixth line," Simakov requested anxiously, sticking his head through the window. "We don't seem to be getting any reaction on it."

Two boys were busy making a kind of placard out of a piece of plywood. Ladygin's group arrived.

At last the scouts came in with reports. Kvakin's gang was assembled on the common outside the garden of No. 24.

"Time to start," said Timur. "Get ready, boys!"

He released the wheel and pulled a rope. Slowly the company's flag rose and rippled over the old barn in the uneven light of the moon that was shuttling in and out of the clouds. This was the signal for battle.

A file of a dozen boys crept along the fence of No. 24. Halting in the shade, Kvakin said:

"Everybody's here but Figure."

"He's smart," someone remarked. "I'll bet he's in the garden already. He always barges in first."

Kvakin removed two previously loosened boards from the fence and climbed through. The others followed him. Alyosha remained in the street to keep watch.

Five heads peeped out from the nettle-and-weed-filled ditch on the other side of the road. Four of them disappeared again. The fifth—Kolya Kolokolchikov's—did not follow immediately, but a hand reached up and slapped it on the crown, and his head, too, vanished from sight.

Alyosha, the sentry, looked around. All was quiet, and he stuck his head through the hole in the fence to see if he could hear what was going on inside the garden.

Three boys crept out of the ditch. The next moment the sentry felt strong hands gripping his arms and legs, and before he could cry out, he was yanked back from the fence.

"Geika!" he muttered, raising his head. "Where'd you come from?"

"Never mind," hissed Geika. "Better hold your tongue! Or I'll forget that you stood up for me."

"Okay," agreed Alyosha, "I'll shut up." Whereupon he immediately and unexpectedly gave a shrill whistle.

His mouth was clapped shut at once by Geika's broad palm. Hands grabbed him and dragged him away.

The boys in the garden heard the whistle. Kvakin spun around. The whistle was not repeated. Kvakin peered into the darkness. He thought he saw the bushes in the corner of the garden moving.

"Figure!" he called in a low voice. "That you hiding there, you fool?"

"Kvakin! There's a light!" somebody shouted suddenly. "Look out, here they come!"

In the bushes behind him at least a dozen flashlights were switched on. They advanced quickly on the raiders, confusing and blinding them.

"Fight 'em, don't run," cried Kvakin, reaching into his pocket for an apple and hurling it at the lights. "Grab the torches and twist their arms off! It's Timur!"

"Timur is here and so am I!" Simakov yelled as he leapt out from behind a bush.

Another dozen or so boys bore down on them from the rear and flanks.

"Oho!" yelled Kvakin. They've got a regular army here! Run for the fence, fellas!"

The ambushed band made a panic-stricken rush for the fence. Jostling and bumping into one another, the boys tumbled out into the road and fell straight into the arms of Ladygin and Geika.

The moon had completely disappeared behind a cloud. Only voices were to be heard in the darkness:

"Lemme go!"

"Leave me alone!"

"Hands off! Hey!"

"Quiet, everybody!" Timur's voice rang out. "Don't knock the prisoners around! Where's Geika?"

"I'm here!"

"Take them away!"

"Suppose they won't go?"

"Frog-march 'em!"

"Lemme go, you filthy rats!" someone whined.

"Who was that?" Timur demanded furiously. "Aha, you can dish it out but you can't take it! Geika, give the order and get a move on!"

The prisoners were led to the empty booth on the fringe of the market square and pushed inside one after another.

"Bring Kvakin over here to me," Timur ordered.

Kvakin was led up.

"Ready?" asked Timur.

"All ready."

The last prisoner was shoved into the booth, and the door was bolted and locked.

"Run along," Timur told Kvakin. "You're just a joke. Nobody's afraid of you and nobody needs you."

Kvakin stood looking down, expecting a beating.

"Run along," Timur repeated. "Take this key and let your friend Figure out of the chapel."

Kvakin did not move.

"Let the fellas out or lemme in with them," he growled.

"No," said Timur, "that's over and done with. You're finished with them and they're finished with you."

A cacophony of whistles and catcalls followed Kvakin as he slowly walked off, hunching his shoulders. Ten paces away, he stopped and straightened up.

"I'll beat the life out of you!" he shouted savagely at Timur. "I'll smash you single-handed. To a pulp!" After which he plunged into the darkness.

"Ladygin, you and your five can go," said Timur. "What's your next assignment?"

"No. 22, Bolshaya Vasilkovskaya—stack the logs."

"Fine. Get to work!"

A whistle blew at the station nearby. A suburban train had pulled in, and the passengers would soon be coming from the station. Timur began to hurry.

"Simakov, you and your five—what's yours?"

"No. 38, Malaya Petrakovskaya." He added with a laugh, "Same as usual: buckets, barrel, and water. S'long!"

"Fine, get to work! Well, and now people are coming this way. The rest can go home. Quick now!"

Katyusha
Mikhail Isakovsky and Matvei Blanter (1938)

ONE OF THE FEW SOVIET MASS SONGS THAT ACHIEVED INTERNATIONAL RENOWN, "KATYUSHA," WITH MUSIC BY BLANTER AND WORDS BY ISAKOVSKY, WAS AN ADAPTATION OF FOLK MOTIFS — THE RECRUITMENT LAMENT — TO THE TOPICAL THEME OF RED ARMY MEN SERVING IN THE SOVIET FAR EAST DURING THE BORDER TENSIONS WITH JAPAN. IT REFLECTS AN UNABASHED MILITARISM PRESENT IN MOST POPULAR SONGS OF THE LATE 1930s. THE FAMOUS MORTAR ROCKET WAS GIVEN ITS NAME AND IT BECAME A GIGANTIC SONG HIT DURING THE WAR, WITH ANTI-GERMAN LYRICS. IT WAS THUS USED WITH GREAT EFFECTIVENESS IN THE FILM *FATE OF A MAN* (1957).

КАТЮША

Расцветали яблони и груши,
Поплыли туманы над рекой.
Выходила на берег Катюша,
На высокой, на берег крутой.

Выходила, песню заводила
Про степного сизого орла,
Про того, которого любила,
Про того, чьи письма берегла.

Ой ты, песня, песенка девичья,
Ты лети за ясным солнцем вслед
И бойцу на дальнем пограничье
От Катюши передай привет.

Пусть он вспомнит девушку простую,
И услышит, как она поет,

KATYUSHA

Spring is gay with pear and apple
    blossoms,
Wreaths of mist along the river creep,
And Katyusha wanders by the river,
On the bank, upon the rocky steep.

There she wanders singing of the eagle,
Brave and strong, from whom she had
    to part,
He's the youth that Katyusha loves so
    dearly,
And his letters lie against her heart.

O you song, you song so sweet and
    tender,
Fly the path the sun will take above,
Reach the youth who guards the distant
    border,
Tell the soldier of Katyusha's love.

Let him dream about their days
    together,
Hear her song about the river sweep.

From *Russkie-sovetskie pesni, 1917–1977* (Moscow: Khudozhestvennaia literatura, 1977), p. 89.

Пусть он землю бережет родную,
А любовь Катюша сбережет.

Let him keep good watch along the
  border,
And his heart Katyusha's love will keep.

WARTIME PARODY

Разметались головы фашистов.
Целовала Катя «фрицев» в лоб.
Как причмокнет—от фашистов чисто,
Даже нечего запрятать в гроб.

Fascist skulls careened around all over,
Katya'd kissed the Fritzes on the brow.
When her lips smack—from the Nazis
  nothing's
Left to shove even into the grave.

Обнимай, «Катюша», фрицев чаще,
Ревновать нам, «Катя», не к лицу.
Гитлер тоже о тебе скучает,
Выходи навстречу подлецу.

Hug those Fritzes, Katya, even harder,
Jealousy, dear, is not our cup of tea.
Even Hitler is longing for your kisses,
Why not show the rascal a good time.

Загляни Адольфу в волчьи очи,
Приголубь бандита, приласкай,
Пожелай ему загробной ночи
И по ветру кости разметай.

Gaze into the wolfish eyes of "Dolfie,"
Hug the bandit, snuggle up to him,
Say "Goodnight," and sweet dreams
  forever
Then you'll scatter his bones unto the
  wind.

Эх ты, «Катя», «Катенька»,—подружка,
Угощай непрощенных гостей,
Выдай им украинских галушек
И московских щей погорячей.

Hey you, "Katya," "Katyenka," our
  dearest,
Serve our uninvited guests your best,
Fill their plates up with some cabbage
  dumplings
And pour the borscht as hot as they can
  take.

From *Russkii fol'klor velikoi otechestvennoi voiny* (1964), p. 323.

If Tomorrow Brings War
Vasily Lebedev-Kumach and the Pokrass Brothers (1938)

FROM THE 1938 FILM OF THE SAME NAME BY YEFIM DZIGAN,

ABOUT THE ADVENTURES OF A TEAM OF TANK-DRIVING BROTH-

From *Pesni strany sovetov*, ed. Boris Turganov (Moscow: Khudozhestvennaia literatura, 1940), pp. 88–90.

ERS DURING THE COMING WAR WITH FASCISM. THE SELF-CONGRATULATORY BRAVURA OF THIS FILM, AND OTHERS OF ITS TYPE, WAS PARTLY RESPONSIBLE FOR RUSSIAN UNPREPAREDNESS IN JUNE 1941 — NOTE THE GUSHING PRAISE FOR VOROSHILOV, WHO PROVED HIMSELF DISASTROUSLY IGNORANT OF MODERN WARFARE. NEVERTHELESS, THE LYRICS WERE UPDATED (WITH VERBS PUT IN THE PAST TENSE) DURING THE WAR, AND MAINTAINED THEIR POPULARITY. MUSIC BY THE POKRASS BROTHERS AND WORDS BY LEBEDEV-KUMACH.

ЕСЛИ ЗАВТРА ВОЙНА

Если завтра война, если враг нападет,
Если темная сила нагрянет,
Как один человек, весь советский народ
За свободную родину встанет!

Припев:
На земле, в небесах и на море,
Наш напев и могуч и суров,
Если завтра война, если завтра поход,
Пусть сегодня к походу готов.
Если завтра война, если завтра поход,
Пусть сегодня к походу готов.

Если завтра война, всколыхнется страна,
От Кронштата до Владивостока,
Всколыхнется страна, велика и сильна,
И врага разобьем мы жестоко.

Припев.

Полетит самолет, застрочит пулемет,
Загрохочут железные танки.
И линкоры пойдут, и пехота пойдет,
И помчатся лихие тачанки.

Припев.

IF TOMORROW BRINGS WAR

If tomorrow brings war, if the foe
    should attack,
If the forces of dark are at hand,
The Soviet nation as one will strike
    back,
Will arise for a free motherland.

Refrain:
O'er the land, in the air, on the ocean,
Our resolute song will declare:
If tomorrow brings war, if the campaign
    begins,
Be prepared for the battle today.
If tomorrow brings war, if the campaign
    begins,
Be prepared for the battle today.

If tomorrow brings war, the country will
    rise
From Kronshtat to Vladivostok,
The country will rise, mighty and great,
And cruelly crush the foe.

Refrain.

Then airplanes will soar, machine-guns
    will roar,
And the iron tanks go to battle.
Battleships will sail, and the infantry
    march,
And the daring tachankas will rattle.

Refrain.

Мы войны не хотим, но себя защитим—
Оборону крепим мы недаром.
И на вражьей земле мы врага разгромим
Малой кровью, могучим ударом!

Припев.

Подымайся, народ, собирайся в поход,
Барабаны, сильней барабаньте!
Музыканты, вперед! Запевалы, вперед!
Нашу песню победную гряньте!

Припев.

В целом мире нигде нету силы такой
Чтобы нашу страну сокрушила.
С нами Сталин родной, и железной
    рукой
Нас к победе ведет Ворошилов!

Припев.

We do not want a war, but we'll stand in
    defense,
We strengthen our force for tomorrow.
We will rout out the foe on his very own
    land,
Scant the bloodshed but mighty the
    blow.

Refrain.

So rise up, people, rise, be prepared to
    march forth,
Strike up, drums, play the march loud
    and strong!
Musicians, march on! Brave singers,
    march on!
Ring out our victory song.

Refrain.

In the world there's no force that is up
    to the task
Of bringing destruction to our land.
Our Stalin's with us, and victory will
    come
From the guidance of Voroshilov's iron
    hand.

Refrain.

Three Tank Drivers
Boris Laskin and the Pokrass Brothers (1937)

FROM THE FILM *THE TRACTOR DRIVERS*, DIRECTED BY IVAN PY-
RIEV, THIS SONG IS ONE OF THE MANY REFERENCES IN POPULAR
CULTURE TO THE GROWING TENSION ON THE MANCHURIAN BOR-
DER BETWEEN THE SOVIETS AND THE JAPANESE. THE SAME SONG-
WRITING TEAM ALSO WROTE "THE TANK DRIVERS' MARCH."
BOTH SONGS LINK TANK-WAR TECHNOLOGY TO TRACTORI-
ZATION.

From *Krasnoarmeiskie pesni* (Moscow: Gos. voennoe izd-vo, 1937), pp. 142–143.

ТРИ ТАНКИСТА

На границе тучи ходят хмуро,
Край суровый тишиной объят.
У высоких берегов Амура
Часовые родины стоят.

Там заслон врагу готовят прочный,
Край суров, отважен и силен,
Там стоит в тайге дальневосточной
Огневой ударный батальон.

В нем живут, и песня в том порука,
Нерушимой, крепкою семьей
Три танкиста, три веселых друга,
Экипаж машины боевой.

На траву легла роса густая,
Полегли туманы у реки.
В эту ночь решили самураи
Перейти границу у тайги.

Но глаза разведки видят точно,—
И пошел, командою взметен,
По родной земле дальневосточной
Броневой ударный батальон.

Мчались танки, ветер подымая,
И по сопкам лязгала броня.
И летели наземь самураи
Под напором стали и огня.

И добили—песня в том порука—
Всех врагов в атаке огневой
Три танкиста, три веселых друга—
Экипаж машины боевой.

THREE TANK DRIVERS

Thunderclouds have gathered on the
    border,
The perimeter is in silence's embrace.
On the bluffs above the Amur River
Sentries of the homeland have been
    placed.

There they build a barrier for their foe.
The region's tough, courageous, and
    brave,
In the Far Eastern taiga stands
An armored strike battalion.

There they live—and singing
    guarantees it—
As a tight, unbroken family:
Three tank drivers, three fun-loving
    buddies,
Crewmates in a vehicle of war.

On the grass the dew has settled thickly,
O'er the river the mist is hovering.
On this night the samurai decided
To cross the border into the taiga land.

But the scout's eye sees all their
    positions,
And the armored strike battalion
Goes in action, spurred on by an order
Along the Far East ground that they call
    home.

The tanks rush by, whipping up a
    tailwind,
And the armor clanks atop the hills.
And the samurai come crashing
    earthwards
Under pressure of the fire and steel.

There they nabbed—singing
    guaranteed it—
All their foes in this hot attack,
The three tank-drivers, three fun-loving
    buddies,
Crewmates in a vehicle of war.

Legend of Voroshilov

(1939)

KLIMENT, OR KLIM, VOROSHILOV (1881–1969) WAS ONE OF STA-
LIN'S CHIEF HENCHMEN AND SHARED SOME OF THE DICTATOR'S
GLORY AS LEADER OF THE ARMED FORCES (1925–40) AND AS FEL-
LOW HERO IN THE OFFICIALLY SPONSORED AND CREATED LEG-
ENDS ABOUT THE TSARITSYN (LATER STALINGRAD) CAMPAIGN
IN THE CIVIL WAR. HERE HE IS MYTHOLOGIZED IN A FOLKLIKE
TALE OF A CHILD'S RESCUE, WHERE VOROSHILOV IS DEPICTED AS
EXCEPTIONALLY BRAVE AND ALSO A MASTER ORGANIZER.

We fought our way out of the village and into the steppe. Commissar Voroshilov rushed up to the baggage train and asked sternly: "Where have the bread carts gone to?"

Indeed, two carts were missing. Each of them contained forty loaves of rye bread and lots of grain. Truly, it was a heavy loss. What was to be done now? It was impossible to send anybody to the village to fetch them, and just as impossible to leave them, too. So Voroshilov summoned the women and quick-witted lads together and dashed off with them to the village.

It was a dark night. Dogs howled and shooting went on from all sides.

In one of the yards they found the carts. With their own hands they wheeled them to the camp, a distance of two kilometers.

Happening to look around, Voroshilov saw a woman alongside him straining herself. She breathed heavily as she pushed at a wheel. She was pregnant.

Voroshilov grew angry at her, for he had summoned only the strong and able. Pushing aside the bread and grain, they laid the pregnant woman on the cart, and rolled on to the camp.

At dawn the woman gave birth to a daughter. The child was born healthy, cheerful and bawling.

Hot battles raged on the way to Tsaritsyn. Voroshilov didn't shut his eyes even a moment for a wink of sleep. He was always on his feet, clean-shaven and neat. He would call a meeting and report so clearly that everything he said is remembered even now. You fought with more courage because you knew what you were shedding your blood for in the steppes.

Once, during a battle, Klim came galloping up on his horse. Glancing at the baggage train he asked: "Where is the family with the child?"

Translated as "Red Army Folklore," in *International Literature*, no. 2 (1939), pp. 66–68.

"A shell killed the horse, smashed the cart to pieces and killed the father and mother," he was told.

"And the child?" asked the commissar.

"The child remained under the cart."

He spurred his mettlesome horse and galloped along the field straight toward the enemy, two Lugansk men following him. The Whites saw three riders dashing straight at them, and they ceased fighting. Voroshilov came galloping up to the smashed cart and halted his horse. He threw the reins to one of the Lugansk comrades, and in the twinkling of an eye had seized the child and was off like a bird. The deceived Whites began firing, but it was too late.

In the camp he gave the child to the women. "Take care of her," he said. "Feed her."

"What shall we give her to eat?" they asked.

"Try to get a goat," replied the commissar and rode off.

The women surrounded the orphan, trying to amuse her.

"Kind folk, what is her name?" asked one.

"I heard him call her Gul-gul," answered one of the Lugansk men.

They laughed and named the girl "Gul-gul."

In the Cossack villages they found a goat. They fed the child with its milk. They guarded the goat from bullets, and hid it in the trenches during battles. It followed the camp to Tsaritsyn. And the girl grew up at the front.

History of the C. P. S. U. (Short Course)
(1939)

THE NOTORIOUS FALSIFIED HISTORY OF THE PARTY AND THE REVOLUTION UPON WHICH GENERATIONS OF SOVIET STUDENTS WERE NURTURED. IN THIS TYPICAL SELECTION, STALIN'S ROLE IN EVENTS IS MAGNIFIED, THOSE OF TROTSKY ARE EITHER IGNORED OR TREATED AS TREASON, THE SCALE OF ALLIED INTERVENTION IS EXAGGERATED, THE WHITES ARE DEMONIZED, AND THE COLLEAGUES OF LENIN IN THE REVOLUTION ARE ACCUSED OF ESPIONAGE AND OTHER CRIMES.

History of the Communist Party of the Soviet Union (Bolsheviks): Short Course (New York: International Publishers, 1939), pp. 236–239.

EXTENSION OF INTERVENTION. BLOCKADE OF THE SOVIET COUNTRY. KOLCHAK'S CAMPAIGN AND DEFEAT. DENIKIN'S CAMPAIGN AND DEFEAT. A THREE MONTH RESPITE. NINTH PARTY CONGRESS

Having vanquished Germany and Austria, the Entente states decided to hurl large military forces against the Soviet country. After Germany's defeat and the evacuation of her troops from the Ukraine and Transcaucasia, her place was taken by the British and French, who dispatched their fleets to the Black Sea and landed troops in Odessa and in Transcaucasia. Such was the brutality of the Entente forces of intervention that they did not hesitate to shoot whole batches of workers and peasants in the occupied regions. Their outrages reached such lengths in the end that after the occupation of Turkestan they carried off to the Transcaspian region twenty-six leading Baku Bolsheviks—including Comrades Shaumyan, Fioletov, Djaparidze, Malygin, Azizbekov, Korganov—and with the aid of the Socialist-Revolutionaries, had them brutally shot.

The interventionists soon proclaimed a *blockade* of Russia. All sea routes and other lines of communication with the external world were cut.

The Soviet country was surrounded on nearly every side.

The Entente countries placed their chief hopes in Admiral Kolchak, their puppet in Omsk, Siberia. He was proclaimed "supreme ruler of Russia" and all the counter-revolutionary forces in the country placed themselves under his command.

The Eastern Front thus became the main front.

Kolchak assembled a huge army and in the spring of 1919 almost reached the Volga. The finest Bolshevik forces were hurled against him; Young Communist Leaguers and workers were mobilized. In April 1919, Kolchak's army met with se-vere defeat at the hands of the Red Army and very soon began to retreat along the whole front.

At the height of the advance of the Red Army on the Eastern Front, Trotsky put forward a suspicious plan: he proposed that the advance should be halted before it reached the Urals, the pursuit of Kolchak's army discontinued, and troops trans-ferred from the Eastern Front to the Southern Front. The Central Committee of the Party fully realized that the Urals and Siberia could not be left in Kolchak's hands, for there with the aid of the Japanese and British, he might recuperate and retrieve his former position. It therefore rejected this plan and gave instructions to proceed with the advance. Trotsky disagreed with these instructions and tendered his resignation, which the Central Committee declined, at the same time ordering him to refrain at once from all participation in the direction of the operations on the Eastern Front. The Red Army pursued its offensive against Kolchak with greater vigor than ever. It inflicted a number of new defeats on him and freed of the Whites the Urals and Siberia, where the Red Army was supported by a powerful partisan movement in the Whites' rear.

In the summer of 1919, the imperialists assigned to General Yudenich, who headed the counter-revolutionaries in the north-west (in the Baltic countries, in the vicinity of Petrograd), the task of diverting the attention of the Red Army from the Eastern Front by an attack on Petrograd. Influenced by the counter-revolutionary agitation of former officers, the garrisons of two forts in the vicinity of Petrograd mutinied against the Soviet Government. At the same time a counter-revolutionary plot was discovered at the Front Headquarters. The enemy threatened Petrograd. But thanks to the measures taken by the Soviet Government with the support of the workers and sailors, the mutinous forts were cleared of Whites, and Yudenich's troops were defeated and driven back into Estonia.

The defeat of Yudenich near Petrograd made it easier to cope with Kolchak, and by the end of 1919 his army was completely routed. Kolchak himself was taken prisoner and shot by sentence of the Revolutionary Committee in Irkutsk.

That was the end of Kolchak.

The Siberians had a popular song about Kolchak at that time:

Uniform British,	Uniform in tatters,
Epaulettes from France,	Epaulettes all gone,
Japanese tobacco,	So is the tobacco,
Kolchak leads the dance.	Kolchak's day is done.

Since Kolchak had not justified their hopes, the interventionists altered their plan of attack on the Soviet Republic. The troops landed in Odessa had to be withdrawn, for contact with the army of the Soviet Republic had infected them with the revolutionary spirit and they were beginning to rebel against their imperialist masters. For example, there was the revolt of French sailors in Odessa led by André Marty. Accordingly, now that Kolchak had been defeated, the Entente centered its attention on General Denikin, Kornilov's confederate and the organizer of the "Volunteer Army." Denikin at that time was operating against the Soviet Government in the south, in the Kuban region. The Entente supplied his army with large quantities of ammunition and equipment and sent it north against the Soviet Government.

The Southern Front now became the chief front.

Denikin began his main campaign against the Soviet Government in the summer of 1919. Trotsky had disrupted the Southern Front, and our troops suffered defeat after defeat. By the middle of October the Whites had seized the whole of the Ukraine, had captured Orel and were nearing Tula, which supplied our army with cartridges, rifles and machine-guns. The Whites were approaching Moscow. The situation of the Soviet Republic became grave in the extreme. The Party sounded the alarm and called upon the people to resist. Lenin issued the slogan, "All for the fight against Denikin!" Inspired by the Bolsheviks, the workers and peasants mustered all their forces to smash the enemy.

The Central Committee sent Comrades Stalin, Voroshilov, Ordjonikidze and Budyonny to the Southern Front to prepare the rout of Denikin. Trotsky was removed from the direction of the operations of the Red Army in the south. Before Comrade Stalin's arrival, the Command of the Southern Front, in conjunction with Trotsky, had drawn up a plan to strike the main blow at Denikin from Tsaritsyn in the direction of Novorossisk, through the Don Steppe, where there were no roads and where the Red Army would have to pass through regions inhabited by Cossacks, who were at that time largely under the influence of the White Guards. Comrade Stalin severely criticized this plan and submitted to the Central Committee his own plan for the defeat of Denikin. According to this plan the main blow was to be delivered by way of Kharkov–Donetz Basin–Rostov. This plan would ensure the rapid advance of our troops against Denikin, for they would be moving through working class and peasant regions where they would have the open sympathy of the population. Furthermore, the dense network of railway lines in this region would ensure our armies the regular supply of all they required. Lastly, this plan would make it possible to release the Donetz Coal Basin and thus supply our country with fuel.

The Central Committee of the Party accepted Comrade Stalin's plan. In the second half of October 1919, after fierce resistance, Denikin was defeated by the Red Army in the decisive battles of Orel and Voronezh. He began a rapid retreat, and, pursued by our forces, fled to the south. At the beginning of 1920 the whole of the Ukraine and the North Caucasus had been cleared of Whites.

During the decisive battles on the Southern Front, the imperialists again hurled Yudenich's corps against Petrograd in order to divert our forces from the south and thus improve the position of Denikin's army. The Whites approached the very gates of Petrograd. The heroic proletariat of the premier city of the revolution rose in a solid wall for its defence. The Communists, as always, were in the vanguard. After fierce fighting, the Whites were defeated and again flung beyond our borders back into Estonia.

And that was the end of Denikin.

The defeat of Kolchak and Denikin was followed by a brief respite.

When the imperialists saw that the Whiteguard armies had been smashed, that intervention had failed, and that the Soviet Government was consolidating its position all over the country, while in Western Europe the indignation of the workers against military intervention in the Soviet Republic was rising, they began to change their attitude towards the Soviet state. In January 1920, Great Britain, France, and Italy decided to call off the blockade of Soviet Russia.

This was an important breach in the wall of intervention.

It did not, of course, mean that the Soviet country was done with intervention and the Civil War. There was still the danger of attack by imperialist Poland. The forces of intervention had not yet been finally driven out of the Far East, Transcaucasia and the Crimea. But Soviet Russia had secured a temporary breathing space and was able to divert more forces to economic development. The Party could now devote its attention to economic problems.

During the Civil War many skilled workers had left industry owing to the closing down of mills and factories. The Party now took measures to return them to industry to work at their trades. The railways were in a grave condition and several thousand Communists were assigned to the work of restoring them, for unless this was done the restoration of the major branches of industry could not be seriously undertaken. The organization of the food supply was extended and improved. The drafting of a plan for the electrification of Russia was begun. Nearly five million Red Army men were under arms and could not be demobilized owing to the danger of war. A part of the Red Army was therefore converted into *labor armies* and used in the economic field. The Council of Workers' and Peasants' Defense was transformed into the *Council of Labor and Defense,* and a *State Planning Commission* (Gosplan) set up to assist it.

Such was the situation when the Ninth Party Congress opened.

The congress met at the end of March 1920. It was attended by 554 delegates with vote, representing 611,978 Party members, and 162 delegates with voice but no vote.

The congress defined the immediate tasks of the country in the sphere of transportation and industry. It particularly stressed the necessity of the trade unions taking part in the building up of the economic life.

Special attention was devoted by the congress to a single economic plan for the restoration, in the first place, of the railways, the fuel industry and the iron and steel industry. The major item in this plan was a project for the electrification of the country, which Lenin advanced as "a great program for the next ten or twenty years." This formed the basis of the famous plan of the State Commission for the Electrification of Russia (GOELRO), the provisions of which have today been far exceeded.

The congress rejected the views of an anti-Party group which called itself "The Group of Democratic-Centralism" and was opposed to one-man management and the undivided responsibility of industrial directors. It advocated unrestricted "group management" under which nobody would be personally responsible for the administration of industry. The chief figures in this anti-Party group were Sapronov, Ossinsky and Smirnov. They were supported at the congress by Rykov and Tomsky.

The Chuvash Peasant and the Eagle
Recorded in the Chuvash Autonomous Soviet Socialist Republic (1937)

PURPORTEDLY A LEGEND OF THE CHUVASH, A TURKIC-SPEAKING PEOPLE WHO RESIDE ALONG THE MIDDLE VOLGA, THIS FRAGMENT OF "FOLKLORE FOR STALIN" CONTAINS FAMILIAR INGREDIENTS: THE CULT OF STALIN, FOLK MOTIFS, ECHOES OF THE FABULIST IVAN KRYLOV, AND A UTOPIAN PICTURE OF THE SOVIET KOLKHOZ.

Translated in *International Literature,* no. 12 (1937), pp. 45–47.

In a Chuvash village there lived a peasant family, an old man, his old wife and their three sons. They lived in dark poverty.

"Woe is me," says the old man. "I starve and I see my family starve. What can I do?"

And he thought of the old fairy tale he had been told in childhood, that described how happiness had been lost to the Chuvash people. In the beginning of the world when happiness was being distributed to the peoples, the first Chuvash, the ancestor of the Chuvash people, took too long putting on his straw sandals and arrived after the distribution was all over. Thus the Chuvash people lost their share of happiness.

The old man thought: There is nothing for the three boys here. Let them go seck happiness.

Andry was the name of the youngest son. He was the one who found happiness.

He set out, and he walked and he walked on the road he had chosen, till he came to where the road divided. There at the fork of the road stood a signpost on which were two inscriptions: "Go right; meet a bear. Go left; meet an eagle."

Andry did not know which way to choose. At last he decided to take the road to the left, the road to the eagle.

He walked two days and on the second day he saw a strange thing. Before him there was a big board. On the board was a shining sun. And on the sun perched a large eagle.

"Andry, where are you going?" asked the eagle.

"My father sent me to seek happiness," said Andry. "We cannot endure the hunger and misery of our life."

The eagle called Andry over to him. And he said: "Andry, happiness is not a thing that lies on the road. One must know how to get it. Here, take a stick with you and return to the village, on your way you'll meet a bear. Don't be afraid of him. Hit him with your stick until he is dead. Then disembowel him. Out of his belly will fall a golden box. If you open it, inside you will find happiness."

Andry did what the eagle advised. He killed the bear, opened him up and took out the golden box. Out of the box jumped a sheep and a pig.

Joyfully Andry went home, driving before him the sheep and the pig and thinking he had found happiness.

Andry lived in his village for awhile. Life was better, but happiness was still far away.

So he decided to seek it again. Once more he went on the road to the left where the eagle perched on the sun. When he arrived the eagle said to him:

"Andry, friend, where are you bound for this time?"

And Andry told him everything.

"All right, Andry," says the eagle, "here's another stick. Use it well. On your way back you will meet a wolf. Do to him what you did to the bear. Beat him; kill him; disembowel him. Take out the box you will find inside him. In that box is what you seek."

Andry did as the eagle said. When he opened the box, out jumped a cow and a horse.

"Ah, now I will be happy at last," thought Andry, and home he went skipping with joy.

And he lived in his village for awhile and life was better, much better, but still happiness was far away. So he decided to go searching again.

A third time he came to the eagle and told how things were with him.

"This time you will meet a fox," said the eagle. "Kill it and on the spot where it dies you will find happiness."

Andry went and did as he was told. At the very edge of his village he met the fox. He killed it. When he looked up from the slain animal he did not recognize the village of his childhood. It was a new village, clean and wonderful. The buildings were smart. There were big barns full of grain and seeds, big stables and cowsheds. And on the main building was written a great word: "kolkhoz."

So the poor Chuvash, Andry, found happiness at last. He had killed the bear, the tsar; the wolf, the landlord; and the fox, the kulak. And the eagle who showed the poor Chuvash the way was—Stalin!

March of the Enthusiasts
Anatoly DAktil and Isaac Dunaevsky (1940)

ANOTHER MOVIE HIT BY DUNAEVSKY, THIS ONE FROM *RADIANT ROAD* (OR *BRIGHT PATH*, 1940), A PRODUCTION-CINDERELLA STORY, STARRING LYUBOV ORLOVA AS THE CLEANING GIRL TURNED INVENTOR.

МАРШ ЭНТУЗИАСТОВ

В буднях великих строек,
В веселом грохоте, в огнях и звонах,
Здравствуй, страна героев,
Страна мечтателей, страна ученых!

Ты по степи, ты по лесу,
Ты к тропикам, ты к полюсу
Легла родимая, необозримая,
Несокрушимая моя.

MARCH OF THE ENTHUSIASTS

In the everyday work of great building,
In the merry rumble, the flames and
    the peals,
Hello, you country of heroes,
A country of dreamers, a country of
    thinkers.

Across the steppe, across the forests,
From the tropics all the way to the pole,
You spread out, my boundless
    homeland,
My indestructible land of birth.

From *Russkie-sovetskie pesni, 1917–1977* (Moscow: Khudozhestvennaia literatura, 1977), pp. 33–34.

Нет нам преград ни в море, ни на суше,
Нам не страшны ни льды, ни облака.
Пламя души своей, знамя страны своей
Мы пронесем через миры и века!

Нам ли стоять на месте!
В своих дерзаниях всегда мы правы,
Труд наш есть дело чести,
Есть дело доблести и подвиг славы.
К станку ли ты склоняешься,
В скалу ли ты врубаешься,—
Мечта прекрасная, еще неясная,
Уже зовет тебя вперед.

Создан наш мир на славу.
За годы сделаны дела столетий,
Счастье берем по праву,
И жарко любим, и поем, как дети.
И звезды наши алые
Сверкают, небывалые,
Над всеми странами, над океанами
Осуществленною мечтой.

Нет нам преград ни в море, ни на суше,
Нам не страшны ни льды, ни облака.
Пламя души своей, знамя страны своей
Мы пронесем через миры и века!

On sea or land, we know no obstacles,
We fear not icebergs, not the clouds.
The flame of our heart, the flag of our
     country
We carry across worlds and ages!

Is it for us to stand in place?
We are always right in our daring,
Our work is a matter of honor,
A matter of valor and glorious exploit.
Whether you're leaning over a
     workbench,
Or cutting out stone from a wall,
A dream of wonderment, still unclear to
     you,
Is calling you ever ahead.

Our world was created wonderfully.
The work of centuries has been done in
     years,
We grasp our happiness by rights,
We love with gusto, and sing like
     children.
And our stars of scarlet
Glitter, like never before,
Above all other countries, and the
     oceans
Like a dream that has come true.

On sea or land, we know no obstacles,
We fear not icebergs, not the clouds.
The flame of our heart, the flag of our
     country
We carry across other worlds and ages!

Anecdotes

A factory director comes up to an office worker and asks sternly: "Comrade Niko-laev, why were you late for work today?"
"Forgive me, I overslept."
"That's no excuse, you could have slept at work." [4:20]

For anecdote sources, see *Blue Blouse Skit,* above.

Marx: Being defines consciousness.
Stalin: Beating defines consciousness. [5:127]

The Lord God noticed that something terrible was happening in Russia. He sent Jesus Christ to discover what was the matter. Time passes, and Jesus hasn't returned. The Lord sends an angel to find Christ. The angel comes back with a message:

Arrested. Heading for interrogation. Christ.

The Lord sends the prophet Ilya to save him. He doesn't return either. The messenger angel comes back with another note:

Also arrested. The Prophet Ilya.

Finally, to make sure that the job is done right, the Lord sends Moses. A telegram soon arrives from him:

Alive and healthy. People's Commissar Petrov. [4:29]

Various projects for a Pushkin monument are presented for Stalin's judgment.
The first project: Pushkin reading Byron.
Stalin says: "The project is historically accurate, but politically false; where's the general line?"
The second project: Pushkin reading Stalin.
"The project is politically accurate, but historically false: when Pushkin was alive, Stalin hadn't written any books."
The third project was judged to be historically and politically accurate: Stalin reading Pushkin.
When the monument was finally put up, there were slight changes made: it showed Stalin reading Stalin. [5:183]

Riddle: Stalin, the Politburo, and their entire retinue are cruising along the Volga on a steamship. Suddenly, the ship begins to sink. If it goes down instantly, who will be saved?
Answer: The peoples of the USSR. [4:61]

Stalin's pipe is missing. He calls the NKVD and orders them to find it. In two hours, he finds it himself in his own boot. He calls the NKVD back: "Don't bother, I found it."
"Forgive us, Comrade Stalin, but we've already arrested ten people for stealing your pipe."
"Let them go."
"We can't, they've all confessed." [4:73]

The mummy of an unknown pharoah is discovered in Egypt. Nobody could determine which pharoah it was, so specialists were invited from the USSR to assist.
Soon they informed their colleagues: "It's Ramses XVIII."
They asked the Russians how they arrived at that conclusion: "The bastard confessed." [5:264]

Three prisoners meet in a transit camp. The first says: "I've been in jail since 1929, because I called Karl Radek a counterrevolutionary."

The second: "I've been here since 1937, because I said that Karl Radek wasn't a counterrevolutionary."

The third: "Excuse me, but I'm Karl Radek." [4:105]

At the 18th Party Congress in 1939, someone sneezes during Stalin's speech.
Stalin demands, "Who sneezed?"
Silence.
"Give every tenth delegate ten years in a labor camp." The delegates are counted off, and every tenth is led away.
"Who sneezed?" Silence.
A brave delegate finally stands and admits, "I did."
Stalin answers, "God bless you." [5:184]

An Indian magician comes onstage at an international magicians' competition. He shows an open palm. "Nothing there. Puff! (he blows on his hand)—an egg! Puff! A chicken! Puff! Nothing left!"

An American appears. "Nothing in my hand. Puff!—a chunk of iron. Puff!—a wheel! Puff!—an automobile! Puff!—nothing left!"

The Soviet magician comes out. "Nobody there. Puff!—a local party secretary! Puff!—regional party boss! Puff—Central Committee secretary! Alacazam! Nobody's there!" [5:111]

In 1940, Hitler asks Stalin for help in destroying London. Stalin offers one thousand Soviet apartment managers. [5:82]

III.

Russia
at
War

My Beloved

E. Dolmatovsky and M. Blanter (1939)

Music by Matvei Blanter, one of the most prolific mass-song composers of the 1930s and 1940s. In 1939, Soviet forces were engaged in the conquest of eastern Poland, in conjunction with Hitler; and then in the Winter War with Finland in 1939–40. The theme of a girl back home standing at the gate with a kerchief is a modern adaptation of recruitment laments.

МОЯ ЛЮБИМАЯ

Я уходил тогда в поход,
В далекие края.
Платком взмахнула у ворот
Моя любимая.

Второй стрелковый храбрый взвод
Теперь моя семья.
Поклон-привет тебе он шлет,
Моя любимая.

Чтоб дни мои быстрей неслись
В походах и боях,
Издалека мне улыбнись,
Моя любимая.

В кармане маленьком моем
Есть карточка твоя,
Так, значит, мы всегда вдвоем
Моя любимая.

MY BELOVED

I marched off on the long campaign,
Into a distant land.
You waved your kerchief from the gate,
My beloved girl.

The Second Rifles brave platoon
Is now my family.
It salutes you with a bow,
My beloved girl.

To help my days pass quickly by,
In battles and at march,
Smile to me from far away,
My beloved girl.

In my little pocket there
Is a snapshot of you.
So that we'll together be,
My beloved girl.

From *Russkie-sovetskie pesni, 1917–1977* (Moscow: Khudozhestvennaia literatura, 1977), p. 286.

The Blue Kerchief

Jerzy Peterburgsky and Yakov Galitsky (1940)

THE KERCHIEF HAS NOW BECOME THE MAIN EMBLEM OF LOVE
AND SEPARATION IN THIS WARTIME SONG, WHICH ATTAINED IM-
MEDIATE AND ENDURING FAME AS SUNG BY KLAVDIA SHUL-
ZHENKO AT THE FRONT AND IN BESIEGED CITIES. GIVEN HERE IS
THE VERSION FOR MALE VOICE.

СИНИЙ ПЛАТОЧЕК (1941)

Синенький скромный платочек падал с опущенных плеч.
Ты говорила, что не забудешь ласковых радостных встреч.
Порой ночной мы распрщались с тобой...
Нет прежних ночек! Где ты, платочек, милый, желанный, родной!

Письма твои получая, слышу я голос родной.
И между строчек синий платочек снова встаст прсдо мной.
И мне не раз снились в предутренний час
Кудри в платочке, синие ночки, искорки девичьих глаз.

Помню, как в памятный вечер падал платочек твой с плеч,
Как провожала и обещала синий платочек сберечь.
И пусть со мной нет сегодня любимой, родной,
Знаю, с любовью ты к изголовью плачешь, платок голубой.

Сколько заветных платочков носим мы в сердце с собой!
Радости встречи, девичьи плечи помним в страде боевой.
За них, родных, любимых, желанных таких
Строчит пулеметчик за синий платочек, что был на плечах дорогих!

THE BLUE KERCHIEF

The modest blue kerchief dropped from your neck in despair.
You told me you'd always remember our tender and joyous time shared.
In the dark of the night I bid you goodbye...
Those nights are gone! Where are you, kerchief, so precious, close, and desired!

From a private collection.

When I get your letters, I hear your voice calling my name.
Between the lines, your kerchief of blue rises before me again.
And I often dream in the hour before the dawn...
Of curls in your kerchief, tender blue nights, the sparks of your maidenly eyes.

I remember the memorable evening when the kerchief fell from your neck,
How you saw me off, and promised to keep the blue kerchief until I came back.
And so what if my dearest, my loved one, is not with me today,
I know you cry in your pillow with the blue kerchief in your embrace.

How many kerchiefs have cherished places kept for them in our hearts!
We remember those meetings and maidenly shoulders amidst the hardship of war.
It's all for our loved ones, our nearest and dearest that we go to war,
The machine-gunner fights for the blue kerchief that those dear shoulders wore.

Wait for Me

Konstantin Simonov (1941)

SIMONOV (1915–1979), POET, PLAYWRIGHT, AND NOVELIST,
SERVED AS CORRESPONDENT FOR THE MILITARY PAPER *RED STAR,*
ALONG WITH EHRENBURG AND OTHER PROMINENT WRITERS. HIS
LOVE POEM WAS HEARD ON THE RADIO THROUGHOUT THE WAR,
RECITED BY MILLIONS AS THOUGH IT WERE A PRAYER, REPEATED
BY WOMEN AS TEARS STREAMED DOWN THEIR FACES, AND
ADOPTED BY MEN AS THEIR OWN EXPRESSION OF THE MYSTICAL
POWER OF A WOMAN'S LOVE. IT WAS PRODUCED FOR STAGE AND
CINEMA AND SET TO SEVENTEEN DIFFERENT MELODIES.

Wait for me, and I'll come back,
But wait with might and main.
Wait throughout the gloom and rack
Of autumn's yellow rain.
Wait when snowstorms fill the way,
Wait in summer's heat,

Wait when, false to yesterday,
Others do not wait.

Wait when from afar at last
No letters come to you.
Wait when all the rest have ceased

Translation by Dorothea Prall Radin in *Russian Literature since the Revolution,* ed. Joshua Kunitz (New York: Boni and Gaer, 1948), pp. 787–788.

To wait, who waited too.
Wait for me and I'll come back.
Do not lightly let
Those, who know so well the knack,
Teach you to forget.

Let my mother and my son
Believe that I have died;
Let my friends, with waiting done,
At the fireside,
Lift the wine of grief and clink
To my departed soul.
Wait, and make no haste to drink,
Alone amongst them all.

Wait for me and I'll come back,
Defying death. When he
Who could not wait shall call it luck
Only, let it be.
They cannot know, who did not wait,
How in the midst of fire
Your waiting saved me from my fate.
Your waiting and desire.
Why I still am living, we
Shall know, just I and you:
You knew how to wait for me
As no other knew.

—Konstantin Simonov,
Western Front, July 1941

Smolensk Roads
Konstantin Simonov (1941)

HERE SIMONOV SKILLFULLY EVOKES RELIGIOUS EMOTIONALISM
AND THE SACRED PAST OF ANCIENT RUSSIA — A THEME THAT FIT
IN LATER WITH THE OFFICIAL SOFTENING OF ANTIRELIGIOUS
POLICY AND CLEARLY MATCHED THE DEEPLY AUTHENTIC MOODS
OF POPULAR PATRIOTISM THAT THE WAR AUGMENTED.

To A. Surkov

You remember, Alyosha, the roads of Smolensk province,
And how the evil rains poured down and gave no rest,
And milk in jars was offered by tired women
Who hugged each jar like a babe against the breast.

How they quietly wiped their tears and whispered to God
"Lord, save them," praying, as we rolled,
And again described themselves as the wives of soldiers
As the custom was in great Russia of old.

Measured by tears rather than versts, and lurching,
The paths wound into the hillocks, lost in space,
Villages, villages, villages, with churchyards,
As if all Russia had met in this huddled place,

Translated by Jack Lindsay in *Soviet Literature,* no. 6 (1967), pp. 143–144.

As if behind each village-bound, all day,
Protecting the living with the cross of their hands,
Our great-grandfathers in village *mirs* were praying
For the unbelieving heirs of their broad lands.

I see my country—I think you know it, Alyosha—
Not in the townhouses where time idled by,
But in the hamlets with their simple crosses
On Russian graves, where our forefathers lie.

Not vainly, I trust, has war borne me along
These village-ways, to hear with anguished heart
The wail of the widow and the women singing,
And learn for the first time here the country-part.

You remember near Borisov the wooden shack,
The girls lamenting the dead man day and night,
The grey-haired woman in the velvet jacket,
The old man dressed for meeting death, in white.

What could we say to them? How console their tears?
But the old woman knew why we looked so stern,
And read and answered our grief, "Now go my dear ones,
And we'll be waiting here when you return."

Aye, we'll be waiting, all the cornfields rustled,
Waiting for your return, the forests cried.
Alyosha, I heard them in the midnight hush,
The voices always echoing at our side,

And so, as the Russian custom ordered, grimly
The homes were burned and the heavy winds were grey;
Before our very eyes, our comrades, dying
Tore their shirts down the front, the Russian way.

So far we've come in safety through the bullets,
Though thrice I thought I'd seen my last of earth.
How proudly have I come to know in fullness
The loved and bitter country of my birth.

Proud that it's destined for my death-bed,
Proud that a Russian mother gave us to the day,
And proud that Russian women bid us proud farewell
With threefold kisses, in the Russian way.

                                    Kandalaksha, November, 1941

Scout Pashkov

Aleksei Surkov (1941)

THE LINE OF LITERARY POLITICS UNDER STALIN COULD USUALLY
BE TRACED BY THE PROGRESS OF THE POLITICALLY ATTUNED
SURKOV. ELECTED HEAD OF RAPP (1928) AND FIRST SECRETARY
OF THE WRITERS' UNION IN 1953, SURKOV SPENT THE WAR AS A
FRONT-LINE CORRESPONDENT. HIS ROUGH-CUT VERSE WAS IM-
MENSELY POPULAR IN THE TRENCHES: HE WAS CONSIDERED THE
SOLDIERS' POET, AS OPPOSED TO SIMONOV, WHO WAS THE OFFI-
CERS' FAVORITE.

Looks like my scouting that night was no good,
And my cunning that night was a laugh,
For they caught me red-handed right there in the wood,
And they dragged me away to their staff.
With a Parabello stuck in my eye.
   "Bastard," they said, "don't lie!
     Many Reds in those trees?"
     "Like the sands in the seas."
   "Many guns?"
     "You can count if you try."
Here a sergeant got sore and started to slog
With his rifle, a ticklish tool.
   "Answer our questions, you son of a dog!
     Enough of your playing the fool!
     Don't try," said the guy, "to get funny with us.
     Out with it now! Don't stall!
     Tell the truth and you'll be free and there won't be a fuss.
     Keep it back, and you're dead—that's all."
If they beat you to putty and throw you about,
I'm telling you, brother, it hurts.
The price was sure high, but I figured it out, ·
And decided to take my deserts.
Then they twisted my arms—once again—and again—
And they battered my shoulders and back.

Translated by Margaret Wettlin in *Soviet Literature,* no. 1 (1947), p. 49.

It isn't so nice to remember what then—
I don't want to remember the rack.
But the big guy—he sees that the torture's the bunk,
So he figures he'll do it up brown,
Shoves a spade in my hand, "Get going, you skunk!"
And they usher me out of the town.
There I dug me a bed in the earth with these hands
While their rifle butts prodded for fun.
You can be a bum shot, yet your bullets will land
In a fellow who hasn't a gun.
They gathered around my bed in the ground.
And their shots at that range were a cinch.
The number of bullets I took in the face
Was easily one to the inch.
I fell on my face in the hole I had made.
With a sizzling under my shirt.
An officer gave me a blow with a spade
Where the lead in my shoulder-blade hurt.
They dug me in tight and left me alone
With that weight pushing down on my chest.
I wiggled a leg, got a cramp in the bone,
Couldn't breathe for the clay, as I guessed.
But to go and pass out in that grave—what the hell!
Better flirt with your fate, the old witch.
So I gathered the strength—where from I can't tell,
And tried to get out of that ditch.
I turned myself over. I clawed at the clay.
I felt my body. I wasn't dead!
There at my feet the coffin lay,
There at my head the stars were spread.
I kissed the dirt and crawled away
To the woods where my pals were collected.
 At half past ten I was pickled in clay,
 At eleven I resurrected.
I felt O.K. on the following day.
My first funeral wasn't so bad.
So I pointed my tommy gun over the way,
And gave my grave-diggers all that I had.

Western Front. 1941

Holy War

Vasily Lebedev-Kumach and Aleksandr Aleksandrov (1941)

THIS SONG, WRITTEN ONE DAY AFTER THE GERMAN INVASION AND RUSHED ONTO THE AIRWAVES, GENERATED THE GREATEST EMOTIONAL REACTION DURING THE WAR (MUSIC BY GENERAL ALEKSANDR ALEKSANDROV, FOUNDER OF THE RED ARMY ENSEMBLE; WORDS BY VASILY LEBEDEV-KUMACH). THE CUMULATIVE EFFECT OF ALL THE VERSES WAS AUGMENTED BY A MELODY THAT ASCENDS AND DESCENDS MAJESTICALLY IN A MINOR KEY TO A MARCH RHYTHM IN AN UNUSUAL ¾ TIME.

СВЯЩЕННАЯ ВОЙНА	HOLY WAR
Вставай, страна огромная, Вставай на смертный бой С фашистской силой темною, С проклятою ордой.	Arise, oh my colossal land, Stand for this mortal war, Against the fascist forces sinister, Against the cursed horde.
Припев: Пусть ярость благородная Вскипает как волна— Идет война народная, Священная война.	Refrain: Let our avenging anger surge, Our noble fury soar; For this war is a people's war, It is a Holy War!
Дадим отпор душителям, Всех пламенных идей, Насильникам, грабителям, Мучителям людей!	We'll beat back all the murderers, The carriers of strife, The killers of ideals high, The torturers of life.
Припев: Не смеют крылья черные Над родиной летать, Поля ее просторные Не смеет враг топтать.	Refrain: Their black wings shall not dare to fly Above the motherland. The rank feet of the enemy Won't trample on our lands.
Припев: Гнилой фашистской нечисти Загоним пулю в лоб,	Refrain: We'll drive our bullets through the skulls Of the rotten fascist fiends,

From *Russkie-sovetskie pesni, 1917–1977* (Moscow: Khudozhestvennaia literatura, 1977), p. 188.

Отродью человечества	And for the scum of humankind
Сколотим крепкий гроб!	We'll make the coffin strong.
Припев (дважды)	Refrain (twice)

Tanya

Pavel Lidov (1942)

THE LEGEND OF THE PARTISAN TEENAGER ZOYA KOSMODEMYAN-
SKAYA, WHO WAS TORTURED AND HANGED BY THE GERMANS
EARLY IN THE WAR, WAS STAMPED INTO THE MEMORIES AND DE-
VOTIONAL LIFE OF WARTIME RUSSIA — AND FOR DECADES BE-
YOND — IN TALE, POEM, DRAMA, RADIO PLAY, PHOTO, STATUE,
AND MOVIE. IN DEPICTING THE SUFFERINGS OF THE MARTYR
ZOYA, KNOWN AS "TANYA," LEV ARNSHTAM'S FILM ZOYA (1944)
COPIES VIRTUALLY EVERY DETAIL OF THE FOLLOWING NEWSPA-
PER ACCOUNT.

In the early days of December 1941 in Petrishchevo, near the city of Vereya, the Germans executed an eighteen-year-old Moscow Komsomol girl who called herself Tatyana.

Moscow was in its gravest danger then. The vacation districts around Golitsyno and Skhodnya became battlefields, and Moscow sent a corps of daring volunteers across enemy lines to help partisan detachments take the fight to the enemy rear.

That was when someone in Petrishchevo cut the Germans' field communication lines. The stables of the local military unit and the seventeen horses in it were destroyed soon after. A partisan was captured the next evening.

From talking with soldiers, the Petrishchevo collective farmers discovered how the partisan had been captured. The partisan had infiltrated an important military base. The partisan wore a cap, a fur coat, and quilted cotton snow-pants, and a shoulder bag. Approaching the target, the partisan holstered a pistol, took a gasoline-filled bottle from a bag, poured the gas out, and bent down to strike a match.

Pravda, 26 January 1942, p. 2.

At that moment, a sentry sneaked up and seized the partisan's arms from behind. The partisan managed to shove back the German and draw the revolver, but didn't get off a shot. The soldier knocked the weapon away and raised an alarm.

The partisan was taken to a hut where the officers lived, and where they discovered that it was a young girl, tall and slender, with big dark eyes and dark hair cut short and combed back.

The owners of the house were sent into the kitchen, but they still heard how the officers questioned Tatyana and she answered without pause, "No," "I don't know," "I won't tell you," "No"; how straps whistled through the air, how they lashed her body. In a few minutes a tender young officer leapt into the kitchen, put his head in his hands, and sat with eyes and ears shut tight till the interrogation ended.

The owners of the house counted two hundred blows, but Tatyana did not utter a sound. After the beating she still answered: "No," "I won't tell you," only her voice was more muffled than before.

After the interrogation, Tatyana was taken to Vasily Aleksandrovich Kulik's hut. By now she no longer wore her boots, hat, or warm clothing. The convoy brought her dressed only in her undershirt and shorts, and she walked barefoot through the snow.

As they led her into the dimly lit house, the owners saw a huge black and blue mark on her brow and abrasions on her hands and feet. The girl's hands were tied behind her back with a rope. Her lips were bitten, bloody, and swollen. She had probably bitten them while the Germans tried to beat a confession out of her.

She sat down on a bench. A German stood guard by the door. There was another soldier with him. From their berth on the stove,[1] Vasily and Praskovya Kulik watched the prisoner. She sat calmly and motionlessly, and asked for something to drink. Vasily Kulik came down from the stove and approached the water bucket, but the sentry pushed him away.

"You also vant trouble?" he asked maliciously.

The soldiers quartered in the hut stood around the girl and made loud fun of her. Some poked her with their fists, others held lit matches up to her chin, and someone scraped a file across her back.

The soldiers had their fun and went back to their quarters to sleep. The sentry put his rifle on his shoulder and ordered Tatyana to get up and go outside. He walked along the street right behind her, with his bayonet practically jabbing her back. Then he yelled "Zu rück!" and marched the girl in the other direction. Barefoot, wearing nothing but her underclothes, she walked on the snow until her tormentor himself shuddered and decided it was time to get back under the warm roof.

The sentry guarded Tatyana from ten in the evening until two in the morning, and every half-hour to an hour he would take her back out on the street for fifteen to twenty minutes. Finally, the monster was relieved. A new sentry took his post. The poor girl was allowed to lie down on a bench.

---

1. Russian peasant huts are centered around a large earthen stove, used for heating and cooking, which has sleeping berths on top.

Seizing the proper moment, Praskovya Kulik struck up a conversation with Tatyana. "Who are you?" she asked.

"What's it to you?"

"Where are you from?"

"Moscow."

"Are your parents alive?"

The girl did not answer. She lay motionless till morning without a word more, without even a moan, although her feet were frostbitten and could not have caused her anything but pain.

Nobody knows whether she slept that night and what she thought about as she lay surrounded by enemies.

That morning soldiers began to build a gallows in the middle of the village.

Praskovya tried to speak with her again. "Was that you yesterday?"

"Me. Did the Germans catch fire?"

"No."

"A shame. What did burn?"

"Their horses. They say some weapons burned too."

Officers came at ten. The senior officer asked Tatyana in Russian: "Tell me, who are you?"

Tatyana did not answer.

"Tell me, where is Stalin?"

"Stalin is at his post," answered Tatyana.

The owners of the house did not hear how the interrogation continued—they were ordered out of the room and allowed back only when the interrogation was over.

Some of Tatyana's things were brought over from headquarters: her jacket, pants, socks. Her hat, fur coat, and boots had disappeared—the junior officers had already split them among themselves. There was also her travel bag holding the gasoline bottle, matches, pistol cartridges, sugar, and salt.

Tatyana was dressed, and her hosts helped her pull socks onto her frostblackened feet. The gasoline bottle and a board with "Partisan" written on it were hung on Tatyana's chest. This was how she was led out onto the square where the gallows stood.

The place of execution was surrounded by ten horse soldiers with sabers bared. More than a hundred German soldiers and a few officers stood around them. Local residents were ordered to attend the execution, but only a few came, and some of those quietly went back home after standing a few minutes, so as not to witness the horrible spectacle.

Two macaroni boxes were stacked under a noose hanging from the crossbeam. Tatyana was lifted onto the boxes and the noose was placed around her neck. One of the officers focused his Kodak on the gallows: Germans love to photograph executions. The commandant signaled the soldiers acting as hangman to wait.

Tatyana used the opportunity to turn to the collective farmers and yell in a loud and pure voice: "Hey, comrades. Why are you looking so sad? Be brave, continue the struggle, beat the Germans, burn them, poison them!"

The German standing next to her waved his arm as if he wanted to hit her or shut her mouth, but she knocked his hand away and continued: "I'm not afraid to die, comrades. It's a great joy to die for your country."

The photographer shot the gallows from far away and close up, and then got in position for a side shot. The hangmen glanced restlessly at the commandant, who yelled to the photographer: "Hurry up!"

Then Tatyana turned toward the commandant and addressed him and the German soldiers: "You can hang me now, but I'm not alone. There are two hundred million of us, you can't hang us all. My vengeance will be taken for me. Soldiers! Before it's too late, give yourselves up, victory will be ours anyway! My vengeance will be had for me."

The Russians standing on the square were crying. Some turned their backs so they wouldn't see what must happen next.

The hangman pulled on the rope, and the noose tightened around Tanya's neck. But she pulled the noose back with her hands, stood up on her toes, and yelled with all her strength: "Farewell, comrades! Don't fear, keep up the struggle! Stalin is with us! Stalin will come!"

The hangman kicked the bottom box with the steel toe of his boot, and it scraped along the slippery packed snow. The top box dropped down and struck the earth with a hollow thud. The crowd lurched back. There was a short wail that died out and echoed against the edge of the forest.

She died a prisoner of the enemy on a fascist rack, without betraying her sufferings by a single sound, without betraying her comrades. She accepted the death of a martyr like a heroine, like the daughter of a great people that cannot be broken. May her memory live eternally!

. . . On New Year's Eve drunken fascists surrounded the gallows, pulled the clothes off the hanged girl, and vilely outraged her body. She hung in the middle of the village one more day, stabbed and cut by daggers. On the evening of January 1 the fascists ordered the gallows sawed down. The village elder called his people together, and they hacked a pit in frozen ground away from the village.

Tanya was buried without honors, outside the village under a weeping birch tree, and a blizzard covered the grave with snow. Those for whom Tanya had opened the westward road with her breast on a dark December night soon arrived.

When they halt for shelter, fighting men will come bow to the earth before her ashes and to say a heartfelt Russian thank-you. To the father and mother who bore her into the world and raised her a heroine; to the teachers who educated her; to the comrades who forged her spirit.

Her undying glory will reach all corners of the Soviet land, millions of people will think about a distant snowy grave with love, and Stalin's thoughts will go to the graveside of his faithful daughter.

Western Front, January 26

The Front

Aleksandr Korneichuk (1942)

KORNEICHUK (1905–1972) WAS AN ALMOST UNIVERSALLY DE-
SPISED OPPORTUNIST OF THE PEN IN STALIN'S TIME (SEE JOKE
ABOUT HIM BELOW). HIS PLAY, WARNING AGAINST AN OLD-
FASHIONED WARRIOR MENTALITY IN A MODERN WAR OF TECH-
NOLOGY, WAS A TRANSPARENT DIG AT CIVIL WAR HEROES SUCH
AS VOROSHILOV AND BUDYONNY, BLAMING THEM FOR THE DISAS-
TERS OF THE WAR'S FIRST YEAR. THEY WERE SOON REPLACED BY
YOUNGER PROFESSIONAL OFFICERS, WHO INTRODUCED THE TI-
TLES AND EPAULETS OF THE TRADITIONAL OFFICER CORPS.

Gorlov, Commander of the Front[1]
Gaidar, Member of the Military Council
Blagonravov, Chief of Staff of the Front
Ognev, Army Commander
Kolos, Cavalry Unit Commander
Orlik, Chief of Army Political Division
Udivitelny, Chief of Reconnaissance of the
　Front
Miron Gorlov, Commander's Brother,
　Director of an Aviation Plant

Sergei Gorlov, Commander's Son,
　Guards Lieutenant
Svechka, Guards Colonel
Krikun, Special Correspondent
Khripun, Chief of Front-line
　Communications
Commanders, officers, staff, Red Army
men, guests

ACT ONE, Scene Two

A room in the house where GORLOV *is billeted. The stage is empty, but a lot of noise
is heard coming from the next room, where the guests are assembled. They are toasting*
GORLOV. *Enter* MIRON *and* GAIDAR. MIRON *puts glasses and a bottle of wine on
the table and begins to pour out.*

MIRON: Come on, we might as well have another.
GAIDAR: Thanks very much, but I don't drink.
MIRON: You were drinking at dinner.

Excerpted from *Four Soviet Plays* (Hutchinson & Co. Ltd., 1944), pp. 22–38, 49–58.
1. Korneichuk illustrates his themes by means of "talking names": Gorlov = throat (perhaps neutral in
that there are good and bad Gorlovs in the play); Blagonravov = moral; Ognev = fire (as of a gun);
Kolos = wheel; Orlik = little eagle; Udivitelny = surprising; Svechka = candle.

GAIDAR: Lemonade. I've been on the wagon a long time now. My heart's a bit tricky, you know.

MIRON: I'll have to have one by myself then. All the best. (*Enter* SERGEI GORLOV, *Lieutenant of the Guards. He has a wine-glass in his hand.*)

SERGEI: Uncle Miron! Hey, that's not nice, swiping a bottle from the table and running off with it like that! Come on, hand it over!

MIRON: (*Filling his glass.*) Lay off it, Sergei, you'll get drunk.

SERGEI: Don't be too rough on me, I never drink when I'm in the line. I always give my vodka ration to Chekalenko. He's our Artillery Commander. But I feel like getting drunk tonight—if only in your honor. I've told my apostles how you taught me to fish and once gave me a hiding. I remember it all. (*He embraces* MIRON.)

MIRON: Your apostles?

SERGEI: That's what I call my gunners. They're real apostles, they work miracles every day.

MIRON: Apostles! (*He laughs.*) Not bad!

SERGEI: Comrade Member of the Military Council, don't you think I've got a good uncle?

MIRON: Now then, Sergei.

SERGEI: No, come on. Tell me.

GAIDAR: Yes, very good.

SERGEI: There you are! Everybody says so, including my apostles. They've taken a fancy to you. They have honestly. I'm not fooling. Guardsman's honor.

MIRON: What do you want to tell your Guardsmen a lot of nonsense about your civilian uncle for? You'd much better talk to them about their own job.

SERGEI: Oh, we like talking about civilian life after we've been in action. I know everything about everybody in my battery. And they know everything about me. We're a regular family. Do you know who's the father?

MIRON: The Political Commissar?

SERGEI: No, Chekalenko, the Battery Commander. He's over forty and fat as butter, with a mustache like a fox's brush. But put him out in a really nasty open spot and he's like a lion. He tells the funniest stories. Come over and see our battery and meet the apostles: Ostapenko, Shayametov, Bashlykov, Vasya Sokol. They're an absolutely tip-top bunch. (*Voices in the next room are heard:* "To the health of the Commander of the Front!" *Shouts of* "Hurrah" *and the clinking of glasses.*)

SERGEI *shakes his head.*

I'm not going to drink his health.

MIRON: Why not?

SERGEI: I've drunk my father's health enough already. But I don't wish to drink to him as Commander of the Front tonight. So there! Don't look so disapproving, Comrade Gaidar. I wouldn't say it anywhere else. I know how to behave. The Commander must be respected and obeyed without question. But I just don't feel like drinking his health tonight and that's all there is to it. And now Guards Lieutenant Sergei Gorlov, it's time for you to hit the hay.

GAIDAR: Not a bad idea.

SERGEI: O.K. O.K., I'm going. But I want to say this. Why isn't my Commander, Major-General Ognev, at this party? Do you know why? When I asked my father, he went off the deep end. He doesn't like Ognev. Shall I tell you why? He doesn't want to realize that my Commander, Major-General Ognev, is quite as good a man as...

MIRON: Chapaev?

SERGEI: No.

MIRON: Bagration?

SERGEI: No.

MIRON: Suvorov?[2]

SERGEI: Don't you dare.

GAIDAR: Who then? (*A pause.*)

SERGEI: Well, anyway he's Vladimir Ognev. That's what you've got to realize. But that stubborn old father of mine can't see beyond his own nose... Ah, it's a shame. (*He wipes his eyes.*) It's a damned shame.

He throws down his glass and goes out. The sound of a guitar comes from the next room. Somebody sings softly.

MIRON: I bet you find my brother a bit difficult to work with?

GAIDAR: Well, yes, I suppose I do. I'm a civilian, you see. Before the war I was a civil servant, so it really is rather difficult for me. One has to learn all about this business of modern warfare, and it's not like it was in the civil war, you know. It's all so much more complicated.

MIRON: Tell me candidly, do you think my brother really knows how we've got to fight nowadays?

GAIDAR: Well, he's had a lot of experience in the civil war, of course, and he's got his generals well in hand. He fights as well as he can, you know.

MIRON: He fights as well as he can . . . As well as he can? But what about as well as he ought to fight? How long will it take him to reach that stage?

GAIDAR: (*Laughing.*) That's what we're all waiting for.

MIRON: Yes, but should you?

GAIDAR: Should we what?

MIRON: Wait. Waiting is a difficult and costly business.

GAIDAR: There's nobody else to take over.

MIRON: Isn't there? What about Ognev?

GAIDAR: He's certainly talented, but he's so young.

MIRON: (*Laughing.*) Never took part in the civil war and hasn't got many medals, I suppose?

---

2. Bagration and Suvorov, Russian military commanders of 1812 and the 1790s, respectively.

GAIDAR: Unfortunately that still counts before everything else with some of the High Command. No matter how brilliant a young commander may be, if he didn't take part in the civil war with them they simply don't recognize him. They may pat him on the back in public, but in reality they look down on him. It's quite a job to convince them.

MIRON: Well, don't stand for any more of it. Declare a new war on those ignoramuses who don't know how to fight the modern way.

GAIDAR: But you can't do that now.

MIRON: Why not? Remember what happened in industry. In the beginning a lot of our factories and combines were run by managers with an honorable past and plenty of prestige—old comrades who boasted of their callused hands, their foghorn voices and bluff manner of speaking, but they knew nothing about the technical side, and what's more they refused to learn. They hadn't the faintest idea how to run a factory. They couldn't move a step without babbling about their proletarian origin, but they didn't want to learn, they didn't want to broaden their minds. And what was the result? The factories couldn't have worked worse, because almost everywhere the people in charge were "authority-struck," self-opinionated ignoramuses, and if the Central Committee hadn't changed the tune very sharply and put engineers, technicians and people who knew their jobs at the head of the factories the workers would have said: "If you can't run the show properly, go to hell with your precious authorities." That's a fact. And no matter how loudly the ignoramuses yelled, nobody backed them up. The people love leaders who know the job and can think, they clamor for them.

GAIDAR: Yes, but you know it's all much more complicated now. A really drastic change here might cause a complete breakdown. You've got to use subtler methods. The enemy's on our territory. We've got to put up with people more trying than your brother if we're going to liberate our country.

MIRON: O.K. Carry on. But I bet you'll soon get sick of it. I've declared war on my brother to-day. I'm only here for two days, but I'm going to give the old buffalo the works.

GAIDAR: (*Laughing.*) How?

MIRON: If the guests had arrived an hour later they wouldn't have found a plate left to eat off. My brother flung one of the dishes on to the floor with such a crack it made sparks fly. (*He laughs.*)

Enter the Commander's ADJUTANT.

ADJUTANT: Comrade Gaidar.

GAIDAR: Yes, what is it?

ADJUTANT: Moscow has just rung through. You're to attend the Defense Committee in the Kremlin at 6:30 tomorrow evening. Here's the text of the message. (*He hands* GAIDAR *a sheet of paper.*)

GAIDAR: Tell 'em to get a plane ready for 7:30 sharp tomorrow morning.

ADJUTANT: Very good.

He goes out.

MIRON: Pity it's not the day after tomorrow. We could have flown together.

GAIDAR: Yes. I should have liked that. I'll get the Commander to come out.
He goes into the next room.

MIRON: (*Filling his glass with wine.*) Plenty of guests, but nobody to drink with.
(*Raising the glass.*) Here's to you, Valya darling, anyway. . . . (*He drinks.*)

Enter GORLOV and GAIDAR.

GORLOV: (*Laughing.*) Look at this brother of mine, swigging all by himself! I'm
fond of the beggar even if he has set himself up as a military critic.

MIRON: You wait a minute. You're going to get it hot and strong from me as soon
as your guests are out of the way.

GORLOV: Careful. You're not behind the lines now, you're at the front. And I'm
the Commander. If I give the order, you'll find yourself in the guardroom
before you can say knife. (*He laughs out loud.*)

MIRON: The member of the Military Council will protect me.

GORLOV: How? A member of the Military Council may lodge a protest, of course.
That I admit. But if the Commander's worth his salt, then the Lord God
Himself won't help you.

MIRON: Oh, pipe down, you old buffalo! You've been spoiled, you old devil, that's
your trouble.

GORLOV: Be careful, Miron! Better watch your step. You can't monkey around
with me, you know. Come on. All the best! (*He takes the glass and drinks.*)

GAIDAR: Gorlov, I've been ordered to Moscow. I've got to be at the Defense
Committee at half-past six tomorrow evening.

GORLOV: You alone?

GAIDAR: Yes.

GORLOV: All right—off you go tomorrow morning.

GAIDAR: We must have a word together first. I'll get my things ready now. Come
round to my place in an hour's time.

GORLOV: All right. I'll be there as soon as they've left.

GAIDAR: (*To MIRON.*) All the best. I hope you're still here when I come back.

MIRON: I'll be seeing you in Moscow, anyway. I'll be at the Defense Committee
myself. Hope you have a good trip.

GAIDAR: Thanks. (*He goes out.*)

*GORLOV goes after him. After a pause, the guests enter holding their glasses. There are
some civilians amongst them, including MESTNY and GRUSTNY. MAJOR-GENERAL
KHRIPUN enters at the head.*

KHRIPUN: Where's the Commander? We're going to toast him.

MIRON: He'll be back in a minute.

KHRIPUN: Then I propose we drink to the brother of our beloved Commander. Your brother's a brilliant commander. I'd go so far as to call him a genius. He's the favorite of the army. And we're quite sure you are worthy of him. Here's to you.

MIRON: (*Smiling.*) Steady on. I'm a very insignificant chap, you know.

Enter the COMMANDER.

KHRIPUN: Ah, here he is! Comrade Commander, we are fortunate enough to have with us tonight that distinguished artiste, Grustny, who is now going to say a few words and sing our favorite song to wind up the party. Silence for the one and only Grustny. (*He hands him the guitar.*)

GORLOV: Cut out the speech. Let's have the song right away.

GRUSTNY: Allow me, half a minute. I simply can't tell you how happy I am. The three months I've spent with you at the front have made a new man of me— toughened every fiber of my body and inspired me with the titanic emotions of love and hatred. . . .

MIRON: Listen, Grustny! You don't want to spoil that golden voice of yours with a speech. Sing, man, sing.

VOICES: Sing, sing. We don't want a speech.

MESTNY, *the chairman of the Town Soviet, rushes forward with a glass in his hand.*

MESTNY: As chairman of the Town Soviet, I protest. I won't allow our intellectuals to be sat on like this. Grustny, go on with your speech.

GRUSTNY: (*Wiping his eyes with his handkerchief*) Tell you what. I'll express my emotion in song. (*He sits down on a chair, plays the guitar and then sings:* "Otvori potikhonku kalitku" [Open the gate quietly]).[3]

Shouts of "Bravo! Bravo!" GRUSTNY *bows.*

MESTNY: Bravo! That was splendid. Come on, let's dance. (*He squats down and kicks out his legs in a Russian dance.*)

GORLOV: You'll really have to excuse me, my dear guests. I've got some work to do.

MESTNY: So have we. I'll be working till morning, doing my utmost for the front. Now, come on, civilians, three cheers for our great Commander and strategist who's saved our town from the Fascists, Lieutenant-General Gorlov!

The civilian guests shout: "Hurrah!" run up to GORLOV *and shake his hand.* MESTNY *tries to kiss him.*

---

3. Vadim Kozin made this gypsy romance a hit in the late 1930s.

GORLOV: I'm very grateful to you, civilian comrades, and also to my military colleagues, for all the kind things you've said, but there are one or two remarks I'd like to make. You know the kind of chap I am. I always speak my mind. In the first place, it's not correct to say, as many of you have been saying tonight, that the whole series of great, I might even say historic, victories on my front depend only on myself as Commander. That's not true at all.

MESTNY: (*Shouting.*) No, no. You're wrong. You're wrong!

GORLOV: Shut up, Mestny. Our victories also depend on the courage of the troops.

MESTNY: Yes, yes, you're right, you're right!

GORLOV: And in the second place, there's another thing I disagree with. You've also talked a lot of high falutin' nonsense about my being a brilliant commander, a genius even. But I'm just a simple, ordinary chap. I began my military career after finishing at my "university"—the local village school. And I haven't been to any other universities whatsoever. I didn't learn to wage war in military academies, but in action. I'm no theoretician. I'm an old war-horse. The other day a foreign correspondent said: "As a commander, General Gorlov is not to be judged by ordinary standards." These bourgeois specialists can't understand how Gorlov, a son of the soil, who's neither academician nor theoretician, is beating the vaunted German Generals, who are both. (*He laughs.*)

Applause. Voices shout: "Bravo!"

MESTNY: Gorlov is beating them and he'll go on beating them, because he expresses the spirit of our people. (*Applause.*)

GORLOV: That's right, Mestny. That's right. You've hit the nail on the head. The spirit of our people is simple and sincere. "Leave me alone and I'll leave you alone. But if you start playing around with me, you'd better watch out." The spirit is what counts in an army commander. So long as he's full of guts, there's nothing to be afraid of. Aren't I right? *Voices: "Yes, you're right." "That's right."* (*Applause.*) I'm not used to sitting long hours in a study racking my brain over maps. War's not a staff college. The main thing is to search out the enemy and go for him wherever you find him. Get on with the job. Never mind about the theoretical discussion. Aren't I right? *Voices: "That's right! That's the way!"* (*Applause.*) Unfortunately, some of my Generals still fail to understand this simple truth. I've got one or two book-strategists who keep chattering about military culture. We've got to knock all that nonsense out of their heads.

MIRON: That's just where you're wrong. Our trouble is we still have too many ignorant commanders who don't understand modern warfare. You can't win this war on courage alone, you've got to know how to fight the modern way, and you've got to learn how to do that. Civil war experience is not enough.

GORLOV: There you are, you see. Even my own brother starts chattering about culture. Now I ask you, what the devil has culture to do with war, which is its exact opposite? Our trade is the roughest of all—you can't fight in cultural kid gloves. Well, Comrades, thank you again for your generous sentiments. Better get some sleep now, and we soldiers will get on with the job. Aren't I right, Khripun?

KHRIPUN: Absolutely.

MESTNY: Let's have one more drink and then we'll do our utmost for the front. (*He fills his glass and drinks.*)

GRUSTNY: (*To* GORLOV.) Might I have your autograph?

GORLOV: Yes, if you like. (*He writes his signature.*)

GRUSTNY: Thank you. This is the happiest day of my life. Good night.

ALL: Goodnight, General. Good night.

They go out. From the corridor comes the sound of voices: "What a man!" "He's clever, you know, he's clever." "There's a real army commander for you."

MESTNY'S VOICE: (*Off.*) He's saved our town.

MIRON: (*Closing the door.*) Phew! At last!

GORLOV: Fine bunch, eh?

MIRON is silent.

What are you thinking about?

MIRON: I'm thinking: God Almighty, when will our country see the last of fools, ignoramuses, grovelers, nincompoops and toadies?

GORLOV: At it again! Never mind, think as much as you like. Thought killed the turkey-cock, as they say down our way.

He laughs out loud and goes into the next room.

MIRON: That's right! It's too late to think. We've got to smash these conceited ignoramuses, smash them to pieces and replace them as quickly as possible with new, young, talented men. If we don't our great cause may be lost.

ACT TWO, Scene One

OGNEV's H.Q. A large room still showing traces of German looting. A heap of battered books in a corner. When the curtain rises the ADJUTANT is standing near a table on which are several telephones, going out of the window. Enter KOLOS.

KOLOS: Started snowing again.

ADJUTANT: Time it stopped.

KOLOS: So that their planes can dive-bomb my horses? Don't be a bloody fool!

ADJUTANT: Sorry, General.

KOLOS: Where's General Ognev?

ADJUTANT: In the Square. (*Points.*)

KOLOS: (*Looking out of the window.*) What's all that crowd doing?

ADJUTANT: Funeral. They've just brought in the bodies.

KOLOS: Were they soldiers?

ADJUTANT: No, civilians shot by the Germans. The General's been out there—trying to identify his father.

KOLOS: Yes, the old man stayed on, didn't he?

ADJUTANT: This used to be his house.

KOLOS: (*Picking up books and looking at them.*) All about geography.

ADJUTANT: He was a schoolmaster. The Germans shot sixty people just outside the town the day before yesterday. Apparently they had a lot of fun with them. Most of the faces are slashed to pieces. The locals say old Ognev was one of them. They say he marched to execution at the head. Barefoot. No hat. Singing. They were all singing.

KOLOS: Singing, eh?

ADJUTANT: The General'll tell you all about it. The Germans took their boots away.

KOLOS: We'll take the hide off those bastards.

Enter OGNEV. *He sits down silently at the table, and rests his head on his hand.*

OGNEV: (*Quietly.*) Grigory... Grigory...

KOLOS: What's the matter, Volodya?

OGNEV: I couldn't recognize him. I couldn't recognize my own father. They mutilated every one of them, the beasts! What a frightful sight! Bodies riddled with bullets and slashed to pieces. Eyes gouged out. There they lie, but they marched out proudly singing. "Be brave, comrades, keep in step,"[4] that's what they sang. And those beasts tortured them for it.

KOLOS: Take it easy, Volodya. Take it easy, old chap. It's all over now.

OGNEV: He used to sit at this very window late into the night. A little old man in spectacles, coughing, and correcting his pupils' exercise books. For forty years he taught the children geography. He always longed to go and see the Pamirs, "The Roof of the World." I promised him to take him. (*A pause.*) He told everybody the Germans wouldn't get any further because his son was near here and he wouldn't let the Germans get his home town and the house where he was born. He was waiting for me—dear old father, you didn't know how hard it was for me. You didn't believe it. Yes, you expected something better from me.

The sounds of a Funeral March come softly from the square. OGNEV *gets up and looks out of the window.* KOLOS *gets up.*

They're filling in the grave. Good bye, Father. Good bye. They'll know you again, old schoolmaster. They'll know you again in your son, I swear this over your grave: you'll hear my revenge through the earth and then you'll forgive me, you dear, good old man.

---

4. "Smelo, tovarishchi, v nogu," a march famous from the Revolution.

KOLOS: Volodya! (*He embraces him.*)

The sounds of the Funeral March grow louder. Farewell volleys resound. Enter the AD-JUTANT.

ADJUTANT: General Ognev, a major from G.H.Q. has arrived.
KOLOS: Let him wait a bit.
OGNEV: No, tell him to come in. (*He sits down at the table.*)

The ADJUTANT goes out. Enter the MAJOR.

MAJOR: Major Gusakov from G.H.Q.
OGNEV: Sit down.
MAJOR: Dispatch for you. (*He hands him the dispatch.*)

OGNEV unseals it and reads.

KOLOS: You must be frozen.
MAJOR: (*Shakes his head.*) Matter of fact, we had a pretty hot time getting here.
OGNEV: Tell the Chief of Staff I thank him for his warning, which is exactly what I drew his attention to before operations began.

He hands the dispatch to KOLOS, who reads it.

KOLOS: When we warned him he didn't take any notice. Now it's too late he sends us a dispatch. Well, I suppose that's something.
OGNEV: Tell me, is G.H.Q. in touch with the tank corps yet?
MAJOR: I don't think so. I don't know for certain.
OGNEV: Where was it yesterday?
MAJOR: I've no information about that.
OGNEV: Is General Orlov asleep? The Germans have already got our corridor under fire.
MAJOR: I've found that out all right. But why Orlov is asleep, search me.
OGNEV: You don't seem to know much, do you? What the hell have you come here for? What are you? A Staff Officer or just a dispatch rider?
MAJOR: My orders are to hand you the dispatch and go straight.
OGNEV: (*Interrupting*) Oh, I see! Hand over the dispatch and to hell with us, eh? You've got to get back. So that's it, is it?
MAJOR: General Ognev, I'm afraid I have some rather unpleasant news for you. It was only with the greatest difficulty that I managed to get through to you at all. The corridor no longer exists. I was under enemy mortar fire the whole way and they damned nearly got me. I suppose you know you're cut off and surrounded?
OGNEV: What?

MAJOR: No doubt about it.

OGNEV: Stand up.

The MAJOR stands up. OGNEV looks at him with contempt.

Report yourself to the town commandant in the house opposite and tell him I've ordered you to be put under arrest.

MAJOR: But, General Ognev, I'm the representative of G.H.Q. Staff.

OGNEV: Silence! Carry out my orders!

MAJOR: Very good.

He goes out.

KOLOS: I thought you were going to sock him one. What a wretched creature.

OGNEV: If he wasn't from G.H.Q. I'd sock him so hard he'd never use that word again.

Enter the CAPTAIN, who is O.C. Communications for OGNEV's force.

CAPTAIN: Code message, Comrade Commander.

OGNEV: (*Taking and reading it and handing it to KOLOS*) How are communications?

CAPTAIN: The gunfire's a hindrance and the Germans are making a hell of a row in the ether, but we're holding on.

OGNEV: (*To KOLOS.*) How do you like that?

KOLOS: Beats me altogether.

CAPTAIN: May I go?

OGNEV: Yes.

The CAPTAIN goes out.

KOLOS: Either the Commander of the front doesn't understand anything at all or else he doesn't want to understand. We're to dig ourselves in here and wait. Wait for what?

OGNEV: Till the Germans bring up everything they've got. Then it's ten to one he'll say: "How did you damned fools manage to get caught in spite of all my efforts to bash sense into your heads? Why didn't you use your eyes? What d'you expect me to do for you now?"

KOLOS: That's just about what he will say, the old rhino. Damn him! How on earth did he get this way?

OGNEV: All limited people are like that. As soon as they get authority they become infatuated with themselves and their only pleasure is to throw their weight about. So, of course, they always trying to bash sense into people's heads.

The telephone rings. He picks up the receiver.

Yes—where are you? All right. Come round.

KOLOS: Who was that?

OGNEV: That was Orlik, Chief of our Army Political Department. The crazy devil nearly got killed yesterday. As it was, he was hit in the arm by a shell splinter. He always charges right in the hottest spots.

KOLOS: I thought he was your philosopher.

OGNEV: He's clever all right. He used to be a Political Instructor. Speaks two languages fluently. I always call him Professor.

KOLOS: And he's tough as well?

OGNEV: I'll say he is! He may look thin and wear glasses, but that guy can stand up to anyone.

KOLOS: My Commissar's called Strategistov, a strapping hulk of a fellow. I had a hell of a job finding a horse up to his weight. He's not so hot at brainwork, but he certainly knows how to ride. He's a born horseman, absolutely devoted to them.

OGNEV: (*Laughing.*) Strategistov—what a priceless name; where did you unearth him from?

KOLOS: I didn't. He was wished on me. I've nicknamed him Hoof. It seems to suit him better.

OGNEV: Does he mind?

KOLOS: Lord, no, he's got a sense of humor.

Enter ORLIK. His arm is bandaged.

OGNEV: Orlik, you devil—I've got a bone to pick with you. What do you mean by going into action with the third battalion? As chief of our Political Department, you're not supposed to act recklessly.

ORLIK: Well, you see, Comrade General, it was like this. Division Intelligence reported that enemy agents were trying to stir up trouble in the third battalion, starting dangerous talk.

OGNEV: Who was it? Some of our people?

ORLIK: Yes. The Commissar of the battalion was a very vigilant comrade, super-vigilant in fact. He discovered everything double quick time and immediately reported it to the authorities. By the time it reached me it was all over. Two men were at the bottom of it, and can you beat it, both of them had been decorated.

OGNEV: What! What sort of things had they been saying?

ORLIK: Oh, very dangerous talk (*Laughs.*) You'll scarcely believe it, but they said the Battalion Commander and the Political Instructor were regular gentlemen, who'd got their own private chef and guzzled enough for five people while the enlisted mess was a damned disgrace. The men gave the cook a hiding because he always gave them such filthy stew.

You needn't write it down. I've raised such a hell of a row in the battalion that it'll be a long time before they forget it. Both the Political Director and the Commander.

OGNEV: The rats! Make me out a short report and I'll sign it. I'll add a ruling that in future all commanders are forbidden to have any food until the men have had theirs.

ORLIK: That's the stuff. I'll do it right away.

KOLOS: Now tell us, how did you manage to get into the thick of it? How did you get wounded?

ORLIK: (*Laughing.*) Learning that I was going to make such an important address to the men, the Germans decided to launch an attack.

KOLOS: And then?

ORLIK: Well, I couldn't very well say to the men: "You buzz off and do your fighting, Comrades, and when you've finished I'll come back and go on with my talk."

KOLOS: And then I suppose you went into the attack shouting "Hurrah for the Motherland!"?

ORLIK: Not me! Their Commander has a voice like a trumpet. I joined up with the trench mortar boys. They even let me have a go. My mines went over all right. Admittedly the Battery Commander flew into a rage and said: "You something, why the flaming hell can't you shoot quicker!" I gave up after that and let a gunner take over.

OGNEV: I think you did very well.

ORLIK: I didn't mind his cursing me. Anyway, he was quite right. Hey, is there any answer from the Commander of the front?

OGNEV: (*Going to the door and calling to the* ADJUTANT.) Tell the Chief of Staff to come in.

VOICE: (*Off.*) Very good.

OGNEV: Read that.

He hands the message to ORLIK, *who reads it.*

KOLOS: Do you understand what this means?

ORLIK: Probably it means the Tank Corps is coming here.

OGNEV: You can forget about the Tank Corps. The whole front is searching all over the place for it.

ORLIK: Why?

KOLOS: Don't you know what sort of communications we've got? They've reported me dead and buried twice already.

ORLIK: It's partly your own fault.

KOLOS: Why? One of my radio stations has been bombed and the other is out of action. I need twenty-two, not two.

ORLIK: How many have you got now?

KOLOS: Oh, I'm all right now. I gave Khripun a hell of a shake up and got the stuff straight away. It's always the same story here. They won't deal anything out, even though the stores are full to bursting. They all hang back and hum and haw until you get hold of them by the throat and squeeze them till their eyes bulge out of their sockets. Then they fork out and even sing your praises afterwards. They're just like the merchant in the old days: You could be at death's door in front of his eyes and he'd pretend he didn't see you, but if you grabbed him by the beard he'd open up his money-bags, bow down to the ground and thank you into the bargain.

Enter the CHIEF OF STAFF *and* COLONEL SVECHKA.

CHIEF OF STAFF: I've brought Colonel Svechka along. The situation is getting complicated.

OGNEV: Has the ski patrol returned?

SVECHKA: Yes, they're back and they've done the job.

OGNEV: Fine They've been pretty quick! Report, please.

SVECHKA: (*Pulling out a map.*) Now this, where my finger is, is the Communard State Farm. From here that's about...

OGNEV: Thirty-three miles. Go on.

SVECHKA: A group of about a hundred and fifty tanks has been discovered.

OGNEV: Just a second. (*He marks his map.*) Well?

SVECHKA: This morning an S.S. Division and two hundred tanks arrived at the village of Sinitsino east of the farm. Another column of about two regiments is on its way there. This movement was reported to our scouts by a guerrilla detachment. Two of them have arrived.

CHIEF OF STAFF: I've just had a talk with them.

OGNEV: What sort of detachment? How big is it?

CHIEF OF STAFF: About fifty men.

OGNEV: Locals?

CHIEF OF S.: Yes.

OGNEV: Do they know the roads?

CHIEF OF S.: They could walk along them blindfold. These men have given us extremely valuable information. It appears that the Germans have built a new road leading from the river to Kolokol station. (*He indicates it on his map.*) Here it is. They commandeered the entire population and made them work on it day and night. Over three thousand people died of cold or were shot on this road.

OGNEV: I make it eighteen miles away.

CHIEF OF S.: That's right. They've built strong bridges along the road, but at present they're not using it for transport. Probably for fear of being spotted by our reconnaissance planes.

OGNEV: Very likely. Go on.

SVECHKA: That's all. At 11.20 hours our scouts discovered enemy units here, and at 12.00 at the collective farm.

CHIEF OF S.: Divisional Commander Yakovenko has just reported that his scouts have discovered an enemy movement from Kolokol towards our corridor.

OGNEV: How many?

CHIEF OF S.: One division and about seventy tanks.

OGNEV: Where exactly?

CHIEF OF S.: At 15.40 they were here. (*Points to map.*)

OGNEV: And now it's 16.00.

CHIEF OF S.: That's right.

OGNEV: (*To* SVECHKA.) What's it like up your way beyond the farm?

SVECHKA: Quiet. Enemy concentration's very weak. If you give the order, I'll push on right up to the river.

OGNEV: Oh, no you don't. That's just what they're praying for. You're too far advanced as it is. You may get a visit from their tanks this evening, and your position's lousy. I order you to withdraw and join up with us here immediately. All our forces have got to bunch together in a fist. Cover your withdrawal with artillery and aircraft in the proper manner, so that the enemy don't mess up your rear. Come and report the execution of the order at 19.00 hours. Off you go.

SVECHKA: Very good, Comrade Commander. But it won't be an easy job to transfer a complete division in three hours. Look at the distance. Let's see: how many miles . . .

OGNEV: (*Interrupting.*) Don't reckon in miles, man, we've got to reckon in seconds now. You'll report at 18.30 instead of 19 hours, if you stand here any longer, you'll find yourself reporting at . . .

SVECHKA: O.K., Comrade Commander. I'll report at 18.30. (*Exit.*)

OGNEV: (*Looking at the map, measuring with a pair of compasses and making a note.*) Ah, that's good. Now I see their little game. Ugh, what swine those Germans are!

CHIEF OF S.: They've planned it all very neatly.

OGNEV: Who?

CHIEF OF S.: The German Command. Look how cunningly they're moving.

OGNEV: Cunning be damned! Why it's child's play. If the German Command had made the sort of mistake our Commander made the day before yesterday I'd have wiped out forces three times the size of ours. There's nothing cunning in what they're doing. On the contrary, they're very slow at taking advantage of our stupidity, very slow. What's Gorlov's strategy worth now, eh? His Tank Corps has gone and got itself stuck somewhere on these God-forsaken roads, while the Germans have been building a brand new road right under our noses that nobody knew anything about. Gorlov said there were no tanks, but there they're complete with infantry rushing at us as bold as brass. They've blocked our corridor while Orlov was fast asleep. I bet at this moment they're having a full dress rehearsal of how they're got to shout to us tomorrow morning: "Russ Kaput. Surrender Russians, you're surrounded." But we're going to give 'em a smashing answer. (*He looks at the map.*)

A pause.

KOLOS: Not so sure about the smashing.

ORNEV: Oh, I am. (*Looking at the map and making a note.*) Aren't you, Orlik?

ORLIK: You bet.

OGNEV: What I like about you, Professor, is your healthy, intelligent optimism. Look here, boys. Look at the map. The enemy have withdrawn their garrison from Kolokol in order to trap us. They've sent half their tanks against us and the other half is engaged with our Tank Corps somewhere miles away on the roads. It's simply a matter of foot-slogging, as dear old Suvorov used to say, foot-slogging and forced marches and popping up where the Germans least expect us. We'll leave two regiments in the town, all our dear little heavy guns, and four squadrons of cavalry as a blind. There you are, Fritz, it's in the bag. The army's standing waiting for your pincers. We'll ask you, Professor, and your Guards to hang on to this convenient hillock only for twenty-four hours. As soon as it gets dark the rest of us (*turns to* KOLOS), including your dear little horses, will creep out on to the new road and charge like hell at the back gates of Kolokol. By the time we've got the station, the German tank will have to make a pretty quick withdrawal, but it will be too late then. All their stores of petrol, shells and food will have fallen into our hands and we'll bayonet the hell out of them in their own fortifications. How about it? Have a look at the map and unload your criticisms. (*A pause.*) What's the matter, old man. You're looking like an undertaker.

KOLOS: (*Looking at the map.*) Comrade Commander, you've put forward a very risky proposal. I must have time to think it over.

OGNEV: Two picked squadrons of our toughest men will lead the vanguard. They'll knock out the sentries and to give it the finishing touch, we'll dress up our men in German uniforms. Fortunately, we've taken enough prisoners for that.

ORLIK: I don't think we ought to use enemy uniforms. That's the kind of low-down trick the Fritzes play on us.

OGNEV: I think we're crazy to fight honestly against an enemy who's up to every dirty trick in the game. They trick, and we don't answer with anything. Suvorov stressed the importance of cunning in warfare, but some of our home-grown generals have forgot all about it. The only answer to cunning is more cunning.

KOLOS: (*Turning away from the map, to the* CHIEF OF STAFF.) What's your opinion?

CHIEF OF S.: There's no other way.

OGNEV: Hey, you can cut that out. I'm not suggesting this operation because there's no other way out.

CHIEF OF S.: I didn't make myself clear. I consider it's the best we can do under the circumstances.

KOLOS: It's awfully risky. Suppose they guess our move?

OGNEV: That's just why nobody must be told where we're going. Our most dangerous enemies at present are spies and gossip. And they're all over the place, even in our army.

KOLOS: Really?

OGNEV: Of course they are. The Germans are past-masters at monkey business.

CHIEF OF S.: We'd better put forward our proposal to the Commander of the Front in code.

OGNEV: Oh, no, we won't.

KOLOS: Why not?

OGNEV: He'd waste hours "hammering sense into my skull" and we'd miss the bus.

ORLIK: Not very good form, is it.

OGNEV: I know, but all this "good form" will drive me crazy. I've had just about enough! Gorlov got us into this mess. Let's get out of it with honor; that'll be the best thing for him as well. Come on, Chief of Staff. Write out the order. Firstly . . .

Enter OGNEV's Chief of Communications.

CAPTAIN: Code telegram from the Commander of the Front. (*He delivers it.*)

> OGNEV *reads it. The pencil snaps in his hand and falls on the table.* ORLIK *goes over and reads in silence.*
> OGNEV *comes out quickly from behind the table, which is near the door, and hands it to* KOLOS *who reads it and passes it on to the Chief of Staff.*

OGNEV: Well, what have you got to say?

> KOLOS *is silent.*

> Answer me! (*A pause.*) Say something. (*He snatches the telegram out of the hands of the Chief of Staff.*) What does it mean?

KOLOS: The Commander of the Front suggests an immediate withdrawal to our initial position. True, he asks whether you have any objections, but that's only a matter of form. In one hour this suggestion will become an order.

OGNEV: I know all about that. I can read.

KOLOS: Well, there we are, orders are orders, we shall have to fight our way back.

OGNEV: That's obvious. But in the first place, it's not yet an order. It's still a suggestion. In the second place it's incorrect in conception and altogether disastrous. He tells us to fight our way back. What for? Where's the Tank Corps? He says it's had rather a battering and can't help. That's a lie. It's wiped out. And now it appears that my army is going to get a battering.

KOLOS: We'll be able to fight our way back.

CHIEF OF S.: The Commander wants to straighten the line and he's decided to withdraw.

OGNEV: Oh, go to hell! The ravens are already circling. First he makes us advance and it doesn't work. Now he wants us to withdraw at any cost. Surely there must be an alternative? I haven't been sacrificing my men breaking down the German defenses merely to fight my way back again. My army's going to live and fight and win! We can do it and we're damn well going to do it. (*Enter* CAPTAIN.)

CAPTAIN: A code telegram from Gaidar, member of the Military Council of the front. From Moscow. (*He hands it over.*)

OGNEV: (*Reads it and his face lights up.*) This is terrific! There's still some justice in the world after all. Listen—Moscow gives a free hand. We're to act according to our plan. That means we attack. Never mind about the Commander's suggestion.

KOLOS: Really?

OGNEV: Yes, and here's another "really" for you. I asked Gaidar to submit both our plan and Gorlov's to the proper quarter in Moscow. Now Gaidar tells me that Moscow approves of our plan and Gorlov has been informed accordingly.

KOLOS: (*Joyfully.*) That's fine! Well, let's get going right away and burn up the Germans till we scorch the very skies.

OGNEV: That's the stuff. . . .

ACT THREE

Gorlov's Headquarters. Morning a few days later. Enter ADJUTANT. *He arranges a water jug on the table, lays out pencils and sharpens them. Special Correspondent* KRIKUN *can be seen through the open door.*

KRIKUN: (*Standing in the doorway.*) Do you think the Commander will be here soon?

ADJUTANT: I doubt it. He's been up all night at Communications. I expect he'll go to his quarters and turn in. He's got to sleep sometime.

KRIKUN: Think he'll look in here on the way?

ADJUTANT: You never know. You can wait.

KRIKUN: It's really most unfortunate. I'll have Moscow phoning through in half an hour. I've got to let them have an article on the heroic death of the Commander's son.

ADJUTANT: Let them have it, then.

KRIKUN: Well you see, the trouble is my article ends up like this. Listen. (*He takes out the article and reads aloud.*) "He met his death in front of my eyes, this magnificent young man, the worthy son of his father. Through the thunder of the gun-fire, I heard his last gallant words: 'Tell my father I die calmly in the knowledge that he will take vengeance on those bloody reptiles for my death.'" If only I could get a few words from his father. This is the sort of thing I want from him. (*Reading.*) "The old General sat with bowed head for a long time after hearing of the death of his beloved son. When at last he raised his head, there were no tears in his eyes—no, not one! His eyes glowed with the sacred fire of vengeance. In a firm voice he said: 'Sleep in peace, my son. Don't worry. I will avenge you. I swear it on the honor of an old soldier.'" Don't you see, if I could only check up on it right away, I'd have the scoop of a lifetime. But what can I do? Moscow will be ringing any minute now. What do you think? Could I check up on it by 'phone?

ADJUTANT: I don't know how you'll check up on the Commander's eyes over the 'phone. We aren't wired for television, you know.

KRIKUN: My dear fellow if I only wrote about what I saw, I'd never be able to do my daily piece. My stuff wouldn't be anything like so popular. My editor insists on an article from me every day. Our readers have got used to me. The paper can't come out without Krikun. All the others are green with envy. They're always telling my editor how lucky he is. They say they'd willingly exchange their whole staff of special correspondents for one Krikun.

ADJUTANT: Yes, you certainly know how to churn it out. I read your stuff every day. It's slick all right.

KRIKUN: Well, what's to be done? How do I call up the Commander?

ADJUTANT: You can't ring him there.

KRIKUN: (*Glancing at the clock.*) I'm late already. I'll send it over as it stands. I don't suppose the Commander will object. What do you think? After all, it's a lovely piece of writing.

ADJUTANT: Not bad.

KRIKUN: I must rush off and send it. Be seeing you. (*He goes out.*)

Enter BLAGONRAVOV *and* UDIVITELNY.

BLAGONRAVOV: Hasn't he come?

ADJUTANT: Not yet.

BLAGONRAVOV: He 'phoned up and said he was on the way. (*He sits down.*)

The ADJUTANT *goes out.*

UDIVITELNY: Who could have expected we'd lose the tank corps? I can't get over it. All our information indicated...

BLAGONRAVOV: What information! We never had any proper information. That's the whole trouble.

UDIVITELNY: The way you talk anyone would think we hadn't got an Intelligence Service.

BLAGONRAVOV: That's exactly what I do think—so far as our front is concerned. The front-line units see what the enemy's doing—as far as the first hillock. But what's beyond that they have to guess. If it wasn't for the air force, we'd know absolutely nothing. But air reconnaissance can't do everything. Besides it always needs checking.

UDIVITELNY: Blagonravov, I'm surprised at you. The daily reports I prepare for you so that...

BLAGONRAVOV: (*Interrupting.*) I've decided not to read them. Look here, we've had enough of this. We've got to take serious steps—otherwise we'll be court-martialled. Proper intelligence is always fifty per cent of any success, sometimes even a hundred. Any fool can tell you that. But here we are groping about like a lot of blind men. It's absolutely scandalous.

UDIVITELNY: (*Surpise.*) You seem to imply that we're...

BLAGONRAVOV: Fools, of course we're fools. I'm a fool because I work with you. As for you, well, that's just the way you were born.

UDIVITELNY: Comrade Chief of Staff, I'd have you know the Commander has a different opinion of my work and he's known me a good many years. I protest. Besides, I've been decorated.

BLAGONRAVOV: I know what the Commander thinks of you. As for your decoration that was simply a misunderstanding.

UDIVITELNY: Aha, so you think the Government made a mistake in decorating me?

BLAGONRAVOV: Yes, I do. They've made two mistakes. The first was when they decorated you. And the second mistake is that they still haven't stripped us of our decorations and disgraced the pair of us publicly.

He goes out.

UDIVITELNY: (*Takes out a note-book and writes in it.*) Government making a mistake. Government's made two mistakes. Our intelligence service is rotten. Now what else did he say? Aha! (*A pause.*) He called me a fool. It's a plain case of defeatism. You wait a bit. You'll soon find out what sort of Intelligence Officer I am. (*Takes up the telephone receiver.*) Get me Ivanov. Ivanov this is Udivitelny. When's the next meeting of the Party Bureau? Today? Good. I've got a little matter that needs looking into. Listen, I suppose you don't remember what sort of family Blagonravov comes from? Aha! The son of a deacon, eh? No wonder... Yes... That's all. I'll be there. (*He puts down the receiver.*) (*Enter the* COMMANDER.) Morning, Comrade Commander.

GORLOV: Morning. Phew, I've got a splitting headache. Haven't slept a wink the whole night.

UDIVITELNY: How can you, Ivan? You know your health is precious to the whole country.

GORLOV: Never mind. What have you got?

UDIVITELNY: This is for you. (*He hands him a paper.*)

GORLOV: Good. I'll have a look at it later on.

UDIVITELNY: Comrade Commander, I think you ought to know that Blagonravov is adopting a very bad attitude.

GORLOV: How's that?

UDIVITELNY: He's discontented with everything and everybody. Looks like defeatism. He says...

GORLOV: (*Interrupting.*) Never mind him! You know what these people are like? When the Commander's doing well, they toady to him, strut about like roosters and lap up decorations. But as soon as anything goes wrong, you can't see 'em for dust. They're scared of the responsibility. I know their petty little souls. It's always due to the same thing; they're soft, they've never been through the mill. How can you expect them to be tough?

UDIVITELNY: How right you are. Take me, for instance. Although I didn't work very long in a factory, only three years and two weeks, I just know that I've got enough proletarian instinct to last me all my life. But you take some men—they're cultured, they've been to universities, but take a good look at them and you know they're not the real thing.

GORLOV: Obviously. They've got culture on the surface but they're no good inside.

Enter BLAGONRAVOV. UDIVITELNY *goes out.*

BLAGONRAVOV: Read this. (*He hands over a paper.*) If there are no corrections, I'll have it coded at once. They've rung up twice from Moscow. They're asking for details.

GORLOV: (*Reading.*) Yes. All right. Hmm... Oh, no! (*He makes a mark with a pencil.*)

BLAGONRAVOV: (*Looking.*) Why not?

GORLOV: What's the matter with you? Have you taken leave of your senses? Who was in command of our Tank Corps? Balda. A damned fool. That's why he was beaten. And it must be reported honestly.

BLAGONRAVOV: All the same, I think...

GORLOV: (*Interrupting.*) I'm not interested in what you think. It's going to be exactly as I want it. (*He reads on.*) Oho, here's another discovery. Why have you promoted Ognev to the position of Alexander the Great all of a sudden and that old creeper Kolos into a Suvorov?

BLAGONRAVOV: It doesn't say that, but they've done their job brilliantly—Kolokol has been taken.

GORLOV: And who are they, I'd like to know? Where do we come in? Whose orders were they acting on?

BLAGONRAVOV: That's just the point. They acted on a plan of their own which was right in the teeth of your orders. And they had Moscow's consent.

GORLOV: I'm going to inquire into that. That's why I've sent for them. I'm not going to allow the Command of the front to be overruled. Anyway, there's no reason why young pups should get their heads turned. Ognev's an upstart as it is. This'll completely ruin him. No! (*He crosses it all out.*) You will kindly do it all over again and bring it to me in an hour's time.

BLAGONRAVOV: Excuse me, Comrade Commander, but I can't go on working with you any longer. (*Excitedly.*) I request to be released. I've had to make this decision because...

GORLOV: (*Interrupting.*) Wait a minute! The ship isn't sinking yet and it doesn't intend to. But you're on the run already like a rat. You're not going to get away with it, my friend. I'll have the pants off you first. Then I'll have your hide. After that I might begin to think about chucking you out.

BLAGONRAVOV: Comrade Commander!

GORLOV: Enough! That's all! Go and carry out my order.

BLAGONRAVOV: I... I... I can't.

GORLOV: Don't you stutter, or I'll make you go on stuttering for the rest of your life. You know what my temper's like, I don't go in for psychology.

BLAGONRAVOV goes out. Enter ADJUTANT.

ADJUTANT: Major-General Ognev and Major-General Kolos are here as you ordered.

GORLOV: Let 'em sit outside and wait.

ADJUTANT: Very good. He goes out.

GORLOV: (*Taking up the telephone receiver.*) Get me Khripun. Is that you, Khripun? Listen. Come over to me at once. We'll have lunch together. More brandy, eh? Bring it along. (*He replaces the receiver.*)

Enter MIRON GORLOV.

MIRON: Good morning, Ivan. Have you been up at Communications all night?

GORLOV: Yes. Are you going?

MIRON: Yes. Plane's ready to take off now. I can't wait for the weather any longer. I'll have to take my chance.

GORLOV: It seems to be a bit bitter to-day.

MIRON: I'll make it somehow, Ivan, I never dreamt we'd have such a sad parting.

GORLOV: Yes, I loved Sergei. (*A long pause.*)

MIRON: He was so cheerful, so spontaneous. I just can't bring myself to realize...

GORLOV: It can't be helped. War is war.

MIRON: I know how you feel, Ivan. I don't know whether we'll meet again soon, but perhaps... That's why I've made up my mind. Please forgive me, but I've got to tell you some bitter home-truths. I've simply got to.

GORLOV: Come on then, out with it.

MIRON: You know, brother, you mustn't fool yourself or the Soviet State. Let's face it. You don't know your job and you're unable to command the front. It's not the job for you. Times are different. In the civil war you fought almost without artillery, but the enemy didn't have so much either. You fought without aircraft, without tanks and without scientific technique. To-day you've got to know all that inside out. But you know very little about it. In fact, you don't know anything about it at all. Turn it in, old boy. Turn it in for your own sake, understand. We're building machines for the front day and night. The best machines in the world. And what for? So that half of them can be lost because you're so darned inefficient and out-of-date? What shall I tell the workers when I get back to the factory? What shall I say to the engineers? They haven't left the shops since the first day of the war. They're heroes, like the men in the front line! I can't conceal from them the fact that their precious work and all our fine technical productions are being misused at the front owing to your ignorance. Ivan, try to understand before it's too late. Otherwise they'll sack you.

GORLOV: (*Interrupting.*) Stop! (*He presses the button.*)

Enter the ADJUTANT.

ADJUTANT: At your service.

GORLOV: This civilian is now going to the aerodrome. See him off to the plane.

ADJUTANT: Very good, Comrade Commander. This way, please.

Long pause.

MIRON: Don't bother about me. I know my way all right. You'd better stay with the Commander. I think he'll soon have to be seen off himself.

He goes out.

ADJUTANT: Excuse me, Comrade Commander.

GORLOV: Well?

ADJUTANT: Major-General Ognev asks you to see him immediately or else make a definite appointment. He's got to go and be bandaged.

GORLOV: What's he got to have bandaged now? Is it his head again?

ADJUTANT: No, it's his right arm.

GORLOV: All right, let them come in.

ADJUTANT: Very good.

He goes out. Enter OGNEV and KOLOS in full dress uniform.

OGNEV: We've come as you ordered. (*A pause.*)

GORLOV: So I see. Are both of you cripples?

KOLOS: Only Major-General Ognev. I'm all right.

GORLOV: What have you dressed up like this for? (*To* KOLOS.) You look as if you'd been twirling your mustaches all night. Perhaps you think we're going to congratulate you and give a banquet in your honor? If so you're damned well mistaken, do you understand?

OGNEV: We knew you'd say that, Comrade Commander.

GORLOV: Did you indeed?

KOLOS: That's right.

GORLOV: Well then, sit down, sit down. Let's have a nice little heart-to-heart talk.

OGNEV and KOLOS sit down.

Who's going to begin? Come on, Ognev. You've had more responsibility so you've got more to answer for. Well? (*A pause.*) Why don't you say something?

OGNEV: I'm waiting for questions.

GORLOV: The devil you are. Very well, then, why didn't you carry out my orders?

OGNEV: We acted in accordance with our own plan with Moscow's permission. You know that. Kolokol Station has been captured and the entire German force smashed. Our plan turned out to be correct.

GORLOV: In that case what am I doing here? Do I command this front or don't I?

OGNEV is silent.

See here, Ognev. What's on your mind? What do you want of me?

OGNEV: Only one thing—that you should give up the command of the front.

GORLOV: (*To KOLOS.*) Aha, and that's what you want, too, my old friend?

KOLOS: That's right.

GORLOV: Now I see your little game.

Enter GAIDAR.

How are you, Gaidar? You've come at the right moment.

GAIDAR: How are you, Gorlov? Hullo, Ognev. (*He shakes hands with everybody.*) I've been delayed in Moscow. (*To OGNEV and KOLOS.*) I'm very glad to find you two here. Congratulations on your brilliant victory.

GORLOV: Better go steady with the congratulations.

GAIDAR: Why?

GORLOV: Do you know what he has just said?

GAIDAR: What?

GORLOV: Repeat it. Let the Member of the Military Council hear you.

A pause.

Got your tail down, have you?

OGNEV: Comrade Member of the Military Council, I declare that there is no proper command on our front.

KOLOS: That's right.

GORLOV: You heard?

A long pause.

GAIDAR: Yes. I heard. (*To OGNEV and KOLOS.*) Go and wait outside for a few minutes, will you?

OGNEV: Very good.

They go out.

GORLOV: (*Writing.*) I'll show the . . .

GAIDAR: What are you doing?

GORLOV: Won't be a minute. You'll see it when you sign it. (*Writing.*) I'll bang some sense into their heads. They won't forget this as long as they live. Here, sign it.

GAIDAR: (*He takes the paper, tears it up without reading it and throws it away.*) We've had enough of banging sense into people's heads, Comrade Gorlov. It's time you took a rest from this hard work. Here's Moscow's order for your retirement. Read it. (*He hands him the order. GORLOV reads it. A long pause.*) You're a brave man and devoted to our great cause. That's all very fine and they respect you for it. But it's not enough to win this war. To do that you've got to know how to fight the modern way. You've got to know how to be able to learn from each new experience. You've got to know how to raise up new, young commanding cadres instead of keeping them under. Unfortunately you haven't got that capacity. Of course, technical knowledge and the capacity to wage war are things that can be acquired. To-day you lack them. Tomorrow you may be able to acquire them provided that you've got a strong desire to learn, to learn from experience and to develop yourself. But that's just what you haven't got. Are our old army-leaders capable of developing themselves and mastering the technique of modern warfare? Of course they are. They're just as capable as the young men, perhaps even more so, if only they're willing to learn from experience and don't regard this as beneath their dignity. There's a good old proverb which says: "You can learn as long as you live." But the whole trouble with you, that is to say with some of you old army-leaders, is that you don't want to learn. You're so infected with conceit you think you know all there is to know. That, Comrade Gorlov, is your chief failing.

GORLOV: (*Stands up. A long pause.*) Then I suppose it was you who arranged for my retirement?

GAIDAR: Unfortunately it wasn't. I've worked smoothly with you. I've signed and sealed and discussed with you, but I never allowed anything to interfere with the friendly relations between us. In fact, I haven't been giving a real Party lead. They gave me a dressing down that I'll remember for the rest of my days. And I thoroughly deserved it.

GORLOV: I'm obliged to you for your frankness. Well, orders are orders. As a soldier, I'm accustomed to obey them. We'll see how you get on without me. (*He puts on his cap and greatcoat.*) You'll regret this, but it'll be too late then.

GAIDAR: It's no use trying to frighten us. Bolsheviks aren't easily frightened. Nobody is indispensable. Lots of people have tried to frighten us, but they've been discarded on history's rubbish heap long ago. The Party remains strong as steel.

A pause.

GORLOV: And may I ask to whom you order me to hand over command?

GAIDAR: You'll be informed later. We shall send for you.

GORLOV: Very good.

He salutes and goes out by the side door. The telephone rings. GAIDAR picks up the receiver.

GAIDAR: Hullo, yes? Krikun? You're the special correspondent? Wait a bit. You were the guy who criticized our front-line paper for publishing an article on Communications? Then get this straight. This is Gaidar, member of the Military Council of the front, speaking. Listen! You get the hell out of here, do you understand? If you're found hanging around on the territory of our front tomorrow, I'll make you squeal like a weasel. (*He hands down the receiver.*)

Enter MAJOR-GENERAL KHRIPUN, carrying a large parcel.

KHRIPUN: So you're back, Gaidar. Well, how goes it? Has the Commander gone out?
GAIDAR: He's coming right away. (*He presses the button.*)

Enter the ADJUTANT.

GAIDAR: Ask Major-General Ognev, Commander of the front, and Major-General Kolos to come in.
KHRIPUN: You mean General Gorlov, don't you?
GAIDAR: I mean exactly what I said. Carry out the order, please.
ADJUTANT: Very good.

He goes out.

KHRIPUN: What's the meaning of all this? (*The parcel drops out of his hands. There is a crash of broken bottles.*)
GAIDAR: (*Going up to him.*) What's this?
KHRIPUN: A little drop of brandy. How very unfortunate. We might have drunk to the health of the new Commander. Oh, well, there's more where this came from.
GAIDAR: Clear up that mess and then clear out.
KHRIPUN: Very good, very good, very good! (*He picks up the parcel and hurries out.*)

Enter OGNEV, followed by KOLOS.

GAIDAR: Major-General Ognev! It gives me great pleasure to hand to you on behalf of Comrade Stalin this order appointing you Commander of the front. (*He hands the order to OGNEV. OGNEV reads it. So does KOLOS.*)
OGNEV: But I'm so young.
GAIDAR: Stalin says that talented young generals have got to be promoted more boldly to leading positions on a level with the veteran commanders, and that the men to be promoted are those who are capable of waging war in the

modern way, not in the old-fashioned way, men who are capable of learning from the experience of modern warfare, capable of growing and developing.

KOLOS: Volodya, my dear chap. I beg your pardon. (*He straightens himself up.*) Comrade Commander of the front, take a look at an old man like me, and you'll realize how right it is. (*He embraces* OGNEV.)

THE END

Vasily Tyorkin

Aleksandr Tvardovsky (1942–1945)

VASILY TYORKIN BECAME A WARTIME FOLK HERO TO THE TROOPS BECAUSE OF HIS EARTHY LANGUAGE, HIS CENTER OF WARMTH AND COMEDY AROUND THE FIELD MESS, HIS SKEPTICAL ATTITUDE TOWARD OFFICIAL HEROISM, AND HIS UNALLOYED AUTHENTICITY. READ OVER THE RADIO BY DMITRY ORLOV, THE POEM WON A HUGE AUDIENCE DURING THE HARD WINTER OF 1942. TVARDOVSKY (1910–1971), A MAN OF PEASANT STOCK, WAS A WAR CORRESPONDENT AND LATER BECAME FAMOUS AS THE EDITOR OF *Novyi Mir.*

BIVOUAC: CHAPTER I

"He had genius, some old chap:
Found a way of boiling
Soup with never spill or slop
While the kitchen's rolling.
First, soup piping hot, and then
Kasha for your mess-tin.
Yes, he was a bright old man,
There can be no question!

"Dish us out a spoonful more.
Here, let's have another!
This is not my only war,

It's my second, brother!
One more dab—it's only fair."

Cook is slightly startled.
"Well, we've got a right one here.
This new lad's an eater."
Slaps some extra on his plate,
Growls, but not in anger,
"Better join the Navy, mate,
If you're always hungry."

"Thanks, but that would never do.
Tyorkin in the Navy.
Let me be a cook like you.

Translation from *Vassili Tyorkin: A Book about a Soldier,* trans. Alex Miller (Moscow: Progress Publishers, 1975), pp. 13–25, 251–263.

Always in the gravy."
And he sits beneath a tree,
Shoulder hunching over.

"One of us!" the lads agree,
Winking at each other.

All the regiment now snores
Full of evening rations,
Number One Platoon ignores
Army Regulations.
Leaning up against a tree,
See Vasily Tyorkin
Dishing out most generously
Wisdom and makhorka.[1]

"No need for preliminaries;
I'm not one of your recruits,
And I've worn out in the service
Many a pair of Army boots.
Brand-new uniforms and rifles,
Straight off to the front, that's you.
But can any of you soldiers
Tell me what's a *sabantu?*"

"*Sabantu?* Dunno. Or maybe
It's Mongolian for booze?"
"Don't show up your ignorance, matie.
There's three sorts of *sabantus*.
Air-raid warning. Helter-skelter
To the nearest ditch for shelter.
You'll survive it. Don't get blue.
That's a **little** *sabantu*.

"Have a breather. Get some food down.
Smoke. So that's an air raid! Pooh!
Then old Jerry starts a showdown
With a mortar *sabantu*.

"This time, all those bangs and whizzes
Really scare the pants off you.
But remember, brother, this is
Just a **medium** *sabantu*.

"*Sabantus* teach you a lesson.
Fritz gets rough and so should you.
Quite a different proposition
Is a **super-***sabantu*."

———————
   1. Shag tobacco.

Tyorkin pauses here, delaying,
Cleans his mouthpiece for a bit.
Winks at someone, as if saying,
"Just a moment. Wait for it!.."

"Up you get as day is dawning,
Take a look and—suffering cats!
German tanks—a thousand—coming..."
"German tanks—a thousand? Rats!"

"Listen, would I fool you, brother?
No sense trying anyway."
"How come all those tanks together?"
"Well, all right. Five hundred, say."
"Still too many tanks. You've blundered.
Needn't try to scare us, son."

"Say, three hundred, or two hundred...
Well, if you insist—just one."

"Like it tells you on the poster,
'Don't dash into scrub or grain!'
Though your tank may look a monster,
He's stone-deaf and blind, that's plain."

"Sure! Down in a ditch you're lying,
And your heart goes pit-a-pat.
Since he can't see where he's going,
Suddenly he'll squash you flat.

"Don't show off your ignorance, matie,
Don't talk such a lot of rot.
Sabantu seems nothing, maybe,
But a word—and yet, and yet

It can smack you on the noddle
Otherwise known as the bonce.
(Got some baccy, anybody?)
We'd a laddie with us once."

And they hang on every word
Scared to lose a minute
Good to have a wag like him
Serving with the unit.

In the forest dark and grim,
When the cold winds bite you,
Good to have a lad like him
Marching there beside you.

And they ask him, all polite
"Tell another yarn which
We could end on for the night
Vasily Ivanych."

Still the night and damp the ground
Campfire embers fading...

"No lads. Time for kipping down
Organise your bedding."

Face half-buried in his arm,
Flat out on his stomach
Tyorkin settles, snug and warm
On a grassy hummock.

Damp his heavy greatcoat feels.
Fine rain drizzling lightly;
Sky for roof and trees for walls
Tree-roots hurting slightly.

But he never gives a sign
That he's feeling restless.
You would think him bedded down
On a feather mattress.

Then he gives his coat a hitch,
Since his back feels colder;
Silently, he starts to bitch,
Just like any soldier.

On the damp ground lying prone,
Very tired and weary,
Just as in his bed at home
Sleeps my gallant hero.

Cold or hungry, he's adept,
Sleeping to some purpose;
Catching up when underslept,
Storing up a surplus.

But there's one thing, while he's resting,
Spoils his sleep some nights at least:
And that's how he left the Western
Border-line, retreating East.

How he trudged, did Private Tyorkin,
Through his homeland in retreat,
Verst on verst, with tunic soaking,
Aching heart and aching feet.

Vast and boundless is our homeland,
And no matter where you stray,
It is yours, it's your own land,
You belong there anyway.

Tyorkin snores. There's no more to it.
He just takes things as they come.
"I belong, and well I know it.
Russia needs me. Here I am!"

Sleep. Forget the summer's sorrow.
Worrying's no good to you.
Maybe dawn will bring tomorrow
Yet another *sabantu*.

And the men sleep on the ground
Underneath the pine trees,
While the rain comes drizzling down
On the lonely sentries.

Pitch-black night. The sentry there
Stands in some dejection.
Then he grins from ear to ear
At some recollection.

Sleep is banished right away.
Yawning turns to laughter.

"Now that Tyorkin's come to stay,
Things'll be much better."

Tyorkin, who might he be, pray?
No need to be chary:
He's a fellow, you might say,
Rather ordinary.

Still, he's really quite a lad,
Got something about him.
There's no Army company
Or platoon without him.

Is he handsome of aspect?
No need to be chary:
We must answer with regret,
Frankly, no, not very.

Not so tall as soldiers go;
But true hero's mettle
During the Karelian show
He displayed in battle.

And we really don't know why
(Not that we would meddle)
Vasya Tyorkin's bravery
Didn't rate a medal.

Shall we give this one a miss?
It would be much fairer
Just to say that the Honors List
Had a printer's error.

Never mind what's on your chest,
Look ahead and keep abreast!

June—called up. July—in action.
Tyorkin's in the wars again.

"Contrary to expectation,
Still no bullet with my name.

"In the fighting I was wounded
By a fragment—just a nip.
And three times I was surrounded,
And three times I gave the slip.

"And though feeling mildly nervous,
I've come through (and it was dire)
Indirect and cross, as well as
Overhead and triple fire.

"To the long route-march accustomed,
Often on the dusty road
I've been partially dispersed, and
I've been partially destroyed."

But he's still
Alive and kicking:
Kitchen—camp-site—battle station.
Gaily eating, drinking, smoking,
Whether waiting or in action.

When you think you can't be winning,
Don't give up, but look ahead.

This is only the beginning,
Now the story starts instead.

DEATH AND THE SOLDIER: CONCLUSION

As the battle din receded
Over the hills and far away,

Tyorkin, lonely and unheeded,
In the snow abandoned lay.

Blood and snow to ice had hardened
Underneath him. Stealthily,
Death stooped over him and whispered:
"Soldier, come along with me.

"I am now your own dear true-love,
And we haven't far to go.
I shall make the blinding blizzard
Hide your trail with sifting snow."

Tyorkin shuddered as he froze there
On his ice-encrusted bed.
"I don't need you here, Kosaya,[2]
I am still alive, not dead."

Laughing, Death stood lower, saying:
"Here, young fellow, that will do.
Though you live, your hours are
    numbered.
I know better far than you.

"As I passed, my deathly shadow
Touched your cheeks so young and fair,
And you haven't even noticed
How the snow is settling there.

"Do not fear my shades of darkness,
Truly, night's no worse than day..."

"What d'you mean? Just what exactly
Are you after, anyway?"

Here Death almost seemed to falter.
And she even half withdrew.
"I ask little, almost nothing...
This is what I want of you:

"Just a token of agreement
That you're weary of this world,
That you pray for Death to free you..."

"Sign my name then, in a word?"
Death fell thoughtful:
"You could say that—
Sign for everlasting peace."
"Go! I sell my life more dearly."
"Don't you bargain, lovey, please!

_____
2. Death the Squint-Eyed. Female in Russian.

"What's the use? Your strength is failing."
Death drew closer, bent down low.
"What's the use? Your lips are freezing.
Cold your teeth..."
"The answer's: No."

"Just look yonder. Night is falling.
And the skyglow heralds frost.
There's no point in freezing slowly,
While my precious time is lost..."

"I can wait."
"You foolish fellow.
You can only come to harm.
I could wrap you up in sheepskins
And you'd be forever warm.

"Ah, you trust me! Look, you're weeping.
Now you feel more drawn to me."

"Lies! It's from the cold I'm crying,
And not from your sympathy."

"Happiness or pain—what matter?
Savage is this frost. The snow
Swirls across the open meadow.
No, they'll never find you now...

"Even if they come to fetch you,
It will be too late. You'll freeze.
You'll be sorry that they didn't
Leave you here to die in peace."

"Death, you play a cat-and-mouse game."
Painfully he turned away.
"Me, I want to go on living.
I'm still much too young to die."

"Get up, then! You'll still regret it,"
Death continued with a leer.
"Start again from the beginning—
Cold, fatigue, pain, dirt and fear...
Friend, just give a simple verdict:
Is all that worth struggling for?"

"Verdict? There's no court of justice
Where a man can sue a war."

"Worse—you'll miss your home and family,
You'll be simply worried sick."

"First of all, I'll get the job done:
Beat the Hun. And then go back."

"Granted. But suppose you do, then?
What's the point in it for you?
All the land's been stripped stark naked,
Ravaged, looted, plundered, too.
Just a shambles..."

"I'm a worker.
I'd pile in and get things done."
"No house left."
"I'd build a new one."
"And no stove..."
"I'd soon make one.
Jack-of-all-trades out of boredom,
Game for anything—that's me."

"Let a poor old woman finish:
If you've lost an arm, maybe,
Or in some such way been crippled,
Even you will cease to care."

For the Man, this argument with
Death was more than he could bear.
Still the blood was flowing freely,
And his limbs were growing stiff.

"Listen, Death, I might be willing,
But there's just one single *if*."

Tortured by the cruellest yearning,
Lonely, helpless, weakening,
Half beseeching, half reproaching,
Tyorkin started bargaining:

"Better and worse men than I am
May have lost their lives in war,
But, when all the fighting's over,
Will you grant me one day more?"
On that day of celebration,
Festival of world renown,
May I hear the victory salvo
Thunder over Moscow town?
Will you let me join the living
As they throng the streets outside?

Tap a certain cottage window
In my native countryside?
When my folks step through the doorway,

"Death, O Death, before I go,
May I say a word of greeting?
Half a word?"
"The answer's *No*."

Tyorkin shuddered as he froze there
On his ice-encrusted bed.

"Then be gone from me, *Kosaya*,
I am still alive, not dead.

"I shall weep, shall howl with torment,
Die forgotten in this field,
But of my own will and choosing,
Know that I shall never yield."

"I'll never find you a purer motive,
If you'll give the sign. Fair's fair."

"Wait! They're coming for me. Searching.
From the hospital."
"Fool! Where?"
"Yonder, down that snowy footpath..."

Death laughed long, as at a joke.
"That's the burial detail coming."
"Never mind. They're living folk."

Soft snow crunching, two approaching,
Clang of crowbar hitting spade.

"Here's another one. We'll never
Get 'em done by nightfall, mate!"

"And the day's been heavy going.
Mate, give us a twist of shag.
Let's sit down here on this dead 'un,
And we'll have a crafty drag."

"Would be better if we ate first—
Cabbage soup—a mess-tin full."
"And a snifter from a hip-flask."
"More than that—A good long pull."
"Two long pulls."
                    Albeit feebly,
Tyorkin found his voice and said:
"Just get rid of that old woman,
I am still alive, not dead."

Both men stare. Would you believe it!
He's alive, as they can see.

"How about that?"
"Get him back to
Hospital immediately."

"Happens one time in a thousand!"
But they take it in their stride.
"One thing if it's just a body—
This here's got a soul inside."

"Only just."
"Say that again, chum!
You're near frozen stiff, you know.
We'd have sent you to the People's
Commissar for Down Below."

"That'll do. Don't keep him waiting.
Chop his coat free. Careful, mind!
Lift him up."
                    And then Death muttered:
"Still, I'll follow on behind.

"Yokels, both of them; they're used to
Duties of a different kind.
Fools!" she thought. "They'll jolt and jar
    him.
In the end, he'll still be mine."

Two stout belts and two long shovels.
And two greatcoats, end to end.
"Soldier, careful with your comrade."
"Off we go. Chin up, my friend!"

And the two men somehow manage
Not to shake him needlessly.
With solicitude they bear him,
While Death tags along close by.

And the road's no road, but rather
Virgin land waist-high in snow.
"Hey, it's time you had a breather,
Fellers..."
                    "Ah, but don't you know,
My dear fellow," says one bearer,
"There's no need to worry, mate.
You're a live 'un that we've got here.
Dead, you would be twice the weight."
Then his friend:
"That's common knowledge.

Live 'uns hurry," added he.
"But a dead 'un, he's already
Home—wherever that may be."

It depends on how you see it,
They decided in the end.
"Here, you've only got one mitten.
Take mine while it's warm, my friend."

As she watched them from the sidelines,
Death was forced to think, at length:
"Why, they're thick as thieves together,
All the living. It's their strength.
I can only strike a bargain
When they're on their own, and so,
I suppose I must postpone it."

And Death, sighing, let them go.

Dark Is the Night
N. Bogoslovsky and V. Agatov (1943)

THE 1943 MOVIE *TWO WARRIORS* STARRED MARK BERNES AS A
BUBBLY AND TALKATIVE "SOUTHERN" TYPE AND BORIS ANDREEV
AS THE STRONG AND SILENT ARCHETYPICAL GREAT RUSSIAN (A
ROLE HE REPEATED IN MANY FILMS). DURING THIS BATTLEFIELD-
CUM-ROMANCE FILM, BERNES SANG "DARK IS THE NIGHT" IN THE
DUGOUT AGAINST THE BACKGROUND OF HIS FELLOW SOLDIERS.
THE CONTRAST BETWEEN THE DARK AND DANGEROUS WAR ZONE
OF THE STEPPE AND THE PICTURE OF WIFELY FIDELITY AT HOME
FAR AWAY FIT PERFECTLY WITH THE MELODY. THOUGH IT WAS
DENOUNCED AFTER WAR FOR ITS "ESCAPISM AND TAVERN MELAN-
CHOLY," THIS CLASSIC SONG IS SUNG EVEN TODAY.

ТЕМНАЯ НОЧЬ

Темная ночь, только пули свистят по степи,
Только ветер гудит в проводах, тускло звезды мерцают
В темную ночь ты, любимая, знаю, не спишь,
И у детской кроватки тайком ты слезу утираешь.

Как я люблю глубину твоих ласковых глаз,
Как я хочу к ним прижаться сейчас губами!

From *Russkie-sovetskie pesni* (Moscow: Khudozhestvennaia literatura, 1977), p. 391.

Темная ночь разделяет, любимая, нас,
И тревожная, черная степь пролегла между нами.

Верю в тебя, в дорогую подругу мою,
Эта вера от пули меня темной ночью хранила...
Радостно мне, я спокоен в смертельном бою,
Знаю, встретишь с любовью меня, что б со мной ни случилось.

Смерть не страшна, с ней не раз мы встречались в степи.
Вот и сейчас надо мною она кружится.
Ты меня ждешь и у детской кроватки не спишь,
И поэтому знаю: со мной ничего не случится.

DARK IS THE NIGHT

Dark is the night, only bullets careen cross the steppe,
On the wires the wind plays its song, while the stars glitter dimly.
I know, my love, you don't sleep in the dark of the night.
And you secretly wipe your tears back near the baby's cradle.

Oh how I love the deep regions of your gentle eyes,
How I long to press my lips upon those eyes.
Dark is the night, and it keeps us, my love, far apart,
The perilous steppe, wreathed in black, stretches out between us.

My faith in you, oh beloved friend of my heart,
Is a faith that has saved me from death by an enemy's bullet.
Life is a joy—I can face mortal battle and know,
Know that you'll greet me with love, whatever should happen.

I fear not death, we have met many times in the steppe,
Even now she is circling above me.
You'll wait for me, and won't sleep while by the crib.
And so I am sure that nothing will happen to me.

Conversation with a Neighbor
Olga Berggolts (1941)

THE POETRY AND MEMOIRS OF BERGGOLTS STAND AS MONU-
MENTS TO THE HARD BLOCKADE WINTER IN 1941–42 LE-

From *The Road to the West: Sixty War Poems,* chosen and translated by Alan Moray Williams and Vivian de Sola Pinto (London: Frederick Muller Ltd., 1945), pp. 25–27.

NINGRAD. READ OVER THE RADIO, HER VERSE FORTIFIED CIVIL
SPIRIT DURING THE CRUSHING FAMINE, AND INSPIRED PEOPLE
THROUGHOUT THE COUNTRY. HUMAN LOYALTY THAT TRAN-
SCENDED CLASS BOUNDARIES AND STOIC ENDURANCE DEFINED
THE WARTIME EXPERIENCE FOR SURVIVORS, AND MADE THIS TER-
RIBLE TIME THE FORGE OF IDENTITY FOR A GENERATION.

December the Fifth, 1941. Fourth month of the blockade. In the preceding weeks air-raid alerts had lasted anything from ten to twelve hours. The Leningrad bread ration averaged 125 to 250 grams.

Dariya Vlasievna, my next-door neighbor,
Let us sit down and talk, we two.
Let's talk about the days of peace,
The peace that we all long for so.

Nearly six months now we've been fighting,
Six months of battle's roar and whine.
Cruel are the sufferings of our nation,
Your sufferings, Dariya, and mine.

O nights of shriekings and of rumblings
And bombs that ever nearer fall,
And tiny scraps of rationed bread
That scarcely seem to weigh at all...

To have survived this blockade's fetters,
Death daily hovering above,
What strength we all have needed, neighbor,
What hate we've needed—and what love!

So much that sometimes moods of doubting
Have shaken even the strongest will:
"Can I endure it? Can I bear it?"
You'll bear it. You'll last out. You will.

Dariya Vlasievna, wait a little:
The day will come when from the sky
The last alert will howl its warning,
The last all-clear ring out on high.

And how remote and dimly distant
The war will seem to us that day
We casually remove the shutters
And put the black-out blinds away.

Let the whole house be bright with lights then,
Be filled with Spring and peacefulness.
Weep quietly, laugh quietly, and quietly
Exult in all the quietness.

Fresh rolls our fingers will be breaking,
Made of dark rye-bread, crisp and fine,
And we'll be drinking in slow sips
Glasses of glowing, crimson wine.

And to you—to you they'll build a statue
And place on the Bolshoi Square;
In firm, imperishable steel,
Your homely form they'll fashion there.

Just as you were—ill-fed, undaunted,
In quickly gathered clothes arrayed;
Just as you were when under shell fire
You did your duties undismayed.

Dariya Vlasievna, by your spirit
The whole wide world renewed shall be.
The name of that spirit is Russia.
Stand and be bold then, even as She.

Good Is Stronger Than Evil
Vasily Grossman (1944)

ANOTHER OF THE GREAT WARTIME LITERARY JOURNALISTS, GROSSMAN (1905–1964) SERVED WITH *RED STAR* AND WROTE WARTIME STORIES SUCH AS THIS ONE, WHICH EVOKES THE BEAUTIES OF THE DENSE BELORUSSIAN FORESTS (THICKER WITH PARTISANS THAN ANY OTHER REGION) AND THE BEREZINA RIVER MADE FAMOUS IN 1812 BY NAPOLEON'S RETREAT. GROSSMAN LATER BECAME BITTER TOWARD SOVIET LIFE AND WROTE A VERY DIFFERENT ACCOUNT OF WAR IN *LIFE AND FATE,* WHICH REMAINED UNPUBLISHED IN HIS LIFETIME.

Translated in *VOKS*, no. 7 (1944), pp. 11–14.

Frequently, on a winding front-line road, in the course of a brief halt, in a momentary encounter with a passerby, in a brief conversation at a village well with the sun-dried crane creaking monotonously, you suddenly see and hear a wonderful thing; you catch a fleeting glimpse of the marvel of the human soul, its strength, its kindness, and its greatness. Sometimes you may hear the homely wisdom of a soldier or a villager, or a canny old woman. Sometimes you may see a sight that brings involuntary tears to your eyes, or a situation that keeps you laughing for days. How much poetry, how much beauty there is in these transient pictures glimpsed in a forest clearing, in the tall rye, under the bronze trunks of pine trees, on the sandy bank of a little river at break of day, in the glow of a sunset, in the light of the moon. And sometimes the sight you see will shake you, will drain the blood from your heart, and you will know that the fearful memory will haunt you forever, until the very hour of your death.

But the surprising, the dreadful thing is that the moment you sit down to write your story, for some reason or other all that you have lived through and have seen refuses to let itself be put down on paper. You write about a tank corps, about heavy artillery, about a break in the enemy's defenses, and suddenly you see an old woman conversing with a soldier, or a young pony standing on unsteady legs near the body of its slain mother, or bees swarming on the branch of a young apple tree in a hot village while a barefoot old Belorussian crawls out of a slit-trench where he has been hiding from enemy shells and begins to tend the bees, while the other villagers watch him. How much can be read in the sad, thoughtful eyes of these people! In such trifles is revealed the soul of the people. In them is reflected the war with all its triumphs and torment, and its glory won through much suffering.

The Belorussian landscape is both like and unlike the Ukrainian landscape, and similarly like and unlike are the countenances of the Belorussian and Ukrainian peasant.

The Belorussian landscape is a sad watercolor in gentle, restrained tones. Everything that is here can be found in the Ukraine as well—the marshes, streams, orchards, forests, groves, red sands, and the dust on the roads. But the Ukrainian landscape lacks the dull sadness. Ukrainian faces lack the Belorussian pallor, and their clothes are not so uniformly gray and white. The Belorussian land is more miserly and marshy. Nature here has not yielded so many flowers, such fertility and abundance; the people do not express such gaiety and color in faces and clothing.

But sometimes when you see a group of Belorussian partisans emerging from the forests weighted down with grenades, with German tommy-guns in their hands and cartridge belts around their waists, you see how rich the Belorussian people are in love for their land and for liberty.

Our truck drove into a village. A few women in white kerchiefs, some urchins, an old man without a cap were standing about a lad in a torn jacket who had placed a German tommy-gun on the ground beside him and was digging the earth with a pick-ax. We supposed he was digging a grave.

We had already seen innumerable white crosses crudely stuck into the earth without even a first layer of dust to mar their newness. We had seen innumerable open graves and tall, bearded old men of Biblical solemnity bearing coffins in their hands. By these white crosses and open graves we had followed the route of the Germans.

We wondered whom this lad was burying—a sweetheart, or perhaps a sister?

But it was not death that had brought the people together here. In 1941, just after his graduation from elementary school, this village youth had buried his textbooks and gone to the woods to join the partisans. Today, three years later, he was digging his books out again. Was not this a beautiful symbol: a partisan lad who laid his tommy-gun in the dust raised by advancing armies that he might retrieve the soggy yellow pages of a schoolbook. His name was Anton. Let the Belorussian academicians, the writers and professors hasten to him. He is waiting for them.

Our machine was already driving on—hastening to catch up with the advancing division. But how could we hope to find our old Stalingrad friend here, in the dust and the smoke, amid the roar of engines, the grinding of caterpillar treads, the creaking of long baggage trains—moving westward, and in the eastward-moving stream of barefooted children and women in white kerchiefs now returning home after having been driven off by the Germans.

In order to avoid stops and inquiries, people told us an easy way to identify the division we were looking for: harnessed to one of the wagons of the artillery regiment was a camel named Kuznechik (Grasshopper). This native of Kazakhstan had traveled the whole way from Stalingrad to Berezina. The liaison officer always looked first for Kuznechik if they were in search of the staff, and they advised us to likewise find the staff, which was moving night and day.

We laughed at their advice and rode on.

In this vast stream everything might seem strange to the outsider, and he might feel himself lost amid these thousands of strange people. But after a while, this outsider would note with surprise that all those who were moving ahead were acquainted with each other.

Here was an infantry lieutenant leading his platoon by a side path. He waved a hand to a young man in a helmet and overalls sitting astride a self-propelled gun, and the latter smiled back to him, shouting a remark that was lost in the noise of the caterpillar treads. Here was a transport man in a faded cap, with eyebrows, lashes and mustache gray with dust, shouting to the driver of a towing car, as dusty and begrimed as himself. The driver, although he heard nothing, nodded his head in reply.

And the two lieutenants who were riding with us in our truck kept commenting as they pointed to passing automobiles:

"There's the Major from the anti-tank regiment in that jeep. Anichka, don't lean over, you'll fall off. Look, there's Lyuba from the liaison company. Goodness, how fat she's gotten! Nikitin, are you out of the hospital and back again so soon?"

For three years these people had been fighting shoulder to shoulder, and their friendship became evident in these momentary encounters. It was a friendship of blood binding together all these dusty, rowdyish, sunburned officers, sergeants, corporals, and privates with medals and wound stripes on their breasts.

We drove into a forest. At once everything seemed hushed as our truck followed the narrow path. Under the spreading boughs of huge oak trees stood three attractive women. Bright sun spots and the shadows of filigreed foliage fell on their heads and shoulders. How lovely was this quiet summer hour, but how bitterly did these women weep at a chance remark uttered by our driver: "How's life treating you, ladies?"

In almost every village we heard of the grief endured by Belorussian mothers.

About two weeks before the battles, the Germans began to gather together all the village children from eight to twelve years of age. They said they were going to teach them. But soon it became common knowledge that the children were being kept in camps behind barbed wire. Their mothers began coming to them from miles around.

"The mothers yearned toward the children and the children clung to the wires," one woman told us.

Then the children suddenly disappeared. Where were they? What had happened to them? Were they slain? Driven off into slavery? Or, as some had it, were they being kept near hospitals for German officers so that their blood could be transfused to wounded Germans?

How to console inconsolable grief?

A few hundred meters further on we saw two fleet shadows disappear among the trees: two girls who had been picking berries were scampering away in fright.

"Hey, there, don't be afraid," our driver called out. "We're not Germans!"

The girls emerged from their hiding place. Covering their mouths with their kerchiefs, they watched our machine pass and held out their baskets full of berries to us.

Again we entered a forest. The first thing we saw was a brown camel harnessed to a cart. This was the famous Kuznechik. A crowd of German prisoners was being led in the opposite direction. The camel turned its ugly head with pendant lips toward them, evidently attracted by the unaccustomed color of their clothes, or by an unfamiliar scent. The camel driver shouted to the convoys: "Give us a couple of Germans. Kuznechik will eat them!" They told us that when under fire, Kuznechik hid in shell and bomb craters. He had already earned three wound stripes and the Stalingrad Defense Medal. Kapramanyan, the commander of the artillery regiment, promised Kuznechik's driver a reward if he brought Kuznechik to Berlin. "Your whole chest will be covered with medals," the commander said seriously, only his eyes smiling.

Following the road indicated by Kuznechik, we drove up to the division we were looking for. I found that many old acquaintances were no longer in the Gurtiev division. Many were gone whom I should never forget because of our personal friendship. Others who were missing would long be remembered for the exploits which had made them famous. Gurtiev himself had perished in the taking of Orel: with his own body he had shielded Commander Gorbatov from an exploding shell. Gorbatov's cap had been spattered with Gurtiev's blood. But I found Colonel of the Guards Svirin, artilleryman Fugenfirov, and sapper Ryvkin still there.

New young men had come to take the places of the departed, and the indomitable spirit of the fallen lived on in them. It was the custom here to present young heroes with the arms of the Stalingraders. Gurtiev's pistol was presented to this son—a lieutenant. The pistol of the daring sapper Brysin was now being worn by his friend Dudnik.

During one battle we were witnesses to the friendship binding those who fought together at Stalingrad. A liaison man came running over to us shouting: "Fugenfirov has been killed at the artillery observation point!" Svirin clutched his head and groaned, and the faces of the people about us paled. Everyone sorrowfully repeated, "No, no. It cannot be!" Fifteen minutes later the news came that Fugenfirov was safe and sound.

Once during the battle for Stalingrad a liaison man named Putilov crawled out to repair the communication lines leading to headquarters. He was gravely wounded, but before he died he clinched the ends of the wires together between his teeth, so that communications could be reestablished through his dead body. Today the spool on which Putilov's wire was coiled is presented like a banner or an order to the best liaison men of the division. And it struck me that the wire spliced by the dead Putilov at the Barricades factory in Stalingrad stretches from the Volga to the Berezina, from Stalingrad to Minsk, across the whole of our vast country like a symbol of the unity and fraternity that abides in our army and among our people.

We spent the night in the forest, in the tent of the division's medical-sanitary battalion. In the morning we saw orderlies carrying a wounded man from one medical tent to another. At the feet of the wounded man lay two kittens rocking sedately to the movement of the stretcher. When we entered the tent we found the wounded lying on stretchers and on the grass, watching a girl orderly teasing the kittens with a fir twig. The kittens did everything expected of them in such cases—they crawled stealthily on their stomachs, advanced belligerently with upthrust, bushy tails, leapt into the air. They collided with each other in the air, rolled on their backs, waved their tails.

I looked at these wounded who had just come from the battlefield. Their tunics and linen were torn and stained with black blood. But their gray, pallid faces were smiling. They were watching something important and significant. They had seen death, and now they were seeing life: for this scene spoke to them of their homes, of their childhood, and of their children. It distracted their attention from suffering and blood.

The girl orderly was the only one who was not smiling. She was busy practicing medicine. It required much tender and subtle feminine solicitude for her to carry this live medicine on the constant marches to positions nine or ten kilometers from the battlefield, just to bring a smile to pale lips.

Captain Ametistov, one of the old-timers in the army, told me that many of the men in Gorbatov's troops were passionately fond of animals. One of the generals carries a dove along with him which "drinks tea," thrusting its bill first into a piece of sugar and then into a saucer of water set before it. The tank commander has a pet porcupine and a tom cat. In the regiments there are trained squirrels and dogs with wounded and healed paws. One commander has even trained a fox which runs away to the forest during the day but comes back to him every night.

And again I wondered what these trifles expressed. A mere whim? The desire for amusement? Or did they not rather express man's transcendent love of life, of nature, of the world, wherein it is free man's duty to destroy the dark forces of evil and be ever a kind and wise master?

We drove into Bobruisk while part of the city was still in flames and the rest lay in smoking ruins.

The road to Bobruisk is the road of vengeance. Our machine had difficulty making headway through the burned and twisted remains of German tanks and self-propelled guns. People were walking over the bodies of the Germans. Bodies—hundreds and thousands of them—paved the road, lay in ditches, under pines, in crumpled ryefields. There were places where vehicles rode right over dead bodies, so thickly did they cover the ground. The dead were continually being buried, but there were so many of them that it was impossible to dispose of them all in one day. It was wearisomely hot that day. Not a breath of wind stirred, and people trudged on and on, holding handkerchiefs to their mouths and noses. The cauldron of death was boiling here. Vengeance—stern, terrible vengeance laid down their arms but had tried to break through to the west along roads cut off by Soviet troops. It was vengeance against those who had drenched the whole earth in the blood of women and children, who had burned and destroyed peaceful dwellings.

At the entrance to flaming Bobruisk, on the low, sandy bank of the Berezina, sat a German soldier wounded in both legs. Raising his head, he gazed at the tank columns crossing the bridge, at the artillery and the self-propelled guns. A Red Army man approached him and dipped a tin into the water. He gave him a drink and walked back to the bridge.

Unbidden, the thought came to mind of what the German would have done in the summer of 1941, when the panzer columns of the Nazi troops crossed this bridge to the east, if one of our men had been sitting wounded on the sandy bank of the Berezina. We know what he would have done. But we are people, and this is why we have vanquished the beasts. The Nazis destroy women, children, and wounded. In that lies their ruin. The highest law of life has sentenced them to destruction. The day is near when the court of the world will sit in judgment upon darkness; when good will prevail over evil. The day of absolute vengeance is near.

Again the road, dust, streams, fields, the barking of tommy guns in the woods.

In a dark, shell-torn shed, the first interrogation of German generals captured the previous evening was in progress. Those being interrogated were Lieutenant-General Haine, commander of the Sixth Division, and the famous executioner, formerly successively commandant of Orel, Karachev, and Bobruisk, Major General Adolph Haman. Here, in this shed, was the end of the "sack."

Haine had an elongated, bald skull. He was in ordinary soldier boots. He wiped the sweat from his red face, smiled, and nodded his head. His voice was hoarse, either from a cold or from the quantities of schnapps with which he had buttressed his courage during his wanderings through the forest. He was verbose and vague in speech, perhaps because he was still drunk, or perhaps because his powers of reasoning and expression were limited. I recalled how a captive German captain had complained only a few hours previous about the unusually low mental level of the

German generals; Hitler had put Nazi corporals in place of experienced generals. And listening to Haine's confused, dull speech, I thought, "The Nazi Hauptmans and Ober-Leutnants[1] certainly have just cause for complaint."

Now Adolph Haman began to reply. He was a short, squatty old man with a big, red face and heavy jowls. Hitler had decorated him with ten or eleven orders and marks of distinction. They hung on his ponderous chest and his ponderous stomach and his ponderous side. It was unpleasant to look at Haman.

There was nothing about his hands, his eyes, his hair, and his speech to distinguish him from other men. But the sight of this man called up images of the disinterred grave where lay the hundreds and thousands of bodies of women and children who had been buried alive, bodies in which anatomists found sand in the lungs. You remembered the ruins of Orel, the city which he had blown up on August 4, 1943; Karachev, which he had wiped off the face of the earth; and Bobruisk, which was still smoking.

It was in this same bass voice to which we were listening that he had given orders to his incendiaries; it was with this same puffy hand that he had signed the order for the mass extermination of helpless children and old people. No, it was fearful to breathe the same air with this inhuman human. As is customary with criminals, he denied everything—his mass murder of Jews, his mass execution of guerilla fighters, his having driven off the population, and the use of violence in general. Only once, in Orel he thought it was, he had had a man executed for a murder committed in jealousy. Had he blown up Orel? Well, everyone knew that he was a soldier and merely obeyed the orders of Schmidt, Commander of the Second Tank Army. Yes, yes, and in Karachev, too, he had merely obeyed the orders of his superiors. And in Bobruisk. Suddenly he stole a quick, frightened glance at his interrogators, the glance of a practiced rogue and assassin, the glance of a coward.

With what disgust, with what morbid curiosity, that lanky tommy-gunner in green puttees and heavy shoes looked at him! No, it was a good thing that the first interrogation was brief and that Haman was already being taken to the rear.

Eleven months ago, at a meeting in Orel, General Gorbatov called upon his men to avenge the destruction of the city by apprehending its destroyer. The Red Army men had carried out his orders.

Our machine sped ever onward through the thick forests. Bobruisk was already far behind us and Minsk was close up ahead. And everything we saw, everything that momentarily flashed before our eyes and disappeared from view, but that would always remain in our memories, everything confirmed our belief that good triumphs over evil, that light is stronger than darkness, that in a just cause man always proves stronger than beasts.

July 1, 1944
First Belorussian Front, *Krasnaya zvezda*

---

1. Captains and first lieutenants.

Immortal

Aleksandr Fadeev (1943)

FADEEV (1901–1956) WAS A CONTROVERSIAL SOVIET LITERARY
FIGURE WHO HEADED THE WRITERS' UNION IN THE REPRESSIVE
YEARS 1946–1954. HE COMMITTED SUICIDE IN 1956. HIS MOST
FAMOUS NOVELS ARE *THE ROUT* (1927), A CIVIL WAR TALE, AND
THE YOUNG GUARD, FOR WHICH THIS PIECE WAS A PRELIMINARY
SKETCH WRITTEN ORIGINALLY FOR RADIO. IT IS BASED ON A REAL
EVENT AND REAL PEOPLE — THE KOMSOMOL UNDERGROUND OF
KRASNODON — ALTHOUGH FADEEV'S TEENAGED CHARACTERS
ARE GREATLY IDEALIZED. AFTER THE WAR, THE AUTHOR HAD TO
REVISE THE BOOK SEVERAL TIMES TO MEET PARTY MANDATES;
BUT IT REMAINED POPULAR AND WAS THE SUBJECT OF A WELL-
KNOWN MOVIE (1948), IN WHICH THE TOUGH KID SERGEI TYU-
LENIN (PLAYED BY SERGEI GURZO) BECAME A KIND OF CULT
HERO FOR URBAN YOUTH.

"Entering the ranks of the Young Guard, I solemnly swear before my comrades-in-arms, before my much-afflicted homeland, before the entire nation:

"I will unquestioningly fulfill any task assigned me by a senior comrade.

"I will keep all that concerns my work in the Young Guard the deepest secret. I swear to take merciless revenge for all our burned, razed cities and villages, for the blood of our people, for the thirty heroic miners who died martyrs' deaths. And if my life must be sacrificed for that vengeance, then I will surrender it without a moment's hesitation.

"Blood for blood! A death for a death!"

This oath of loyalty to the motherland and to fight to the last breath for its liberation from the German aggressors was given by members of the underground Komsomol organization the Young Guard in the city of Krasnodon, Voroshilovgrad Region. They swore it in the fall of 1942, standing across from one another in a small hut, while a piercing autumn wind howled above the enslaved and devastated lands of the Donbass. The small city was wrapped in fog; Germans were billeted in the miners' homes. That night traitorous policemen and Gestapo executioners plundered the apartments of citizens and ran wild in the torture chambers.

Pravda, 15 September 1943, p. 3.

The oldest of those who took the oath was nineteen, and the main organizer and inspiration, Oleg Koshevoi, was only sixteen.

During our people's worst tribulations, the youngest generation of those who fight for the freedom and happiness of our homeland repeated an oath that had reverberated many years before from the tribune of the Second Congress of Soviets.

"We swear to you, Comrade Lenin, that we will spare no effort to fulfill this, your testament, with honor."

The open Donets steppe is grim and unhospitable, particularly in the late autumn, or the winter, with its icy winds, when clods of the black earth freeze together. But this is our Soviet earth, steeped in our blood, settled by the mighty and glorious clan of coal miners, which gives energy, light, and warmth to our great motherland. The freedom of this land was defended by its best sons, headed by Klim Voroshilov and Aleksandr Parkhomenko, during the Civil War. It gave birth to the wonderful Stakhanovite movement, which transformed the face of our land. Soviet man has penetrated the depths of the Donets earth, and powerful factories have sprouted upon its inhospitable face. There are the pride of our technical thought, socialist cities bathed in light, and our schools, clubs, theaters, where Soviet man has bloomed and revealed his spiritual strength. And this same ground was trampled by the enemy, the German degenerates. They went along it like a tornado, like the plague, plunging cities into darkness, turning schools, hospitals, clubs, and nurseries into barracks, into stables, into Gestapo torture chambers.

Fire, rope, bullets, and the axe—the terrible weapons of death—became the constant companions of Soviet people. Soviet people were doomed to torments unthinkable from the viewpoint of human reason and conscience. It's enough to say that in the city park of Krasnodon the Germans buried thirty miners alive for refusing to register with the German "employment bureau." When the city was liberated by the Red Army and they began to dig up the victims, they were still standing up in the ground: first the heads were uncovered, then the shoulders, trunks, arms.

Innocent people were forced to leave their homes, to hide. Families were broken up. "I bade my father farewell, and tears streamed from my eyes," says Valya Borts, a member of the Young Guard. "It was as if an invisible voice were whispering: 'This is the last time you'll see him.' He left, and I stood there until I couldn't see him anymore. This man had a family, his own corner, shelter, children, and then, like a stray dog, he must wander. How many people have been tortured, how many shot!"

Young people, who avoided registration by every means possible, were taken by force and sent off to slave labor in Germany. Truly heart-rending scenes could be seen then on the streets of town. The rough shouts and curses of the police mixed with the sobbing of fathers and mothers who had their sons and daughters torn away from them.

And with the terrible poison of a lie, spread by vile little German papers and leaflets, about the fall of Moscow and Leningrad, and the death of the Soviet order, the German degenerates tried to corrupt the hearts of Soviet people.

People of the older generation who stayed in Krasnodon to organize the struggle against the German occupiers were soon exposed by the enemy, and they perished or were forced to hide. The weight of organizing the struggle fell on the shoulders of young people. Thus, in the fall of 1942 the underground organization Young Guard was formed.

This was our Soviet youth—the same that grows around us and is brought up in Soviet schools and Pioneer detachments, Komsomol organizations. The enemy tried to exterminate the spirit of freedom in them, the joy of creative work that the Soviet system inculcates. And in answer to that, young Soviet people proudly held their heads high.

Freedom-loving Soviet music. It is closely linked with Soviet youth, and always echoes in its heart.

"Once Volodya and I were going to visit Grandpa in the village of Sverdlovka. It was pitch black outside. German transport planes were flying overhead. We're walking through the steppe. Nobody around. So we sing "The dark hills are sleeping. A young man walked into the Don Steppe." Then Volodya says: "I know where our soldiers are.""

"He began to give me the report. I threw myself on him and hugged him."

These simple memories of Volodya's sister Osmukhina cannot be read without emotion.

The organizers and leaders of the Young Guard were Oleg Vasilevich Koshevoi, born 1926, Komsomol member from 1940; Ivan Aleksandrovich Zemnukhov, born 1923, Komsomol member from 1938; and Sergei Gavrilovich Tyulenin, born 1925, Komsomol member from 1941. Soon the three patriots drew new members into the organization: Ivan Turkenich, Stepan Safonov, Lyuba Shevtsova, Ulyana Gromova, Anatoly Popov, Nikolai Sumsky, Volodya Osmukhin, Valya Borts, and others. Oleg Koshevoi was elected commissar. The staff designated Ivan Vasilievich Turkenich, a Komsomol member since 1940, as commander.

These young people, who had never known the old order and, naturally, had no underground experience, managed in a few months to disrupt the work of the German subjugators and inspired the resistance of Krasnodon and the surrounding villages: Izvarino, Pervomaika, and Semeikino, where branch organizations were formed. The organization grew to seventy people, then numbered over one hundred: the children of miners, peasants, and civil servants.

The heritage of the great, immortal revolutionary school of Lenin and Stalin can be felt in the organization's character, in its methods, and in its common spirit. The Young Guard distributed hundreds and thousands of leaflets; in bazaars, in the movie theater, in the club. Leaflets turned up at police headquarters and even in the pockets of policemen. The Young Guard set up four radio receivers and informed the population of the daily Inform-Bureau reports.[1]

Despite the restrictions of underground existence, members were inducted into the Komsomol, temporary mandates were handed out, membership fees were collected. As the Soviet army approached, an armed uprising was prepared, and weapons were attained in a variety of ways.

At the same time, shock groups conducted diversions and terrorist acts.

On the night of November 7, Ivan Turkenich's group hanged two policemen. On

---

1. The national information bureau.

the chest of the hanged men they left a sign: "This fate awaits every treacherous dog."

On November 9, on the road from Gundorovka to Gerasimovka, Anatoly Popov's group destroyed a light transport with three high German officers.

On November 15, Viktor Petrov's group liberated seventy-five soldiers and commanders of the Red Army from a concentration camp in the village of Volchansk.

In the beginning of December, Moshkov's group burned three gas trucks on the road from Krasnodon to Sverdlovsk.

A few days after that operation, on the road from Krasnodon to Rovenki, Tyulenin's group undertook an armed attack on guards herding five hundred head of cattle requisitioned from the local residents. They destroyed the convoy and scattered the herd across the steppe.

Members of the Young Guard who were assigned by the staff to take jobs in German offices delay their work through clever maneuvers. Sergei Levashov, who works in the garage, puts three trucks out of order, one after the other; Yury Vitsenovsky causes several accidents in the mine.

On the night of December 5, a valiant troika of Young-Guardists—Lyuba Shevtsova, Sergei Tyulenin, and Viktor Lukyanchenko—conducted a brilliant operation: they set fire to the German employment bureau. The destruction of the bureau and all its documents saved several thousand Soviet people from being herded to Germany.

On the night of November 6, organization members hung red flags on the school building, on the former consumers' union, on the hospital, and on the tallest tree in the city park. "When I saw the flag on the school," says M. A. Litvinova, a resident of Krasnodon, "an instinctive joy and pride came over me. I woke the children and quickly ran across the street to see Mukhina. I found her standing in her underclothes on a windowsill with tears streaming down her gaunt cheeks. She said: 'Maria Alekseevna, this was done for us, the Soviet people. They remember us, our own people haven't forgotten us.'"

The police uncovered the organization because they had enlisted too broad a circle of young people, among whom some were less steadfast.

But undergoing the terrible tortures that the savage enemy inflicted on members of the Young Guard, the moral temperament of our Soviet motherland's young patriots was revealed in untold strength, a temperament of such spiritual beauty that it will inspire many generations of young people to come.

Oleg Koshevoi. A marvelous organizer despite his youth. Dreaminess was combined in him with exceptional practicality and efficiency. He was the inspiration and initiator of a series of heroic enterprises. Tall, broad-shouldered, he breathed strength and healthiness, and took part in many of the most daring attacks on the enemy. When he was arrested, his unshakable contempt enraged the Gestapo. They seared him with hot irons and stuck needles in his body, but his unshakable will never abandoned him. After each "interrogation," gray locks appeared in his hair. His hair was completely gray when he went to his execution.

Ivan Zemnukhov, one of the best-read and educated members of the Young Guard, was the author of a number of remarkable leaflets. His appearance was clumsy, but his spirit was strong, and he was universally loved and respected by the young people. His oratorical powers were famous; he loved poetry and wrote it himself (as, by the way, did Oleg Koshevoi and many other members of the Young Guard). In the torture chamber Ivan Zemnukhov suffered the most beastly agonies and tortures. They hung him up in a noose connected to the ceiling by a special block-and-tackle, poured water over him when he passed out, and hung him up again. Three times a day they beat him with a whip made of electrical cord. The police kept at him for testimony, but they got nothing. On January 15 he and other comrades were thrown down mineshaft #5.

Sergei Tyulenin. This small, nervous, active adolescent was temperamental and desperately daring. He took part in many desperate enterprises and personally destroyed more than a few of the enemy. "He was a man of action," his surviving comrades characterize him. "Didn't like braggarts, chatterboxes, or loafers. He would say: 'You'd be better to do something, let others tell stories about you.'" Sergei Tyulenin was not only tortured cruelly himself, he had to watch his old mother being tortured. But like his comrades, Sergei Tyulenin didn't break.

Here's what Maria Andreevna Borts, a Krasnodon schoolteacher, says about the fourth member of the Young Guard staff, Ulyana Gromova: "She was a tall girl, a well-built brunette with curly hair and a pretty face. Her dark, piercing eyes were strikingly serious and intelligent. She was serious, sensible, intelligent, and educated. She never got angry, like others, and never cursed her torturers. 'They think they can hold their power by terror,' she would say. 'Stupid people! Can you really turn the wheel of history back.'"

The girls asked her to read them "Demon."[2] She said, "With pleasure! I love 'Demon.' What a wonderful poem. Just think, he rebelled against God himself!" It grew completely dark in the room. She began to read in her pleasant, melodic voice. Suddenly, the quiet of dusk was broken by a wild wail. Gromova stopped reading and said: "It's beginning!" The moans and cries grew stronger. The room was as quiet as a graveyard. It continued for a few minutes. Turning to us, Gromova read with a firm voice:

> Sons of the snow, sons of Slavs,
> Why has your courage fallen?
> Why? Your tyrant will perish,
> As all tyrants have before.

Ulyana Gromova underwent inhuman tortures. They hung her up by her hair, carved a five-pointed star in her back, burned her body with a red-hot iron and sprinkled the wounds with salt, sat her on a hot stove. But even in the face of death her spirit never fell, and using the Young Guard code, she tapped out words of encouragement to her friends on the other side of the wall. "Friends! Don't despair! Our soldiers are coming. Stand firm. The hour of liberation is near. Our soldiers are coming. Our soldiers are coming..."

---

2. A romantic poem by Mikhail Lermontov (1814–1841).

Her friend Lyuba Shevtsova was assigned by the staff to be a scout. She established communications with the Voroshilovgrad underground and visited there several times a month, showing extraordinary ingenuity and daring. Wearing her best dress, acting like a "hater" of Soviet power, the daughter of an important industrialist, she penetrated the circles of German officers and stole important documents. Shevtsova was tortured longer than the others. The municipal police got nothing from her and sent her on to the county police sector in Rovenki. There they drove needles under her nails and carved a star on her back. A person of extraordinary *joie de vivre* and spiritual strength, she sang songs on the way back to her cell after the interrogation to aggravate her torturers. Once when she was being tortured and heard the sound of a Soviet plane, she suddenly laughed and said: "Our boys are casting their vote."

On February 7, 1943, Lyuba Shevtsova was shot.

Thus, having kept their vow to the end, the majority of the Young Guard perished; only a few people survived. They went to their death singing Lenin's favorite song, "Tormented by Oppressive Bondage."[3]

Their deeds and moral stature powerfully expressed the best features of people tempered in the Leninist-Stalinist forge. They revived the characteristics of our nation's best people: Dzerzhinsky, Kirov, Ordzhonikidze, and many other glorious Bolsheviks.

The Young Guard was not a unique or exceptional phenomenon on the territory taken by the German occupiers. Proud Soviet people fight back everywhere. And although members of the Young Guard fell in battle, they are immortal, because their spiritual character is that of the new Soviet man, of the people of the land of socialism.

Eternal memory and glory[4] to the Young Guardists—heroic sons of the immortal Soviet people!

Let the blood-stained German dogs tremble before the final judgment—it will strike them no matter where they try to hide from their crimes!

---

3. A prerevolutionary exile song popular with revolutionaries.
4. A phrase from the Orthodox funeral rite.

The Night before Battle
Aleksandr Dovzhenko (1944)

WRITTEN UNDER THE THREAT OF DEFEAT BY THE GERMANS, THIS STORY BY THE UKRAINIAN DOVZHENKO, MORE FAMOUS AS A FILM DIRECTOR, MODERNIZED THE MYTH OF TOLSTOY'S *WAR AND*

Translated in *Soviet Short Stories* (London: Pilot Press, 1944).

PEACE. AN ARROGANT FOREIGN AGGRESSOR, RETREAT INTO THE
DEPTHS OF RUSSIA, AND THE STOIC PATIENCE OF THE SIMPLE
PEOPLE (EMBODIED HERE, AS IN *WAR AND PEACE,* BY A PEASANT
NAMED PLATON) ALL REMINDED RUSSIANS THAT VICTORY WAS
STILL POSSIBLE, PERHAPS EVEN FOREORDAINED. THE STORY ALSO
HAD A MORE PROSAIC TASK: SHIFTING BLAME FOR THE DISASTER
FROM STALIN'S LEADERSHIP TO MILITARY COWARDICE.

"Comrade Commander, tomorrow you're leading us over the top. Now we here, all of us—both the veterans who've been in it for a long time already, and the youngsters, like Ovcharenko here, who are going into their first battle—know that there'll be hot fighting to-morrow and that some of us will never come back. That's right, isn't it?"

Ivan Drobot, a young tankman with an extremely pleasant and modest face, was obviously excited. "Right," answered their famed commander, Petro Kolodub, Hero of the Soviet Union. "Go on, Drobot, what did you want to say?"

"I wanted to ask you, even though they write about you in all the papers and talk about you at meetings as a man who is fearless and tireless, especially as, you'll pardon me for saying, you don't look too strong and are certainly not a giant, I wanted to ask you what is the source of all these things they say about you—and we ourselves know for a fact that you'd come out of hell itself with flying colors; you see, we want you to tell us what you're like, to tell us just unofficially, as if there wasn't a war at all. What is your fighting, or rather, so to say, inner, secret? Maybe I haven't expressed myself very clearly—please excuse me."

Drobot reddened after his long and confused question. It seemed to him that he had expressed himself most unclearly, and this upset him completely.

"No, it's quite clear, Drobot. You put it very well, and expressed yourself most delicately. I'll be only too glad to answer you, especially since I do really have a secret."

Everyone, and there were about thirty officers and men in the dug-out, drew round him and settled down for a long and interesting talk. Their commander knew how to tell a story. They were a splendid lot of men, and Petro Kolodub had become very much attached to them. Putting down his pipe, he waited a moment until there was complete silence.

"It was on the Desna River," began the famous captain, smiling at his memories. "Yes... To put it in a nutshell, an ordinary Ukrainian fisherman, a simple old man in no way different from thousands of others in our Ukraine, turned my whole soul inside out."

"Who among us who came through the whole brunt of last year's German invasion will ever forget that old man? Remember last autumn? Every river was the scene of a regular drama, and the ferrymen were like good river spirits. They were brave, these old men, stern and fearless of death. But they seemed to have some sort of a grudge against us crowding there at the crossings. Sometimes their dislike for us... well, there just seemed to be no end to it. Isn't that so?"

"That's a fact," sighed someone in the dugout.

"Anyway, here's the story."

Captain Kolodub shifted his position so that he was sitting crosslegged—a favorite pose of his ever since the days when he had been a shepherd lad—and, putting his hands on his knees, he looked straight in front of him at his men.

The air in the dug-out was thick with smoke. The men sat in the dim light in every possible position, leaning against one another. They were all different, yet all of one family. All of them were united by the unforgettable and inimitable feeling that in time of war brings your hearts closer together in the face of daily danger, a feeling that remains the finest memory throughout the rest of your life.

The years will roll by, wounds will heal, enemy graves will be plowed under, razed cities and villages will be rebuilt, and much of what happened will become confused in the grey heads, will become tales told and retold, but one thing will remain fixed for all time and never to be forgotten—the lofty and noble feeling of comradeship and brotherhood among the men who fought the German madness and wiped it from the face of the earth.

"We were withdrawing, out of touch with one another, without artillery, retreating eastward day and night. At any moment the enemy pincers might close on us. We carried the wounded on our backs, felt with them, damned everything under the sun, and kept going farther. To tell the truth, there were even some among us who shot themselves in desperation and pride. There were some who threw down their arms and with bitter curses crawled to their cottages, without heart to pass them by."

Kolodub fell silent, lost in thought. Then he continued: "There were only a few of us—fifteen all told, a few tankmen whose machines had been crippled, machine-gunners, political officers, two ground mechanics, a wireless operator, and even a colonel. At that time I was commander of a tank that had remained with the Germans, its motor wrecked. Before the war I had been a gardener who liked to sing songs and was fond of the girls, that's about all I guess."

Captain Kolodub laughed so infectiously here, and at the same time with such irony, that everyone in the dug-out laughed with him.

"We were completely played out. Our legs refused to carry us any further, and it was getting dark. Ahead of us, beyond the village, was a big river. Some of us could not swim. And the Germans were not far off. Someone pointed out the house of the ferryman.

"'Running are you, you sons-of-bitches,' asked Old Man Platon Pivtorak as he came out of the shed with an oar, a net and a wooden bucket. 'I've sure ferried plenty of you across already. Plenty—and all of you strong, healthy, young, and all of you moaning: *Ferry us across, oh, ferry us across...* Savka!' he shouted over to the neighboring cottage. 'Come on, Savka. We've got to take 'em across—seems they're still running. Ha! Come on, hurry up. It's the last of 'em, I hope.'

"Savka came out of his house and stared at us with pretended surprise. He must have been seventy, if he was a day. He was short and had a clipped beard. He looked an awful lot like the icon of St. Nicholas, if you can imagine St. Nicholas with a filthy cap pulled over his ears and a pretty well earth-colored sweater that hung on him like a father's jacket hangs on a kid.

"After Old Man Savka, a sturdy looking youngster came out with a pair of oars.

"'Eh-e-e! Look here, my boys, something cockeyed somewhere,' said Old Man Savka regarding us slyly. 'Your uniforms are new, and look at your shiny leather cases and your belts. Ekk, and you're young yourselves. Maybe you're not heading in the right direction, eh?'

"'Come on, now. Quit it,' said Platon.

"We started out.

"'Don't fret, there's a rowboat all right, and a good one at that,' I whispered to Boris Troyanda, who was always in more of a hurry than any of the others. He could not swim.

"'Do you think they'll take us across? I think we've got to keep our eyes peeled,' said Troyanda, trying to keep a check on his uneasiness.

"'I can't make it out. What're they running for like that?' said Old Man Platon to Savka as they walked down to the river, for all the world as if we weren't there at all.

"'Why're they so scared of dying? Once there's a war on, you don't have to be afraid of death. If you're fated to die, there's no getting away from it anywhere.'

"'Uh-huh!' agreed Savka. 'As the saying goes: there's no hiding from it in a pond and no ducking out of sight behind the oven.'

"'They're not in it heart and soul, the spoiled brats,' said Platon angrily. 'Now take my Levko. Look at how he gave it to those what-do-you-call-'ems at Khalkin-Gol![1] Wiped 'em out to a man! Did you read his letter? He's Colonel Levko Pivtorak now, I understand! But this trash, they're not even men.'

"We walked in silence along the narrow path through the dense willow grove. The old fishermen walked ahead with their nets and oars, deliberately, as if they were setting out on one of their regular fishing trips, apparently completely oblivious to the artillery fire and the roar of enemy aircraft—in a word, all those German fireworks that had tortured us so during all the last days of painful retreat simply did not exist for them.

"'Look here, grand-dad, couldn't you walk a little faster?' Troyanda asked Platon.

"Platon made no reply.

"Restraining himself, Troyanda repeated his question in Ukrainian.

"'No, I can't,' replied Platon. 'Why the devil are the lot of you in such a tearing hurry all of a sudden? I'm too old to be walking fast. I've done all my fast walking.'

"'I say, where is the river? Is it far?'

"'Here it is.'

"And indeed the willow grove came to an abrupt end and we walked out onto the clean sandy shore. Before us lay the broad, quiet Desna. On the opposite shore was

---

1. An anti-Japanese engagement in 1939 on the Manchurian-Mongolian border.

a steep bank, and further to the right again sand and a willow grove. Beyond that was a dark forest, while over the river and back of the woods loomed an evening sky the like of which I had never seen before in all my life.

"The sun had set some time ago. But its rays still rose over the horizon, lighting up the huge masses of cloud moving from the West over the entire sky. The clouds were heavy and somber, altogether inky below, while the very tops, the crowns so to say, almost directly over our heads, seemed to have been dipped in violent blood-red and yellow paint.

"Grandiose, silent streaks of lightning flashed almost incessantly among the huge clouds. And all this was reflected in the water, so that it seemed as though we were not standing on the earth, and as though there were no river, but only some sort of gloomy space between the clouds where we hovered, lost in its enormity like grains of sand.

"The sky was out of the ordinary. It seemed as though nature had entered into a compact with events and was warning us with menacing signs. The fish feared such a night, and surged into the shallows at the shores. Somewhere above us, just under the clouds, German rockets were flaring aloft, writhing like snakes. It was light. The livid gleam of the sinister cloud-tops shed a glow. Guns were thundering in the distance. We stood motionless. There was something solemn and oppressive all about us. We fell silent and stood there in bewilderment, as if we were on the brink of some momentous event.

"'Well, pile in. We'll take you across. What're you standing there for?' asked Platon. He was already near the boat with his oar.

"'We'll take you across all right, and there you'll have to shift for yourselves. You couldn't take care of yourselves so I guess we'll see about getting you over. Running... well, run, devil take your souls. Where do you think you're going? Didn't you ever see a boat before, soldier?' thundered the old man at one of us. We got into the boat in silence, each of us plunged in his own gloomy thoughts.

"'Are you ready, Savka?'

"'Go ahead.'

"'Look at how the clouds've gathered. Akh! What's it all about? Like the Day of Judgment, eh?'

"Old Man Platon stared at the sky and spat on the palms of his hands. Then he took up his oar, and with a mighty push shoved off from the shore. Savka and his grandson took the oars at the side. The boat was old and roomy, all over tar and warped with age.

"I sat beside Platon, gazing at the quiet river and at the shore, at the lowering clouds overhead on the background of the grim sky. I felt as though I were being ferried across to the other world. Shame and despair, an inexpressible sorrow and many other feelings filled and twisted my heart. Farewell, my beautiful Desna!

"Platon's voice roused me from my reveries. He was continuing his conversation with Savka, a conversation that was insulting and bitter for us to hear. Apparently something was bothering him, something that he wanted to think out to the end. It was as if he were thinking aloud:

"'God only knows what it's all about. This morning a fellow comes into my house armed to the teeth, with straps on him, and, let me tell you, not any kind of straps, brand new ones.' 'Uh-huh!' came Savka's voice from behind me.

"'And all that cost a pretty penny.'

"'Uh-huh!'

"'*Get up,*' says he, '*and take me across. You've slept long enough now.*' Three nights I've not slept a wink, but I ferried him over.

"'Yes, not long ago, just before it got dark, Mitrofan and I took a party across. One of them, devil take him, wore glasses, like that one sitting beside you. Rigged up in shiny new straps, too, he was; and waving his revolver about besides, and shouting. '*Take me across,*' he says, '*and make it snappy.*' That's God's honest truth. And as for himself he was shaking all over and his eyes popping out like a fish's, he was that scared. There's a pretty picture for you, may God have mercy on it all.

"'The devil only knows what to make of it.'

"'Yes. Then his comrades butted in. '*What're you insulting the old man for?*' they said. They all but knocked the stuffing out of him. And then everything was quiet. Like now. You just think of it...' Platon broke off and listened to the guns. 'Listen to that! I guess the Germans'll be showing up pretty soon.'

"The German heavy guns were thundering. Frightened wild ducks flew by overhead. '*Take us across, Old Man,*' mimicked Platon angrily.

"'Uh-huh!' Savka broke in. 'And they don't know that in war if you're fated to die then there's no squirming out of it, and no boat will save you. If a bullet won't get you then a louse will, and war will have its own. Over to the left! There's a strong current here.'

"'I am bearing to the left. If my Levko were here with his regiment he would never be retreating, not he. He would turn the boat back and pitch into them, he would!' said Platon, pulling at his oar furiously. 'He wouldn't be running!'

"'Uh-huh! My Demid's like that too. You could burn him with fire or cut him to shreds, but he wouldn't retreat. Not like these here!' said Savka. 'All they think of is saving their skins, and you mark my words the result will be that we'll be spitting blood for a long time to come. After all, we'll have to take it all back again!'

"'Yes, we'll have to,' caught up Platon. 'Can't even begin to think how much land we'll have to take back again. And all that means spilled blood!'

"I looked at Platon and listened with agitation to every word he said. The old man believed in our victory. To me he was the living and formidable voice of our courageous people.

"'But you see, our unit was obliged to withdraw,' began the Colonel tentatively.

"'Rubbish! you simply couldn't fight! That's what I think about your retreat,' said Platon. 'What does it say about war in the Field Regulations? D'you know? It says: If you're aiming at a target, hate what you're aiming at.'

"'And where's your hate?' asked Savka.

"'Yes! And you're afraid to die. That means that you haven't any live hatred in you. None at all!' Platon was all but shouting and had stopped rowing.

"We did not know what to answer.

"'Oh, something's floating down the river. Is it one of ours or a Fascist?' asked Platon as he stretched out his oar to pull in the floating body.

"'A Fascist. May the cholera get you! You're floating already, are you? Ekh, look where he's got to. The Desna! Managed to do it, the pig. And all you people do is ponder and feel miserable. This is no time for feeling miserable.'

"'I tell you, Old Man, I hate Fascism with all my soul!' shouted Troyanda, even rising in his seat with the force of his emotion.

"'Well, that means you've got a small soul,' said Platon. 'There are all sorts of souls, my boy. Some are deep and swift, like the Dnieper, others are like the Desna here, and there is a third sort, that is like a puddle, and sometimes not even a puddle but just a wet spot, like what's left by a bull, if you'll excuse my saying so.'

"'Well, and what if your soul's big but you're nervous?' said Troyanda, taking offence and at the same time angry with himself. He was a witty and resourceful lad, but suddenly he could find nothing to say and all his resourcefulness seemed to have evaporated into thin air.

"'If you're afraid, you just chain yourself to the machine gun and let the enemy have it as long as you're alive, without saying a word,' said Platon. 'Leave it to those who remain among the living to decide later what sort of a nervous person you were. Otherwise it comes out that you've got lots of hatred in you, but even more nervousness and love of yourself. That's why you come running: "Take us across, Old Man!" And you waste your hatred on something else. What's it worth if you don't even know how to die?'

"'Not everyone knows how to do that,' mumbled Troyanda, who hadn't a leg to stand on by now.

"'That's just the trouble. And everyone should know this when the enemy is pushing. Everyone has to eat bread and knows how. And all that you've learned to do is to wag your tongues.'

"'Ho-oo, there! Give us a boat! H-e-ey!' came from the shore we had left.

"'Some more nervous souls hollering away! The Germans can hear them! Can't even wait quietly,' said Savka.

"We continued a while in silence. Platon began to pull hard on his oar. It was obvious that he wanted to say something else, to give vent to his dissatisfaction.

"'Just imagine, Savka, what Stalin thinks of all this. After all, he depended on them, like I do on my Levko, and here they come with their *Old Man, take us across!*'

"'Did you hear Comrade Stalin's speech?' asked Troyanda.

"'No, I didn't,' replied Platon softly and sighed.

"'Yes,' said Savka, 'just think how many years Stalin has been teaching them, Platon. And they're running. Right now he is saying: *What,* he says, *are you doing? Stand firm, don't you dare run! The further you run, the more blood will be spilled. And not only your soldier blood, but the blood of mothers and children.* That's the kind of speech he made!'

"'Comrade Stalin never said that,' declared Troyanda pedantically.

"'Well, if he didn't, he will,' said Savka. 'What does Stalin say? He says what the people think, that's what he says.'

"'I don't know how you feel about it, Savka,' said Platon, 'but, as for me, not only Hitler, but the devil himself couldn't drive me away from the Dnieper or the Desna.'

"'That's easy said, grand-dad. You should wait until you've seen a tank or two,' began Lieutenant Sokol in justification.

"'What if I should?' Platon interrupted him, evidently having no desire to hear us out. 'How many times can this here tank kill you? In any case it's you that will have to smash them, not me. I've done my share of fighting in my day. Now take my Levko at Khalkin-Gol, have you heard what he did to those what-do-you-call-'ems?... Tanks!...' snorted Platon. 'A good stout heart is stronger than any tanks. It always was, is, and will be!'

"I simply couldn't bear to listen to his conversation any longer, so painful was it. He seemed to me at that moment a cruel and unjust old man.

"'Do you really think, grand-dad, that it isn't hard for us? Do you really think that pain and regret aren't tearing our souls, torturing and searing our hearts with the fires of hell?' I flung at him.

"'What's there for me to be thinking about?' retorted Platon, looking straight at me. 'Think yourself! Life belongs to you now, not me. I only want to tell you before you leave: you're pouring your drinks from the wrong bottle. What you're drinking, I see, is sorrow and regret. There's no earthly use to that. It's not your drink, my boys. That's drink for women. What you soldiers need to drink today is the strong drink of wrath against the enemy, yes, a fiery rage. That's your drink. Moaning and groaning are not for you. Being sorry eats into a person like a worm. The people who win through are those who are quick to action and in a passionate rage, not those who go around being sorry!' said Platon and lapsed into silence. He had finally given utterance to his thought. That was his truth. Stern and handsome, he sat there majestically, staring straight in front of him, over our heads.

"Just then a shell fell not far away, raising a huge spout of water.

"'Ho! It'll stun the fish,' came Savka's voice.

"'It'll stun them all right,' said Platon. 'The winter before last they died because of the terrible frosts, couldn't get enough air to breathe. Now the Germans are feeding them with grenades. Everything living in the world, even in the rivers, they're wiping out now... Well, here we are.'

"The boat scraped gently on the river sand. I got out on the bank utterly devoid of feeling and at the same time somehow completely different, new. It was as if the Desna had swallowed up my sorrow, my regret, the desolate despair of the retreat. I looked around me. Great fires were flaring beyond the Desna. And the fiery conflagration somehow lit up my heart in a new way. An intolerable flame fired my whole being. It seemed to me at that instant that if I rushed back to the Desna the very waters would part before me. It's something I shall never forget. We began to take our leave of the old men, hastening into the underbrush.

"'Hold on a minute,' said Platon as he leaned on his oar. 'What do you want us to tell the Fascists? How shall we meet them, how look them in the eye?'

"'Tell them that we shall return. Don't fret, Old Man, we'll come back,' said Troyanda in an endeavor to put heart into him. Platon looked right through Troyanda and spat lightly.

"'Ho-o o-ho-o-o! He-e-ey, there! Let's have the boat!' came from the other shore.

"'Goodbye, and thanks,' said my fellow-travellers softly as they plunged into the willow grove.

"'Get along with you,' said Savka indifferently. Platon said nothing.

"We entered the willow grove. I walked behind the others, thinking of Old Man Platon. Thanks be to him, I thought, that he had no pity upon us, that he did not sprinkle our path with tears, that he struck fire from my heart in the night. Why, I thought the question to myself, are you so bitter and sour at times? And then suddenly I stopped short. Then I turned and ran back to the Desna.

"There was something I had to tell Old Man Platon in farewell. I dashed down to the shore.

"Platon was standing at the water's edge with his oar, like some ancient prophet, motionless, evidently looking after us.

"'Goodbye, grand-dad. Forgive us for not having safeguarded your old age,' I said, choking on the words. 'We shall never...'

"'Beat it! Get out of my sight,' said Platon, not even glancing at me. Over his wrinkled, swarthy cheeks the tears coursed and fell into the Desna.

"That, my friends, is all. That is my whole secret," said Captain Kolodub and lit his pipe. A deep sigh came from the men in the dug-out.

"Now I am a hero of the Soviet Union. I've done for quite a number of the enemy. Many of them I shot down during attacks and no few I've crushed under caterpillar tracks. There have been times, if you'll believe me, when I've felt nauseated at the crunching of German bones. And I've been in a tight fix myself more than once. But wherever the fighting may be, no matter how the enemy whirlwind may storm around me, nothing can ever extinguish the flame that Old Man Platon once kindled in me in that boat. What do our lives mean? What does our blood mean, when our whole country, our whole people is suffering?" The Captain's voice rang like a tocsin.

"When we are in the fight, it seems as if I have a hundred hands, and my wrath and hatred is multiplied a hundred times over!"

Captain Kolodub laughed shortly.

"And yet there is nothing in life I would like so much as to go to the Desna after the war to see Old Man Platon."

"And to tell him that he was mistaken, Comrade Hero of the Soviet Union. Good evening, everybody! How're tricks?" came the jaunty voice of Boris Troyanda from the door. He had been standing there for the past half hour.

"And to take my hat off to Old Man Platon for what he taught me," said the Captain as if he had not heard the newcomer. There was not a sound in the dug-out. No one moved, as if the thoughts of all the tankmen were still far away on the Desna.

"No, Comrade Captain, you won't take your hat off to Old Man Platon," sighed a young tank man.

Everyone turned round to the speaker. It was Ivan Drobot. He was standing in the farthest corner of the dug-out. Somehow he seemed to have been particularly moved by the Captain's story.

"Old Man Platon, Comrade Captain, is no longer among the living," said Drobot. "As soon as you went off into the willow grove and Old Man Platon and Savka returned to their own side, the Germans came running up. They beat the old man terribly for having ferried you across, and wanted to shoot him, when orders came for them to cross to the other shore immediately. Just a stroke of luck. They crammed into the boat. Old Man Platon rowed them out into the middle of the Desna and then he said: 'Savka, forgive me.' 'And you forgive me, too, Platon!' Savka said to him. 'And may God forgive me!' At that they suddenly raised their oars, threw themselves to the right and capsized the boat. Everything went down: machine-guns, the Germans and the old men. Only I managed to swim to our shore."

"And who are you?" Captain Kolodub asked softly.

"I am Savka's grandson. I was the one at the second oar."

"Stand!" came the order from Kolodub.

Everyone rose. For a long minute the family of soldiers stood in silence.

The Captain was pale and solemn. He stood with closed eyes. Then slowly he sank to one knee and everyone followed his example.

"Are you ready for battle?" asked Kolodub, and seemed to tower before the men just as Old Man Platon had towered on the Desna bank.

"We are ready for anything!"

Silence filled the dug-out. It was quiet in the trenches too. Only far away on the horizon the bright sword of a searchlight flashed through the sky.

The Justication of Hate
Ilya Ehrenburg (1942)

EHRENBURG (1891–1967) WAS A PROLIFIC JOURNALIST AND NOVELIST WHO PASSED THROUGH DOZENS OF TRIALS AND SURVIVED THE PURGES, THE SPANISH CIVIL WAR, AND THE FALL OF PARIS TO THE GERMANS. IN WARTIME RUSSIA, HE BECAME THE BEST-KNOWN VOICE OF HATRED TOWARD THE GERMAN ENEMY — HIS CHARACTERIZATIONS OFTEN DESCENDED INTO OUTRIGHT RACISM. HERE ALL OF EHRENBURG'S PERSUASIVE ORATORY IS ON DISPLAY AS HE HOLDS UP PICTURES OF CHEERY PREWAR MOSCOW WITH ITS FIREWORKS IN GORKY PARK, THE WARTIME DEEPENING OF EMOTIONS, THE BONDAGE OF PEOPLE UNDER ARMS, AND THE BARBARISM OF THE GERMANS.

From *We Carry On: Tales of the War,* trans. David Fromberg (Moscow: FLPH, 1942).

Of all the Russian writers the Nazi ideologists show the most forbearance towards Dostoevsky. The scenes of moral torment depicted by the great Russian writer are to the Nazis' liking. The fascists, however, are not very discerning readers; to grasp the genius of Dostoevsky who, in delving into the darkest recesses of the human soul illuminates it with the light of compassion and love, is something beyond them. One German "critic" wrote in a magazine article: "Dostoevsky is the justification of torture." Stupid and vile words. The Hitlerites are making an attempt to justify Himmler by Dostoevsky. They are powerless to understand the self-sacrificing nature of Sonya, the benignity of Grunya. To them the Russian soul is a sealed book.

The Russian by nature is gentle, passionate, easily pacified, ready to understand and forgive. Many French writers of memoirs mention how the Russian soldiers who were in Paris after the defeat of Napoleon carried water for the French women, played with their children, shared their meals with the poor of Paris. Even in those black years when Russia was attacked by a foreign foe the Russians always adopted a benevolent attitude towards prisoners of war. After the defeat of the Swedes at Poltava, Peter the Great had a kind word for the war prisoners. Sauvage, an officer in Napoleon's army, writes in his memoirs of 1812 that the Russians are "good-natured children."

Some ten years as I happened to be in the Transylvanian town of Oradea Mare. What surprised me was the number of people in the stores, cafés and workshops who understood Russian. Many of the inhabitants of this town, it appeared, had been taken prisoner by the Russians during the first World War. All of them had the most pleasant memories of the years they spent in Siberia or Central Russia and spoke at great length about the kind treatment and sympathetic attitude of the Russians. Time and again at the beginning of this war I saw our men chatting peacefully with war prisoners, sharing their tobacco and food with them. How did it happen then that the Soviet people came to abhor the Nazis with so implacable a hatred?

Hatred was never one of the traits of the Russians. It did not drop from the skies. No, this hatred our people now evince has been born of suffering. At first many of us thought that this war was like other wars, that pitted against us mere human beings dressed only in different uniforms. We were brought up on the grand ideas of human fraternity and solidarity. We believed in the force of words, and many of us did not understand that opposing us were not human beings but frightful, loathsome monsters, and that the principles of human brotherhood imperatively demand that we deal ruthlessly with the fascists, that with the Hitlerites one can speak only in one tongue—the tongue of shells and bombs.

The Russians have a song and in it the people have expressed their attitude towards just and unjust wars: "Wolfhounds are justified where cannibals are not." It is one thing to destroy a mad wolf, it is another thing to raise one's hand against a human being. Now every Soviet man and woman knows that we have been attacked by a pack of wolves.

A savage may smash the most exquisite statue, a cannibal may feast on a world-famous scientist who happens by chance to land on an island inhabited by cannibals. But the German fascists are civilized savages and conscientious cannibals.

Looking recently through the diaries of German soldiers I found that one of them who, it appeared, took part in the Klin pogrom, was fond of music and particularly "admired" Chaikovsky. Desecrating the house of the composer that man knew what he was about. Ravaging Novgorod the Germans wrote long winded dissertations on the "architectural beauties of Naugart"—that's how the Germans call Novgorod.

In the pockets of one dead German our men found a pair of baby's knickers spattered with blood and a photograph of his own children. He murdered a Russian child but his own children he undoubtedly loved. To them murder is not a manifestation of an unsound mind but a premeditated act. After slaughtering thousands of children in Kiev one Nazi wrote: "We are annihilating the offspring of a terrible tribe."

Of course, there are good and bad men in the ranks of the German aggressors; but the point is not the psychic qualities of this or that Nazi. The German "good fellows"—those who at home give way to sentimentalities, give pickabacks to the kiddies and feed the German cats with morsels of their rationed hamburgers, murder Russian children with the same pedantry as do the bad Germans. They murder because they have come to believe that only people with German blood are worthy of living on this earth of ours.

At the beginning of the war I showed one Nazi war prisoner a leaflet. This was one of the first leaflets we published and it breathed with the naiveté of a man who had been roused from bed in the dead of night by German bombs. The leaflet stated that the Germans had made a wanton attack on us and were conducting an unjust war. The Hitlerite read it through and shrugged his shoulders: "That does not interest me in the least," he said. The question of justice did not interest him in the least: he was out for Ukrainian pork. It had been dinned into his ears that wars of aggression were a means of making something. He was out for "vital territory" for Germany and "booty" stockings for his wife.

What astounded us was the businesslike and efficient manner in which the Germans robbed. This was not the perniciousness of individual marauders but the flagrancy of a hoodlum soldiery—the principle on which Hitler's army is built. Every German soldier is materially interested in the robber campaign. Personally I would write a very short leaflet for the benefit of Hitler's soldiers, a leaflet containing only five words: "You won't get any pork." This is all they are capable of understanding, all that actually interests them.

In the diaries of the Germans one can find a record of what they rob; they keep an account of the chickens they gobble up and the number of blankets pilfered by them. They pillage and steal without any qualms of conscience as though it was not live people they were stripping but gooseberry bushes. If a woman refuses to hand over her baby's dress to a German soldier—he'll threaten her with his rifle. And if she dares to defend her property—he'll murder her. He does not consider it a crime: he'll as soon murder a woman as go into a forest and break twigs—without thinking twice about it.

Forced to retreat the Hitlerites consign everything to the flames: to them the Russian noncombatant population is as much an enemy as the Red Army. To leave a Russian family without a roof over their heads is considered a military achievement by them. At home, in Germany, they are forced to toe the line, they will not so much as throw a match on the floor or dare to walk on the grass in a public square. In our country they have trampled underfoot entire regions, defiled entire cities, turned museums into latrines and converted schools into stables. This is done not only by clodhoppers from Pomerania or herdsmen from the Tyrol, it is being done by assistant professors, writers, "doctors of philosophy," and "learned counsels" reared by Hitler.

When our Red Armymen—our collective farmers of yesterday—saw for the first time, in the Moscow or Tula regions, entire villages in which only the chimney stacks and dovecotes remained, they thought of their own villages on the Volga or in Siberia. They saw women and children exposed to the bitter frosts, robbed by the Germans of every bit of clothing. And a savage hatred gripped hold of them.

One German general, ordering his subordinates to show no mercy to the civilian population, added: "Sow fear in the midst." Fools and dolts—they do not understand the Russian nature. They sowed not fear but the wind that will reap the storm.

Now everybody in our country knows that this war does not in any way resemble the wars that went before it. For the first time our people have found pitted against them not human beings but vile, malicious monsters, savages, armed with everything, that modern science can give, fiends who act according to rules and regulations and refer to science, for whom the slaughter of infants in arms is the last word of statecraft.

Hate did not come to us easily. Entire cities and regions, hundreds of thousands of human lives—this was the price we paid for it. But now our hatred is ripe, it no longer goes to the head like young wine, it has become cold and deliberate. We have realized that the world is too small a place to hold both us and the fascists. We have realized that there can be no question of compromising or coming to terms, that the question at issue is plain and simple: our right to exist.

And having learnt to hate, our people have not lost the good inherent in them. Need one mention that what they have been through has quickened their hearts. One cannot think without emotion of the mothers of large families who, in our trying times, are adopting orphans and sharing their last with them.

I recall to mind young Lyuba Sossunkevich, a military feldsher. Under enemy fire she rendered first aid to the wounded. The dugout was surrounded by Germans. Revolver in hand she fought single-handed against a dozen German soldiers, defended the wounded men under her charge and saved them from the inhuman treatment and torture that would have been their lot.

Or take the modest work of another Russian girl—Varya Smirnova—who under rifle and trench mortar gun fire delivers letters to the very front lines, guarding them as something most precious. She said to me: "It's only natural... after all everybody's so anxious to get a letter. Life would be so dismal without letters from home."

But the Russians do not evince a deep concern only for their own people. They understand the sufferings of other people, too. What profound human sympathy emanates from the declaration of the women of much-suffering Leningrad to the women of London. How many times have the Red Armymen questioned me about the sufferings of desecrated Paris. I happened to be present once when the Red

Armymen were listening to a newspaper report telling how the Nazis had doomed the people of Greece to death from starvation, and one of the men, a collective farmer from Saratov region, said: "It's a real calamity. Everywhere it's the same. We've got to wipe out those Fritzes as quickly as possible so as to help people."

Our hatred for the Hitlerites is dictated by love—love of our country, love for man, love for humanity. And in this is the force of our hatred. In this is its justification. Coming to grips with the Hitlerites we see how blind hatred has destroyed Germany's soul. We are far from such hatred. We hate each and every Hitlerite because he is a representative of a misanthropic principle, because he is a convinced murderer, a robber on principle, we hate every one of them for everything they have singly and jointly done in our country and in other countries, for the tears of the widows, for the blighted children's lives, for the dreary caravans of refugees, for the fields trampled underfoot, for the millions of lives and the fruits of years of highly creative labor they have destroyed.

We are fighting not against human beings, but against robots who resemble human beings but do not have a grain of humanism in them. Our hatred is so much stronger because in appearance they look like human beings, because they can laugh, because they can pat a horse or a dog, because in their diaries they indulge in introspection and because they have taken on the guise of human beings and civilized Europeans.

We often use words changing their original meaning. It is not of base hatred that our people dream of calling for vengeance. It is not for this that we brought up our boys and girls that they should stoop to the level of the atrocities perpetrated by the Nazis. Never will our Red Armymen murder German children, set fire to Goethe's house in Weimar or to the libraries in Marburg. Vengeance—that means paying one back in one's own kind, to speak to one in one's own tongue. But we do not have a common tongue with the fascists.

What we are yearning for is not vengeance but justice. We are out to destroy the Hitlerites so that the principle of humanity shall again flourish on the earth. We rejoice at life in all its variegated and intricate forms and aspects, the native traits of nations and people. There is sufficient room for everybody on this earth of ours. And the German people, too, shall live, having purged themselves of the monstrous crimes of the Hitler decade. But even the widest latitudes have their boundaries: just now I do not want to think or speak about the future happiness of a Germany rid of Hitler—such thoughts and words would be out of place and insincere as long as millions of Hitlerites are running amok on our soil.

Soviet State Anthem

(1944)

In June 1943, Stalin decided to replace the "Internationale" (which in turn had replaced the old tsarist anthem, "God Save the Tsar" in 1918) with a new national anthem or state hymn. After a massive competition among writers and composers, the "Internationale" became the Party hymn, and the melody of the old Party hymn (composed by General Aleksandrov) was put to the words of Sergei Mikhalkov, children's writer, and Garold El-Registan, an Uzbek poet. It was first broadcast on New Year's Day, 1944.

Союз нерушимый республик свободных
Сплотила навеки Великая Русь!
Да здравствует созданный волей народов
Единый могучий Советский союз.

Припев:
Славься отечество наше свободное,
Дружбы народов—надежный оплот!
Знамя советское, знамя народное
Пусть от победы к победе ведет.

Сквозь грозы сияло нам солнце свободы,
И Ленин великий нам путь озарил.
Нас вырастал Сталин—на верность народу,
На труд и на подвиги нас вдохновил.

Припев.

Мы армию нашу растили в сраженьях,
Захватчиков подлых с дороги сметем!

Unbreakable union of freeborn republics,
Great Russia has welded forever to stand!
Created in struggle by the will of the people,
United and mighty, our Soviet land.

Refrain:
Sing to our Fatherland, glory undying,
Bulwark of peoples, in brotherhood strong.
Flag of the Soviets, people's flag flying,
Lead us from triumph to triumph on!

Through tempests the sunrays of freedom have cheered us,
Along the new path where great Lenin did lead,
Be true to the people, thus Stalin has reared us,
Inspired us to labor and valorous deed!

Refrain.

Our Army grew up in the heat of grim battle,

Мы в битвах решаем судьбу поколений,
Мы к славе Отчизну свою поведем!

Barbarian invaders we'll swiftly strike
    down.
In combat the fate of the future we
    settle,
Our country we'll lead to eternal
    renown!

Припев.

Refrain.

Anecdotes

A German called Goebbels a pig. The German was accused of three crimes:
1. Disturbing the peace.
2. Slandering a government official.
3. Divulging a state secret.

—In *Crocodile,* taken from the London *New Statesman*[1]

A collector of rare photographs in Munich told a friend:
"My collection is missing one picture, which I'd give half my life for."
"Which one?"
"A photo of Mussolini's widow standing by Hitler's casket."[2]

—*Crocodile*

Stalin asks Roosevelt on the telephone: "Why are the Lend-Lease shipments being held up?"
Roosevelt: "The longshoremen are striking for more money."
Stalin: "Don't you have police in your country?" [5:185]

Roosevelt, Churchill, and Stalin are driving through the Crimean countryside after the Yalta conference. Suddenly, a bull blocks the road. Roosevelt gets out and asks the bull to clear the road. No result. Churchill gets out and tries to sway the bull with his eloquence, but the result is the same. Finally, Stalin gets out and whispers something in the bull's ear. The bull instantly rears up and races away.
Roosevelt and Churchill ask Stalin what he said. "It was simple," he replied. "If he didn't move, he'd be sent to a kolkhoz." [5:186]

What were the worst things to come out of the victory over Germany?
(1) The Red Army saw Europe. (2) Europe saw the Red Army. [5:294]

For anecdote sources, see *Blue Blouse Skit,* above.
1. This Goebbels joke was later recycled as a Khrushchev joke, and told by Khrushchev himself.
2. The Mussolini's widow joke is the revision of an anecdote first told about Lenin and his comrades, then later about Stalin and Beria.

IV.

The Postwar Era

Cossacks of the Kuban

N. Pogodin (1949)

THE PROLIFIC POGODIN WROTE THIS SCRIPT FOR THE MOST FA-
MOUS STALINIST POSTWAR FILM, RELEASED AT A TIME OF SEVERE
SHORTAGES AND THE RAVAGES OF RECOVERY, AND DIRECTED BY
IVAN PYRIEV — MASTER OF THE GLOSSY RURAL MUSICAL COMEDY.
IT IS A HORSE OPERETTA ABOUT COSSACK COLLECTIVE FARMERS
COMPETING IN A "COUNTRY FAIR" VENUE (LIKE RODGERS AND
HAMMERSTEIN'S *STATE FAIR*, 1945) AND A COUPLE OF STANDARD
LOVE PLOTS (DASHA SHELEST-KOVYLEV, VORON-PERESVETOVA).
ISAAK DUNAEVSKY'S BRIGHT SCORE MAKES THIS A LIGHT-
HEARTED FROLIC. BUT FROM THE OPENING CHORUS AMID FIELDS
OF GRAIN TO THE TRADE PAVILIONS AND BOOTHS BULGING WITH
CONSUMER GOODS, *COSSACKS* GAVE A DISTORTED PICTURE OF
THE ECONOMIC LIFE OF RURAL RUSSIA. AS THESE EXCERPTS SUG-
GEST, THE SIMPLE PLOT TWISTS AROUND THREE TENSIONS: A
CONTEST BETWEEN TWO COLLECTIVE FARMS, A DIFFICULT LOVE
BETWEEN THE CHAIRMAN AND CHAIRWOMAN OF THOSE FARMS,
AND THE LOVE OF DASHA FOR A MEMBER OF THE OPPOSING FARM.

The market fair.

The cloudless blue sky of the Kuban steppe in autumn. On the broad square of
a large district center, almost next to the river, solid rows of gaily decorated shops,
tents, temporary stores, and large trade pavilions rise against the background of a
grain elevator.

Flags and transparent banners, colorful balloons, vivid posters, powerful radio
speakers, a carousel, the white circus tent.

People fill the square with holiday costumes; noise and joyful shouts can be
heard.

Cossack hats, caps, military headgear, berets, and colored kerchiefs flash brightly
amid the rows of still-unopen shops and stores. People examine items in the shop
windows.

Excerpted from the scenario in *Izbrannye sovetskie kinostsenarii* (Moscow, 1951), pp. 441–442, 452–455.

Plyasov and Kovylev, young Cossacks from the Testament of Ilich[1] kolkhoz, hurry through the crowd. They are looking for someone.

"There she is—there!" Plyasov stops his friend.

"Where?" asks Kovylev.

"There, can't you see?"

"Nope."

"You're not looking in the right place. Look at the tribune."

"I see, it's her."

The district's most eminent citizens mount a beautifully decorated tribune rising over the central square. They include Dasha, the leading milkmaid of the Red Partisan kolkhoz; Peresvetova, chairwoman of the Testament kolkhoz; Voron, chairman of the Red Partisan and Dasha's guardian; district soviet chairman Stepan Koren; a military man; and five or six other people. The market hum quiets down.

"Let's get closer," Kovylev says impatiently, and pushes his way forward. Plyasov follows him. Their places are immediately taken by elderly kolkhoz peasants, including Marko Danilovich Dergach, one of the oldest chairmen.

District soviet chairman Koren approaches the tribune microphone.

"Dear comrades! Allow me to give you joyful news. Our district was the first in the entire Kuban to deliver its grain consignment to the state in time."

The square, packed full of people, was swept by loud applause.

"Never have our steppe lands," continued Koren, "yielded such a rich and abundant harvest as in this year. How did this miracle happen? Where is the magical spring that made the arid lands of our district so fertile? Or perhaps it was all luck? Or the Lord God himself helped us? No, dear comrade grain growers. This miracle was worked by you!"

Tan faces of kolkhozniks, men and women. They listen closely to the words spoken to them.

"You labored well," says Koren. "You worked gloriously and harmoniously. And so today we may boldly congratulate ourselves on this great victory. The promise made by us to our great leader, Comrade Stalin, has been met with honor."

The entire square in joyful and thunderous applause. . . .

Kovylev and Plyasov applaud, staring at the tribune, where Dasha Shelest stands and applauds too.

"We have given our motherland 146,000 tons of beautiful Kuban wheat above the plan! Each hectare averaged twenty-six centners of grain. You are wealthy people! You have something to trade with, and something to buy with at this market fair. Dear friends!" continued Koren. "We now open our market fair! This year's fair will be special, there will be more than just selling and purchasing. No! It is a great people's holiday of inspired labor, a summation of socialist competition; it is a review of our artistic efforts, of sports and horse races. I wish you success, happiness,

---

1. Referring, of course, to Lenin's historical legacy, not to his notorious will—then unknown to the public.

and fun! For the happy Soviet people, and for our father and friend Comrade Stalin—hip, hip, hoorah!"

A powerful "Hoorah" thunders across the square.

The band strikes up a march. Caps and hats are tossed high in the air above the square.

A huge red flag rises into the blue sky.

The market fair is open.

Clusters of colorful balloons float above the heads of the crowd.

A stream of people bustles along noisily. A march is played. . . .

The large auditorium is packed full of kolkhozniks in holiday dress.

A girl's choir on a stage against the backdrop of a picturesque garden. Lyuba and Dasha lead the singing from the middle of the choir. Backstage stands Mudretsov, dressed in high style, directing in time with the choir, unbeknownst even to himself.

Peresvetova and Voron sit in the first row and listen to the singing. Voron leans over slightly and says softly: "I gaze at you, and my heart again strikes notes of trepidation."

"What sort of notes?" smiles Peresvetova.

"Of trepidation," whispers Voron, leaning even more closely toward Galina Yermolaevna [Peresvetova], and he tries to take her hand, but Peresvetova takes it back delicately.

"Do listen... they sing well."

"But who is that singing? That's my link leader," whispers Voron, pointing at Dasha, who is leading the song and smiling at Kovylev and Plyasov standing offstage.

Tuzov, a young Cossack from Red Partisan, watches them and whispers a command in the ear of Fedya, his friend: "Fedya, don't let them out of your sight."

"Who do you think you're talking to," Fedya growls.

"Shhh... and make sure to stick around in case anything happens."

"Who do you think you're talking to," Fedya growls even more loudly. "They won't..."

"Shhh..." Tuzov clamps his mouth shut and, looking around timorously, meets Plyasov's mocking gaze.

"They're stepping up the surveillance," Plyasov tells his friend quietly and turns toward Dasha and Lyuba, who are singing the song's final couplet.

The choir finishes the song in perfect synchrony. Thunderous applause erupts.

The girls dash off the stage.

Kovylev and Plyasov, standing offstage and applauding, grab the girls.

"Wonderful! Terrific! Fantastic!" they say, each topping the other in their congratulations.

"Step back, young men!" sounds a stern voice, and Mudretsov appears and cavalierly ushers the boys away from the girls. "The audience is calling you back," he firmly commands the singers.

Dasha and Lyuba go back out onstage with the rest of the choir.

The auditorium greets them with applause.

The girls bow and walk offstage. Mudretsov takes their place. He is conducting the program.

"The dancers of the Red Partisan kolkhoz will now perform a Kuban-Cossack dance," announces Mudretsov.

"That's my director, Mudretsov," Voron tells Peresvetova with satisfaction, smoothing his mustache, "a top-notch fellow! There's not another director like him!"

The dancers dash out onstage in smart Cossack costumes. Tuzov rounds out the row.

"That's my horse breeder," shouts Voron. "A dashing fellow. There's not another horse breeder like him!"

"Don't boast so much, Gordei Gordeich," Peresvetova interrupts him. "Your director, your horse breeder! I don't like it when you boast."

"You don't like it?" asks Voron.

"I don't like it!"

"I'll keep that in mind," mumbles Voron and turns back to the stage.

The dance is at full throttle.

All the evening's performers are crowded together backstage. Dasha is standing near the group of girls, and next to her is Kovylev. Fedya's powerful figure towers over them threateningly. Mudretsov stands at Dasha's side. He watches the dancers enraptured, occasionally giving Dasha and Kovylev a worried glance.

Tuzov dances wonderfully. Dasha shifts her gaze from Tuzov to Kovylev. Their eyes meet. She bashfully turns away.

Casting a crafty glance at Mudretsov and Fedya, who are absorbed in the dancing, Dasha gives Kovylev's sleeve a tug, crouches quickly, and backs away, with Kovylev following, and they disappear.

Glancing in Dasha's direction and not spotting her, Mudretsov looks around in confusion and races off after them. He runs down the stage stairs and bumps into Plyasov. Plyasov has a bayan—he is getting ready for his performance.

"Where's your friend?" Mudretsov attacks him.

"What do you need him for?"

"He's stolen our Dasha."

"Well, good for him!"

"It's all your doing!" Mudretsov threatens him. "Where's our girl?"

"The girl is seeking her happiness!" Plyasov answers with a broad gesture. "And it's useless to try and stop her."

"Don't you get me off the track."

"And don't you get me all riled up. I have a solo coming up."

Mudretsov wants to say something back, but the auditorium breaks out in applause, and he dashes onstage.

To the sound of the applause, Tuzov and the ensemble finish the dance handsomely and with great effect.

"What beauty! What bravado!" shouts Voron, applauding, and looks around proudly. "Dergach, Marko! You see! I trained them!"

"You're boasting again, Gordei Gordeich," Peresvetova says quietly.

Voron is chagrined.

"O-kay, I won't do it."

Mudretsov onstage. He clears his throat, and announces the soloist: Plyasov, the Testament of Ilich accordionist.

The audience is animated.

"Well, now it's your people's turn," Voron tells Peresvetova patronizingly. "We'll see now."

Plyasov onstage. Putting his fingers to the strings, he strikes the first chords of a classical variation. His face reflects inspiration and triumph.

The noise in the auditorium dies out.

Koren is sitting with a group of district political workers. He listens attentively.

"Food for the soul," Voron says dreamily, and glancing at Peresvetova, he gingerly leans toward her.

"Oh, Galina Yermolaevna," he whispers, "I'll steal you away."

"What was that? I can't hear," asks Peresvetova in a whisper.

"I'll steal you away. I'll put you on my horse and take you away to our kolkhoz." Plyasov continues playing.

Evening.

The wind flutters autumn leaves in the orchard.

"What wonderful music," Dasha says quietly to Kovylev.

"That's my friend playing," he answers. "We work together in the horse barn."

"What's your position?"

"I'm a horse breeder."

"So young! And him?"

"Andrei's my assistant. We have a lot of mares. A whole herd."

"We also have a lot. I'm a link leader," Dasha continued. "I work with grain. Wheat."

"I know that."

"Oh, the harvest was difficult this year. There wasn't much snow. It was bitter cold. The winds were strong, and all our winter crops almost froze. And what didn't we think of doing: we put up screens, earth banks. Then it rained and rained all summer. The grain was ripe, it's bending under its own weight, but we couldn't harvest it. You just wanted to cry."

"I understand. It's hard work."

"Not really. It's not so much hard as it's stressful."

"Do you remember, Dasha, how we met?"

"I remember," smiled Dasha. "You met me—and then forgot me."

"How can you! I was searching for you."

"You searched, but you didn't find me. That must mean you didn't search very well."

"Why are you saying that? I thought about you all the time. And yesterday, when I suddenly saw you..."

"You didn't even say a word."

"How could I? We hadn't even been properly introduced."

"Well, now we have," Dasha laughed merrily.

The Story of a Real Man
Boris Polevoi (1947)

POLEVOI (1908–1981) FOUGHT THROUGH THE WAR AS A MAJOR ON GENERAL KONEV'S STAFF. HE WAS TRAINED AS A JOURNALIST, AND THIS SHOWS IN MOST OF HIS WORKS. *THE STORY OF A REAL MAN* (NOVEL, 1946; RADIO PLAY AND MOVIE, 1947), BASED ON A REAL EVENT, IS A CLASSIC OF SOCIALIST REALISM, VIVIDLY WRITTEN, AND CHARGED WITH SUSPENSE. THE HERO'S EVENTUAL TRIUMPHAL RECOVERY AFTER LOSING HIS LEG PROVIDED YOUTH WITH AN EXAMPLE OF UNDEFEATABLE DETERMINATION. GENERATIONS OF YOUNG PEOPLE THRILLED TO THE JACK LONDON–LIKE WILDERNESS SEQUENCES IN THE OPENING PAGES (EXCERPTED HERE) AND THE DOGFIGHTS AGAINST THE GERMANS IN THE SKIES OVER RUSSIA.

Pilot Alexei Meresyev had been caught in a double pair of "pincers." It was the worst thing that could happen to a man in a dog fight. He had spent all his ammunition when four German aircraft surrounded him and tried to force him to proceed to their base without giving him a chance to dodge or change his course.

It came about in this way. A flight of fighter planes under the command of Lieutenant Meresyev went out to escort a flight of "Il's"[1] that was to attack an enemy airfield. The daring operation was successful. The Stormoviks,[2] "flying tanks," as the infantry called them, almost scraping the pine tree tops, stole right up to the airfield, where a number of large transport Junkers were lined up. Suddenly diving out from behind the grey-blue pine forest, they zoomed over the field, their machine-guns and cannons pouring lead into the heavy transport planes, showering them with rocket shells. Meresyev, who was guarding the area of attack with his flight of four, distinctly saw the dark figures of men rushing about the field, saw the transport planes creeping heavily across the hard-packed snow, saw the Stormoviks return to the attack again and again, and saw the crews of the Junkers, under a hail of fire, taxi their craft to the runway and take them into the air.

Excerpts from a translation by Joe Fineberg (Progress Publishers, 1958).

1. Ilyushin bombers.

2. From *shtyurmovik* (storm troop or shock troop, an infantry term from World War I): Soviet fighter plane.

It was at this point that Alexei committed his fatal blunder. Instead of closely guarding the area of attack, he allowed himself to be "tempted by easy prey," as airmen call it. He put his craft into a dive, dropped like a stone upon a slow and heavy transport plane that had just torn itself off the ground, and found delight in stitching its motley-colored, rectangular, corrugated duralumin body with several long bursts from his machine-gun. He was so confident that he did not trouble to see the enemy craft hurtle to the ground. On the other side of the field another Junkers rose into the air. Alexei went after it. He attacked—but was unsuccessful. His stream of tracer bullets trailed over the slowly rising enemy plane. He banked round sharply and attacked again, missed again, overtook his victim again, and this time sent it down away over the forest by furiously firing several long bursts into its broad, cigar-shaped body. After bringing down the Junkers and circling twice in triumph over the spot where a black column of smoke was rising out of the heaving, green sea of endless forest, he turned his plane back to the German airfield.

But he did not get there. He saw his three planes fighting nine "Messers,"[3] which had evidently been called up by the commander of the German airfield to beat off the attack of the Stormoviks. Gallantly hurling themselves at the Germans, who outnumbered them three to one, the airmen tried to keep the enemy away from the Stormoviks. They drew the enemy further and further away, as black grouse do, pretending to be wounded and enticing hunters away from their young.

Alexei was so ashamed that he had allowed himself to be tempted by easy prey that he could feel his cheeks burning under his helmet. He chose a target and, clenching his teeth, sped into the fray. The target he had chosen was a "Messer" that had separated itself somewhat from the rest and was evidently also looking for prey. Squeezing all the speed he possibly could out of his plane, Alexei hurled himself upon the enemy's flank. He attacked the German in accordance with all the rules of the art. The grey body of the enemy craft was distinctly visible in the weblike cross of his sight when he pressed his trigger, but the enemy craft slipped by unharmed. Alexei could not have missed. The target was near and was distinctly visible in the sight. "Ammunition!" Alexei guessed, and at once felt a cold shiver run down his spine. He pressed the triggerbutton again to test the guns but failed to feel the vibration that every airman feels with his whole body when he discharges his guns. The magazines were empty; he had used up all his ammunition in chasing the "transports."

But the enemy did not know that! Alexei decided to plunge into the fight to improve at least the numerical proportion between the combatants. But he was mistaken. The fighter plane that he had unsuccessfully attacked was piloted by an experienced and observant airman. The German realized that his opponent's ammunition had run out and issued an order to his colleagues. Four "Messerschmidts" separated from the rest and surrounded Alexei, one on each flank, one above and one below. Dictating his course by bursts of tracer bullets that were distinctly visible in the clear, blue air, they caught him in a double pair of "pincers."

---

3. Messerschmidt—German fighter plane.

Several days before, Alexei heard that the famous German Richthofen air division had arrived in this area, Staraya Russa, from the West. This division was manned by the finest aces in the fascist Reich and was under the patronage of Goering himself. Alexei realized that he had fallen into the clutches of these air wolves and that evidently, they wanted to compel him to fly to their airfield, force him to land and take him prisoner. Cases like that had happened. Alexei himself had seen a fighter flight under the command of his chum, Andrei Degtyarenko, Hero of the Soviet Union, bring a German observer to their airfield and force him to land.

The long, ashen grey face of the German prisoner and his staggering footsteps rose before Alexei's eyes. "Taken prisoner? Never! That trick won't come off!" he determined.

But do what he would, he could not escape. The moment he tried to swerve from the course the Germans were dictating him, they barred his path with machine-gun fire. And again the vision of the German prisoner, his contorted face and trembling jaw, rose before Alexei's eyes. Degrading animal fear was stamped on that face.

Meresyev clenched his teeth tightly, opened the throttle of his engine as far as it would go and, assuming a vertical position, tried to dive under the German plane that was pressing him to the ground. He managed to break loose from the convoy, but the German airman pressed his trigger in time. Alexei's engine lost its rhythm and every now and again missed a beat. The entire craft trembled as if stricken with mortal fever.

"I'm hit!" Alexei managed to plunge into the white turbidness of a cloud and throw his pursuers off his track. But what was to be done next? He felt the vibrations of the wounded craft through his whole body, as if it were not the death throes of his damaged engine but the fever of his own body that was shaking him.

Where was the engine damaged? How long could the plane keep in the air? Would the fuel tanks explode? Alexei did not think these questions so much as feel them. Feeling as if he were sitting on a keg of dynamite with the fuse already alight, he put his craft about and made for his own lines in order, if it came to that, to have his remains buried by his own people.

The climax was sudden. The engine seized and fell silent. The aircraft slid to the ground as if slipping down a steep mountain side. Beneath it heaved the forest, like the grey-green waves of a boundless ocean. "Still, I won't be taken prisoner," was the thought that flashed through the airman's mind when the nearest trees, merged in a continuous strip, raced under the wings of his craft. When the forest pounced upon him like a wild animal he cut off the throttle with an instinctive movement. A grinding crash was heard and everything vanished in an instant, as if he and the machine had dived into a stretch of dark, warm, thick water. . . .

Evidently, in the autumn, or more probably in the early winter, the fringe of this forest had been a defence line which a Soviet Army unit had held, not for long perhaps, but stubbornly, unto death. Blizzards had covered up the earth's wounds with a layer of snowy cotton wool; but even beneath that layer the eye could still trace the line of trenches, the hillocks of wrecked machine-gun emplacements, the endless shell craters, large and small, stretching to the feet of the mutilated, be-headed or blasted trees at the forest edge. Dotted over this lacerated field were a number of tanks painted in the motley colors of pike's scales. They stood frozen to the snow, and all of them—particularly the one at the extreme end which must have been turned over on its side by a grenade, or a mine, so that the long barrel of its gun hung to the ground like an exposed tongue from the mouth—looked like the carcasses of strange monsters. And all over the field, on the parapets of the shallow trenches, near the tanks, and on the edge of the forest, lay the corpses of Soviet and German soldiers. There were so many that in some spots they lay piled up on top of each other; and they lay in the very same frozen postures in which death had struck them down in battle only a few months before, on the border-line of winter.

All this told Alexei of the fierce and stubborn fighting that had raged here, told him that his comrades-in-arms had fought here, forgetting everything except that they had to check the enemy and not let him pass. At a little distance, near the edge of the forest, at the foot of a thick pine which had been decapitated by a shell, and from whose tall, mutilated trunk yellow, transparent resin was now oozing, lay the bodies of German soldiers with smashed-in skulls and mutilated faces. In the middle, lying across one of the enemy bodies, was the prostrate body of a huge, round-faced, big-headed lad without a greatcoat, in just a tunic with a torn collar; and next to him lay a rifle with a broken bayonet and a splintered, blood-stained butt. Further on, on the road leading to the forest, halfway out of a shell crater at the foot of a young, sand-covered fir-tree, lay the body of a dark-skinned Uzbek with an oval face that seemed to have been carved out of old ivory. Behind him, under the branches of the fir-tree, there was a neat stack of grenades; and the Uzbek himself held a grenade in his dead, upraised hand, as if, before throwing it, he had taken a glance at the sky and had remained petrified in that pose. And still further on, along the forest road, near some motley-colored tanks, on the edges of large shell craters, in the foxholes, near some old tree stumps, everywhere lay dead bodies, in padded jackets and trousers and in faded green tunics and forage-caps pulled over the ears; bent knees, upraised chins and waxen faces gnawed by foxes and pecked by magpies and ravens protruded from the snow.

Several ravens were circling slowly over the glade and this suddenly reminded Alexei of the mournful but magnificent picture of "The Battle of Igor" reproduced in his school history book from the canvas of a great Russian artist.[4]

"I might have been lying here like them," he thought, and again the sense of being alive surged through his whole being. He shook himself. The rough grindstones were still turning slowly in his head, his feet burned and ached worse than before, but he sat down on the bear's carcass, now cold and silvery from the dry snow that powdered it, and began to ponder what to do, where to go, how to get to his own forward lines.

When he was thrown out of his aircraft he had lost his map case, but he could vividly picture the route he had to take. The German airfield, which the Stormoviks had attacked, lay about sixty kilometers west of the forward lines. During the air battle his men had drawn the enemy about twenty kilometers east away from the

---

4. The motif is from Viktor Vasnetsov's *After Prince Igor's Battle with the Polovtsy* (1880).

airfield, and, after escaping from the double "pincers," he himself must have got a little farther to the east. Consequently, he must have fallen about thirty-five kilometers from the forward lines, far behind the forward German divisions, somewhere in the region of the enormous tract of forest land known as the Black Forest, over which he had flown more than once when escorting bombers and Stormoviks in short raids on near-by German bases. From the air this forest had always looked to him like a boundless green sea. In clear weather it heaved with the swaying tops of the pine trees; but in bad weather, enveloped in a thin, grey mist, it looked like a smooth, dreary waste of water with small waves rolling on the surface.

The fact that he had fallen into the middle of this huge forest had a good and bad side. The good side was that he was unlikely to meet any Germans here in the virgin forest, for they usually kept to the roads and towns. The bad side was that his route, though not long, was very difficult; he would have to push through dense undergrowth, and was not likely to meet with human aid, to get shelter, a crust of bread, or a cup of something warm to drink. His feet... would they carry him? Would he be able to walk?

Both his feet were useless. Evidently, when he was thrown out of the cockpit of his aircraft, something must have caught his feet and shattered the bones of the instep and toes. Under ordinary circumstances, of course, he would not have dreamed of attempting to stand up on feet in such a frightful condition. But he was alone in the depths of a virgin forest, in the enemy's rear, where to meet a human being meant not relief, but death. So he resolved to push on, eastward, through the forest, making no attempt to seek convenient roads or human habitation; to push on at all costs. . . .

Alexei felt himself growing weaker from exertion and pain. Biting his lips, he continued to push on and reached a forest road that ran past a wrecked tank, past the dead Uzbek holding the grenade, and into the depths of the forest, eastward. It was not so bad hobbling on the soft snow, but as soon as his foot touched the wind-hardened, ice-covered, humped surface of the road, the pain became so excruciating that he dared not take another step and halted. He stood, his feet awkwardly apart, his body swaying as if blown about by the wind. Suddenly a grey mist rose before his eyes. The road, the pine-trees, the greyish pine tops and the blue, oblong patch of sky between them vanished. He was in his airfield, by a fighter, his fighter, and his mechanic, lanky Yura, his teeth and eyes, as always, glistening on his unshaven and ever smutty face, was beckoning him to the cockpit, as much as to say: "She's ready, off you go!" Alexei took a step towards the plane, but the ground swayed, his feet burned as if he had stepped upon a red-hot metal plate. He tried to skip across this fiery patch of ground onto the wing of his plane, but collided with the cold side of the fuselage. He was surprised to find that the side of the fuselage was not smooth and polished, but rough, as if lined with pine bark. But there was no fighter; he was standing on the road, stroking the trunk of a tree.

"Hallucinations? I am going out of my mind from the concussion!" thought Alexei. "It will be torture, going by this road. Should I turn off? But that will make the going slower." He sat down on the snow and with the same short, resolute wrenches pulled off his fur boots, tore open the uppers with his teeth and fingernails to make them easier for his fractured feet, took off his large, fluffy angora woollen scarf, tore it into strips, which he wound round his feet, and put his boots on again.

It was easier to walk now. But it is not quite correct to say walk: not walk, but move forward, move forward carefully, stepping on his heels and raising his feet high, as one walks across a bog. After every few steps his head swam from pain and exertion. He was obliged to halt, shut his eyes, lean against the trunk of a tree, or sit down on a snow hummock to rest, conscious of the acute throbbing of the blood in his veins.

And so he pushed on for several hours. But when he turned to look back, he could still see the sunlit turn of the road at the end of the forest cutting where the dead Uzbek lay like a small dark patch on the snow. Alexei was extremely disappointed. Disappointed, but not frightened. It made him want to push on faster. He got up from the hummock, tightly clenched his teeth and moved on, choosing close targets, concentrating his mind upon them—from pine-tree to pine-tree, from stump to stump, from hummock to hummock. And as he moved on he left a winding, irregular track on the virgin snow on the deserted forest road, like that left by a wounded animal.

Children's Verse
Sergei Mikhalkov (1946)

THESE POEMS ARE REDOLENT OF THE SUNNY AND SANCTIMONIOUS OPTIMISM OF THE POSTWAR ERA. THEY HARK BACK TO THE 1930s JOY OF INDUSTRIAL ACHIEVEMENT AT A TIME OF PROFOUND ECONOMIC DEPRIVATION.

THE ONLY COUNTRY IN THE WORLD

There're many countries in the world,
But the Soviet country
Stands alone among the others
On the mighty planet Earth.

Beyond the border of our country
You will find no other land,
Where everyone can go to school,

ALL THIS IS OURS

Take a good look all around,
All this is ours, it's all for us;
All the mountains and the meadows...
For miles around are woods and fields,
And it's all the people's land,
No matter where your foot might fall!
 The gardens flower not for lords,

"Slovo izbiratelia," *Pravda,* 10 February 1946, p. 2; "Ty posmotri po storonam," *Pionerskaia pravda,* 2 November 1951, p. 2, as excerpted in F. A. Fridliand and M. F. Robinson, *Chteniia* (Moscow: Uchpedgiz, 1950), pp. 5–7.

Where everyone is given work,
Where everyone has equality.

If in many other countries,
Under foreign governments,
Those who dictate all the laws
Do not plow or sow the fields,
But own the granaries and silos
And live upon the work of others—
It's the opposite where we live!
Everything our homeland has
Is possessed by all the people.
They keep the books on fields and woods
Meadows, pastures, and the waters,
Mineshafts, minepits, factories.
As a lesson for other nations
The people run them all themselves.

So we have the right to say
That nobody can name for us
Another power in all the world,
Or another nation there,
Where the reins of power are held
Not by bankers and their money,
But by simple master-workers
And the leaders of kolkhozes.

They flower only for us!
And no count lives in the manor,
But schoolchildren live!
And the grain pours from the sacks
Not into the merchant's granary.
And Dneproges[1] belongs
Not to a private owner.
   We sow our wheat and forge our
      arms
   We dig the coal out of the mines,
   Pipe the gas into our homes.
   Both the coal and the rye,
   The gas, the home in which you live
   And all around—is all for us!
Everything the factories make,
Everything the plants produce,
That makes our Motherland so proud,
That makes the might our enemy fears,
All this is ours, it's all for us
Eternally! Forever!

---

1. The Dnepr Hydro-Electric Station.

The Russian Question
Konstantin Simonov (1947)

SIMONOV'S PLAY, WHICH WAS MADE INTO A MOVIE THAT SAME YEAR, WAS ONE OF THE SUBTLER WORKS OF THE COLD WAR ERA. IT SHOWED A NATURAL AFFINITY BETWEEN TWO NATIONS THAT WAS CORRUPTED BY THE AMERICAN YELLOW PRESS (NOTE THE HEARST-LIKE CHARACTER OF MACPHERSON) AND THE POWER OF CAPITALIST MONEY. THE PICTURE PLAYED ON A STILL-LIVING AF-

---

Excerpted from a translation by Eve Manning and Sergei Kozelsky, *Soviet Literature,* no. 2 (1947), pp. 2–6.

FECTION FOR THE WARTIME ALLY WHILE PRESENTING THE STAN-
DARD GOVERNMENT LINE.

Macpherson—owner and editor of a large New York paper and part owner of a number of other papers; sixty years of age, but looks much younger.

Gould—part owner of a large newspaper in San Francisco and also one of the editors of Macpherson's paper; about forty years of age. Limps slightly. Rough in his manner playing "the man of the people."

Smith—correspondent of Macpherson's paper, the same age as Gould, and his old schoolmate.

Preston—editor of the foreign department of Macpherson's paper; forty-five years of age.

Hardy—Reporter on Macpherson's paper; forty years of age.

Murphy—correspondent of one of the Hearst papers; forty-six years of age. Careless in his dress. Never completely drunk, but always slightly intoxicated.

Jessie—pretty woman of thirty-three who looks younger.

Place—New York. Time—winter, spring 1946.

ACT I. SCENE I

Macpherson's private office in his newspaper building. A large room, with little furniture—a desk, several armchairs. Only ornament—photographs hanging in a row above the oak paneling that lines the lower part of the walls. Over the desk—a huge photograph of an old two-story house.

Enter Jessie, comes to the table, takes papers and newspaper galleys from a folder and arranges them on the desk. The telephone rings.

JESSIE (at the telephone): Hello... no. He'll be back in a quarter of an hour. (A knock at the door.)

JESSIE: Come in.

GOULD (entering): You here? What an unpleasant surprise.

JESSIE: Unpleasant—why?

GOULD: Back from the army and everything just the same as it was in '41.

JESSIE: I'm just pinch-hitting for Miss Bridge. She's gone on her vacation.

GOULD: Relations strictly business with the chief?

JESSIE: Strictly business.

GOULD: H'm—he's getting old, all right.

JESSIE: So am I.

GOULD: I wouldn't say so. We left the Philippines last February—so it's only a year.

JESSIE: Yes.

GOULD: But all the same, you look better in a dress than in a WAC uniform.

JESSIE: Maybe.

GOULD: What about a kiss—for old times sake?

JESSIE: No.

GOULD: OK. When do you quit?

JESSIE: At ten.

GOULD: The Bromley Club at eleven, OK?

JESSIE: No, I'm busy.

GOULD: May I ask, with whom?

JESSIE: You may. I think that Harry...

GOULD: Harry Smith?

JESSIE: Yes. I think Harry's going to ask me to supper tonight.

GOULD: But he only flew in from Japan last night!

JESSIE: Yes, I know. I met him at the airport.

GOULD: Office sent you?

JESSIE: No. (A pause) They say your wife's not very pretty.

GOULD: She isn't.

JESSIE: And so rich that private detectives keep her informed of what you're doing.

GOULD: Possible.

JESSIE: Did you finally buy that San Francisco paper?

GOULD: Not quite. Forty percent so far. You know, it's God's truth, when I got married I was really sorry that it was she that was rich and not you.

JESSIE: I believe you. Is she very unattractive?

GOULD: Very.

JESSIE: You've got my sympathy.

GOULD: I believe you. Where's the chief?

JESSIE: At a lunch for the Russian newspapermen. He'll be here in ten minutes.

GOULD: Oh. Harry. May I smoke?

JESSIE: Of course.

GOULD: (lighting a cigar) Only flew in last night. Fast work.

JESSIE: Not so fast. We met in Tokyo.

GOULD: Ah... that's right. I'm getting thick. Does he know about me?

JESSIE: No. I never thought of you when he was there. And in general.

GOULD: Other people might tell him.

JESSIE: Not very likely. He doesn't like that sort of talk.

GOULD: But he loves you?

JESSIE: I think so.

GOULD: And you? Only tell the truth. In '41 you liked him less than you did me.

JESSIE: That's right. But now I like him much better than you. And then I've gotten older and wiser. And I want to get married.

GOULD: The chief wants to send him to Russia.

JESSIE: Yes, I know. I typed the draft contract for Harry's book yesterday. I guess you had a finger in that pie.

GOULD: Yes, it was my idea. And my draft.

JESSIE: Well—I guess that would take Harry away for about three months.

GOULD: About that. That is—if he goes.

JESSIE: He'll go, all right.

GOULD: Of course. Last year he began to lose ground. If he doesn't do something to pick up his reputation, and do it quick, he won't be making more than 500 a month soon. And I'm afraid that wouldn't look much like a happy marriage for you.

JESSIE: He'll go.

GOULD: I'm not so sure of it. He used to have some goofy ideas of his own about Russia.

JESSIE: I'm not bothering about his ideas or the Russians, or what he writes about them. I want my own home, my own children and a little happiness for myself. I'm sick of being somebody's baby doll. He'll go.

GOULD: Where did you get the idea of marrying him? In Japan?

JESSIE: Just about.

GOULD: And clinched it?

JESSIE: Yesterday.

GOULD: When you were typing my draft contract for his book? Looks as though I've got the silly part of marriage broker.

JESSIE: Looks like it. But why silly?

GOULD: Well, after all. Nearly three years we... You ought to be grateful to me.

JESSIE: I am

GOULD: Cigarette?

JESSIE: I've stopped smoking. Harry doesn't like it.

GOULD: Oh, then it really is serious.

JESSIE: Yes, it's very serious.

MACPHERSON (entering): How do, Jack.

GOULD: All right, Charlie, then: only admit that it's not just because you're naturally democratic that you like people to call you "Charlie."

MACPHERSON: Is that so?

GOULD: Yes. You're just trying to be young. "Charlie" sounds younger than "Mr. Macpherson." Right?

MACPHERSON: Maybe. But you don't have to say it when ladies are present.

JESSIE: May I go?

MACPHERSON: Yes, you can do anything you wish. She's leaving, Jack, doesn't want to work for me.

JESSIE: Mr. Macpherson, I've explained to you...

MACPHERSON (interrupting): Yes. You don't need to explain it a second time. Run along now, Jessie.

(Exit Jessie)

MACPHERSON: I'm getting old, Jack. Yesterday I suggested that when Miss Bridge comes back, Jessie could change places with her and stay with me. Like it used to be... No. She likes the City desk better. I'm getting old... Smith'll be here in a quarter of an hour.

GOULD: Well, how were the Russians?

MACPHERSON: The newspapermen? I quite forgot them. (Into the telephone) Mike! Send me Hardy, and in five minutes.

PRESTON (to Gould): Well, they've got their heads on their shoulders. (Laughs) At lunch they replied to a hundred impolite questions of ours with a hundred very polite jabs. And when we got up, they asked Bill Crosby, who was host, to allow them to shoot one more parting question—what did he consider to be the difference between a lunch and a press conference? Crosby was on the spot, all right.

(Enter Hardy)

MACPHERSON: Hardy, when you go to the Russians' last press conference tomorrow, get in one last question—are the rumors true that they brought money with them to finance our coal strike?

HARDY: But...

MACPHERSON: What?

HARDY: They'll only shrug their shoulders.

MACPHERSON: Of course. And you'll write that the only reply the Russians could give was an embarrassed shrug, or something of that sort. It's your job to dope it out. That's all.

HARDY: OK. (Exit)

GOULD: Isn't that a bit too obvious for a serious paper?

MACPHERSON: Doesn't matter. Everybody knows Hardy's a mudslinger. It'll sound quite natural coming from him.

GOULD: Maybe you're right.

MACPHERSON: You mean I'm not quite gaga yet?

GOULD: Not quite.

MACPHERSON: What d'ya mean, not quite?

GOULD: I mean, that wasn't quite what I wanted to say. It's that you're taking a firmer stand every day. I like that.

MACPHERSON: So do I. And I think I like it even more than you. (Slams his fist on the desk) A fine old-fashioned desk. Even for a man playing along new lines, it's pleasant to sit at an old-fashioned desk like this. Right?

GOULD: Sure.

MACPHERSON: Yes, sure. But unfortunately you'll have to wait. Unfortunately it was I and not you who started this job thirty years ago in that old wreck (pointing to the photograph of the house over the table.) Too bad. The sacred right of private property.

GOULD (walking around the office): Aha, an old friend come to light again.

MACPHERSON (approaching and looking at a photograph of Mussolini): Yes. Well, what about it? Ever since the poor devil was hanged head down in Milan, he's most certainly been dead. Speak no ill of the dead. He autographed it when I was in his Rome palace in '33. Look at that autograph. One of the best in my collection.

GOULD: And the other gentleman?? Still in the safe?

MACPHERSON: For the present. There are rumors that he's still alive. Too early to hang him yet.

GOULD: I think you'd be quite safe.

MACPHERSON: No, it's still too early.

GOULD: You're too much afraid of the future. That's the trouble with you.

PRESTON (entering): Here I am. How are you? Hello Jack.

GOULD: Hello.

MACPHERSON: What have you got about Russia today, Bill?

PRESTON: U.P. gave us fifty lines by Harner on the Russians in Vienna. Harner praises the Russians. Don't know whether to use it or not.

MACPHERSON: Sure we'll use it. Unlike Hearst, we keep our information objective. Put it on page 16. No closer. What else?

PRESTON: Wippman's article on Russian expansionist plans and five or six more items of that sort.

MACPHERSON: Give it all. We're objective. Put Wippman on the front page, the rest no further than the sixth. What else?

PRESTON: What else? A crazy Italian report about Russian aircraft over Eritreia. But that's just crap.

MACPHERSON: Headline it on page one.

PRESTON: But the Russians will deny it tomorrow.

MACPHERSON: Well what if they do? We'll put it on page twenty. Five lines. They always write short denials. Millions of people'll read the report, and ten thousand the denial.

PRESTON: I don't like this business.

MACPHERSON: What's that?

PRESTON: You're interfering with the work of my department. I'm used to running my own show.

MACPHERSON: Sorry, you're right Bill, and I'm very sorry. But you don't seem to get me these days.

PRESTON: I got you all right a month ago. You've changed this month.

MACPHERSON: Of course I have. You'll have to understand that. Well, so long.

PRESTON: Goodbye. (Exit)

GOULD: Smith'll be along in three minutes.

MACPHERSON: Yes. Well, I guess he'll just have to fall in line. Thirty thousand for a series of articles and a book with a guaranteed sale. I tell you, if I didn't need it so badly I wouldn't pay him a cent over fifteen. He'll agree. Things are pretty bad with him. He hasn't written anything for nearly a year and hasn't made a dollar.

GOULD: Why hasn't he been writing?

MACPHERSON: I got two letters from him—in Okinawa in Japan. Post-war lunacy. He thought that as soon as peace was signed, there'd be cooing doves and blooming roses everywhere. But the world's the same as it always was. And that just drove him nuts. He told me he couldn't write anything till he understood what was going on in the world. To hell with that anyway—he'll go.

GOULD: He's thinking of marrying Jessie.

MACPHERSON: So that's it? Now I understand. Well, it's a pity but it's a good thing at the same time. He'll go all right. Jessie's not the right girl for life in a shack.

SMITH (entering): How do you do, chief. Hello Jack. (shakes hands)

MACPHERSON: Sit down Harry.

SMITH: There. But if you don't mind my asking—what's all the hurry about? I got a shaking over the Pacific that's turned my guts inside out.

MACPHERSON: And I'm afraid that now you'll have to take a shaking over the Atlantic.

SMITH: What do you want me to do?

MACPHERSON: Russia.

SMITH: Russia? You know I've been having insomnia this last month and for the first time in my life, I started reading our worthy paper nights. Judging by your new political line, I guess there's not much sense in picking me for Russia.

MACPHERSON: First of all, thanks for reading my paper at last. And secondly, I've decided that considering my new line, it's precisely you that I want to send to Russia.

SMITH: You're getting me mixed up with Jack, chief.

GOULD: Don't be a fool. After the books I wrote about Russia, they would be idiots to let me in again. And unfortunately, they're not idiots.

SMITH: But after the book I wrote about Russia only an idiot could advise the chief to send me of all people to Russia now, considering his new line.

GOULD: Thanks. But you've got it all balled up as usual. I'll just show you why it's not I, but you who's the idiot.

SMITH (settling himself comfortably in his armchair): That's interesting. It's something I've been wondering about all my life. The fact's plain enough, but the reason's not very clear.

GOULD: You're an idiot because you don't know anything about dialectics. Dialectics is a science showing how everything constantly moves and changes.

SMITH (interrupting): Splendid. I never acquired wisdom so quickly in my life.

GOULD (continuing): So you see, if you approach the question dialectically... (Smith takes out a notebook and writes something) What are you doing?

SMITH: Taking it down: "dialectically."

MACPHERSON (reproachfully): Harry!

SMITH: Don't be angry, chief. That's all. I'm all attention.

GOULD (continuing): Then your 1942 book praising Russia ought to help you write quite a different book about Russia now. The kind of book we need.

SMITH: What do you mean we?

MACPHERSON: People who think we don't need communism in America.

SMITH: I'm one of them. Live and let live—the Russians have their own ways, we have ours. Well, what next?

GOULD: Next is that you should go to Russia again and write the whole truth about it.

SMITH: But I wrote the whole truth then.

GOULD: No.

SMITH: Hey! Take it easy!

GOULD: What did you write? That the Russians are brave soldiers, that they held

Stalingrad heroically, that their airmen rammed the Germans, that their women are snipers. And are you going to tell me that that's the whole truth about Russia?

SMITH: Everything I wrote was the truth.

GOULD: And has it not occurred to you that now, when those brave soldiers have got to the heart of Europe and Korea, when those airmen are flying over Vienna and Port Arthur, that this truth isn't turned against the Germans anymore, but against us?

SMITH: I've read all that in our worthy newspaper.

GOULD: And you think the Russians won't go any further?

SMITH: On the contrary, first they'll conquer Europe, then America, then Australia. Then the Antarctic... Of all the bunk!

GOULD: Bunk? Did you ever read Marx's *Communist Manifesto?* And Lenin's *Imperialism, the Last Stage of Capitalism*—note the last. Did you read it or not?

SMITH: No, I never read it, and what's that got to do with all this, anyway?

GOULD: And then...

MACPHERSON: Hold your horses, Jack. Get on with your conversation without me, I've got to go. Take my advice, Harry, and listen to Jack. He'll tell you what we both think. And now just a couple of words. You'll fly in two weeks. Time— three months. The book—a month after you're back. Part'll go as articles in the paper. Publication is guaranteed. Success guaranteed. Thirty thousand dollars guaranteed. Your answer here by midnight tomorrow. Say yes, and you get my first check for seven thousand five hundred. Think it over. Goodbye. (Exit)

SMITH: Seventy-five hundred bucks! Not bad for a first advance. The amount makes me think I have to write something pretty vile for you.

GOULD: No. You'd just have to remember the demands of the times. And our present views on Russia, summarized here (takes a newspaper from his pocket and gives it to Smith) in my article. It's not written in such brilliant style—you know I don't go in for that. But some of the ideas and maybe the names, even, might come in handy.

SMITH: "Ten Reasons why the Russians want War." That's impossible.

GOULD: When did you leave Russia?

SMITH: In December '42.

GOULD: And now it's February '46.

SMITH: All the same, they just can't want war.

GOULD: Well, maybe not just now. Let's say even that they don't want it now, I'm not afraid of crossing my "t's." I myself stand for an immediate preventive war against world communism. The Communists are fanatics, and the Russians are double fanatics as Russians and Communists. Believe me, if they think they can make the world accept their ideas nothing'll stop them.

SMITH (clutching his head): Stop. Be quiet.

GOULD: I'm right.

SMITH: Possible. Everything is possible. I don't understand any more in this crazy post-war world. Bombs, espionage, Iran, Korea, Trieste, blocs, unions! Was that what I was thinking about when I was in the Sahara, when I was lying in the mud at Okinawa, when they were taking splinters out of me in New Guinea? Was it all just for that? I can't breathe, I can't write, I can't think. I came with ten dollars in my pocket and I drank it all in order to stop thinking. (Lights a cigarette and suddenly calms down.) I don't know if I want to write that book. I froze with them at the front near Gzhatsk. I drank vodka with them in the trenches. I saw Russian children who'd been hanged, and even if all you say is true, I can't write that book. Find someone else.

GOULD: Think it over till tomorrow.

SMITH (rising): Think, think. What's there to think about? Of course, the way things are with me, I ought to go. It's crazy not to go. But I can't (pause). Listen. Lend me a hundred dollars—I need it today. I'll earn it somehow and pay you back.

GOULD: Maybe you'd like more?

SMITH: No, a hundred.

GOULD: Here. (Presses a bell)

JESSIE (entering): Yes?

GOULD: First of all, Jessie, we're going. (Nods at the telephone)

JESSIE (sitting down): All right. I'll be here.

GOULD: Secondly, tell the boss that I'll call him up and Smith'll give his reply at midnight tomorrow. Well, and thirdly, bye.

JESSIE: So long.

SMITH: So long, Jessie.

JESSIE: So long.

(Gould goes out first. Smith stops in the doorway.)

SMITH: Jessie.

JESSIE: Well, dear?

SMITH: Ten-thirty at the Press Bar, OK?

JESSIE: All right, dear. (Smith exits. Jessie rises, walks about the room.) Yes dear... of course dear... very dear... For three months... Well, what of it, another three months to wait for happiness. That's not so much for a woman who (looks in the mirror) between ourselves, strictly between ourselves, is thirty-three.

CURTAIN

The Man Who Did the Impossible
Gennady Fish (1948)

THIS SKETCH BY FISH (1903–1971) TYPIFIES THE POPULARIZA-
TION OF SOVIET AGRICULTURAL SCIENCE, WHICH WAS SCARRED
BY THE FALSIFICATIONS AND VENDETTAS OF TROFIM LYSENKO
(1898–1976). BUILDING ON THE WORK OF AMATEUR BOTANIST
I. V. MICHURIN (1855–1935), LYSENKO REJECTED DARWINISM
IN FAVOR OF A THEORY OF THE INHERITABILITY OF ACQUIRED
TRAITS. ELEVATING NURTURE OVER NATURE, HE CONDEMNED OP-
PONENTS FOR THEIR ANTIMATERIALISM. THIS PIECE IS A TYPICAL
BLEND OF PSEUDOSCIENCE AND PRODUCTIVITY SERMON WITH
FOLK AND ETHNIC MOTIFS.

> The agricultural history of all times and nations has
> found an entirely new model for farmers in the person
> of the kolkhoznik, who does battle with the elements
> using the wonderful weaponry of technology, and
> modifies nature with the intent of transforming it.
>   —I. Michurin

We head toward the Uil River. It's hot here in the arid plains of Kazakhstan. They
say it's forty degrees Celsius in the shade. But where can you find it, that shade,
when there's not a tree or bush around. If only a breeze would blow. But just let it,
and immediately you'll repent of your wish. Dust, dust, and sand. Wormwood,
camel thorn, and then more sand. It crunches between your teeth, gets into every
pore, forces you to squint, and makes things seem even hotter. And suddenly, in
this scorched steppe, many kilometers in the distance, a tall white building rises
like a mirage, like an enormous snowdrift. The lancet arch leading inside is dark,
promising coolness, and on both sides stone steps twist around the enormous white
building and lead upwards, as if onto a tribune. You can see the Uil from here.

"What's that building that looks like the tombs of ancient Eastern sovereigns?"

"Right here, on the very spot where he gathered his harvest, they built him a
sepulcher!" the guide says triumphantly.

"Who?"

"Read the inscription."

Cast in an iron plaque above the entrance is: "To Chaganak Bersiev."

He was a nomad. His forebears had wandered the immense desert of the Aktyu-

---

Excerpted from "Narodnaia akademiia," *Novyi mir,* no. 9 (1948), pp. 187–195.

binsk region. That's how it was long ago and not too long ago. Chaganak Bersiev had worked for a bai[1] six years as a farmhand. Then he quit. The Kazakhs were livestock breeders since time immemorial. But Chaganak was attracted to the earth. Herding his stock toward the Emba River for the summer, he turned the layers of virgin ground with a wooden plowshare, sowed millet, built a chigir,[2] harnessed his shabby camel, and watered his small field. When the Kazakhs abandoned their nomadic life during the Great Turning Point,[3] chose permanent lands for themselves, laid out auls,[4] Chaganak was already more than fifty years old. He was one of the first aul members to join the kolkhoz. The new aul—the first permanent settlement—pitched its tents on the banks of the Uil. Its twisting waters flow along steppe lands overgrown with wormwood that are as flat as a tablecloth, lacking mountains and hills. The kolkhoz was named "Kurman" in memory of the Bolshevik commissar Slamgali Kurmanov, who expelled the nationalists, the ancestral chiefs Dosnukhamedov, from the Uil.

Chaganak was a rank-and-file kolkhoz member, but everyone could see that he loved working on the land, which the former nomads were not used to, and that he understood plant life. They elevated him to the important position of mirab: waterman. He worked five years as mirab, driving the weary camel around in circles, pumping water with the antediluvian chigir. But how much land can you water with a chigir?!

"If we want to work the land, then let's sow like respectable kolkhozniks," said Chaganak at a general meeting. "Otherwise sixty households will spend the whole summer picking away at some six hectares. Even if the crops grow well, how many can we feed like that?! The sky is drier than the earth itself in our region."

On his suggestion, the kolkhoz obtained an oil engine and a pump. This did not happen without some argument. And it wasn't easy to get the engine. People said: The first big steppe wind will cause a sandstorm that will cover the machine, grind down the tiny parts, and ruin the pump!

"We'll protect it!" argued Chaganak, and he remembered meeting a group of prospecting geologists in a nomad encampment. There for the first time in his life he had seen a motor-driven pump. This vision became his dream.

From 1935 on, an eighteen-horsepower "Red Progress" oil engine, the first on the Uil, sputtered and pumped up enough water to irrigate forty hectares. There was no lack of fuel. Pits were dug in the sun-parched steppe fifteen kilometers from the kolkhoz. A thick, dark liquid trickled into the pits like water into a well. Pure oil. The Kurman kolkhoz drew fuel for its "Red Progress" from these oil pits.

Nobody had ever heard of the illiterate Chaganak before he was fifty, but now everyone suddenly discovered that he was a smart worker, a quick-witted and wise talker, a wonderful storyteller, that he could put together a song or make a merry

---

1. Wealthy Central Asian landowner.
2. A cattle-driven water pump.
3. *Velikii perelom*—the years of industrial drive, collectivization, and cultural revolution, ca. 1928–1932.
4. Villages.

joke like Nasreddin,[5] and that he loved to have guests. People came from all around to hear him talk. And people with an argument would come and ask him to settle it.

But he could be found in his tent only in the evening. He spent the whole day in the fields. He looked after the millet, watched the mechanic Yegalsiev work, and talked to his peer, the mirab Ali Bek Magombetov, about the best time to irrigate.

"Our neighbors don't have a pump, yet they're already done," the chairman told him. "It's already past time to do it."

"I don't care when we're supposed to do it, I care about the millet!" Chaganak answered stubbornly. "It has to be given water when it wants it and as much as it wants, not all the time. So it doesn't get pampered."

"But when does it want to be watered?"

"That's what I keep trying to find out. I water plots in different ways and compare them."

Harvesting still hadn't begun, the millet hadn't ripened, and already he was walking the field, choosing millet clusters that had ripened earlier than the others and taking them home. He spent long nights picking through each separate grain. The local people had sown the "Uilyan White" variety of millet. But it was only called a variety; it ripened at different times, and the spikes were different: some spread out, some grew in a clump. There were plenty of yellowish grains among the white. So from every plot Chaganak took the spikes (why does he need them, the neighbors wondered) that matured earlier than the others. At home, hidden from everyone else (he would never show others something that wasn't completed), he spent long hours selecting the ripest, largest grains from the spikes.

"It's more productive growing in a clump than spread out," he said.

Chaganak put aside the grains he selected for next year's seed, for sowing. And every year, Bersiev's millet crop became fuller and heavier. And he, the link leader, the "millet director," became the kolkhoz's leading figure. More important than the chairman, because the millet grown by his link fed the entire Kurman kolkhoz. People even came from neighboring kolkhozes to get some of the miraculous seeds. He gave seed to his in-law, Kashken Sokurov from the "Zhanakodam" (New Way) kolkhoz, to his pupil Zaura Baimuldinova from the "Kemerchi" kolkhoz, to his competitor Azima Bektemova, and to many others who came from far away to seek his knowledge. These seeds were better than others, and his knowledge was real, for by 1939, Chaganak Bersiev's link was averaging twenty-five and a half centners—153 poods—for thirty-two hectares! And still he kept choosing seeds and creating a new variety.

He loved to receive guests from distant and nearby auls. He spoke with them about life, about the harvest. But guests have to be received properly. Good hospitality makes the conversation more memorable. Mutton bishbarmak! You might be offered such fare in any Kazakhstan aul. But fresh fish—now that's not such a common dish. The old man bought a dragnet, and when he knew ahead of time that

---

5. Khodza Nasreddin, legendary wise man and wit of the Near and Middle East and Middle Asia. Also known as Haji Nasreddin, Bu Adam, Afandi, Mullah.

company would be coming, he would go to the Uil. When he'd return, the net would be full of slippery silver fish. Drinking it down with an endless supply of tea or bouza—an excellent libation—the host and his guest would sit on the felt rug and have long conversations about life. They'd talk about their kolkhozes, about their children. The little ones would crawl around the yurt. Conversation would shift to their older children. Everyone would slip in a boast about his own. Chaganak had something to talk about here too. His son Makhmud was finishing college that year, not just anywhere, but in the renowned city of Rostov. He would be a railroad engineer. His other son was in the army, and his daughter Akzhiben was in a technical school. In a year she would become a teacher. If someone had told him this when he was a nomad of the vast desert, would he have believed it? But whatever was discussed as they sat drinking tea on the rug, conversation would eventually come around to millet.

"Millet is a living thing," Chaganak told Kashken Sokurov and Yevgeny Aleksandrovich Malyugin, the director of VIR's* Aral station. "It's like a little baby that you can make into a fearless warrior or a wily mullah. Here I'm sowing it on an irrigated plot and giving it as much water as it wants. If you do that from year to year, it will become as pampered as an only child. Spoiled. At the first difficulty it encounters it will droop and die. No! I don't want to bring up a mollycoddle, but a brave warrior. I don't want my efforts to shield my beloved son from life's storms. I want to send these seeds"—he holds out large, white millet grains—"into the big world. After two years of watering I'll plant them in a bogar.** I gave him more strength, more endurance, I raised him, and now let him make his own way, let him forge himself, let him become a warrior! And then next year—I'll take the best of what grew in the bogar to my bosom like a beloved son returning from his wanderings and sow it on an irrigated plot."

This is what Chaganak Bersiev said and did.

"Aksakal,[6] do what progressive science teaches us. Cultivating plants was what Michurin did," said Malyugin.

Back then there was a bitter discussion about the possibility of consolidating useful hereditary traits by altering growing conditions and upbringing.

Official Western science said that heredity cannot be altered. It is constant and unchanging. Pure lineage was the best way to develop new varieties, using the Johannsen method. The Michurinists believed that by changing growing conditions it was possible to develop new plant strains that could be transmitted hereditarily. What seemed to be a purely theoretical dispute had enormous practical significance. Partisans of "classical" Western genetics wrote: "Suppose a high-yield wheat variety is developed somewhere. A seed farm selects it, plants it in its fields, and then distributes the new seeds. Some of these descend from good plants while others descend from impoverished plants. This circumstance, as we well know, has ab-

---

* All Union Plant-Growing Institute.
** An unirrigated field.
6. Wise man, elder.

solutely no significance, inasmuch as the descendants of each will be identical...
The same holds true for livestock breeding."*

The Mendelist-Morganist theory of the irrelevance of growing conditions for species development has deeply penetrated seed-farm selection practices. High-quality seed production was based on the assumption that growing conditions cannot influence species. Soil was not fertilized properly. No attention was paid to plowing depth. They limited their efforts to preventing the introduction of other seed types. In the *Handbook for Seed Farm Brigadiers,* followers of "classical" genetics taught that agrotechnical conditions cannot help improve a species.** Everything that Chaganak Bersiev did from year to year to improve his millet strain contradicted "classical world genetics" and fully confirmed the correctness of our national, Michurinist theory. Chaganak Bersiev's work coincided with the Michurinists' battle to develop and improve local varieties. This was what Michurinist scholars were asking for. And this was what the talented self-taught master Bersiev did with unprecedented art and skill, bringing glory to his people.

In 1940, Chaganak got 125 centners of millet per acre from a high-yield plot of 3.25 acres. For the entire 32 hectares of land he averaged 87.5 centners.

Seven hundred fifty poods of grain per hectare! That was a world-record millet harvest.

To this day nobody under any circumstance has harvested as much grain from a field. No grain culture—not wheat, not rye, not barley, not rice, not oats, not even corn has yielded such a crop! Yet it was no miracle, because Chaganak's competitor Azima Bektenova, link leader of the Khobdinsky district's Rosa Luxemburg kolkhoz, averaged 636 poods from 2.7 hectares. Chaganak had supplied her with seeds. . . .

But was this truly the limit? When he came to Moscow (to receive an Order of Lenin) and met with Academic Lysenko, this was what Chaganak Bersiev wanted to talk about.

"What is the harvest limit, what is the end of the road we're following?"

"The great Soviet scientist Williams," said Lysenko, "determined a maximum grain harvest of two hundred centners. He calculated the strength of sunshine and figured out how much of that strength plants could use. Although some called Williams's figures baseless fantasies, I am convinced he was right. But we're talking theoretically. Nobody until now has reached the level determined by Williams. You've surpassed anyone else in the history of agriculture."

"Aha!" said Chaganak Bersiev. "I roll the ground flat before sowing. And then I roll it again afterwards. But the regional agronomist got scared. He said I was doing it wrong."

"That's what he was taught. The old textbooks didn't allow it. They thought that two rollings lost too much moisture, no matter where and when. But it's not true

---

* Yu. A. Filippchenko, *Genetics and Its Significance in Livestock Breeding* (Moscow: Selkhozgiz, 1931), p. 46.
** *Handbook for Seed Farm Brigadiers,* 2nd rev. ed. (Moscow: Selkhozgiz, 1935), pp. 5–7.

anywhere and anytime. If there are strong winds, unrolled ground dries more quickly than rolled ground. When you roll the earth after sowing, the moisture reaches the seeds from below. No, you did the right thing. It's what the Academy recommends."

"Well," continued Chaganak, and his eyes glittered gaily from beneath his thick, black, mossy eyebrows, "then the agronomist said to fertilize the ground. And not only with chemical fertilizers, but with cow and sheep manure and bird droppings. We steppe nomads have never done that. It's messy, somehow."

"That's because when you were nomads you were always sowing on virgin land. And anyway, how can a nomad collect manure? Fertilizer is necessary. Turn it into the soil along with the chemical fertilizer. Here the agronomist was right. Tell me, how do you cultivate the millet?"

Chaganak explained it in detail, and the academician listened attentively and nodded his head in agreement. Chaganak read approval in his eyes.

In the year that the fascist armies fell upon our homeland, Bersiev's link harvested an average of 155.8 centners from four hectares. The rest of the land also yielded more than the year before.

It was a bitter autumn. The enemy raced toward Moscow and rampaged near Leningrad. The Kazakhs collected gifts for the Leningrad front. Three hundred fifty poods of grain were Chaganak Bersiev's personal gift. A delegation was given the task of bringing the freight train filled with gifts, and old Chaganak was part of it. Leningrad was under the blockade. The train with gifts from Kazakhstan was received in Moscow by the Leningrad regional party secretary. Several cars were shipped off to the Seventh Army, which was holding the front at Svir.

It was a snowy winter. Birds froze to death in flight. Pines cracked from the forest cold. In February, before Red Army Day, I had an opportunity to accompany the Kazakhstan delegates to a division camped near Svir. The steppe dwellers stared at the unfamiliar forests. Their beards and brows were covered with frost, and icicles hung from their mustaches. They covered their mouths and noses with their sleeves to keep from breathing the cold air. The delegates stopped soldiers to shake their hands. They pinched their fur jackets and boots to check the quality, and they were satisfied that the soldiers were dressed warmly. A meeting between the delegates and the division's best snipers took place in a village club. The snipers promised the delegates that they would shoot the enemy even more savagely. The delegates promised to work even harder in the rear to bring about victory. But when they gave figures for the harvest gathered that year by Chaganak Bersiev, I thought the translator had made a mistake. The figures were simply amazing. Then he stood himself. An old Kazakh with sunken cheeks, completely bald, he began to speak in a singsong and spoke faster and faster as he went along, caught up in his own speech. The other delegates nodded in time with his words, even the translator, who was already exhausted by speeches and translating.

"It takes many days on a horse and on a train to reach the front. When you count the kilometers—the war seems far away. But look into yourself and you'll see it's there, in your heart, in your thoughts and dreams. Look around, it's in your aul, in your work and the work of all Kazakhs. Where are our men, strong and agile? They're fighting the Germans. And my son is one of them. Women have taken up men's work in our steppe. Our Kazakh women tend the horse herds, lead the sheep flocks into the steppe, plow and grow our bread. Work churns and boils in their able hands. The Kazakh woman works at the call of her heart; her labor helps victory. There is an old woman, Zhaika Isengalieva, in my link; there are young girls: Akbal Beroizova, Zhonelu Zhumagazieva. They never give less than twice the norm. Even the oldest folk have rediscovered their former strength. Mirab Ali Bek Magombetov, a member of my link, is the first to volunteer for any useful job. Nobody does more or better than he does. Indberli Issengaliev, our pump-station mechanic, doesn't lag behind him. I myself am old in years. I'm in my sixties, and I never let my hands rest for a moment. Our sons have left for the front; who will take care of them? Who will give them bread, meat, leather for their boots? Me, their old father. There are heroes sitting before me now. Here on the frozen earth, among the wild forests, fight calmly, win the war. We will do everything in the rear to make sure you want for naught. In Moscow I heard about the exploits of twenty-eight Panfilov Guard soldiers.[7] That was a Kazakh division. And there was Kazakhs among the heroes. I heard how they stood firm to the death, protecting Moscow with their body and spirit. And my eyes wept tears when I heard the bitter news of how the young and great-spirited warriors had died. My heart was radiant with the knowledge that sons of the Kazakh nation are among Stalin's unconquerable soldiers. Old men tell that when Tamerlane threatened one city with war, the citizens asked their wise man: "How can we build an unbreachable wall against him?" He answered: "The wall will be stronger than any army if its mortar is mixed with the blood of a young man who has volunteered to sacrifice his life for the city." And then all the city's young men answered the elders' call. Looking at them, the wise man said: "The city that has such citizens, such warriors, needs no walls. It is unconquerable." I don't know if there was such a city or whether it was a legend. But I know that there are such cities now: Moscow and Leningrad! Comrades, you here are fighting like the Panfilov Guard soldiers. Drive the Germans from our land. And here, before you soldiers, Stalin's warriors, I give my word, I swear that with every year of my life I will gather ever greater harvests for the good of our Motherland!"

At night we returned to army headquarters along a snowy forest road. A day later, the delegation left for Kazakhstan.

In 1942, when the Germans approached the Volga near Stalingrad, Chaganak Bersiev's sons fought the enemy alongside the hero-city's defenders, and he himself did battle for Stalingrad on the fields of Kazakhstan. He harvested an average of 175 centners of millet from 6 hectares. And the average yield for the entire 38 hectares was 105 centners! As the Stalingrad operation was coming to a close, Chaganak Bersiev received a telegram from Comrade Stalin thanking him for the

---

7. Ivan Panfilov, an officer who, with 27 of his men, died heroically defending Moscow in 1941. Many stories and plays about them were written during and after the war (e.g., *Volokolamsk Chausée*).

50,000 rubles that the aksakal, the ex-farmhand, had contributed toward military equipment. Chaganak dictated a letter to be published in a newspaper for Kazakh front-line soldiers. He took upon himself the obligation of gathering an even bigger harvest. Others called it bravado.

"Hold on to what you've done, Chaganak, or else you'll let it slip away. You've risen high already!" they said.

"You've taken on a heavy burden," others argued.

"Was it any easier in Stalingrad?" he would answer.

His competitor friends came to visit him. Those who had responded to his challenge. There were Zaure Baimuldina, Sokurov, and Ashimbaev from the Irgiz district. They talked among themselves for a long time, and then as they were leaving, Chaganak gave each some seed millet. He didn't try to keep it from them, he was glad to share—let mankind's happiness spread.

He found some ground, and the most learned soil scientist couldn't have chosen better. A forty-hectare plot in the Uil floodlands with deep topsoil. Scientists investigated the soil later and discovered it was virgin land that had been a sheep pasture for many years, and that the newly formed top layer was well fertilized with humus. Black earth–type soils were buried beneath the shallow top layer. Evidently, this had once been a river bed of the capricious Uil, which periodically changes its course.

Over the winter, the entire link picked out seeds that weighed not the usual five grams but seven to eight per thousand. This work was as painstaking as could be. They plowed to a depth of twenty centimeters. They fertilized. And Chaganak, knitting his brow, gave the four hectares of land set aside for a record crop a supplementary enrichment of sheep manure.

The link installed a fine, dense irrigation network on the plot. They dug central canals and smaller branches off it so that the millet was grouped in a checkerboard pattern. Every square was surrounded by a dirt bolster. It was difficult work. The people labored without let-up. Everyone in Bersiev's link dug up eighteen cubic meters a day, every day. They removed six thousand cubic meters of dirt during the spring. They fed the millet twice: before they watered the plot, they spread fertilizer in the ditches. And the record plot received a supplement of bird droppings and wood cinder.

"Well, how did the millet tell you when it wants to drink?" the chairman asked Chaganak.

"I guessed myself. Lysenko told me, and my heart told me too: a man wants to drink when it's hot, but when it's cold he's in no hurry. What you drink without rushing is more pleasant and useful. I think it's the same with crops. Last year, the plots that were watered in the cool evening or morning grew up strong, while crops watered during the heat of day failed."

The "Red Progress" roused the steppe with its clatter at sunrise. By day it was silent, and then it coughed to life again at sunset.

Chaganak toured his fields on a kolkhoz steppe horse. From a distance it seemed he was floating atop the millet, like on the ocean, because the horse could not be seen. That was how tall the Kurman kolkhoz's millet grew.

It was during July of that summer [1943] that our army routed the Germans at the Kursk Salient. Absorbing every bit of news from the ever-distant front, Chaganak Bersiev's link began gathering the crops. The harvest was glorious. The spikes were strong. The grains were full and heavy. Each cluster had up to fifteen hundred grains, and some even three thousand. Chaganak did not wait for the millet to ripen over the entire plot. They harvested selectively. They reaped without waiting for the lower part of the clusters to ripen. The upper half might scatter, and only the "beard" would be left. The lower halves ripened nicely in the sheaves. They reaped with sickles. Fallen clusters were gathered by hand. They threshed the grain with rollers. Nothing was lost.

A commission was called to write out a certificate of crop yield.

They weighed it and then checked the scales. Then they checked the weights.

"Weigh it again!" said Chaganak, and he remembered he had given a kolkhoz woman a bucket of millet the day before.

Even he had not expected such a triumph. From each of the record plot's 4 hectares, 201 centners—1,206 poods—had been gathered. The link had threshed 2,848 centners of millet from its entire 36-hectare field, or 80 centners per hectare.

Chaganak Bersiev thought, "The harvest was bigger than the great Williams fore-saw," and he ordered a telegram sent to Moscow, to the Academy.

"How many poods per person?" asked the old mirab Ali Bek Magombetov.

The kolkhoz accountant calculated the figure and rechecked it. In all, 17,088 poods had been gathered, and there were ten workers in the link. That meant each person's labor had brought in more than 1,708 poods.

"And don't you forget that we—Chaganak's link—also till four hectares of vege-tables, potatoes, and melons," the old mirab admonished.

"How could anyone forget that!"

Twenty-nine hundred poods of millet above plan. Almost three carloads above the amount due reckoning by labor days.

The link presented the premium to the advancing Red Army. Thus, the battle for millet was part of our unstoppable attack.

On the day fireworks exploding over Moscow announced that Kiev, mother of Russian cities and capital of the Soviet Ukraine, had been liberated from the occupi-ers and returned to life, Chaganak was handed a letter from Moscow. The president of the Lenin Academy of Agricultural Sciences congratulated the aksakal for his world-record harvest.

"Our millet is food even for science," Chaganak said, smiling.

In the spring of 1944, Chaganak Bersiev visited Moscow for the last time. The Soviet Army had routed the Nikopol Army Group and reached the Black Sea near Odessa. Seed millet traveled along with the advancing army. Many fields had stood empty under the Germans, and late spring was too late to sow spring wheat. Wher-ever possible, the virgin lands were immediately sown with a late wartime crop: millet.

Chaganak Bersiev returned to the Academy again. Passing the cloakroom, he climbed up to the third floor, and taking the sheepskin coat from his shoulders, he laid it on the silk-upholstered reception room couch, much to the secretary's amazement. He walked over the door of the president's office and opened it. When he saw that the academician was in, he took off his galoshes and entered the office in thick woolen socks. According to Kazakh custom, that was how one entered the home of an elder.

The president of the Academy rose to greet him and seated him next to himself.

"How are your wife and children, how are things in the kolkhoz?" the academician asked, looking into the eyes of his guest.

The guest inquired as to the health of his host's family, and about scientific affairs.

Chaganak's beard and mustache had turned completely white; only the mossy eyebrows above his sunken eyes were as black as before.

"I was convinced that millct is the highest-yielding crop," said the academician, "and you proved it. You did what was considered impossible. Now professors who don't want life to leave them behind will have to rewrite their textbooks."

Affection glowed in the look he directed at the old man. The aksakal said:

"I was the leader, and now thousands of Kazakhs are following in my footsteps. They're even passing me. Uksukbai Ashambaev, a link leader from the Irgiz district, harvested 206 centners (of course, the plot was smaller), my in-law Sokurov brought in 203 centners, and a neighbor woman of mine, the link leader of the "Kemerchi" kolkhoz, averaged 175 centners for five hectares. I began it, and thousands of people have taken up, multiplied, and spread my experience, my methods. It fills my heart with pride and adorns my final years. And if it is granted me to prolong my days, I plan to bring even greater glory to my home Kurman next year."

"How will you do that?"

"We received an average of six grams of grain per spike. What can we do to make it weigh eight? I thought for a long time and decided to sow four kilograms less per hectare, to sow a chessboard pattern over the entire field so that each bush gets an equal amount of sunlight. I'll put down bird droppings and sheep manure everywhere. And then it seems I've discovered yet another secret. In early spring, a wind blows up from the Caspian. It seems to me that millet sown before that wind gives lower yields than millet sown after. What's your advice?"

"It's not for me to give you advice," was the academician's sincere answer. "It's I who have something to learn from you."

They talked about many other things as well, and at the end of the conversation Lysenko presented Chaganak Bersiev with his book *Work in the Days of the Great Patriotic War,* and wrote on the title page:

> To my dear, respected comrade Chaganak Bersiev
>
> The greatest scientists determined that the grain yield of one hectare cannot exceed two hundred centners. The calculations were based on the quantity of solar energy absorbed by vegetation. You have exceeded these calculations with your harvest, showing that harvests depend on man.
>
> Glory to the best of the best masters of this unprecedented harvest. I wish you good health for many years to come.
>
> April 6, 1944
>
> TROFIM LYSENKO

Later, when his guest was leaving, Lysenko escorted him out into the reception area. To the secretary's surprise, the president, who was not known for pleasantries, walked over to the couch, picked up the sheepskin coat, gave it to the old man, who had meanwhile pulled on his boots, and helped him into it.

"So send me some winter-wheat seeds that won't be scared of our bitter cold! I'll do my best to make sure that wheat gives a good harvest in our desert."

"I'll send some," Lysenko promised as they parted. And the rest of that day was joyful and radiant for him. But he never had the opportunity to fulfill his promise. That spring, in May, Chaganak Bersiev died at home, surrounded by friends in the aul of Ashi-Uil, in the Kurman kolkhoz.

In Moscow, an obituary was printed in the newspaper *Socialist Agriculture*. Academicians and professors considered signing it an honor.

The fame of the man and his feat of labor, of his world-record harvest and his contributions to science, spread widely across the steppes, deserts, and cities of Kazakhstan. In the city park of Aktyubinsk, a memorial bust stands high on a pedestal. An inscription carved on a sheaf of millet on the pedestal reads:

Chaganak Bersiev
1881–1944

Passersby stop and gaze at the wise aksakal's energetic features. Kazakh bards compose songs about their compatriot.

The tall white mausoleum in the steppe, lovingly built by Kazakh masters, also tells of Bersiev's noble glory. But his glory was not put to rest by melodious songs, the statue, or the stone monument. It is alive. The scientific workers of VIR's Aral experimental station—the enthusiastic conqueror of deserts E. A. Malyugin, who discovered methods of trench cultivation, and A. I. Milovzorov—have developed two new state-certified varieties from samples of Bersiev's grain: Bersievan, in honor of Chaganak, and Guards' (it grows higher than a man), in honor of the twenty-eight Panfilov Guards and Bersiev's vow. All local kolkhozes use those varieties, and every spring the new shoots freshen and spread the memory of Chaganak. It lives and flourishes in the widespread Bersiev movement that grows by the year. In 1947 in the Aktyubinsk region alone there were 700 high-production Bersiev links. The Bersiev movement has spread throughout Kazakhstan.

Is there a glory more alive than that whose seeds sprout in the fields every year, than that which today inspires thousands of noble hearts, thousands of working hands?

Academician Lysenko was demonstrating the results of his experiments on the hearing of fleas. He sat a flea on his right hand and ordered: "Jump to the left!"

The flea jumped over to his left hand. He gave another command: "Jump to the right!"

Again, the flea obediently jumped.

Then the scientist carefully tore the hind legs off the flea and commanded again: "Jump to the left!" But the flea didn't budge.

He moved the flea back to the other hand and ordered, "Jump to the right!" But that didn't help either.

"We can consider it dialectically and scientifically proven," said Lysenko, "that along with its legs, the flea loses its hearing." [4: 106]

[For anecdote sources, see *Blue Blouse Skit*, above.]

Cavalier of the Gold Star
Semyon Babaevsky (1948)

BABAEVSKY (1909–) WAS ONE OF THE MAJOR "POETS" OF POST-
WAR RECONSTRUCTION. TO AN OUTSIDER, *CAVALIER* IS DEADLY
DULL, AND SUFFERS FROM THE DOCTRINE OF *UNCONFLICT-
EDNESS*; BUT IT WAS POPULAR WITH RUSSIAN READERS, BECAUSE
IT DEALT WITH TOPICAL ISSUES, ABOVE ALL THE RETURN TO CI-
VILIAN LIFE OF WAR-HARDENED SOLDIERS. A MOVIE WAS MADE IN
1950 BY THE TALENTED DIRECTOR YULY RAIZMAN, STARRING A
FINE ACTOR, SERGEI BONDARCHUK; AND IT WAS MADE INTO AN
OPERETTA IN THE SAME YEAR. THE QUESTIONS APPENDED TO
THIS SELECTION, DESIGNED FOR SCHOOLCHILDREN, SUGGEST
THE VALUES THE AUTHORITIES WANTED PUPILS TO DERIVE FROM
THIS KIND OF LITERATURE.

IN STAVROPOL

The pilot circled, as if wishing to show his passengers the whole of Stavropol. Bazaars packed with people, a spacious square, thoroughfares with green parks in the middle, the outskirts with their dusty streets, all flew by under his wings. The pilot waggled his wings over the city center and then went in for a landing. He landed so lightly that he did not even stir a sleeping passenger. Sergei touched his travel companion on the shoulder and said, "Get up!"

"We're there?" the passenger said sadly, rubbing his eyes. "It seems I dozed off for a moment." He swung his right foot out the door and jumped to the ground. "It's six kilometers to the town center."

"I hadn't given it a thought yet," Sergei answered. "We can walk if we have to."

"Why walk? Ride with me. I'm about to call a car."

He went off to use the dispatcher's telephone, and Sergei stretched out face up on the grass. Soon his companion joined him and also lay down on the grass, saying that the car had left the garage. He drew a large paper bundle from his briefcase and offered Sergei a piece of rice and egg pie.

"My wife wrapped it up for the road," he said. "I work in Stavropol, but I live in Pyatigorsk. It's a nice convenience. Actually, it's more my family that lives there."

They ate the pie and talked. Sergei discovered that his chance companion was one of the region's leaders, that he thought of himself as an old inhabitant of Stavropol, but that his wife had fallen in love with Pyatigorsk.

"She doesn't want to leave Kavminvod,"[1] he complained. "It's just bad luck."

Sergei talked about himself and his reason for coming to Stavropol.

"That's great!" his companion said open-heartedly. "I'd be glad to help you." He was already addressing Sergei like an old friend. "Listen here: come straight to my office tomorrow. Today is already lost, but tomorrow come first thing in the morning and I'll help you. In any case, write down my phone number. Write down all three. Why three? It's a technical convenience." He laughed. "One's busy, you call the next. Call and ask for Nikolai Nikolaevich. That'll be me. And here's my car."

A black MK sedan appeared on a yellow hilltop.

"Where are you headed?" Nikolai Nikolaevich asked Sergei. "The hotel? Wonderful. Then we'll take you to the hotel."

AT NIKOLAI NIKOLAEVICH'S

At the doorway where Sergei entered the red building, a strapping police sergeant stood with a snappy bearing. He saluted according to the book and politely informed him that the Bureau of Passes was right next door. It was here that the telephone numbers Sergei had jotted down the day before came in handy. Without thinking, he dialed the first number and heard Nikolai Nikolaevich's pleasant bass voice in the receiver.

"Oh, Sergei Timofeevich! Come on up, my friend. I've been waiting for you some time now."

A pass was written out, the police sergeant saluted again, and Sergei climbed up to the third floor. Nikolai Nikolaevich came out of his office. Once they had exchanged greetings, he embraced Sergei and led him along a soft carpet to a table in his spacious office.

"So, let's get down to work," he said. "Where are your preliminary drafts? Give them here, let's take a look."

He took the notebook from Sergei's hand and began to read attentively. His fresh, smooth-shaven face seemed kind and attentive.

"A superb plan," Nikolai Nikolaevich said when he'd finished reading. "We'll type up copies and let specialists familiarize themselves with it."

"Won't that take too long?" asked Sergei.

"Why should it?" Nikolai Nikolaevich smiled. "Don't be in a rush. Such things aren't done quickly."

Nikolai Nikolaevich pressed a button as white as a bayan[2] keyboard, and a girl appeared in the doorway. Nikolai Nikolaevich asked her to take the notebook to the typing pool and get eight copies made.

"That amount will be enough, I imagine," he said, turning to Sergei.

Sergei nodded. The girl left, Nikolai Nikolaevich pressed another button—this

---

1. Caucasus Mineral Waters.
2. Accordion-like folk instrument and symbol of Russian national culture.

one brown, not white—and soon the office was entered by a young man in a military uniform without epaulets, just two rows of campaign ribbons. This was the instructor. Nikolai Nikolaevich introduced him to Sergei and ordered him to get in immediate touch with the specialists and send them copies of the village of Ust-Nevinsky's Five-Year Plan. While Nikolai Nikolaevich explained to the instructor what he had to do and how, Sergei thought about how his notebook would be going all over the city, and that he didn't know when it would return. Sergei couldn't stand it: he wanted to finish everything today or at the latest tomorrow. After he had let the instructor go, Nikolai Nikolaevich comforted Sergei: "We'll have their answers tomorrow, and then no other consultations will be necessary."

There and then he gave orders for the unrestricted issue of passes to Sergei for the duration of his stay in the city, and for the issue of coupons for the closed cafeteria.

The next day Sergei was already acknowledging the police sergeant's salute as something due him and again climbed up to the third floor.

Nikolai Nikolaevich invited Sergei into his office. His face looked severe. He said they'd have to wait another day or two.

Two days passed. The morning Sergei once again entered Nikolai Nikolaevich's office, he was joyfully informed: "Well, Sergei Timofeevich, everything is going well. The specialists have approved the Five-Year Plan of Ust-Nevinsky. And there's one more bit of good news."

"What's that?" Sergei practically shouted.

"Here's what!" Nikolai Nikolaevich could not contain a smile. "I've sent your plan on to our deputy in the Supreme Soviet, Andrei Petrovich Boichenko. I went to his office yesterday. He was familiar with the plan and very much approved of it. He asked you to drop by for a chat."

The deputy would receive him the next morning.

VISITING THE DEPUTY OF THE SUPREME SOVIET

As he thought about his coming visit to the deputy, Sergei prepared a long speech in his mind, as if he were speaking on the Five-Year Plan to a large audience. Perhaps, having heard his report, Andrei Petrovich Boichenko would say: "Aren't you asking too much, Comrade Tutarinov?"

"Not in the least," Sergei would say. "Actually, it's very little. Look at the plan. It's only what is absolutely necessary."

"I have seen and read your plan. But who put down such inordinately large figures? Sixteen railcars of construction lumber. And that's only for one village. A bit much... Perhaps you can get by for the time being without the electrical station and movie theater?"

"Absolutely not," Sergei would object. "How is it possible without an electrical station? And the movie theater..."

"You can't build everything at once. We still have lots of time!"

In his mind, Sergei proved to the deputy that reducing the number of new construction projects was impossible, that Ust-Nevinsky had suffered greater losses under German occupation, and that its collective farms had the resources and the labor.

"And don't other villages have the resources and labor?" the deputy would ask.

"Of course, that's true. But don't forget, Comrade Deputy, that besides the materials and labor, we also have the burning desire to build. Here I've come to you, and you must in turn give us your support."

But the conversation began not at all as Sergei had imagined it would. Andrei Petrovich stood up from his chair, stretched out his hand to Sergei, and, smiling, invited him to sit. He was tall and lean; his dark-gray suit of military cut did not sit well on him. His wide belt was loose, not at all like a soldier's, and his collar was unbuttoned. Andrei Petrovich watched Sergei closely, and the gaze of his gray eyes seemed austere and even a bit stern. His aged face was smoothly shaven.

"So tell me, how was it you quarreled with Khokhlakov?" Boichenko asked, and his eyes had a merry glimmer.

"Did he come to make a complaint?"

"No. Kondratiev was here."

"There was no quarrel." Sergei got up. "Fyodor Lukich, if you have to know, amazes and annoys me. You can't look at life like that. This is how it was..."

"Don't," Andrei Petrovich interrupted him. "Kondratiev told me. And don't you worry, I've known Fyodor Lukich for a long time, and I've already told Kondratiev that we will support Ust-Nevinsky. So let's go over your plan together. Why don't you sit a bit closer."

Sergei moved his chair over. Andrei Petrovich opened up the folder. Sergei got hot. He began to sweat. It seemed to him that even a tank had never been so stuffy, no matter how hot it was outside.

"These three collective farms have different grain harvest plans. Isn't the soil the same?"

"Let me explain." Sergei wiped his red face with a kerchief and bent over the table. "The soil is the same. But look at these figures: the Budyonny Collective Farm can already harvest thirty centners of wheat per hectare, while the Voroshilov and Kochubei collective farms get no more than eight to ten. The chairman of the Budyonny farm, Stefan Petrovich Ragulin, a proud and willful old man, hates his neighbors for that, particularly Artamashov, chairman of the Voroshilov Farm. When he found out that the Voroshilovites and Kochubeians had planned twenty-five centners of grain for the third year of the Five-Year Plan, he immediately put down forty, and the figure was unanimously accepted at a general meeting of his collective farm. Forty centners is a lot, of course. It will be tough for the Budyonny people, but I know that Ragulin wants to show Artamashov how to fight for a harvest."

"Will he succeed?"

"If we help him, yes," Sergei said confidently. "You don't know Ragulin. He's persistent. Whatever he dreams up, he'll do."

"Then we have to help him every way we can," said Andrei Petrovich. "To collect that much grain per hectare is praiseworthy, and it's worth all the work."

Then he asked Sergei detailed questions about the livestock development plan, paying particular attention to the Voroshilov kolkhoz's horse-breeding farm, where they proposed to build three stables and a veterinary clinic.

"Why so much for one farm?"

"There's quite a battle behind those stables," said Sergei. "Ivan Atamanov, who directs the farm, insisted on his own plan, and I had to agree with him. If only you knew that Atamanov! A born horseman. He served in the Pliev Cavalry during the Patriotic War,[3] and was awarded six battle orders. He fights his battles hard. We couldn't but satisfy his request. Beyond that, there weren't any disputes about the number of pigs and sheep. Each collective farm has the same."

After that they looked over the figures for orchards, vineyards, beehives, poultry, and market gardening. Andrei Petrovich sat silently in deep thought. Sergei thought his silence had stretched on a bit long, and he felt hot.

"How powerful is the station?"

"Approximately two hundred kilowatts," Sergei answered, feeling how his damp shirt stuck to his back. "That will be entirely enough power for us."

"Good. We'll approve your plan and pass a special resolution in the Regional Committee Bureau, so that other villages follow your example. But I must give you a warning."

Andrei Petrovich again sank into thought, and Sergei heaved a sigh of relief. It felt as if the windows had opened and let in cool air.

"Yes, I must warn you... To put together and confirm a Five-Year Plan is, of course, important, but it's only the beginning, the first step. Fulfilling it is the main task. A successful resolution requires much effort and selfless labor. You cannot forget that, Sergei Timofeevich, you can't forget." Andrei Petrovich stared at Sergei as if seeing him for the first time. "You're a military man, you'll easily understand me if I use this example. We'll consider Ust-Nevinsky a regiment. This regiment is well armed, its junior and senior officers are excellent, its sergeants are experienced, and its soldiers, of course, are brave and well trained. Furthermore, in the last fifteen years the regiment has withstood more than one test, has won more than one battle. And now it's given birth to a daring idea: to take the enemy fortress by storm and thus show other regiments how such tasks should be resolved. The staff has worked out an operations plan, and I must say it's a superb and daring plan. The general has willingly approved and confirmed such a plan. What else needs to be done?"

Andrei Petrovich again turned his attention to Sergei.

"I know," said Sergei. "But let me talk about a tank unit."

"That's fine with me."

"The people and equipment must be readied." Sergei even grinned. "That shouldn't be any problem."

"That's correct. It's now that we have to get our people and materials ready. People will decide the outcome of the battle. We have to think about them. It's important not only that Ivan Atamanov ardently pursued this matter and defended the interests of his farm, but that every brigadier and link leader—the sergeants

---

3. World War II.

and corporals—understands it himself and can explain it to the collective farmers, how and what they should do in the struggle to fulfill the Five-Year Plan. There are political workers, agitators, Communists, and Young Communists in the regiment. And Ust-Nevinsky has them too. The village's Five-Year Plan must be the banner for their political and party work. I've already talked about this with Kondratiev; he'll help you, but the responsibility is still yours. And how are things on the material side? Is everything all right? No, far from it. What will reinforce the desire of the Budyonny farmers to harvest forty centners of grain per hectare? You have to think about that, too. Just wishing it isn't enough. And construction materials? All right, we'll provide cement and iron from the regional supplies, but don't count on anything more. Don't forget about bricks and stucco. The first thing to do is to speed up construction of the brick factory and straighten out the production of stucco. Without that you can't even dream of any construction. And what will cover the buildings? Straw or reeds won't do. So you have to think right away about the local production of tile. Find the tools and a specialist—I do know that the clay near you is excellent. And lumber? It's impossible to count on lumber coming from the outside. Your only option is to find a local supply. And there is such a possibility. In the hills, in the Chubuksunsk Ravine, there's a ready supply of lumber that was set aside for military purposes but has now been handed over to us. But that lumber will have to be floated down the river; there's no other way you'll bring it out.

"The Chubuksunsk Ravine?" Sergei asked. "I was there and saw the lumber. Give it to us and we'll float it out."

"So we will," said Andrei Petrovich. "And not only will we give you sixteen railcars' worth, we'll give you everything you can manage to get to the banks of Ust-Nevinsky."

The conversation did not last much longer. After all questions had finally been taken care of, Boichenko got up, went to the window, and stared silently for a while at the steppe blanketed in a sultry haze.

"When are you leaving for home?" he asked.

"If I had wings I'd fly off right now!" said Sergei.

"Why do you need wings?" Boichenko smiled and approached Sergei. "I understand that you've sprouted wings; that's fine, but it would be better to drive. Go over to Nikolai Nikolaevich right now. I'll call and tell him what else needs to be done, and come by here again at the end of the day. I'm planning to go to your region, and I'll take you to Ust-Nevinsky myself."

RAFTING TIMBER

The log-float began in the morning. Dawn had not yet broken, not a single mountaintop had lit up with the sun's reflection, but Prokhor had already roused the encampment. The unaccustomed freshness of the morning made people shiver. Ivan Atamanov, Gritsko, and Mitka Kushnaryov tossed off their shirts and ran to the river to wash, just to show that they had seen even colder mornings on the front. Irina lit the fire, set up a tripod, and hung a bucket, the bottom blacked by soot, to boil. The young widow Glasha sat down by the fire. She pulled a small, square hand mirror from her bosom and set to prettying herself, looking at her sleepy, slightly puffy face. Prokhor bustled about the ravine, and everyone understood by looking at him that log-floating was nothing new to him and that if Prokhor hadn't been there, nobody would have known what to do with the tall woodpiles lit by the dawn. He selected a spot on the bank to slide the logs into the water, ordered Varya and Glasha to quickly yoke the bulls, gave instructions to the brigadiers about where to place their people. It was already light in the ravine. "Why does he keep running around? It's time to start," thought Sergei. Tossing off his overcoat, he took a crowbar from under the wagon and called over Atamanov, Gritsko, and two other fellows. They scrambled up on top of the pile, shoved their crowbars under logs, and began work. Logs fell to the ground with a groan. Varya and Glasha led the bulls up; instead of a wagon shaft there was a long chain, thick as a hand. Mitka Kushnaryov made a deep notch on the thick end of a log, wrapped the trunk with the chain, and the bulls, straining, dragged the log to the river.

New logs were dragged up to the river. Each pine was straighter than the last, each beech thicker. The bulls strained so hard they fell to their knees. The chain was stretched so tight it rang. Shouts rang out: "Gee-up, whip that bald devil hard!" Or more friendly: "Go, go, everyone to-ge-ther!" And again logs crawled toward the river, and again the thuds of trunks falling from the pile floated through the ravine. On Prokhor's orders the logs were stacked along the bank in several rows. The sun rose somewhere beyond the mountains, the tops of a distant forest flared up with a pink flame, and the ravine was filled by a bright light pouring from the sky.

Work went merrily.

"Hey, Varenka, heart of mine," yelled Mitka, "don't you dance around in front of the bulls! You're getting in their way."

"She's scared of the taskmaster, that's why she keeps hopping out front."

"Take Glasha, she's not scared of the bulls; she even promised Mitka some treats."

"Gritsko, get down from the pile and show Varya how to act around bulls. You're an expert."

"He'll show her."

"Ha, ha, ha."

"Let's go. Lift it up!"

"To-ge-ther!"

"Up, up!"

Setting his crowbar to the next log, Sergei felt happy. "Just like friends," he thought. "It's hard work, but everyone's laughing and joking." He was particularly happy with his partner Gritsko. Broad-shouldered and big-chested, he lifted his end of the log easily and kept glancing at Varya. He both pitied and laughed at her when he saw the tears in her eyes as she pulled at the stubborn bulls' bridle. "She's so pretty," thought Gritsko, "and the bulls won't listen to her."

"Varya, take the rod to them, the rod," he advised the girl.

Gritsko took off his shirt. The muscles played in his arms and back. Following Varya with a tender look, he bent down and grabbed a log with passion, as if it were a bull he had to break. Watching Gritsko, Sergei thought, "He's a healthy one! If he pushed himself he could toss the log down by himself."

The shouting and laughter lasted all day long. Lunchtime was also noisy. They all ate together on the grass. They ate a lot, in haste, like it was a race.

By their merry and flushed faces, Sergei could tell that the loggers' mood was superb: "We put together a good team," he thought. "With such a tight team we can throw more lumber into the river than Savva will be able to get out of the water before it floats by."

STARTING UP THE HYDROSTATION

When the sun had gone behind the horizon and the stars of the dark June night played above the Kuban, the people gathered around the hydrostation to wait. The final preparations could be seen going on: lanterns flickered, silhouettes moved across the electrical station's high, dimly lit windows, someone with a lantern in hand ran up the steps to the floodgate. A winch-chain rattled on the floodgate, and with a muted gurgling the water burst into the throat of a pipe, struck the blades of the turbine, and a light timidly sputtered on in the machine room. A spinning flywheel could be seen through a window, and Viktor walked around the motor, listened closely, and bent over a turbine with what seemed to be a quiet question. When Sergei and Kondratiev approached the hydrostation doors, the crowd fell silent: everyone understood that what they had been waiting for had begun. Sergei and Kondratiev stooped before the red ribbon stretched across the doors.

"Ready!" yelled Viktor, looking at Irina, who was standing by the sluice gate. "Turn up the engine!"

The scissors glistened and Sergei cut the ribbon. Irina closed the knife switch. At that moment a blinding glow parted the darkness, and it became as light as day around the little building. The orchestra struck up, exclamations and "Hurrahs" rang out, hats went flying, hankies were waved. Irina closed another switch, the village was pierced by light, and those gathered saw Ust-Nevinsky outfitted more brightly and beautifully than ever before. Fires blazed above Ust-Nevinsky, sparking and flaring up, and illuminated the satin green of its gardens, its square, streets, and alleys; lightbulbs burned atop poles, from the windows of huts streamed light brighter than anyone had ever seen.

"Number three!" yelled Viktor.

Irina closed the third switch. Then a glow like the dawn stretched from Ust-Nevinsky into the steppe and climbed in the direction of the villages of Belaya Mechet, Krasnokamenskaya, Rodnikovskaya, and Yaman-Dzhalga, and it seemed to people that these fires illuminated that beautiful future that lay on their path.

These excerpts were translated from *Our Native Literature: Stories for Sixth-Graders* [*Rodnaia literatura, Khrestomatiia dlia 6 klassa*] (Moscow: Sredniaia shkola, 1950), where they were accompanied by the following "questions and assignments":

1. List the main points of the Five-Year Plan of Ust-Nevinsky. What branches of the economy are to be developed?
2. How did the regional leaders react to the plan? How was Sergei Timofeevich received?

3. What must be done to fulfill the Plan? Support your answer with quotations from the text.
4. What are the outstanding characteristics of Soviet leaders that can be found and shown in Nikolai Nikolaevich and Boichenko?
5. Tell about the log-float. How does the author convey the mood of the loggers? Why was the work so joyful?

Stilyaga

D. Belyaev (1949)

A HAM-HANDED SATIRE FROM THE HUMOR MAGAZINE *CROCO-DILE*, IN THE SERIES "OBSOLETE TYPES." THE *STILYAGI* WERE CERTAINLY NOT INVENTED BY THE SATIRIST, NOR WERE THEY OBSOLETE. YOUNG GIRLS AND BOYS, SOME THE CHILDREN OF THE MOSCOW ELITE, OTHERS ORPHANED BY THE WAR, TURNED TO AMERICAN JAZZ AND MOVIES AND OTHER WESTERN ARTIFACTS FOR A SENSE OF IDENTITY AND DIFFERENTNESS IN THE POSTWAR YEARS. THEIR CLOTHING, MUSICAL TASTES, AND SUBCULTURE MARKED THEM AS THE ALIENATED YOUTH OF THE LATE 1940s AND 1950s.

Last summer, an agronomist friend and I were wandering across a field of rye.

Suddenly I noticed an ear of rye that stuck out sharply from the masses of grain. It was taller and swayed proudly above them.

"Look," I said to the agronomist, "what a strong and beautiful ear. Maybe it's a special variety?"

The agronomist pitilessly tore off the ear and handed it to me. "Feel it: this beautiful ear won't yield a single grain. It's a parasite ear; it sucks moisture and everything else from nature, but doesn't give grain. The common folk call it an empty-head. There are also flowers

Krokodil, 10 March 1949, p. 10.

like that in nature—degenerate mutants. They often look very pretty, but they're empty and barren inside. Just like the ear of rye."

"A stilyaga ear," I exclaimed.

It was the agronomist's turn to be surprised: "What was that?"

"Stilyaga," I repeated and told the agronomist the following story.

A literary evening was going on in the student club. After business had been taken care of and the dance was beginning, a young man appeared in the doorway. He looked incredibly absurd: the back of his jacket was bright orange, while the sleeves and lapels were green; I hadn't seen such broad canary-green trousers since the days of the renowned bell-bottoms;[1] his boots were a clever combination of black varnish and red suede.

The young man leaned against the doorway and with a uniquely casual motion put his right foot on the left, revealing his socks, which looked as though they were stitched together from an American flag—that's how bright they were.

He stood and surveyed the room with a scornful squint. Then the young man walked over in our direction. When he reached us, we were enveloped by such a strong smell of perfume that I involuntarily thought: "He must be a walking signboard for Tezhe."[2]

"Aha, stilyaga, you've graced us with your presence! And why did you miss the report?" asked one of my companions.

"Give me five!" answered the youth. "I was consciously late: I was scared the yawning and boredom would bust my jaws. Have you seen Mumochka?"

"No, she hasn't appeared yet."

"That's a shame, there's no one to dance with."

He sat down. But how he sat down! He turned the back of the chair forward, wrapped his legs around it, stuck his boots between the legs, and in some improbable manner turned his heels out with the clear intent of showing off his socks. His lips, eyebrows, and thin mustache were made up, and the most fashionable lady in Paris would have envied his perm and manicure.

"How'ya doing, stilyaga? Spending all your time in the ballet studio?"

"The ballet's a thing of the past. I cast off. I'm stuck on the circus now."

"The circus? And what will Princess Maria Alekseevna say?"[3]

"Princess? Maria Alekseevna? And what sort of bird is that?" asked the young man in stupefaction.

Everyone laughed.

"Oh, stilyaga, stilyaga! You don't even know Griboyedov."

About that time a girl appeared in the room who looked as if she had fluttered straight off the cover of a fashion magazine. The young man howled out for everyone to hear: "Muma! Mumochka! Here, kitty, kitty!"

---

1. Popular in the 1920s and early 1930s.
2. A Soviet perfume maker.
3. From Griboyedov's classic comedy *Woe from Wit* (1824).

He crooked a finger at her. Not at all offended by his conduct, she fluttered over to him.

"Shall we stomp one out, Muma?"

"With pleasure, stilyaga!"

They went to dance.

"What a strange young man," I turned to my neighbor, a student. "And a strange last name: Stilyaga. This is the first time I've heard it."

My neighbor laughed.

"That's not a last name. That's what such types call themselves, in their own birdy-words. As you can see, they've worked out their own style of clothing, speech, and manners. The most important part of their style is not to resemble normal people. And as you see, their efforts take them to absurd extremes. The stilyaga knows the fashions all over the world, but he doesn't know Griboyedov, as you've discovered yourself. He's studied all the fox trots, tangos, rumbas, and lindy hops in detail, but he confuses Michurin with Mendeleev, and astronomy with gastronomy. He's memorized all the arias from *Sylvia* and *Maritza*,[4] but doesn't know who wrote the operas *Ivan Susanin* and *Prince Igor.* Stilyagas aren't alive as we understand the word, but they flutter above life's surface, so to speak. Take a look for yourself."

I had long ago noticed that, whatever ordinary dance music—a waltz or krakowiak—was playing, the stilyaga and Mumochka were doing some sort of horribly complicated and absurd movements, something in between a can-can and the dance of the savages from the Land of Fire.[5] Their ecstatic exertions had them twisting around in the very center of the circle.

The band fell silent. Stilyaga and Mumochka came over. The scent of perfume was mixed with the bitter smell of sweat.

"Tell me, young man, what is the dance you're dancing called?"

"Oh, Mumochka and I worked on that dance for half a year," the youth explained with self-satisfaction. "It chicly harmonizes body rhythm with eye expression. Take note that we—me and Muma—were the first to heed the fact that not only foot movement but facial expression is the most important part of dancing. Our dance consists of 177 vertical leaps and 192 horizontal pirouettes. Each leap and pirouette is accompanied by a distinct smile unique to that leap or pirouette. Our dance is called the 'stilyaga de dri.' Do you like it?"

"And how," I answered in the same tone. "Even Terpsichore[6] will faint from ecstasy when she sees your 177 leaps and 192 pirouettes."

"Terpsichore? Is that what you said? What a chic name! Who is she?"

"Terpsichore is my wife."

"Does she dance?"

---

4. Operettas of the Hungarian composer Imre Kálmán (1882–1953). Very popular and watchable (*Silva* was made into a film during the war), to some in postwar Russia they were ideologically suspect because of their foreign origin and lightness of genre. The following two operas, by Glinka and Borodin, respectively, are commendable for their high tone and their Russian origin.

5. From Stravinsky's *The Firebird* (1910), disdained for its "decadent" modernism.

6. The muse of dance.

"It stands to reason. And how! In St. Vitus' Dance[7] she used 334 leaps and 479 pirouettes."

"St. Vitus' Dance? Wow! Even I never heard of that dance."

"You're kidding. But it's the most popular dance in the court of the French king, Heinrich Heine."[8]

"But I heard somewhere that France doesn't have a king," Mumochka timidly objected.

"Muma, clam up!" remarked the stilyaga with an air of superiority. "Don't manifest your bad upbringing. Everyone knows that Heinrich Heine isn't only a king, he's a French poet."

The group's Homeric laughter drowned out his words. The stilyaga thought it was meant for Mumochka and laughed loudest of all. Muma was embarrassed, blushed, and got angry.

"Mumochka, don't get all puffed up. Wipe that frown off and let's go stomp out a stilyaga de dri."

Muma smiled, and they resumed their twisting.

"Now do you know what a stilyaga is?" the student asked. "As you see, it's a fairly rare type, in this case the only one in the room. But would you believe there are guys and girls who envy the stilyagas and mumochkas?"

"Envy? That abomination?" exclaimed one of the girls with indignation. "Personally, I'd like to spit."

I also wanted to spit, and walked over to the smoking room.

---

7. A disease.
8. German poet of the nineteenth century.

Michurin's Dream
From a story by V. Lebedev (1950)

MICHURIN WAS A POPULAR SCIENCE FIGURE ROUGHLY EQUIVALENT TO THE AMERICAN LUTHER BURBANK IN THE 1930S. USED BY LYSENKO TO LEGITIMIZE NON-DARWINIST BIOLOGY, HE ALSO PROVIDED SUITABLE MODELS FOR SOVIET SCHOOLCHILDREN.

One day some schoolchildren visited Michurin. They were scared to walk into his big garden. They had heard many things about this "garden of wonders." Above

---

From F. A. Fridliand and M. F. Robinson, *Chteniia* (Moscow: Uchpedgiz, 1950), pp. 80–81.

the gate hung a board with the inscription: "We cannot wait for nature's favors; our job is to take them."

The garden was silent, though busy people could be seen working quietly along the shady paths. Only the honeybees and bumblebees were buzzing, and birds were chattering in the trees.

"How can we meet Ivan Vladimirovich?"[1] the children whispered to the watchman.

"Go along that path to the right," he said, "and then turn to the left. You'll see a bench under a big apple tree. Ivan Vladimirovich loves to sit there when he's resting."

The children went where he told them: first straight, then to the left, and they saw: a gray-haired old man with a small, pointed beard was sitting hunched over on a bench under a big apple tree. On his head was a bright felt hat. He was wearing a loose, light jacket and holding a thin iron wand.

The children were scared to go up to him; they crowded together some distance away and quietly pushed one another: "You go first..." "No, you go."

Michurin heard them, turned around, and gestured to them with his iron wand: Come here, don't be frightened. The children gathered their courage and went up to Ivan Vladimirovich. One of them, a bit older, stepped forward and said: "Show us, please, the most important thing in your garden, Ivan Vladimirovich."

Michurin thought for a moment: "The most important thing, you say? All right, I'll show you! Only there's a condition, children: you yourselves must guess what it is."

Michurin showed them apples hidden under gauze caps. "These apples are called Pepins," he explained. "And these are Bellefleurs," he continued, showing them some huge apples that weren't yet ripe.

He showed them Beret pears, which melt in the mouth like butter, and plums as big as an egg, and "Northern Beauty" cherries, which are so big that you can't put more than two in your mouth at once.

He showed them his apricots, and grapes impervious to frost. Finally, he brought the children back to the bench where they had first seen him, sat down, rested his hands on the wand, his chin on his hands, and looked ahead with a faint smile showing through his beard, asking them again: "All right, children, what's the most important thing in my garden?"

The children were silent and didn't know what to answer.

They looked in the direction that Michurin was looking and saw two peculiar trees: one had leaves like a bird-cherry tree, the other like a mountain ash. The fruit on both was black and shiny like wild cherries, yet on the first tree it hung in bunches, and on the other in bristle-like rows.

Michurin stared at these trees, barely glancing sideways at the children: so when will they say what they think?

Vasya again gathered his courage and asked: "Are they the most important thing in your garden, Ivan Vladimirovich?"

---

1. I.e., Michurin.

Michurin burst out laughing and clapped Vasya on the shoulder. "Well done," he said, "You guessed. And do you know what sort of trees they are? The first, on the right, is a bird-cherry, and the second, on the left, is a mountain ash."

"How is that? Bird-cherries have small berries, and mountain ashes should have red berries when they're ripe, orange before they ripen."

"So I decided to make them like this," Michurin protested. "You all know how many wild bird-cherry and mountain ash trees we have. Yet they're of little use or enjoyment for mankind: only the bird-cherry is pretty when it blooms, and children can make garlands of mountain ash berries in the autumn. But I dream," Michurin continued, "not only that there will be more apples, pears, and plums in our motherland's gardens, but that the bird-cherry and mountain ash can become useful to mankind. I decided to make them as good as their sister, the cherry."

The children tried the berries of both. On the new bird-cherry, the berries were still a bit bitter, and Ivan Vladimirovich let the children try only one apiece. But he let them have as many sweet ashberries as they wanted.

As they were leaving, Michurin told them: "Everyone comes here to see miracles. They expect miracles as if I were a wizard. But this is not magic... Everyone can do the same thing, maybe even better. But the fact that they come to look is good in itself. They'll look, learn, and then try themselves."*

---

* Michurin was renowned for the quote: "We cannot expect charity from nature. Our task is to take our bounty from her." An anecdote of the time went: "We cannot expect charity from nature after what we've done to her."

To Stalin from the Peoples of the World
(Through the Halls of Gifts to Joseph Stalin)
Boris Polevoi (1950)

IN DECEMBER 1949, ON THE OCCASION OF STALIN'S SEVENTIETH BIRTHDAY, THE PUSHKIN MUSEUM IN MOSCOW, HOME TO A SUPERB COLLECTION OF WESTERN ART, WAS CLEARED FOR AN EXHIBIT OF GIFTS TO THE GREAT LEADER FROM THE ADMIRING MASSES OF THE WORLD. AUTOCRATIC SYMBOLISM AND KITSCHY TASTE DID NOTHING TO IMPEDE POPULAR INTEREST; FOREIGN OBSERVERS JUDGED IT THE MOST ADMIRED DISPLAY OF POSTWAR RUSSIA, AND RECORDED THE AWE OF RAPT VISITORS.

VOKS Bulletin, no. 61 (1950), pp. 79–82.

Stalin! No name is nearer or dearer to the millions of Soviet people—the builders of Communism.

Stalin! No name is more respected and esteemed by the laboring millions in the People's Democracies, liberated from fascist fetters by the valiant Soviet Army and now happily laying the foundations of Socialism.

Stalin! The eyes of all the common men and women the world over, of all those who cherish freedom and true democracy, of all those who hate war and dream of durable and lasting peace, are now turned to him with hope.

This great love of the Soviet people and of the millions of rank-and-file toilers inhabiting our planet for the leader of the Soviet people and the best friend of all progressive humanity is strikingly reflected at the exhibition of gifts presented to Joseph Stalin.

These gifts, sent from all parts of the Soviet land, from all, even the most outlying, corners of the globe, differ vastly in form and content. Side by side with magnificent masterpieces of folk art, the works of the finest weavers, rug makers, chasers, carvers, embroiderers, and bookbinders are simple, even naive articles. But all the objects displayed here are gifts that come straight from the heart. Deep love of Stalin guided the hands that fashioned them. The people who made these gifts put into them some of the warmth of their hearts, the flame of their souls, their dreams and their hopes.

The first halls exhibit the gifts of the working people of the Soviet land, and may be said to represent materialized landmarks in the history of the socialist state, in the history of the growing friendship of the peoples, in the history of the victories of socialism.

Next to the first electric motor turned out by the workers of one of the country's plants lies a piece of the first rail section produced in a newly built steel mill.

One cannot view these material proofs of the development and victories of socialist industry without feeling thrilled.

Some of the gifts are amazing for the craftsmanship they show. Thus, the workers of the Geofizika Optical Plant sent Stalin a microscope and slide of their own workmanship. The slide bears finely executed portraits of Lenin and Stalin, each three-hundredths of a square millimeter in size. This remarkable gift, just like the piece of rail section, the plain chunk of coal from a new coalfield, like the working model of a locomotive of a new make, or the hundreds of other similar articles, shows that the Soviet people dedicate all their labor victories, all their achievements, to Stalin.

Numerous showcases display letters to the great leader from the various peoples of the Soviet republics. These letters differ vastly in form and content. Some have been embroidered on silk or linen by the skillful hands of expert needlewomen, some are contained in caskets and cases of the finest workmanship. Their most valuable adornment, however, is that each line breathes of the peoples' friendship for Stalin.

I should like to cite here the shortest and most modest of all this multitude of letters—a letter which came together with a gift to Stalin from the Orochi people, one of the smallest nationalities inhabiting the Soviet country. The gift consisted of a pair of moccasins, gloves, and soft slippers. The letter, enclosed in a folder of birch bark, made by loving hands, tells that in tsarist Russia the Orochi had almost died out, their population then just barely exceeding three hundred. Now this small nationality, rescued by the Socialist Revolution, has been regenerated. Its people enjoy equal rights with all other Soviet citizens and are avidly drinking from the fount of socialist culture. "No trace remains of the shacks and shanties we used to live in. Today we live in comfortable cottages. The inside walls of many of our cottages have been plastered and painted." Like all the peoples of the great Soviet Union in sending their modest presents, the members of this tiny people, saved from extinction, celebrate the Stalinist national policy and its great author.

2

Inspection of the gifts sent to Stalin during the Great Patriotic War invariably arouses deep emotion in visitors. During the grim years when in a tense duel with the shock forces of fascism the Soviet Army was deciding the fate of its country, the eyes of all humanity were turned with hope to Stalin, who was in command of the Soviet front and rear. The wartime gifts reflect the thought and feelings of Soviet patriots who were ready to give their all for their great Motherland.

Here is an ordinary album sent to Stalin by the soldiers and officers of the Stalingrad front. Its photographs recall episodes of that great epic battle, the crowning point of military art. Another album contains photographs of the legendary "road to life," built on Stalin's orders across icebound Lake Ladoga, in order to bring relief to besieged Leningrad. Then there are skillfully executed models of Soviet heavy guns and tanks, of the famous Katyusha and other weapons which the Soviet rear sent in abundance to its Soviet Army.

And how many modest gifts are here from individual persons, gifts revealing the honest, loyal hearts of Soviet patriots! Thus, seventy-three-year-old A. S. Pavlova, formerly a schoolteacher and now a pensioner, sent Stalin a silver matchbox with the following letter: "To the wisest leader of our valiant Red Army, to the leader and teacher of all peoples, in gratitude for driving from Moscow the fiercest and most perfidious enemy of all mankind—Hitler."

Guards Sergeant-Major Igor Nikolsky sent Stalin a lovingly and intricately fashioned tobacco box, made of transparent plexiglass. On the lid is a picture of the Order of Victory, and on the bottom a map of the route followed by the Soviet Army in its victorious advance to Berlin. Next to it lies this soldier's simple and heartfelt letter.

"A participant of the war, who has traveled its hard road from beginning to end, I wish to send you my thanks for our victory. The tobacco box is made out of a piece of a downed German plane. I am not a jeweler. My tools were an awl, a penknife, a drill, and a brush; my workshop was the open air. I made it as best I could. The box holds neither gold nor jewels, but only the boundless love of a Russian soldier for his leader, Generalissimo Stalin. Please accept this gift from a soldier of the Great Patriotic War. I have written my thoughts, and given of my best."

Looking at this tobacco box, at the cigarette holders, cigarette cases, pipes, bas-reliefs, and busts of the leader made by Soviet soldiers in their rare hours of respite from active fighting, one feels the mighty force of the boundless love the Soviet soldiers and all the Soviet people evince for their country, for their leader, for their Bolshevik Party, a force which has made the Soviet people invincible.

Among the gifts fashioned by the hands of plain Soviet people are many specimens of marvelous craftsmanship. A bouquet of flowers carved out of wood by a vocational school pupil; a beautiful chessboard and chessmen representing personages from the great battle fought by the Russian people on Lake Peipus—which it took an old Tula workman five years to make; a delicately wrought vase, carved out of a block of anhydrite; a portrait of Joseph Stalin of remarkable workmanship, embroidered in silk by a twelve-year-old girl from a children's home in Minsk—all these are samples of a highly developed folk art, an art which has flowered in the USSR under the sun of the Stalin Constitution.

3

The new halls of the museum are of no less interest. These contain gifts from foreign friends, sent to Stalin from all corners of the world.

Under Stalin's leadership, the victorious Soviet Army saved the world from the threat of fascist enslavement. The great Soviet power, the mightiest and strongest in the world, is now a stronghold of peace on earth. The eyes of all the laboring people are turned with hope to the Soviet people and its leader, whose bright genius serves as a beacon to the whole of toiling humanity. All this has found vivid expression in the numerous gifts received by Joseph Stalin from his friends abroad.

Here we see certificates testifying to Stalin's election as an honorary citizen of Prague, Budapest, Sofia, and many other cities, and also as an honorary citizen of the Rumanian People's Republic. Here, too, are letters from the laboring population of the People's Democracies, thanking Stalin for liberating them from the fascist yoke and expressing their love, loyalty, and respect. Some of the letters lie on stacks of bound volumes whose pages are closely filled with signatures. Illiterate people, who were unable to sign their name, left an impress of their fingers under the letter. A letter from the inhabitants of North Korea bears more than 16 million signatures!

Striking gifts have been sent to Stalin by the people of the new China. A big photograph of Mao Tse-tung hangs in one of the halls. The portrait bears the following inscription in Chinese, in the hand of the leader of the Chinese people:

"To our Leader, Comrade Stalin
From Mao-Tse-tung."

Next to it is a big, colorful umbrella, embroidered in silk and adorned with a fringe of ribbons. The deft hands of many Chinese needlewomen embroidered this umbrella with scenes showing Manchurian guerrillas helping units of the Soviet

Army to rout the Japanese imperialists. The umbrella also bears the following significant inscription embroidered in silk: "A gift to the great Soviet military leader Stalin in token of gratitude for the rout of the Japanese imperialists by your heroic Red Army, in recognition of its great, immortal deed—the liberation of Manchuria."

Here in these halls, where, after all, only a fraction of the gifts sent to Stalin from all parts of the globe are displayed, one sees the infinite variety of ways in which laboring mankind expresses its love for its great leader.

Here you find a letter from the people of India, written on a single grain of rice, wishing Stalin long years of health for the benefit of all toiling humanity; the headdress of an Indian war chief sent as a gift to the greatest warrior, Joseph Stalin, elected an honorary chief of the Indian tribes; a bullet-pierced copy of *The History of the CPSU (B)*, printed illegally in Albania during the war. An unknown Albanian guerrilla fighter had carried this book in his breast pocket until his last hour, when the fascist bullet that struck him down pierced the book, too. Here there is a relic of the fighters in the Hungarian Revolution of 1848–49—an old-fashioned flask sent to Stalin by Young Pioneers of Budapest. Here, too, are highland axes—symbol of courage and heroism—sent by the partisans of Czechoslovakia; and nearby a cane with a knob fashioned like a lion's head skilfully carved out of ivory—a present from a Negro from South Africa.

All these numerous gifts, sent as tokens of heartfelt gratitude and supreme devotion, are striking proof of the noble sentiments which the laboring people throughout the world harbor for the Soviet people and their great leader.

Pavlik Morozov
Stepan Shchipachov (1950)

THIS LATTER-DAY REVIVAL OF THE POWERFUL MYTH OF MORO-
ZOV (SEE MIKHAIL DOROSHIN, "PAVLIK MOROZOV" [1933],
ABOVE) WAS AWARDED A STALIN PRIZE FIRST CLASS IN 1950. IT
REFLECTS CHANGING VALUES, PARTICULARLY A REVERENCE FOR
HIERARCHY AND THE FAMILY (REPRESENTED HERE BY THE FIG-
URES OF STALIN AND THE MOTHER), THAT WERE ALIEN TO EAR-
LIER VERSIONS — AND GAINSAYED THE SPIRIT OF THE ORIGINAL
MYTH. SHCHIPACHOV (1899–1980) WAS A PROLIFIC AND WIDELY
READ SOVIET POET.

Excerpted from Stepan Shchipachev, *Stikhi i poemy* (Moscow, 1950), pp. 190–209, 214–225.

CHAPTER II. THE GRAIN CONVOY

The window of Tatyana Morozova's
House opens onto the lane.
A January blizzard buffets
The cherry tree that it frames.

A nighttime walker will notice:
Though the village has long been in bed,
The golden point of Morozova's
Window is shining again.

Pavlik is engrossed in his reading—
A leader the children all love.
His mother's asleep, and his brothers
Roma and Fedya are too.

Tomorrow he has to wake up
Again at the break of day,
But tonight he follows young Danko
On a walk through the forests and mists.

The gray-eyed, skinny young fellow
Has read through Gorky's whole book.
Pavel Vlasov's been Pavlik's
Companion now for some time.[1]

Fear was a stranger to Vlasov.
Surrounded by enemies, he
Hid his red banner under
His jacket, next to his heart.

Believing fervently, fearlessly,
In the people and the right of his cause,
He entered a Pioneer's daydreams
Off in the distant taiga.

Let the wind whistle,
The light
That flared in his heart won't go out:
To stand up for the truth—there's no
    better
Path to be taken in life.

Tree upon tree... from the Urals
To the gray tundra and seas.
The village was lost in the forests,
With the stars and the blizzard above.

Just try to gaze over, imagine
Those expanses and all of that snow,
Where, buried in snowdrifts, the taiga
Lumbers along like a bear.
Where blizzards weave between hamlets,
Leaving a trail with their claws.

Another short winter's day
Comes in the wake of sunrise.

The wind whips the snowflakes along;
They have a long road ahead.
For thousands of kilometers, snow
Whips up in a billow of smoke.

And in it—near Oryol or Kungur—
Wherever paths wind through ravines,
Golden-haired village boys can still
Have their skulls broken for them,
Or, close to a village soviet,
Potshots are still taken at windows
Where the midnight oil burns...
But there is only one truth in this world.

The days and the weeks go on by,
And for their thousands of sins,
The blizzards sweep the roads clean
Behind the dekulakized peasants.

And in this terrible weather,
Given wings by success,
The country inexorably advances
Toward its socialist goal.

Day and night in the tractor plant,
The conveyor hurries along,
An old-time worker carefully
Drives a tractor from the belt.
"You're needed in the fields. At first
Things won't be easy for you."
He lays a hand on its run-board,
Like it was the shoulder of a friend:
"Don't let me down. Take care!
You're destined to plow up this life."

The cruel northern weather
Takes open space in control,

---

1. Pavel Vlasov and Danko are heroes of two of Gorky's more revolutionary works, *Mother* and *The Heart of Danko*.

And bursts from 1931
Into 1932.

The fluffy snowdrifts billowed,
Ground winds threw dust in the face.
Sentries stand in their sheepskins
Guarding the Kremlin's ancient gates.

The flying smoke of the snowstorm
Swirls and flares over walls.
Above, a red banner flutters,
Like a heart beating loud in its chest.

Stalin is still in his office
Bending over a map. He
Has marked off each site in construction,
And each district's come under his eye.
His finger has touched on the Urals,
The blue Dnepr, whose stony cascades
Will soon be deep underwater.
The gray clouds of smoke from his pipe
Twist into rings and disperse
Above the high peaks of Altai,
The Kuzbass and Karaganda.
The country lies in his purview,
With its villages and all its towns.

The road to the city of Tavda
Has been covered in places by snow.

The horses are covered in hoarfrost.
Cheeks have turned white in the cold.
The convoy of grain makes its way through
The swirling confusion of snow.

Snowflakes whipped up by the biting
Wind whip tears from their eyes.
Pavlik sits on a wagon
With his feet rolled up under the hay.

His mother gave Pavlik her fur coat
To keep him warm on the road.

The high road ahead of the convoy
Is swept and buffed smooth by the wind
To lighten the load for the horses
Who are covered with sweat in the cold.

Above the first wagon, and Pavlik,
A red flag is whipped by the wind.
It flutters—and the heart feels warmer

Close to the trail of its flame:
Remember, the flag's the same color
As the flag on the high Kremlin walls.

Pavlik straightened his legs
And leapt from the sleigh to the ground.
To the side, along the roadway,
The snow and the ground wind blew
    strong.

Steam swirls over the convoy.
Pavlik waddles along.
Just like Uncle Yegor, he beats
His mittens together for warmth.

Uncle Yegor's the best!
He has a beard, and he's big,
He's quick with an honest word,
And always does what is right:
He tells you whatever he thinks,
Without going easy on anyone.
Even the Kulikanovs
Have begun to be frightened of him.

Yegor would never curse Motya
Because she's a Pioneer girl.
He's even happy his daughter
Is such a good one. The road
To Tavda is hard, and you can't
Get used to such cold winter days:
Pavlik walks behind the first wagon,
Uncle Yegor follows the next.

And then, perhaps, on the fifteenth
Wagon, the one way in back,
Auntie Natalya is sitting
With her feet wrapped up in a mat.

Her hands are hardened and calloused:
For twenty years in a row,
She worked the Kulikanovs' fields
Until the night fell.

The Kulikanovs have
A big house
With an iron roof,
Their fences tower above the others,
Their gate has a crown carved from wood,
Curtains hang in their windows.
And to the envy of neighborhood boys,

In the middle of their front yard
Is a mountainous slide of ice.

The convoy horses are tired.
They walk with heads hanging low.
In her mind, Natalya
Goes back through the years and days.
She sits, urging on the horses,
Dusted white by the flying snow.

Kulikanov's a clever one. Still
They found the grain that he'd hid.

They looked in the haystacks, and dug up
The barn, and then the front yard.
Finally Pavlik remembered
To look in the mountain of ice.

Why should they need such a slide,
He asked: they don't go sledding
    themselves,
They don't let the local boys on it,
And at home they have only girls.

Dropping his mittens, he poked it
With a crowbar he had in his hands,
And onto the snow, wheat grains trickled
Out of the hole like blood.

Auntie Natalya remembered
It all like it was happening again,
But it seems that all her memories
Were no longer than the long road ahead.

Natalya fell asleep more than once,
And sang more than once on the way.
The tiny red spot of the flag
Could be seen on the wagon ahead.

CHAPTER III. MOTHER AND FATHER

Winter roared out with its blizzards,
And, feeling the joy of the earth,
Spring brought the rains from the south
And passed through the fields of black
    dirt.

The water ate away at the final
Pockets of snows in ravines.
With carts creaking off down the roadways,
The exertions of sowing arrived.

Pavlik's out plowing:
There's an acre
Of land on a low patch of ground,
Where there's a cluster of aspen
Whose leaves they had raked in the fall.

A brown-haired young fellow, barefoot,
In canvas trousers, he walked
Along his private allotment,
Following his fidgeting plow.

The day would seem shorter with Father,
The ground wouldn't pull at the plow,
They could work together till sunset.
But his father's no longer around.

Pavlik can't even hear
About his father these days
Without his eyebrows furrowing,
Without a sad change in his face.

He remembers many offenses,
But most offensive of all
Was the time that his father shouted
At him when his mother was home:

"Get out, you Communist vermin!"
He grabbed the kerchief on his chest:
"They'll string you up on a cross-post
By this red collar, just wait!
The Kulikanovs haven't forgotten..."
Only his mother knows
How that night in the dusky barn
Pavlik wiped tears from his eyes.

And not because his father's
Carping had wearied the boy,
But because the family's father
No longer belonged in his home.

Pavlik would have liked to walk
Alongside him, his face aglow.
He would like to be proud of his father
In front of his Pioneer squad.

From the year before last, Trofim
Was chairman of the village soviet.

At meetings, Trofim heaped praise
On Soviet power,
But the kulaks

Considered him theirs
For all his trying.

More than just Kulikanov
Hid grain all around, in pits
And stacks of straw, but Trofim
Pretended not to see it.

Rogov—who doesn't he know!—
Lived in Bolshie Dubki,
And owned the water mill:
The whole district was in his hands.

It churned and worked by the river,
Wheat flour covered it white.
Once it was owned by the kulaks,
Now it belonged to the people.

But early one Sunday morning,
Rogov burned down the mill.
High in the autumn darkness
Λ red comb of fire leapt up.

Where it had been standing
Was a pile of ash and silence.

Once when he was a bit tipsy,
Rogov let it slip to Trofim.
It might have been drink, or the moment,
But both kept it under their hats.

Rogov's house stuck out onto
The road, but it had settled
Noticeably. And Rogov, too,
Became stooped and went bald.

He took to reading churchly books.
Cockroaches scurried in the corner.
The icons' saintly visages
Were dark, as dark as his soul.

Rogov's fingers have a tremor
From the years and homebrew drink.
A Finnish knife with many notches
Lies behind the icon stand.

Rogov is waiting for something.
But time goes by on its own.
Trofim has his post taken from him,
And then he is brought up on trial.

A brown-haired young fellow, barefoot,
In canvas trousers, he walked
Along his private allotment
Following his fidgeting plow.

The shirt on his sweaty back
Billows in the wind like a sail.
How delicious the smell of the earth!
It's glad for the coming of spring.

The mist beneath the slanting rays
Grows thin, crawling through a gully.

Tatyana brings her son
His breakfast
Bundled in a clean linen cloth.

She hurries, slipping on the path:
"He probably is starved by now."
She's wearing a polka-dot jacket
With gathers high on the chest.

There's woods ahead, then the fields
With putrid swampland in the brush.
But in the area, Tatyana
Has trodden about every path.

Not anywhere, but here misfortune
Had come upon her more than once.
The bitter years she spent in marriage
Have laid their shadows round her eyes.

She remembers how she sat down at
The noisy table in her best dress
Together with Trofim,
Flustered by her happy fate.

But afterwards, her face grew dark.
She awaited happiness in vain:
That night it didn't go home with her
From the wedding table.

Slowing her step a bit,
Tatyana tries to remember
Trofim neither drunk nor rude,
But she finds no such memory.

She walks between the cedars.
The springtime air is still damp.
She mounts a hillock, and her sleeves
Are filled up by the breeze.

Beyond the hill in the morning blue,
Where the path led onto the road,
Tatyana's eyes revealed some aspen,
And a cherry-tree-filled ravine.

Her ear can make out a sound:
"Hey, get a move on!" Pavlik,
Big-headed and thin, presses
Gnedukha, his horse, through a furrow.

Tatyana looks: the cherry trees
Cast a shadow on the field,
And she wipes back a tear: "Pasha
Handles the plow just like a man."

She hails him. And with a smile
She walks along the plowed earth.
The soil sticks to her sandals,
But it doesn't seem heavy at all.

· · · · · · · · · · · ·

The disk of the burning sun
Stands high above the forest.
The horned plow lies still in the field,
Tired out by the iron.

Gnedukha hangs her sleepy head
Gazing at the moist earth.

And Pavlik has already washed up
With cold water from the stream.
The radiant edge of the clouds
Peeks over a pine forest spit.

A haze hangs over the field.
On the clean linen cloth sit
Boiled eggs, a pinch of salt,
And slices of fresh rye bread.

The brown-haired young fellow,
Who looks so much like his mother,
Sits down to eat on grass
That has almost dried in the sun.

Tatyana, satisfied, sits.
(The cherry tree waves a branch
Like a towel). He's a schoolboy,
But he's become the man of the house.
Fedya and Roma are little,
But this one has grown. For us two

Things will be easier: the house
Won't come down around our ears.

On this gray morning, the mother
Sits with her son on the cloth.
But even while eating, Pavlik
Is thinking thoughts of his own.

He loves it out in the field,
The sounds of the cedars and pines!
His hand slows down as it reaches
Out for the last pinch of salt.

From the newspaper scrap, in which
The fragments of salt had been wrapped,
Wafted the smell of the steppeland
Expanses, and April's gray mists.

In a photo, Pasha Angelina
Is driving a tractor,
Plowing.

"Mama, lookit, this is
A tractor. Look at it here!"
He gave her the scrap of newspaper,
Smoothing it out with his hand.
With his brow stubbornly furrowed,
Pavlik looks at his mother.
"Mama, we'll soon have our own:
We can plow with a tractor,
And then we can chuck those kulaks
Straight to hell through the door."
His mother's sad gaze answered:
"Don't buck the tide, my son,
They won't take pity on you."
"Mama, the entire country
Has kolkhozes. And Stalin's for it.
So what do I have to fear?
Just let them try to touch me,
Things won't turn out like they want..."

Snowdrifts of white cherry blossom
Had taken the gully in thrall.

From it wafted a springtime
Dampish chill. In the shade
A crust of ice hadn't melted
From the gnarled roots of the trees.

CHAPTER IV. THE TRIAL

Springtime's passed too.
Yet at moments
The teeth of the harrow
Caked with clods of black earth
Suddenly bring back the spring.

The days grow long,
The nights shorter,
Filled with the scent of grass.

Haymaking's around the corner.
July is stifling with its heat.
The village lies along the highroad
With its single street.

The scythes in every household
Are whetted and put into shape.
Soon they will bathe in the dewdrops
Of the morning mowing.

In the noontime heat, today
The assize court convenes.

The people fill the schoolhouse,
They crowd in the doorways and halls.
The old men standing around say
They've not seen suchlike in their day.

The people squeeze one another,
Wiping the sweat from their faces.
Drunken obscenities ring out:
Danilka holds court on the porch.

In the overcrowded classroom,
Lit by the sun and the truth,
Trofim is made to answer
Before Soviet power.

For people he knew, and strangers,
He wrote out falsified chits.
Shamelessly,
He shoved handfuls
Of crumpled cash in his case.

And, maybe, these same kulaks,
Armed with soviet chits,
Have traveled Russia, and somewhere

Cripple machines on the factory floor.
But by their chits they're poor peasants.

He listens to the witnesses sullenly,
Seated for all to see.
Without watching her husband, Tatyana
Gives the court her testimony.

She would have responded to all
The questions, if only her grief
Didn't burn in her breast, or if
She could hide her tears from the rest.

The short, bespectacled chairman
Of the court stood up to speak:
"Would you please invite the witness
Pavel Morozov to the stand."

A noise, like the rustling of leaves,
Passed down the rows: "Will he really
Help bring down his father?"
Yegor, the hunter, although
Not much of a talker, stepped in:
"His courage won't fail, he'll go,
Although the kulaks, like wolves,
Have had their eye on him some time.
Look—they're in the first row."
From a cloud of tobacco smoke,
Someone hollowly answered:
"Still, it's his father. A pity.
It's one thing to lodge a complaint,
But a trial's a serious thing.
He'll have to rethink it, I bet."

Pavlik strode over the threshold,
Without lowering his eyes.
He wasn't entering the classroom
Today just to sit through a lesson,
But, prepared for anything,
He approached the assize court
With the word of a Pioneer,
Openly, for everyone to hear.

The brown-haired young fellow removes
His cap, and waits for the questions.

"Are you Pavel Morozov?"
"Yes."

"The son of Trofim Morozov?"
"Yes."

So the examination would be short.
The chairman of the court led it:
"Did your father bring strangers
Home with him at night?"
"Yes.
In the wintertime, when blizzards
Had blown for a week in a row,
Sometimes they sat with my father
By a table at the front of the house,
Everyone said: 'We'll pay money,'
And Daddy scratched his head.
I saw from where I was sleeping
How he wrote out the chits on some
    forms."
"He's lying, citizen judges!
Some evil people incited him
To go against his own father.
The villains want nothing more than
To cover me over with shame."

Pavlik's cheeks have turned crimson,
His father fills him with shame:
Here all the kids from the Pioneer
Detachment have come to watch,
He feels the beat of their hearts.
And his father turns his eyes
Away from his glance.

Father is a word to be treasured!
There's affection and sternness in it.

It is with this word that the people
Express the whole of their love
For Stalin, who has accomplished
A turnabout with his whole life.

Living under your father's roof
With your little brothers and mom
Is bitter, if you can't use this word
To name your very own dad.

The young man searches for answers
To the questions, not for the judge,
But he wants to answer himself
How he should live in this world.

As if by a banner, he stands straight
And conceals naught from the judge.
From the wall, inside a thin frame,
Stalin looks down upon him.

Hearing out Pavlik, the chairman
Of the court rises again.
The heat
And a forest fire's smoke
Have filled the air since daybreak.

There hasn't been such a sultry
Summer in memory.
And on top of that, somewhere
The forests are in flame.

CHAPTER VI. THE COMMUNISTS

It's late.
Above the black woods,
The great moon rises,
Filled with crimson light,
As if just taken from the forge.

Where the path runs into a field,
Nestling up to a neighboring fence,
The ramshackle hut of Yegor,
His uncle the hunter, stands.

The pelts of freshly killed wolves
Are hung from the rafters to dry.
Yegor is gloomy and silent
From the time he's spent in the taiga.

The lonely days flew on past him,
Swept by the rain and the snow.
He buried his wife. He and Motya,
His daughter, live on alone.

Reddish moonlight was pouring
Through the window from across the
    roofs.
Motya can't sleep, she just listens.
"Pavlik's been gone for so long.
You know that he's scared of the kulaks,
That's probably why he won't come."
Motya isn't sleepy today,
Although she won't let father know.

On the other side of an old screen,
By an oil lamp's light, by himself,
Zimin's[2] bent over his reading,
Leaning his chin on his hand.

He's back from his hunting, and Yegor
Is also not sleeping tonight.
To the tiniest screw, he has wiped down
His shotgun with kerosene.

The floor creaks under his feet.
Yegor goes over to Motya.

"In this last day, I think,
A chill has come in. Well, sleep tight."
Two light-brown braids on the pillow
Lie apart on her father's hand.
"If only your mother were living,
Life would be happier for you."
Tired, he sat on the bench
And began to take off his boots.
They came off. Just as he put
The boots on the stove to dry out,
The sound of some steps could be heard,
And a knock on the bolted shutters.

Yegor went out in his bare feet
And opened the door. "Well, come in."
An autumn chill followed Pavlik
Into the hut through the door.
The hinges creaked plaintively,
And Pavlik strode into the silence.
"Uncle Yegor, I've come
On business to see Comrade Zimin.
Is it all right now?"
"Oh, you night owl!
You're impatient. It's a quarter
To twelve. And he's tired—
So don't stay too long."

Too quiet to be heard,
The fly-blown cuckoo clock
Ticks away in the quiet.

The hands on the clock face
Came together and parted again.

The host climbed up on the sleep bench:
"It seems our guest won't go soon."

Somewhere, the dogs set to barking,
And the rooster crowed from his perch.
Night finds the road toward daybreak
Following the polar star.

The village was closed by a circle
Of forests and the paths made by wolves.
Wordlessly hearing out Pavlik,
Zimin turned dark and morose.

"Lie down and rest some... I'll soon
Be back from phoning to town."

Running through the door, he stuck
His arms in his leather jacket.
The village stretched down the high road
For a kilometer or two.

A chilly wind from the north,
The stars and the light of the moon,
And shadows fall black from the walls
In the cold, dead light.

Zimin walks through the village,
And a stooping shade can barely
Keep up with him.
Together with it,
Zimin hastens his step.
He passes the watchtower.
And the flag
Hangs dark above the soviet.

The midnight air is transparent,
And Zimin sees: way up high,
Soaring toward the cold stars,
The flagstaff with its red flag.

From the staff, almost invisible,
Through darkness and forest groves
A thin copper wire runs along
The telegraph poles to Tavda.

For thousands of versts, our native
Unforgiving land stretches on.

---

2. A Communist sent to the village to organize collectivization.

The thin copper wire runs along
To Moscow and the Kremlin itself.

Though Pavlik was not in his own home,
He lay down to sleep on a bed
By the shaky table. And slumber
Forbade him to get up again,
Weighing him down like a mountain:
Not a stir
Of a hand or a foot,
With the flame of an oil lamp guarding
His peace like the eye of an owl.

Filled with the freshness of nighttime,
Zimin returned.
He walked on his tiptoes
So the floor wouldn't creak
From his steps.

He takes a seat by the young boy...
Pavlik's breathing is deep,
His forehead is broad and receding.
A light-brown lock falls on it.

"So this is how Communists grow up.
They grow strong here, on the farm,
And maybe from these distant forests
He'll reach the Kremlin tribune.
He might even see Comrade
Stalin..." Zimin thought it a pity
To disturb the sleep of the boy.
"Let him sleep. I'll read for a while."

CHAPTER VII. PICKING BERRIES

The forest leaves had scattered,
Thinned in the golden autumn.
The cranberries in the mossy bogs
Had been nipped by frost.

But the cranberries had ripened late,
They didn't mind the cold.
Their juices had gotten sweeter still
Beneath the white hoarfrost.

In the local berry places
They are carried along forest paths
Red, in buckets,
Intermingled with frost.

And in September the bears
Gorge themselves on cranberries.

Pavlik and his brother Fedya
Roused themselves at dawn.

They took the empty buckets,
Rattled the door ring,
And set off briskly down
The path,
Their faces to the sun.

Little Fedya is happy,
His eyes won't leave his brother.
With the rising of the sun
He is going
To the field for the first time.

He goes together with Pavlik,
Measuring the paths with their steps:
His big brother Pavlik's in fourth grade,
And he's not in any at all.
Pavlik is first in his squad,
And Fedya would join up too,
But the Pioneers tell him
That he still has to grow a bit.

Sometimes he hardly can see
The path as it races ahead.
The bushes shake off the frost,
And the leaves crunch under their steps.

Pavlik walks on... All roads,
His whole life still lies ahead,
He walks with a long stride,
His kerchief aflame on his breast.

And right where the path forks off,
Where a willow grows thick in the gully,
Danilka and some older man
Are standing in the bushes.

They stand concealed.
The boys
Can't see through the bushes,
And happy Fedya is trotting
Just to keep up with his brother.

But right where the bushes grew higher,—
Rustling the frozen leaves,

Danilka stepped out to meet them,
Clenching the grip of his knife.

He stepped on the path—You won't pass.
His knife has more than one notch.

. . . .

The sun is already high in the sky.
The frost
On the rooftops has long ago thawed.
Tatyana stares through the window
Waiting for her children.

Never before had she feared so
For her children.
She got up, stood a bit on the porch,
And sat by the window again.

"Natalya went gathering later,
She was walking with sore feet,
And yet she's back. Maybe
Natalya saw the boys."

She ran out through the gate,
And she saw: Danilka was walking home
Not by the straight road, not
By the street, but through back yards.

"Why is he, that convict,
Trying to skirt our houses?"
Her heart shuddered with fear:
"The scoundrel long ago threatened..."

She went to Natalya's. From Natalya
To Yegor. Not a sight of the kids.

Without feeling the ground, Tatyana
Runs along an overgrown back street.

Danilka's woman is washing
His shirt by the door. She wasn't
Expecting strangers. The suds
On the rim of the washtub are red.

Tatyana could see the water
Was darkened by the washed-off blood.
The old woman made a fuss,
But too late to hide the traces.

Tatyana's eyes were glued
To the shirt, and the dark stains on it.

She staggered back in horror
And raced out through the door.

She passed the school and smithy.
No longer seeing a thing,
She ran glancing up at the sun.
It shone black in the sky.

And the leaves, redder than copper,
Fly down upon the dead.
Fedya won't have to worry
About joining the Pioneers.

Dry grass was clinging
To a crewcut child's head.
The deep blue of the north
Was frozen in unclosed eyes.

And amid the willows
And the slender young oaks,
Pavlik lies,
Face down,
His fists clenched tight.

He fell on the leaf-strewn ground,
Like a soldier on the front line.

EPILOGUE

Autumn winds fill the forests.
The kolkhoz village threshes.
A Pioneer is dead. But sometimes
Death has no power in this world.
Pioneer bugles trumpet
This truth throughout the country:
On the mountain slopes of Artek,
And in the forested regions,
Where, despite bad weather,
Motors sing through the taiga,
The years haven't gone to waste:
Our country has become different.
The wooded land of the steppe
Is in the hands of the people,
And our kids know of kulaks
Only by reading in books.
Tractors and horses harmonize,
Combines stir up the dust.
Our kolkhoz fields stretch from

The Carpathians to Japan
Under the pale northern sky.
For all the country to see,
The early harvest is trucked out
Of the kolkhoz to Tavda.
The dust kicked up by the truckers
Billows above the high road.
On the roof of the first truck's cabin
A red banner flaps in the wind.
Evergreens, aspens, birches—
A customary taiga sight.
Sitting beside his father
Is a boy with light brown hair.
The father is driving. The boy,
Tilting the cap to his brow,
Sits in the cabin,
Not just any way,
But right to go for a spin.
He's leaving the Pioneers' village
With the red convoy of trucks.
The wind batters into the window,
The road, white from the dust,
Hemmed in by the forest,
Lies straight and narrow ahead.

His kerchief, the ends tied together,
Blazes like a flame on his chest.
There's much he'll do in his lifetime:
A Pioneer leader, a bugler.
On the path opened up to the people
He will enter Communism young.
And if a just cause should summon
Him to stand in battle, he will
Bravely, scornful of dying,
Defend his dear motherland.
What won't he see in his lifetime!
He'll show up in the Kremlin some day...
A Pioneer is dead. But sometimes
Death has no power in this world.
No power! Look in the cabin
At the young boy sitting there,
When he raises his eyebrows,
Or furrows them with a frown.
In the Red Presnya[3] Pavlik
Stands by the flagstaff in bronze.
An example for the brave at heart,
A companion to Pioneers
He will be for the ages to come.

---

3. A working-class district of Moscow.

In the Heart of Russia

Konstantin Paustovsky (1950)

PAUSTOVSKY (1892–1968), OFTEN ASSOCIATED WITH THE SOFT
LINE OF SOVIET LITERATURE, WAS LOVED FOR AN ABILITY TO
AVOID FORMULAS AND TO SPEAK TO READERS' CONCERNS. THIS
STORY DEVELOPS THEMES PRESENT IN KONSTANTIN SIMONOV'S
"SMOLENSK ROADS" (1941) AND IN THE "VILLAGE PROSE"
SCHOOL OF THE 1960S AND 1970S: THE UNIQUE RUSSIAN SPIRIT,
FOUND NOT IN ITS CITIES BUT IN THE COUNTRYSIDE, WITH ITS

Based on a translation in K. Paustovsky, *Selected Stories* (Moscow: Progress Publishers, 1967), pp. 397–415. Originally in *Ogonek,* no. 31 (1950), pp. 21–24.

SLOWER WAYS, GENTLER UNDERSTANDING OF HUMAN NATURE,
AND TOLERANCE OF ECCENTRICITY.

Once in a while every writer feels like writing a story without bothering about
any of the "iron" laws or "golden" rules set out in handbooks on composition.

These rules are wonderful, of course. They channel the writer's hazy ideas into
a current of precise thought and guide them along to their final conclusion, the
completion of a book, just as a river carries its water to the broad mouth.

Obviously not all the laws governing literature have been neatly tabulated. There
are many effective ways and means of expressing ideas which have not yet been formulated.

An experimental film about rain appeared some twenty years ago in Moscow. It
was shown exclusively to people connected with the film industry because it was felt
that the ordinary public would be bored by such a picture and leave the cinema
wondering what it was all about.

The film showed rain from every imaginable angle. Rain on the black, oily asphalt
of the town, in the treetops, during the daytime and at night, heavy rain, rain absolutely pelting down, drizzling rain, rain with the sun out, rain on a river, when each
drop dug a tiny crater in the calm water as it fell, and bounced away, glittering and
ringing; air bubbles in puddles, wet trains racing through the fields, enveloped by
the locomotive steam; a belt of rain over the coast.

There was a great deal more as well, which I will not go into here. The film
remained fresh in my mind for a long time and made me much more acutely aware
of the poetry of ordinary rain than I had been before. Like many other people I
had noticed the fresh smell of a dusty road after a rainfall, but I had never listened
carefully to the sound of rain nor perceived the dull, pastel coloring of rainy air.

What could be better for a writer, and every writer must always be a poet as well,
than the discovery of new fields of poetry right beside him that enrich people's
perception, understanding, and memory of things?

All this is simply a way of justifying myself for departing from the strict demands
imposed on me by the subject of this story.

So, then, the morning on which this story opens was cloudy but warm. The broad
meadows were drenched with night rain, so that there was a glistening drop of water
on each corolla, and the whole great host of plants and bushes gave off a sharp,
bracing odor.

I was walking over the meadows to a rather mysterious little lake. To the sober
eye there was nothing at all mysterious about it, but it always left people with a
feeling of something enigmatic. Try as I might, I could not put my finger on the
reason for this.

For me the air of mystery lay in the fact that the water in the lake was crystal clear
but at the same time had the color of wet tar with a faint greenish tinge. According
to the accounts of ancient, garrulous old kolkhoz workers, carp the size "of a samovar tray" lived in this watery blackness. Nobody had ever succeeded in catching

them, but occasionally there would be a flash of bronze disappearing with a nick of the tail deep down in the lake.

A sense of mystery comes from expecting something unknown and out of the ordinary. And, indeed, the height and denseness of the vegetation around the little lake made you think that there must be something unusual and fatally curious concealed in it: a dragonfly with red wings, a blue ladybird with white spots, or the poisonous flower of the oleaster with a juicy stalk as thick as a man's arm.

And all this really was there, including huge yellow irises with sword-like leaves. They were reflected in the water, and for some reason, their reflection was always surrounded by shoals of minnow like pins drawn to a magnet.

The meadows were completely empty. There were still a couple weeks to go before haymaking. In the distance I saw a small boy in a faded artilleryman's cap that was obviously too large for him. He was holding a bay horse by the bridle and shouting. The horse was jerking its head and lashing its coarse tail at the boy, trying to shake him off like a horsefly.

"Hey, Uncle!" cried the boy. "Uncle! Come here!" It was an insistent call for help. I turned off the path and went over to the boy.

"Uncle," he said, gazing at me boldly with an imploring glance. "Give me a leg up onto the gelding. I can't make it on my own."

"Who do you belong to?" I asked.

"The druggist," he replied.

I knew that the village chemist, Dmitry Sergeevich, had no children, and I was somewhat surprised at the boy's reply.

I lifted him up, at which the gelding immediately took fright and began to shy away from me with mincing steps, trying to keep an arm's length between us. "Ee, yer a wicked devil!" said the boy reproachfully. "Bundle o' nerves. Let me grab hold of the reins and then give me a lift up. He'll never let you like that."

The boy grasped the reins and the horse calmed down immediately, almost as if it had dozed off. I lifted the boy onto its back, and it just went on standing, head bowed, looking as though it intended to remain in the same spot all day. It even gave a faint snore. Then the boy gave it a sharp kick in its bloated, dusty flanks with his bare heels. The gelding hiccuped with surprise and broke into a lazy, swinging gallop in the direction of the sandhills beyond Beaver Creek.

The boy kept on bobbing up and down, waving his elbows and digging his heels into the gelding's flanks. I realized that all this hard work was obviously the only way of keeping the gelding on the go.

A green, silt shadow lay on the lake, tucked away in the steep banks, and in this shadow the broom, itself silver, sparkled with silvery dew.

A small gray bird in a red jacket and yellow tie sat on a branch of broom making a staccato, pleasant rattling sound without opening its beak. I stood for a while marveling at this bird and its enjoyable pastime, then made my way down to the water, where I knew the irises should be in bloom.

A town girl called Masha who was very fond of plants had come to stay with us from Moscow after her school exams, and I had decided to pick her a bunch of nice flowers. But since there are no nasty flowers, I was faced with the difficult task of choosing which ones to give her. In the end I decided to take one flower and one branch of all the plants which made up the dense, sweet-smelling, dew-covered thickets around the lake.

I looked around me. The meadowsweet was already blooming in fragile, yellowish clusters. Its flowers smelled like mimosa. It was almost impossible to carry them all the way home, especially in windy weather, but I cut a branch anyway and lay it under a bush to keep it from wilting quickly.

Then I cut some swordlike leaves of sweet flag, which gave off a strong, spicy smell. I remembered that in the Ukraine the women strew sweet flag over the floor before big holidays, and its pungent aroma lingers in their homes almost until winter.

The first green cones had appeared on the arrowhead covered all over with soft needles. I took a branch of this as well.

Then I managed, with some difficulty, to hook a strand of frog's-bit out of the water with a dry branch. The petals of its white flowers with reddish centers were as thin as cigarette paper and wilted at once, so I had to throw them away. Using the same branch, I hooked some flowering water buckwheat. Its pink panicles stood above the water like little round thickets.

I could not manage to reach the white lilies and did not fancy undressing and wading into the lake, because your legs would sink into its silty bed up to the knees. Instead I decided to take a flower on the bank with the somewhat crude-sounding name of *susak,* whose flowers were like tiny umbrellas blown inside out by the wind.

Large patches of innocent blue-eyed forget-me-nots peeped out from the banks of mint. Further on, behind the hanging loops of brambles, a wild young mountain ash with tight clusters of yellow blossoms was blooming on a slope. Tall red clover mingled with cow vetch and bedstraw, and above this happy union of flowers rose a giant thistle. It stood firmly up to its waist in grass, looking like a knight in armour with thorny plates at the elbows and knees.

The warm air vibrated and swayed over the flowers, nearly all of which revealed the striped belly of a wasp or bee buried in their petals. Butterflies fluttered about like obliquely falling white and lemon-colored leaves.

Further still was a dense wall of hawthorn and eglantine. They were so closely entwined that it looked as though the bright red flowers of the eglantine and the white, almond-smelling blossoms of the hawthorn were miraculously growing on the same bush.

The eglantine stood proudly facing the sun, arrayed in its best attire and covered with a large number of sharp buds. Its blooming coincided with the shortest nights—our Russian, northern-like nights, when the nightingale sings in the dew all night long, a greenish glow never leaves the horizon, and at the darkest point it is still so light that you can see the craggy tops of the clouds clearly in the sky. Here and there on their snowy steepness glimmer flecks of pink from the sun. And a silver airplane flying at a great height sparkles above the night like a slowly flying star, because at that height the sun is already shining.

When I arrived home, all scratched by eglantine and stung all over by nettles, Masha was pinning a piece of paper to the gate, on which was written in printed letters:

> Oh, there's dust along the roadside
> And there's mud along the way.
> If you wish to come inside now
> Kindly wipe your feet first, pray.

"Ho ho!" I said. "So you've been to the chemist's shop and seen that notice on his door?"

"Ooh, what lovely flowers!" Masha exclaimed. "Really smashing! Yes, I did go to the chemist's. And I met someone really nice there. His name is Ivan Stepanovich Kryshkin."

"Who's he?"

"A boy. Really different from the rest."

I grinned. If there's anyone I know inside out, it's the local village boys. I can confidently say, after many years of experience, that these noisy, restless compatriots of ours all possess one really unusual feature. A physicist might define it as "all-penetrability." These boys are "all-penetrating," or in archaic, high-falutin' language, "omnipresent."

In the most forsaken corner of a forest, lake, or marsh I would always find these boys engaged in the most multifarious and sometimes startling activities.

This is to say nothing of the time when I met them on a freezing, misty September morning at sunrise, shivering with cold in the wet alder thickets on the bank of a remote lake twenty miles from the nearest house.

They were sitting, concealed in the bushes with their homemade fishing rods, and the only thing that betrayed their presence was the familiar sound of snuffling noses. Sometimes they hid so well that I did not notice them at all and would give a start when I suddenly heard a hoarse, pleading whisper behind me: "Give us a worm, Uncle!"

The boys' inexhaustible imagination and curiosity brought them to all these remote parts where, as the writers of adventure stories like to put it, "man's foot has rarely trod."

I am quite certain that if I arrived at the North Pole or, say, the Magnetic Pole, I would be sure to find a young lad with a fishing rod sitting there by a hole in the ice, snuffling and watching for a cod to appear, or hacking a piece of magnet out of the ground with a broken knife.

As this was the only remarkable feature of theirs with which I was acquainted, I asked Masha: "What's so really different about your Ivan Stepanovich Kryshkin?"

"He's eight," she answered, "but he goes around collecting all sorts of medicinal plants for the chemist. Valerian, for instance."

From the rest of her account it transpired that Ivan Stepanovich Kryshkin bore a remarkable resemblance to the boy I had helped onto the old gelding. Any remaining doubts on this point disappeared when I heard that Kryshkin had appeared outside the chemist's with a bay gelding, and that on being fastened to the fence this gelding had promptly fallen fast asleep. But Ivan Stepanovich Kryshkin had gone into the chemist's and handed him a sack of valerian picked out beyond Beaver Creek.

The only point that remained obscure was how Ivan Stepanovich Kryshkin had managed to pick the valerian without getting off the gelding. But then I discovered that he had arrived leading the horse by the reins, and realized that he had ridden as far as the valerian and returned on foot.

It is now high time for me to turn to the subject of my story, the chemist Dmitry Sergeevich—or perhaps not so much to him as to the subject of a person's attitude toward his work, which has been occupying my mind for some time.

Dmitry Sergeevich was utterly devoted to pharmacy. Talking to him convinced me that the popular assumption that certain occupations are uninteresting is a prejudice born of ignorance. After that I began to find pleasure in everything in the village chemist shop, from the clean smell of freshly scrubbed floor boards and juniper to the misted bottles of fizzy Borzhom mineral water and the white pots on the shelves, bearing the label "venena"—poison!

According to Dmitry Sergeevich, nearly all plants contain either medicinal or poisonous juices. The problem was to extract these juices, determine their properties and the use to which they can be put.

A great deal, of course, was discovered a long time ago, for instance, the action on the heart of infusions obtained from lilies of the valley or foxgloves and the like. But there were still thousands of plants that had not been studied, and Dmitry Sergeevich saw this task as the most fascinating occupation in the world.

That summer he was engaged in extracting vitamins from young pine needles. He would make all of us drink a scalding green infusion prepared from them, and although we grimaced and protested, we were compelled to admit that it was most effective.

One day Dmitry Sergeevich brought me a heavy tome to read—a pharmacopoeia. I cannot remember its exact name. This book was as absorbing as the most brilliantly written novel. It contained a description of the properties of a multitude of plants—not only herbs and trees, but moss, lichen, and mushrooms—which were at times really amazing and unexpected. It also gave detailed instructions on preparing medicines from these plants.

Each week Dmitry Sergeevich contributed a short article to the local district newspaper on the medicinal properties of plants, such as some perfectly ordinary plantain or mushroom. These articles, which he referred to for some reason as essays, were printed under the general heading "In the World of Friends."

I used to see them cut out of the newspaper and pinned up on the wall in people's houses and was able to recognize from them the specific ailment which an inhabitant of that particular house was suffering from.

There was always a crowd of little boys in the chemist's shop. They were Dmitry Sergeevich's main suppliers of herbs. They spared no efforts, going off to the most remote parts, such as Horsetail Bog, for instance, or even beyond the distant, oddly named Chancellery Creek, where hardly anyone ever went and those who did returned with tales of waste ground covered with shallow silted lakes and tall thickets of sorrel.

The boys asked nothing in return for gathering the herbs except babies' rubber pacifiers, which they would blow up, straining hard and getting red in the face, and then tie with a piece of tape so that they looked like "flying bubble" balloons. The "balloons" did not fly, of course, but the boys carried them around all the time, sometimes tying them to their fingers with pieces of string and making a sinister buzzing sound, or simply bonking each other on the head with them, enjoying the delightful popping sound which accompanied this pastime.

It would not be fair to think that the boys spent most of the day idling around enjoying themselves. It was only in the summer holidays, and even then by no means every day, that they were free to play around. Most of the time they spent helping the grown-ups graze the calves, gather brushwood, cut willow bark, bank up potatoes, mend fences, and keep an eye on the younger children when the grown-ups were not there. The worst of it was that the little ones could barely walk, and they had to carry them everywhere on their backs.

The two people whom the village boys loved most of all were Dmitry Sergeevich and an old man nicknamed Scrap.

Scrap used to appear in the village once a month, sometimes even less frequently. He would shuffle along lazily in a dusty loose overall beside his old horse and cart, trailing a rope whip on the sandy ground and crying mournfully: "Bring out your rags, old galoshes, horns, and hooves!"

On the front of Scrap's cart there was a magic box made of ordinary plywood, with the lid hanging open. Suspended from nails on the lid there were lots of brightly colored toys—whistles, yo-yos, celluloid dolls, transfers and skeins of bright embroidery cotton. As soon as Scrap appeared in the village, little boys and girls would rush out from all the houses, jostling and tripping over each other, dragging along their younger brothers and sisters, with old sacks, worn-out homemade slippers, broken cows' horns, and all sorts of old junk. In return for the rags and horns Scrap would hand out new toys, the paint on them still fresh, and would conduct long conversations and sometimes arguments about them with his young suppliers.

Grown-ups never brought anything out for Scrap—this was the exclusive privilege of the children.

Dealing with children clearly develops many good qualities in people. Scrap had a severe, even frightening appearance, with his shaggy head, bristly cheeks, and purple nose peeling from the sun and wind. His voice was loud and coarse. But in spite of these menacing features, he never sent the children away empty-handed. Only once did he refuse to take two completely decrepit tops from a pair of boots belonging to her father which were brought to him by a little girl in a faded red sarafan.

The girl's head seemed to shrink into her shoulders, and she walked slowly away from Scrap's cart to her house as if she had been beaten. The children gathered around Scrap suddenly fell silent, wrinkling their brows, and some of them began to snuffle.

Scrap rolled himself a thick cigarette, appearing not to notice the weeping girl or the children who were stunned by his cruel action. He licked down the edge of the paper slowly, lit the cigarette, and then spat. The children remained silent. "What's the matter with you?" said Scrap angrily. "Don't you understand? I'm doin' a job for the state. Don't you go bringin' me a load o' rubbish. I need stuff that can be used in industry. Get me?"

The children said nothing. Scrap took a deep drag on his cigarette and said, without looking at them: "Bring her back, then. Off you go. Starin' at me as if I was a monster!" The children flew off like a flock of frightened sparrows to the house of the girl in the red sarafan. She was dragged back flushed and embarrassed, her eyes still brimming with tears. Scrap examined the boot tops ostentatiously, threw them on the cart, and handed the girl the best, brightest doll with plump crimson cheeks, rapturously round, deep blue eyes, and chubby outstretched fingers.

The girl took the doll shyly, hugged it to her thin chest, and laughed. Scrap shook the reins, the old horse flattened back its ears, settling into the shafts, and the cart creaked its way on along the sandy road.

Scrap walked beside it, looking as severe and coarse as ever, not saying a word. Only after he had passed a good twenty houses did he cough and start his long, drawn-out cry: "Bring out your rags, horns, hooves, and old galoshes!" Gazing after him, I reflected that there were few less attractive occupations than being a rag and bone man, but this person had managed to turn it into a source of delight for the kolkhoz children.

Another interesting fact was that Scrap went about his work with a certain inspiration, ingenuity, and concern for his boisterous young suppliers. He managed to get a fresh batch of toys from his superiors for each trip around the villages. The spectrum of Scrap's toys . . . was varied and fascinating.

It was a great event in the village when Scrap, at the request of Dmitry Sergeevich, brought bronze fishing hooks as a form of payment for those boys who collected medicinal herbs for the chemist, ticking them off on a special sheet of quarto paper. Ivan Stepanovich Kryshkin received ten hooks for services rendered.

The hooks were distributed in reverent silence. As if in response to some silent command, the boys took off their caps, which had all seen better days, and began to stick the hooks into the lining with tremendous care and concentration. This was the most reliable hiding place for all their treasures.

In Russia we have all grown accustomed to the idea that a person of unassuming, modest appearance may prove to be quite outstanding and unusual. The writer Leskov was particularly aware of this, owing to the fact that he knew his country inside out and loved it with every fiber of his being, having traveled its length and breadth and been the bosom friend and confidant of hundreds of our ordinary people.

Dmitry Sergeevich's modest appearance, which, to put it humorously, was striking for its lack of anything remarkable, concealed an indefatigable explorer in his field, a truly humane person who made high demands on himself and those around him. Beneath Scrap's unprepossessing exterior beat a warm, kind heart. Moreover, here was a person of imagination who applied it to his seemingly trifling occupation.

While I was reflecting on this, I remembered an amusing incident which happened in these parts to me and a friend. We had gone to fish on the Old Kanava, which is a narrow forest stream with swift-flowing brown water. This stream is buried deep in the forest far from human habitation, and reaching it is quite a difficult business. First you travel forty kilometers on the narrow-gauge railway, and then it is another thirty kilometers or so by foot.

There are large carp in the eddying pools on the Old Kanava, and this was what we were after.

We returned the following day, reaching the station in the quiet forest twilight. There was a strong smell of turpentine, sawdust, and cloves. It was August, and yellow leaves had begun to appear here and there on the birch trees. These leaves now lit up in turn with the rays of the dying sun.

The small train arrived with lots of empty goods trucks. We got into the truck with the most people—women with baskets of cowberries and mushrooms, and two shabby, unshaven hunters sitting by the open doors of the truck, dangling their legs and smoking.

At first the women chatted about village affairs, but soon the magical charm of the forest dusk invaded the carriage and they fell silent with a sigh. The train emerged into the meadows, and the quiet sunset became visible in all its glory. The sun sank into the grass, mist, and dew, and not even the noise of the train could drown the chirping and warbling of the birds in the bushes along the track. Then the youngest woman began to sing, gazing at the sunset with eyes of burnished gold. She sang a simple Ryazan folksong, and some of the other women joined in.

When they had finished, the scruffy hunter with puttees made out of an old army greatcoat said in a low voice to his companion: "How about us singing, eh, Vanya?"

"Why not," answered his companion.

The two scruffy men began to sing. One of them had a rich, light bass. All of us were stunned by the ease and power of this remarkable voice.

The women listened to the singers, shaking their heads with amazement. The youngest one began to weep quietly, but nobody even turned in her direction because hers were tears of intense admiration, not of pain or grief.

When the singers stopped, the women began to bless them and wish them long life and happiness for the rare pleasure they had given. We also sat in long silence, stunned by the singing.

We asked the singer who he was, and he replied that he was bookkeeper on a collective farm from beyond the Oka River. Then we tried to persuade him to come to Moscow so that eminent singers and professors from the Conservatory could hear him sing. "It's a crime to hide yourself away with a voice like that, letting your talent go to waste," we told him. But the hunter simply smiled shyly and persistently refused.

"Go on!" he said. "How could I sing opera with my untrained voice! Besides, I've passed the age to go gallivanting around taking risks like that. I've got my house and garden in the village and a wife with children at school. Go to Moscow, indeed. Are you joking? I was there three years ago, and all the hullabaloo made my head ache from morning to night. I couldn't wait to get back home to the Oka."

The small engine gave a shrill whistle—we were approaching our station.

"Listen," my friend said firmly to the hunter. "We've got to get out now, but I'll give you my Moscow address and telephone number. You must be sure to come. I'll introduce you to all the right people."

He tore a leaf out of his diary and rapidly scribbled down his address. The train had already stopped at the station and was now puffing hard, preparing to resume its journey.

The hunter read what was written on the paper in the fading light and asked: "You're a writer, aren't you?"

"Yes, I am."

"Of course. I've read your work. Delighted to make your acquaintance. But allow me to introduce myself—Ozerov, soloist at the Bolshoi. In the name of all that's holy, please don't take offense at my little joke. The only thing I can plead in defense of it is that this is a fortunate country indeed when people are so kind and solicitous to one another." He laughed. "I'm referring, of course, to your eagerness to help a collective-farm bookkeeper become an opera singer. And I'm sure that if I had really been a bookkeeper, you would have stopped me from wasting my voice. Thank you!"

He shook our hands warmly. The train moved off, and we were left perplexed on the wooden platform. It was only then that we remembered Dmitry Sergeevich saying that the singer Ozerov came back every summer to his large native village on the Oka not far from us.

But now it's time for me to finish this story. I can see that I have caught the habit of "going on" from the local old men and got carried away like the ferryman Vasily. Whenever he starts to tell a story, it always reminds him of another one, which leads on to a third and then a fourth. There's really no end to it.

My aim was a simple one: to relate a few ordinary incidents that reveal the talent and warmth of the Russian character. And we will talk about the outstanding incidents another time.

Aviation

From *The Great Soviet Encyclopedia* (1953)

EXCERPT FROM AN ENCYCLOPEDIA ARTICLE AT THE VERY END OF THE STALIN EPOCH AND AT THE PEAK OF THE COLD WAR. IT STRESSES NATIVE RUSSIAN GENIUS AND PRECOCITY IN SCIENTIFIC INVENTION (THOUGH NOT ALWAYS IN TECHNICAL AND IN-

---

Bol'shaia sovetskaia entsiklopediia, glav. redaktor S. I. Vavilov, 2. izd. (Moscow: Izd. Bol'shaia sovetskaia entsiklopediia [1949–1958]), vol.1, pp. 90–94.

DUSTRIAL OR MILITARY APPLICATION). MANY OF THE CLAIMS ARE CORRECT, BUT THE TONE OF THE ARTICLE IS DEFENSIVE AND REFLECTS THE CULTURAL LINE OF THE PERIOD, WHICH EXALTED THINGS RUSSIAN OVER ALL ELSE.

Aviation (from the Latin *avis*—bird) is: (1) a means of air travel on machines heavier than air; (2) an organization or service using machines heavier than air for flight; (3) military aviation (the air force), one of the main types (categories) of the state's armed forces.

Types of heavier-than-air flying machines include the airplane, helicopter, autogyro, ornithopter, and glider. The airplane is currently the most prevalent type of heavier-than-air flying machine. . . .

The great Russian people have made outstanding contributions to world aviation history. Russia is the homeland of the hot-air balloon, the helicopter, the airplane, the homeland of aerodynamics and *progressive ideas in airplane and motor construction, and the homeland of the theory of jet propulsion and aerobatics.*

The earliest attempts to establish the theoretical possibility of air flight were made by Leonardo da Vinci, whose observations of bird flight inspired him to conceive the ideas of flying on heavier-than-air machines, of the helicopter, and of the parachute. But credit for the further development of his theoretical ideas and their realization belongs to Russians.

In 1731 in Ryazan, the scrivener Kryakutnoi created the world's first hot-air balloon and made an ascent in it. A hot-air balloon was built in another country only in 1783, by the Montgolfier brothers (France). M. V. Lomonosov was the first to establish the principles of flight for heavier-than-air bodies, and in 1754 he built a working model of a helicopter with two propellers turned by a clock spring.

Work in aviation received broader development in the nineteenth century. In the 1840s the inventor A. Snegirov proposed the construction plan for a dirigible equipped with a variable-angle aileron. In 1866, N. M. Sokovnin made plans for a hard-body dirigible with a 5,250 cubic meter volume and a reactive engine. The German F. Zeppelin made his plans for a similar dirigible only in 1895. In 1869, A. N. Lodygin developed the first plans for and began construction of a helicopter ("electroplane") with a cylindrical electric engine and two propellers (one for ascent, and one in place of a rudder). This idea was copied abroad many years later by Petrozzi and Carman. A large contribution to the development of aviation was made by D. I. Mendeleev, who conceived of a stratospheric balloon and devised plans for its construction in 1875. The first foreigner to construct a stratospheric balloon was Picard in 1931. In 1887, Mendeleev ascended 3,350 meters in the balloon to observe a solar eclipse. Mendeleev defined the future significance of aviation with great foresight. His "On the Resistance of Liquids and on Aeronautics" (1880) served as one of the fundamental guides for work in shipbuilding, aeronautics, airplane construction, and ballistics. M. A. Rykachov's investigations of the atmosphere's upper layers and the lifting power of air propellers in the 1860s and 1870s were also important works. In "Initial Inquiry into the Lifting Power of a Propeller Revolving in Air" (1871), Rykachov anticipated similar studies conducted by the Frenchman Eiffel (1910). In 1888, the great Russian investigator E. S. Fyodorov did a precise mathematical analysis of the potential use of air propellers for flying machines. In the early 1880s, Russian work in aviation attained broad scope. The first Russian aviation journal was published in January 1880 in St. Petersburg: *The Aeronaut,* which aided the development of technical thought and exerted a great influence on the development of aviation science. The Russian Aeronautic Society was founded on November 21, 1880, with the aim of developing the science and art of aeronautics in general; the establishment of the most advantageous means of air transport; the realization of projects for flying machines, the perfection of the latter, and their practical application; and the popularization and propagation of the science and art of aeronautics by all means possible. Between 1870 and 1900 alone, more than 180 works on questions of flying were published in Russia. The works of the Russian scientists M. V. Lomonosov, M. A. Rykachov, E. S. Fyodorov, and particularly Mendeleev laid deep theoretical foundations for solving the problem of conquering the air.

This complex problem was for all practical purposes solved by the Russian designer and inventor A. F. Mozhaisky, who built the world's first airplane [see picture]. The notion of constructing a heavier-than-air flying machine came to Mozhaisky in 1855 as he was studying the flight of birds. He later built several kites with large ailerons that he flew many times, and he determined the size of an aileron needed to lift a man into the air. Mozhaisky built several model airplanes that gave good test results. In 1877 he presented the Central Bureau of Engineering with the model of an aircraft. On the orders of the War Ministry, a commission manned by Professor Mendeleev, Lieutenant General Zverev, Professor Petrov of the Engineering Academy, Bogoslovsky of the Technological Committee, and the military engineer Struve studied the plan and noted that "in his project, Mozhaisky works from suppositions that are presently recognized to be the most correct and conducive to good results." While continuing work on his projects, Mozhaisky received a patent for the airplane from the Department of Trade and Manufacture on November 3, 1881. In the summer of 1882, on a military field in Krasnoe Selo near Petersburg, Mozhaisky's airplane was tested, and it completed the world's first flight. The plane was flown by I. N. Golubev.

The Russian people also contributed other innovators to the field of aviation. A series of model gliders was developed in the 1890s by V. V. Kotov. In 1896 he published an article, "The Construction of Airplanes." After that, Kotov prepared *Airplanes That Soar in the Sky* with a preface by Mendeleev. Kotov first proposed bending wings for lateral stability in flight. In 1894, K. E. Tsiolkovsky published "The Airplane or Birdlike (Aviational) Flying Machine," with designs for a monoplane with a streamlined form, developed a theory for its flight, gave flight specifications, and proposed a successful solution to the question of an engine. Tsiolkovsky was also

The airplane of A. F. Mozhaisky (1882)

the inventor of the autopilot, an automatic aircraft guidance device. Tsiolkovsky proposed and devised the construction of an autopilot in 1898 (see his "Elements of Air Ships and Their Construction," 1898). Great advances in the construction and practical testing of gliders were made by the Russian engineer S. S. Nezhdanovsky. He built and demonstrated large flying models of airplanes equipped with propellers of a type that was used only ten years later for dirigibles. Russian inventors made enormous contributions to engine construction. In 1879, Mozhaisky proposed an internal-combustion engine for airplanes (two-cylinder, double-action) with direct fuel injection (this is attested by the chief naval mechanical engineer's Report No. 405 to the Ministry on May 14, 1879). The first aviation engines were mounted on Mozhaisky's airplane in 1881. Steam engines built to his new designs in 1885 at the Baltic Ship Plant gave 50 horsepower with a specific gravity of 4.9 kilograms per h.p., which at the time was considered a very high index; the engines were the lightest and most powerful. In 1888, the Russian inventor O. S. Kostovich built an internal-combustion engine of about 30 h.p. (a patent was granted November 4, 1892). Its design was distinguished by its novelty and daring. At the beginning of the twentieth century, Russian engineers devised new gasoline engines of original design. In 1916, A. A. Mikulin and B. S. Stechkin built a 300 h.p. engine.

By the 1890s there were attempts to build airplanes in other countries, too. The first of a number of airplanes that rose into the air (unmanned) was designed by Phillips (1892). In 1898, tests were conducted on the for those times gigantic airplane of Hiram Maxim, an engineer. His plane had a surface area equivalent to 372 square meters and weighed 3,640 kilograms (including fuel, water, and three men); its two steam engines could muster 360 h.p. The airplane circled a specially built rail for takeoff. During testing, Maxim's airplane, which carried three passengers, barely rose into the air before losing its equilibrium and falling. The American professor Langley built a tandem monoplane with a 50 h.p. gasoline motor. During tests the airplane rose into the air from a catapult, but it crashed immediately. The French designer Clément Ader built an aircraft (the "Avion") resembling a bat. After flying three hundred meters (1897), the Avion fell and crashed. Work on the problem of heavier-than-air flight was done by the German engineer Otto Lilienthal, who initially tried to build an aircraft with wings that flapped in imitation of birds (ornithopter). In "The Flight of Birds as a Basis for Aviation" (1889), he followed the Russian investigator of bird flight Arendt (1874) and the English designer G. Phillips (1885) in posing the question of the great lifting power possessed by curved surfaces. Using curved wings in 1891, he accomplished a sliding flight of thirty-five meters with a takeoff from six meters above ground. During the next five years, he completed more than two thousand flights on gliders (with balance poles) of his own construction. On August 9, 1896, Lilienthal died when his glider crashed from twenty meters up. Gliding was pursued in Europe by the French captain Ferber and in the United States by the brothers Wilbur and Orville Wright. After mastering glider flight, W. and O. Wright built an airplane that they flew on December 17, 1903 (twenty-one years after Mozhaisky's flight). The Wright Brothers' airplane had a 16 horsepower engine weighing more than 82 kilograms. The first flight lasted 3.5 seconds, and the airplane flew 32 meters. In 1905–1906 in France, Santos-Dumont and Ferber flew airplanes they built themselves. In 1906, the Dane Ellehammer completed a flight on an airplane of his own construction equipped with an 18 h.p. engine.

A decisive influence on the development of world aviation was exerted by the Russian scientists N. E. Zhukovsky and S. A. Chaplygin, who created the world's first scientific school of aerodynamics, which greatly advanced aviational science. More than 180 fundamental works on mechanics, hydromechanics, and aerodynamics belong to Zhukovsky's pen. His first works in the field of aviation were "On the Theory of Flying" (1890) and "On the Soaring of Birds" (1892). Zhukovsky was the founder of flight dynamics as a special discipline within aviational science. In 1911 he published *The Theoretical Foundations of Aeronautics*, which has been studied by several generations of aviation engineers, and which even today is a standard reference for anyone working in aerodynamics. In collaboration with Chaplygin, Zhukovsky developed the wing profile type now called the Zhukovsky Profile. His name

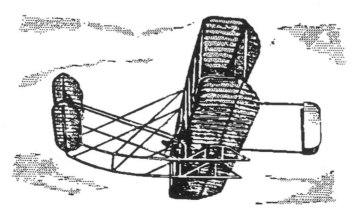

The Wright Brothers' airplane

has also been given to the NEZ[1] propeller, a highly rational form that he established and created in practice. In 1902 at Moscow University, Zhukovsky built a wind tunnel, one of the first in Europe. In 1904 in Kuchino, near Moscow, the world's first aerodynamics institute was founded, whose scientific director was Zhukovsky. V. I. Lenin called Zhukovsky "the father of Russian aviation." Chaplygin was the founder of a new branch of science, gas dynamics, and the originator of high-speed aerodynamics. His works were published in many countries and advanced the development of world aviational science. Thanks to the works of Zhukovsky and Chaplygin, *Russia was the homeland of aerodynamics and became the world leader in developing scientific-theoretical aviational thought.* Zhukovsky and Chaplygin helped educate and form the greatest contemporary Soviet aviation scientists and designers. From 1908, air clubs, voluntary aeronautic circles, and organizations began appearing one after another in Russia. The All-Russian Air Club was organized in Petersburg in 1908.

By the twentieth century, aviation experienced significant progress in other countries, made possible by the firm scientific foundation created by Russian scientists and an increased material base. Whereas the first airplane flights had gone no longer than ten seconds or farther than 100 to 200 meters, an airplane in 1908 could stay aloft for more than two hours. In 1908, pilots risked flights away from their aerodromes. In 1909, the Frenchman Louis Bleriot completed a flight across the English Channel in twenty-seven minutes (32 km). In 1910, the first Aviation Week (April 25–May 2) was celebrated in Russia. The Russian pilot N. E. Popov reached an altitude of 600 meters in competition (foreign pilots went no higher than 150 m in that competition). In 1911, the Russian pilot G. V. Alekhnovich flew a Russian airplane with only a three-and-a-half-hour supply of gas and oil on board on the Petersburg-Gatchina-Petersburg route (100 km) at a record speed of 92 km per hour and set a new record by maintaining an altitude of 500 m for nine minutes. In 1911–1912, flights were made on the routes Petersburg-Moscow (Vasiliev), Berlin-Petersburg (Abramovich), Sevastopol-Petersburg (Dybovsky and Andreadi), and others. The renowned Petersburg-to-Kiev flight was made in the summer of 1914. The 700 km from Petersburg to Orsha were covered nonstop in eight hours. The return route from Kiev to Petersburg was traversed in thirteen hours. This was a new world record. The first Russian pilots to master airplane flight were M. N. Yefimov, N. E. Popov, A. A. Vasiliev, B. I. Rossinsky, S. I. Utochkin, G. V. Alekhovich, L. M. Matsievich, and others.

The realization of long-distance flight was also made possible by the development of aeronavigation. A large role in the creation and development of aeronavigation was played by Russian scientists. A series of flight orientation devices was invented. Flight maps were published. The use of special compasses for air navigation became widespread.

The speed with which aviation developed in the early twentieth century is attested to by the index of records. In 1908, the record for flight duration was two hours eighteen minutes; in 1912 it was thirteen hours seventeen minutes. The speed record of 80 km per hour in 1909 grew to 170 km per hour in 1912. The flight altitude

---

1. [N. E. Z]hukovsky.

The Ya. M. Gakkel airplane

record in 1909 was 510 m, and in 1913 it was already 5,610 m. By 1909, many countries began to build the first aircraft factories.

From 1905 to 1914, many talented and original aircraft inventors and designers worked in Russian aviation. In 1910, B. I. Yuriev designed a helicopter. This machine solved basic tasks of steering, safe takeoff, and gradual motion for the first time in the world. Ya. M. Gakkel achieved significant success in the creation of airplanes. In 1910 he built a biplane that demonstrated high technical capabilities in a 1911 military plane competition. An outstanding event in the history of aircraft construction was the 1913 construction of the "Russian Knight" heavy multi-engine airplanes at the Russo-Baltic Factory in Petersburg, and its later improved version "Ilya Muromets,"[2] which were the forerunners of today's heavy bombers. On May 13, 1913, the Russian Knight successfully completed its test flights, and on August 2, 1913, it set a world record by staying in the air for one hour fifty-four minutes with seven passengers.

In a ten-passenger flight, the Ilya Muromets attained an altitude of 2,000 m, which was registered as a world record for passenger transport to high altitude. On June 5, 1914, the airplane carried six passengers in the air for six hours thirty-three minutes. This was a new world record. At that time, no country in the world had an airplane rivaling the Ilya Muromets for load capacity, activity range, and equipment. The large two-engine hydroplane built in 1914 by the American Curtiss had a load capacity only half that of the Ilya Muromets. A large airplane built in 1915 by Siemens-Schuckert (Germany) also could not compare with the Ilya Muromets. The Ilya Muromets's motor placement was used widely in other countries. The Russian mechanical engineer V. A. Slesarev designed in 1913 and built in 1915 the world's largest two-engine biplane, the "Sviatogor," with an air weight of 6,500 kg, 50 percent of which was working load. *At the beginning of the First World War, Russia was the only country with heavy multi-engine airplanes.* In 1913, the Russian designer D. P. Grigorovich created a "flying boat" hydroplane; in 1913–14 he built several flying boats— the seaplanes M-1, M-2, and M-4. In 1914 he built the hydroplane M-5 (a two-seat biplane with a 100 h.p. engine), with a speed of 108 km per hour and the relatively low landing speed of 68 km per hr. Grigorovich successfully put pontoons on the

---

2. Named for a medieval knight of Russian folk tales. It was designed by Igor Sikorsky—no doubt not mentioned here because he emigrated in 1919 and became a major figure in the American aviation industry.

G. E. Kotelnikov
parachute

Ilya Muromets. In England, practical designs for hydroplanes were made no earlier than 1914 (Sopwith, Short). In 1913, the engineer N. R. Lobanov designed the first special airplane skis, allowing for safe takeoff and landing on snow. In 1911 the Russian inventor G. E. Kotelnikov invented the world's first packable parachute (RK-1).

Thus, Russian scientists, engineers, and inventors, working on the creation of flying machines, pioneered solutions to the basic problems of aviation. However, the decrepitude of Russia's bourgeois-landowner system, the incompetence of its tsarist rulers, and the country's technico-economical backwardness did not allow the initiatives of Russian innovators in aeronautics and aviation opportunities broad practical development. Innovators were given no support. Tsarist functionaries fawning before fancy foreigners ignored the discoveries and inventions of their Russian compatriots. Many valuable works by Russian scientists and inventors were credited to foreigners. Only the Great October Socialist Revolution gave designers, scientists, engineers, inventors, and rationalizers limitless opportunities for creative work and the realization of their projects.

The sort of nationalism represented here inspired a whole series of anecdotes:
Question: Who discovered the electric razor?
Answer: Ivan Petrovich Sidorov, in the trashbin behind the American Embassy. [5:340]

Why are Russians the greatest inventors of all?
Because they can even invent inventors. [5:341]

[For anecdote sources, see *Blue Blouse Skit*, above.]

Anecdotes

The matches were ready to burn with shame for the factory that produced them, but they couldn't. (*Crocodile*)

After the war, an Armenian living in France decided to return to the homeland. He agreed with a friend staying behind that he would write him a letter praising Soviet Armenia. If the letter was written in black ink, that would mean everything was fine, but if it was written in green ink, that would mean it was a lie.

Soon, the Armenian in Paris received a letter, written in black ink, which enthusiastically praised the new Yerevan, his friend's new house, and the wonderful life he had found. It continued, "You can get absolutely anything here, except for green ink." [4:98]

For anecdote sources, see *Blue Blouse Skit*, above.

One day in 1946, a huge crowd of Jews suddenly appeared on Red Square. There were all sorts: men and women, young and old, big-city and provincial. The surprised Muscovite asked them: "Who are you?"

"We're the Jews from all the anecdotes. The generals' wives took our places." [4:94]

Question: Who would be the physicists and mathematicians in an anti-world?
Answer: The anti-Semites. [5:414]

Stalin decided to find out just how obedient his people were. He announced a National Day of Ass-Kissing to take place on Red Square, the object of which would be his own back end. Propaganda explained what the holiday signified and how much enthusiasm the people should show.

The day arrived, with a magnificent parade of workers crossing the square in neat columns, carrying banners, posters, and portraits of the "greatest of the great." The behind of the nation's "beloved son and father" glistened in the sun as he assumed the appropriate position in front of St. Basil's Cathedral. The people formed an orderly line, and each person in turn approached the "Father of the Peoples," kissed his brilliant behind, and walked away.

The Beloved looked around: everywhere reigned order, organization, and calm—complete obedience.

Suddenly, no more than twenty steps away, pandemonium could be heard: shouts, curses, scandal, and tussling. NKVD men instantly ran over. One group formed a wall around the leader; another raced over to suppress the rebellion. A couple of well-placed blows, and order was reinstated. An NKVD officer returned.

Stalin asked, "What happened?"

"Everything's all right, Joseph Vissarionovich, that was just the Academy of Sciences trying to cut in front." [4:89]

A fortuneteller comes to a village. The peasants all ask her the same question: "When will Soviet power end?"

"It's hard to say," the fortuneteller says. "I can't answer for less than a hundred rubles."

They all chip in and give her a hundred. Still, she shakes her head. "It's a very hard question. Give me another hundred." When the peasants had managed to find that much money and pay her, she demanded yet another hundred. Finally, the peasants had enough. They surrounded her and threatened reprisal unless she gave the money back.

The fortuneteller calmly said: "And there's your answer. Soviet power will end the moment you do the same thing to the government." [4:101]

There was an original column marching in the May Day demonstration. It consisted of Abkhazian, Georgian, and other centenarians, who carried the placard: "Thank you, dear Stalin, for our happy childhood."

Stalin is a little confused. He stops the column and says: "But I wasn't around back then."

"That's precisely why our childhoods were happy." [4:105]

A peasant comes to the city with a sack of money after the currency reform of 1947. He puts the sack in a corner and goes to find out where he can exchange the old money for new. When he returns, he finds the money strewn on the floor and the sack gone: the thieves have taken everything of value. [5:58]

In Eastern Europe, the most important postwar Soviet invention is thought to be the cross-breeding of a giraffe with a cow. The new animal eats in the fraternal countries and is milked in the Soviet Union. [4:132]

At an international agricultural conference, the Soviet representative announced that Soviet farmers take four harvests a year. When skeptical delegates asked for an explanation, he continued: "It's simple: one harvest in Poland, one in Hungary, another harvest in Czechoslovakia, and the last in the Soviet Union." [4:134]

An American and a Russian soldier are chatting in Berlin. The American says: "We have a democracy. If I feel like it, I can go to Washington, see President Truman, and say Truman is an idiot."

The Soviet soldier says: "So what? I can go to the Kremlin, see Stalin, and tell him Truman is an idiot too." [4:110]

Question: Why do Soviet doctors remove tonsils through the anus?
Answer: Because nobody dares open his mouth. [5:105]

There are four passengers in an airplane in 1946, during the Greek civil war: an American, an Englishman, a Frenchman, and a Greek. The pilot suddenly opens the door and says: "The motor's not working. One of you will have to jump out so we don't crash."

The Frenchman gets up, says, "Vive la belle France!" and jumps.

Several minutes later, the pilot comes back again and says, "Someone else has to jump too."

The Englishman gets up, says, "Long live merry olde England," and jumps.

Several minutes later, the pilot comes back again and says, "Someone else has to jump."

The American stands up, says, "Long life to the United States of America," lifts the Greek, and throws him out the window. [4:113]

The East German president Wilhelm Pieck asks the postmaster about the success of a stamp bearing his portrait. Embarrassed, the postmaster answers, "It's not doing very well."

"Why's that?"

"They say it doesn't stick to the envelope."

"Do you mean the glue is no good?"

"No, we used the best glue, it's just that everyone keeps spitting on the wrong side." [4:122]

Beria reports to Stalin that the NKVD has arrested a man who looks like he could be Stalin's twin, and asks what he should do.

"Shoot him."

"Maybe we should just shave his mustache?"

"OK, I guess that would do as well." [5:187]

A worker races into the director's office and shouts: "Comrade Director, the head of personnel hanged himself in the closet!"

"Did you cut him down yet?"

"No, he's still alive." [5:265]

SELECTED BIBLIOGRAPHY

Art into Production: Soviet Textiles, Fashion, and Ceramics. Oxford, 1984.

Avins, Carol. *Border Crossings: The West and Russian Identity in Soviet Literature, 1917–1934.* Berkeley, 1983.

Baburina, Nina. *The Soviet Arts Poster: Theatre, Cinema, Ballet, Circus, 1917–1987.* Penguin, 1990.

Borland, Harriet. *Soviet Literary Theory and Practice during the First Five-Year Plan.* New York, 1950.

Bowers, Faubion. *Entertainment in Russia.* Edinburgh, 1959.

Bowlt, John. *Russian Art of the Avant Garde.* New York, 1985.

Brown, Edward J. *Mayakovsky: A Poet in the Revolution.* Princeton, 1973.

Clark, Katerina. *The Soviet Novel: History as Ritual.* Chicago, 1985.

Dunham, Vera. *In Stalin's Time: Middleclass Values in Soviet Fiction.* Cambridge, England, 1976.

Eastmann, Max. *Artists in Uniform.* London, 1934.

Elliott, David. *New Worlds: Russian Art and Society, 1900–1937.* New York, 1986.

Fitzpatrick, Sheila, ed. *Cultural Revolution in Russia, 1928–1931.* Bloomington, 1978.

Fitzpatrick, Sheila; Alexander Rabinowitch, and Richard Stites, eds. *Russia in the Era of NEP: Explorations in Soviet Society and Culture.* Bloomington, 1991.

Garrard, John and Carol. *Inside the Soviet Writer's Union.* New York, 1990.

German, Mikhail. *Art of the October Revolution.* New York, 1979.

Gleason, Abbott; Peter Kenez; and Richard Stites, eds. *Bolshevik Culture: Experiment and Order in the Russian Revolution.* Bloomington, 1985.

Gorchakov, Nikolai. *The Theater in Soviet Russia.* Trans. Edgar Lehrmann. New York, 1957.

Gray, Camilla. *The Russian Experiment in Art, 1863–1922.* New York, 1986.

Groys, Boris. *The Total Art of Stalinism: Avant Garde, Aesthetic Dictatorship, and Beyond.* Trans. Charles Rougle. Princeton, 1992.

Günther, Hans, ed. *The Culture of the Stalin Period.* London, 1990.

Gurevich, P. S., and V. N. Ruzhinov. *Sovetskoe radioveshchanie: stranitsy istorii.* Moscow, 1976.

Harper, Samuel. *Civic Training in Soviet Russia.* Chicago, 1929.

Ianovskii, Mark. *Iskusstvo operetty.* Moscow, 1982.

Ikonnikov, Andrei. *Russian Architecture of the Soviet Period.* Moscow, 1988.

Jelagin, Jury. *Taming of the Arts.* Trans. N. Wreden. New York, 1951.

Journal of Decorative and Propaganda Arts. Winter 1989. Issue devoted to early Soviet art.

Kenez, Peter. *The Birth of the Propaganda State: Soviet Methods of Mass Mobilization, 1917–1929.* Cambridge, England, 1985.

———. *Cinema and Soviet Society, 1917–1953.* Cambridge, England, 1992.

Lane, Christel. *Rites of Rulers: Ritual in Industrial Society.* Cambridge, England, 1981.

Lawton, Anna, ed. *The Red Screen: Politics, Society, and Art in Soviet Cinema.* London, 1992.

Lodder, Christine. *Russian Constructivism.* New Haven, 1983.

London, Kurt. *The Seven Soviet Arts.* London, 1937.

Maguire, Robert. *Red Virgin Soil: Soviet Literature in the 1920s.* Princeton, 1968.

Mally, Lynn. *Culture of the Future: The Proletkult Movement in Revolutionary Russia.* Berkeley, 1990.

Miller, Frank. *Folklore for Stalin: Russian Folklore and Pseudofolklore of the Stalin Era.* Armonk, 1990.

Miller, Jack. *Jews in Soviet Culture.* New Brunswick, 1984.

Mrazkova, Daniela, and Vladimir Remes. *Early Soviet Photographers.* Oxford, 1982.

Nielsson, N. A., ed. *Art, Society, Revolution: Russia, 1917–1921.* Stockholm, 1979.

Patrick, George Z. *Popular Poetry in Soviet Russia*. Berkeley, 1929.

Powell, David E. *Anti-Religious Propaganda in the Soviet Union*. Cambridge, 1975.

Robin, Regine. *Socialist Realism: An Impossible Esthetic*. Stanford, 1992.

Rosenberg, William, ed. *Bolshevik Visions: First Phase of the Cultural Revolution in Soviet Russia*. Ann Arbor, 1984.

Segel, Harold. *Twentieth Century Russian Drama: From Gorky to the Present*. New York, 1979.

Starr, S. Frederick. *Red and Hot: The Fate of Jazz in the Soviet Union*. New York, 1983.

Stites, Richard. *Revolutionary Dreams: Utopian Vision and Experimental Life in the Russian Revolution*. New York, 1989.

———. *Russian Popular Culture: Entertainment and Society since 1900*. Cambridge, England, 1992.

Stites, Richard, ed. *Culture and Entertainment in Wartime Russia*. Bloomington, 1995.

Taylor, Richard. *Film Propaganda: Soviet Russia and Nazi Germany*. New York, 1979.

———. *The Politics of Soviet Cinema, 1917–1929*. Cambridge, England, 1979.

Timasheff, Nicholas. *The Great Retreat: The Growth and Decline of Communism in Russia*. New York, 1946.

Trotsky, Leon. *Problems of Everyday Life*. New York, 1924.

Tumarkin, Nina. *Lenin Lives! The Cult of Lenin in the Soviet Union*. Cambridge, 1983.

Uvarova, Elena, ed. *Russkaia sovetskaia estrada*. 3 vols. Moscow, 1976–81.

von Geldern, James. *Bolshevik Festivals, 1917–1920*. Berkeley, 1993.

White, Stephen. *The Bolshevik Poster*. New Haven, 1988.

Yershov, Peter. *Comedy in the Soviet Theater*. New York, 1956.

Youngblood, Denise. *Soviet Cinema in the Silent Era, 1917–1935*. Ann Arbor, 1985; rpt., Austin, 1991.

Zorkaya, Neya. *The Illustrated History of Soviet Cinema*. New York, 1989.

JAMES VON GELDERN is Associate Professor of Russian at Macalester College and author of *Bolshevik Festivals.*

———•———

RICHARD STITES is Professor of Russian History at Georgetown University and author of *The Women's Liberation Movement in Russia: Feminism, Nihilism, and Bolshevism, 1860–1930; Revolutionary Dreams: Utopian Vision and Social Experiment in The Russian Revolution;* and *Russian Popular Culture: Entertainment and Society since 1900.*

Designer: SHARON L. SKLAR
Copyeditor: JANE LYLE
Typesetter: GRAPHIC COMPOSITION, INC.
Printer and Binder: THOMSON-SHORE, INC.
Typeface: NEW BASKERVILLE AND BENGUAIT